JOB

Adventures in the Land of Uz!

God
thundereth
marvellously with
His voice; great things doeth
He, which we cannot comprehend!

JOB

Adventures in the Land of Uz!

JEFF ADAMS

Published by Reality Living Publishing, Inc.
5460 Blue Ridge Cut-off
Kansas City, Missouri 64133
816-358-1515

Printed in the United States of America
Library of Congress 93-090212
ISBN 0-9643021-3-6

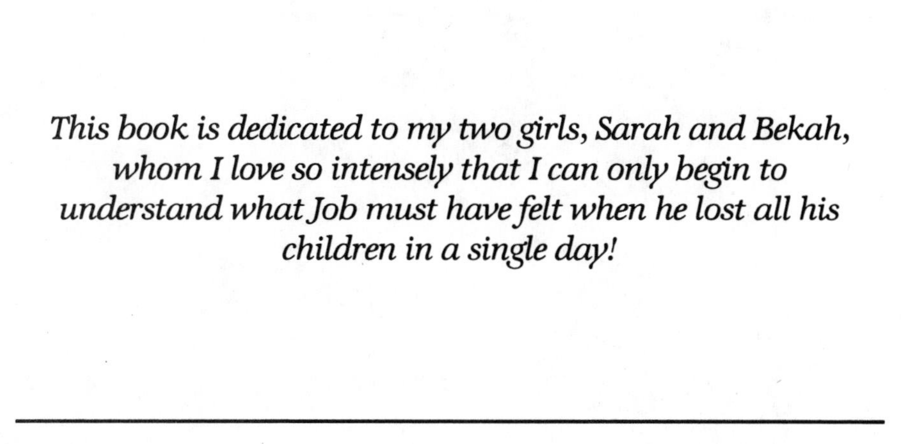

This book is dedicated to my two girls, Sarah and Bekah, whom I love so intensely that I can only begin to understand what Job must have felt when he lost all his children in a single day!

CONTENTS

Acknowledgments 11

Preface 13

1. Adventures in the Land of Uz 17
   Understanding the Context • Utilizing the Application
2. Star Wars Comes to Earth 45
   The Character of Job • The Challenge from God • The Campaign of Satan
3. When Life Falls Apart 67
   Continued Dialogue • Concentrated Attack • Chilling Counsel • Committed Friends
4. Man Without a Clue 85
   Job Curses His Day • Job Considers an Ageless Question • Job Contemplates Death • Job Continues His Questions
5. Killing with Kindness 107
   Background Study • Beginning Remarks • Basic Thesis • Bold Vision
6. The Eloquent Ramblings of Eliphaz 123
   Mistaken Thesis • Misapplied Truth • Millennial Type
7. Man at the Edge of Despair 141
   The View from the Cross Venting His Impatience • Viewing the Cross • Verbalizing His Misery
8. Bildad Takes Off the Gloves 159
   Attack on Job • Appeal to the Fathers • Application to Antichrist • Argument to Job
9. The Patience of Job 177
   Acknowledgment of Bildad's Truth • Acknowledgment of God's Wonders • Job's Seven "If's" • Anxiety of Job's Dilemma • Appeal to God's Mercy
10. Zophar Joins the Fray 201
   Zophar's Perverse Attack • Zophar's Probing Philosophy • Zophar's Pat Answer

11. Job Rises to His Own Defense 217
Absence of Wisdom • Illustration of Wisdom • Source of Wisdon

12. Job Probes the Nature of Life 235
Charges Against His Counselors • Confession of Faith • Confession of Life's Futility

13. Eliphaz Steps Back into the Ring 259
Confrontational Jabs • Coming Judgement

14. The View from the Cross 277
Venting His Impatience • Viewing the Cross • Verbalizing His Misery • Vexing His Counselors

15. Eyes Bigger than the Brain 299
Protest of Bildad • Potrait of Antichrist • Preview of Tribulation

16. Third Time's the Charm! 315
Tired Reaction • Threefold Representation • Tried Redeemer • Tremendous Reality

17. The Long Shadow of "the Wicked" 337
Checkmate in Uz • Content of Prophecy • Collapse of Antichrist • Consequences of Rebellion

18. Lessons from Frustration 357
Confronted Counselors • Concerned Questions • Coming Judgment

19. When Counselors Engage in Slander 373
Counseling Without Listening • Prophesying Without Understanding

20. Desperately Seeking God 395
Seeking for God • Setting Forth Faith • Seeing Forward Through the Ages

21. Final Serve and Volley 415
Fact and Question • Questions and Conclusion • Questions and Cosmology • Job's Cosmology

22. Job's Aching Heart 433
Refusing to Budge from His Righteousness • Responding to His Counselors • Revealing More Prophecy • Relating the Value of Righteousness and Wisdom

23. Job's Last Stand 451
Powerful Questions • Past Blessings • Present Problems • Personal Righteousness

24. The Explosion Of Elihu 477
Elihu's Anger Reaches the Boiling Point • Elihu's Justification for Speaking Reveals His Motivation • Elihu's Authorship is Seen in His Preamble • Elihu's Audacity Shines Through His Words • Elihu's Analysis Depicts Job's Condition • Elihu's Arguments Detail God's Communication with Men

25. The Counselor Who Was So Smart He Did No Good 497
The Conclusions of Elihu • The Confidence of Elihu • The Counsel of Elihu

26. The Man Who Presumed to Speak for God 517
God's Treatment of His Own • God's Treatment of the Lost • God's Terrible Glories • God's Tribulation Activities

27. The World's Most Difficult Examination 545
Questions About Words Without Knowledge • Questions About Creation • Questions About the Waters • Questions About the Sun's Light • Questions About Strange Places • Questions About the Weather • Questions About the Heavens • Questions in General

28. Lessons from God's Zoo 569
Pregnant Goats and Hinds • Wild Asses • Peacocks and Ostriches • Horses and Grasshoppers • Hawks and Eagles

29. Nothing Left to Say 589
Job's Day in Court • Speechless Before the Bench • Mystery of Behemoth

30. The Legacy of Leviathan 607
The Mystery Revealed • The Mystery Examined

31. When You Don't Have All the Answers 623
Nothing to Add • Nothing to Answer • Nothing to Lose

ACKNOWLEDGEMENTS

No honest author can claim originality. I am indebted to the many men of God whose books and sermons, and even casual conversations about the Book of Job, have long stirred up within me a desire to explore its depths.

Ken and Pat Bretches have edited every book I have written. It's wonderful to have people who know what you want to say even when you don't. Their dedication to this project has involved countless hours of laborious work.

I can't imagine doing this project without another husband and wife team—Mark and Cathy McGaughey. If you judge a book by its cover, give credit to Mark. His cover design for Psalm 119: A Journey Into the Heart of God drew rave reviews. Some people even enjoyed what they read! And Cathy, what could I say about her? Starting as my secretary, she has been with me from the very beginning of this commentary project, and has become so much more than "just a secretary." She now functions as a very capable executive assistant who manages every aspect of this book's production. I just write this stuff, folks. She makes the books!

The wonderful people of the Kansas City Baptist Temple give me the freedom and support to make this project a reality. This is an extension of our local church and ministry, not just a personal project. Many have helped in various ways. Some have volunteered to proof read skillfully, a tedious task indeed! Others have helped more than they could ever know just by their encouragement and enthusiasm.

And, of course, my dear wife has endured more than her share of trials as all this has come together. Putting up with my occasional frustrations, frequent interruptions in our lives and my constant study has not been easy. She deserves so much better, but has trusted God for grace to put up with me.

PREFACE

This is a book for adventurers. It is not for the fearful or weak-hearted. We are about to embark on a journey to the land of Uz where we will discover some strange things, indeed! Yet more than what we learn from ancient Uz, we will learn some remarkable things about ourselves.

Before our journey begins, let me set some ground rules. You need to know what to expect. Let me tell you what kind of book this is. This is the second installment in the *Reality Living Commentary Series.*

A commentary is just that—a commentary. It should be no means be considered authoritative. The only absolute authority that God has given to man is the Bible. This is a commentary on the infallible words of God, attempting to explain, analyze and apply them to the contemporary life of man on this planet.

Commentaries come in many different types and styles. Some commentaries are written by those who do not believe that God's Word is man's final authority. They criticize, correct and cast doubt upon the Word of God. Since Paul says in 1 Corinthians 2:14 that the Word of God is to be spiritually discerned, it is evident that one who does not hold to the infallibility and inerrancy of Scripture will not provide a positive impact upon our spiritual lives. Others commentaries are doctrinally correct, yet so heavy, dry, technical and otherwise inaccessible to the average pastor or Bible student as to be practically worthless. They have their place, and are written by scholars for scholars. Still other commentaries are so shallow they are not much more than simple devotional guides. They give a brief overview, often skipping those difficult verses that drive students to the commentaries in the first place.

The *Reality Living Commentary Series* is written to occupy the middle ground between these extremes. One day I overheard my secretary talking to someone about the first volume in the series, *Psalm 119: Journey Into the Heart of God*. To describe the book's style, she said, "It's a (conversational commentary.) He writes just like he's right beside you, talking to you and explaining the Bible verse by verse." I like that.

Indeed, this book was written with the goal of being a "conversational commentary." It is not simply a transcription of messages I preached on the Book of Job. I wrote with the mental image of explaining the book of Job to a friend, a younger pastor or a serious Bible student. I have tried to make it flow as smoothly as possible, to be non-threatening and easy to read.

Our text is the English Bible, King James Version. I have read a number of the critical commentaries, am aware of the major issues and questions, yet see no need to abandon what has been the standard Bible in the English-speaking world for almost 400 years. Its eloquence has defined our language; its accuracy has held true and its power has stretched men's souls and strengthened their spirits.

My burden for this approach also stems from my personal testimony. Meeting the Lord Jesus Christ as a college student, I had an insatiable appetite for the Word of God. I had no bible college background, no knowledge of Greek or Hebrew and no one to sit down with me and spend hours answering my questions. Beginning to preach and teach within months of my conversion, I was desperate to learn the Bible.

I found my teachers on shelves. The Bible was the object of my attention, but some of the centuries' greatest Bible teachers made up my faculty. Frequently visiting Christian bookstores, I was attracted to those commentaries written by men with a pastor's heart. I wanted someone to challenge me, to convict me and to convince me of the truth and power of the Bible. I looked for those who were not afraid to tackle the thorniest issues, the most difficult verses, even if their conclusions were less than certain. I discovered I could learn from all different personalities and opinions—even those with whom I disagreed.

Years later I would move on to secure a more proper theological pedigree, but I never forgot how I really learned the Bible—by sitting at the feet of men who knew God's Book, believed it and lived it. Having followed this path for over a quarter of a century, I have a great desire to pass along whatever God has entrusted to me. I pray that these words will find a place in the hearts of fellow adventurers.

I will not criticize or correct God's Word. The Bible will be the basis for our conversation and we will maintain our commitment to its truth. Even the difficult verses will be dealt with, though I make no claim to have all the answers. I will go out on a limb to suggest what God would have us see, knowing that not everyone will agree. All I ask is that you prayerfully consider what I have to say. If my comments stray from the boundaries of the Bible, stick with the Bible. I do hope, though, to stimulate your mind, to excite you, to force you to think in new directions. Above all, I will try to create a written atmosphere that will facilitate God's Spirit using these words to touch your heart.

1

ADVENTURES IN THE LAND OF UZ

There was a man in the land of Uz, whose name was Job;
and that man was perfect and upright, and one
that feared God, and eschewed evil.

Job 1:1

FOR SEVERAL YEARS I HAVE BEEN A RESIDENT OF THE STATE OF Missouri, but I was born in neighboring Kansas. Growing up in the Sunflower State, we had few claims to fame, except wheat and the Wizard of Oz—a story that has captivated hearts around the world. While visiting other countries people sometimes ask me if I know Dorothy!

We are about to visit the land of Uz. I can't promise you Munchkins and a yellow-brick road, but there will be extra-terrestrial beings and a road called the "circuit of heaven." Don't look for the Wicked Witch of the West or even a good witch. However, you will meet demons and angels, and there WILL be a tornado. Add to this a fire-breathing sea monster, and other exotic creatures, and you have a fascinating journey ahead of you. Welcome to the incredible adventures of Job.

Many "serious Bible students" dismiss Job as simply a fine story containing some valuable moral lessons. I believe that Job is a foundational book of the Bible, necessary to any comprehensive understanding of God's Word. With a genuine grasp of this book, you will see things in the Bible perhaps you never imagined before. I also believe that the study of this book will answer some very practical questions about life and its many adversities.

Before we begin this adventure in Uz, we must address some preliminary tasks. We must first determine the context of the words in this book that we are about to study. Next we will see the historical, doctrinal and devotional applications of the book of Job. Finally, we must set the necessary background to properly understand. These are introductory issues that must be understood before embarking upon our verse-by-verse journey through the land of Uz. To be honest with you, this chapter would normally bear the title "Introduction," and not be listed as a chapter. If I did that, you might not read this, and that would mean you would be in danger of taking my words out of context. It is not my intention to deceive you, but it is my conviction that you will not properly understand what I am about to say unless you clearly see my presuppositions. Now, don't skip right on to the next chapter. Just sit back, relax and consider what I have to say. After all, you may disagree so totally I will save you the bother of reading the rest of the book!

UNDERSTANDING THE CONTEXT

Fundamental to any serious Bible study is the need to take the words of Scripture within their proper context. We don't appreciate someone taking our words out of context in order to twist the sense of what we meant to say. God's words also must be taken within the context. He meant to give them.

CONTEXT AND THE CANON OF TRUTH

Even beginning Bible students are usually aware of their need to consider the context of the sentence, the paragraph, and even the book itself, as they study to find the true meaning of what God has spoken. I believe there is a broader kind of context still—the big picture—that sees the position of the book within the context of the "canon" (not something that shoots cannon balls, but the order and content of Scripture, from the Greek word meaning "standard" or "rule").

A careful student notices a book's position in the canon, or whole of Scripture, as he approaches the study of that book. It makes a difference, for example, whether the book is in the Old Testament or the New Testament. In the New Testament we approach the Gospels differently than we do the epistles, the letters written by Paul, John and Peter. To begin with, Hebrews 9:16 says, *"For where a testament is, there must also of necessity be the death of the testator."* The New Testament properly does not begin until the death of Christ, the *"testator."* This is not to suggest that the four Gospels be taken out of the New Testament arrangement of books, only that we remember that these books are TRANSITIONAL in nature. They form the bridge from Old to New Testament.

The epistles, some of which are written to specific churches, such as in Corinth and Ephesus. They speak directly to the church in this present age, whereas the Gospels include a definite Jewish flavor that we must consider, without automatically applying every word directly to the church. All Scripture is written FOR us, but not necessarily TO us. For example, the Bible tells us that God promised a piece of geography to Israel. This is in the Bible FOR our edification. (Romans 15:4; 1 Corinthians 10:6,11) This is not speaking TO us to give us claim to a piece of real estate in the Middle East. Context is all-important to understanding the Bible.

The Book of Acts is also transitional—it bridges the gap between a church first comprised of Jews, to a church primarily of gentiles. Though Ephesians explains that there is neither Jew nor gentile in Christ, we must consider the Jewish makeup of the early church to understand properly what is happening. Paul takes a Jewish vow in Acts, something few evangelists would do today. Many early believers thought a person must first become a Jew to be born again, or later thought that once a person was born again it would be necessary for them to then become a Jew to grow spiritually.

These are some issues Acts deals with in that period of transition, and they illustrate the importance of a book's location in relationship to the rest of the Bible. Before jumping into a book and stripping out the verses, we must ask where that book is in relationship to the rest of Scripture.

I believe that God left His imprint in the very arrangement of the books of Scripture. This statement will be met with a chorus of protests from those who remind us that men collected and arranged the canon. The truth is that God has allowed men to participate in the process, while never relinquishing His control. After all the councils and arguments have faded into the drab, gray colors of history, the Bible stands in living technicolor just as God intended from the beginning.

The arrangement of the books of the Bible IS important, and ultimately affects the way we approach our study of Job. What can we say about the order of books in the Bible?

God is not a God of chance, or a God of chaos (1 Corinthians 14:33), He is a God of order, Who has used men to arrange the books of the Bible just as He wishes. Am I saying that the book order in the Bible is INSPIRED? No. Certainly not in the same sense that He breathed (or "inspired") His words into the human authors of Scripture. (2 Timothy 3:16) I am contending that God has never lost control of His words, nor any part of the historical process that has delivered these words to us today.

God is the Author of the Bible, but He employed human beings as His writing instruments. These men were not robots, or God's dictaphone, but God used their background, personality, style and experience to say exactly word-for-word what He wanted to say. (Matthew 5:18; Proverbs 30:5) That unfathomable paradox—the Heavenly Author directing each and every word of the human authors—is the great mystery of the inspiration of Scripture. (2 Peter 1:20-21) It should be no stretch of faith to believe that a God, Who is so powerful and so concerned to faithfully communicate His words to men, would likewise divinely supervise their transfer from ancient times to the present.

Why would God deliver His Word to men, then not preserve it into our present age?

I believe that God has controlled every step along the way in transmitting His inspired words from the first to the twenty-first century, including the order of the books in the Bible. Even the difference in the order of books between the Hebrew Bible and the Christian's Old Testament shows evidence of God's singular influence over man's handling of His Word. Though the Hebrew Scriptures and our present Old Testament are identical in content, the order of books is different, and some of them are combined into single volumes in the Hebrew text.

While both begin with the five books of the law, the Hebrew canon ends with 2 Chronicles. (Chronicles is one volume in the Hebrew and two volumes in our present Bible, though the content is identical). Chronicles ends with a mandate for Jews to return to Jerusalem from their captivity.

"Now in the first year of Cyrus King of Persia, that the word of the LORD spoken by the mouth of Jeremiah might be accomplished, the LORD stirred up the spirit of Cyrus king of Persia, that he made a proclamation throughout all his kingdom, and put it also in writing, saying, Thus saith Cyrus king of Persia, All the kingdoms of the earth hath the LORD God of heaven given me; and he hath charged me to build him an house in Jerusalem, which is in Judah. Who is there among you of all his people? The LORD his God be with him, and let him go up." (2 Chronicles 36:22-23) This is precisely what we see the Jews doing today—going up to Jerusalem.

In our present Old Testament the last book is Malachi, which ends with a striking prophecy of the Second Coming of Christ. *"But unto you that fear my name shall the Sun of righteousness arise with healing in his wings; and ye shall go forth, and grow up as calves of the stall."* (Malachi 4:2)

God's final word to Jews—"Go up to Jerusalem." God's final Old Testament word to New Testament believers—"Christ is coming again." Coincidence? You could call it that if you like, but the more I study the Bible, the more amazed I am at how everything fits together with divine purpose. The intricacy of its connections are only surpassed by the simplicity and depth of its message. Whatever you think of this simple example, I believe that there are riches awaiting those who approach God's Word with reverence, anticipation and the presupposition that it is true.

Your heart attitude as you read the Bible will determine what you receive from the Bible. Some see the Word as though they were looking at an ancient artifact that was once produced by human beings, and then buried in layers of culture, language, myth and superstition through the centuries. They see it as an object with cracks and faded colors to be analyzed, catalogued and put on display, useful in the modern world only for occasional tidbits of wisdom.

The real truth about the Bible is that you can scrutinize it from any angle you want, and it will withstand the examination. You can prove its historical validity, demonstrate its trustworthiness, locate its places on a map, and make genealogical charts of its characters. Yet the Bible is more than an ancient artifact; it is the living Word of the living God!

More than a loose collection of ancient writings, patched together in a hodgepodge, coincidental manner, the Bible is the logical, ordered communication of God to mankind.

CONTEXT AND THE CYCLES OF TRUTH

God used Semitic people to write the Bible, and they flavored it with oriental thought patterns. The Western mind usually thinks in a linear fashion, from beginning to end, while the oriental tends to think in spiraling cycles and recurring themes. It's not that one is right and the other wrong. They are just different.

Recurring cycles of God's dealings with mankind can be detected throughout the Bible. Solomon reminds us in Ecclesiastes 1:9 that, "*The thing that hath been, it is that which shall be; and that which is done is that which shall be done: and there is no new thing under the sun.*" One of God's favorite vehicles is to teach us the future by way of the past.

The exodus was more than the simple, historical account of God's rescue of the Hebrews from the oppression of Egypt. The use of this story by New Testament writers makes it clear that God intended to use it to illustrate His desire to rescue all men from the oppression of sin and the world, and lead them into the fullness of the life He has prepared for those who believe. We will later see that God also uses the exodus to illustrate events that are yet future.

The Bible is a whole, not merely a collection of unrelated entities. Even from Old Testament times Bible students have marvelled at the intricate web of relationships that binds together the five books of Moses, called the Pentateuch. There is a flow of God's thought, a progression of His purposes, and it all illustrates His dealings with us today.

The Book of Job fits into one of these cyclical patterns that appear in the Word of God. To see this pattern we have to go back to the books of Kings and Chronicles. Perhaps you have noticed that these books cover the same material. Obviously the emphasis is different, but there is much duplication. Convinced that God does not waste space in His Bible, we must seek a valid purpose in His repeating this material twice. Why does God include both these books in the Bible? What is He saying by repeating the same account twice?

Kings and Chronicles relate the deterioration of the kingdom, and the consequence of sin that resulted in the destruction of the Temple and the dispersion of the Jews. Through Kings and Chronicles, God reminds us twice that the Temple was destroyed and the people dispersed.

Those of us who have the vantage point of history know that the Temple has suffered two destructions, followed by the dispersion of God's people. The first time was at the hands of Nebuchadnezzar in 586 B.C., followed by 70 years of captivity in Babylon, with many other Jews heading for Egypt and different points of the ancient world. The returning Jewish remnant rebuilt the Temple, as told in the books of Ezra and Nehemiah. The Temple was enlarged by Herod before the time of Christ. Then, Roman armies under the leadership of Titus again destroyed the Temple in 70 A.D. Since then the Jewish people have been dispersed around the world. By telling us the story of the Temple's destruction twice, could it be that God was illustrating two coming destructions of the Temple on His prophetic calendar?

Following the destruction of the Temple in 70 A.D., the next prophetic event that relates to God's people is the return of the Jews to their land, as prophesied by so many Old Testament prophets. Interestingly, the book that follows Chronicles is Ezra, which relates the story of Jews returning to the land as the result of a decree given by a gentile king who ruled a vast world empire.

We already saw the last words of 2 Chronicles, which mention Cyrus of Persia, who would play a crucial role in God's plan to bring His people back to the land. Listen to the first words of Ezra. *"Now in the first year of Cyrus king of Persia, that the word of the LORD by the mouth of Jeremiah might be fulfilled, the LORD stirred up the spirit of Cyrus king of Persia, that he made a proclamation throughout all his kingdom, and put it also in writing, saying, Thus saith Cyrus king of Persia, The LORD God of heaven hath given me all the kingdoms of the earth; and he hath charged me to build him an house at Jerusalem, which is in Judah. Who is there among you of all his people? his God be with him, and let him go up to Jerusalem, which is in Judah, and build the house of the LORD God of Israel, (he is the God,) which is in Jerusalem."* (Ezra 1:1-3)

Here is a gentile king, who becomes God's instrument to bring the Jews back to the land. Could it be that the book of Ezra also is a prophetic picture of the later return of God's people to the land following two destructions of the Temple and two dispersions of the Jews? However you answer that question, the facts of history speak for themselves, revealing that the modern return of Jews to their homeland follows a number of remarkable parallels to the way it happened in Ezra's day. A gentile king who boasted of his worldwide influence issued the decree that opened the door for Jews to return to Palestine in Ezra's day.

In the 19th century, the modern Zionist movement gained momentum with the work of Austrian journalist, Theodore Herzl, who convened the first Zionist Congress in 1897. Following World War I, England administered the protectorate of Palestine.

The Balfour Declaration of 1917 promised British support for the formation of the Jewish national homeland in Palestine. It was issued under the authority of a gentile king, the King of England, who was the sovereign of a monarchy that had long boasted that the sun never set upon the British Empire. Are the parallels between the King of Persia and the King of England mere coincidence, or is God still playing a role in history?

Some have observed that World War I prepared the land for the Jews, while the World War II prepared the Jews for the land. After World War II, the Jews made up a significant population in Palestine. Their dream of a homeland in the ancient land of their ancestors had become a reality. Yet the war left the Jews unprotected amidst hostile neighbors. Boundaries needed to be defined. In 1948 the unthinkable happened—these Jews once again formed the nation of Israel.

Although some may call it pure chance, the very next book of the Bible after Ezra is the Book of Nehemiah. Ezra told the story of the Temple's reconstruction, but the rebuilding of the wall of the city of Jerusalem is the subject of the Book of Nehemiah. Ezra told the story of the Temple's reconstruction, but the city was defenseless. There were no walls or boundaries. Nehemiah describes the building of the walls, and setting up of boundaries and defenses, just as our generation has witnessed the establishment of Israel's borders and defenses.

The next event on God's prophecy program is the rapture of the church, to be followed by God's direct dealings with the Jews in a seven-year period of tribulation. Again, there is a fascinating parallel to be seen in the book order of our Old Testament.

The next book in the order of Scripture is the Book of Esther. Esther describes the removal of a gentile queen, Vashti, who is then replaced by a Jewish queen, Esther, and includes the story of a seven-day wedding feast. We are presently waiting for the primarily gentile bride of Christ, the church, to be replaced on earth by the restored bride of Jehovah, the nation of Israel. God will once again deal directly with his people, the Jews, as Paul affirms in his remarkable explanation found in Romans 9-11. The Bible also foretells a coming wedding feast when Christ and His bride are united.

Following the story in Esther of the removal of this gentile queen and replacement with a Jewish queen, comes the book we are considering—the Book of Job. If ever there was a book that deals with tribulation, it is Job. The very next item on God's agenda following the rapture of the church and His return to deal directly with Israel, is a seven-year period of tribulation.

It is worth noting that Psalms follows Job, where the prominent figure is David. Most of the book of Psalms is the chronicle of David's heart during his rise to the throne. This pictures the Lord Jesus Christ, the Son of David, sitting on the throne of His millenial glory.

Again, you can call this order mere chance, coincidence, or wildly speculative musings on my part. You have the right to believe what you will. However, I believe that the placement of Job within the context of Scripture is no accident, and that God has so framed this book to give us a most incredible prophetic picture of the Jew in the coming Tribulation.

You may never have considered the progression I have outlined, but even the internal factors in the book of Job itself, parallel the biblical prophecies of the Tribulation. We will look at these parallels in greater detail as we move on to consider the application of the book's contents.

UTILIZING THE APPLICATION

Earlier we discussed the foundational rule of Bible study—context. There is another important precept of Bible study that needs to be considered at this point in our preparatory study of Job. It is the principle of application.

Scripture says what it means, and means what it says. Our job is not to find some hidden symbolic value or to spiritualize the text in order to apply it to whatever situation strikes our fancy. Our job is to see WHAT it says, and learn to apply it.

The application of Scripture is threefold: historical, doctrinal and devotional (personal). Our study of Job will depend upon establishing these three applications consistently throughout our study.

HISTORICAL APPLICATION

Scripture is, first of all history. The Bible is a book about real people and real events. There are some parables and other literary vehicles in the Bible, but real people events. There are some parables and other literary vehicles in the Bible, but real people speak them to apply in real circumstances. The Bible is not just a collection of religious sayings and proverbs. The Bible is an historically accurate book whose veracity can be proven. It tells of a God who controls history.

The first task of any serious Bible student is to learn what the Bible really says. To accomplish this goal, one must determine the historical context and see the application of biblical truth that was made in the time in which the passage was written.

In our study of Job, despite any fascinating parallels between this book and the Tribulation to come, we must never stray from the fact that Job was a real person. This book is not just an interesting Hebrew drama. Job is not a mythological character or a symbolic representation. This man, whose name means "one persecuted," lived on the same earth we do.

Ezekiel spoke of him in the same context as other historical people. *"Though Noah, Daniel, and Job, were in it, as I live, saith the Lord GOD, they shall deliver neither son nor daughter; they shall but deliver their own souls by their righteousness."* (Ezekiel 14:20) So did James. *"Behold, we count them happy which endure. Ye have heard of the patience of Job, and have seen the end of the Lord; that the Lord is very pitiful, and of tender mercy."* (James 5:11)

Shortly we will see how Job can possibly be identified in the genealogical tables of Genesis. In spite of modern attempts to discredit the veracity of the book, Bible students have always identified Job with the period of the early Hebrew patriarchs in the late eighteenth century B.C.

This makes the book of Job the oldest book in the Bible from a chronological sense, though it is not the first to appear in the canon. The Jews have a tradition that Moses took the early accounts of the book and committed it to writing. Whatever the case, the book is the oldest we have.

When we consider the ages of those who lived before the flood, it is possible that Noah could have known people who knew Adam. Imagine the information that Noah would have received about creation and the early stages of man's history on earth. After the flood Noah lived until just a few years before the birth of Abraham. The significance of this is that Job could very well have spoken with those who conversed with Noah. Job was just a few generations removed from the creation. Seen from this perspective, the creation was no more ancient history to Job, than the Civil War is to us.

It is no wonder that Job offers more information about the creation than any other book in the Bible. Job is the book where God Himself lays down the foundational truths of His cosmology—the nature and principles of the universe. It also offers some fascinating insights into God's ways of communicating with man before the written Word.

DOCTRINAL APPLICATION

Doctrine means teaching. In everything God says, He aims to teach us something.

Earlier I commented that the exodus account is a picture of things that were to come. God is the master Teacher. He uses things we do understand to teach us things we don't understand. Like a father patiently leading a small child through a book of colorful pictures, God takes us by the hand through the Old Testament to show us a picture book of people just like us and of a Savior just like Him. He teaches us the intangible truth of the New Testament by comparing it to the tangible accounts of real people in history who shared the same problems and challenges we do.

Paul makes this truth clear to the Corinthians. *"Moreover, brethren, I would not that ye should be ignorant, how that all our fathers were under the cloud, and all passed through the sea; And were all baptized unto Moses in the cloud and in the sea; And did all eat the same spiritual meat; And did all drink the same spiritual drink: for they drank of that spiritual Rock that followed them: and that Rock was Christ. But with many of them God was not well pleased: for they were overthrown in the wilderness. NOW THESE THINGS WERE OUR EXAMPLES, to the intent we should not lust after evil things, as they also lusted. Neither be ye idolaters, as were some of them; as it is written, The people sat down to eat and drink, and rose up to play. Neither let us commit fornication, as some of them committed, and fell in one day three and twenty thousand. Neither let us tempt Christ, as some of them also tempted, and were destroyed of serpents. Neither murmur ye, as some of them also murmured, and were destroyed of the destroyer. NOW ALL THESE THINGS HAPPENED UNTO THEM FOR ENSAMPLES: and they are written for our admonition, upon whom the ends of the world are come.*" (1 Corinthians 10:1-11) (Author's emphasis)

Paul taught the same truth to the Romans. Speaking of the Old Testament Scriptures he said, "*For whatsoever things were written aforetime were written for our learning, that we through patience and comfort of the scriptures might have hope.*" (Romans 15:4)

Preachers who fail to understand this truth either avoid the Old Testament altogether, or bore their people to death with archaeological oddities. Failure to understand how God uses the Old Testament to teach doctrine makes the Old Testament about as interesting as day-old oatmeal.

Paul constantly looked to the Old Testament to illustrate the deep things of God that he wished to communicate. The ways he employed the Old Testament scriptures reveals just how shallow our contemporary understanding has become. In Paul's same letter to the Corinthians he was establishing why he had a right to have expected some financial support from them. He recognized their immaturity, though, and put food on the table through his tent-making trade. He lists several reasons why he had every right to have expected financial help. One of them is a quotation from Deuteronomy 25:4.

"*Who goeth a warfare any time at his own charges? who planteth a vineyard, and eateth not of the fruit thereof? or who feedeth a flock, and eateth not of the milk of the flock? Say I these things as a man? or saith not the law the same also? For it is written in the law of Moses, Thou shalt not muzzle the mouth of the ox that treadeth out the corn. Doth God take care for oxen?*" (1 Corinthians 9:7-9)

Notice what he says immediately afterwards, admonishing them to open their eyes to the doctrinal truth of the Old Testament. "*Or saith he it altogether for our sakes? FOR OUR SAKES, NO DOUBT, THIS IS WRITTEN: that he that ploweth should plow in hope; and that he that thresheth in hope should be partaker of his hope.*" (1 Corinthians 9:10) (Author's emphasis)

In effect he is saying, "Do you think all God had in mind was to write about oxen to a group of Jews? Don't you understand that He was painting us a picture? Don't you see that He wrote these things for us?" Alas! Some people see only oxen.

Let us hasten to add that this understanding isn't a license to run through the pages of the Old Testament gathering up any text that strikes your fancy to use as a pretext for your personal opinions—precisely the approach used by Origin of Alexandria in the third century of Christianity. He established what is called the allegorical (or symbolic) method of biblical interpretation. For centuries preachers and Bible teachers have ripped verses from their historical and doctrinal moorings, using them to bolster their private agendas.

So many have erred so greatly with their fanciful flights to worlds unknown on the magic carpets of Scripture verses isolated from their contexts, that we are presently witnessing the pendulum swing to the opposite pole. There are those who now reject anything but the purely historical value of Scripture, daring only to tack on a neat moral truth or two as food for thought.

While soundly rejecting the "allegorical method of biblical interpretation," one cannot strip the Bible of allegory. For example, Paul uses allegory in Galatians 4, taken directly from the pages of the Old Testament. He uses the real historical women, Sarah and Hagar, to teach about law and grace.

The Lord Jesus, in one of His many debates with the religious leaders of His day, appealed to Moses. *"Do not think that I will accuse you to the Father: there is one that accuseth you, even Moses, in whom ye trust. For had ye believed Moses, ye would have believed me: for he wrote of me."* (John 5:45-46) Moses did write about Jesus, but you will not find a single direct reference to Him in all five books of Moses. The only way to understand Jesus' words is to see that Moses wrote of Him in word pictures, in type and in symbol.

Once we lay hold of this truth, the Old Testament opens like Ali Baba's cave to reveal wonderous riches. When Moses wrote of the bronze serpent raised on the wooden pole, he was writing of Christ on the cross made sin for us. Jesus defined this picture in John 3:14. When Moses wrote of Abraham offering up his only son Isaac, whom he loved, he was really giving us a figure of God the Father offering up His only begotten Son, whom He loves. That this is a figure is clearly defined in Hebrews 11:19. When Moses wrote of the passover that eventful night in Egypt, Paul tells us he was really writing about Christ, our passover. (1 Corinthians 5:7).

Here is the key: We know these figures and types because they are confirmed as we compare Scripture with Scripture. In his first letter to the Corinthians, contrasting worldly wisdom to God's wisdom as revealed in the Bible, Paul taught that this was the method the Holy Spirit uses to teach us the deep things of God, *"comparing spiritual things with spiritual."* (1 Corinthians 2:13)

If Job is nothing more than an ancient Hebrew morality play, why should we bother continuing our study? However, if you believe that God is at work in the pages of Job, there is much adventure that awaits us.

There will doubtless be those who think I have gone too far. I make no claim to infallibility. Of loving God's Word I am guilty! But as we look for our Lord on each page, I will make every attempt to show you how Scripture interprets Scripture to the believing heart.

In those moments when my raw excitement carries me away on billowy puffs of imagination and speculation, I will dutifully try to inform you, and label my speculation clearly. My intention is not to lead you astray or entice you with some strange doctrine, but to stretch your mind, your imagination, your spirit and your creativity as we travel together through this wonderful book.

Having attempted to expose my presuppositions, we return to our book of Job. We have established that Job is history. In presenting this history, God is writing for us *"upon whom the ends of the world are come."* (1 Corinthians 10:11) The Bible clearly teaches that the church will not go through the seven-year great Tribulation. However, as believers, we do suffer tribulation now. In Job, God gives us an incredible illustration of believers in tribulation. If ever anyone qualified for enduring tribulation it was Job! Remember that the next major event on God's prophetic calendar is a seven-year period we often call the "Tribulation" which will fall upon this earth. Some of the prophecies in the Book of Revelation are incredible and probe the limits of our imagination. To help us understand, God has given us the story of a man named Job. More than a simple story about his trials, Job is a wonderful picture of the coming time of Tribulation, and helps us to better understand the future.

As you approach the Book of Job, consider the picture that is drawn. The parallels between what happened to Job and the prophecies of the coming time of Tribulation are too many to be mere coincidence. In this introduction, let me suggest some of those parallels. As we move through our study we will encounter them at every turn. Do not take my word for it, but prayerfully consider the evidence of Scripture.

The story of Job takes place in the land of Uz, exactly where the faithful remnant of Jews will be hidden during the Tribulation. Uz always has a connection with Edom in the Bible, and the famous "Petra" (from the Greek word for "rock") is in Edom, the refuge God has prepared for His people. We will consider more details about the land of Uz later in this chapter.

Job sits in his misery for seven days, while his friends look on speechless. In the coming Tribulation the Jews will suffer at the hands of the Antichrist for a seven-year period. The world will be powerless to help, and most will genuinely believe that they are only getting what they deserve. Don't think that World War II did away with antisemitism.

Actually, the "Great Tribulation" is the last half of the seven years, though we often apply the word "Tribulation" to the entire period. The first three and a half years are a time of false peace, when the Antichrist comes into power through a brilliant series of treaties that brings peace to the Middle East, and structures a disarmament. (Daniel 8:11-14,25, 9:27; Isaiah 28:18)

At midpoint of this seven-year period the Antichrist breaks his treaty with Israel, and in the reconstructed Jewish Temple declares himself to be God. This is the abomination spoken of by Daniel. (Daniel 9:27; 8:13-14; 11:31; Matthew 24:15) These last three and a half years are of world war and great destruction. The Book of Revelation counts it as a period of 42 months. (Revelation 11:2) Chapter divisions in the Bible were not added until several hundred years ago, and most people may not believe that God had anything to do with it. But it is interesting to notice that Job has 42 chapters.

We have already mentioned another parallel. Job follows the books that picture a taking away (rapture) of a gentile queen, a wedding feast and then a Jewish queen is placed on the throne.

Job makes an interesting comment in Job 17:6. *"He hath made me also a byword of the people; and aforetime I was as a tabret."* Job's identification of himself as a *"byword"* to the people reminds us of a prophecy pronounced upon Israel more than once. Just as Job's trials caused him to become a byword for trials, Israel's tribulation due to sin also will result in the same designation. We first see it in Deuteronomy 28:37, when God warns Israel of the consequences of disobedience. *"And thou shalt become an astonishment, a proverb, and a byword, among all nations whither the LORD shall lead thee."*

This is a warning that God repeated to Solomon. *"Then will I cut off Israel out of the land which I have given them; and this house, which I have hallowed for my name, will I cast out of my sight; and Israel shall be a proverb and a byword among all people."* (1 Kings 9:7) The same truth appears in Psalm 44:13-14. *"Thou makest us a reproach to our neighbours, a scorn and a derision to them that are round about us. Thou makest us a byword among the heathen, a shaking of the head among the people."* (Psalm 44:13-14)

Very few people can boast that the Devil himself has personally persecuted them, but Job could. He was the direct target of Satan. This is also a figure of what will happen to Israel in the time of Tribulation. Israel will be attacked by the very Devil.

In Revelation 12 the woman represents the nation of Israel: *"And the great dragon was cast out, that old serpent, called the Devil, and Satan, which deceiveth the whole world: he was cast out into the earth, and his angels were cast out with him. And I heard a loud voice saying in heaven, Now is come salvation, and strength, and the kingdom of our God, and the power of his Christ: for the accuser of our brethren is cast down, which accused them before our God day and night. And they overcame him by the blood of the Lamb, and by the word of their testimony; and they loved not their lives unto the death. Therefore rejoice, ye heavens, and ye that dwell in them. Woe to the inhabiters of the earth and of the sea! for the devil is come down unto you, having great wrath, because he knoweth that he hath but a short time. And when the dragon saw that he was cast unto the earth, he persecuted the woman which brought forth the man child."* (Revelation 12:9-13)

At the end of the book of Job, Job's captivity is turned, and he receives double all that he lost. In a similar way, the captivity of Israel will be turned around after the purging of the Tribulation, and will be restored to the position of blessing.

PERSONAL APPLICATION

The Bible is history. God uses that history to teach us by example those intangible doctrines that are hard to grip with our finite minds. These are two primary levels of biblical application. There is a third, and without it, the first two are merely academic. The truth that we distil from the Bible must then be applied to our personal lives. The Bible is about life. Its purpose is to change our lives. The third level of biblical application is to apply what you have learned to your daily life.

In our study of Job we will make every attempt to understand what really happened in Job's life, and to comprehend the precise meaning of everything that is said. Simultaneously, we will seek God's doctrinal teaching each step of the way. We will make note of the many similarities between Job's trial and the trial that is yet to come upon this world. Most importantly, we will listen to the Spirit of God as He teaches us to deal with the very real trials that we face each day.

Many have stated that the Book of Job answers the question "why do good people suffer bad things?" Nothing could be further from the truth! The Book of Job never answers this question directly.

Job was a good man who suffered a series of incredible calamities. As Job's friends began to speak, apparently the one idea they held in common was that Job's suffering had to be the result of some hidden, unconfessed sin in his life. They reasoned that no one could suffer like this without having done something to deserve it.

Young Elihu patiently waited until the older men had their say. He quickly criticized them for their errant views, but really had nothing new to offer himself. He also concluded that God was just, and clearly would not allow something like this to happen to someone who did not deserve everything he got.

Job goes through various stages of despair and frustration, yet desperately holds on to his integrity and faith in God. When God finally speaks, He has absolutely nothing to say about the reason for Job's trials. Instead, He gives Job an incredible lesson on creation. Never does He explain to Job Satan's role in all his trials. Not once does He answers why, nor will we.

When God gives Job a chance to respond, this man who had complained that he wanted a chance to speak to God has nothing to say.

The real message of Job is that when good people suffer bad things, they sometimes never learn the real reason, or the true story of what has happened to them. Some things are simply beyond our understanding. The emphasis of Job is not to answer WHY bad things happen to good people, but to show good people how to realistically and biblically deal with those trials.

The book also has other valuable lessons for practical Christian living. We will see some very important principles of biblical counseling. We will also see how NOT to do biblical counseling by the negative example of Job's counselors. Job establishes both the foundation and the realistic limits of biblical counseling.

Finally, Job gives a fantastic glimpse into the arena of spiritual warfare. We actually see conversation between God and Satan. We learn that our lives can be greatly affected by powers beyond our sight and beyond our control.

UNCOVERING THE BACKGROUND

We have examined the context and the applications of the study of Job. Another ingredient must be added to this mixture before we embark on our journey to the land of Uz. Background questions of authorship, date and location must be dealt with.

AUTHOR

Many theories deal with the authorship of Job. Some see Job himself as the author. We have already mentioned a Jewish tradition associating

Moses with committing the book to its present written form. There is no formal announcement within the book itself affixing authorship.

The only internal evidence of authorship appears in Job 32 as Elihu begins his discourse. Up to this point the book has been written entirely in third person narrative. The first verses of Elihu's speech follow the same pattern. After his initial explosion of words, the three counselors are speechless, taken by surprise that this young man would have the courage to speak in such a bold fashion. *"They were amazed, they answered no more: they left off speaking."* (Job 32:15)

Then, describing his reaction to the scene, Elihu speaks in first person singular, as though he were the author of these words. *"When I had waited, (for they spake not, but stood still, and answered no more;) I said, I will answer also my part, I also will shew mine opinion."* (Job 32:16-17) This is the only appearance of first person narrative in the book.

Although the authorship of Job will continue to be debated until Christ returns, the only internal evidence points to Elihu as the human author. The most important issue, though, is that Job was a real person, and that the events described are history, no matter who put the words down in writing.

DATE

While discussing the historical application of Job, we noted that the book was written in the era of the Hebrew patriarchs, and that possibly Job could be identified in the book of Genesis. Let's examine this further in our attempt to set the date for the writing of Job.

We just referred to Elihu. In the same chapter, Job 32, we learn a little about his background. *"Then was kindled the wrath of Elihu the son of Barachel the Buzite, of the kindred of Ram: against Job was his wrath kindled, because he justified himself rather than God."* (Job 32:2)

Elihu was a Buzite. The Buzites were descendants of Buz, mentioned in Genesis 22:21. *"Huz his firstborn, and Buz his brother, and Kemuel the father of Aram."* These words appear in the listing of the children of Nahor, brother of Abraham. Elihu, then, would be from people who originated in the area of Ur of the Chaldees.

Information concerning Job's counselors appears in Job 2:11. *"Now when Job's three friends heard of all this evil that was come upon him, they came every one from his own place; Eliphaz the Temanite, and Bildad the Shuhite, and Zophar the Naamathite: for they had made an appointment together to come to mourn with him and to comfort him."* (Job 2:11)

Zophar's ancestry is difficult to identify, but the ancestry of the other two appears in Genesis. Bildad is a Shuhite. *"Then again Abraham took a wife, and her name was Keturah. And she bare him Zimran, and Jokshan, and Medan, and Midian, and Ishbak, and Shuah."* (Genesis 25:1-2) Shuah is the father of the Shuhites, and the son of Abraham by his second wife, Keturah.

So far we know that the principal characters of the story come from those who lived after the birth of Abraham. Eliphaz is identified in Job 2:11 as a Temanite. His ancestry also can be traced to Genesis 25. *"Hadar, and Tema, Jetur, Naphish, and Kedemah."* (Genesis 25:15) Tema is father of the Temanites, and is a descendant of Ishmael, the son born to Abraham by Sarah's maid, Hagar. None of these men are considered Hebrews, yet all can be traced to the same period shortly following Abraham, and in the same geographical region.

Several names in Genesis have been suggested as being the same Job of the Book of Job. Remember that biblical words sometimes have different spellings according to the method of transliteration, or the form of the name. Even today, sometimes John is called Jack. My middle name is Geoffrey, sometimes written Jeffrey or some other way.

The best possibility for Job is the name found in Genesis 36:33. *"And Bela died, and Jobab the son of Zerah of Bozrah reigned in his stead."* This is still in the era of the patriarchs. Thus, with enough time having passed since Abraham for the Buzites, Shuhites and Temanites to have developed, this list in Genesis 36 is of the kings of Edom. Jobab (Job?) is a king of Edom.

This is completely consistent with the statement of Job 1:3 that Job was "one of the greatest men of the east." It also would be a literal explanation of Job's words in Job 19:9. *"He hath stripped me of my glory, and taken the crown from my head."* Not only do these facts fit the case, but if Job was indeed a king of Edom, we would understand why he was in Uz. Edom, as we will soon see, is in Uz!

The name Job also appears in Genesis 46:13. *"And the sons of Issachar; Tola, and Phuvah, and Job, and Shimron."* Some have proposed that this is the Job of the book that bears the same name. Though the spelling is the same, this suggestion presents some difficulties. As a son of Issachar, what would he be doing in Uz, which is in Edom? The sons of Issachar lived in the land given to Abraham, not in Edom, which occupied by the descendants of Esau, the brother of Jacob, a grandson of Abraham. If Job were a Jew from the days of Issachar, why would there be no direct reference to Jews in the Book of Job? How would this son of Issachar have risen to become "one of the greatest men of the east?"

The best alternative is to see Jobab as the biblical Job, king of Edom, and one of the greatest men of the east. This would place Job squarely in the late 1700's to 1800 B.C.

Modern critical scholarship seeks to deny this early date, since it does not fit in with their other rearrangements of Scripture. Not willing to accept any legitimate predictive prophecy, or true divine inspiration of Scripture, they have their hands full trying to twist and corrupt the Word of God to fit their own private ideologies. (I use the word "ideology" because "theology" has to do with God, and very little of what modern Bible critics say has to do with God.)

Examining the literature, the objections to this early date begin with the argument that the language of the book is too advanced for 1800 B.C. This reasoning, of course, follows the assumption that no one could be as "advanced" as modern man. We have evolved, after all! How could primitive man of 1800 B.C. have been so sophisticated?

With this argument the critics rejected Moses as the author of the Pentateuch. Scholars once believed that man could not even write in 1800 B.C. Robert Dick Wilson and others embarrassed them early in this century, as the finds of archeology definitely proved that man was writing very well in 1800 B.C., with language more sophisticated than most of our "modern" languages.

Others object that the book could not have been written in the days of the Patriarchs, because there are too many references to the Mosaic law, such as the sacrifices mentioned. What references to Mosaic law? There are only IMAGINED references. The scholars' reasoning has no foundation other than assumption. For some reason (prejudice) they imagine that every reference to sacrifice is a reference to the Mosaic law. They have forgotten that Cain and Abel understood a system of sacrifice given by God centuries before Moses. Noah and Abraham, and many others, offered sacrifices ages before Moses.

Some point to the Hebrew word *"torah"* in Job 22:22. But the word simply means "law," not MOSAIC law, any more than the word "law" in English always refers to the law of Moses. The scholarly attempts to reject an early date of Job merely reflect their personal prejudice. Their arguments have no more substantiation that the claim that "Job is not primitive enough to have been written in 1800 B.C." Such a statement is purely speculative, and has not a shred of evidence.

The real reason critical scholars don't want to accept the true dates and authorship of biblical books, is because they don't want to accept the accuracy of prophetic and historical statements made under the inspiration of the Holy Spirit. If they accept the validity of what the Bible says, they also must accept the implications of what the Bible says about their personal lives and sin.

PLACE

Next, we consider the setting of this book, the land of Uz. Like Job's friends, the land of Uz can also trace the origins of its name back to the book of origins, Genesis. *"And the children of Aram; Uz, and Hul, and Gether, and Mash."* (Genesis 10:23) This verse places Uz, for whom the land is named, as a descendant of Shem through Aram. A second mention of Uz is in Genesis 36:28, but this Uz is probably named for the first one. Please note that the context of Genesis 36 connects Edom, Esau and mount Seir, which are all the same. Before the mention of "Uz" in verse 28, we have this statement earlier in the context, *"Thus dwelt Esau in mount Seir: Esau is Edom."* (Genesis 36:8)

A survey of the Old Testament substantiates the claim connecting Uz with Edom. Lamentations 4:21 is clear. *"Rejoice and be glad, O daughter of Edom, that dwellest in the land of Uz; the cup also shall pass through unto thee: thou shalt be drunken, and shalt make thyself naked."*

Uz is also "Idumea," the site of Petra ("rock"), where God will hide His faithful remnant during the last half of the Tribulation. On a map this area is to the southeast and southwest of the Dead Sea, which today would overlap the border between Israel and Jordan.

There has been much talk about "Petra" in recent years, due to the increased awareness of biblical prophecy. The biblical foundation for this is God's promise to prepare a place for the faithful remnant in the Tribulation. This place is the place of the "rock."

Earlier we spoke of the prophecy in Revelation 12 where we see that Israel will be persecuted by the Devil in the Tribulation. Let's go back to a verse just before the portion we quoted. *"And the woman fled into the wilderness, where she hath a place prepared of God, that they should feed her there a thousand two hundred and threescore days."* (Revelation 12:6) Verse 14 of Revelation 12 is also relevant. *"And to the woman were given two wings of a great eagle, that she might fly into the wilderness, into her place, where she is nourished for a time, and times, and half a time, from the face of the serpent."*

In these verses notice that God has a place prepared for Israel. It is *"her place."* She is nourished there for a *"time, and times, and half a times,"* which is to say "three and a half years," the last half of the Tribulation. Why is she *"nourished?"* Revelation 13:16-17 tells us that no one could buy or sell without the mark, or the name of the beast. God will need to nourish this remnant of His people, since they will not be able to buy or sell.

How will God nourish His people, who have fled to the place He has prepared for them in the wilderness? Several passages in biblical prophecy connect Israel in the coming time of Tribulation to Israel in the time of the exodus. *"Therefore, behold, I will allure her, and bring her into the wilderness, and speak comfortably unto her. And I will give her her vineyards from thence, and the valley of Achor for a door of hope: and she shall sing there, as in the days of her youth, and as in the day when she came up out of the land of Egypt."* (Hosea 2:14-15)

Ezekiel saw the same thing. *"As I live, saith the Lord GOD, surely with a mighty hand, and with a stretched out arm, and with fury poured out, will I rule over you: And I will bring you out from the people, and will gather you out of the countries wherein ye are scattered, with a mighty hand, and with a stretched out arm, and with fury poured out. And I will bring you into the wilderness of the people, and there will I plead with you face to face. Like as I pleaded with your fathers in the wilderness of the land of Egypt, so will I plead with you, saith the Lord GOD. And I will cause you to pass under the rod, and I will bring you into the bond of the covenant: And I will purge out from among you the rebels, and them that transgress against me: I will bring them forth out of the country where they sojourn, and they shall not enter into the land of Israel: and ye shall know that I am the LORD."* (Ezekiel 20:33-38)

Again, the connection with the exodus is in Micah 7:14-15. Here the element of feeding is added, and linked with the exodus. *"Feed thy people with thy rod, the flock of thine heritage, which dwell solitarily in the wood, in the midst of Carmel: let them feed in Bashan and Gilead, as in the days of old. According to the days of thy coming out of the land of Egypt will I shew unto him marvellous things."*

We can now understand how this Jewish remnant can survive for three and a half years of Great Tribulation, when no one will be allowed to buy or sell without the mark of the beast. God will provide for them exactly as He did in the exodus, with manna from heaven.

Armed with this understanding, let's go to the words of Christ in His famous Mount Olivet Discourse, where He explains to His Jewish disciples how it will be for Israel in the time of the Tribulation. *"When ye therefore shall see the abomination of desolation, spoken of by Daniel the prophet, stand in the holy place, (whoso readeth, let him understand:) Then let them which be in Judaea flee into the mountains: Let him which is on the housetop not come down to take any thing out of his house: Neither let him which is in the field return back to take his clothes. And woe unto them that are with child, and to them that give suck in those days! But pray ye that your flight be not in the winter, neither on the sabbath day: For then shall be great tribulation, such as was not since the beginning of the world to this time, no, nor ever shall be.*" (Matthew 24:15-21)

The direct references to Judaea and the sabbath day have no meaning for the church, and enable us to see that these words apply directly to the Jewish remnant. At midpoint in the Tribulation, the Antichrist will declare himself to be God, and he will do so in the rebuilt Jewish Temple. (2 Thessalonians 2:1-4) This is the abomination spoken of by Daniel the prophet. (Daniel 9:27; 11:31) This is the sign for the remnant to flee to the place in the "rock" that God has prepared for them.

This "rock" in the Idumea wilderness (Uz) appears several times in Scripture. (Judges 1:36; Isaiah 42:11) For the purposes of our study of Job we need to remember that this "rock" is in the land of Uz, which is in Edom, or Idumaea.

Obadiah, one of the Minor Prophets, wrote his prophecy against Edom. Here, he reveals the pride of Edom, thinking that her place in the rock was impregnable. "*The vision of Obadiah. Thus saith the Lord GOD concerning Edom; We have heard a rumour from the LORD, and an ambassador is sent among the heathen, Arise ye, and let us rise up against her in battle. Behold, I have made thee small among the heathen: thou art greatly despised. The pride of thine heart hath deceived thee, thou that dwellest in the clefts of the rock, whose habitation is high; that saith in his heart, Who shall bring me down to the ground? Though thou exalt thyself as the eagle, and though thou set thy nest among the stars, thence will I bring thee down, saith the LORD.*" (Obadiah 1-4)

Not only has the Lord humbled Edom since Obadiah's time, He will use that very "rock" to hide His people in the Tribulation. Fittingly, it is the place of the rock that serves as Israel's hiding place, for this rock points to THE Rock, the Lord Jesus Christ, who will rescue them as their Savior and Messiah. Visiting them in Edom at the time of His second coming, He will lead them down the King's Highway and across the Jordan River, just as Joshua (the name is identical with Jesus, transliterated from Hebrew instead of Greek) did centuries earlier.

Fulfilling the types of the exodus, Jesus will "touch down" on the Mount of Olives, just as the angels promised in Acts 1:11.

Isaiah foresaw the victorious Savior returning down the same road Joshua had trod centuries earlier. "*Who is this that cometh from Edom, with dyed garments from Bozrah? this that is glorious in his apparel, travelling in the greatness of his strength? I that speak in righteousness, mighty to save.*" (Isaiah 63:1)

The rock in Edom pictures the coming Rock of Israel. *"The LORD is my rock, and my fortress, and my deliverer; my God, my strength, in whom I will trust; my buckler, and the horn of my salvation, and my high tower."* (Psalm 18:2) Twenty-four times in the Psalms this figure of the rock appears.

No other portion of the Bible is more definitive about the Rock of Israel, than Deuteronomy 32. *"He is the Rock, his work is perfect: for all his ways are judgment: a God of truth and without iniquity, just and right is he."*

In the verses that follow, notice the prophetic reference to the Rock, and that the Rock connects with Israel in the wilderness and the same figure of the eagle that also appears in Revelation 12:14 and Obadiah 4.

"When the most High divided to the nations their inheritance, when he separated the sons of Adam, he set the bounds of the people according to the number of the children of Israel. For the LORD's portion is his people; Jacob is the lot of his inheritance. He found him in a desert land, and in the waste howling wilderness; he led him about, he instructed him, he kept him as the apple of his eye. As an eagle stirreth up her nest, fluttereth over her young, spreadeth abroad her wings, taketh them, beareth them on her wings: So the LORD alone did lead him, and there was no strange god with him. He made him ride on the high places of the earth, that he might eat the increase of the fields; and he made him to suck honey out of the rock, and oil out of the flinty rock." (Deuteronomy 32:8-13)

In the past, Israel deserted its Rock. This why the Jews have been dispersed around the world, and will be purged in the Tribulation.

"But Jeshurun waxed fat, and kicked: thou art waxen fat, thou art grown thick, thou art covered with fatness; then he forsook God which made him, and lightly esteemed the Rock of his salvation. They provoked him to jealousy with strange gods, with abominations provoked they him to anger. They sacrificed unto devils, not to God; to gods whom they knew not, to new gods that came newly up, whom your fathers feared not. Of the Rock that begat thee thou art unmindful, and hast forgotten God that formed thee.

"And when the LORD saw it, he abhorred them because of the provoking of his sons, and of his daughters. And he said, I will hide my face from them, I will see what their end shall be: for they are a very froward generation, children in whom is no faith. They have moved me to jealousy with that which is not God; they have provoked me to anger with their vanities: and I will move them to jealousy with those which are not a people; I will provoke them to anger with a foolish nation. For a fire is kindled in mine anger, and shall burn unto the lowest hell, and shall consume the earth with her increase, and set on fire the foundations of the mountains. I will heap mischiefs upon them; I will spend mine arrows upon them. They

shall be burnt with hunger, and devoured with burning heat, and with bitter destruction: I will also send the teeth of beasts upon them, with the poison of serpents of the dust. The sword without, and terror within, shall destroy both the young man and the virgin, the suckling also with the man of gray hairs.

"I said, I would scatter them into corners, I would make the remembrance of them to cease from among men: Were it not that I feared the wrath of the enemy, lest their adversaries should behave themselves strangely, and lest they should say, Our hand is high, and the LORD hath not done all this. For they are a nation void of counsel, neither is there any understanding in them. O that they were wise, that they understood this, that they would consider their latter end! How should one chase a thousand, and two put ten thousand to flight, except their Rock had sold them, and the LORD had shut them up?" (Deuteronomy 32:15-30)

There is a danger. There is another "rock" that is not THE Rock. *"For their rock is not as our Rock, even our enemies themselves being judges. For their vine is of the vine of Sodom, and of the fields of Gomorrah: their grapes are grapes of gall, their clusters are bitter: Their wine is the poison of dragons, and the cruel venom of asps."* (Deuteronomy 32:31-33)

Jesus identified Himself as the Rock in Matthew 16:18. Yet this verse has been a source of controversy for centuries, as the Roman Catholic church claims that Peter was the Rock upon which the church was built. This would be strange, since Peter himself used that same figure in his first epistle to show that the church is built upon Christ.

"To whom coming, as unto a living stone, disallowed indeed of men, but chosen of God, and precious, Ye also, as lively stones, are built up a spiritual house, an holy priesthood, to offer up spiritual sacrifices, acceptable to God by Jesus Christ. Wherefore also it is contained in the scripture, Behold, I lay in Sion a chief corner stone, elect, precious: and he that believeth on him shall not be confounded. Unto you therefore which believe he is precious: but unto them which be disobedient, the stone which the builders disallowed, the same is made the head of the corner, And a stone of stumbling, and a rock of offence, even to them which stumble at the word, being disobedient: whereunto also they were appointed." (1 Peter 2:4-8)

Deuteronomy gave us the understanding of this controversy by warning us of a false "rock" connected with a biting, bitter wine, quite different from the sweet new wine that pictures the shed blood of Christ. Satan has counterfeited everything God does. If Jesus Christ is the Rock, you can be sure the there will be "another rock."

If you are not part of the Jewish remnant in the Tribulation, you'll never have to worry about fleeing to Edom to the place of the rock. You CAN, however, find refuge in THE Rock. The Lord Jesus Christ is the ONLY refuge from sin and death. He is the only ROCK who can nourish His people, and protect them from the attacks of the world. Are YOU standing on THE Rock?

Even a discussion of the land of Uz brings us face to face with biblical prophecies of the coming Tribulation. As we go through the Book of Job we will witness strange happenings in the land of Uz, things that are shortly to be repeated in many particulars.

The book of Job will amaze you with the startling accuracy of the Bible. You will see things written in Job, centuries before Christ, that "modern science" has only recently discovered.

If the Bible is right about such things as science and creation, it is right about your life. Make sure that your feet are firmly planted upon the Rock.

2

STAR WARS COME TO EARTH

And said, Naked came I out of my mother's womb, and
naked shall I return thither; the LORD
gave, and the LORD hath taken away;
blessed be the name of the LORD.
In all this Job sinned not, nor charged God foolishly.

Job 1:21-22

THE STORY WE ARE ABOUT TO SEE IS WILDER THAN ANY SCIence fiction thriller. We will find it exceedingly difficult to believe that the scene unfolding is actually real. Yet we already dealt with the historical veracity of the book of Job in the first chapter, and we will accept these words as God's words, the words He wants us to have. Everything within us will cry out to see this as a parable, a mythological representation, or a moral drama. However, the real power and meaning of this book will not be clear until we understand that Job is a real person just like us.

The opening verses of this book deal with Job's character. He is not a faceless person; he is a genuine human being with a great heritage, family, interests and personality. The midsection of the chapter is a challenge that God throws out to Satan about Job's character. The Devil accepts the challenge, and the final portion of the first chapter details the campaign he carries out against Job.

THE CHARACTER OF JOB

1 "There was a man in the land of Uz, whose name was Job; and that man was perfect and upright, and one that feared God, and eschewed evil.
2 And there were born unto him seven sons and three daughters.
3 His substance also was seven thousand sheep, and three thousand camels, and five hundred yoke of oxen, and five hundred she asses, and a very great household; so that this man was the greatest of all the men of the east.
4 And his sons went and feasted in their houses, every one his day; and sent and called for their three sisters to eat and to drink with them.
5 And it was so, when the days of their feasting were gone about, that Job sent and sanctified them, and rose up early in the morning, and offered burnt offerings according to the number of them all: for Job said, It may be that my sons have sinned, and cursed God in their hearts. Thus did Job continually." (Job 1:1-5)

PERFECT MAN

In the first chapter we researched the land of Uz and made the connection with Edom, and "Petra," where the Jewish remnant will be hidden by God in the Tribulation.

That Job was *"upright"* (Job 1:1) or righteous, and that he *"feared God and eschewed evil"* as Job 1:1 continues, presents no problem. These are common topics in the study of the Bible, and especially of the Old Testament.

That Job is *"perfect"* (Job 1:1) is a tremendous stumbling block. We are not even finished with the first verse before a theological controversy brews. The source of difficulty is our needless and erroneous insistence upon linking the adjective "sinless" to "perfection" every time it rolls off our lips, as though the two words are inseparable. We imagine that Job must be on a spiritual plane not accessible to mere mortals. It is no wonder we think of him as a figure in a moral drama and not as a real person.

"Sinless perfection" is not a biblical phrase. It is not a biblical concept when applied to man on earth in any dispensation. The idea of "sinless perfection" is the product of bad doctrine. Job was a good man; but he was not sinless. He offered sacrifices! If he were "sinless," this would not be necessary.

Noah is also a *"perfect"* man. Pay careful attention to the context of these words. *"But Noah found grace in the eyes of the LORD. These are the generations of Noah: Noah was a just man and perfect in his generations, and Noah walked with God."* (Genesis 6:8-9) Like Job, Noah is *"just"* or *"upright"* and is *"perfect."* Noah's designation as *"perfect"* is tightly connected to God's grace in this context.

In the Old Testament being "perfect" is the result of righteous living (being "just" or "upright") and the grace of God. In Job 1:1 this is precisely the description of Job's perfect condition—*"one that feared God, and eschewed evil."* The same definition appears in verse 8 in the discussion between God and the Devil. *"And the LORD said unto Satan, Hast thou considered my servant Job, that there is none like him in the earth, a perfect and an upright man, one that feareth God, and escheweth evil?"* (Job 1:8)

Job makes it clear by his own usage of the word *"perfect,"* that it does not mean "sinless perfection." *"If I justify myself, mine own mouth shall condemn me: if I say, I am perfect, it shall also prove me perverse. Though I were perfect, yet would I not know my soul: I would despise my life."* (Job 9:20-21)

Though God testifies that Job is perfect, Job's humility does not allow him to think of himself as fitting that designation. Even if he were perfect, Job says here in chapter 9, he would still have to reckon with his sinful human nature. Job has no "sinless perfection" in mind.

The Hebrew word translated "perfect" is *"tamin"* and means "without blemish." This should cause the serious Bible student to think of Christ's care for His bride, the church. *"Husbands, love your wives, even as Christ also loved the church, and gave himself for it; That he might sanctify and cleanse it with the washing of water by the word, That he might present it to himself a glorious church, not having spot, or wrinkle, or any such thing; but that it should be holy and WITHOUT BLEMISH."* (Ephesians 5:25-27) (Author's emphasis)

Perfection has an even clearer definition in the New Testament. We find it in Paul's second letter to Timothy. *"All scripture is given by inspiration of God, and is profitable for doctrine, for reproof, for correction, for instruction in righteousness: That the man of God may be perfect, throughly furnished unto all good works."* (2 Timothy 3:16-17)

This passage is a wealth of information on the biblical precept of perfection. The final clause of verse 17 defines *"perfect"* as *"throughly furnished unto all good works."* We also see that this equipping to do God's work is the result of God's Word working in our lives. In short, perfection never means "sinless" in the Bible.

Though he did not live in a state of "sinless perfection," the wonderful testimony in verse 1 reminds us that Job is in some ways a picture, or type, of the Lord Jesus Christ. Christ, the only sinless human being since Adam, was also personally attacked by the Devil. Adam, another prophetic picture of Christ, was perfectly sinless before his fall, and was also personally stalked by the god of this world himself.

This is a good moment to store in our minds a bit of information that will be dealt with many times later in the book. Job appears in this book as a figure of three things—the Jew in Tribulation, Christ on the cross, and the lost man in hell. These three figures will crop up repeatedly in our study, and it will be all but impossible to distinguish between them. In fact, they are intimately related. Christ suffered our hell on the cross. All hell is let loose on earth in the Tribulation, and lost man goes to hell because he refuses to accept the substitutionary death of Christ. We will observe how many times it is difficult to separate these three images, due to this common thread that connects them.

PROLIFIC FATHER

2 "And there were born unto him seven sons and three daughters." (Job 1:2)

Verse 2 lists the number of Job's children, and there are a total of ten. Ten children clearly qualifies Job for a "full quiver award." There may be more here than meets the eye. Ten is a number often associated with fullness or completeness of order. For example, Nebuchadnezzar's dream in Daniel 2 shows an image depicting the history of gentile nations. The ten toes of the image picture the great gentile empire of Antichrist in the time of the *"fullness of the gentiles."* (Romans 11:25) The same ten-nation confederacy is symbolized by ten horns in Daniel's vision of the beast. (Daniel 7:7,20,24) The tribulation of the flood came in the days of Noah, the tenth generation from Adam. (Genesis 5) In the coming Tribulation, the nation of Israel is symbolized by ten virgins in that time of the *"fullness of the gentiles."* Whatever the case, Job is a gentile in his fullness, and his family is full and complete.

POWERFUL CITIZEN

3 "His substance also was seven thousand sheep, and three thousand camels, and five hundred yoke of oxen, and five

hundred she asses, and a very great household; so that this man was the greatest of all the men of the east." (Job 1:3)

We also saw in the first chapter the best possibility of identifying Job in the book of Genesis is as Jobab in Genesis 36:33. This would make him a king of Edom, and explains his great wealth described in Job 1:3.

Many liberal and even some evangelical theologians teach that wealth is oppressive and evil. Rather than emphasizing a relationship with God, they preach a salvation that is more a liberation from oppression and poverty. The other extreme is the television evangelist preaching a "name it, claim it" gospel, which teaches that all who truly have faith will be blessed with wealth and prosperity.

The biblical truth reveals the error of both these extremist views. Wealth or fame do not necessarily mean carnality. Nor does poverty insure spirituality. A poor man is often as materialistic as the greediest capitalist. Both have their focus on material things—one because he constantly wants more, and the other because he doesn't have anything.

Job's extreme wealth and influence in no way mars his testimony. Abraham accumulated great wealth. David, the man after God's own heart, was not a pauper but a king, though he did experience times of need in his life. Daniel rose to great power in both the Babylonian and Persian empires. In the New Testament Lazarus and Joseph of Arimathaea were wealthy men who were friends of Jesus. Luke 8:3 speaks of wealthy women who ministered to Jesus out of their substance.

PROTECTIVE PATRIARCH

Proof of Job's character follows the listing of his wealth. Job was a concerned parent.

4 "And his sons went and feasted in their houses, every one his day; and sent and called for their three sisters to eat and to drink with them.

5 And it was so, when the days of their feasting were gone about, that Job sent and sanctified them, and rose up early in the morning, and offered burnt offerings according to the number of them all: for Job said, It may be that my sons have sinned, and cursed God in their hearts. Thus did Job continually." (Job 1:4-5)

"Every one his day" is a reference to birthday celebrations. Job lamented *"his day,"* and defined it as his birthday. The Bible defines its own words when we compare Scripture with Scripture. *"After this opened Job his mouth, and cursed HIS DAY. And Job spake, and said, Let THE*

DAY perish WHEREIN I WAS BORN, and the night in which it was said, There is a man child conceived." (Job 3:1-3) (Author's emphasis)

Job probably worried that his children might get carried away in the celebration festivities and would sin. Like any good parent he worried about his kids.

Despite Job being a gentile, don't miss his knowledge that the only way to God is through a substitutionary sacrifice. This has nothing to do with the Mosaic law, as these actions take place centuries before Moses. Remember what we saw in the first chapter. Cain and Abel understood the principle of substitutionary sacrifice. So did Noah, Abraham, and the great priest Melchizedek, who was a gentile.

This is the testimony of Job—he was a rich and influential man, and a godly man. He was born a sinner like every other human being since Adam. He wrestled with the same problems we all do, except that he was exceptionally good at applying his faith to practical living. Job is a wonderful example of a God-fearing man, and one that James holds up for us to follow in James 5:11.

However, the life of this great and godly man is about to fall apart at the seams. Yet, he has done nothing to deserve it.

THE CHALLENGE FROM GOD

6 "Now there was a day when the sons of God came to present themselves before the LORD, and Satan came also among them.

7 And the LORD said unto Satan, Whence cometh thou? Then Satan answered the LORD, and said, From going to and fro in the earth, and from walking up and down in it.

8 And the LORD said unto Satan, Hast thou considered my servant Job, that there is none like him in the earth, a perfect and an upright man, one that feareth God, and escheweth evil?

9 Then Satan answered the LORD, and said, Doth Job fear God for nought?

10 Hast not thou made an hedge about him, and about his house, and about all that he hath on every side? thou hast blessed the work of his hands, and his substance is increased in the land.

11 But put forth thine hand now, and touch all that he hath, and he will curse thee to thy face.

12 And the LORD said unto Satan, Behold, all that he hath is in thy power; only upon himself put not forth thine hand. So Satan went forth from the presence of the LORD." (Job 1:6-12)

THE SONS OF GOD

The first item we must deal with is the identity of the *"sons of God"* (Job 1:6) Adam was the *"son of God,"* but only bears that title in the genealogy of Luke 3:38. Following Adam's fall in Genesis 3, no other human being in the Old Testament is ever called the "son of God." God speaks of the Jews as his sons and daughters in Isaiah 43:6, and Hosea 1:10 prophesies a future day when God will restore Israel, and will call them His sons. Yet the specific phrase *"the sons of God"* appears only in Job and in Genesis 6.

Job 2:1 repeats the scene we see in 1:6. *"Again there was a day when the sons of God came to present themselves before the LORD, and Satan came also among them to present himself before the LORD."*

Job 38:7 is the third reference to *"the sons of God"* in Job. God has just spoken to Job out of the whirlwind. His words do not reveal the answer for Job's suffering, but declare the greatness of God in creation.

"Then the LORD answered Job out of the whirlwind, and said, Who is this that darkeneth counsel by words without knowledge? Gird up now thy loins like a man; for I will demand of thee, and answer thou me. Where wast thou when I laid the foundations of the earth? declare, if thou hast understanding. Who hath laid the measures thereof, if thou knowest? or who hath stretched the line upon it? Whereupon are the foundations thereof fastened? or who laid the corner stone thereof; When the morning stars sang together, and all the sons of God shouted for joy?" (Job 38:1-7)

These sons of God are not Christians, nor are they Old Testament saints. They are witnesses who saw God lay the foundations of earth.

Job is written in poetic form. In the Hebrew language poetry finds expression in parallelism, as opposed to the rhyme and meter that predominates in English poetry. In parallelism, the author places parallel thoughts side by side to contrast, complement or complete each other. In Job 38:7 we are not to imagine that the morning stars are one class of beings and the sons of God another. The parallel sentence construction and the context implies that the morning stars are the sons of God.

The word *"stars"* in the Bible often represents angels. This is clearly the case in Revelation 1:20, in the symbolism of the first chapter of the Apocalypse. *"The mystery of the seven stars which thou sawest in my right hand, and the seven golden candlesticks. The seven stars are the angels of the seven churches: and the seven candlesticks which thou sawest are the seven churches."* There are several instances in Revelation where *"stars"* appear, and the context clearly shows that the word does not mean literal stars, but angels.

To identify these sons of God with angels is completely consistent with the only other reference to *"the sons of God"* outside the Book of Job in Genesis 6. The identity of these *"sons of God"* is an important and hotly debated issue. To understand it fully we need to divert briefly from the study of Job and grasp correctly the significance of the events of Genesis 6. This knowledge will greatly help our understanding of Job.

"And it came to pass, when men began to multiply on the face of the earth, and daughters were born unto them, That the sons of God saw the daughters of men that they were fair; and they took them wives of all which they chose. And the LORD said, My spirit shall not always strive with man, for that he also is flesh: yet his days shall be an hundred and twenty years. There were giants in the earth in those days; and also after that, when the sons of God came in unto the daughters of men, and they bare children to them, the same became mighty men which were of old, men of renown. And God saw that the wickedness of man was great in the earth, and that every imagination of the thoughts of his heart was only evil continually. And it repented the LORD that he had made man on the earth, and it grieved him at his heart." (Genesis 6:1-6)

Again, it is the identification of *"the sons of God"* that poses a problem. The thought that angels could have sinned by cohabiting with human women, and producing mutant *"giants,"* is just too much for some theologians to swallow. Never mind that this revelation would explain the origin of much mythology by cutting off the layers of embellishment and pointing to the germ of truth that caused the legends.

A major problem in understanding the Bible is that many theologians of liberal persuasion believe that the "Judeo-Christian religious tradition" is merely the direct result of an evolution of the pagan religions of Israel's neighbors. However, God's truth, clearly expressed in Romans 1, is that Israel's pagan neighbors became pagan because they rejected God's truth that was revealed to them from the beginning. The story in Genesis 6 ties together some loose ends of myths, religions and legends that have been left dangling through the ages.

The standard line of so-called "scholars" in our modern, so-called enlightened age is that the *"sons of God"* were the godly descendants of

Seth, while the *"daughters of men"* were the ungodly descendants of Cain. This teaching says that these young men of Seth married the daughters of Cain and produced men who were "famous," and were giants in a figurative sense, not literal.

I will do nothing to dispel the "narrow-minded" label that many have pinned on me, since I will show you why I believe there cannot be two opinions on this issue. While some of my good friends disagree, my dogmatic assertion is that there is only the clear teaching of the Bible and the opinion of those who don't want to accept it.

We have already established that the phrase *"the sons of God"* only refers to angels in Job, which was written not long after the Flood. The only other time the phrase appears in the Old Testament is shortly before the Flood. If there WAS a "godly line of Seth," why don't some of these godly people get on the Ark? The only godly man God saw was Noah.

Carefully see that Genesis 6:1-2 forms a single sentence. Then, notice that the very grammatical structure of that sentence makes a distinction between the *"men"* who began to multiply on the face of the earth in verse 1, and *"the sons of God"* who took wives of the daughters of men in verse 2. The contrast makes *"the sons of God"* different from *"men."*

Another anomaly is that it is only the *"sons"* of Seth who marry the *"daughters"* of Cain, if we follow the popular reasoning. Why was there no mixture of sexes on both sides of the line? Why don't some of the DAUGHTERS of Seth marry some young men of Cain? Were the godly daughters of Seth so ugly that no son of Cain would marry them? When there is intermarriage of two groups of people, there is generally a mixture of sexes on both sides.

The conclusive proof offered by those who claim that *"the sons of God"* could not possibly be angels, is that angels are sexless. Everyone knows that! Why just look at all the Medieval art! Angels are cute little things with baby faces, wings, a halo, often floating on fluffy clouds playing a harp—but they are neuter! If they cite any biblical evidence, it is what Jesus said in Matthew 22:30. *"For in the resurrection they neither marry, nor are given in marriage, but are as the angels of God in heaven."*

A close look at this verse shows that it says nothing of the kind. This verse does NOT say angels are sexless. It only says that angels don't marry. Many unmarried people would highly object to the title of "sexless." Also, the reference here is to the *"angels of God in heaven,"* not the angels that came to earth shortly before the Flood.

Another problem with the "godly line of Seth" theory, is a phrase that appears in verse 4. *"There were giants in the earth in those days, AND AFTER THAT, when the sons of God came in unto the daughters of men, and they bare children to them, the same became mighty men which were of old, men of renown."* (Genesis 6:4) (Author's emphasis)

If the "godly line of Seth" was eliminated in the Flood, as God says, then how did these giants come about *"AFTER THAT?"* David established his fame by slaying a giant, who was a literal giant, not a figurative one. Examine the detailed and measured descriptions of giants in the following verses: Numbers 13:33; Deuteronomy 3:11; Joshua 17:15; 2 Samuel 21:16; 1 Chronicles 20:4. The best explanation is simply to believe what the Bible says—angels engaged in sexual relationships with human women, both before and after the Flood.

There are three passages in the New Testament that imply this sexual sin by angels. *"And the angels which kept not their first estate, but left their own habitation, he hath reserved in everlasting chains under darkness unto the judgment of the great day. Even as Sodom and Gomorrha, and the cities about them in like manner, giving themselves over to fornication, and going after strange flesh, are set forth for an example, suffering the vengeance of eternal fire."* (Jude 6-7)

This passage links the sin of these angels to the sexual sins of Sodom and Gomorrha, specifically *"going after strange flesh."* In Genesis 6 they are *"the sons of God."* Here, they are *"angels."*

There are references to this event in both of Peter's epistles. *"For Christ also hath once suffered for sins, the just for the unjust, that he might bring us to God, being put to death in the flesh, but quickened by the Spirit: By which also he went and preached unto the spirits in prison; Which sometime were disobedient, when once the longsuffering of God waited in the days of Noah, while the ark was a preparing, wherein few, that is, eight souls were saved by water."* (1 Peter 3:18-20)

Without getting into other questions raised by this passage, we will note that Christ preached to the *"spirits in prison."* The word *"spirits"* occurs without a qualifying adjective only to refer to angels or demons. Otherwise it is specified, such as "man's spirit," or "God's spirit."

The passage in Jude 6-7 spoke of imprisoned angels. 1 Peter 3:18-20 sets the time as *"when once the longsuffering of God waited in the days of Noah, while the ark was a preparing."*

Before leaving this passage, we must avoid the temptation to think that Christ's preaching to these imprisoned spirits is a second opportunity to be saved, as some have taught. 1 Peter 3:19 does NOT say He preached the Gospel to these spirits. The word translated here as *"preached"* means preaching in the sense of "proclamation," as in proclaiming His victory over the forces of hell, not "evangelizing."

Peter also speaks of this same incident in his second epistle. Again, these angels that sinned appear in the same context with the Flood and with Sodom and Gomorrha.

"For if God spared not the angels that sinned, but cast them down to hell, and delivered them into chains of darkness, to be reserved unto judgment; And spared not the old world, but saved Noah the eighth person, a preacher of righteousness, bringing in the flood upon the world of the ungodly; And turning the cities of Sodom and Gomorrha into ashes condemned them with an overthrow, making them an ensample unto those that after should live ungodly." (2 Peter 2:4-6)

When we simply believe what the Bible says, it is obvious that the sons of God are angels, some of whom sinned by cohabiting with human women both before and after the Flood, producing mutants of unusual size and strength. You can believe the theory of your choice, or you can accept at face value the clear statements of Scripture, confirmed no less than three times in the New Testament.

Believing the Bible, literally as it was written, will prepare you for the near future. Jesus said, *"But as the days of Noe were, so shall also the coming of the Son of man be. For as in the days that were before the flood they were eating and drinking, marrying and giving in marriage, until the day that Noe entered into the ark, And knew not until the flood came, and took them all away; so shall also the coming of the Son of man be."* (Matthew 24:37-39)

Could it really be possible that we will see a repeat of this visitation of *"the sons of God"* to earth in the last days before the Second Coming? Interpreting Nebuchadnezzar's dream, Daniel gives us this interesting information concerning the ten-nation revived Roman Empire of the Antichrist. *"And whereas thou sawest iron mixed with miry clay, THEY SHALL MINGLE THEMSELVES WITH THE SEED OF MEN: but they shall not cleave one to another, even as iron is not mixed with clay."* (Daniel 2:43) (Author's emphasis) This statement is admittedly enigmatic, but leaves room for thought in light of the other passages we have examined.

THE STATUS OF SATAN

This long detour I have taken has been to show that *"the sons of God"* are angels. With this background we return to our text. *"Now there was a day when the sons of God came to present themselves before the LORD, AND SATAN CAME ALSO AMONG THEM."* (Job 1:6) (Author's emphasis)

The word Satan comes from the Hebrew word for "adversary." The Greek equivalent is "Devil." This is precisely the description of the Devil.

"Be sober, be vigilant; because your adversary the devil, as a roaring lion, walketh about, seeking whom he may devour" (1 Peter 5:8)

Now we DO have a problem! How can the essence of evil, the very Devil, come into the presence of a holy God? Again, we are hampered by the images in our minds, planted there by what we have been taught, what we have always thought, or what we have imagined. Many imagine Satan coming boldly into the Holiest of Holies in the Heavenly Temple to stand in the presence of God Almighty. This is NOT necessarily what Job 1:6 says. The sons of God and Satan are coming *"before the Lord."* Often in the Old Testament God appears in the person of the pre-incarnate Christ, the second person of the Trinity. The voice of the Lord God walked with man in the Garden of Eden. (Genesis 3:8) The only "voice" that "walks" is the WORD of God. (John 1:1-3) The Lord appeared to Abraham in Genesis 18.

To say that Satan came before the Lord could mean he came into the presence of the Lord Christ during one of His appearances on earth or anywhere in the universe, not necessarily in the throne room of heaven. Even at that, there are many questions left unanswered by this scene. It could have even been before God's throne in Heaven! Let me acknowledge that I don't begin to understand all the many implications of this verse. I only ask you to keep an open mind, and not allow yourself to be locked into preconceived ideas. Wherever this exchange took place, God's opening question to Satan provides some interesting cross-references. *"And the LORD said unto Satan, Whence comest thou?"* (Job 1:7)

The Lord Jesus Christ asked a similar question of Judas when He was betrayed. *"And Jesus said unto him, Friend, wherefore art thou come? Then came they, and laid hands on Jesus, and took him."* (Matthew 26:50)

Pilate asked the Lord the same question. *"And went again into the judgment hall, and saith unto Jesus, Whence art thou? But Jesus gave him no answer."* (John 19:9)

This is exceedingly interesting, because Pilate KNEW where Jesus was from in an earthly sense. When they had first brought the Lord before him, Pilate would not deal with the case because he discovered that Jesus was from Galilee and therefore out of his jurisdiction. He sent him to Herod. (Luke 23:6-7)

Now, in John 19 Jesus again stands before Pilate due to the incredible events of those few hours. Pilate is in a quandary. He doesn't want to crucify Jesus. His wife has warned him about a dream she had, and begged him not to have anything to do with Jesus. Pilate has already spoken to the restless crowd outside, which is growing in number. Three times he declares to them that he has found no fault in Jesus. Jesus has confirmed to Pilate that He is King of the Jews, but that His kingdom is not of this world. All this is brewing in Pilate's head and heart when he retreats from the crowd to go again into the judgment hall where Jesus is being held. He is afraid—afraid of the Jews, and afraid that he is dealing with something far beyond his understanding. He has just one question for Jesus. *"Whence art thou?"* "Where are you REALLY from?" He knew that Jesus was from Galilee (Luke 23:6-7). This time the Lord does not answer. Soon, the One who knew no sin would become sin for us.

How ironic that God greets Satan with the same question. "Where are you coming from?"

The last half of verse 7 gives Satan's response.

7 "And the LORD said unto Satan, Whence comest thou? Then Satan answered the LORD, and said, From going to and fro in the earth, and from walking up and down in it." (Job 1:7)

This is the same information given in 1 Peter. *"Be sober, be vigilant; because your adversary the devil, as a roaring lion, WALKETH ABOUT, seeking whom he may devour"* (1 Peter 5:8) (Author's emphasis)

The earth is Satan's domain, his sphere of influence, his kingdom. *"In whom THE GOD OF THIS WORLD hath blinded the minds of them which believe not, lest the light of the glorious gospel of Christ, who is the image of God, should shine unto them."* (2 Corinthians 4:4) *"Wherein in time past ye walked according to the course of this world, according to THE PRINCE OF THE POWER OF THE AIR, the spirit that now worketh in the children of disobedience"* (Ephesians 2:2) (Author's emphasis)

In tempting Christ, the Devil offered the kingdoms of this world. *"Again, the devil taketh him up into an exceeding high mountain, and sheweth him all the kingdoms of the world, and the glory of them; And saith unto him, All these things will I give thee, if thou wilt fall down and worship me. Then saith Jesus unto him, Get thee hence, Satan: for it is written, Thou shalt worship the Lord thy God, and him only shalt thou serve."* (Matthew 4:8-10)

The Lord responded to the temptation with the Word of God, quoting from Deuteronomy, yet He never questioned Satan's claim to the kingdoms of this world. He knew that Satan is the god of this world, having taken the earth by virtue of Adam's sin.

In the ancient world, walking up and down through a piece of land with one's shoes on was a symbol of ownership. In Genesis 13 God tells Abram to walk through the land. God gave the land to him as a gift, and Abram was now to appropriate that land grant. *"Arise, walk through the land in the length of it and in the breadth of it; for I will give it unto thee."* (Genesis 13:17)

This principle of appropriation by walking with shoes on through the land also plays an important role in Joshua. Joshua receives his instructions from the Lord in the first chapter. *"Every place THAT THE SOLE OF YOUR FOOT SHALL TREAD UPON, that have I given unto you, as I said unto Moses."* (Joshua 1:3) (Author's emphasis) Even animals stake out the parameters of their territory.

This explains the strange command that Joshua receives from the *"captain of the LORD's host,"* who was the pre-incarnate Christ, when He appears to Joshua to instruct him about taking Jericho.

"And it came to pass, when Joshua was by Jericho, that he lifted up his eyes and looked, and, behold, there stood a man over against him with his sword drawn in his hand: and Joshua went unto him, and said unto him, Art thou for us, or for our adversaries? And he said, Nay; but as captain of the host of the LORD am I now come. And Joshua fell on his face to the earth, and did worship, and said unto him, What saith my lord unto his servant? And the captain of the LORD'S host said unto Joshua, Loose thy shoe from off thy foot; for the place whereon thou standest is holy. And Joshua did so." (Joshua 5:13-15)

God tells Moses the same thing in Exodus, when He appears to him out of the burning bush. *"And he said, Draw not nigh hither: put off thy shoes from off thy feet, for the place whereon thou standest is holy ground."* (Exodus 3:5) In both of these cases, Joshua and Moses were to take off their shoes to acknowledge that they were on holy ground, ground that did not belong to them.

In a spiritual sense, there is a great lesson here. Though you have been given *"all spiritual blessings in heavenly places in Christ"* (Ephesians 1:3), you will never possess more than your WALK appropriates. You must rise up and walk in the blessings God has given you.

In Job, Satan's walking to and fro, up and down in the earth, was a symbol of his ownership. The earth is Satan's sphere of operation. This, of course, does not nullify the sovereignty of God. God has allowed Satan's presence and control in this world, using him as His instrument. As Creator, God can remove this "squatter" any time He wishes. God paid the price and filed his deed when the Lord Jesus Christ died on the cross and triumphed by bursting forth from the tomb!

THE SUMMONS OF GOD

The next words God speaks to Satan are among the most incredible words ever recorded.

8 "And the LORD said unto Satan, Hast thou considered my servant Job, that there is none like him in the earth, a perfect

and an upright man, one that feareth God, and escheweth evil?" (Job 1:8)

Look at what is said! God mentions Job's name first! This is not Satan's challenge to God, this is God's challenge to Satan. God has confidence in Job. He says there is none like him *"in the earth,"* although there is one greater than him in Heaven—the Lord Jesus Christ. This shows that there is no temptation in our lives not allowed by God.

"There hath no temptation taken you but such as is common to man: but God is faithful, who will not suffer you to be tempted above that ye are able; but will with the temptation also make a way to escape, that ye may be able to bear it." (1 Corinthians 10:13) God is not going to allow you to be tempted above that you are able, because there is no temptation that He has not allowed.

Satan is merely God's delivery boy. He delivers our trials so that we might be made strong in the Lord. Consider Paul's *"thorn in the flesh."* Paul calls it *"the messenger of Satan." "And lest I should be exalted above measure through the abundance of the revelations, there was given to me a thorn in the flesh, the messenger of Satan to buffet me, lest I should be exalted above measure. For this thing I besought the Lord thrice, that it might depart from me. And he said unto me, My grace is sufficient for thee: for my strength is made perfect in weakness. Most gladly therefore will I rather glory in my infirmities, that the power of Christ may rest upon me. Therefore I take pleasure in infirmities, in reproaches, in necessities, in persecutions, in distresses for Christ's sake: for when I am weak, then am I strong."* (2 Corinthians 12:7-10)

Not only do we see that this thorn was Satan's messenger, we see how God used it (and Satan) to build up Paul in the grace of God. This is the same reason God allowed Satan to attack Job, and the same reason you and I have trials in this life.

Satan's answer to God in Job is caustic.

9 "Then Satan answered the LORD, and said, Doth Job fear God for nought?

10 Hast not thou made an hedge about him, and about his house, and about all that he hath on every side? thou hast blessed the work of his hands, and his substance is increased in the land.

11 But put forth thine hand now, and touch all that he hath, and he will curse thee to thy face." (Job 1:9-11)

In essence Satan is claiming that Job just serves God for what he can get. Why wouldn't Job serve God? Just look at the big house he lives in, the riches he has, his beautiful family. Take all that away, and Job will curse

God just like anyone else. This is Satan's line of argument. God has made a hedge about Job. Take away that hedge, and Job's world will come tumbling down. It won't be long before Job will curse God, Satan implies.

This is consistent with the picture of the Devil as the accuser of the righteous that we have in the Book of Revelation. *"And I heard a loud voice saying in heaven, Now is come salvation, and strength, and the kingdom of our God, and the power of his Christ: for the accuser of our brethren is cast down, which accused them before our God day and night."* (Revelation 12:10)

This glimpse into the realm of spiritual warfare should be a sobering reminder of the impact this unseen, ongoing war can have on our own lives. Whether or not we recognize it, this warfare touches our lives daily. More sobering still is God's response to Satan in the next verse.

12 "And the LORD said unto Satan, Behold, all that he hath is in thy power; only upon himself put not forth thine hand. So Satan went forth from the presence of the LORD." (Job 1:12)

God gives Satan permission to attack! God is saying, "Give him your best shot." In this case Satan only executes the options given directly by God, Who brought the issue up for discussion in the first place.

This insight is chilling. The immature believer might be genuinely frightened. To balance this, we must remember the following truth. *"Forasmuch then as the children are partakers of flesh and blood, he also himself likewise took part of the same; that through death he might destroy him that had the power of death, that is, the devil."* (Hebrews 2:14)

God only USES the Devil. Praise God, He can and DOES LIMIT the Devil! In this verse He places limits on what Satan can do. *"Only upon himself put not forth thine hand."* (Job 1:12)

CAMPAIGN OF SATAN

13 "And there was a day when his sons and his daughters were eating and drinking wine in their eldest brother's house:
14 And there came a messenger unto Job, and said, The oxen were plowing, and the asses feeding beside them:
15 And the Sabeans fell upon them, and took them away; yea, they have slain the servants with the edge of the sword; and I only am escaped alone to tell thee.

16 While he was yet speaking, there came also another, and said, The fire of God is fallen from heaven, and hath burned up the sheep, and the servants, and consumed them; and I only am escaped alone to tell thee.

17 While he was yet speaking, there came also another, and said, The Chaldeans made out three bands, and fell upon the camels, and have carried them away, yea, and slain the servants with the edge of the sword; and I only am escaped alone to tell thee.

18 While he was yet speaking, there came also another, and said, Thy sons and thy daughters were eating and drinking wine in their eldest brother's house:

19 And, behold, there came a great wind from the wilderness, and smote the four corners of the house, and it fell upon the young men, and they are dead; and I only am escaped alone to tell thee.

20 Then Job arose, and rent his mantle, and shaved his head, and fell down upon the ground, and worshipped,

21 And said, Naked came I out of my mother's womb, and naked shall I return thither: the LORD gave, and the LORD hath taken away; blessed be the name of the LORD.

22 In all this Job sinned not, nor charged God foolishly." (Job 1:13-22)

SATAN'S BLITZKRIEG

Satan marshals his forces, orders his attack, and sends it forth simultaneously in waves against the different segments of Job's vast holdings. In a matter of minutes, Job is going to receive word of an unimaginable calamity.

The first wave of attack begins.

13 "And there was a day when his sons and his daughters were eating and drinking wine in their eldest brother's house:

14 And there came a messenger unto Job, and said, The oxen were plowing, and the asses feeding beside them:

15 And the Sabeans fell upon them, and took them away; yea, they have slain the servants with the edge of the sword; and I only am escaped alone to tell thee." (Job 1:13-15)

The Sabeans came from Sheba, a grandson of Abraham, listed in Genesis 25:3. They are Satan's tool to destroy not only Job's oxen and asses, but also the servants working with them.

Before this lone servant can even finish providing Job the details of the attack, another servant arrives, torn and tattered.

16 "While he was yet speaking, there came also another, and said, The fire of God is fallen from heaven, and hath burned up the sheep, and the servants, and consumed them; and I only am escaped alone to tell thee." (Job 1:16)

The fire that falls from heaven reminds us again of the Tribulation aspect of this story. When the Jews are under attack in the Tribulation, the false prophet will bring down fire from heaven. "*And he doeth great wonders, so that he maketh fire come down from heaven on the earth in the sight of men.*" (Revelation 13:13) The false prophet will be attacking GOD'S sheep and servants.

The final remains of Job's empire vanish under another attack.

17 "While he was yet speaking, there came also another, and said, The Chaldeans made out three bands, and fell upon the camels, and have carried them away, yea, and slain the servants with the edge of the sword; and I only am escaped alone to tell thee." (Job 1:17)

The Chaldeans are the forerunners of the Babylonians. Babylon will also play a prominent role in the coming Tribulation. As a result of these disasters, Job goes from riches to rags in a matter of minutes. As if this were not enough to shake anyone's faith, the next news Job receives rocks him to the very core of his being.

18 "While he was yet speaking, there came also another, and said, Thy sons and thy daughters were eating and drinking wine in their eldest brother's house:

19 And, behold, there came a great wind from the wilderness, and smote the four corners of the house, and it fell upon the young men, and they are dead; and I only am escaped alone to tell thee." (Job 1:18-19)

The text says the great wind "*smote the four corners of the house,*" which would imply a tornado. Rather than a hurricane-like wind that blows from a single direction, those of us who live in Midwest know that what this servant describes is what actually happens in a tornado. Speaking of winds, remember that winds will also have a crucial part in the Tribulation. (Revelation 7:1) Again, we note the prophetic imagery of this book.

I have never lost a child. I have been with those who have. To imagine what it must be like to receive such news is beyond me. I have known people who have lost two children simultaneously in an accident. Again, I can't comprehend how horrible that must be. Job has just lost his entire fortune. Yet, before he can even digest the news, another runner arrives to tell him that all of his children are dead—ten children!

What were you saying about YOUR problems? I can't think of anyone, except Christ Himself, who has suffered to this degree—losing ALL he had. Even when I read the account in 2 Corinthians 11:23-28 of all Paul suffered, Job's case seems incomparably worse. Beat my body. Put me in jail. Deprive me of food. Betray me. Threaten me. But to tell me that ALL . . . ALL of my children have been wiped out in a single blow—that's a pain I wonder if I could bear.

JOB'S BACKBONE

Job's reaction is a graduate-level course for all of us about how to deal with calamity.

20 "Then Job arose, and rent his mantle, and shaved his head, and fell down upon the ground, and worshipped,

21 And said, Naked came I out of my mother's womb, and naked shall I return thither: the LORD gave, and the LORD hath taken away; blessed be the name of the LORD.

22 In all this Job sinned not, nor charged God foolishly." (Job 1:20-22)

Analyzing each element of this response, first notice Job's humility. Tearing his clothing, shaving his head and falling down on the ground was the proper Oriental way to express extreme humility and anguish.

Mordecai did the same when he learned of Haman's plot to exterminate the Jews. *"When Mordecai perceived all that was done, Mordecai rent his clothes, and put on sackcloth with ashes, and went out into the midst of the city, and cried with a loud and a bitter cry."* (Esther 4:1)

The absence of this reaction by His people provoked God to address them through His prophet, Micah. *"Make thee bald, and poll thee for thy delicate children; enlarge thy baldness as the eagle; for they are gone into captivity from thee."* (Micah 1:16)

Next, Job did a truly remarkable thing. He worshiped God. He did not complain. He did not question. He did not get angry. He worshipped the God of Heaven.

In churches we often speak of having an "11 o'clock worship service." Even in the best of churches, it rarely is a true worship service. The word "worship" first appears in Genesis 22, as Abraham is taking his beloved son, Isaac, up on the mountain to offer him as a sacrifice to God. Abraham doesn't understand God's plan any more than Job, but he determines to obey God. He says, *"Abide ye here with the ass; and I and the lad will go yonder and worship, and come again to you."* (Genesis 22:5)

To worship God is to meet with Him on such a level, and with such a sacrifice, that you come away from that experience totally transformed. Only when all the distractions of life have been stripped away can we meet with God to worship Him. The proper response when our life falls apart is to worship Him.

With humility and worship, Job opens his mouth to bless the name of the Lord. It is in this prudent and proper use of the tongue that Job can avoid its evil use to curse God. *"In all this Job sinned not, nor charged God foolishly."* (Job 1:22)

We could summarize Job's response by saying that he displayed the proper attitude and the proper control of his tongue. Our natural reaction in calamity is to affix blame with our mouth. God's alternative is to have us use our mouth to praise, worship and bless.

The Scripture has many examples of this teaching. Here are a few of them. *"In the multitude of words there wanteth not sin: but he that refraineth his lips is wise."* (Proverbs 10:19) *"The wicked is snared by the transgression of his lips: but the just shall come out of trouble."* (Proverbs 12:13) *"Whoso keepeth his mouth and his tongue keepeth his soul from troubles."* (Proverbs 21:23) This is why David prayed, *"Set a watch, O LORD, before my mouth; keep the door of my lips."* (Psalm 141:3)

Humility, worship, and using your mouth to bless, not to curse—this is the way to deal with calamity. It is not the world's way, but it is the biblical way. How would YOU handle calamity?

Could God have as much confidence in YOUR character as He did in Job's? This chapter is a tremendous challenge. If you want to ready yourself in the Word, and in your walk with God, so you can face any situation that life throws your way, you can make the example of Job a guide for your life.

3

WHEN LIFE FALLS APART

Then said his wife unto him, Dost thou still retain
thine integrity? curse God, and die.
But he said unto her, Thou speakest as one of the
foolish women speaketh. What? shall we receive
good at the hand of God, and shall we not receive evil?
In all this did not Job sin with his lips.

Job 2:9-10

JOB, THE MAN WHO HAD EVERYTHING, SITS ATOP THE SMOLDER-ing ruins of his life. In about the time it would take to empty the magazine of an automatic weapon, he learned that all he owned was lost. His live-stock, his holdings and his servants are gone. Before he can absorb that information, another messenger breathlessly tells him that his ten chil-dren have all died in a natural disaster.

Few men could handle this news with the grace displayed by Job. Many have put a bullet in their brain for far less. How would YOU handle such calamities?

Remember what we have already learned. Besides being a true story, Job paints a picture of the coming Tribulation. The story also gives us in-sight into the spiritual war that still rages. Job is a pawn in an exchange between God and Satan, and he does not even realize it.

There is another thing we must always remember in the study of this book: contrary to popular opinion, the book does NOT answer the ques-tion "Why do bad things happen to good people?" Often good people NEVER completely understand WHY tragedies like this happen. Though we can sometimes point to some good things God does through our trials, we often have questions that will never be fully answered. This book, and this chapter in particular, focuses on HOW TO DEAL WITH CALAMITY, or "what to do when life falls apart."

With what we saw in the previous chapter, you would think that Job has suffered all he can take. We saw in 1 Corinthians 10:13 that God will not tempt us more than we can bear. Surely Job has reached the limit of what he can bear! Not so. Round Two is ready to begin. Again, we are in God's presence to hear the continued dialogue between God and Satan.

CONTINUED DIALOGUE

1 "Again there was a day when the sons of God came to present themselves before the LORD, and Satan came also among them to present himself before the LORD.
2 And the LORD said unto Satan, From whence comest thou? And Satan answered the LORD, and said, From going to and fro in the earth, and from walking up and down in it.
3 And the LORD said unto Satan, Hast thou considered my servant Job, that there is none like him in the earth, a perfect and an upright man, one that feareth God, and escheweth evil? and still he holdeth fast his integrity, although thou movedst me against him, to destroy him without cause. (Job 2:1-3)

We have covered this ground before, in Job 1:6-7. The Lord's opening words to Satan in Job 2:3 are also the same up to the middle of the verse. *"And the LORD said unto Satan, Hast thou considered my servant Job, that there is none like him in the earth, a perfect and an upright man, one that feareth God, and escheweth evil?"* (Job 2:2-3a) Again, God brings up the subject of Job.

Now, the new material begins. God knows that Satan has attacked Job with fierce intensity, and says, *"and still he holdeth fast his integrity, although thou movedst me against him, to destroy him without cause."* (Job 2:3b)

A tiny phrase within this statement holds an important key for understanding the significance of all this—*"without cause."* This is a key phrase of Scripture. There are several such phrases that point to a particular truth each time they appear. This phrase, *"without cause,"* has a special, prophetic relationship to the Lord Jesus Christ.

Shortly before His crucifixion, the Lord gives His disciples instruction concerning the persecution they would surely receive. He points out that the servant is not greater than the master, and that if the world persecuted Him, it would persecute His disciples. Then, He explains that this is the fulfillment of Old Testament prophecy. *"But this cometh to pass, that the word might be fulfilled that is written in their law, They hated me WITHOUT A CAUSE."* (John 15:25) (Author's emphasis)

The words in the law that Jesus refers to are probably from Psalm 69. This psalm is without question a Messianic prophecy. Psalm 69:9 is the verse the disciples remembered when Jesus cleansed the Temple in John 2:13-17. Psalm 69:21 prophesies giving Him vinegar and gall when He was on the cross. Psalm 69:4 fulfills John 15:25. *"They that hate me without a cause are more than the hairs of mine head: they that would destroy me, being mine enemies wrongfully, are mighty: then I restored that which I took not away."* (Psalm 69:4)

Yet the Lord could just as well have been thinking of Psalm 35. *"Plead my cause, O LORD, with them that strive with me: fight against them that fight against me. Take hold of shield and buckler, and stand up for mine help. Draw out also the spear, and stop the way against them that persecute me: say unto my soul, I am thy salvation. Let them be confounded and put to shame that seek after my soul: let them be turned back and brought to confusion that devise my hurt. Let them be as chaff before the wind: and let the angel of the LORD chase them. Let their way be dark and slippery: and let the angel of the LORD persecute them. For WITHOUT CAUSE have they hid for me their net in a pit, which WITHOUT CAUSE they have digged for my soul."* (Psalm 35:1-7) (Author's emphasis)

Or, He could have had Psalm 109 in mind. *"Hold not thy peace, O God of my praise; For the mouth of the wicked and the mouth of the deceitful are opened against me: they have spoken against me with a lying tongue. They compassed me about also with words of hatred; and fought against me WITHOUT A CAUSE. For my love they are my adversaries: but I give myself unto prayer. And they have rewarded me evil for good, and hatred for my love."* (Psalm 109:1-5)

The truth of this prophecy, appearing three times in Psalms, was also verified by a lost man—Pontius Pilate. Three times in John (18:38 and 19:4,6) Pilate declared that he found no fault in Christ.

The significance of God's use of this same phrase in Job cannot be overstated. He is the Author of these words everywhere they appear in the Scripture. Every word He speaks is measured. There can be no serious doubt that God intends for Job to be a picture of the Lord Jesus Christ.

Consider also the fact that this same Devil would stand before One greater than Job almost two thousand years later. He would again be giving Him his best shot. He would be doing everything in his power to cause the sinless One to curse God, and he would be no more successful than he had been with Job.

There is an idea that we mentioned in the last chapter that bears repeating. Job pictures at least three things simultaneously—the Jew in Tribulation, Christ on the cross, and the lost man in hell. The Tribulation images thus far have been unmistakable. This cross-reference to Christ is also obvious. Very shortly the imagery of the lost man in hell will come through just as clearly.

Satan has a ready answer.

4 "And Satan answered the LORD, and said, Skin for skin, yea, all that a man hath will he give for his life.

5 But put forth thine hand now, and touch his bone and his flesh, and he will curse thee to thy face." (Job 2:4-5)

The Devil's words are caustic and sardonic, yet they are completely true. They can be historically documented. When a man's body comes under attack, when the pain level becomes intolerable, most men will do anything—betray their colleagues, betray their country, or even curse God.

Traveling in Romania shortly after the revolution of 1989, I heard much discussion among believers about how to handle those who had denied their faith under the pressure of torture. During the years of oppression many had held true to their faith, even while imprisoned and tortured. Others did not display the same strength.

Such a situation is not new. History tells of many soldiers of the cross who stood bravely in the face of unspeakable torture and excruciating pain. Literally millions have died as martyrs for their faith. Yet there have been countless others who have buckled under such pain.

Permission is granted for Satan to take Job through the "chamber of horrors." Again we see that nothing happens without God's permission. The only limitation is for Satan to spare Job's life.

6 "And the LORD said unto Satan, Behold, he is in thine hand; but save his life." (Job 2:6)

Be careful not to miss the devil's objective. Satan believes he can get Job to curse God to His face.

In the midst of the tremendous doctrinal and prophetic gems that appear in this passage, there are some vital lessons for every believer to learn and apply to life. We must constantly bear in mind that there are things that happen to us "without cause," simply because God has given Satan permission to try our faith.

The proper response for the New Testament believer is that given by Peter. *"For what glory is it, if, when ye be buffeted for your faults, ye shall take it patiently? but if, when ye do well, and suffer for it, ye take it patiently, this is acceptable with God. For even hereunto were ye called: because Christ also suffered for us, leaving us an example, that ye should follow his steps: Who did no sin, neither was guile found in his mouth: Who, when he was reviled, reviled not again; when he suffered, he threatened not; but committed himself to him that judgeth righteously."* (1 Peter 2:20-23)

This passage is a textbook on how to suffer biblically. We must first be certain that we are suffering *"without cause."* Many believers are suffering from the consequences of their own sin.

Notice in the above 1 Peter passage the connection to keeping the mouth free from sin—*"neither was guile found in his mouth . . . reviled not again . . . he threatened not."*

We saw this in Job's response in the previous chapter. *"Then Job arose, and rent his mantle, and shaved his head, and fell down upon the ground, and worshipped, And said, Naked came I out of my mother's womb, and naked shall I return thither: the LORD gave, and the LORD hath taken away; blessed be the name of the LORD. In all this Job sinned not, nor charged God foolishly."* (Job 1:20-22)

The other essential element of a biblical response seen in 1 Peter is an unshaken commitment to the righteousness of God, *"but committed himself to him that judgeth righteously."* (1 Peter 2:23)

Is this how YOU handle calamity in your life? It is definitely not your natural response. It CAN be your response, if you turn to God in the time of trouble to lay hold of His matchless grace. You may never understand the "WHY" of your trouble, but Job and Jesus give us the example of "HOW" to respond.

Job's response to Satan's attack is as solid as the foundation of a mighty "skyscraper." It is precisely this solid, well-anchored response that enables Job later to reach "new heights" that few men have reached.

"After this opened Job his mouth, and cursed his day. And Job spake, and said, Let the day perish wherein I was born, and the night in which it was said, There is a man child conceived." (Job 3:1-3)

Satan's objective was for Job to curse God to His face. Instead, Job curses the day of his birth. Even when chided by his wife, he refuses to curse God.

CONCENTRATED ATTACK

7 "So went Satan forth from the presence of the LORD, and smote Job with sore boils from the sole of his foot unto his crown.

8 And he took him a potsherd to scrape himself withal; and he sat down among the ashes." (Job 2:7-8)

Armed with God's permission, it doesn't take Satan long to launch his attack on Job's body. It has been difficult to imagine all Job suffered with the loss of his wealth and his ten children. To add this physical attack seems beyond comprehension. Remember that none of this could have happened without God's permission.

Job has lost everything, including his good health. From head to toe his body is covered with boils. Don't miss the Tribulation aspect of this physical condition. When Moses explained to Israel the consequences of disobedience, he gave them a somber warning. *"Then the LORD will make thy plagues wonderful, and the plagues of thy seed, even great plagues, and of long continuance, and sore sicknesses, and of long continuance. Moreover he will bring upon thee all the diseases of Egypt, which thou wast afraid of; and they shall cleave unto thee. Also every sickness, and every plague, which is not written in the book of this law, them will the LORD bring upon thee, until thou be destroyed."* (Deuteronomy 28:58-61)

In a literal, yet future, sense, the final fulfillment of this is what we find in Revelation 16. *"And the first went, and poured out his vial upon the earth; and there fell a noisome and grievous sore upon the men which had the mark of the beast, and upon them which worshipped his image."* (Revelation 16:2)

I am not suggesting that this physical attack against Job was the consequence of his disobedience, or that he is a type of those who take the mark of the Beast. This was the unfounded theory of his three counselors, as we will see in great detail.

The point here in this passage is merely to see another Tribulation element that appears in the story of Job. When an Old Testament story, character or object foreshadows a New Testament truth, it does not necessarily mean that every detail corresponds. Some types or pictures are more complete than others. One of the features of the book of Job is the way it presents Tribulation images, yet not every detail of Job is a picture of the Tribulation.

In the time of the Exodus, one of the ten plagues against Egypt was boils upon the Egyptian men. Exodus is a prophetic book, in the sense that it points to many events of the Tribulation shortly before the Second Coming. The plagues upon Egypt reappear in the Book of Revelation. When Job is covered with boils, he curses the day of his birth. In the Tribulation, men who receive this plague of boils curse God and die. *"And blasphemed the God of heaven because of their pains and their sores, and repented not of their deeds."* (Revelation 16:11) Job is one in a million.

From a purely human viewpoint, it is hard to see how Job's condition could be more miserable. He scrapes his oozing sores with a potsherd (a piece of broken pottery), and sits down *"among the ashes."* In the Bible this action of sitting down among the ashes is symbolic of abject grief.

In predicting the ruin of Tyre, Ezekiel spoke of the reaction of Tyre's inhabitants. *"And shall cause their voice to be heard against thee, and shall cry bitterly, and shall cast up dust upon their heads, they shall wallow themselves in the ashes."* (Ezekiel 27:30)

When Jonah finally got God's message to Nineveh, the king reacted with the proper attitude of repentance. *"For word came unto the king of Nineveh, and he arose from his throne, and he laid his robe from him, and covered him with sackcloth, and sat in ashes."* (Jonah 3:6)

Job has been reduced to ashes. In his case, however, it is through no fault of his own. Who has possibly fallen farther, faster? Could this be the same man described in Job 1:3?

"His substance also was seven thousand sheep, and three thousand camels, and five hundred yoke of oxen, and five hundred she asses, and a very great household; so that this man was the greatest of all the men of the east." (Job 1:3)

Before leaving this section, we must make an important distinction. Although Satan attacks Job's body, not all sickness is the result of Satanic attack. There are other causes of sickness in the Bible.

While Job's boils are definitely the result of supernatural attack, sin is another valid biblical reason we sometimes get sick. This was the warning God gave to His people in the time of the Exodus.

"And said, If thou wilt diligently hearken to the voice of the LORD thy God, and wilt do that which is right in his sight, and wilt give ear to his commandments, and keep all his statutes, I will put none of these diseases upon thee, which I have brought upon the Egyptians: for I am the LORD that healeth thee." (Exodus 15:26)

Sometimes we get sick simply because we violate principles of natural law. Adding sugar to the gas tank of your car will cause serious problems. In like manner, chewing on lead-based paint can have terrible consequences for a baby. A steady diet of pizza three times a day will not provide your body with the nutrients needed to maintain good health.

In John 9 there is the story of Jesus healing a man who had been blind from birth. Like Job's counselors, Jesus' disciples were certain there must be sin somewhere. Yet this sickness was for the glory of God.

"And as Jesus passed by, he saw a man which was blind from his birth. And his disciples asked him, saying, Master, who did sin, this man, or his parents, that he was born blind? Jesus answered, Neither hath this man

sinned, nor his parents: but that the works of God should be made manifest in him." (John 9:1-3)

There are times when God uses sickness as His instrument to bring us close to Him. This was Paul's experience.

"And lest I should be exalted above measure through the abundance of the revelations, there was given to me a thorn in the flesh, the messenger of Satan to buffet me, lest I should be exalted above measure. For this thing I besought the Lord thrice, that it might depart from me. And he said unto me, My grace is sufficient for thee: for my strength is made perfect in weakness. Most gladly therefore will I rather glory in my infirmities, that the power of Christ may rest upon me. Therefore I take pleasure in infirmities, in reproaches, in necessities, in persecutions, in distresses for Christ's sake: for when I am weak, then am I strong." (2 Corinthians 12:7-10)

There is yet another reason for sickness. Sometimes God uses sickness as a way to get us to Heaven.

There is much bad teaching on sickness today. Some believe that every time we get sick, we are out of God's will. They look for the sin in our lives that brought on the illness.

Others go further. They find demonic influence in all sickness. They rebuke the "flu demon," cast out the "sore throat demon," and command the "demon of cancer" to leave.

As well-meaning as such individuals may be, they show their ignorance of Scripture. There are plainly several possible causes of sickness in the Bible. Job was attacked by the Devil in a physical way. You may, or may not be similarly attacked.

CHILLING COUNSEL

9 "Then said his wife unto him, Dost thou still retain thine integrity? curse God, and die.

10 But he said unto her, Thou speakest as one of the foolish women speaketh. What? shall we receive good at the hand of God, and shall we not receive evil? In all this did not Job sin with his lips." (Job 2:9-10)

Just about the time we think Job has endured as much as is humanly possible, we see that Satan has not finished. What more could happen to Job? He has lost his earthly possessions, lost his ten children simultaneously, and sits on an ash heap covered from head to toe with repugnant, oozing, raw boils. Is it really conceivable that anything else could happen?

Job's condition reminds me of what God said about Israel in Isaiah 1. There was nothing more God could do to Israel than what He had already done.

"Why should ye be stricken any more? ye will revolt more and more: the whole head is sick, and the whole heart faint. From the sole of the foot even unto the head there is no soundness in it; but wounds, and bruises, and putrefying sores: they have not been closed, neither bound up, neither mollified with ointment. Your country is desolate, your cities are burned with fire: your land, strangers devour it in your presence, and it is desolate, as overthrown by strangers. And the daughter of Zion is left as a cottage in a vineyard, as a lodge in a garden of cucumbers, as a besieged city." (Isaiah 1:5-8)

God is saying, "I have beaten you from the top of your head to the bottom of your feet. There's no place left to hit you!"

Job is in the same condition. What's left for Satan to hit? Only one spot remains, and that is precisely where the Devil takes his aim. At the precise moment Job needs some encouragement, some tender loving care from his "help meet," from his life partner, just look at what comes out of his wife's mouth. *"Then said his wife unto him, Dost thou still retain thine integrity? curse God, and die."* (Job 2:9)

Isn't this all he needs? His own wife lashes out at him with poison on her tongue. In the third verse God pointed out to the Devil that Job still held fast to his integrity. Now, it is his wife who prods him to drop this integrity, curse God and die. Who do you suppose has been talking to her? She even uses the same vocabulary from the debate between God and Satan.

When the man will not fall despite repeated blows, Satan makes a beeline for the man's weakest link—his commitment to a woman. Here, Job's wife reminds us of another famous wife who led her husband to sin—Eve.

Unsuccessful in getting to us, the Devil will zero in on those closest to us. In Matthew 16 Peter was used as the Devil's instrument immediately after confessing Christ to be the Son of the living God.

Adam's wife tempted him to sin. Job's wife tempted him to sin. In the Tribulation there will be a false bride of Christ, the church of the Antichrist, which will induce men to sin. (Revelation 17:1-6)

None of us can imagine Job's grief and anguish. Just as Job's sufferings are infinitely removed from our experience, they are infinitely less than the suffering endured by the One Job foreshadows, the Lord Jesus Christ.

Our Lord was falsely accused (like Job), beaten to a bloody pulp and exhausted, and large spikes were driven through His hands and feet. His body hanging limp from the cross, fighting for every breath, our Savior furthermore had to endure the weight of the world's sin. What more indignation could He possibly suffer?

"And they that passed by reviled him, wagging their heads, And saying, Thou that destroyest the temple, and buildest it in three days, save thyself. If thou be the Son of God, come down from the cross. Likewise also the chief priests mocking him, with the scribes and elders, said, He saved others; himself he cannot save. If he be the King of Israel, let him now come down from the cross, and we will believe him. He trusted in God; let him deliver him now, if he will have him: for he said, I am the Son of God. The thieves also, which were crucified with him, cast the same in his teeth." (Matthew 27:39-44)

To hear words of scorn from his wife must have hurt Job almost as much as the scorn hurt by Christ as He hung on the cross. Yet Job's response was correct, and worthy to be our example. *"But he said unto her, Thou speakest as one of the foolish women speaketh. What? shall we receive good at the hand of God, and shall we not receive evil? In all this did not Job sin with his lips."* (Job 2:10)

Job does not understand why he is suffering, but he DOES understand God. He has placed his faith firmly in the sovereignty of God. The meaning, although not Job's exact words, echo through the centuries, and find expression through the mouth of Jeremiah, as he laments the destruction of Jerusalem. *"Who is he that saith, and it cometh to pass, when the Lord commandeth it not? Out of the mouth of the most High proceedeth not evil and good? Wherefore doth a living man complain, a man for the punishment of his sins? Let us search and try our ways, and turn again to the LORD. Let us lift up our heart with our hands unto God in the heavens."* (Lamentations 3:37-41) Jeremiah gives us a classic example of how the Old Testament saint responded to tragedy.

As New Testament believers, we have received concrete instruction from the Apostle Paul about how we should respond to the things in our lives we don't fully understand.

"And we know that all things work together for good to them that love God, to them who are the called according to his purpose." (Romans 8:28)

Though we do not understand the reason for the things that happen to us, we can be certain that God will use them for good. However, there IS a condition—if we are firm in our love for Him, and in our commitment to conform to His purpose. Sometimes, this is the ONLY option available to us in the dark moments of life.

These words in Romans were not mere theory to Paul. He lived them. When he was imprisoned in Rome, he could not possibly understand all that God was doing. Even in his imprisonment, people took advantage of him, taunted him, and tried to make things worse. He explains both the situation and his response to it to the Philippians.

"Some indeed preach Christ even of envy and strife; and some also of good will: The one preach Christ of contention, not sincerely, supposing to add affliction to my bonds: But the other of love, knowing that I am set for the defence of the gospel. What then? notwithstanding, every way, whether in pretence, or in truth, Christ is preached; and I therein do rejoice, yea, and will rejoice." (Philippians 1:15-18)

Paul didn't know everything that was happening. Yet he knew that as long as he kept his focus on the preaching of Christ, God would see to the details, whatever the intentions of his enemies might be.

With an economy of words, James put the Book of Job into proper perspective. *"Behold, we count them happy which endure. Ye have heard of the patience of Job, and have seen the end of the Lord; that the Lord is very pitiful, and of tender mercy."* (James 5:11)

Job NEVER understood all that happened to him, but he patiently endured. The key is to see *"the end of the Lord."* In other words, we are to focus our attention on the Lord's end—His purpose, and not our own.

God had a purpose in all that was happening in Job's life, even though Job did not understand it all. We must remember that God also has a purpose in the things that happen to us. With our complete Bible, we have an advantage that Job never had. Though we still will not understand all the details and how it all fits together, we can hold to the words that Paul wrote to the Romans. These words don't explain the details, but they help us see God's end.

"And not only so, but we glory in tribulations also: knowing that tribulation worketh patience; And patience, experience; and experience, hope: And hope maketh not ashamed; because the love of God is shed abroad in our hearts by the Holy Ghost which is given unto us." (Romans 5:3-5)

COMMITTED FRIENDS

11 "Now when Job's three friends heard of all this evil that was come upon him, they came every one from his own place; Eliphaz the Temanite, and Bildad the Shuhite, and Zophar

the Naamathite: for they had made an appointment together to come to mourn with him and to comfort him.

12 And when they lifted up their eyes afar off, and knew him not, they lifted up their voice, and wept; and they rent every one his mantle, and sprinkled dust upon their head toward heaven.

13 So they sat down with him upon the ground seven days and seven nights, and none spake a word unto him: for they saw that his grief was very great." (Job 2:11-13)

Job had been a man of incredible wealth. Besides his riches, he had something money could not buy—three friends! Life's disasters help us to know who our friends really are. Undoubtedly Job had many more "friends" before his money disappeared.

It has been said that a man can have many "acquaintances," but is rich indeed if he has two or three friends. Despite their harmful counsel, at least they cared enough to come and sit with Job in the ashes for seven days.

Most of us have a problem keeping our mouths shut. These men did it for seven days. This was not that unusual in ancient culture, but it is still remarkable to think of caring enough to sit with someone for seven days without saying anything.

When Ezekiel arrived as God's messenger to the Jews in captivity, he did the same thing. *"Then I came to them of the captivity at Telabib, that dwelt by the river of Chebar, and I sat where they sat, and remained there astonished among them seven days."* (Ezekiel 3:15)

A great problem in offering help to those in need today is thinking that we have to SAY something. Part of my job as a pastor has involved visiting with people in moments of disaster—those moments when life falls apart. Early in my ministry I felt an artificial obligation to say something. I imagined that it was my job to offer great pearls of wisdom that would magically transform the moment, and cause the cloud of doom to blow away with the freshness of my wisdom.

I have learned that often the best response to those in the midst of great pain is wordless. Most people in time of calamity are neither in any state of mind to listen well nor are they capable of rational thinking. The greatest message we can give at such a time is that we genuinely care. There is no way that we could ever explain all that God is doing through these difficult times, so why try? Later, there will be a time for talk, a time for questions, and time to reinforce biblical truth. Initially, the best response is often with the mouth shut.

The purpose Job's friends had in coming is stated in verse 11. They had come *"to mourn with him and to comfort him."* From a human standpoint, we can imagine that their intentions were the best. However, once they all began to collectively share their ignorance about why they thought all this had befallen Job, things began to deteriorate rapidly. This is not unlike what happens at many committee meetings!

Verse 12 contains a remarkable statement. As they drew near to their old friend, they looked directly at Job, yet they *"knew him not."* Job's physical condition, aggravated by his grief, had twisted his features so that he was beyond recognition, even by his friends.

Years ago I came back to the United States for a short visit from our home in El Salvador. I received news that the pastor who had baptized me and been my mentor in the early years of my ministry was dying of a brain cancer. I arranged my travel plans to visit him in his hospital room.

Though this man had been like a father to me, I would never have recognized him! His head was swollen to twice its normal size and his features were marred beyond my recognition. I will never forget the initial shock of seeing him in that miserable condition. Job's friends must have experienced the same feeling.

Remember that something far deeper is being pictured here. We must never lose sight of the fact that Job represents several pictures simultaneously—the Jew in Tribulation, lost man in hell, and Christ on the cross. Consider the prophecy of Isaiah as he looked through the ages and saw Christ on the cross after His repeated beatings. *"As many were astonied at thee; his visage was so marred more than any man, and his form more than the sons of men."* (Isaiah 52:14)

In keeping with the Tribulation theme that underlies the book of Job, we can say that the seven days and seven nights Job's friends sat with him figuratively points to the seven years of Tribulation, as we discussed in the first chapter.

Even assuming these historical men had the best of intentions, their appearance and tormenting words must point to corresponding figures in the Tribulation. Whom could these three men represent prophetically? Interestingly enough, there is a satanic trinity that appears during the Tribulation as revealed in the Book of Revelation. This is pure speculation on my part, but it is interesting to see again in Revelation the appearance of three characters who torment with pious words, as though they were God's representatives.

The satanic trinity I refer to appears in Revelation 13, where we first see the Antichrist (called the "beast"), the false prophet (the other beast), and the Dragon (also defined as "Satan" and the "Devil" in Revelation 12:9). It is in Revelation 16 that we learn that these individuals are empowered by demonic spirits, who give them miraculous powers to amaze men and thereby bring men under their spell, setting up the campaign of Armageddon. *"And I saw three unclean spirits like frogs come out of the mouth of the dragon, and out of the mouth of the beast, and out of the mouth of the false prophet. For they are the spirits of devils, working miracles, which go forth unto the kings of the earth and of the whole world, to gather them to the battle of that great day of God Almighty."* (Revelation 16:13-14)

Like the trio in the Book of Job, they channel men into God's wrath by deceiving them with signs and wonders. Also like in Job, they will give the appearance of being God's ambassadors. Even if Job's friends serve the Devil's purpose, this does not detract from their sincerity in an historical sense. The Devil very rapidly can use even the most sincere humans as his instruments.

In Matthew 16 Peter had just made his great confession of faith—*"And Simon Peter answered and said, Thou art the Christ, the Son of the living God."* (Matthew 16:16) Moments later, Satan took over control of Peter's mind and mouth, prompting him to rebuke the Lord for speaking of the coming crucifixion. The Lord Jesus turned around, looked squarely in Peter's eyes, and rebuked THE DEVIL in Peter.

"But he turned, and said unto Peter, Get thee behind me, Satan: thou art an offence unto me: for thou savourest not the things that be of God, but those that be of men." (Matthew 16:23)

We have already observed how quickly Satan moved in on Job's wife, using her as his tool in his continued campaign against Job. When her counsel to *"curse God and die"* failed, Satan quickly altered his plan and used Job's friends.

These three friends of Job have come to mourn with him and comfort him. Very soon, and probably without awareness on their part, they also became spokesmen for the very Devil, speaking 99% truth, with just enough error mixed in to prompt Job to collapse under the weight of their words, curse God and die. Job weakens, his knees buckle and quiver, and he comes to the very edge, yet he still holds fast to his integrity. He does NOT curse God, nor does he admit to some "secret sin."

In the Tribulation, the three figures that form the satanic trinity play a prominent role in provoking men to sin. They do this through fair and reasonable words, through signs and wonders, and through the power of the demonic spirits that control them. Like Eve, like Job's wife, and like Job's three friends, they are used as the Devil's instruments.

Another phrase in verse 11 is worthy of comment. Announcing the arrival of the three friends, the text says *"they came every one from his own place."* This same phrase is employed to speak of the destination of Judas Iscariot.

In the first chapter of Acts, Peter calls attention to the vacancy in the Twelve left by the suicide of Judas. Two men are chosen who have been with the apostles from the beginning of Jesus' ministry. Peter leads them in prayer, asking God to show them which of the two he has chosen.

"And they prayed, and said, Thou, Lord, which knowest the hearts of all men, shew whether of these two thou hast chosen, That he may take part of this ministry and apostleship, from which Judas by transgression fell, that he might go TO HIS OWN PLACE." (Acts 1:24-25) (Author's emphasis)

Judas Iscariot was an individual who allowed himself to become not only the instrument of the Devil, but allowed himself to become inhabited by the Devil. See what Jesus said about him. These are strong words!

"Jesus answered them, Have not I chosen you twelve, and one of you is a devil? He spake of Judas Iscariot the son of Simon: for he it was that should betray him, being one of the twelve." (John 6:70-71)

Later Christ would say in His prayer to the Father, *"While I was with them in the world, I kept them in thy name: those that thou gavest me I have kept, and none of them is lost, but the son of perdition; that the scripture might be fulfilled."* (John 17:12)

The significance of calling Judas the *"son of perdition"* is that the same phrase also designates the Antichrist. Paul writes to the Thessalonians using the same phrase.

"Let no man deceive you by any means: for that day shall not come, except there come a falling away first, and that man of sin be revealed, THE SON OF PERDITION; Who opposeth and exalteth himself above all that is called God, or that is worshipped; so that he as God sitteth in the temple of God, shewing himself that he is God." (2 Thessalonians 2:3-4) (Author's emphasis)

In the middle of the Tribulation, a strange thing occurs. John describes demonic monsters released from the bottomless pit. *"And they had a king over them, which is the angel of the bottomless pit, whose name in the Hebrew tongue is Abaddon, but in the Greek tongue hath his name Apollyon."* (Revelation 9:11) The same Greek word *"apollyon"* is the one translated *"perdition"* in 2 Thessalonians 2:3.

Could Judas Iscariot, totally possessed by the Devil and called the *"son of perdition"* by Christ, be reserved *"in his own place"* to come forth again in the Tribulation? Is God signaling another Tribulation parallel in the Book of Job by telling us that these three friends came *"every one from his own place?"* (Job 2:11)

These and many other questions and speculations await us as we continue our adventures in the land of Uz. We must be careful to hold fast to those things that can be proven and allow God to expand our thinking in those things that tantalize our thoughts and stretch us. Many questions will remain unanswered. Yet, again we remember the theme of this fascinating book—that there are many things in this present life that will remain unanswered. Our responsibility is to deal with them biblically, hold fast to our integrity, and commit our lives to Him that judges righteously.

4

MAN WITHOUT A CLUE

For the thing which I greatly feared is come upon me,

and that which I was afraid of

is come unto me.

Job 3:25

JOB HASN'T MOVED. HIS LIFE HAS SHATTERED LIKE A CHINA CUP on a tile floor. His clothes torn, and his shaved head covered with hideous sores that stretch down to the soles of his feet, Job picks up a broken piece of pottery from the ash heap where he sits. He uses it to scrape at layers of scab, pus and dirt all over his body.

For seven days he has sat expressionless, numb from the incalculable pain of simultaneously losing his children and all he owned. Three friends have come to mourn with him and to comfort him. They have not said a word because there are no real answers. Silently, they sit through seven sunsets, while no one dares to speak. Yet Job's friends can't help coming to certain conclusions as they continually review the circumstances in their minds.

Job is a man without a clue about why all this has happened. His grief is so great he cannot speak. There is no one to blame, no excuses to give.

From an unseen vantage point, untold numbers of spectators watch the drama with great interest. Much more is at stake than Job's life. God has challenged the Devil to test Job's integrity. Satan has retorted that Job will curse God to His face. Angels and demons alike stand breathlessly awaiting Job's first words.

For seven long days and nights, Job has uttered not a word since he answered his wife's urging to curse God and die. *"But he said unto her,*

Thou speakest as one of the foolish women speaketh. What? shall we receive good at the hand of God, and shall we not receive evil? In all this did not Job sin with his lips." (Job 2:10)

How much more can he take? Usually when a man is left without a clue as to the reason for his tragedy, he curses God. This is why Satan had been so confident in accepting God's challenge.

Seven days have come and gone. Suddenly, there is movement. Job is lifting his head. He is moving his mouth as if to speak. His friends train their eyes upon him, as thousands of spirit-beings gaze steadily earthward. Will Job curse God?

JOB CURSES HIS DAY

1 "After this opened Job his mouth, and cursed his day.
2 And Job spake, and said,
3 Let the day perish wherein I was born, and the night in which it was said, There is a man child conceived.
4 Let that day be darkness; let not God regard it from above, neither let the light shine upon it.
5 Let darkness and the shadow of death stain it; let a cloud dwell upon it; let the blackness of the day terrify it.
6 As for that night, let darkness seize upon it; let it not be joined unto the days of the year, let it not come into the number of the months.
7 Lo, let that night be solitary, let no joyful voice come therein.
8 Let them curse it that curse the day, who are ready to raise up their mourning.
9 Let the stars of the twilight thereof be dark; let it look for light, but have none; neither let it see the dawning of the day:
10 Because it shut not up the doors of my mother's womb, nor hid sorrow from mine eyes." (Job 3:1-10)

Job doesn't curse God; he curses the day of his birth! He still holds fast to his integrity. The third chapter of Job is a monologue in which Job gives us the first indication of what is going through his mind in response to his incredible calamity. It is also a chapter filled with fascinating prophetic utterance and symbol, tracing the book's role as a picture of the future Tribulation.

The last phrase of Job 3:3, *"There is a man child conceived,"* points us to a similar phrase in Revelation 12: *"And there appeared a great wonder in heaven; a woman clothed with the sun, and the moon under her feet, and upon her head a crown of twelve stars: And she being with child cried, travailing in birth, and pained to be delivered. And there appeared another wonder in heaven; and behold a great red dragon, having seven heads and ten horns, and seven crowns upon his heads. And his tail drew the third part of the stars of heaven, and did cast them to the earth: and the dragon stood before the woman which was ready to be delivered, for to devour her child as soon as it was born. And she brought forth a man child, who was to rule all nations with a rod of iron: and her child was caught up unto God, and to his throne."* (Revelation 12:1-5)

The symbolism in Revelation 12 is too close to the dream of Joseph in Genesis 37:9 to be coincidence. *"And he dreamed yet another dream, and told it his brethren, and said, Behold, I have dreamed a dream more; and, behold, the sun and the moon and the eleven stars made obeisance to me."* (Genesis 37:9)

Joseph is a beautiful type of Christ, and the man God used to preserve Jacob and his other eleven sons so that the twelve tribes of Israel could flourish into a nation. There are eleven stars in Genesis 37, as opposed to twelve in Revelation 12, because Joseph is one of the stars, and he is doing the talking. Revelation 12 tells us that the woman is a symbol ("wonder"), and she gives birth to a *"male child."*

The *"male child"* of Revelation 12 has an obvious reference to the Lord Jesus Christ, since He will *"rule all nations with a rod of iron"* (Revelation 12:5), as prophesied in Psalm 2:9. Israel is consistently symbolized by the figure of a woman, the wife of Jehovah, in the Old Testament. (Isaiah 54:1-6; Jeremiah 3:1-14)

Yet something else is happening in Revelation 12. As is common in biblical prophecy, there is a double fulfillment. The *"man child"* is also a picture of Israel's spiritual rebirth in the 144,000 witnesses, 12,000 from each tribe. This symbolic use of painful birth in tribulation is common among the prophets.

Isaiah saw this day when Israel would come to life: *"Before she travailed, she brought forth; before her pain came, she was delivered of a man child. Who hath heard such a thing? who hath seen such things? Shall the earth be made to bring forth in one day? or shall a nation be born at once? for as soon as Zion travailed, she brought forth her children."* (Isaiah 66:7-8)

Jeremiah also saw a strange picture: *"Ask ye now, and see whether a man doth travail with child? wherefore do I see every man with his hands on his loins, as a woman in travail, and all faces are turned into paleness? Alas! for that day is great, so that none is like it: it is even the time of Jacob's trouble; but he shall be saved out of it. For it shall come to pass in that day, saith the LORD of hosts, that I will break his yoke from off thy neck, and will burst thy bonds, and strangers shall no more serve themselves of him: But they shall serve the LORD their God, and David their king, whom I will raise up unto them."* (Jeremiah 30:6-9)

Jeremiah himself is a prophetic picture of the 144,000 Jewish witnesses in the time of the Tribulation. Jeremiah is the only man in the Bible specifically commanded by God not to marry (Jeremiah 16:2), and he corresponds to these 144,000 witnesses.

"These are they which were not defiled with women; for they are virgins. These are they which follow the Lamb whithersoever he goeth. These were redeemed from among men, being the firstfruits unto God and to the Lamb." (Revelation 14:4)

Putting this information together makes it even more significant that Jeremiah utters a cry very similar to Job's words.

"Cursed be the day wherein I was born: let not the day wherein my mother bare me be blessed. Cursed be the man who brought tidings to my father, saying, A man child is born unto thee; making him very glad." (Jeremiah 20:14-15)

"Wherefore came I forth out of the womb to see labour and sorrow, that my days should be consumed with shame?" (Jeremiah 20:18)

The similarity of these words is striking, and totally lost on those who fail to see the Tribulation application of Job. Even Jeremiah's name means "Jehovah will cast out." The weeping prophet also suffered unspeakable tribulation, making him a fitting type of Israel in Tribulation, just like Job.

Yet in the midst of such prophetic riches, we must not fail to remember the great truth of the historical battle between God and the Devil. Job does NOT curse God. He curses the day he was born. Please don't think that such a statement would imply a lapse of faith, or root of bitterness. If you had suffered what Job suffered, what would YOU have said? Would YOU still hold fast to your integrity, and keep you lips from sinning?

The key phrase in Job 3:3, *"a man child conceived,"* led us into a discussion of the various prophetic implications. There is another key phrase in Job 3:4 that we must consider—*"that day."* Whenever it appears in Scripture, it refers directly or indirectly to that coming day when the Lord Jesus Christ will return to this earth in judgment, and establish His kingdom. It is sometimes called *"the day of the LORD."*

Look at what Job says about that day. Historically, Job is referring is to the day of his birth. Yet just as the message of Job 3:1-2 transcended

Job's birthday to point to a future fulfillment, so do these words that follow.

A DAY OF DARKNESS

3 "Let the day perish wherein I was born, and the night in which it was said, There is a man child conceived.
4 Let that day be darkness; let not God regard it from above, neither let the light shine upon it." (Job 3:3-4)

Job counts his birthday as a day of darkness and night. The testimony of Scripture is also unanimous that the coming *"day of the LORD"* will be precisely that way. Consider the evidence.

"Woe unto you that desire the day of the LORD! to what end is it for you? the day of the LORD is darkness, and not light. As if a man did flee from a lion, and a bear met him; or went into the house, and leaned his hand on the wall, and a serpent bit him. Shall not the day of the LORD be darkness, and not light? even very dark, and no brightness in it?" (Amos 5:18-20)

Zephaniah saw the same vision. He saw a coming day of great darkness.

"That day is a day of wrath, a day of trouble and distress, a day of wasteness and desolation, a day of darkness and gloominess, a day of clouds and thick darkness." (Zephaniah 1:15)

Paul understood this prophecy of darkness and echoes these Old Testament prophets in his words to the Thessalonians concerning the Second Coming of Christ.

"But of the times and the seasons, brethren, ye have no need that I write unto you. For yourselves know perfectly that the day of the Lord so cometh as a thief in the night." (1 Thessalonians 5:1-2)

Remember that Paul is not talking about the rapture of the church. That was discussed in 1 Thessalonians 4:13-18. He begins chapter 5 talking about the Second Coming, and says that it will be associated with *"the night."*

John completes the prophetic picture in the Revelation.

"And I beheld when he had opened the sixth seal, and, lo, there was a great earthquake; and the sun became black as sackcloth of hair, and the moon became as blood." (Revelation 6:12)

Later he adds, *"And the fifth angel poured out his vial upon the seat of the beast; and his kingdom was full of darkness; and they gnawed their tongues for pain."* (Revelation 16:10)

Even had we not laid the foundation in the first chapter, we should see by now the many parallels to the coming Tribulation. We will have more to say about that time of darkness, but there is another phrase that we need to examine before moving on to the following verses. Verse 5 is the object of our attention.

A DAY OF DEATH

5 "Let darkness and the shadow of death stain it; let a cloud dwell upon it; let the blackness of the day terrify it." (Job 3:5)

This is the first time in the Bible that *"the shadow of death"* appears, and it will play a prominent role in the chapters to follow. Let's group together the several references to *"the shadow of death"* in the Book of Job.

"Before I go whence I shall not return, even to the land of darkness and THE SHADOW OF DEATH; A land of darkness, as darkness itself; and of THE SHADOW OF DEATH, without any order, and where the light is as darkness." (Job 10:21-22) (Author's emphasis)

"He discovereth deep things out of darkness, and bringeth out to light THE SHADOW OF DEATH." (Job 12:22) (Author's emphasis)

"My face is foul with weeping, and on my eyelids is THE SHADOW OF DEATH." (Job 16:16) (Author's emphasis)

"For the morning is to them even as THE SHADOW OF DEATH: if one know them, they are in the terrors of THE SHADOW OF DEATH." (Job 24:17) (Author's emphasis)

"He setteth an end to darkness, and searcheth out all perfection: the stones of darkness, and THE SHADOW OF DEATH." (Job 28:3) (Author's emphasis)

"There is no darkness, nor SHADOW OF DEATH, where the workers of iniquity may hide themselves." (Job 34:22) (Author's emphasis)

"Have the gates of death been opened unto thee? or hast thou seen the doors of THE SHADOW OF DEATH?" (Job 38:17) (Author's emphasis)

In a book that has such an obvious connection prophetically to the Tribulation, there must be prophetic importance to this thing called *"the shadow of death."* What could it possibly be?

If you have taken a tour of the "Holy Land," you might have had a tour guide point out to you one of the deep valleys to the north of Jerusalem. They probably used one of these valleys to illustrate "the valley of the shadow of death." There are valleys so deep, they have limited exposure to sunlight. Some link one or another of these valleys to David, and other shepherds, who led their flocks through this dangerous and imposing valley. This tradition goes back a long way, and there certainly are some dark valleys. Remember, however, that Job was not a Palestinian shepherd. He lived in the land of Uz, not north of Jerusalem.

Perhaps this understanding of the Tribulation connection of the "*shadow of death*" will throw new light on familiar Scriptures that we have taken for granted. Could the famous Twenty-third Psalm have a prophetic application?

"*Yea, though I walk through the valley of THE SHADOW OF DEATH, I will fear no evil: for thou art with me; thy rod and thy staff they comfort me.*" (Psalm 23:4) (Author's emphasis)

This is not the only time in the Psalms that we find this phrase.

"*Though thou hast sore broken us in the place of dragons, and covered us with THE SHADOW OF DEATH.*" (Psalms 44:19) (Author's emphasis)

"*Such as sit in darkness and in THE SHADOW OF DEATH, being bound in affliction and iron.*" (Psalm 107:10) (Author's emphasis)

Notice in these last two verses the Tribulation elements "*dragons,*" and "*affliction and iron.*" We will meet them again in our journey through Job and explain them further. We're not finished yet. The prophets also employ the same phrase, and in the same Tribulation context.

"*The people that walked in darkness have seen a great light: they that dwell in the land of THE SHADOW OF DEATH, upon them hath the light shined.*" (Isaiah 9:2) (Author's emphasis)

This prophecy, partially fulfilled in Christ's first coming (Matthew 4:16), will be finally fulfilled in His Second Coming.

Jeremiah saw it also. "*Neither said they, Where is the LORD that brought us up out of the land of Egypt, that led us through the wilderness, through a land of deserts and of pits, through a land of drought, and of THE SHADOW OF DEATH, through a land that no man passed through, and where no man dwelt?*" (Jeremiah 2:6) (Author's emphasis)

"*Give glory to the LORD your God, before he cause darkness, and before your feet stumble upon the dark mountains, and, while ye look for light, he turn it into THE SHADOW OF DEATH, and make it gross darkness.*" (Jeremiah 13:16) (Author's emphasis)

Amos is another witness. He saw the same thing in a Tribulation context. "*Seek him that maketh the seven stars and Orion, and turneth THE SHADOW OF DEATH into the morning, and maketh the day dark with night: that calleth for the waters of the sea, and poureth them out upon the face of the earth: The LORD is his name.*" (Amos 5:8) (Author's emphasis)

Zacharias, the father of John the Baptist, prophesied concerning John's ministry of preparing the way of the Lord. He called Jesus the "*dayspring from on high,*" and also saw the infamous "*shadow of death.*"

"*Through the tender mercy of our God; whereby the dayspring from on high hath visited us, To give light to them that sit in darkness and in THE SHADOW OF DEATH, to guide our feet into the way of peace."* (Luke 1:78-79) (Author's emphasis) What could not be fulfilled due to the Jews' rejection of their Messiah will be fulfilled following the *"shadow of death"* that will cover the land when that *"dayspring from on high," "the day star,"* (2 Peter 1:19) and the *"Sun of righteousness"* (Malachi 4:2) arises in the Second Coming.

What is the big deal? What is being talked about? Why does this phrase, *"the shadow of death,"* keeping recurring in the prophecies surrounding the Tribulation and the Second Coming of Christ?

When dealing with future events, we must remember that we are limited by our imperfect understanding, and by our ability to mentally conceive what has not yet occurred. The "Campaign of Armageddon" is really a "World War III," possibly a nuclear exchange on a large scale. Could it be that the *"shadow of death"* refers to the resulting radioactive cloud that would spread the pallor of death on all who came under its shadow?

Notice the connection with a *"cloud"* in Job 3:5. *"Let darkness and the shadow of death stain it; let A CLOUD dwell upon it; let the blackness of the day terrify it."* (Job 3:5) (Author's emphasis) Certainly a large nuclear exchange would result in a cloud of debris that would darken the light of the sun and the moon, and would spread its radioactive sickness and death on everyone who is openly exposed to the shadow of the cloud.

A DAY THAT DOESN'T COUNT

Job's words in verse 3:6 are enigmatic.

6 "As for that night, let darkness seize upon it; let it not be joined unto the days of the year, let it not come into the number of the months." (Job 3:6)

We have already established that *"that day"* is really a time of darkness and of night. Job seems to use day and night interchangeably in this passage. Remember that the beginning of a new "day" is always at night. The Jewish day begins at six o'clock in the evening. From the first chapter of Genesis God began reckoning a day as *"evening and morning,"* and in that order. (Genesis 1:5,8,13,19,23,31) Even in our modern society our "day" begins right at the stroke of midnight.

What Job is saying in Job 3:3-4 is that he wishes that his day of birth simply "not count." He doesn't want it to be numbered as a day that belongs to a month of the year. Surely those who experience the wrath of God during the Tribulation will feel the same way.

All we can say about that coming time is that it will be very special. It cannot be counted as a "normal" time. It will be a time of transition from the "day of grace" to the "day of the Lord." Jesus said, *"For then shall be great tribulation, such as was not since the beginning of the world to this time, no, nor ever shall be."* (Matthew 24:21)

This theme of agony continues into verses Job 3:7-8, but there is an added dimension. Here, Job speaks of those who curse the day and mourn.

A DAY OF CURSING

7 "Lo, let that night be solitary, let no joyful voice come therein.
8 Let them curse it that curse the day, who are ready to raise up their mourning." (Job 3:7-8)

Job has already cursed his day and now calls on others to curse it. The coming day is the "day of the Lord," and there will be those who will curse it. Difficult as it may be to believe, men's hearts will be so hardened they will curse the very God who alone holds the way to life. In the middle of the incomprehensible anguish of the Tribulation, Revelation 16:9 is representative of mankind's attitude. Instead of eagerly awaiting the dawning of the Sun of righteousness, they emphatically curse the God of glory. *"And men were scorched with great heat, and blasphemed the name of God, which hath power over these plagues: and they repented not to give him glory."* (Revelation 16:9)

Lost men on earth will also be ready to mourn the apparent assassination of the Antichrist (Zechariah 11:17; Revelation 13:3,12), who will miraculously appear to come to life, as his lifeless body is animated by the very Devil. (Revelation 13:12,15)

In Job 3:9, Job's words echo those of men in the Tribulation, who live a night that, for them, will never end.

A DAY OF HOPELESS EMPTINESS

9 "Let the stars of the twilight thereof be dark; let it look for light, but have none; neither let it see the dawning of the day." (Job 3:9)

With all that Job has suffered, it is easy to understand why he would say this, why he thinks the dawn will never come, that there would be no light at the end of the tunnel. Imagine what it will be like for those who live to see the forces of Hell let loose upon the earth! Yet for all of that, they will still not repent, but curse the very God who can save them.

The dense darkness that had dominated these opening verses of Job 3 is reminiscent of the plague of darkness that fell upon Egypt in the Exodus.

"And the LORD said unto Moses, Stretch out thine hand toward heaven, that there may be darkness over the land of Egypt, even darkness which may be felt. And Moses stretched forth his hand toward heaven; and there was a thick darkness in all the land of Egypt three days: They saw not one another, neither rose any from his place for three days: but all the children of Israel had light in their dwellings." (Exodus 10:21-23)

The plague of darkness in the Exodus is a prophecy of the coming darkness of the Tribulation, and it is reflected prophetically in Job's experience. Many people are amazed at how much prophecy dominates the Exodus. All of the plagues that Moses brought upon Egypt reappear in the Tribulation.

This is why I am personally convinced that Moses and Elijah are the two witnesses who appear in the Tribulation. Along with the facts that Moses and Elijah are the two who appear with Christ on the Mount of Transfiguration (Matthew 17:1-3), consider this: Elijah never died but was transported to heaven in a chariot of fire by a whirlwind (2 Kings 2:11). And the archangel Michael and the Devil fought over the body of Moses (Jude 9). Also consider the following passage in Revelation 11.

"And I will give power unto my two witnesses, and they shall prophesy a thousand two hundred and threescore days (three and a half years), *clothed in sackcloth. These are the two olive trees, and the two candlesticks standing before the God of the earth.* (Zechariah 4:11-14) *And if any man will hurt them, fire proceedeth out of their mouth, and devoureth their enemies* (Moses and Elijah are the only Old Testament figures who called fire down upon their enemies. Numbers 16:31-35; 2 Kings 1:10): *and if any man will hurt them, he must in this manner be killed. These have power to shut heaven, that it rain not in the days of their prophecy* (Elijah did this. James 5:17): *and have power over waters to turn them to blood, and to smite the earth with all plagues* (Moses did this. Exodus 7-12), *as often as they will. And when they shall have finished their testimony, the beast that ascendeth out of the bottomless pit shall make war against them, and shall overcome them, and kill them. And their dead bodies shall lie in the street of the great city, which spiritually is called Sodom and Egypt, where also our Lord was crucified. And they of the people and kindreds and tongues and nations shall see their dead bodies three days and a half, and shall not suffer their dead bodies to be put in graves."* (Revelation 11:3-9) (Author's notes)

A DAY OF SORROWFUL BIRTH

10 "Because it shut not up the doors of my mother's womb, nor hid sorrow from mine eyes." (Job 3:10)

Job continues his woeful complaint, lamenting his sorrowful birth. Again we have a Tribulation theme—the sorrowful birth. Anguish and the horrible pain of the Tribulation accompanies the rebirth of the nation of Israel. This thread is wound through both Testaments.

Jeremiah looked into the future to see the judgment of God that will yet come upon God's people. Just a few verses after speaking of the "*shadow of death*" (Jeremiah 13:16), he speaks of the terrible pain of "*that day.*"

"*What wilt thou say when he shall punish thee? for thou hast taught them to be captains, and as chief over thee: shall not sorrows take thee, as a woman in travail?*" (Jeremiah 13:21)

Micah also compared the pain of the Tribulation Jews to that of a sorrowful and painful birth.

"*Now why dost thou cry out aloud? is there no king in thee? is thy counsellor perished? for pangs have taken thee as a woman in travail. Be in pain, and labour to bring forth, O daughter of Zion, like a woman in travail: for now shalt thou go forth out of the city, and thou shalt dwell in the field, and thou shalt go even to Babylon; there shalt thou be delivered; there the LORD shall redeem thee from the hand of thine enemies.*" (Micah 4:9-10)

Paul also understood this figure, and used it himself to speak of the conditions surrounding the Second Coming.

"*For when they shall say, Peace and safety; then sudden destruction cometh upon them, as travail upon a woman with child; and they shall not escape.*" (1 Thessalonians 5:3)

All of us know what it is to go through times of grief and anguish in life. Some could even identify with Job's cursing of his day of birth. Yet surely no one has ever expressed it as eloquently, as completely and prophetically as Job did.

JOB CONSIDERS AN AGELESS QUESTION

11 "Why died I not from the womb? why did I not give up the ghost when I came out of the belly?

12 Why did the knees prevent me? or why the breasts that I should suck?" (Job 3:11-12)

Job's reference to the knees speaks in Old Testament terms of knees that are ready to hold a newborn child. Similar words appear in Genesis 30:3 and 50:23. The next phrase, of course, points to the mother's breasts ready to nurse. In contemporary terms Job is simply saying, "Why was I ever born?" How many of us in times of total frustration and despair have cried out this very question?

When Job says *"why did I not give up the ghost when I came out of the belly?"* he uses the word ghost as synonymous with "spirit." In the King James Version of the New Testament, "Holy Ghost" (KJV) is another way of saying "Holy Spirit." Linguistically they are translations of the same word, with the different words in the translation emphasizing different aspects of the Spirit. A "ghost" is an appearance, and "Holy Ghost" emphasizes that the Holy Ghost is the Person of God in His appearance as God's Spirit. "Holy Spirit" points more to the Spirit's function or ministry. I mention this so that you will realize that the old English use of the word ghost did not exclusively speak of things that haunt old houses. "Giving up the ghost" is still a common idiomatic expression for death in our English language today. Few, however, realize that it is taken directly from the King James Bible.

Job questions why he just couldn't have given up the *"ghost,"* or spirit, when he emerged from the womb. There is good understanding of the birth process and the nature of life on Job's part.

Consider the great importance of Genesis 2:7 to understanding the uniqueness of human life.

"And the LORD God formed man of the dust of the ground, and breathed into his nostrils the breath of life; and man became a living soul." (Genesis 2:7)

Having said that He was going to create man in His own image (Genesis 1:26), God shows us man's three-fold nature in this verse. God formed man's BODY out of the dust of the ground. God breathed His breath (SPIRIT) into man's nostrils, and man became a living SOUL.

This same equivalency between God's breath in man's nostrils, and man's God-given life was clearly understood in Job's day.

"All the while my breath is in me, and the spirit of God is in my nostrils." (Job 27:3)

"The Spirit of God hath made me, and the breath of the Almighty hath given me life." (Job 33:4)

Earlier in this chapter, in our discussion of verses 1-3, we saw how Jeremiah used words that were very similar to Job's. We commented how Jeremiah is a prophetic picture of the 144,000 witnesses in the Tribulation, and that it was therefore fitting that we should observe some parallels. Now, compare Job's comments in verses 11 and 12 with these words of Jeremiah.

"Wherefore came I forth out of the womb to see labour and sorrow, that my days should be consumed with shame?" (Jeremiah 20:18)

JOB CONTEMPLATES DEATH

13 "For now should I have lain still and been quiet, I should have slept: then had I been at rest,
14 With kings and counsellors of the earth, which built desolate places for themselves;
15 Or with princes that had gold, who filled their houses with silver:
16 Or as an hidden untimely birth I had not been; as infants which never saw light.
17 There the wicked cease from troubling; and there the weary be at rest.
18 There the prisoners rest together; they hear not the voice of the oppressor.
19 The small and great are there; and the servant is free from his master." (Job 3:13-19)

It is a short step from asking "Why was I born?" to questioning the very value of life itself. In verses 13-19, Job muses on the nature of death. He wistfully reflects on how much better off he would be dead. This is dangerous talk, if it is serious, and would alarm one's friends to hear it. In Job's case we need to remember what he has just experienced, and make some allowances. Small wonder it is that he is desperate, depressed and full of anguish!

THE NATURE OF DEATH

13 "For now should I have lain still and been quiet, I should have slept: then had I been at rest." (Job 3:13)

Job pictures the Old Testament saint in death as being *"at rest."* It is interesting that in Jesus' story of the rich man and Lazarus in Luke 16, Lazarus never answers, never responds. It is the rich man in Hell who is doing all the desperate questioning. In 1 Samuel 28 Saul visited the witch at Endor. Whether you believe that Saul spoke to a demon imitating Samuel, or that God permitted Samuel himself to return from death to give a message to Saul, it is interesting that the first words reputedly spoken by Samuel are, *"Why hast thou disquieted me, to bring me up?"*

Job longs for a state of rest. He understands that the Old Testament believer is at rest in death, and would far prefer that to the misery he was living. He never threatens suicide, nor discusses that option, but is honest enough to express the genuine feelings of his heart, that he would be better off dead than alive.

These verses reveal that Job had a very mature understanding of death. He goes on to expound that death knows no social boundaries—it is the common denominator of mankind. Add the next two verses to the one we just considered.

THE NEIGHBORS IN DEATH

13 "For now should I have lain still and been quiet, I should have slept: then had I been at rest,
14 With kings and counselors of the earth, which built desolate places for themselves;
15 Or with princes that had gold, who filled their houses with silver." (Job 3:13-15)

The kings and counsellors (government officials) Job mentions certainly never intended to build *"desolate places"* for themselves, but death exposed the naked reality of the emptiness of their palaces, their gold and their silver. Job was one of them. He had everything a man could want in this life. He's not even dead yet, and still his places are *"desolate."*

Job could easily understand the wisdom of Christ's words in Matthew 6.

"Lay not up for yourselves treasures upon earth, where moth and rust doth corrupt, and where thieves break through and steal: But lay up for yourselves treasures in heaven, where neither moth nor rust doth corrupt, and where thieves do not break through nor steal." (Matthew 6:19-20)

There is a sense in which Job is fortunate to come to this realization while he is still alive. Most men, who have spent their energy in life amassing great fortunes, never discover until it is too late that one day their place will be desolate. Scripture is filled with warning about the coming desolation.

"Be not afraid of sudden fear, neither of the desolation of the wicked, when it cometh." (Proverbs 3:25)

"Yet the defenced city shall be desolate, and the habitation forsaken, and left like a wilderness: there shall the calf feed, and there shall he lie down, and consume the branches thereof." (Isaiah 27:10)

"For thus saith the Lord GOD; When I shall make thee a desolate city, like the cities that are not inhabited; when I shall bring up the deep upon thee, and great waters shall cover thee." (Ezekiel 26:19)

"But I scattered them with a whirlwind among all the nations whom they knew not. Thus the land was desolate after them, that no man passed through nor returned: for they laid the pleasant land desolate." (Zechariah 7:14)

Not only does death encompass kings and counselors, it reaches even the unborn.

THE NAMELESS IN DEATH

16 "Or as an hidden untimely birth I had not been; as infants which never saw light." (Job 3:16)

In wishing he had never been born, Job knows that infants who are aborted or miscarried have the same *"rest"* as do the dead saints. Paul uses the figure of *"untimely birth"* in 1 Corinthians.

"And last of all he was seen of me also, as of one born out of due time." (1 Corinthians 15:8)

We saw in the first part of this chapter how Jeremiah was a picture of the 144,000 witnesses in the Tribulation. Paul is another such picture. Like Jeremiah Paul carried on his ministry without marrying. Like Jeremiah, he was a Jew who had a prophetic voice to the nations. As such, he was *"born out of due time."*

Apart from the recurring Tribulation themes, the truth expressed in Job 3:16 should be a source of great comfort for parents who have lost infants *"which never saw light,"* for whatever reason. The obvious and literal meaning is that they never *"saw light,"* in the sense of never having been born. Spiritually, they are free to go to heaven because they never rejected God's Light (they never saw Christ, the Light of the world). Christ's finished work in His death, burial and resurrection covers the penalty of their sin nature.

THE NEUTRALIZING EFFECT OF DEATH

More important truth about the state of the believing dead in the Old Testament emerges in the last three verses of this section of Job 3.

17 "There the wicked cease from troubling; and there the weary be at rest.

18 There the prisoners rest together; they hear not the voice of the oppressor.

19 The small and great are there; and the servant is free from his master." (Job 3:17-19)

Here is why Job knows he'd be better off dead. The weary can be at rest there, because *"the wicked"* aren't there to trouble them. Again we see that the Old Testament believer is *"at rest"* in death.

There is a very practical application in these words. The wicked don't bother anyone in death; they are in Hell. The believers don't bother anyone in death; they are *"at rest."* When you hear people talking about being bothered by someone's "ghost," you can be certain that if there has been any contact with the "spirit world," it is with an imitating demon, not with a deceased person.

Job says, *"there the prisoners rest together."* (Job 3:18) Why would the believing saints of the Old Testament be called *"prisoners?"* This is really quite consistent with the teaching of the rest of the Bible, and manifests an incredible depth of understanding on Job's part.

In the Old Testament, although God could "forgive" sin because of a man's faith in God's Word, the legal act of "redemption" could not be accomplished, since Christ had not yet shed His blood. Sin must be legally dealt with in a definitive manner. That was to take place on the cross. God explained this to Moses.

"And the LORD passed by before him, and proclaimed, The LORD, The LORD God, merciful and gracious, longsuffering, and abundant in goodness and truth, Keeping mercy for thousands, forgiving iniquity and transgression and sin, and that will by no means clear the guilty; visiting the iniquity of the fathers upon the children, and upon the children's children, unto the third and to the fourth generation." (Exodus 34:6-7)

God was busy *"forgiving iniquity,"* but *"that will by no means clear the guilty"* until the Lamb of God had shed His blood on the cross. Though some have questioned the translation of this last phrase, the same construction is used in Nahum 1:3, where the context clearly supports that sense of the explanation I have just given. This is why the Old Testament saint at death went to *"Abraham's bosom"* (Luke 16:22), or also called *"paradise"* (Luke 23:43). There they would wait until redemption was complete.

Paul explained to the Ephesians what happened when Jesus rose from the dead.

"Wherefore he saith, When he ascended up on high, he led captivity captive, and gave gifts unto men." (Ephesians 4:8)

These Old Testament *"prisoners"* were held in *"captivity"* until the work of redemption took place on the cross.

Paul was quoting from the Psalms.

"Thou hast ascended on high, thou hast led captivity captive: thou hast received gifts for men; yea, for the rebellious also, that the LORD God might dwell among them." (Psalm 68:18) It is in death that the *"prisoners"* are free from the *"voice of the oppressor"* (the Devil).

Job 3:19 is another reminder of how death is life's common denominator. *"The small and great are there; and the servant is free from his master."* (Job 3:19)

JOB CONTINUES HIS QUESTIONS

20 "Wherefore is light given to him that is in misery, and life unto the bitter in soul;
21 Which long for death, but it cometh not; and dig for it more than for hid treasures;
22 Which rejoice exceedingly, and are glad, when they can find the grave?
23 Why is light given to a man whose way is hid, and whom God hath hedged in?
24 For my sighing cometh before I eat, and my roarings are poured out like the waters.
25 For the thing which I greatly feared is come upon me, and that which I was afraid of is come unto me.
26 I was not in safety, neither had I rest, neither was I quiet; yet trouble came." (Job 3:20-26)

THE QUESTION OF MERCY

An amazing feature of the Book of Job is how almost every basic question of life seems to emerge in its pages. I will be pointing them out as we go along, but here is one of the all-time classics.

20 "Wherefore is light given to him that is in misery, and life unto the bitter in soul;
21 Which long for death, but it cometh not; and dig for it more than for hid treasures;
22 Which rejoice exceedingly, and are glad, when they can find the grave?
23 Why is light given to a man whose way is hid, and whom God hath hedged in?" (Job 3:20-23)

We would say it this way: "Why doesn't God put the miserable out of their suffering?" As a pastor, I have heard this question often, and have been tempted to ask it myself. Sometimes the pain we are asked to bear seems unbearable. If God were truly loving, wouldn't He just put such people out of their misery? It is certainly easy to see why Job would speak this question.

Even with our advantage of having seen the great spiritual battle raging behind the scenes in Job, it is still impossible for us to satisfactorily answer this question. There are just too many factors involved, and much information we don't yet have available. While this great devotional question remains largely unanswered, there is another Tribulation application we must note. In that time of inconceivable suffering that looms in the future, there will be a time when the misery is so great that men will WANT to die, and yet cannot. *"And in those days shall men seek death, and shall not find it; and shall desire to die, and death shall flee from them."* (Revelation 9:6)

It is hard to imagine such a time, when men will be in such agony they will seek death, and *"death shall flee from them."* Look at how the suicide rate has escalated in modern society, as many have taken "the easy way out." Can anything be worse than to want to die, and yet not be able to die?

This is only a foretaste of Hell. If lost man simply ceased to exist, dying without Christ could conceivably be bearable. Yet the Bible nowhere teaches annihilation. The horrible reality of Hell is that man CONTINUES TO EXIST FOREVER! Men without Christ will be subjected to a torture more intense than any yet devised by man. The worst of all is that it never lets up, never goes away.

Don't fail to notice the irony of verse 23. *"Why is light given to a man whose way is hid, and whom God hath hedged in?"* (Job 3:23) In Job 1:10, Satan accused God of keeping Job behind a *"hedge"* of protection. Now, Job realizes the terrible truth that he is *"hedged in"* by God for being the object of Satan's full assault.

Job is so consumed, he is reduced to animalistic sounds. *"For my sighing cometh before I eat, and my roarings are poured out like the waters."* (Job 3:24)

His choice of words is interesting—*"roarings"*—considering that Job is a type of Christ in many respects, he represents the *"Lion of the tribe of Juda"* (Revelations 5:5) in distress. David, also a type of Christ, could identify with Job's lion-like roarings.

"When I kept silence, my bones waxed old through my roaring all the day long." (Psalm 32:3)

THE FEAR FACTOR

Job concludes his opening monologue.

25 "For the thing which I greatly feared is come upon me, and that which I was afraid of is come unto me.

26 I was not in safety, neither had I rest, neither was I quiet; yet trouble came." (Job 3:25-26)

Often our fears become self-fulfilling prophecies. This statement of Job's gives us some real insight into his inner being. We must remember the pressure which Job feels. But if what Job says is true, we have the first real indication of an impending problem in his life. Despite his godly character, his righteousness and all we observed earlier, Job has some hidden fears in his life.

There is only one valid fear in a man's life—the fear of the Lord. A man who genuinely fears God will fear nothing else. Perhaps there are some areas of Job's life that need some polishing. Perhaps this is one of the objectives God has in mind as He subjects Job to this intense testing.

"For God hath not given us the spirit of fear; but of power, and of love, and of a sound mind." (2 Timothy 1:7)

We do know that the refinement of our character, the growth of our inner man, is the purpose that God wants to realize in our lives.

"And not only so, but we glory in tribulations also: knowing that tribulation worketh patience; And patience, experience; and experience, hope: And hope maketh not ashamed; because the love of God is shed abroad in our hearts by the Holy Ghost which is given unto us." (Romans 5:3-5)

When the *"love of God is shed abroad in our hearts,"* fear is driven away. John put it this way:

"There is no fear in love; but perfect love casteth out fear: because fear hath torment. He that feareth is not made perfect in love." (1 John 4:18)

What are YOU afraid of? Be careful that your fear does not become self-fulfilling! Learn to fear God, and you will have nothing and no one else to fear.

5

KILLING WITH KINDNESS

Behold, thou hast instructed many, and thou hast strengthened the weak hands.
Thy words have upholden him that was falling, and thou hast strengthened the feeble knees.
But now it is come upon thee, and thou faintest; it toucheth thee, and thou art troubled.

Job 4:3-5

JOB HAS BROKEN THE SILENCE. HE HAS SUCCESSFULLY RESISTED the temptation to curse God, cursing instead the day of his birth. You can be sure that the Devil is cursing God by this time! He has hit Job with the full force of his fury, and thus far has been unsuccessful.

What you will see in the following chapters is Satan's change of strategy, from direct to indirect, from blatant to subtle. He will be using Job's friends as his instruments to continue attacking Job. No doubt they are totally unaware of how the Devil is using them, just like the average church-going Christian today.

Satan is a master at what he does. Here, he takes the only three men who cared enough about Job to come and visit him in his affliction, and uses them to wage psychological warfare. Your biggest battles will be when Satan gets hold of your brothers and sisters in Christ, the members of your own church, and uses them to get to you.

So far, Job is holding up well under the circumstances. His mental state may not be the healthiest, perhaps, but how would YOU deal with what Job has experienced? If you detected some frustration, depression, anxiety and other emotional ills in Job's opening monologue, you must give him some slack. The fact that he has not cursed God is impressive enough.

Just as remarkable is the restraint of his three friends, who for seven days have been patiently sitting at his side without saying a word. Now that Job has loosened up the emotional log jam that had blocked his throat for the past week, these men feel the liberty to voice their views also. What would YOU say in such a situation, after you had seven days to think about it?

Eliphaz is the first to speak. Within the context of Middle Eastern culture, this implies that he is the eldest and perhaps most prestigious of the three. His words, and those of his companions, will give us plenty to consider about biblical counseling. Eliphaz show us what NOT to do and say.

The conversation will rapidly deteriorate, but he chooses his first words with great care. He will give the appearance of piety and great spiritual insight, but his words will cut right to the heart. He will be killing Job with his kindness.

BACKGROUND STUDY

1 "Then Eliphaz the Temanite answered and said." (Job 4:1)

We have already learned that Eliphaz is a native of the land of Edom, called here "Uz." He is a contemporary of the children of Esau and Jacob, and is NOT a Jew, nor are any of the characters of this book. We must continue to remind ourselves of this fact. Finding this story in the Old Testament, we have the tendency to automatically assume that everyone here is a Jew.

The Temanites descended from Tema, as we learn in Genesis 25:15. That same passage shows that Tema was one of the twelve princes of Ishmael, the son of Abraham with Hagar, Sarah's concubine.

Somewhere in history, the Temanites appear to have mixed with the descendants of Esau, since they are well-established in the land of Edom (Uz) when this story takes place. The study of human history is an impossibly-twisted knot of various lines of people cross-breeding to produce new groups of people. This tendency of man to mix with other people groups is further evidence of the miracle of how the Jews have maintained their identity as a people through the ages.

Genesis emphasizes the total identification of Edom with Esau. *"Now these are the generations of Esau, who is Edom."* (Genesis 36:1) *"Thus dwelt Esau in mount Seir: Esau is Edom."* (Genesis 36:8) This is where Uz is located, and it is therefore not surprising to read in Genesis 36 that Eliphaz is a son of Esau.

"And these are the generations of Esau the father of the Edomites in

mount Seir: These are the names of Esau's sons; Eliphaz the son of Adah the wife of Esau, Reuel the son of Bashemath the wife of Esau. And the sons of Eliphaz were Teman, Omar, Zepho, and Gatam, and Kenaz." (Genesis 36:9-11)

The Eliphaz in Genesis is probably the same Eliphaz we find in Job. The same passage tells us he named his firstborn Teman, perhaps in honor of Tema of Genesis 25:15. This further implies the connection between Tema, Esau and the Temanites, of whom Eliphaz counted his lineage. This is probably why he is a Temanite instead of an Edomite. He is the son of Esau, and it would be later that this people would grow to the size and strength to go by the name of Edomites.

Whatever the case, there is no doubt that Teman is closely connected to Edom.

"Concerning EDOM, thus saith the LORD of hosts; Is wisdom no more in TEMAN? is counsel perished from the prudent? is their wisdom vanished?" (Jeremiah 49:7) (Author's emphasis)

"Thus saith the LORD; For three transgressions of EDOM, and for four, I will not turn away the punishment thereof; because he did pursue his brother with the sword, and did cast off all pity, and his anger did tear perpetually, and he kept his wrath for ever: But I will send a fire upon TEMAN, which shall devour the palaces of Bozrah." (Amos 1:11-12) (Author's emphasis)

BEGINNING REMARKS

"You're probably not going to like this, but . . ." Have you ever used this famous line? Have you ever had it used on YOU? It's much more fun to use it on someone else! This is precisely how Eliphaz begins his remarks.

2 "If we assay to commune with thee, wilt thou be grieved? but who can withhold himself from speaking?" (Job 4:2)

Who, indeed, could "*withhold himself from speaking*" for seven days? This is almost humorous!

Now that Eliphaz DOES speak, he has much to say. There is something we must establish right now. MOST of what Eliphaz says is true. As we work through the next chapters and the discourses of Job's friends, we will see that almost everything they say is the truth. We can confirm the truth of their words as we compare it to the rest of Scripture. We will see that it is consistent with God's revealed truth.

These men know a lot of the things of God. Eliphaz's problem in particular, and the problem of all three in general, is not TRUTH, but TIMING and TACT.

Here is a great principle of counseling—the biblical counselor must learn to keep his mouth shut at times, even when what he has to say is true.

The Bible is filled with truth, but sometimes a particular truth does not apply to a specific situation. We will see this often in Job. What the men say is true. It simply does not apply in Job's situation. Also, it is possible to say the right thing at the wrong time. Job's counselors will also make this mistake. They will speak the truth, but they will be off in their timing.

There is an important truth in 1 Corinthians 14:32. *"And the spirits of the prophets are subject to the prophets."* (1 Corinthians 14:32)

Paul makes this statement in dealing with the abuses of spiritual gifts occurring in the Corinthian church. We see the same type of abuse today when people exclaim, "I just couldn't help it! The Spirit was upon me, and I just had to say it." All type of foolishness is blamed on the Holy Spirit. He is often the excuse for any spontaneous, flighty, idiotic behavior that backfires.

The point Paul makes is that when God gives someone a gift, or an anointing, He also gives the common sense and the self-discipline to use it correctly. If God has given to you truth and understanding, He will also give you the common sense, decency, and self-control to speak that truth at just the right time, and in just the right spirit.

In Job 4:3-4, Eliphaz gives Job a compliment. Remember, though, that the title of this chapter is "Killing With Kindness." In effect, Eliphaz is setting up for a "slam-dunk."

3 "Behold, thou hast instructed many, and thou hast strengthened the weak hands.

4 Thy words have upholden him that was falling, and thou hast strengthened the feeble knees." (Job 4:3-4)

Job was obviously a strong man who had been a help and encouragement to many. No one seems ready to question this statement. Remember, Job was the *"greatest of all the men of the east."* (Job 1:3) Yet Job was a man who used his wealth and influence to make a positive difference in the lives of others.

Looking forward to the coming of Messiah, Isaiah cries, *"Strengthen ye the weak hands, and confirm the feeble knees."* (Isaiah 35:3) In the New Testament, the author of Hebrews, using Isaiah's words, instructs us about dealing with those who have been subject to chastening. *"Where-*

fore lift up the hands which hang down, and the feeble knees." (Hebrews 12:12)

Job did this. Eliphaz confirms it. But watch out! Here it comes!

5 "But now it is come upon thee, and thou faintest; it toucheth thee, and thou art troubled." (Job 4:5)

In other words, "What's wrong, Job? You have been the great and wise counselor. Can't you give yourself the same advice you've given to others?"

Does this sound familiar? It should. Remember that Job is a prophetic picture of the Lord Jesus Christ in His sufferings on the cross. Jesus knew ahead of time that this accusation would be hurled in His face.

"And he said unto them, Ye will surely say unto me this proverb, Physician, heal thyself: whatsoever we have heard done in Capernaum, do also here in thy country." (Luke 4:23)

This prophecy, as all other biblical prophecies, was exactly fulfilled. Hanging on the cross, these were the words He heard:

"He saved others; himself he cannot save. If he be the King of Israel, let him now come down from the cross, and we will believe him." (Matthew 27:42)

Eliphaz is getting right to the point. He doesn't waste much time moving in for the kill. You would think that after seven days of meditation, Eliphaz could have chosen more encouraging words. Having slapped Job right where it hurts, Eliphaz now lays out his basic thesis.

BASIC THESIS

6 "Is not this thy fear, thy confidence, thy hope, and the uprightness of thy ways?
7 Remember, I pray thee, who ever perished, being innocent? or where were the righteous cut off?
8 Even as I have seen, they that plow iniquity, and sow wickedness, reap the same.
9 By the blast of God they perish, and by the breath of his nostrils are they consumed." (Job 4:6-9)

REAPING WHAT IS SOWN

Eliphaz, as the other men will affirm also, is convinced that Job is reaping the consequence of personal sin. When he says *"is not this thy fear?"*, Eliphaz is saying that Job is afraid of the wages of sin.

Job expressed fear in Job 3:25-26. *"For the thing which I greatly feared is come upon me, and that which I was afraid of is come unto me. I was not in safety, neither had I rest, neither was I quiet; yet trouble came."* (Job 3:25-26)

He again mentions his fear in chapter 23. *"Therefore am I troubled at his presence: when I consider, I am afraid of him."* (Job 23:15)

Eliphaz's basic thesis is rooted in what is sometimes called the "law of sowing and reaping." Paul stated it memorably in Galatians.

"Be not deceived; God is not mocked: for whatsoever a man soweth, that shall he also reap. For he that soweth to his flesh shall of the flesh reap corruption; but he that soweth to the Spirit shall of the Spirit reap life everlasting." (Galatians 6:7-8)

You will also find this truth in Proverbs, and even in Hosea.

"He that soweth iniquity shall reap vanity: and the rod of his anger shall fail." (Proverbs 22:8)

"Ye have plowed wickedness, ye have reaped iniquity; ye have eaten the fruit of lies: because thou didst trust in thy way, in the multitude of thy mighty men." (Hosea 10:13)

Eliphaz feels very secure in his premise, because the law of sowing and reaping is absolute. There are no exceptions. The problem, however, is that it does not apply here.

Even nature teaches this. Sometimes things grow up that you have NOT sown. We call them weeds! This is what Job is reaping—weeds. He has not sown them, but he is reaping them. This happens to all of us. You WILL reap what you sow. There will also be times in your life when you reap trouble and sorrow which you did NOT sow.

Before moving on, notice carefully the wording of verse 9. *"By the blast of God they perish, and by the breath of his nostrils are they consumed."* (Job 4:9)

Now, compare this with words of Paul and Isaiah. *"And then shall that Wicked be revealed, whom the Lord shall consume with the spirit of his mouth, and shall destroy with the brightness of his coming."* (2 Thessalonians 2:8)

"But with righteousness shall he judge the poor, and reprove with equity for the meek of the earth: and he shall smite the earth with the rod of his

mouth, and with the breath of his lips shall he slay the wicked." (Isaiah 11:4)

Both verses appear in a Tribulation context. We establish again the Tribulation application of Job. Over and again we see the same words, same phrases, same pictures and same context. Job is a prophetic picture of Tribulation, drawn by the Spirit of Almighty God, using the historical events of Job's life to illustrate a coming time so that it's worse than we can imagine.

ROARING OF THE LIONS

The next verses are enigmatic, as Eliphaz takes us on a safari, mentioning lions no less than five times.

10 "The roaring of the lion, and the voice of the fierce lion, and the teeth of the young lions, are broken.

11 The old lion perisheth for lack of prey, and the stout lion's whelps are scattered abroad." (Job 4:10-11)

Where did these lions come from, and why does Eliphaz mention them? What do they represent? I can't answer all the questions that arise from these verses, but we do need to examine this issue of lions.

We all know who it is that goes about "*as a roaring lion.*"

"*Be sober, be vigilant; because your adversary the devil, as a roaring lion, walketh about, seeking whom he may devour.*" (1 Peter 5:8)

Even casual students of the Bible also know that the Lord Jesus Christ is the "*Lion of the tribe of Juda.*" (Revelation 5:5)

An interesting feature of these two verses is that the five mentions of "lion" are each separate Hebrew words. This seems strange to us, since there is only one "lion" in our English language. Generally, when something plays an important role in the daily life of a people, their language tends to have multiple words to designate various species or types of the same thing. Eskimos, for example, have several words for "snow." Thinking about it, even in our culture we speak of a "wet snow," a "dry snow," or "snow flurries." Rather than use adjectives, the Eskimos have different words to refer to the different kinds of snow.

Historians tell us that lions were once common even in certain areas of Europe and the Middle East. Today, we associate them only with the continent of Africa. With lions a reality of daily life, it is not surprising that the Hebrews had various words that could be translated as "lion."

Job's context prophetically is in the time of the Tribulation. Do these lions represent Satan, the Lord Jesus Christ, or something else? Because of the Tribulation prophecy in Job, when mapping out the itinerary of our safari, we need to hunt for lions that also appear in a Tribulation context. Our first stop will be in the seventh chapter of Daniel.

"In the first year of Belshazzar king of Babylon Daniel had a dream and visions of his head upon his bed: then he wrote the dream, and told the sum of the matters. Daniel spake and said, I saw in my vision by night, and, behold, the four winds of the heaven strove upon the great sea. And four great beasts came up from the sea, diverse one from another. The first was like a lion, and had eagle's wings: I beheld till the wings thereof were plucked, and it was lifted up from the earth, and made stand upon the feet as a man, and a man's heart was given to it." (Daniel 7:1-4)

In this vision Daniel sees a succession of gentile kingdoms that will come upon the earth, as interpreted by the angel in Daniel 7:17. There are many ideas about the historical identification of these gentile empires. This is not a commentary on Daniel, and I will not add my ideas to the pile at this time. I mention this passage to show that lions in the Bible represent more than the Devil ("a roaring lion") and Christ ("the lion of the tribe of Judah").

Another prophecy that mentions lions is in Ezekiel. *"Thus saith the Lord GOD; It shall also come to pass, that at the same time shall things come into thy mind, and thou shalt think an evil thought: And thou shalt say, I will go up to the land of unwalled villages; I will go to them that are at rest, that dwell safely, all of them dwelling without walls, and having neither bars nor gates, To take a spoil, and to take a prey; to turn thine hand upon the desolate places that are now inhabited, and upon the people that are gathered out of the nations, which have gotten cattle and goods, that dwell in the midst of the land. Sheba, and Dedan, and the merchants of Tarshish, with all the young lions thereof, shall say unto thee, Art thou come to take a spoil? hast thou gathered thy company to take a prey? to carry away silver and gold, to take away cattle and goods, to take a great spoil?"* (Ezekiel 38:10-13)

Chapter 37 of Ezekiel sets these verses as occurring during the Tribulation, when Israel, armed with a treaty made by the Antichrist, will *"dwell safely"* (38:11), convinced no one will harm her. Chapter 38 describes the movement of gentile nations against Israel. In verse 13, some Bible students link *"Tarshish"* with western Europe, and see the *"young lions"* as the English-speaking nations influenced by the old lions of England and Germany, both of whom employ lions in their national symbols.

Lions also stalk the pages of Nahum.

"Where is the dwelling of the lions, and the feedingplace of the young lions, where the lion, even the old lion, walked, and the lion's whelp, and

none made them afraid? The lion did tear in pieces enough for his whelps, and strangled for his lionesses, and filled his holes with prey, and his dens with ravin." (Nahum 2:11-12)

Three of the "lion words" of Job 4:10-11 appear in Nahum 2, along with yet another. Nahum prophesies against Nineveh, a gentile power, and points to a final fulfillment yet ahead in the *"day of trouble."* (Nahum 1:7)

The older I get, and the more I study the Bible, the less dogmatic I become about my understanding of things to come. I know that the Lord is returning soon, but I am ready to accept my lack of understanding of many aspects of biblical prophecy.

My concern in taking us on this lion safari is not to establish a definitive link between Eliphaz's lions and specific nations, events or persons of the future. The intent is simply to point out that lions keep popping up in prophecy concerning gentile powers in the last days. I have no idea how these lions of Eliphaz relate to specific nations, people or events of the Tribulation. Perhaps there is some corresponding truth, given that Job prophetically illustrates the coming Tribulation. In the historical setting, Eliphaz is probably using the figure of lions to show how Job, a strong lion-like man, has been broken.

Whatever I have come to understand in the Book of Job, I am certain that there is just as much I DON'T understand. My prayer is that this book will jog you from complacency, and cause you to consider Job in a different light. We often go to the Bible blinded by what we have always thought, what we have always heard, or what "they" have always said. I make no claim for absolute understanding; I do claim that God's Word is our only absolute truth. Just as the events of the last few decades have given us greater understanding of biblical passages such as Daniel and Revelation, perhaps as we draw closer to *"that day,"* we will come to understand more about the prophetic pictures of Job.

BOLD VISION

Eliphaz's words reach a climax in the closing verse of this chapter, as he relates a vision that he had. In verses 12-16 he describes an image that he saw, while in verses 17-21 he tells us the message he received. We will look first at what appeared to Eliphaz in this vision.

THE MYSTERY OF THE VISION

12 "Now a thing was secretly brought to me, and mine ear received a little thereof.
13 In thoughts from the visions of the night, when deep sleep falleth on men,
14 Fear came upon me, and trembling, which made all my bones to shake.
15 Then a spirit passed before my face; the hair of my flesh stood up:
16 It stood still, but I could not discern the form thereof: an image was before mine eyes, there was silence, and I heard a voice, saying." (Job 4:12-16)

Today, in many circles this type of statement is supposed to end all argument. When someone claims he has received a vision, a dream, a word of knowledge or other direct revelation from God, there is no more room for discussion. Personal experience has usurped the authority of the Bible among many today who call themselves Christians. "I don't care what the Bible says, I've had this experience!" is the attitude of a growing number of individuals who have been swept away on the waves of a great charismatic "revival." Trusting their "experience" instead of the Bible will deliver a coming generation straight into the hands of a waiting Antichrist.

There is, though, no reason to doubt Eliphaz's experience. In his day there was no written Word to serve as the final authority. God revealed His truth to men in other ways. Dreams and visions were legitimate means of divine revelation.

"And he said, Hear now my words: If there be a prophet among you, I the LORD will make myself known unto him in a vision, and will speak unto him in a dream." (Numbers 12:6)

The Book of Hebrews opens by explaining the change that has occurred in God's revelation to man since Christ finished His redemptive work on the Cross.

"God, who at sundry times and in divers manners spake in time past unto the fathers by the prophets, Hath in these last days spoken unto us by his Son, whom he hath appointed heir of all things, by whom also he made the worlds." (Hebrews 1:1-2)

In ages past God used various methods to communicate His truth to men. Now, in these last days, He speaks to us by his Son, the living Word. Since the living Word is at the right hand of God the Father, He has left us the written Word, *"the mind of Christ."* (1 Corinthians 2:16)

No one present questions Eliphaz on his vision. They accept his words at face value. Job understood that God spoke in this way.

"For God speaketh once, yea twice, yet man perceiveth it not. In a dream, in a vision of the night, when deep sleep falleth upon men, in slumberings upon the bed; Then he openeth the ears of men, and sealeth their instruction." (Job 33:14-16)

Look again at the words of Eliphaz in 4:13. *"In thoughts from the visions of the night, when deep sleep falleth on men."* (Job 4:13) This is what happened to Abraham in Genesis 15. It was through this experience that God confirmed the covenant to Abraham.

"And when the sun was going down, a deep sleep fell upon Abram; and, lo, an horror of great darkness fell upon him." (Genesis 15:12)

The *"spirit"* Eliphaz mentions in verse 15 is obviously an angel. I say this because Hebrews 1:14 says this of the angels: *"Are they not all ministering spirits, sent forth to minister for them who shall be heirs of salvation?"* (Hebrews 1:14)

There is nothing in the message Eliphaz receives through this visiting spirit that is inconsistent with biblical truth. Considering the context of the times, there is no reason to doubt the validity of the experience. Let's examine that message.

THE MESSAGE OF THE VISION

17 "Shall mortal man be more just than God? shall a man be more pure than his maker?
18 Behold, he put no trust in his servants; and his angels he charged with folly:
19 How much less in them that dwell in houses of clay, whose foundation is in the dust, which are crushed before the moth?
20 They are destroyed from morning to evening: they perish for ever without any regarding it.
21 Doth not their excellency which is in them go away? they die, even without wisdom." (Job 4:17-21)

The answer to the two questions in verse 17 is obvious. Of course mortal man is not more just than God! Of course man cannot be more pure than his Maker!

A close examination of verse 18 puts in the time immediately before the Flood. *"Behold, he put no trust in his servants; and his angels he charged with folly."* (Job 4:18) In our study of Job 1, we went into the events of Genesis 6 in some detail, seeing the unnatural union of the *"sons of God"* with the *"daughters of men."* We also saw the phrase *"and also after that"* in Genesis 6:4. This was not the last time that God would have occasion to charge His angels with folly, or to distrust His servants.

It will help to review a couple of New Testament passages to shed light on what Eliphaz is referring to.

"Even as Sodom and Gomorrha, and the cities about them in like manner, giving themselves over to fornication, and going after strange flesh, are set forth for an example, suffering the vengeance of eternal fire." (Jude 7)

"For if God spared not the angels that sinned, but cast them down to hell, and delivered them into chains of darkness, to be reserved unto judgment." (2 Peter 2:4)

An important indicator of the time period in which Job occurs, is the many number of times these men make reference of the events surrounding the Flood. The memory of the Flood was still very much alive, since Noah's sons had only recently died.

In making the prophetic application of this passage, we need to remember that God will again charge His angels with folly. Consider what John saw in Revelation 12. Many assume that this points back to angels that fell with Lucifer, as described in Isaiah 14:12-15. Yet the events of Revelation 12 take place in the time of Tribulation. This is something still future.

"And there appeared a great wonder in heaven; a woman clothed with the sun, and the moon under her feet, and upon her head a crown of twelve stars: And she being with child cried, travailing in birth, and pained to be delivered. And there appeared another wonder in heaven; and behold a great red dragon, having seven heads and ten horns, and seven crowns upon his heads. And his tail drew the third part of the stars of heaven, and did cast them to the earth: and the dragon stood before the woman which was ready to be delivered, for to devour her child as soon as it was born." (Revelation 12:1-4) . . . *"And there was war in heaven: Michael and his angels fought against the dragon; and the dragon fought and his angels, And prevailed not; neither was their place found any more in heaven. And the great dragon was cast out, that old serpent, called the Devil, and Satan, which deceiveth the whole world: he was cast out into the earth, and his angels were cast out with him."* (Revelation 12:7-9)

We are constantly observing a great biblical truth—what will be, has already been. Consider the words of Solomon.

"The thing that hath been, it is that which shall be; and that which is done is that which shall be done: and there is no new thing under the sun." (Ecclesiastes 1:9)

Bringing up the fall of angels sets the stage for the punch line of verse 19. *"How much less in them that dwell in houses of clay, whose foundation is in the dust, which are crushed before the moth?"* (Job 4:19)

Who are those who *"dwell in houses of clay?"* Paul gives the answer.

"But we have this treasure in earthen vessels, that the excellency of the power may be of God, and not of us." (2 Corinthians 4:7)

The point is simple. If God can't trust His angels, why would we think that MAN was worthy of His trust? Eliphaz may have a wrong attitude, but this statement is as true as can be.

Truly our *"foundation is in the dust."* Go back to the words of Genesis. *"And the LORD God formed man of the dust of the ground, and breathed into his nostrils the breath of life; and man became a living soul."* (Genesis 2:7) And again, *"All go unto one place; all are of the dust, and all turn to dust again."* (Ecclesiastes 3:20)

The last phrase of verse 19 is more difficult—*"which are crushed before the moth."* Job uses the figure of a "moth" in chapter 27, as he describes the life of *"a wicked man"* (Job 27:13). *"He buildeth his house as a moth, and as a booth that the keeper maketh."* (Job 27:18)

The image is that of weakness and frailty, a house that is gnawed away, like a moth chewing up a piece of wool. The same transitory frailty is communicated with the figure of the moth in Psalms.

"When thou with rebukes dost correct man for iniquity, thou makest his beauty to consume away like a moth: surely every man is vanity." (Psalm 39:11)

Physical beauty is quickly consumed, just as the moth destroys a garment.

The message of Eliphaz's vision is that man has no solid foundation. He is as vulnerable as a fine, woolen garment before the moth. The entire earth is like this.

"Lift up your eyes to the heavens, and look upon the earth beneath: for the heavens shall vanish away like smoke, and the earth shall wax old like a garment, and they that dwell therein shall die in like manner: but my salvation shall be for ever, and my righteousness shall not be abolished." (Isaiah 51:6)

In verse 20 we read: *"They are destroyed from morning to evening: they perish for ever without any regarding it."* (Job 4:20) Men are dying all around us, every day. Life is cheap. Death is inevitable. It happens to all.

"They perish for ever without any regarding it." Who really cares about the lost that pass into eternity every day? We give lip service to statistics, and we emphasize our ministries, yet very few care about the real men and women who daily fall headlong into a Christ-less eternity.

"Doth not their excellency which is in them go away? they die, even without wisdom." (Job 4:21)

Whatever excellency man has vanishes in the moment of death. The message of Psalm 49 is similar.

"Nevertheless man being in honour abideth not: he is like the beasts that perish." (Psalm 49:12) *"Be not thou afraid when one is made rich, when the glory of his house is increased; For when he dieth he shall carry nothing away: his glory shall not descend after him."* (Psalm 49:16-17) *"Man that is in honour, and understandeth not, is like the beasts that perish."* (Psalm 49:20)

The truth and finality of the last phrase are startling. *"They die, even without wisdom."* What better way to express the doom of lost man?

Wisdom is defined in Job. *"And unto man he said, Behold, the fear of the Lord, that is wisdom; and to depart from evil is understanding."* (Job 28:28)

Lost man never obtains the *"fear of the Lord."* He perishes, never having come to the knowledge of the Lord, never having obtained wisdom. This is true despite great intelligence or a long list of academic degrees.

Phrase by phrase we have analyzed Eliphaz's vision. There is nothing in it to contradict the rest of Scripture. Exactly the opposite is true! This is a wonderful summation of the condition of man without God.

What we have seen in these words is a pattern that will predominate in speech after speech, until God Almighty Himself speaks in chapter 38. These men, with few exceptions, speak the truth. They know their stuff! They have a good amount of information about God and life. What they don't have is the wisdom and discernment to apply it correctly. Eliphaz's vision is wonderfully true! Yet it has nothing to do with Job's condition. It is irrelevant.

After these several thousand years, mankind has not changed, even with all our technology. In a thousand different churches this Sunday, pastors will ascend into pulpits, speaking the great truth of God, yet not having the slightest idea how to make contact with the hurting lives in front of them.

Tragedy stalks men's lives like a serial killer. While few of us suffer to the degree Job suffered, we can all identify with the frustration of not knowing what God is doing in our lives. We meet in the hallways of church, throw Bible verses at each other with reckless abandon, and seldom hit the target of reality.

Learning Bible truth is not that difficult. It equips you to amaze your friends in a game of Bible Trivia. Yet, learning how to effectively and sensitively express the truth of God's Word to those who are hurting is an art that requires the investment of a lifetime, and the anointing of the Spirit of God.

6

THE ELOQUENT RAMBLINGS OF ELIPHAZ

Behold, happy is the man whom God correcteth:
therefore despise not thou the chastening
of the Almighty:

Job 5:17

ELIPHAZ HAS BEEN THE FIRST OF JOB'S FRIENDS TO SPEAK, releasing more than a week's worth of pent-up thoughts and emotions. He is motivated by the best of intentions and fueled with the finest of divine truth. The problem is that he is totally unaware that he is the Devil's instrument to push Job over the edge and curse God.

Based on what we have seen thus far, Eliphaz is ready to lay out his basic thesis. Job's other friends will use the same thesis. They will dress it differently, and give it some new twists, but ultimately they all come back to this single idea—Job would not be suffering like this if it were not for some unconfessed sin in his life.

Job's counselors share one common problem in their approach toward Job—the misapplication of God's truth. It will become increasingly clear that these men have a great deal of true and wonderful information about God and His universe. Indeed, an amazing feature of Job is the high level of knowledge these men possessed, much of which can now be verified by both the Bible and science. Their problem is not a lack of information, but knowing how and when to apply it.

Here is a major problem of those who seek to help others today. The real issue is having the wisdom to know when and where to apply the knowledge you have. The machinery of "Christian counseling" breaks down as great biblical truths are passed back and forth across the table, while precious little communication takes place. Genuine and pressing issues are left undone, while both counselor and counselee are engaged in flaunting their knowledge.

The Bible mentions three qualities in the same breath—wisdom, knowledge and understanding. A tour of Proverbs traces this fascinating trail. You will find these words consistently in the same context. Each one depends on the others. Knowledge alone will not suffice without wisdom regarding how to apply it and understanding when to make it operative.

Remember what has been said in these few words of introduction. They outline things to come. All three men, and Elihu, will hold to the idea that Job has a dark secret sin that must be dealt with. All three and Elihu will display great knowledge, but little wisdom or understanding.

Eliphaz has just explained a vision he received in the night. He continues his speech. We will examine his mistaken thesis, his misapplied truth, and a millennial type that appears in his final words.

MISTAKEN THESIS

1 "Call now, if there be any that will answer thee; and to which of the saints wilt thou turn?" (Job 5:1)

NO MEDIATOR

Eliphaz knows the answer to his question in the first verse before he opens his mouth—Job has NO ONE to turn to. (Not counting God, of course). Yet God has so far been silent. Who could possibly answer Job? Is there some saint on whom he could call?

This is a basic, and valuable bit of theology. If God Himself is not talking, there is no one else to whom he can turn. Can you really imagine Job clutching a Saint Christopher medallion around his neck? Can you visualize him stroking a plastic saint on the dashboard of his car?

Eliphaz knows that there is no qualified mediator between God and man. He states as much himself in his second discourse.

"Behold, he putteth no trust in his saints; yea, the heavens are not clean in his sight." (Job 15:15)

If God puts no trust in His saints, there's not much point in man putting faith in them either.

NO MISTAKE

Seeing that there is no public defender, no attorney, no mediator to step forward and argue Job's case, Eliphaz gets right to the accusation. Job is guilty. There must be sin in his life; otherwise, he would not be suffering these things, or talking like this.

The point Eliphaz makes has to do with the consequences that befall a foolish and silly man. By implication that man is Job.

2 "For wrath killeth the foolish man, and envy slayeth the silly one.

3 I have seen the foolish taking root: but suddenly I cursed his habitation." (Job 5:2-3)

Beneath the innocuous-sounding proverb, here is what is boiling: If Job is really serious about all this "I wish I were dead" talk, he is a foolish and silly man. The idea is that Job is just mad he's been caught, and is suffering the consequence of his sin. If his life were not filled with anger and envy, he would not be wishing he were dead.

A "foolish man" ("a fool") in the Bible is one who rejects God's truth. He may have a high IQ, a Ph.D. and a closet filled with awards, but if he rejects God's truth he is a fool. Solomon said: *"The fear of the LORD is the beginning of knowledge: but fools despise wisdom and instruction."* (Proverbs 1:7)

A valuable study is to follow the word "fool" through the Bible. You will clearly see that being a fool has nothing to do with intelligence or knowledge.

"Yes," says Eliphaz, "your sin has finally caught up with you, Job. You wish you were dead, and I know that you would never say such a thing if your heart were right with God. You're a fool, Job. Your whole life has been motivated by envy. Yes, that's all clear to me now. No wonder you think you'd be better off dead."

It's easy to pontificate when YOU are not the one suffering! "Have YOU ever lost ALL of your ten children in a single day, Eliphaz? Have you ever been totally wiped out financially in a moment of time? Have you ever been reduced to sitting in the city dump, scraping pus from your body with a broken piece of pottery? Eliphaz, do you really think that YOU could endure such a disaster, and still be ready for another rousing chorus of 'I have the joy, joy, joy, joy, down in my heart'?"

Now, here is a scene you surely can visualize. Eliphaz leans forward. His brow wrinkles with the appropriate seriousness of the moment. He slowly opens his mouth, as if to show that he is choosing his words with great care, taking you into his confidence. His eyes meet yours. When the words finally come out, they are loud, but carefully articulated and tinged with the arrogance of "I thought so all along!"

Haven't you ever been on the ground with your breath knocked out, when a dear Christian friend comes along to "help" you by saying, "I saw this coming for a long time?"

Eliphaz says: *"I have seen the foolish taking root: but suddenly I cursed his habitation."* (Job 5:3) Today, he would say something like, "Job, all the while you were accumulating your great wealth and power, I could see this pride of yours taking root. God blessed you, and you turned your back on God. I don't know specifically what you've done, but you have obviously sinned greatly against God to have suffered this calamity. I love you 'in the Lord,' Job, but I've got to take God's side in this, and say 'amen' to this judgment that has come upon your household. It's a tragedy, all right, but nothing you don't deserve. There is no mistake here. God is fair in all He does."

NO MERCY

That these jabs are squarely aimed at Job becomes certain in the following words.

4 "His children are far from safety, and they are crushed in the gate, neither is there any to deliver them.

5 Whose harvest the hungry eateth up, and taketh it even out of the thorns, and the robber swalloweth up their substance." (Job 5:4-5)

Isn't this exactly what happened to Job? Were not HIS children crushed? Wasn't it JOB'S harvest that was destroyed? Were not "ROBBERS" the ones who swallowed up his substance?

Poor Job! Here he is in the very pit of misery, and he is being treated as though he were the personification of evil. Job, the perfect man (Job 1:1,8; 2:3), is held in derision as the fullness of sin. Don't miss this very important point. Don't forget the prophetic implications of this book as related to the coming time of Tribulation.

A definite characteristic of the Tribulation will be the reversal of values. Men will call good, that which is evil, and evil, that which is good. Isaiah warned of this.

"Woe unto them that call evil good, and good evil; that put darkness for light, and light for darkness; that put bitter for sweet, and sweet for bitter!" (Isaiah 5:20)

In that day antichrists will pass for Christ, and those who follow the Christ, will be persecuted and killed. *"Then shall they deliver you up to be afflicted, and shall kill you: and ye shall be hated of all nations for my name's sake. And then shall many be offended, and shall betray one another, and shall hate one another. And many false prophets shall rise, and shall deceive many."* (Matthew 24:9-11) *"Then if any man shall say unto you, Lo, here is Christ, or there; believe it not. For there shall arise false Christs, and false prophets, and shall shew great signs and wonders; insomuch that, if it were possible, they shall deceive the very elect."* (Matthew 24:23-24)

The charge Eliphaz levels against Job can be applied directly to the Antichrist. *"I have seen the foolish taking root: but suddenly I cursed his habitation."* Beyond signifying a man in rebellion against God's truth, the foolish man will someday be personified in the person of the Antichrist. He will be the epitome of evil, wickedness and foolishness. Consider the following:

"I have seen the wicked in great power, and spreading himself like a green bay tree. Yet he passed away, and, lo, he was not: yea, I sought him, but he could not be found." (Psalm 37:35-36)

"Why boastest thou thyself in mischief, O mighty man? the goodness of God endureth continually. Thy tongue deviseth mischiefs; like a sharp razor, working deceitfully. Thou lovest evil more than good; and lying rather than to speak righteousness. Selah. Thou lovest all devouring words, O thou deceitful tongue. God shall likewise destroy thee for ever, he shall take thee away, and pluck thee out of thy dwelling place, and root thee out of the land of the living. Selah. The righteous also shall see, and fear, and shall laugh at him: Lo, this is the man that made not God his strength; but trusted in the abundance of his riches, and strengthened himself in his wickedness." (Psalm 52:1-7)

"But the wicked shall be cut off from the earth, and the transgressors shall be rooted out of it." (Proverbs 2:22)

These passages, and others, all point to the one who will focus all wickedness and evil in a single personality in a moment of history—the Antichrist. They all show that he will be *"cut off."* Although he is speaking long before the above prophecies were recorded in writing, indeed, long before David, Solomon and Isaiah were born, Eliphaz understands the facts of biblical prophecy. He just applies them to the wrong person.

All this makes me tremble at the prospect of entering into a counseling session with an armload of "pat answers." Eliphaz was a decent man with the best of intentions, and knew more about God's truth than most professionally-trained counselors today. He had the right answers but the wrong questions.

Nothing is more dangerous than a well-intentioned Christian, equipped with some good, solid biblical information, yet void of wisdom. When you set out to do good based upon a mistaken thesis, you are doomed to failure, no matter how lofty your motives.

Eliphaz has set the counseling process in motion. He is brilliant, well-educated, influential, pure in motive and armed with great biblical truth. He is certain Job has sinned to bring on this disaster, yet he is WRONG. His thesis is off-target.

MISAPPLIED TRUTH

Now that his basic thesis is on the table, Eliphaz will toss out a series of biblical truths and proverbs to reinforce his case. He will have a great deal of truth to teach but it will all be misapplied. It doesn't make any difference how fast you run, or how many tackles you break, if you're headed toward the wrong goal line.

INEVITABLE TROUBLE

Speaking of eloquence, Eliphaz outdoes himself in the next verses. These words have often been quoted.

6 "Although affliction cometh not forth of the dust, neither doth trouble spring out of the ground;

7 Yet man is born unto trouble, as the sparks fly upward." (Job 5:6-7)

Eliphaz is correct. Though man comes from the ground, from the dust (Genesis 2:7), this isn't the source of our affliction. There are many sources of trouble and affliction mentioned in the Bible, including evil heart attitudes. One example surfaces in James.

"From whence come wars and fightings among you? come they not hence, even of your lusts that war in your members?" (James 4:1) Jesus confirms this: *"For from within, out of the heart of men, proceed evil thoughts, adulteries, fornications, murders, thefts, covetousness, wickedness, deceit, lasciviousness, an evil eye, blasphemy, pride, foolishness: All these evil things come from within, and defile the man."* (Mark 7:21-23)

Another source of trouble and affliction, besides bad heart attitudes, appears in Ephesians and was the source of Job's afflictions. *"Finally, my brethren, be strong in the Lord, and in the power of his might. Put on the whole armour of God, that ye may be able to stand against the wiles of the devil. For we wrestle not against flesh and blood, but against principali-*

ties, against powers, against the rulers of the darkness of this world, against spiritual wickedness in high places." (Ephesians 6:10-12)

While Eliphaz is playing in the dust, he completely misses the real source of Job's affliction—spiritual warfare. There is a spirit world that coexists with our visible world. It is the world of an entire hierarchy of spirit-beings, under the leadership of Satan, who vie to hinder the purposes of God and afflict His children.

Again, Eliphaz is as right as right can be. He just applies the right truth at the wrong time and to the wrong situation.

He does, however, hit the bull's eye in the next verse. *"Yet man is born unto trouble, as the sparks fly upward."* (Job 5:7) Yes, this is a very real problem. Man is BORN unto trouble. There is something wrong with man's birth. He is born with a sin nature.

David understood this truth. *"Behold, I was shapen in iniquity; and in sin did my mother conceive me."* (Psalm 51:5)

This is why man needs to be born again. There is a basic problem with his first birth, his physical birth. This is why he desperately needs a second, spiritual birth. (John 3)

INAPPROPRIATE ADVICE

Now, Eliphaz has some concrete advice for Job.

8 "I would seek unto God, and unto God would I commit my cause." (Job 5:8)

These words of advice are nothing more than pious boasting by Eliphaz. How easy to say what YOU would do, Eliphaz.

Job has already done this! Who could do more than what Job already did? *"Then Job arose, and rent his mantle, and shaved his head, and fell down upon the ground, and worshipped, And said, Naked came I out of my mother's womb, and naked shall I return thither: the LORD gave, and the LORD hath taken away; blessed be the name of the LORD. In all this Job sinned not, nor charged God foolishly."* (Job 1:20-22)

INCOMPREHENSIBLE GOD

9 "Which doeth great things and unsearchable; marvellous things without number." (Job 5:9)

Having missed the mark in his basic thesis and in his advice, Eliphaz retreats to a position of utmost safety—he delivers a powerful sermon on the greatness of God. It is all true, of course. Yet what difference does it make under these circumstances?

His words are delivered with reverent tones of piety. What he says is intended to bring God glory, and it DOES. Yet beneath the surface flows a current of nasty insinuation that Job is merely a man who is getting exactly what he deserves.

What Eliphaz does is a variation on our "prayer-preaching." We really don't pray. We use "prayer" as an excuse to indirectly say those things we don't have courage to say face to face.

Having given Job the advice to seek God and commit his cause to Him, Eliphaz now tells us about this incomprehensible God.

INCREDIBLE WORKS

In verses Job 5:10-16, Eliphaz lists some of the great, unsearchable and marvellous things that God does.

10 "Who giveth rain upon the earth, and sendeth waters upon the fields." (Job 5:10)

Despite all the scientific statements that explain the process, it is GOD who is the source and cause of rain. It rains when God wants it to rain. It doesn't rain when God doesn't want it to rain. He takes that rain water and disperses it through run-off, snow melting, creeks, rivers and floods. There is nothing random about it. Eliphaz probably couldn't predict the weather any better than a modern television weatherman, but he DID understand where rain comes from.

In the coming Tribulation God is going to give a rain that will be a real "gully-washer!" There are many Old Testament prophecies that speak of supernatural rain in the Tribulation. For a quick survey, begin with a Second Coming prophecy in 2 Samuel. *"The Spirit of the LORD spake by me, and his word was in my tongue. The God of Israel said, the Rock of Israel spake to me, He that ruleth over men must be just, ruling in the fear of God. And he shall be as the light of the morning, when the sun riseth, even a morning without clouds; as the tender grass springing out of the earth by clear shining after rain."* (2 Samuel 23:2-4)

We have already remembered Malachi's prophecy of the rising of the Sun of Righteousness. This passage adds that it will be like a sunrise *"after rain."* Psalm 68 is also a Second Coming prophecy. David adds:

"Thou, O God, didst send a plentiful rain, whereby thou didst confirm thine inheritance, when it was weary." (Psalm 68:9)

Joel received the same vision in greater detail.

"Be glad then, ye children of Zion, and rejoice in the LORD your God: for he hath given you the former rain moderately, and he will cause to come down for you the rain, the former rain, and the latter rain in the first month." (Joel 2:23)

There are both former and latter rains in Palestine that regulate the growing cycles. What is different here is that during the Tribulation, both come together in the first month—"raining pitchforks and taxi cabs!"

"Then shall we know, if we follow on to know the LORD: his going forth is prepared as the morning; and he shall come unto us as the rain, as the latter and former rain unto the earth." (Hosea 6:3)

11 "To set up on high those that be low; that those which mourn may be exalted to safety." (Job 5:11)

Eliphaz is sticking to his thesis. Job has a problem with God. If he will just confess his sin and express a proper sorrowful attitude of repentance, God will lift him up again. This is, of course, a solid biblical principle. It does not, of course, apply to Job.

When Joseph was left in the depth of a pit to die, God took him out. Later, he was in the depths of an Egyptian prison. God set him free, and set him on high, as the second ruler in Egypt. David was laying low in Palestinian caves, hiding for his life, when God brought him out, and set him high upon the throne. The Lord Jesus Christ was in the grave, in the heart of the earth, when God brought him forth and set Him at His own right hand in heavenly places.

12 "He disappointeth the devices of the crafty, so that their hands cannot perform their enterprise."

13 "He taketh the wise in their own craftiness: and the counsel of the froward is carried headlong." (Job 5:12-13)

No wonder Job became so wealthy and powerful. He did it all by his craftiness! Now, he is getting just what he deserves.

It is not hard to follow Eliphaz's line of thought. Many subscribe to it today. If a brother in Christ is enjoying a fine life, there must be something wrong! Christians are not supposed to be rich. "He couldn't come by all that honestly, could he?"

Once more the application is off. The biblical truth, however is substantiated by the Scriptures.

Pharaoh tried every trick up his sleeve to prevent Israel from leaving Egypt, but God disappointed his devices. Sanballat and Tobiah schemed to prevent Nehemiah from finishing the walls of Jerusalem, but God disappointed the devices of the crafty. Absalom, David's son, craftily sat in the gate of the city ingratiating himself to the people, and setting the stage for a takeover of his father's kingdom, but again, God disappointed his devices. Even the Devil with all his "wiles" (Ephesians 6:11) will be disappointed, and his hands will not be allowed to perform his diabolical enterprise.

The very craftiness of those "wise" in the ways of the world is the seed of their destruction. Some people are just so smart, they will assure their place in Hell. This is the problem with a legion of philosophers, scientists and self-styled religious leaders who have been so smart, they have imagined themselves smarter than God.

"Froward" (Job 5:13) is an old English word meaning "crooked." The last part of the verse says that when the crooked, the froward of Job 5:13, come together to offer their "wise" counsel, it merely accelerates their movement toward Hell and destruction.

Paul was extremely well-educated. He could play the games of the world system. He had impeccable academic credentials. Yet he refused to trust in the world's wisdom. This was a continual theme in the first chapters of 1 Corinthians. For example, in 1 Corinthians 3:19, Paul says *"For the wisdom of this world is foolishness with God. For it is written, He taketh the wise in their own craftiness."*

Where was it written? Right here in Job 5:13. Stop. This is very important. Paul is quoting the words of Eliphaz as Scripture. Eliphaz is saying the wrong thing at the wrong time to the wrong person. Yet what he says is true. This man KNOWS God's truth. There is nothing wrong with what he says. It's his lack of wisdom and understanding that results in the misapplication of truth, but it IS truth.

The same principle applies to what the other men will say. Their knowledge of God's truth is astounding. Their application of God's truth leaves a lot to be desired. We will see the same thing happen later in this chapter. Other information that Eliphaz gives in this speech is quoted in other parts of the Bible.

14 "They meet with darkness in the daytime, and grope in the noonday as in the night." (Job 5:14)

This is the destiny of the froward in Job 5:13, the crafty—those who think they are smarter than God. When the Sun of righteousness (Jesus Christ) arises with healing in His wings (Malachi 4:2), and the light of His countenance shines brighter than the noonday sun, these "bright" fellows will be left in the dark!

15 "But he saveth the poor from the sword, from their mouth, and from the hand of the mighty.

16 So the poor hath hope, and iniquity stoppeth her mouth." (Job 5:15-16)

These two verses are obviously still awaiting their final and complete fulfillment, which will also happen at the Second Coming of the Lord Jesus Christ. The poor are still waiting to be delivered. Yet the poor have this hope!

Recognizing the prophetic application of these last few verses, we remember that the entire book of Job has a prophetic application—looking forward to the coming time of the Tribulation. The clear, direct and literal application of verses 8-16 is not difficult to see. Yet all these verses also carry some definite prophetic overtones in the context of the future Tribulation.

The rearrangement of people's positions mentioned by Eliphaz in verses 11-13 also has profound Tribulation implications. God's people, the faithful remnant who are brought low by persecution, will be set on high, exalted to safety, and raptured out of the wickedness of antichrist's world. (Psalm 50:1-5; Revelation 11:11-12; 20:4; Isaiah 26:19) Simultaneously, those who sought to destroy God's purposes with the craftiness of their own devices will be disappointed and taken in their own craftiness. (Revelation 12-13, 17-18)

In Job 5:14 the "*darkness in the daytime*" matches many prophetic utterances of that coming day. "*Woe unto you that desire the day of the LORD! to what end is it for you? the day of the LORD is darkness, and not light.*" (Amos 5:18) "*Shall not the day of the LORD be darkness, and not light? even very dark, and no brightness in it?*" (Amos 5:20) "*A day of darkness and of gloominess, a day of clouds and of thick darkness, as the morning spread upon the mountains: a great people and a strong; there hath not been ever the like, neither shall be any more after it, even to the years of many generations.*" (Joel 2:2)

The "*sword*" from which the poor will be saved, according to Job 5:15, is the same one that proceeds out of the mouth of the returning King of kings. "*And out of his mouth goeth a sharp sword, that with it he should smite the nations: and he shall rule them with a rod of iron: and he treadeth the winepress of the fierceness and wrath of Almighty God.*" (Revelation 19:15)

Yes, Eliphaz has many very interesting things to say. Too bad they don't apply to Job. Eliphaz is just getting the prophetic vision warmed up, however. In a burst of prophetic energy, he delivers one of the clearest visions yet, not only of the coming Tribulation, but going even beyond into the establishment of the Millennial kingdom of the Lord.

MILLENNIAL TYPE

The next two verses, Job 5:17-18, state a truth. The truth is that God does use chastening to purify those He loves. Obviously, Eliphaz means to apply this truth to Job, telling him that what has happened to him is for his own purification.

THE TRUTH OF TRIBULATION

17 "Behold, happy is the man whom God correcteth: therefore despise not thou the chastening of the Almighty:
18 For he maketh sore, and bindeth up: he woundeth, and his hands make whole." (Job 5:17-18)

This principle is quoted in two other places in the Bible. Again we learn that what Eliphaz says is God's truth. However, it is misapplied to Job's situation.

"My son, despise not the chastening of the LORD; neither be weary of his correction." (Proverbs 3:11)

"And ye have forgotten the exhortation which speaketh unto you as unto children, My son, despise not thou the chastening of the Lord, nor faint when thou art rebuked of him." (Hebrews 12:5)

Job 5:18 speaks of God's ability to make sore and wound, and to bind up and make whole. The first two chapters of Job illustrate God's wounding and making sore. The last chapter of Job deals with the binding up and making whole. Moses recorded the same truth. *"See now that I, even I, am he, and there is no god with me: I kill, and I make alive; I wound, and I heal: neither is there any that can deliver out of my hand."* (Deuteronomy 32:39) These words of Moses to Israel remind us that this truth is precisely God's motivation as He seeks to purify centuries of Israel's sin in the fires of the coming Tribulation.

Eliphaz was acquainted with this truth hundreds of years before God had Moses commit it to writing. During Job's lifetime, man had no Bible in his hands, but God has never left the world without a witness to His truth.

THE TIMES OF TRIBULATION

19 "He shall deliver thee in six troubles: yea, in seven there shall no evil touch thee." (Job 5:19)

The words Eliphaz speaks in Job 5:19 have a clear and direct application to the Tribulation. "Six . . . yea, seven," or "four . . . yea, five," is a Hebrew poetic device of emphasis. Eliphaz is saying that God will deliver him in seven times of trouble that are to come over him.

Clearly, this transcends the historical person of Job and looks forward to that faithful remnant of Jews, preserved by God in a coming seven-year period of trouble. This is what Daniel saw in his vision of the seventy weeks of years (490 years) determined upon Israel. These seven troubles correspond to the seventieth week, or seven-year period, which is still to be fulfilled. From Artaxerxes' decree to rebuild Jerusalem on March 14, 445 B.C. to the completion of the task under Ezra and Nehemiah, 49 years passed (seven weeks of years). From that point to Christ's triumphant entry into Jerusalem on "Palm Sunday" before His crucifixion was another 434 years (62 weeks of years). The last week, or seven years, are the seven troubles, the time of Jacob's trouble. (Jeremiah 30:7)

"Seventy weeks are determined upon thy people and upon thy holy city, to finish the transgression, and to make an end of sins, and to make reconciliation for iniquity, and to bring in everlasting righteousness, and to seal up the vision and prophecy, and to anoint the most Holy. Know therefore and understand, that from the going forth of the commandment to restore and to build Jerusalem unto the Messiah the Prince shall be seven weeks, and threescore and two weeks: the street shall be built again, and the wall, even in troublous times. And after threescore and two weeks shall Messiah be cut off, but not for himself: and the people of the prince that shall come shall destroy the city and the sanctuary; and the end thereof shall be with a flood, and unto the end of the war desolations are determined. And he shall confirm the covenant with many for one week: and in the midst of the week he shall cause the sacrifice and the oblation to cease, and for the overspreading of abominations he shall make it desolate, even until the consummation, and that determined shall be poured upon the desolate." (Daniel 9:24-27)

THE TRIALS OF TRIBULATION

20 "In famine he shall redeem thee from death: and in war from the power of the sword.

21 Thou shalt be hid from the scourge of the tongue: neither shalt thou be afraid of destruction when it cometh.

22 At destruction and famine thou shalt laugh: neither shalt thou be afraid of the beasts of the earth." (Job 5:20-22)

Eliphaz lists the seven things from which Job will be delivered if he but repents. They are: famine, death, war, the power of the sword, the scourge of the tongue, destruction, and the beasts of the earth.

Every element in Job 5:20-22 is identified with a prophecy of the Tribulation. You need go no further than Revelation 6 to see five of the seven specifically, and all seven by implication. A good concordance will locate many cross-references about these Tribulation prophecies.

THE TRIUMPH AFTER TRIBULATION

The final words of Eliphaz look past the chaos of the Tribulation and the immediate outpouring of God's wrath to the establishment of the Millennial kingdom with Christ seated on the throne of David. Again, every element of these verses can be located with respect to corresponding millennial prophecies.

23 "For thou shalt be in league with the stones of the field: and the beasts of the field shall be at peace with thee." (Job 5:23)

Isaiah saw that day. Isaiah 11 begins with the second coming. "*And there shall come forth a rod out of the stem of Jesse, and a Branch shall grow out of his roots: And the spirit of the LORD shall rest upon him, the spirit of wisdom and understanding, the spirit of counsel and might, the spirit of knowledge and of the fear of the LORD; And shall make him of quick understanding in the fear of the LORD: and he shall not judge after the sight of his eyes, neither reprove after the hearing of his ears: But with righteousness shall he judge the poor, and reprove with equity for the meek of the earth: and he shall smite the earth with the rod of his mouth, and with the breath of his lips shall he slay the wicked. And righteousness shall be the girdle of his loins, and faithfulness the girdle of his reins. The wolf also shall dwell with the lamb, and the leopard shall lie down with the kid; and the calf and the young lion and the fatling together; and a little child shall lead them. And the cow and the bear shall feed; their young ones shall lie down together: and the lion shall eat straw like the ox. And the sucking child shall play on the hole of the asp, and the weaned child shall put his hand on the cockatrice' den. They shall not hurt nor destroy in all my holy mountain: for the earth shall be full of the knowledge of the LORD, as the waters cover the sea.*" (Isaiah 11:1-9)

24 "And thou shalt know that thy tabernacle shall be in peace; and thou shalt visit thy habitation, and shalt not sin." (Job 5:24)

It is impossible to say just how much Eliphaz really understands of the prophetic implications of his words. But there will be a day when God's people will dwell in peace and be free from sin. Scripture is filled with such promises. One classic example is what John saw in the Revelation.

"*And I saw a new heaven and a new earth: for the first heaven and the first earth were passed away; and there was no more sea. And I John saw the holy city, new Jerusalem, coming down from God out of heaven, prepared as a bride adorned for her husband. And I heard a great voice out of heaven saying, Behold, the tabernacle of God is with men, and he will dwell with them, and they shall be his people, and God himself shall be with them, and be their God. And God shall wipe away all tears from their eyes; and there shall be no more death, neither sorrow, nor crying, neither shall there be any more pain: for the former things are passed away."* (Revelation 21:1-4)

The eloquent ramblings of Eliphaz continue.

25 "Thou shalt know also that they seed shall be great, and thine offspring as the grass of the earth." (Job 5:25)

Eliphaz's prophetic promise to Job of numerous and prosperous descendants closely parallels God's many promises to His people. Consider a couple of examples.

"There shall be an handful of corn in the earth upon the top of the mountains; the fruit thereof shall shake like Lebanon: and they of the city shall flourish like grass of the earth." (Psalm 72:16)

"His seed shall be mighty upon earth: the generation of the upright shall be blessed." (Psalm 112:2)

Job 5:26 also looks beyond Job's historical character into the yet future restoration of Israel in the Millennium. *"Thou shalt come to thy grave in a full age, like as a shock of corn cometh in his season."* (Job 5:26)

Job did live a long, full life. We also know that the Scripture prophesies that the long lifetimes that existed before the Flood will again be common when the curse upon creation is lifted during the Millennium. Isaiah saw a time when a person of one hundred years would be just a kid.

"There shall be no more thence an infant of days, nor an old man that hath not filled his days: for the child shall die an hundred years old; but the sinner being an hundred years old shall be accursed." (Isaiah 65:20)

Eloquent ramblings of Eliphaz? Only on the surface. Eliphaz may not have full understanding of the impact of his words, but this is spiritual warfare. There are more things happening here than meet the eye. It's time that we carefully review what is taking place.

On the surface, Eliphaz thinks he has figured out Job's problem, but he totally misses the mark with his thesis that Job has secret sin. Once off target, he continues to fire salvo after salvo of assorted biblical truth in Job's direction, evidently hoping that something might stick that will be of help.

Unknown to Eliphaz, behind the scene Satan is using him in an attempt to push Job over the edge of despair. The Devil doesn't care how much divine truth Eliphaz throws around, if it accomplishes his purpose of frustrating Job.

Now the plot thickens. As if two currents in this stream weren't enough, there is a third. While Eliphaz rambles on, and Satan craftily manipulates his intentions with the goal of destroying Job, God is quietly above the fray, causing every word spoken to be recorded just as He wanted.

In the midst of this spiritual battle God uses the misapplied truth of Eliphaz to paint a prophetic picture of a time of trouble—the Tribulation—that is to come upon His people, Israel. Then, in a section of speech that transcends the historical circumstances, he puts words in the mouth of Eliphaz that describe the coming Millennial reign of the Lord Jesus Christ. What an incredible example of the sovereignty of God!

27 "Lo this, we have searched it, so it is; hear it, and know thou it for thy good." (Job 5:27)

The final words of Eliphaz are almost comical, if it were not for the tragedy of it all. In other words, "Yes, I have examined the evidence, studied it out, and what I've said is exactly the way it is. So listen up, Job, and remember that this is all for your own good."

Eliphaz must have been feeling quite satisfied with himself. Satan, sensing the growing pain and frustration of Job, is also pleased. And, above it all, God is firmly in control, using even the best shots of the enemy to accomplish His purposes, and record for all generations a prophetic picture in a most remarkable book.

7

MAN AT THE EDGE OF DESPAIR

Oh that my grief were throughly weighed,
and my calamity laid in the balances together!
For now it would be heavier than the sand of the sea:
therefore my words are swallowed up.
For the arrows of the Almighty are within me,
the poison whereof drinketh up my spirit:
the terrors of God do set themselves in array against me.

Job 6:2-4

HOW MUCH DOES GRIEF WEIGH? HOW DO YOU WEIGH IT? DO you need a special scale?

We know, of course, that grief is intangible. It does not have mass, and therefore cannot be physically weighed. It is interesting nonetheless to observe that many people who labor under a "load" of grief, actually walk stooped over, as though they were carrying a load of lumber.

JOB WEIGHS HIS GRIEF

1 "But Job answered and said,
2 Oh that my grief were throughly weighed, and my calamity laid in the balances together!
3 For now it would be heavier than the sand of the sea: therefore my words are swallowed up.
4 For the arrows of the Almighty are within me, the poison whereof drinketh up my spirit: the terrors of God do set themselves in array against me." (Job 6:1-4)

HEAVY GRIEF

No one could understand the weighty characteristic of grief better than Job. Have you ever lugged around a bucket of wet sand? Job says his grief is heavier than the sand of the sea. The *"balances"* that Job speaks of refer to scales, in which his grief and calamity could be weighed.

It should be evident that Job is not giving Eliphaz a direct answer to his speech. Job is so absorbed in his own trial, he doesn't attempt to rebut Eliphaz argument for argument. His anxiety is aimless.

Job will again wish for balances in chapter 31, but there it will be to weigh his integrity. *"Let me be weighed in an even balance, that God may know mine integrity."* (Job 31:6)

Who can blame Job for complaining about the weight of his grief and calamity? Have any of us ever approached his level of pain? After all, Job doesn't even know what is happening, or why. He is totally in the dark.

Few individuals in Scripture could identify with Job's intense suffering. One of the few who could approach him would be the Apostle Paul. Consider the trials Paul endured. Here is his own testimony from his second letter to the Corinthians, as he defends his ministry against attacks from self-serving, false teachers.

"Are they ministers of Christ? (I speak as a fool) I am more; in labours more abundant, in stripes above measure, in prisons more frequent, in deaths oft. Of the Jews five times received I forty stripes save one. Thrice was I beaten with rods, once was I stoned, thrice I suffered shipwreck, a night and a day I have been in the deep; In journeyings often, in perils of waters, in perils of robbers, in perils by mine own countrymen, in perils by the heathen, in perils in the city, in perils in the wilderness, in perils in the sea, in perils among false brethren; In weariness and painfulness, in watchings often, in hunger and thirst, in fastings often, in cold and nakedness. Beside those things that are without, that which cometh upon me daily, the care of all the churches." (2 Corinthians 11:23-28)

Perhaps Paul is not quite in Job's league, but he has more experience suffering than most of us. There is a significant difference between Paul's perspective and Job's. Paul is on the Sonshine side of the Cross, and can understand much more than Job ever did.

"Paul, how much does all that affliction weigh?" He gives us the answer here in this same letter to the Corinthians. *"For our LIGHT affliction, which is but for a moment, worketh for us a far more exceeding and eternal weight of glory."* (2 Corinthians 4:17) (Author's emphasis)

What Job would call heavy, Paul called light, because he sees a truth that Job couldn't. Paul sees that God knows every "pound" of our grief, and that He will one day tip the balance in our favor. Whatever affliction we might be asked to suffer, God is going to convert it into *"a far more exceeding and eternal weight of glory."*

What makes Job's affliction heavier is that he thinks he is the target of God's *"arrows."* (Job 6:4) As we have observed before, Job is ignorant of Satan's role in his calamity. Satan has been firing the arrows, yet God has allowed it.

That Job would choose the word *"arrows"* is interesting. God DOES have "poisoned arrows" like those Job mentions here in Job 6:4. David felt the sting of God's arrows. *"For thine arrows stick fast in me, and thy hand presseth me sore."* (Psalm 38:2)

Having felt God's arrows, David prays for God to use them on his enemies. *"Cast forth lightning, and scatter them: shoot out thine arrows, and destroy them."* (Psalm 144:6)

Habakkuk mentions God's arrows also. *"The sun and moon stood still in their habitation: at the light of thine arrows they went, and at the shining of thy glittering spear."* (Habakkuk 3:11)

Zechariah as well sees the same thing in the prophetic context of the Second Coming. *"And the LORD shall be seen over them, and his arrow shall go forth as the lightning: and the Lord GOD shall blow the trumpet, and shall go with whirlwinds of the south."* (Zechariah 9:14)

What makes this doubly confusing is that Satan also has arrows. A primary biblical truth is that Satan attempts to counterfeit EVERYTHING about God.

The psalmist prayed to the Almighty to protect him from the arrows of the mighty. *"Sharp arrows of the mighty, with coals of juniper."* (Psalm 120:4)

Paul also spoke of God's provision against the Devil's arrows. *"Above all, taking the shield of faith, wherewith ye shall be able to quench all the fiery darts of the wicked."* (Ephesians 6:16)

A critical issue in any wartime situation is that of "friendly fire." In the heat of battle, with lead of all shapes and sizes speeding through the air, a soldier must take great care not to hit his own men. Even with the best of intentions, and the most professional training, men are sometimes killed by "friendly fire." A military maxim is that "friendly fire isn't," which means friendly bullets kill just as dead as enemy bullets. Conclusion: keep your head down and dodge ALL bullets and "arrows."

Job can tell you that those arrows hurt, no matter whose they are. Yet that is just the way life is sometimes. We take heavy fire without ever knowing where it is coming from. We may NEVER know, just like Job.

Sometimes we magnify our misery because we are too curious. We want to know who is shooting the arrows, and why. The basic issue is to deal with the arrows, not who is shooting them. That may be impossible to decide with certainty. In Job's case the arrows came from the Devil. Yet God allowed it, and God brought up Job's name first. How do you figure it? Whose arrows are they, really? Don't wear yourself out analyzing the WHO, WHAT, and FROM WHERE. Just deal with it, minimize your losses, keep your head down and get on with life!

In the following verses Job asks a series of four questions. He is not expecting an answer because it is obvious that they all demand a negative answer.

HARD TO STOMACH

5 "Doth the wild ass bray when he hath grass? or loweth the ox over his fodder?
6 Can that which is unsavoury be eaten without salt? or is there any taste in the white of an egg?
7 The things that my soul refused to touch are as my sorrowful meat." (Job 6:5-7)

Through these four rhetorical questions Job is saying, "Would I be complaining like this without cause? When I was well I ate what I wanted. Now, I'm having to take in a steady diet of things that are hard to stomach—sorrow, grief, affliction."

Don't fail to notice Job's use of the word *"soul."* In the Old Testament "soul" is used to speak of a man's whole being, while in the New Testament the word is generally used in a more specific sense. Forgive this diversion, but we will see Job and others in the Old Testament speak of "souls," and it is important you understand what is being discussed. In today's world we generally use the word to speak only on that inner part of our being that is "us." In the Old Testament it has a broader, more inclusive meaning.

New Testament teaching is that a man is a three-part being—body, soul and spirit. (1 Thessalonians 5:23) Man is stillborn spiritually. His spirit is dead because sin is his nature inherited from his father. God provides his being, mind, will, volition, and personality (soul), with sufficient physical life to have opportunity to respond to the Gospel and receive eternal life.

Man's spirit before salvation is dead. Yet death in the Bible never means annihilation, only separation. Lost man HAS a spirit, but it is a DEAD spirit, separated from God's life. Lost man's spirit operates on the same level as his soul, and for that reason there is little practical difference between the two.

In the Old Testament the whole of man is seen as a "soul." While salvation is clearly offered in the Old Testament, the rebirth of man's lost spirit is something made possible only by the finished work of Christ. This is why the idea of being "born again" is a New Testament concept.

Now, because of what the Lord Jesus Christ accomplished in His death, burial and resurrection, man can have a new spirit. This new spirit operates on the level God intended for it. It is man's contact with the spiritual realm. Receiving spiritual information from the spirit, and physical information from the body, the soul of man makes decisions and sets the course of his life accordingly.

"For the word of God is quick, and powerful, and sharper than any two-edged sword, piercing EVEN TO THE DIVIDING ASUNDER OF SOUL AND SPIRIT, and of the joints and marrow, and is a discerner of the thoughts and intents of the heart." (Hebrews 4:12) (Author's emphasis)

HOPELESS HOPING

8 "Oh that I might have my request; and that God would grant me the thing that I long for!

9 Even that it would please God to destroy me; that he would let loose his hand, and cut me off!" (Job 6:8-9)

In a burst of emotional energy Job explodes in verse 8. Job asks God to answer his prayer. What IS that prayer? It is the same thing that he spent most of chapter 3 of Job talking about—Job still thinks he would be better off dead.

Job's thoughts are similar to those offered by many proponents of euthanasia. Where DOES one draw the line before putting someone out of their misery? It's not hard to see why Job would rather just end it all. Yet if someone had ended his suffering, there would have been no double blessing as recorded in the last chapter. We should leave those decisions to God Himself. He is the only One who really knows what is happening.

10 "Then should I yet have comfort; yea, I would harden myself in sorrow: let him not spare; for I have not concealed the words of the Holy One." (Job 6:10)

This theological philosophizing is of no value to Job at this point. All he knows is that his life doesn't seem to be worth living. Job is convinced that death is the only way out.

A devotional application needs to be pointed out here. For every believer who is sick and tired of the afflictions of the flesh, the frustration of life's misery, and all the other many trials of life, the only way out IS death. Let me be quick to add I do not mean physical death here, but the death of the flesh, and death to self.

When the Lord Jesus Christ died on the cross, His death was sufficient to end our slavery to the flesh (Romans 6:6-14). When we accept Him as our Savior, His death is counted as ours. No longer do we have to live as slaves of the flesh. To make this victory continuously effective in our lives we must learn to die to self (Galatians 6:14; Ephesians 4:21-24; Colossians 3:1-4), a decision that needs to be made daily (1 Corinthians 15:31).

Yes, Job's grief was overwhelming. No one could deny him the right to cry out in anguish. Yet do not fail to notice a remarkable testimony placed at the end of verse 10. After expressing again his desire to die, Job said, *"for I have not concealed the words of the Holy One."* (Job 6:10b)

Not only had Job not cursed God, nor foolishly charged Him in all that had happened (Job 1:22), he had *"not concealed the words of the Holy One."* Job correctly understood that this is the major issue, the ONLY issue in life—*"the words of the Holy One."*

This statement is also remarkable for the recognition that even in Job's day there WERE *"words of the Holy One."* Job had no Bible, but he had the *"words of the Holy One."*

Creation began with the words of the Word of God. (John 1:1-3) The essence of all life, of all human history, is how man relates to God's words. In every circumstance the only issue is whether man will believe what God has said.

Job is bruised and bloody from repeated attacks coming from a source yet unknown to him. He is reeling from the blows, both mentally and physically, yet he dares not turn loose of the words of God.

11 "What is my strength, that I should hope? and what is mine end, that I should prolong my life?

12 Is my strength the strength of stones? or is my flesh of brass?

13 Is not my help in me? and is wisdom driven quite from me?" (Job 6:11-13)

Job issues this series of questions to no one in particular. These questions have no answer. His counselors have no answer. They are questions that spring from the misery of an afflicted man. A man still clinging to the words of God, but a man who has lost all hope for his own life. Job is a man of faith, yet he has no hope to hold to for his own immediate future. These questions require no commentary.

HARDENED FRIENDS

14 "To him that is afflicted pity should be shewed from his friend; but he forsaketh the fear of the Almighty." (Job 6:14)

If ever a man needed a friend, that man is Job. Yet Job has some gripes about the type of friendship his counselors are showing.

Job's argument is simple. What's a friend for if not to show pity when his buddy is afflicted? If you can't get pity from your friend, then who is going to give it to you?

Here is Job's complaint about his "friend." *"But he* (the friend) *forsaketh the fear of the Almighty."* (Author's comment) (Job 6:14) Job is saying that when a man refuses to pity his friend, he is forsaking the fear of God. The gist of Job's words is his friend isn't right with God.

The conversation is headed straight downhill. Eliphaz has accused Job of secret sin. Now, Job accuses Eliphaz of not being right with God. Unfortunately many pious-sounding conversations end this way, with a "God is on my side, not yours" argument.

From our New Testament perspective Job has Scriptural basis for his complaint. *"Remember them that are in bonds, as bound with them; and them which suffer adversity, as being yourselves also in the body."* (Hebrews 13:3)

From the beginning we have remarked that the problem with Job's counselors was one of timing and tact, not truth. There is a time for hard love, and we should not hold back from pointing out known sin. Yet we should be very careful to have our facts together before we speak. Eliphaz had not done his homework. Job needs pity, not pious accusations.

Another feature of Job 6:14 we need to observe is the use of the name of God as *"the Almighty."* The Hebrew word is *El Shaddi.* This name appears first in Genesis 17:1 when God confirmed His covenant with Abram, changed his name to Abraham and gave him the sign of circumcision.

El Shaddai appears six times in Genesis, and thirty-one times in Job. In Moses' time it has only three appearances, two of them concerning a gentile priest (Numbers 24:4,16). It is a name that was used in the times of the patriarchs, which is more evidence of the early composition of Job. Had Job been written later, as some scholars claim, it would be more likely that the common name for God in the book would not be "the Almighty," but a name used more frequently in later times.

In the following verses Job amplifies and illustrates his complaint that when you need a friend, he's never there. We will consider the verses in order beginning with Job 6:15.

15 "My brethren have dealt deceitfully as a brook, and as the stream of brooks they pass away." (Job 6:15)

In west Texas, and other arid climates, there are many dry ditches and gullies that spread their fingers throughout the landscape. People who live in a wetter climate often wonder what purpose these breaks in the ground serve.

When it rains, it often comes fast and furiously. The ground is so dry and hard that the water immediately runs off and into these gullies, forming rushing torrents of water. Yet the water disappears as quickly as it came, hence the term "flash flood"—it comes and goes in a "flash." This type of rain storm is known as a "gully-washer." The idea is that friends disappear just as rapidly as water in those dry ditches—"flash friends."

16 "Which are blackish by reason of the ice, and wherein the snow is hid." (Job 6:16)

The brooks Job is thinking of, however, aren't from Texas or New Mexico. Job is thinking about the runoff from snow and ice. Snow is beautiful when it is falling, but soon disappears in dirty, black water and slush. He concludes:

17 "What time they wax warm, they vanish: when it is hot, they are consumed out of their place." (Job 6:17)

Unfortunately, most "friends" are like snow runoff waters. When it gets hot, they are gone.

Those ditches Job has been referring to are empty most of the time. This is why he says,

18 "The paths of their way are turned aside; they go to nothing, and perish." (Job 6:18)

You see them, expect to find water, yet are soon disappointed. Job gives an example of this phenomena in the next two verses.

19 "The troops of Tema looked, the companies of Sheba waited for them.

20 They were confounded because they had hoped; they came thither, and were ashamed." (Job 6:18-20)

Job is thinking of a caravan going from Tema in Edom to Sheba in Arabia. The Temanites were looking for water in those dry ditches, and never found it, because the water was swallowed up by the desert. Those waiting for them in Sheba were confounded and ashamed for their false hope.

We again see a prophetic application. Tema has already been connected with Edom, in our discussion of the background of Job's counselors. Tribulation prophecy mentions both Tema and Sheba. The prophetic idea is that of waiting during in the Tribulation for help that never arrives.

21 "For now ye are nothing; ye see my casting down, and are afraid." (Job 6:21)

Job has concluded that his counselors are a worthless lot, as empty as the dry creek beds he has been using as an illustration.

22 "Did I say, Bring unto me? or, Give a reward for me of your substance?

23 Or, Deliver me from the enemy's hand? or, Redeem me from the hand of the mighty?" (Job 6:22-23)

Job has not asked these men for anything. Job has also not asked these men for protection. All Job wants is some help and understanding, yet so far they have not addressed his problem, except to accuse him of some secret sin.

24 "Teach me, and I will hold my tongue: and cause me to understand wherein I have erred.

25 How forcible are right words! but what doth your arguing reprove?" (Job 6:24-25)

Job comes to the same conclusion that we have been holding to from the beginning—these men have many facts, but don't know how to apply them. If they really know what they are talking about, then Job asks them to point out his specific sin. They cannot, or course, do that, because there is no secret sin. All their arguing proves nothing.

26 "Do ye imagine to reprove words, and the speeches of one that is desperate, which are as wind?" (Job 6:26)

Job has enough presence of mind to realize that it is useless to try to use his words to get a handle on what is happening. We cannot hold Job to his words in this moment of desperate agony. He is just blowing off steam. He is going to say some things in desperation that he wouldn't say except under extreme agony.

This is why we spoke earlier of cutting him some slack. He has just suffered a monstrous calamity. It is enough that he holds to his integrity and to the words of the Holy One. Don't pay attention to every thing he says. This is a good counseling principle for dealing with desperate people.

At the death of a loved one, a divorce, a tragedy, or another stressful happening, people tend to let words fly wildly from their lips. They say things they would not normally say. The worst thing a friend can do is to try to answer or respond to every word. When someone is hurting, sometimes the best thing you can do is just to be there. Simply love them. You don't HAVE to say anything. There will be plenty of time to talk later. "Oh, you don't really mean that!" is the worst thing you can say. Job's integrity is retained when he doesn't take his own life. At the moment of extreme agony the person who says "I wish I could die!" means just that. But that doesn't require the same reaction from you as if he is pouring out pills or loading a pistol.

27 "Yea, ye overwhelm the fatherless, and ye dig a pit for your friend." (Job 6:27)

Job would love to receive some genuine love and understanding from these men, yet it turns out that He is teaching THEM what they should be doing. "Why are you attacking ME?" says Job, "I'm supposed to be your friend."

28 "Now therefore be content, look upon me; for it is evident unto you if I lie.
29 Return, I pray you, let it not be iniquity; yea, return again, my righteousness is in it.
30 Is there iniquity in my tongue? cannot my taste discern perverse things?" (Job 6:28-30)

Finally, Job turns to deal with the only issue that has been put forth—that Job has a secret sin. He pleads with his friends to believe him when he tells them that he has committed no secret sin. He asks them to think it through again. Iniquity is NOT the cause of his suffering.

If Job has a problem, it is his tendency to trust in his own righteousness. It is NOT hidden sin. This is also Israel's present situation—trusting in their own righteousness instead of God's. *"Brethren, my heart's desire and prayer to God for Israel is, that they might be saved. For I bear them record that they have a zeal of God, but not according to knowledge. For they being ignorant of God's righteousness, and going about to establish their own righteousness, have not submitted themselves unto the righteousness of God. For Christ is the end of the law for righteousness to every one that believeth."* (Romans 10:1-4)

JOB CATALOGUES HIS COMPLAINTS

COMPLAINING ABOUT THE BURDEN OF LIFE

1 "Is there not an appointed time to man upon earth? are not his days also like the days of an hireling?" (Job 7:1)

Job understands that there is a day appointed for all men to die, a truth that is found various places in the Scriptures. *"And as it is appointed unto men once to die, but after this the judgment."* (Hebrews 9:27)

Paul spoke the same truth to the Athenians on Mars Hill. *"Because he hath appointed a day, in the which he will judge the world in righteousness by that man whom he hath ordained; whereof he hath given assurance unto all men, in that he hath raised him from the dead."* (Acts 17:31)

However, in this verse, Job is complaining that his life is doomed. What he is saying is simply, "Isn't my number up yet?"

2 "As a servant earnestly desireth the shadow, and as an hireling looketh for the reward of his work." (Job 7:2)

His words in Job 7:2 are just as despondent. In other words, "Just give me what I've got coming to me and let me go," as though he were a common laborer just fired and picking up his final paycheck.

3 "So am I made to possess months of vanity, and wearisome nights are appointed to me." (Job 7:3)

Job simply feels he has no reason to live. Empty days and long, sleepless nights are all he has left.

4 "When I lie down, I say, When shall I arise, and the night be gone? and I am full of tossings to and fro unto the dawning of the day." (Job 7:4)

Anyone who has gone through a time of intense crisis can identify with Job's words in verse 4. The historical and literal meaning of these words is obvious.

Remember that doctrinally Job pictures three almost indistinguishable things—lost man in hell, the Jew during the Tribulation and Christ on the cross. The anguish of those in the coming time of Tribulation is impossible for us to understand. All the forces of hell will be unleashed upon the earth. Men will toss to and fro, wondering when the dark night will ever end. The only Man who could possibly identify with this level of torment is our Lord Jesus Christ, Who suffered our hell for us on the cross.

The only thing more terrible is the plight of lost man in hell, where night has no end, ever! For him the day will never dawn. If hell was just the end of existence it wouldn't be so bad. The hell of hell is lost man's acknowledgement that he has rejected God's love, has no other opportunity, and will suffer the torment of flame and separation from God for ever *"without hope,"* as Job will say in 7:6. We emphasized this truth in our comments on Job 3:20-23.

COMPLAINING ABOUT THE PRESENT REALITY

5 "My flesh is clothed with worms and clods of dust; my skin is broken, and become loathsome." (Job 7:5)

Back to the reality of Job's horror. Verse 5 is another of those verses that is not difficult to understand.

The greatest man in the East is sitting among ashes, his skin broken open by the boils that cover his entire body. The circumstance could not be worse for his medical condition. Parasitic "worms" have taken root in his sores, compounded by dirt. Infection has set in, and he undoubtedly smells. A *"loathsome"* situation indeed!

The reference to *"worms"* has a possible prophetic application. Notice the mention of worms in connection with lost man's final destiny.

"And if thy foot offend thee, cut it off: it is better for thee to enter halt into life, than having two feet to be cast into hell, into the fire that never shall be quenched: WHERE THEIR WORM DIETH NOT, and the fire is not quenched. And if thine eye offend thee, pluck it out: it is better for thee to enter into the kingdom of God with one eye, than having two eyes to be cast into hell fire: WHERE THEIR WORM DIETH NOT, and the fire is not quenched." (Mark 9:45-48) (Author's emphasis)

Psalm 22 is a remarkable prophecy of the crucifixion of Christ. The Gospels give the crucifixion from man's point of view. Psalm 22 is the view from the cross. It gives us the thoughts that ran through our Lord's mind as He hung dying for us. As He bore the burden of hell, He exclaimed, *"But I am a worm, and no man; a reproach of men, and despised of the people."* (Psalm 22:6)

Isaiah even mentions worms as he looks forward to the calm after the storm of God's judgment. *"And they shall go forth, and look upon the carcases of the men that have transgressed against me: for their worm shall not die, neither shall their fire be quenched; and they shall be an abhorring unto all flesh."* (Isaiah 66:24)

What do all these worms mean? Your guess is as good as mine, but I do find irony in this image. Man has concluded that all life began with single cells wonderfully combining into more complex life forms. From amoebas to worms to monkeys to man! From this point of view, man has now evolved into a magnificent masterpiece capable of altering the building blocks of life and ushering in a wonderful kingdom of humanistic glory. But from God's point of view, lost man will be reduced to the level of a slimy worm forever enduring the flames of hell.

6 "My days are swifter than a weaver's shuttle, and are spent without hope." (Job 7:6)

Verse 6 is not a contradiction to the seemingly endless nights of verse 4. Verse 4 emphasized the unspeakable agony that robs one of sleep, while in verse 6 Job comments on the transitory nature of life. He continues this theme in verse 7.

7 "O remember that my life is wind: mine eye shall no more see good." (Job 7:7)

The brevity of life is often contemplated in the Book of Job. Many figures will be used to illustrate how quickly life passes. James said the same thing. *"Whereas ye know not what shall be on the morrow. For what is your life? It is even a vapour, that appeareth for a little time, and then vanisheth away."* (James 4:14)

Job is afraid his life is over, but yet he is afraid also that it isn't. The combination of verses 6 and 7 are interesting. In verse 6 he put forth the truth of life's brevity, while in verse 7 he reminds God of that truth, as if He might forget.

God has not forgotten. Listen to the psalmist. *"For he remembered that they were but flesh; a wind that passeth away, and cometh not again."* (Psalm 78:39)

David mentions life's wind-like quality again in Psalm 103. *"As for man, his days are as grass: as a flower of the field, so he flourisheth. For the wind passeth over it, and it is gone; and the place thereof shall know it no more."* (Psalm 103:15-16)

Although Psalms was written hundreds of years after Job, God never changes, so Job was well aware of the truths expressed in it. Yet he must have forgotten the truth expressed immediately before verses 15 and 16 of Psalm 103. *"Like as a father pitieth his children, so the LORD pitieth them that fear him. For he knoweth our frame; he remembereth that we are dust."* (Psalm 103:13-14)

This is the Old Testament expression of 1 Corinthians 10:13. *"There hath no temptation taken you but such as is common to man: but God is faithful, who will not suffer you to be tempted above that ye are able; but will with the temptation also make a way to escape, that ye may be able to bear it."* (1 Corinthians 10:13)

If these words are true (and we know they MUST be), then Job must have been quite a man! God has allowed him to be tempted above what most of us could handle, yet God knows that in spite of Job's agony of the moment he CAN handle it.

Job isn't convinced at all. He believes it is all over. He is ready to say his goodbyes.

> **8 "The eye of him that hath seen me shall see me no more: thine eyes are upon me, and I am not.**
> **9 As the cloud is consumed and vanisheth away: so he that goeth down to the grave shall come up no more.**
> **10 He shall return no more to his house, neither shall his place know him any more." (Job 7:8-10)**

COMPLAINING ABOUT BEING THE TARGET OF GOD'S WRATH

Job is convinced that God has singled him out for special attention. This is true, as we saw in the very first chapter. However, Job has no idea that what is happening to him is a compliment from God. Not knowing why he has been singled out, Job merely assumes, as most of us would, that God is mad at him. He is wrestling with bitterness in his soul.

11 "Therefore I will not refrain my mouth; I will speak in the anguish of my spirit; I will complain in the bitterness of my soul." (Job 7:11)

Having stated that he will soon be departing this world, Job feels he is entitled to his full share of self-pity. Who could blame him?

The next few verses give further detail of Job's desperation. They explain why Job thinks that he must be the object of God's special attention.

12 "Am I a sea, or a whale, that thou settest a watch over me?" (Job 7:12)

Job compares himself to a *"sea"* or a *"whale"* which he identifies as having a *"watch"* set over them. Does Job understand why God set whales aside from the time of creation?

Consider this fine point from the account of creation. *"And God said, Let the waters bring forth abundantly the moving creature that hath life, and fowl that may fly above the earth in the open firmament of heaven. AND GOD CREATED GREAT WHALES, and every living creature that moveth, which the waters brought forth abundantly, after their kind, and every winged fowl after his kind: and God saw that it was good."* (Genesis 1:20-21) (Author's emphasis)

Of all the life forms God created, He singles out this one. Why would He do this? One good explanation is to consider carefully the following words of the Book of Jonah. *"NOW THE LORD HAD PREPARED A GREAT FISH to swallow up Jonah. And Jonah was in the belly of the fish three days and three nights."* (Jonah 1:17) (Author's emphasis)

God had been watching the whale from the very beginning. He also had set a watch upon the sea. God has some special purposes in the sea. We will learn some interesting things about the sea in Job.

"Or who shut up the sea with doors, when it brake forth, as if it had issued out of the womb?" (Job 38:8) God has placed *"doors"* to mark the limits of the sea. He keeps it in its appointed place.

"Hast thou entered into the springs of the sea? or hast thou walked in the search of the depth?" (Job 38:16) Here is a remarkable statement. We now know that the sea DOES have springs! But how does Job know this? We'll have more to say about the sea later. For now just note that God has put a watch over it, and over whales too.

It is the watch placed upon Job that is the object of our attention, and in verse 13 Job continues his lament. The message of his words is obvious.

13 "When I say, My bed shall comfort me, my couch shall ease my complaint;

14 Then thou scarest me with dreams, and terrifies me through visions:

15 So that my soul chooseth strangling, and death rather than my life.

16 I loathe it; I would not live alway: let me alone; for my days are vanity." (Job 7:13-16)

Again Job goes back to the same theme. His life is not worth living. He looks for rest and comfort and finds terror. The only way out he sees is to die. This is not what he wants, but it's the only way he can think of to escape the vanity of his life.

Poor Job! His despair is perfectly understandable, but what a difference the cross makes. On our side of the cross listen to Paul's attitude concerning life and death. *"For to me to live is Christ, and to die is gain."* (Philippians 1:21)

The reason for this attitude appears in Paul's letter to the Galatians. *"I am crucified with Christ: nevertheless I live; yet not I, but Christ liveth in me: and the life which I now live in the flesh I live by the faith of the Son of God, who loved me, and gave himself for me."* (Galatians 2:20)

In verse 17 Job's despair moves him to ask an age-old question.

17 "What is man, that thou shouldest magnify him? and that thou shouldest set thine heart upon him?" (Job 7:17)

What human being in a moment of quiet contemplation has not pondered this mystery? Why would God be interested in man?

David also posed this question. *"What is man, that thou art mindful of him? and the son of man, that thou visitest him?"* (Psalm 8:4) Again, in Psalm 144 the question appears. *"LORD, what is man, that thou takest knowledge of him! or the son of man, that thou makest account of him!"* (Psalm 144:3)

Then, in the New Testament we find it again. *"But one in a certain place testified, saying, What is man, that thou art mindful of him? or the son of man, that thou visitest him?"* (Hebrews 2:6)

18 "And that thou shouldest visit him every morning, and try him every moment?" (Job 7:18)

Job's statement in verse 18 is an exaggeration, but surely doesn't seem exaggerated to Job.

19 "How long wilt thou not depart from me, nor let me alone till I swallow down my spittle?" (Job 7:19)

In verse 19, Job sings another chorus of "Just let me die now, Lord." He just wants to choke on his last drops of spittle.

20 "I have sinned; what shall I do unto thee, O thou preserver of men? why hast thou set me as a mark against thee, so that I am a burden to myself?

21 And why dost thou not pardon my transgression, and take

away mine iniquity? for now shall I sleep in the dust; and thou shalt seek me in the morning, but I shall not be." (Job 7:20-21)

Job's speech ends with a most remarkable confession. Follow the words closely, and don't think for a moment that Job has finally caved in to Eliphaz's accusation. He still thinks that he has a *"mark"* on him as God's special target. Yet he is now confessing, *"I have sinned."* Job never denies that he is a sinner, just like everyone else. He simply is not going to admit that his calamity is the result of some special, secret, unconfessed sin. Job's problem is his sin nature, not a specific sin.

This is another of the great theological issues found in Job. Man's problem is his SIN, not the specific sins he commits. Man does not go to hell for specific sins, but for the fact that he was born with a sin nature and so he is separated from God.

This is why Christ became man, died in our place and rose again from the dead. He sets us free from our sin nature. He paid the penalty for our SIN. We can still commit specific sins when we yield to that sin nature that still exists. The difference is that now we do not HAVE to sin.

Job knows that he has the same sin nature shared by all the human race. He will NOT admit to having some dark, hidden sin in his life that has brought these horrible trials upon him. He is right.

8

BILDAD TAKES OFF THE GLOVES

Then answered Bildad the Shuhite, and said,
How long wilt thou speak these things? and how long
shall the words of thy mouth be like a strong wind?
Doth God pervert judgment? or doth
the Almighty pervert justice?

Job 8:1-3

THE SECOND OF JOB'S FRIENDS TO SPEAK IS BILDAD THE SHUhite. For seven days he sat patiently with the others. He has listened to the exchange between Eliphaz and Job, and watched the conversation rapidly deteriorate. The strain of seven days filled with emotional stress is beginning to show.

Eliphaz had begun his discourse with tactful words of piety, though they weakly disguised his charge that Job was harboring a secret sin. Bildad, who was a descendent of one of Abraham's sons by Keturah (Genesis 23:2), now sees no reason to pull his verbal punches.

ATTACK ON JOB

1 "Then answered Bildad the Shuhite, and said,
2 How long wilt thou speak these things? and how long shall the words of thy mouth be like a strong wind?
3 Doth God pervert judgment? or doth the Almighty pervert justice?
4 If thy children have sinned against him, and he have cast them away for their transgression;

5 If thou wouldest seek unto God betimes, and make thy supplication to the Almighty;
6 If thou wert pure and upright; surely now he would awake for thee, and make the habitation of thy righteousness prosperous.
7 Though thy beginning was small, yet thy latter end should greatly increase." (Job 8:1-7)

Bildad's opening words aren't hard to understand. *"Then answered Bildad the Shuhite, and said, How long wilt thou speak these things? and how long shall the words of thy mouth be like a strong wind?"* (Job 8:1-2)

Today we would say: "Job, you're full of hot air! How long are you going to keep blowing smoke?"

Bildad quickly gets to his basic thesis, which agrees with Eliphaz. He is convinced that Job and his family deserved what they got.

He lays the groundwork with a rhetorical question. *"Doth God pervert judgment? or doth the Almighty pervert justice?"* (Job 8:3)

The answer is obvious. Of course He doesn't! God is righteous and just in all He does. Yet this has no bearing on Job's situation. This does not mean that Job is getting what he deserves. Bildad's reasoning is as flawed as Eliphaz's. Neither Zophar nor Elihu will improve the logical process. The premise is correct; the conclusion is wrong. God IS just, but Job is NOT getting what he deserves.

Having set up his solid premise, Bildad proceeds to build a crooked house on it. Foundations are important. The psalmist declares, *"If the foundations be destroyed, what can the righteous do?"* (Psalm 11:3)

As believers in Christ we have a solid, immovable foundation. *"According to the grace of God which is given unto me, as a wise masterbuilder, I have laid the foundation, and another buildeth thereon. But let every man take heed how he buildeth thereupon. For other foundation can no man lay than that is laid, which is Jesus Christ. Now if any man build upon this foundation gold, silver, precious stones, wood, hay, stubble; Every man's work shall be made manifest: for the day shall declare it, because it shall be revealed by fire; and the fire shall try every man's work of what sort it is."* (1 Corinthians 3:10-13)

Paul identifies our foundation as Christ Himself, yet warns that we can build badly on that foundation. No matter how solid the foundation, a building of straw will not hold up against hurricane winds.

This is the mistake of Bildad and his colleagues. Their foundation of knowledge of biblical truth is solid and right. It is what they build upon this foundation that is faulty. Their reasoning will not stand, even on such a solid foundation.

Here is a problem that is played out countless times in the hallways of many churches. A sincere believer, armed with a fair amount of biblical truth, sets out to *"comfort"* (Job 2:13) those in need. Knowing that their information is absolutely true, they confidently and sincerely approach their counselee, and then slug him squarely in the gut with the "truth."

Having stated a truth no one could disagree with, Bildad says, *"If thy children have sinned against him, and he have cast them away for their transgression . . ."* (Job 8:4).

Can you possibly imagine how this statement must have hit Job? All of his children had died in a day! This was from a man who came to *"mourn with him and to comfort him."* (Job 2:11) For seven days Bildad has been at his side to show support. Yet the Devil has so influenced Bildad's thought that in the space of a few words, he has told Job to his face that Job is full of hot air, and that the death of his ten children was exactly what they deserved for their sin.

Bildad, of course, has no idea what their sin may have been; he is just certain that they have sinned. Even Job knows of no problem in the lives of his children. He merely offered sacrifices in case there was sin *"in their hearts."*

"And it was so, when the days of their feasting were gone about, that Job sent and sanctified them, and rose up early in the morning, and offered burnt offerings according to the number of them all: for Job said, It may be that my sons have sinned, and cursed God in their hearts. Thus did Job continually." (Job 1:5)

Bildad is a typical, well-intentioned counselor who knows nothing for certain about the case, yet he is certain that his diagnosis is correct. Bildad knew that God is just. Obviously Job's children sinned. Bildad reasoned that hey wouldn't have been killed like that if there were no sin in their lives.

Now, like a good counselor Bildad wouldn't point out a problem without offering the solution, and he has a ready solution. *"If thou wouldest seek unto God betimes, and make thy supplication to the Almighty; If thou wert pure and upright; surely now he would awake for thee, and make the habitation of thy righteousness prosperous. Though thy beginning was small, yet they latter end should greatly increase."* (Job 8:5-7)

He first tells Job to *"seek unto God betimes"* (Job 8:5) *"Betimes"* is an old English word that means "early." In the same breath he accuses Job by implication of not praying. He conditions his solution by telling Job to seek God early, and to *"make thy supplication to the Almighty."*

We have already observed the importance of using this name of God, *"the Almighty."* He IS the Almighty. To whom could Job turn, if not to the Almighty?

Bildad is right. There is no evidence of Job praying up to this point in the story. When hit with such a calamity it is very easy for even the most devout saint to forget to pray. Prayer ought to be a natural, "knee-jerk reaction." Yet, this is not always the case. Physically, a strong blow can sometimes affect our body's reactions. The same is true spiritually.

It would have been much better for Bildad to say something like, "Job, we've been sitting here for seven days trying to figure this thing out. Eliphaz and you were getting a little heated trying to find God's purpose in all this. Yet in all this time none of us have sought the Almighty in prayer. Don't you think it's about time we prayed, and asked God to show us what to do? There are times when we don't even feel like praying, and I can't possibly imagine what you are experiencing after losing your ten children. But I CAN pray for you and with you. Why don't we pray right now?"

Instead Bildad has told Job he is full of hot air, that his kids got what they deserved, and that if he would only pray and seek God early he would find the solution. In verse 6 the finger-pointing continues. *"If thou wert pure and upright; surely now he would awake for thee, and make the habitation of thy righteousness prosperous."* (Job 8:6)

Now, he accuses Job of not being pure and upright. In other words, he is saying that if Job would just get his heart right with God, the Lord would answer him and make him prosperous again. Bildad sounds like a modern day "name it and claim it televangelist" and He confirms this "televangelist" formula of prosperity, "seed-giving" and the like by his words in verse 7. *"Though thy beginning was small, yet thy latter end should greatly increase."* (Job 8:7)

APPEAL TO THE FATHERS

8 "For enquire, I pray thee, of the former age, and prepare thyself to the search of their fathers:
9 (For we are but of yesterday, and know nothing, because our days upon earth are a shadow:)
10 Shall not they teach thee, and tell thee, and utter words out of their heart?
11 Can the rush grow up without mire? can the flag grow without water?
12 Whilst it is yet in his greenness, and not cut down, it withereth before any other herb." (Job 8:8-12)

Bildad speaks these words casually. He puts them on the table as though everyone understood what he was saying. They are anything but commonplace for us today. Yet, they hold incredible implications for us once we consider what Bildad is actually saying.

He is asking Job to enquire of the *"fathers"* of the *"former age."* These *"fathers"* are not the "church fathers" we hear quoted so often. They are not even Abraham, Isaac and Jacob, who were the fathers of the Hebrew people. The events in Job are taking place in the first generations after the Flood. The *"former age"* is a reference to life on the other side of the Flood.

In the first chapter we observed how these men were only a few generations removed from creation. Noah spoke to people who spoke to Adam. These men probably spoke with Shem, Noah's son. If not, they could have done so. He was still alive to give an eyewitness account of the Flood.

No one questions this remark of Bildad. Later, we will see Eliphaz make reference to this former age also. *"Hast thou marked the old way which wicked men have trodden? Which were cut down out of time, whose foundation was overflown with a flood: Which said unto God, Depart from us: and what can the Almighty do for them?"* (Job 22:15-17)

Bildad is encouraging Job to examine the record. God knows how to deal with religious hypocrites. This is why the Flood came. Job should know he can't get away with his sin. If God judged the generations of the former age with the Flood, why should Job think he could hide his sin forever?

Verse 9 is a parenthesis: *"(For we are but of yesterday, and know nothing, because our days upon earth are a shadow.)"* (Job 8:9)

Don't fail to catch the full impact of these words. When Bildad says *"For we are but of yesterday,"* he is saying, "We're the new kids on the block. We were just born yesterday."

He goes on to explain. *"Because our days upon earth are a shadow."* They are a shadow, that is, compared to the wonderfully long lives of those before the Flood, when men lived for 500, 600, even 900 years and more. We see the age of men like Abraham, who died at 175 years of age (Genesis 25:7), and are astonished. Yet the life of Abraham was a mere shadow of his great-great-great grandfather Eber's, who lived 464 years (Genesis 11:15), and from whom the name "Hebrew" is derived, "descendant of Eber."

The further removed from the Flood, the shorter men's lives became. The harmful rays of the sun, which had been filtered out by the earth's atmosphere, now changed the nature of life on this planet due to the radically changed atmosphere.

"Check it out, Job," says Bildad. "Go ahead and talk to those who can remember the Flood. You'll see that God judges those who sin. God has obviously brought judgment upon you, and you have therefore obviously sinned."

Though the Flood had shortened men's lives, it had not destroyed the passed-down, oral tradition that had come from the other side of the Flood. *"Shall not they teach thee, and tell thee, and utter words out of their heart?"* (Job 8:10)

It was this oral tradition, this teaching of God's truth that enabled men to grow spiritually in those days. *"Can the rush grow up without mire? can the flag grow without water?"* (Job 8:11)

When men neglect that tradition they wither up and die. *"Whilst it is yet in his greenness, and not cut down, it withereth before any other herb."* (Job 8:12)

What Bildad and Job take for granted in this conversation seems sensational to us! Imagine being able to talk to Shem, who was still around in the days of Abraham. The Bible did not exist in written form, but the truth of God has always been the truth of God. Job will disagree with much of what his three friends have to say, but he will not debate what all know to be God's truth.

APPLICATION TO ANTICHRIST

13 "So are the paths of all that forget God; and the hypocrite's hope shall perish:
14 Whose hope shall be cut off, and whose trust shall be a spider's web.
15 He shall lean upon his house, but it shall not stand: he shall hold it fast, but it shall not endure.
16 He is green before the sun, and his branch shooteth forth in his garden.
17 His roots are wrapped about the heap, and seeth the place of stones.
18 If he destroy him from his place, then it shall deny him, saying, I have not seen thee." (Job 8:13-18)

The words now coming from Bildad's mouth have an obvious application to his continued attack on Job. Though Bildad does not know it, they also have a prophetic application to a future figure on the prophetic horizon, who will be the personification of all wickedness and sin—the Antichrist.

In the context of the discussion, Bildad is drawing his conclusion that what has happened to Job and his children is only right. They obviously have sinned, and God judged them. He has appealed to the example of the *"former age,"* showing that sin does not go unpunished. Now, he pulls it together in a sweeping statement, which although true, is not applicable to Job. *"So are the paths of all that forget God; and the hypocrite's hope shall perish."* (Job 8:13)

The ultimate hypocrite will be the Antichrist—one so close to the true Christ he will deceive the great multitudes of the world. His path will be the same as *"all that forget God,"* because God makes no exceptions.

His *"hope shall perish."* The same truth is expounded in Proverbs. *"The hope of the righteous shall be gladness: but the expectation of the wicked shall perish."* (Proverbs 10:28)

Even someone who has failed can have hope. What a terrible thing to be totally without hope! Nothing to cling to, no expectation. *"Whose hope shall be cut off, and whose trust shall be a spider's web."* (Job 8:14) The hope and trust of those who forget God will support no more weight than a spider's web. It will all be cut off.

Bildad has more truth for Job. *"He shall lean upon his house, but it shall not stand: he shall hold it fast, but it shall not endure."* (Job 8:15) Job's house will not stand. In other words, Job's descendants will be cut off. No matter what he does, there will be no way to avoid God's judgment. *"It shall not endure."*

This is similar to a prophecy found in Psalm 109. Peter applied these words to another Satanic attempt at antichrist—Judas Iscariot. Peter referred to this psalm in Acts 1:15-20 to explain the need to have another disciple replace Judas. *"Let his days be few; and let another take his office."* (Psalm 109:8)

A few verses later there is a prophecy concerning his descendants. *"Let his posterity be cut off; and in the generation following let their name be blotted out."* (Psalm 109:13)

GREEN TREES AND DRY BRANCHES

As Bildad continues, his words become more ominous, and more direct in their reference to antichrist. *"He is GREEN before the sun, and his BRANCH SHOOTETH FORTH in his garden. His ROOTS are wrapped about the heap, and seeth the place of stones. If he destroy him from his place, then it shall deny him, saying, I have not seen thee.*" (Job 8:16-18) (Author's emphasis)

Again, we see the multilevel intrigue of spiritual warfare. Satan has influenced the thoughts of Job's friends so that they serve as his instruments to push Job over the edge. His "*hope,*" which will be "*cut off,*" is that they will incite Job to curse God. They, of course are operating out of the goodness of their hearts, pushing blindly ahead armed with the same truth of God that later was written down as the Bible, and unaware of the spiritual war raging around them. On another level God molds the very thoughts that Satan puts in their minds, so that the words that come out are God's words—words that perfectly paint a picture of things to come.

Bildad describes the hypocrite as a green branch, or sapling, whose roots are in a precarious place. This is a figure that is used elsewhere to represent the Antichrist.

David expresses a similar thought in Psalm 37. "*Fret not thyself because of evildoers, neither be thou envious against the workers of iniquity. For they shall soon be cut down like the grass, and wither as the green herb.*" (Psalm 37:1-2) A little further in the psalm David's vision becomes more specific. "*I have seen the wicked in great power, and spreading himself like a green bay tree.*" (Psalm 37:35)

Ezekiel saw the same image. Prophesying the ultimate defeat of antichrist and the victory of Christ he said, "*And all the trees of the field shall know that I the LORD have brought down the high tree, have exalted the low tree, have dried up the green tree, and have made the dry tree to flourish: I the LORD have spoken and have done it.*" (Ezekiel 17:24)

The high, green tree that is brought down is a reference to the Antichrist. The low, dry tree is a prophecy of the Lord Jesus Christ, Who is prophesied as the dry rod of Aaron that budded (Numbers 17:8). This picture of Christ as the Branch, flourishing in life that comes forth from the spiritual dryness of Israel, is a key prophetic concept in the Bible. "*And there shall come forth a rod out of the stem of Jesse, and a Branch shall grow out of his roots.*" (Isaiah 11:1)

This Branch is the righteous King. "*Behold, the days come, saith the LORD, that I will raise unto David a righteous Branch, and a King shall reign and prosper, and shall execute judgment and justice in the earth. In his days Judah shall be saved, and Israel shall dwell safely: and this is his name whereby he shall be called, THE LORD OUR RIGHTEOUSNESS.*" (Jeremiah 23:5-6)

He is the Servant. "*Hear now, O Joshua the high priest, thou, and thy fellows that sit before thee: for they are men wondered at: for, behold, I will bring forth my servant the BRANCH.* (Zechariah 3:8)

He is the perfect Man-Priest. "*And speak unto him, saying, Thus speaketh the LORD of hosts, saying, Behold the man whose name is The BRANCH; and he shall grow up out of his place, and he shall build the temple of the LORD: Even he shall build the temple of the LORD; and he shall bear the glory, and shall sit and rule upon his throne; and he shall be a priest upon his throne: and the counsel of peace shall be between them both.*" (Zechariah 6:12-13)

He is the fruit of god's glory and beauty. "*In that day shall the branch of the LORD be beautiful and glorious, and the fruit of the earth shall be excellent and comely for them that are escaped of Israel.*" (Isaiah 4:2)

The contrast to the dry Branch that flourishes is the green branch that God dries up. The classic development of this theme is in Daniel 4, where Nebuchadnezzar is pictured as a green tree in a dream. Let Nebuchadnezzar describe the dream himself.

"*Thus were the visions of mine head in my bed; I saw, and behold, a TREE in the midst of the earth, and the height thereof was great. The tree grew, and was strong, and the height thereof reached unto heaven, and the sight thereof to the end of all the earth: The leaves thereof were fair, and the fruit thereof much, and in it was meat for all: the beasts of the field had shadow under it, and the fowls of the heaven dwelt in the boughs thereof, and all flesh was fed of it. I saw in the visions of my head upon my bed, and, behold, a watcher and an holy one came down from heaven; He cried aloud, and said thus, Hew down the tree, and cut off his branches, shake off his leaves, and scatter his fruit: let the beasts get away from under it, and the fowls from his branches: Nevertheless leave the stump of his roots in the earth, even with a band of iron and brass, in the tender grass of the field; and let it be wet with the dew of heaven, and let his portion be with the beasts in the grass of the earth: Let his heart be changed from man's, and let a beast's heart be given unto him; and let seven times pass over him. This matter is by the decree of the watchers, and the demand by the word of the holy ones: to the intent that the living may know that the most High ruleth in the kingdom of men, and giveth it to whomsoever he will, and setteth up over it the basest of men.*" (Daniel 4:10-17)

Daniel gave the interpretation of this dream, which in a literal, immediate sense was fulfilled when Nebuchadnezzar was stricken for seven years with lycanthropy, or boanthropy, a disease that caused him to become animal-like.

"*The tree that thou sawest, which grew, and was strong, whose height reached unto the heaven, and the sight thereof to all the earth; Whose leaves were fair, and the fruit thereof much, and in it was meat for all; under which the beasts of the field dwelt, and upon whose branches the fowls of the heaven had their habitation: It is thou, O king, that art grown and become strong: for thy greatness is grown, and reacheth unto heaven, and they dominion to the end of the earth. And whereas the king saw a watcher and an holy one coming down from heaven, and saying, Hew the tree down, and destroy it; yet leave the stump of the roots thereof in the earth, even with a band of iron and brass, in the tender grass of the field; and let it be wet with the dew of heaven, and let his portion be with the beasts of the field, till seven times pass over him; This is the interpretation, O king, and this is the decree of the most High, which is come upon my lord the king: That they shall drive thee from men, and thy dwelling shall be with the beasts of the field, and they shall make thee to eat grass as oxen, and they shall wet thee with the dew of heaven, and seven times shall pass over thee, till thou know that the most High ruleth in the kingdom of men, and giveth it to whomsoever he will. And whereas they commanded to leave the stump of the tree roots; thy kingdom shall be sure unto thee, after that thou shalt have known that the heavens do rule."* (Daniel 4:20-26)

Going beyond the immediate fulfillment of this prophecy, it also looks to the antichrist, because Nebuchadnezzar is a type of the Antichrist. Just before telling us of the dream, Nebuchadnezzar described his prosperity in verse 4 by saying, *"I Nebuchadnezzar was at rest in mine house, and flourishing in my palace."* (Daniel 4:4)

The word that is translated *"flourishing"* is also used to describe a green tree. He was flourishing just like a young, green tree in spring. He would soon be cut down.

It is interesting to note the way John the Baptist began his ministry. *"And now also the axe is laid unto the root of the trees: therefore every tree which bringeth not forth good fruit is hewn down, and cast into the fire."* (Matthew 3:10)

Meanwhile, back at Job's ranch . . . (Please pardon the detour, but the serious Bible student must learn that the Antichrist is represented by the figure of a green tree, to be brought low, dried up and cut down by God.) Let's return to Job 8:17-18 again before moving forward.

STRANGE STONES AND PLACES OF PERDITION

"His roots are wrapped about the heap, and seeth THE PLACE OF STONES. If he destroy him from his place, then it shall deny him, saying, I have not seen thee." (Job 8:17-18) (Author's emphasis)

Here is a real puzzle. What on earth is this *"place of stones?"* Perhaps the question should be, "What IN the earth, or what OUT of the earth is this *"place of stones?"*

This is one of those areas of the Bible where we are in danger of getting in over our heads. The Bible IS understandable. There are some things, however, that God has chosen not to reveal to us at this time. In Daniel there is an example of how God sometimes works in this manner. *"And I heard, but I understood not: then said I, O my Lord, what shall be the end of these things? And he said, Go thy way, Daniel: for the words are closed up and sealed till the time of the end."* (Daniel 12:8-9)

Our Lord gives us another example in the Gospel of John. *"I have yet many things to say unto you, but ye cannot bear them now."* (John 16:12)

Some things we just need to ponder, to observe, and to guard in our hearts until God gives us more understanding. Let me give you some cross-references to consider. We will return to the stones later in Job. Now, I only want to start you thinking.

Job himself talks about stones. *"He setteth an end to darkness, and searcheth out all perfection: THE STONES OF DARKNESS, and the shadow of death."* (Job 28:3) (Author's emphasis)

Later, in the same chapter, he said, *"THE STONES OF IT are the place of sapphires: and it hath dust of gold. THERE IS A PATH which no fowl knoweth, and which the vulture's eye hath not seen: The lion's whelps have not trodden it, nor the fierce lion passed by it."* (Job 28:6-8) (Author's emphasis)

God Himself also had some things to say about stones in the Book of Job. Speaking of the Devil he said, *"SHARP STONES ARE UNDER HIM: he spreadeth sharp pointed things upon the mire."* (Job 41:30) (Author's emphasis)

Isaiah knew about these strange stones. Isaiah 34 is one of the most graphic prophetic pictures of hell in the Bible.

"And the streams thereof shall be turned into pitch, and the dust thereof into brimstone, and the land thereof shall become burning pitch. It shall not be quenched night nor day; the smoke thereof shall go up for ever: from generation to generation it shall lie waste; none shall pass through it for ever and ever. But the cormorant and the bittern shall possess it; the owl also and the raven shall dwell in it: and he shall stretch out upon it the line of confusion, and THE STONES OF EMPTINESS." (Isaiah 34:9-11) (Author's emphasis)

Ezekiel 28 is in the context of a prophecy against the king of Tyre. Yet obviously the prophet's words far transcend the mere human king, and point to the spiritual power that controlled him like a puppet. This is a passage that gives us valuable information about the original state of the Devil, when, before his fall, he was the masterpiece of God's created beings.

"Moreover the word of the LORD came unto me, saying, Son of man, take up a lamentation upon the king of Tyrus, and say unto him, Thus saith the Lord GOD; Thou sealest up the sum, full of wisdom, and perfect in beauty. Thou hast been in Eden the garden of God; every precious stone was they covering, the sardius, topaz, and the diamond, the beryl, the onyx, and the jasper, the sapphire, the emerald, and the carbuncle, and gold: the workmanship of thy tabrets and of thy pipes was prepared in thee in the day that thou wast created. Thou art the anointed cherub that covereth; and I have set thee so: thou wast upon the holy mountain of God; thou hast walked up and down in the midst of THE STONES OF FIRE." (Ezekiel 28:11-14) (Author's emphasis)

The place of stones, sharp stones, stones of emptiness, stones of darkness, stones of fire. What could all this possibly mean?

We DO know that the *"place of stones"* in verse 17 appears in context with the Antichrist. In Job 28:3 the *"stones of darkness"* are connected with *"the shadow of death,"* which earlier we learned was an element of the Tribulation. God connects the *"sharp stones"* with the Devil. Ezekiel 28 relates the *"stones of fire"* to the Devil. Isaiah mentioned the *"stones of emptiness"* as being in hell.

Making these connections between the Devil, hell, and these strange stones that keep popping up in the Old Testament, causes us to reexamine the passage in question here in Job 8, and notice another interesting phrase.

"His roots are wrapped about the heap, and seeth THE PLACE OF STONES. If he destroy him from HIS PLACE, then it shall deny him, saying, I have not seen thee." (Job 8:17-18) (Author's emphasis)

This *"place of stones"* is related to *"his place"* concerning a figure of the Antichrist. Armed with this observation we go to the first chapter of Acts. The disciples are gathered in the upper room waiting for the Holy Ghost to descend. Peter brings up the fact that "The Twelve" are now the eleven, since the suicide of Judas Iscariot. Leading the process of asking God for guidance in naming a replacement, Peter relates the story of Judas.

"And they prayed, and said, Thou, Lord, which knowest the hearts of all men, shew whether of these two thou hast chosen, That he may take part of this ministry and apostleship, from which Judas by transgression fell, that he might go to HIS OWN PLACE." (Acts 1:24-25) (Author's emphasis)

For centuries commentators and Bible scholars have noted that unusual phrase, as though there were a special place reserved for Judas. We do understand that he WAS special in the sense that he was a diabolic attempt at Antichrist. He was not just a demon-possessed man, but a man in whom the very Devil was incarnate. *"And after the sop SATAN ENTERED INTO HIM. Then said Jesus unto him, That thou doest, do quickly."* (John 13:27) (Author's emphasis)

In the Book of Revelation we learn that the bottomless pit will be opened during the time of Tribulation. God alone holds the key to this place in the center of the earth (a place in the exact center of the earth would be bottomless, since every direction is up). In Revelation chapter 9 an angel is entrusted with this key. Read the fascinating account of what happens next.

"And the fifth angel sounded, and I saw a star fall from heaven unto the earth: and to him was given the key of the bottomless pit. And he opened the bottomless pit; and there arose a smoke out of the pit, as the smoke of a great furnace; and the sun and the air were darkened by reason of the smoke of the pit. And there came out of the smoke locusts upon the earth: and unto them was given power, as the scorpions of the earth have power. And it was commanded them that they should not hurt the grass of the earth, neither any green thing, neither any tree; but only those men which have not the seal of God in their foreheads. And to them it was given that they should not kill them, but that they should be tormented five months: and their torment was as the torment of a scorpion, when he striketh a man. And in those days shall men seek death, and shall not find it; and shall desire to die, and death shall flee from them. And the shapes of the locusts were like unto horses prepared unto battle; and on their heads were as it were crowns like gold, and their faces were as the faces of men. And they had hair as the hair of women, and their teeth were as the teeth of lions. And they had breastplates, as it were breastplates of iron; and the sound of their wings was as the sound of chariots of many horses running to battle. And they had tails like unto scorpions, and there were stings in their tails: and their power was to hurt men five months." (Revelation 9:1-10)

Now, onto the stage steps a terrible figure, a being of awesome power. He is the *"king"* of these despicable creatures from hell.

"And they had a king over them, which is the angel of the bottomless pit, whose name in the Hebrew tongue is Abaddon, but in the Greek tongue hath his name Apollyon." (Revelation 9:11)

Both the Hebrew word, *"Abaddon,"* and the Greek word, *"Apollyon,"* mean the same thing—"destroyer." Forms of this Greek root are also translated other ways in the New Testament. It forms part of the title that the Apostle Paul gives to the Antichrist. *"Let no man deceive you by any means: for that day shall not come, except there come a falling away first, and that man of sin be revealed, the son of PERDITION."* (2 Thessalonians 2:3) (Author's emphasis)

The word *"perdition"* shares a common origin with the same *"Apollyon"* of Revelation 9:11. It is also the same word used by the Lord Jesus Christ Himself to describe none other than Judas Iscariot. *"While I was with them in the world, I kept them in thy name: those that thou gavest me I have kept, and none of them is lost, but THE SON OF PERDITION; that the scripture might be fulfilled."* (John 17:12) (Author's emphasis)

Could this *"bottomless pit"* be the same place to which Judas Iscariot went, waiting to be reactivated by the Devil in the last days of the Tribulation—*"his own place?"* Could this have any significance to the use of this phrase *"his place"* in Job 8:18 in a context that prophetically prefigures the Antichrist?

ARGUMENT TO JOB

19 "Behold, this is the joy of his way, and out of the earth shall others grow.
20 Behold, God will not cast away a perfect man, neither will he help the evildoers:
21 Till he fill they mouth with laughing, and thy lips with rejoicing.
22 They that hate thee shall be clothed with shame; and the dwelling place of the wicked shall come to nought." (Job 8:19-22)

Without realizing he is caught in the middle of an intergalactic battle between God and Satan, Bildad comes back to earth in these final verses, applying his argument to Job. It is a familiar formula we have heard often before—do good and God will bless you.

This is true, of course. Our problem is understanding the meaning of blessing. Does blessing mean only prosperity? Or, is it possible for God to bless us by teaching faith, patience and spiritual depth through trials?

Bildad has incorrectly identified Job with the same characteristics we see in antichrist. Yet what he says is true of the final doom of that wicked one. His dwelling place shall be reduced to nothing. *"And then shall that*

Wicked be revealed, whom the Lord shall consume with the spirit of his mouth, and shall destroy with the brightness of his coming." (2 Thessalonians 2:8)

The details are put in place in Revelation 19. "*And I saw heaven opened, and behold a white horse; and he that sat upon him was called Faithful and True, and in righteousness he doth judge and make war. His eyes were as a flame of fire, and on his head were many crowns; and he had a name written, that no man knew, but he himself. And he was clothed with a vesture dipped in blood: and his name is called The Word of God. And the armies which were in heaven followed him upon white horses, clothed in fine linen, white and clean. And out of his mouth goeth a sharp sword, that with it he should smite the nations: and he shall rule them with a rod of iron: and he treadeth the winepress of the fierceness and wrath of Almighty God. And he hath on his vesture and on his thigh a name written, KING OF KINGS, AND LORD OF LORDS. And I saw an angel standing in the sun; and he cried with a loud voice, saying to all the fowls that fly in the midst of heaven, Come and gather yourselves together unto the supper of the great God; That ye may eat the flesh of kings, and the flesh of captains, and the flesh of mighty men, and the flesh of horses, and of them that sit on them, and the flesh of all men, both free and bond, both small and great. And I saw the beast, and the kings of the earth, and their armies, gathered together to make war against him that sat on the horse, and against his army. And the beast was taken, and with him the false prophet that wrought miracles before him, with which he deceived them that had received the mark of the beast, and them that worshipped his image. These both were cast alive into a lake of fire burning with brimstone. And the remnant were slain with the sword of him that sat upon the horse, which sword proceeded out of his mouth: and all the fowls were filled with their flesh.*" (Revelation 19:11-21)

Are you confused? To sum up briefly what's happening, Job becomes a target for a challenge match between God and Satan with God's full permission and even His encouragement. Job's three best friends come to mourn with him and comfort him. They end up as Satanic instruments to push Job to curse God. Yet God overrules the designs of the Devil in order to record incredible prophetic pictures of the Tribulation, the Antichrist and other things to come. All at once Job is a picture of Christ on the cross, a lost sinner in hell and God's people in the coming time of Tribulation. At the same time he is target of attacks by his friends whose words prophetically picture the Antichrist.

That's a lot to sort out, and don't feel bad if you're still struggling to keep up with all that is happening. Life is like this. So many things are continually happening on so many different levels that it is difficult, if not impossible, to understand it all.

This is the message of Job—sometimes we just DON'T understand it all. All we can do is keep on trusting God, with complete confidence in His love and goodness, knowing that *"all things work together for good to them that love God, to them who are the called according to his purpose."* (Romans 8:28)

9

THE PATIENCE OF JOB

For he is not a man, as I am, that I should answer him,
and we should come together in judgment.
Neither is there any dayman betwixt us,
that might lay his hand upon us both.

Job 9:32-33

JOB HAS ENDURED THE SPEECHES OF TWO WELL-INTENTIONED friends who have accused him of having secret sin in his life. Bildad, from whom we just heard, began immediately by hitting direct and hard. Most of us would wonder how Job could bear such attacks from a friend, but Job is probably hurting so much that no one could add to his sorrow.

His response to Bildad is a remarkable display of patience and humility. Listening to Job's words of despair, his outbursts of emotion and an occasional tendency to self-pity, it would be easy for us to be judgmental. We are inclined to see such things idealistically, wondering why Job just doesn't trust God and get on with life. This is how most of us view tragedy in someone else's life.

Most of us operate on the level of Job's well-meaning friends, and, furthermore, we have no way to comprehend Job's pain. In all the heartache and agony, we must not lose sight of Job's testimony of patience. Consider James' words. *"Behold, we count them happy which endure. Ye have heard of the patience of Job, and have seen the end of the Lord; that the Lord is very pitiful, and of tender mercy."* (James 5:11)

Don't be tempted to think that Job is so desperate that he has lost his patience. In front of us we have one of the best examples in the book. Remembering Bildad's blistering attack, Job's calm and measured response is remarkable.

James also said, *"Knowing this, that the trying of your faith worketh patience."* (James 1:3) Considering all Job has been through, he is now becoming an expert on patience!

ACKNOWLEDGEMENT OF BILDAD'S TRUTH

1 "Then Job answered and said,
2 I know it is so of a truth: but how should man be just with God?" (Job 9:1-2)

Bildad's accusation was false. There were undoubtedly many things Job could have said to defend himself, and he WILL engage in his own defense occasionally. Here, he chooses to admit the truth of Bildad's words.

This is another reminder of an important aspect of our study. Most of what these men say is true. There is no debate over divine truth, no arguments about what God said or did not say. All share a common theological foundation. All possess abundant information about the ways of God. The only issue is the application of that truth.

We live in a time when the Word of God is being questioned like never before. Even fundamental scholars are echoing the serpent's words, *"Yea, hath God said?"* (Genesis 3) Those of us who hold to the inerrancy and preservation of Scripture are often so embroiled in the defense of God's truth, we often fail to be concerned about its proper application. False application, too, is a ploy of the enemy.

Yet all of these men agree about what God had said. We find words they speak in Job later recorded elsewhere in Scripture as authoritative. While speaking the truth, they were merely off in their timing and application.

Electing to ignore Bildad's personal attack for the moment, Job draws a straight line to life's most basic question. *"How should man be just with God?"* (Job 9:2)

Can there be any question more important? Despite all his information about God and His ways, Job is still wrestling with life's basic issue. How he would have clung to Paul's words in his letter to the Romans! No one ever better nailed down the answer to this question. No man who has read the book of Romans could EVER misunderstand the answer to Job's question.

"Being justified freely by his grace through the redemption that is in

Christ Jesus: Whom God hath set forth to be a propitiation through faith in his blood, to declare his righteousness for the remission of sins that are past, through the forbearance of God; To declare, I say, at this time his righteousness: that he might be just, and the justifier of him which believeth in Jesus." (Romans 3:24-26)

In the Person of the Lord Jesus Christ the grace of God has been clearly and completely revealed for all to lay hold of and be justified freely. Paul explains that God could not simply ignore, or brush away our sin. In the previous verse he established that *"the wages of sin is death."* (Romans 6:23) Were God to change the rules, He would not be just, and, therefore, would not be God. God had no choice but to deal with sin directly and totally.

The solution was for God Himself to become a member of the human race in the Person of Jesus Christ, and to pay our debt of sin Himself. Having done this, He can be the *"justifier of him which believeth in Jesus."* (Romans 3:26)

This is an essential truth, and the spine of Paul's doctrinal framework. Consider, *"Who was delivered for our offences, and was raised again for our justification."* (Romans 4:25) *"And not as it was by one that sinned, so is the gift: for the judgment was by one to condemnation, but the free gift is of many offences unto justification. For if by one man's offence death reigned by one; much more they which receive abundance of grace and of the gift of righteousness shall reign in life by one, Jesus Christ.) Therefore, as by the offence of one judgment came upon all men to condemnation; even so by the righteousness of one the free gift came upon all men unto justification of life."* (Romans 5:16-18)

YOU may have much information about God and the Bible. You may be fluent in "God-speak." But are you absolutely certain that you can answer life's basic question—*"How should man be just with God?"* (Job 9:2) Nothing else matters unless you are positive about your answer. Forget Job for right now. Be concerned for your own eternal destiny, and accept God's gift of redemption through what Christ did on the cross for you. That's the **ONLY** way man can be just with God.

ACKNOWLEDGEMENT OF GOD'S WONDERS

THE GOD OF WONDERS

3 "If he will contend with him, he cannot answer him one of a thousand." (Job 9:3)

Job is simply declaring that there is not one in a thousand who could give an answer to God. This is true. Job will repeatedly express his anxiousness to talk directly with God and work this thing out. Yet in the end of the book God DOES speak directly to Job, and Job has precious little to say. Job has no idea just how true his words are.

This is the same thought that Paul was communicating in 1 Corinthians 2, as he contrasted God's wisdom with the wisdom of the world. He shows how God's wisdom is out of reach for the natural man. In 1 Corinthians 2:14 Paul states that the natural man cannot understand the things of God because they are "spiritually discerned." What mere man could possibly argue with God and win?

Yet in this same passage in 1 Corinthians 2 Paul also reveals why our position and privileges as New Testament believers are infinitely superior to Job's. He quotes from Isaiah 64:4, "*But as it is written, Eye hath not seen, nor ear heard, neither have entered into the heart of man, the things which God hath prepared for them that love him.*" (1 Corinthians 2:9)

Though lost men cannot grasp the things of God, the last part of the verse tells us that God has prepared this wisdom for us who believe. In Job's day God's revelation was not complete.

In the next verse Paul tells us what an astonishing blessing we have received in Christ. "*But God hath revealed them unto us by his Spirit: for the Spirit searcheth all things, yea, the deep things of God.*" (1 Corinthians 2:10)

If Job could be patient in the face of unbelievable tribulation, how much more should WE endure in our own hardships, considering the truth that God has revealed to us through His Spirit. We have much to be thankful for.

4 "He is wise in heart, and mighty in strength: who hath hardened himself against him, and hath prospered?" (Job 9:4)

In verse 3 Job made the point that no one can give an answer to God. Now, he says that no one who is so strong and hardened will win against God.

Proverbs tells us the same thing. "*He, that being often reproved hardeneth his neck, shall suddenly be destroyed, and that without remedy.*"

(Proverbs 29:1) You may have a strong neck, but God will snap it like a twig when He is ready.

This truth ought to be obvious, yet millions of people step into the ring against God every day. In the last several thousand years no one has beat Him. Do you really think you will be the first?

This is why Job brings up this point. He is merely confirming that he is not trying to put one over on God. His friends have accused him of harboring secret sin. Yet Job knows better than to think that he would be the first to get away with unpunished sin before God. Job may have just suffered untold tragedy, but he has not altogether lost his mind!

Having put forth his point, he is now going to amplify it. He will list the mighty wonders and power of God. His purpose is to again show that it would be utter foolishness to think that he could escape God's wrath by hiding some unconfessed sin.

As we work our way through these next verses, we will see Job's incredible scientific understanding. His objective is not to impress us with what he knows, but to illustrate that no one can take on God and win.

THE WONDERS OF GOD

5 "Which removeth the mountains, and they know not: which overturneth them in his anger." (Job 9:5)

In a prophetic sense Job's words parallel those of Isaiah. "*Oh that thou wouldest rend the heavens, that thou wouldest come down, that the mountains might flow down at thy presence; As when the melting fire burneth, the fire causeth the waters to boil, to make they name known to thine adversaries, that the nations may tremble at thy presence!*" (Isaiah 64:1-2)

Perhaps in an historical sense Job was thinking of the cataclysmic upheaval that occurred in the Flood, still fresh in everyone's consciousness. In a prophetic sense what Job and Isaiah saw was that future day when the Lord Jesus Christ returns to set up His eternal kingdom. "*And every island fled away, and the mountains were not found.*" (Revelation 16:20)

Identifying the prophetic reference here is easier than the historical reference. If not the Genesis Flood, to what could he possibly be referring? Consider the next verse, which also has an apocalyptic nature.

6 "Which shaketh the earth out of her place, and the pillars thereof tremble." (Job 9:6)

More than a simple reference to God's control over earthquakes, this verse, coupled with the others in this context, suggest that Job is thinking of a far more destructive and apocalyptic event. Many would see these words in this context as a reference to the Flood.

There is another possibility of an earlier judgment of God that happened before the Flood, and even before the creation of man. I am speaking of the cataclysmic judgment upon Lucifer, the anointed cherub, who dared to think he could be like God, without God.

In an earlier chapter, we have already commented on the fall of the Devil, and how God sometimes addresses him in the Bible through His prophecy against the human, puppet-kings he controls. Look again at these words from Isaiah.

"How art thou fallen from heaven, O Lucifer, son of the morning! how art thou cut down to the ground, which didst weaken the nations! For thou hast said in thine heart, I will ascend into heaven, I will exalt my throne above the stars of God: I will sit also upon the mount of the congregation, in the sides of the north: I will ascend above the heights of the clouds; I will be like the most High. Yet thou shalt be brought down to hell, to the sides of the pit. They that see thee shall narrowly look upon thee, and consider thee, saying, Is this the man that made the earth to tremble, that did shake kingdoms; That made the world as a wilderness, and destroyed the cities thereof; that opened not the house of his prisoners?" (Isaiah 14:12-17)

In this passage we learn the Devil's original name—Lucifer, which means "light-bearer." He was the one who bore the light of the glory of God. His sin was pride, thinking he could ascend to the throne of God, and be like God without submitting to God.

This was the temptation he put to Eve—*"For God doth know that in the day ye eat thereof, then your eyes shall be opened, and ye shall be as gods, knowing good and evil."* (Genesis 3:5) He offered Eve the chance to become like God, without God.

How ironic! To become like God is God's will for every life. *"And we know that all things work together for good to them that love God, to them who are the called according to his purpose. For whom he did foreknow, he also did predestinate to be conformed to the image of his Son, that he might be the firstborn among many brethren."* (Romans 8:28-29)

At issue is not the goal, but the means to the goal. Will it be with, or without God? This is the beginning principle behind the religion of humanism—man striving to become like God, yet without God. This is the heart of all false religion. Now, we know the source of all this false doctrine—Lucifer.

Do not fail to notice the description God gives to him in Isaiah 14:16-17 and that coincides with Job's words in Job 9:6. Lucifer is the one who *"made the earth to tremble . . . that made the world as a wilderness,"* as a consequence of his rebellion against God.

Many scoff at the idea of a calamitous event between Genesis 1:1 and 1:2. Some have said that would imply the existence of a "pre-adamic race" of humans. This is not so. Man was created as described in Genesis One and Two. Yet God already had a group of beings—not a race—but a company of angelic creatures who praised God and did his bidding. God Himself mentions this later in his words to Job.

"Where wast thou when I laid the foundations of the earth? declare, if thou hast understanding. Who hath laid the measures thereof, if thou knowest? or who hath stretched the line upon it? Whereupon are the foundations thereof fastened? or who laid the corner stone thereof; When the morning stars sang together, and all the sons of God shouted for joy?" (Job 38:4-7)

Who were these *"morning stars,"* these *"sons of God?"* We examined this passage in connection with our comments on Job 1, and saw stars defined in Revelation 1:20 as being figures of angels. God says they were praising Him when He laid the foundations of the earth.

Ezekiel offers some clues to who was present in the beginning, in his description of the Devil in his original state. In Ezekiel 12, God gives Ezekiel a prophecy against the human king of Tyrus, who was Satan's instrument. In Ezekiel 28:12-15, God looks past the king of Tyre and begins speaking about Satan directly. God said, *"Thou sealest up the sum, full of wisdom, and perfect in beauty."* (Ezekiel 28:12)

Then, God said of Satan, *"Thou hast been in Eden the garden of God; every precious stone was thy covering, the sardius, topaz, and the diamond, the beryl, the onyx, and the jasper, the sapphire, the emerald, and the carbuncle, and gold: the workmanship of thy tabrets and of thy pipes was prepared in thee in the day that thou wast created."* (Ezekiel 28:13)

So—he was in Eden, was he? This is obviously not the human king of Tyrus! Who IS he? *"Thou art the anointed cherub that covereth; and I have set thee so: thou wast upon the holy mountain of God; thou hast walked up and down in the midst of the stones of fire. Thou wast perfect in thy ways from the day that thou wast created, till iniquity was found in thee."* (Ezekiel 28:14-15)

This is the same Lucifer, the anointed cherub, the one who was on the *"holy mountain of God."* This Lucifer, who was the sum of wisdom and beauty, sinned. When man appeared in Eden, he was already the Devil (Adversary). When did this occur? The only hole in time is between Genesis 1:1 and 1:2. It was a time when the earth trembled and was made a wilderness. The opening verses of Genesis record that time. *"In the begin-*

ning God created the heaven and the earth. And the earth was without form, and void; and darkness was upon the face of the deep. And the Spirit of God moved upon the face of the waters." (Genesis 1:1-2)

Whatever historic reference Job has in mind (or maybe his talk is purely theoretical!) his words remind us of a future restoration, following an unprecedented purification of the cosmos, which will again shake the very position of the earth in space. This is foreseen in a portion of Isaiah known as the "Little Apocalypse."

"*The earth is utterly broken down, the earth is clean dissolved, the earth is moved exceedingly. The earth shall reel to and fro like a drunkard, and shall be removed like a cottage; and the transgression thereof shall be heavy upon it; and it shall fall, and not rise again. And it shall come to pass in that day, that the LORD shall punish the host of the high ones that are on high, and the kings of the earth upon the earth.*" (Isaiah 24:19-21)

Job continues his listing of God's mighty wonders.

7 "Which commandeth the sun, and it riseth not; and sealeth up the stars." (Job 9:7)

Again, it is difficult to match this verse with an historical event that would be in Job's mind. Those who see Noah's Flood in this passage will point to the intense cloud cover as the rains came pouring down, preventing the sun to shine by day, or the stars by night. However, if these words are to be understood in a literal sense, they must have some connection with the fall of Lucifer.

Indeed, whatever Job may be thinking of, there ARE historical events that certify the truth of Job's testimony that God has and will manipulate the movement of the sun and the stars. In Joshua 10:12-14 Joshua spoke to the Lord, and the sun and the moon stood still. Isaiah 38:4-8 also relates how God gave king Hezekiah a sign by causing the sun to go back ten degrees on the sun dial.

Biblical prophecy makes it clear that God will be doing strange things with the sun and moon in the future. On Pentecost, Peter quoted a prophecy from Joel 2:31. "*And I will shew wonders in heaven above, and signs in the earth beneath; blood, and fire, and vapour of smoke: The sun shall be turned into darkness, and the moon into blood, before that great and notable day of the Lord come.*" (Acts 2:19-20)

Whatever is going through Job's mind as he speaks, the major issue in these verses is that God has absolute control over His creation. God has ordered the universe according to physical laws, yet He has, can and will overrule those natural laws at His will.

8 "Which alone spreadeth out the heavens, and treadeth upon the waves of the sea." (Job 9:8)

Some see the first phrase of this verse as a reference to the ever-expanding universe. Before you leap to the conclusion that the second phrase is about the waves of the Atlantic or Pacific, ponder the fact that there are also waters that are not on this planet. *"Praise him, ye heavens of heavens, and ye WATERS THAT BE ABOVE THE HEAVENS."* (Psalm 148:4) (Author's emphasis)

Remember, the sovereignty of God over His creation is the key point of Job's speech in Job 9, and comparative passages are abundant in Scripture.

"The heavens declare the glory of God; and the firmament sheweth his handiwork. Day unto day uttereth speech, and night unto night sheweth knowledge." (Psalm 19:1-2)

"Whatsoever the LORD pleased, that did he in heaven, and in earth, in the seas, and all deep places." (Psalm 135:6)

"And, Thou, Lord, in the beginning hast laid the foundation of the earth; and the heavens are the works of thine hands: They shall perish; but thou remainest; and they all shall wax old as doth a garment; And as a vesture shalt thou fold them up, and they shall be changed: but thou art the same, and thy years shall not fail." (Hebrews 1:10-12)

9 "Which maketh Arcturus, Orion, and Pleiades, and the chambers of the south." (Job 9:9)

Still on his journey through the universe, Job makes this truly remarkable statement. These are the names of constellations. Job is aware of the same constellations, with the same names, that we still see today. Look at a chart of the constellations. The layout of the stars in the constellation in no way suggests the names they have received.

Arcturus is Ursa Major, the "Big Bear, or the "Big Dipper." Check out the stars in this constellation, and try to find a bear. Books have been written to prove that the constellations received their names, not because of any resemblance to the name, but as a memory device to help man to remember a truth they represent. Our church has a ministry called the "Gospel in the Stars," to show people how God has written the Gospel across the skies in the constellations. Through the ages man has passed this truth down from generation to generation, though it has often been perverted.

It is far beyond the scope of this commentary to detail how God has laid out His truth in the heavens. Consider just a few hints from the Psalm 19, whose first two verses we just quoted. We will go farther this time, and I will add some comments.

"The heavens declare the glory of God; and the firmament sheweth his handiwork. Day unto day uttereth speech, and night unto night sheweth

knowledge. (The heavens, night and day show God's work, His speech and His knowledge.) *There is no speech nor language, where their voice is not heard.* (People of all languages can understand this manifestation of God's truth. Romans 1:20.) *Their line is gone out through all the earth, and their WORDS to the end of the world. In them hath he set a tabernacle for the sun, Which is as a bridegroom coming out of his chamber* (the sun is a type of Christ, [Malachi 4:2] and Christ is a Bridegroom), *and rejoiceth as a strong man to run a race. His going forth is from the end of the heaven, and his circuit unto the ends of it: and there is nothing hid from the heat thereof.*" (Psalm 19:1-6) (Author's notes).

Job points to the heavens, naming key constellations, although none is of the twelve major constellations. Arcturus is in the north. Orion is the Hunter (Nimrod), called appropriately by the Arabs "the fool," and associated with the west. Pleiades, is called the Heath, a cluster of seven stars (six are currently visible), representing the daughters of Atlas in pagan mythology. Pleiades is in the east. Then, Job names the chambers of the south. This is possibly a reference to the Clouds of Magellan, or to the entire group of southern constellations which were not even visible from Palestine! How did he know about this constellation? Perhaps these men had more information than "modern" man ever imagined.

In a burst of praise Job declares,

10 "Which doeth great things past finding out; yea, and wonders without number." (Job 9:10)

Paul similarly says, "*O the depth of the riches both of the wisdom and knowledge of God! how unsearchable are his judgments, and his ways past finding out!*" (Romans 11:33)

WONDERING ABOUT GOD

11 "Lo, he goeth by me, and I see him not: he passeth on also, but I perceive him not." (Job 9:11)

So great is God, Job says, that he can't perceive of the scope of His wonders and His person.

Verse 12 brings us to Job's point in listing the wonders of God.

12 "Behold, he taketh away, who can hinder him? who will say unto him, What doest thou?" (Job 9:12)

Job is simply affirming the sovereignty of God, to show that God does what He wants to do, and when He wants to do it. That He has chosen to take away everything Job has is not necessarily a sign of secret sin in Job's life. It is an issue of God's sovereignty. This is one of the most important lessons of the whole Bible—God is God!

Now, Job turns to take a slap at his counselors.

13 "If God will not withdraw his anger, the proud helpers do stoop under him." (Job 9:13)

In Job's mind the *"proud helpers"* are his counselors. No matter how hard they try to pin a sin on Job, they can do nothing to divert God from His course. If God has chosen to pour out His fury upon Job, there is no one who can change it.

14 "How much less shall I answer him, and choose out my words to reason with him?" (Job 9:14)

Job is asking His friends if they really think he is so dumb as to think he could pull one over on God. What could Job possibly say to God to reason with Him, to answer Him, or to argue with Him?

15 "Whom, though I were righteous, yet would I not answer, but I would make supplication to my judge." (Job 9:15)

Job is not admitting secret sin. He is simply acknowledging his sinful nature, as he has already done. (Job 7:20) Even if Job was totally free from his sin nature, he still could not answer God. All he could do would be to throw himself at the mercy of Heaven's court, begging for mercy.

JOB'S SEVEN "IF'S"

The following verses give a series of seven hypothetical situations in which Job shows that he is at the mercy of God's sovereignty. He is going to hold fast to his position that there is no hidden, unconfessed sin in his life that has brought on his calamity.

THE FIRST "IF"

16 "If I had called, and he had answered me; yet would I not believe that he had hearkened unto my voice.
17 For he breaketh me with a tempest, and multiplieth my wounds without cause.
18 He will not suffer me to take my breath, but filleth me with bitterness." (Job 9:16-18)

Job is saying that even if God would speak to him directly, he is so broken he could not comprehend. The weight of his trial is pressing down so hard on his chest, he can't catch his breath. He is in the very grips of bitterness.

Do not fail to pay attention to the key phrases of Scripture. In verse 17 we again find that Job's wounds were *"without cause."* We discussed the prophetic significance of this phrase in connection with Job 2:3, showing that they point to Christ Who suffered for us *"without cause."* (John 18:-38)

Being reminded that Job is a type of Christ hanging on the cross, the fact that Job has difficulty breathing becomes more important. Crucifixion was a slow, agonizingly painful death. The person was hung so that he would have to push up on his nailed feet, gasp for air, and slump back down to rest. This pushing up to breathe could go on for days, until the man was too weak to push himself up again. To hasten death, the executioners often broke the legs of the victim, prohibiting him from using them to push the body upward to breathe. Death was then by asphyxiation.

THE SECOND "IF"

19 "If I speak of strength, lo, he is strong: and if of judgment, who shall set me a time to plead?" (Job 9:19)

The sense of Job's words is that it is useless to see this as a contest of strength. Who could be stronger than God? This is obvious to Job, and is a truth that has been confirmed often in the Scriptures. No matter how strong a man may be, he is never strong enough.

"There is no king saved by the multitude of an host: a mighty man is not delivered by much strength. (Psalm 33:16)

"For my life is spent with grief, and my years with sighing: my strength faileth because of mine iniquity, and my bones are consumed." (Psalm 31:10)

"Thus saith the LORD, Let not the wise man glory in his wisdom, neither let the mighty man glory in his might, let not the rich man glory in his riches." (Jeremiah 9:23)

Nor can Job talk about judgment. If he demands his day in court, how is he going to plead his case? Who could set a time for such a judgment?

Job apparently does not understand the truth that Paul spoke on Mars Hill. *"Because he hath appointed a day, in the which he will judge the world in righteousness by that man whom he hath ordained; whereof he hath given assurance unto all men, in that he hath raised him from the dead."* (Acts 17:31)

THE THIRD "IF"

20a "If I justify myself, mine own mouth shall condemn me." (Job 9:20a)

If Job were to try to justify himself, he would be subject to the same problem that millions face each day—his own mouth would give testimony against him. In other words, he would be telling a lie.

In the first three chapters of Romans, Paul's indictment of man's sinfulness is ample witness of the truth of Job's words. Speaking of gentiles like Job, he said, *"For when the gentiles, which have not the law, do by nature the things contained in the law, these, having not the law, are a law unto themselves: Which shew the work of the law written in their hearts, their conscience also bearing witness, and their thoughts the mean while accusing or else excusing one another;) In the day when God shall judge the secrets of men by Jesus Christ according to my gospel."* (Romans 2:14-16)

Later, he said, *"Their throat is an open sepulchre; with their tongues they have used deceit; the poison of asps is under their lips: Whose mouth is full of cursing and bitterness."* (Romans 3:13-14)

THE FOURTH "IF"

20b "If I say, I am perfect, it shall also prove me perverse.
21 Though I were perfect, yet would I not know my soul: I would despise my life.
22 This is one thing, therefore I said it, He destroyeth the perfect and the wicked.
23 If the scourge slay suddenly, he will laugh at the trial of the innocent.
24 The earth is given into the hand of the wicked: he covereth the faces of the judges thereof; if not, where, and who is he?
25 Now my days are swifter than a post: they flee away, they see no good.
26 They are passed away as the swift ships: as the eagle that hasteth to the prey." (Job 9:20b-26)

Here is another reminder that the context in the Bible is the ultimate indicator of a word's definition. This is the text that helped us to understand the meaning of "perfect" in our study of Job 1. God has already testified that Job was *"perfect."* (Job 1:1,8; 2:3) We learned then the meaning of the word as "complete, equipped, ready, furnished for all good works." We saw the word as it appears in 2 Timothy. *"All scripture is given by inspiration of God, and is profitable for doctrine, for reproof, for correction, for instruction in righteousness: That the man of God may be perfect, throughly furnished unto all good works."* (2 Timothy 3:16-17)

Job also uses the word here to mean "without fault." Even if Job WERE perfect, or without fault, he would still have to contend with his own sin nature. This is the sense of verse 21, and perfectly consistent with the truth of 1 John 1:8. *"If we say that we have no sin, we deceive ourselves, and the truth is not in us."* (1 John 1:8)

The *"He"* that *"destroyeth the perfect and the wicked"* in verse 22 is God. This is what Solomon concluded in Ecclesiastes, as he established death as man's common denominator. *"The wise man's eyes are in his head; but the fool walketh in darkness: and I myself perceived also that one event happeneth to them all. Then said I in my heart, As it happeneth to the fool, so it happeneth even to me; and why was I then more wise? Then I said in my heart, that this also is vanity. For there is no remembrance of the wise more than of the fool for ever; seeing that which now is in the days to come shall all be forgotten. And how dieth the wise man? as the fool."* (Ecclesiastes 2:14-16)

In Job 9:23, the *"scourge"* is the Devil, who slays as the instrument of God's judgment. He is called *"destroyer"* in Exodus. *"For the LORD will pass through to smite the Egyptians; and when he seeth the blood upon the lintel, and on the two side posts, the LORD will pass over the door, and will not suffer the destroyer to come in unto your houses to smite you."* (Exodus 12:23)

He will appear again in the Tribulation. *"And they had a king over them, which is the angel of the bottomless pit, whose name in the Hebrew tongue is Abaddon, but in the Greek tongue hath his name Apollyon."* (Revelation 9:11) As we saw earlier, both the Hebrew *"Abaddon,"* and the Greek *"Apollyon"* translate as "destroyer."

Isaiah saw this *"scourge."* *"Because ye have said, We have made a covenant with death, and with hell are we at agreement; when the overflowing SCOURGE shall pass through, it shall not come unto us: for we have made lies our refuge, and under falsehood have we hid ourselves: Therefore thus saith the Lord GOD, Behold, I lay in Zion for a foundation a stone, a tried stone, a precious corner stone, a sure foundation: he that believeth shall not make haste. Judgment also will I lay to the line, and righteousness to the plummet: and the hail shall sweep away the refuge of lies, and the waters shall overflow the hiding place. And your covenant with death shall be disannulled, and your agreement with hell shall not stand; when the overflowing SCOURGE shall pass through, then ye shall be trodden down by it."* (Isaiah 28:15-18) (Author's emphasis)

This *"scourge"* laughs *"at the trial of the innocent."* We again find ourselves faced with the typology of Job, who prophetically points to Christ—the Innocent One—hanging on the cross while the *"scourge"* laughed. Yet God always has the last laugh. *"I also will laugh at your calamity; I will mock when your fear cometh."* (Proverbs 1:26)

Job shows his usual good insight into God's truth by his statement in Job 9:24. *"The earth is given into the hand of the wicked: he covereth the faces of the judges thereof; if not, where, and who is he?"* (Job 9:24) This shows Job's understanding that God had ceded control over earthly affairs to "the wicked."

When Jesus was tempted by the Devil in Luke 4, the fact that Satan is ruler of this world was an accepted fact of life. *"And the Devil, taking him up into an high mountain, shewed unto him all the kingdoms of the world in a moment of time. And the Devil said unto him, All this power will I give thee, and the glory of them: for that is delivered unto me; and to whomsoever I will I give it. If thou therefore wilt worship me, all shall be thine."* (Luke 4:5-7)

The Lord never debated whether or not all the kingdoms of the world had been delivered unto the Devil. He knew that it was true, and so did Paul. *"In whom THE GOD OF THIS WORLD hath blinded the minds of them which believe not, lest the light of the glorious gospel of Christ, who is the image of God, should shine unto them."* (2 Corinthians 4:4) (Author's emphasis)

Obviously, Job has no consciousness of the implications of this fact for the way it would figure into the temptation of Christ by the Devil. In the historical context Job is complaining that it seems as though God is indifferent to the innocent and oppressed, seeing that He has delivered control of these matters to the wicked. And if He did not do it, who did?

The final two verses of this fourth "if" proposition emphasize the brevity of life. *"Now my days are swifter than a post: they flee away, they see no good. They are passed away as the swift ships: as the eagle that hasteth to the prey."* (Job 9:25-26)

Job compares the brevity of life to the speed of a horse race *("swifter than a post")*, swift ships and an eagle in flight. The Scriptural evidence in support of Job's words is abundant. *"Whereas ye know not what shall be on the morrow. For what is your life? It is even a vapour, that appeareth for a little time, and then vanisheth away."* (James 4:14)

THE FIFTH "IF"

27 "If I say, I will forget my complaint, I will leave off my heaviness, and comfort myself:

28 I am afraid of all my sorrows, I know that thou wilt not hold me innocent." (Job 9:27-28)

Here is what Job is saying: "Don't tell me just to forget it and get on with life. That's impossible." How could Job just forget all that has happened and walk away into the sunset?

Furthermore, even if Job COULD just walk away from it all, he still wouldn't be innocent before God. Remember, Job is NOT confessing to secret sin. He is simply recognizing his place as a fallen man before a just, omnipotent and sovereign God.

Notice also how Job occasionally alternates between addressing his counselors and speaking to God. This is evidenced when he says, "*I know that THOU wilt not hold me innocent.*" (Job 9:28) (Author's emphasis)

THE SIXTH "IF"

29 "If I be wicked, why then labour I in vain?" (Job 9:29)

This sixth hypothetical statement is directed at his friends. If he were harboring some unconfessed sin, why would he be foolish enough to think he could get away with it? Why would Job be working so hard to keep up appearances, if he knew in his heart that he really was concealing secret sin?

THE SEVENTH "IF"

30 "If I wash myself with snow water, and make my hands never so clean;
31 Yet shalt thou plunge me in the ditch, and mine own clothes shall abhor me.
32 For he is not a man, as I am, that I should answer him, and we should come together in judgment.
33 Neither is there any daysman betwixt us, that might lay his hand upon us both.
34 Let him take his rod away from me, and let not his fear terrify me:
35 Then would I speak, and not fear him; but it is not so with me." (Job 9:30-35)

This is truly a salient passage of the Bible. The major message is that self-justification is worthless. Job is confident in his righteous living, knowing assuredly that his trials are not due to unconfessed sin in his life. Yet he also correctly understands that no amount of self-righteousness is sufficient to stand before God. Despite all self-righteousness and good works, Job points to the utter depravity of man. "*Yet shalt thou plunge me in the ditch, and mine own clothes shall abhor me.*" (Job 9:31)

In Job 9:32, Job wishes to communicate with God as he would with a man. "*For he is not a man, as I am, that I should answer him, and we should come together in judgment.*" (Job 9:32) This problem was solved when God became incarnate in the Person of Jesus Christ.

Verse 32 is a craving for an intermediary to argue his case before God. *"Neither is there any daysman betwixt us, that might lay his hand upon us both."* (Job 9:33) A *"daysman"* is an umpire, or a person to set your day in court. Job is continuing his thought from verse 19—*"Who shall set me a time to plead?"* Obviously, this dilemma was also resolved by the incarnation of the Lord Jesus Christ.

Fortunately, we New Testament believers are in a position far superior to Job's. We DO have a mediator. *"For there is one God, and one mediator between God and men, the man Christ Jesus."* (1 Timothy 2:5) And we DO have a representative in court. *"My little children, these things write I unto you, that ye sin not. And if any man sin, we have an advocate* (daysman, umpire, lawyer, mediator) *with the Father, Jesus Christ the righteous."* (1 John 2:1) (Author's comments)

In the last two verses of the chapter Job asks for God to *"take his rod away from me."* (Job 9:34) The Devil is God's *"rod"* that He uses to execute His judgment. Jeremiah defines how God uses the Devil to do His will, using the king of Babylon as his human channel.

"THOU ART MY BATTLE AXE AND WEAPONS OF WAR: for WITH THEE will I break in pieces the nations, and WITH THEE will I destroy kingdoms; And WITH THEE will I break in pieces the horse and his rider; and WITH THEE will I break in pieces the chariot and his rider; WITH THEE also will I break in pieces man and woman; and WITH THEE will I break in pieces old and young; and WITH THEE will I break in pieces the young man and the maid; I will also break in pieces WITH THEE the shepherd and his flock; and WITH THEE will I break in pieces the husbandman and his yoke of oxen; and WITH THEE will I break in pieces captains and rulers." (Jeremiah 51:20-23) (Author's emphasis)

Essentially the same truth appears in the Psalms. *"Arise, O LORD, disappoint him, cast him down: deliver my soul from THE WICKED, WHICH IS THY SWORD." (Psalm 17:13) (Author's emphasis)*

ANXIETY OF JOB'S DILEMMA

1 "My soul is weary of my life; I will leave my complaint upon myself; I will speak in the bitterness of my soul.

2 I will say unto God, Do not condemn me; shew me wherefore thou contendest with me.

3 Is it good unto thee that thou shouldest oppress, that thou

shouldest despise the work of thine hands, and shine upon the counsel of the wicked?" (Job 10:1-3)

Job is at the end of his rope. He cannot stop the torrent of anguish that overflows from his overburdened heart. How could he possibly cease from speaking in the bitterness of his soul? *"My soul is weary of my life; I will leave my complaint upon myself; I will speak in the bitterness of my soul."* (Job 10:1)

He rehearses what he would say to God if he had the chance. *"I will say unto God, Do not condemn me; shew me wherefore thou contendest with me."* (Job 10:2)

Job is only asking that God show him what in the world is happening. This is a biblically valid request. God Himself extended the invitation to, *"Come now, and let us reason together, saith the LORD: though your sins be as scarlet, they shall be as white as snow; though they be red like crimson, they shall be as wool."* (Isaiah 1:18) Job will have his moment with God at the end of the book.

"Is it good unto thee that thou shouldest oppress, that thou shouldest despise the work of thine hands, and shine upon the counsel of the wicked?" (Job 10:3)

Job's bitterness is drawing him dangerously close to the line. Job is the work of God's hands. He is complaining that the counsel of his "friends" is oppressing him at the same time that he is being despised of God. Compare that with the Psalmist who prays on the basis of God's mercy that the Lord would perfect what He had begun, and not forsake the works of His own hands. *"The LORD will perfect that which concerneth me: thy mercy, O LORD, endureth for ever: forsake not the works of thine own hands."* (Psalm 138:8)

APPEAL TO GOD'S MERCY

JOB'S QUESTIONS

Job begins a series of questions for God. He is finally praying! His first question shows that he doesn't feel that God can properly understand what he is going through, since God is not a man. How could God understand the sufferings of a man?

4 "Hast thou eyes of flesh? or seest thou as man seeth?

5 Are thy days as the days of man? are thy years as man's days,

6 That thou enquirest after mine iniquity, and searchest after my sin?" (Job 10:4-6)

Now, of course, this is not an issue. God HAS become a man. *"For we have not an high priest which cannot be touched with the feeling of our infirmities; but was in all points tempted like as we are, yet without sin. Let us therefore come boldly unto the throne of grace, that we may obtain mercy, and find grace to help in time of need."* (Hebrews 4:15-16)

Job continues.

7 "Thou knowest that I am not wicked; and there is none that can deliver out of thine hand." (Job 10:7)

Job knows, and he knows that God knows, that he is NOT wicked. The implication is "Why are you then tearing my life apart, God?" Even if Job WERE wicked, God knows as well as Job that there is no escape from the omnipotent and omnipresent hand of God.

There would be no point in trying to hide sin from God, in other words. The Psalmist said it. *"If I take the wings of the morning, and dwell in the uttermost parts of the sea; Even there shall thy hand lead me, and thy right hand shall hold me. If I say, Surely the darkness shall cover me; even the night shall be light about me."* (Psalm 139:9-11)

8 "Thine hands have made me and fashioned me together round about; yet thou dost destroy me." (Job 10:8)

This is also similar to the message of Psalm 139. *"I will praise thee; for I am fearfully and wonderfully made: marvellous are thy works; and that my soul knoweth right well. My substance was not hid from thee, when I was made in secret, and curiously wrought in the lowest parts of the earth. Thine eyes did see my substance, yet being unperfect; and in thy book all my members were written, which in continuance were fashioned, when as yet there was none of them."* (Psalm 139:14-16)

Job understands that he is God's workmanship. He does not understand why God would want to destroy His own workmanship.

9 "Remember, I beseech thee, that thou hast made me as the clay; and wilt thou bring me into dust again?" (Job 10:9)

The answer to this question is "yes." The only question has to do with when and how. All men eventually return to the dust. We came from dust. *"And the LORD God formed man of the dust of the ground, and breathed into his nostrils the breath of life; and man became a living soul."* (Genesis 2:7) Because of sin, man will return to the dust. *"In the sweat of thy face shalt thou eat bread, till thou return unto the ground; for out of it was thou taken: for dust thou art, and unto dust shalt thou return."* (Genesis 3:19)

Job's questions continue.

10 "Hast thou not poured me out as milk, and curdled me like cheese?" (Job 10:10)

In light of being God's workmanship, Job still cannot grasp why God has turned his life upside down, just like pouring out so much milk to curdle and produce cheese. Job feels that his own life is going through the same curdling process.

Today we say, "Don't cry over spilt milk." Yet it is Job's entire life that is poured out like milk. More than poured out, his life is spoiling before him. How can he help but cry over it?

JOB'S CASE

Having laid this foundation, Job is ready to lay his case before God. Job emphasizes that everything he is results from what God has done, the same truth we reviewed earlier in Psalm 139:14-16.

11 "Thou hast clothed me with skin and flesh, and hast fenced me with bones and sinews.

12 Thou hast granted me life and favor, and thy visitation hath preserved my spirit.

13 And these things hast thou hid in thine heart: I know that this is with thee." (Job 10:11-13)

Job points to body *("skin and flesh," "bones and sinews")*, soul *("life and favour")* and spirit as coming from the heart of God. This is why Job knows it would be impossible for him to get away with sin. This is the source of Job's confusion.

14 f I sin, then thou markest me, and thou wilt not acquit me from mine iniquity.

15 If I be wicked, woe unto me; and if I be righteous, yet will I not lift up my head. I am full of confusion; therefore see thou mine affliction.

16 For it increaseth. Thou huntest me as a fierce lion: and again thou shewest thyself marvellous upon me." (Job 10:-14-16)

Since God is not the Author of confusion, we New Testament believers should immediately be suspicious of the Devil's involvement any time confusion prevails. (1 Corinthians 14:33) Job's affliction was increasing, and he thinks that God is hunting him *"as a fierce lion."* Job is being pursued, but by another lion. It is not the Lion of the tribe of Judah, but the roaring lion in 1 Peter 5:8 that is after him. This is why Job is confused. He can't reconcile this stalking lion with the marvels of God in his life. Job is the victim of spiritual warfare, yet at this point he cannot distinguish between enemy fire and friendly fire.

18 "Wherefore then hast thou brought me forth out of the womb? Oh that I had given up the ghost, and no eye had seen me!

19 I should have been as though I had not been; I should have been carried from the womb to the grave." (Job 10:18-19)

Job returns to the "why was I born" theme. We have seen this too often before.

20 "Are not my days few? cease then, and let me alone, that I may take comfort a little,

21 Before I go whence I shall not return, even to the land of darkness and the shadow of death;

22 A land of darkness, as darkness itself; and of the shadow of death, without any order, and where the light is as darkness." (Job 10:20-22)

All that Job can do is to ask God to let up a little. David made the same request. *"O spare me, that I may recover strength, before I go hence, and be no more."* (Psalm 39:13)

In the final two verses Job is describing hell. Compare the *"land of darkness," "shadow of death"* and *"darkness itself"* with the following Scriptures.

In a parable warning of the danger of hell the Lord said, *"Then said the king to the servants, Bind him hand and foot, and take him away, and cast him into outer darkness; there shall be weeping and gnashing of teeth."* (Matthew 22:13)

In the context of false teachers and prophets Peter wrote, *"These are wells without water, clouds that are carried with a tempest; to whom the mist of darkness is reserved for ever."* (2 Peter 2:17)

Eliphaz will also mention the darkness of hell. *"He believeth not that he shall return out of darkness, and he is waited for of the sword. He wandered abroad for bread, saying, Where is it? he knoweth that the day of darkness is ready at his hand."* (Job 15:22-23) *"He shall not depart out of darkness; the flame shall dry up his branches, and by the breath of his mouth shall he go away."* (Job 15:30)

Hell is associated with both flames and darkness. This is scientifically accurate. The hottest flame gives off no light. No amount of twisting the Scripture can eliminate the reality of hell as Bible doctrine.

Job has acknowledged the truth of Bildad's speech. He has acknowledged the wonders of God, and followed with a series of hypothetical statements. He has poured out the anguish of his soul, and appealed to God for mercy. Yet he still has no answers, no direction and no hope beyond hell itself. He is in the very depths of despair.

Perhaps YOU are in the very depths of despair. You may not be able to answer all of the "why's" and "what's," but you CAN get into the Word of God and discover the truth of 1 Thessalonians 5:18, which says, "*In everything give thanks: for this is the will of God in Christ Jesus concerning you.*" We aren't to give thanks FOR all things, but IN all things, because sometimes God doesn't give us victory OVER the problem, but gives us victory IN the problem. You have so much more light than Job. If HE can hold out, learn patience and keep from cursing God, you can, too.

10

ZOPHAR JOINS THE FRAY

If iniquity be in thine hand, put it far away,
and let not wickedness dwell in thy tabernacles.
For then shalt thou lift up thy face without spot;
yea, thou shalt be stedfast, and shalt not fear:
Because thou shalt forget thy misery,
and remember it as waters that pass away:
And thine age shall be clearer than the noonday;
thou shalt shine forth, thou shalt be as the morning.

Job 11:14-17

ZOPHAR, PROBABLY THE YOUNGEST AND LEAST INFLUENTIAL OF Job's three friends, is the last to take his turn. He has had the benefit of listening to his two colleagues and Job's response. We have watched with horror as these sincere, godly, knowledgeable men have become Satan's pawns in his attack on Job.

While the conversation was heating up, Zophar should have had time to reflect upon the real issues involved, and ask for a call to reason. Instead, he simply follows the lead of those before him and tires to do them one better. Inflexibly wielding the thesis shared by all three, Zophar charges ahead with revival fervor. If the other two have been hard, he will be harder. Rather than examine God's truth for the answer, he uses God's truth out of context to bolster his own argument. He is playing "follow the leader."

Coming to Job with the best of intentions, these men have been unwittingly captured by the Devil. Clawing with his fingernails to keep from falling off the cliff of despair, their friend is in danger of losing his grip. Failing in his direct attacks to move Job to curse God, Satan has convinced these friends that they are doing Job a favor by stomping on his fingers!

Stop!! Let's not be guilty of the same error. Here is an excellent lesson for us to learn as we observe the sad state of Christianity today. Like Job, millions of believers are wounded and hurting. Satan is desperately trying to deliver a knock-out blow to the church. He has thrown everything he has at believers, yet the church marches on. What will the Devil do?

Send in the Christian counselors! Failing in a direct attack, the Devil resorts to using the good intentions of sincere, yet spiritually immature people to undermine those they love most. Satan will use the same strategy he used several thousand years ago. Most men pay no attention to the Bible. They don't understand as Solomon did that *"there is no new thing under the sun."* (Ecclesiastes 1:9)

Many zealous young people today no longer want to be pastors and missionaries. They want to be "Christian counselors," since that is a far more "relevant ministry." They want to address people's REAL needs, help those who are hurting and make a lasting contribution where it counts most. They are sincere. Who do you think would want to use this abundance of good will minus biblical wisdom? Who would benefit by a well-meaning, but misguided army of "Christian counselors"?

Please don't think this is an attempt to minimize the problems people face in everyday life. Using the Bible to deal with the problems of life is to be encouraged! We all need a friend to help us see how God's truth applies to those areas of our lives that hurt so badly that we have a hard time seeing how to apply the Word.

This is an objection to much of what is called "Christian counseling" today, that is nothing more than recycled psychology, done by sincere people who know far more about psychology than they do about the Bible. Armed with their Old and New Testament survey, systematic theology and secular psychology that is "Christianized" with a sprinkling of Bible verses, they eagerly seek out their hurting clients. Not having time to study the Bible as *"a workman that needeth not to be ashamed, rightly dividing the word of truth"* (2 Timothy 2:15), they turn instead to their university or seminary notes.

They have been told that these poor, suffering people really don't understand their problems. Their root problems are buried deep in childhood and environment. Modern, scientific "Christian counseling" has the answer. Rather than seek the face of God, they scan the notes of their professors to sincerely, lovingly, and inflexibly convince the client that THEY, the "Christian counselors," have the true answers.

In these last days before the time of Tribulation, is it any wonder that we see an explosion of mental and emotional problems followed by an army of well-intentioned "Christian counselors?" Is it any wonder that so many believers are in such a mess? Does it seem strange to you that we are shouting at one another, divided and fragmented? If you take to heart Solomon's words that *"there is no new thing under the sun"* (Ecclesiastes 1:9), you will understand that all this is part of a master strategy by a master deceiver. The strategy is succeeding because most churches have stopped teaching their members the Bible, let alone how to *"rightly divide"* it.

Understanding the BIBLICAL issues involved, it is time to turn our attention to the specific words of Zophar. His approach could charitably be classified as DIRECT.

ZOPHAR'S PERVERSE ATTACK

1 "Then answered Zophar the Naamathite, and said,
2 Should not the multitude of words be answered? and should a man full of talk be justified?
3 Should thy lies make men hold their peace? and when thou mockest, shall no man make thee ashamed?
4 For thou hast said, My doctrine is pure, and I am clean in thine eyes.
5 But oh that God would speak, and open his lips against thee;
6 And that he would shew thee the secrets of wisdom, that they are double to that which is! Know therefore that God exacteth of thee less than thine iniquity deserveth." (Job 11:1-6)

Zophar opens by accepting Job's rebuttal as a challenge. *"Should not the multitude of words be answered?"* (Job 11:2a) In other words, "Job, I simply can't let you get by with what you've said."

Then, he gets right to the point. No polite words of introduction for him! *"Should a man full of talk be justified?"* (Job 11:2b) What he is saying is, "Job, you're full of hot air! I can't let you get away with that."

Not satisfied with the bluntness of these words, Zophar pushes the knife in a little deeper and begins to twist it. *"Should thy lies make men hold their peace? and when thou mockest, shall no man make thee ashamed?"* (Job 11:3)

Zophar is calling Job a liar and a mocker. His comments are only building up steam. Apparently Zophar's gift is not mercy.

Zophar has labeled Job a liar, yet it is Zophar who speaks lies. *"For thou hast said, My doctrine is pure, and I am clean in thine eyes."* (Job 11:4) Reflect upon the words of Job. He has said no such thing. Job has confessed his sin nature. (Job 9:20 is just one example.) All that Job has refused to admit is that some secret, hidden sin is the cause of his problems.

Zophar has not been listening. This is a violation of the cardinal rule for anyone who wants to truly help someone else. Zophar is leaping to conclusions. He is hearing only what he wants to hear, and imagining the rest.

Tragically, Zophar did not have the benefit of Solomon's proverbs. Here is a small sampling of wisdom from David's son.

"In the multitude of words there wanteth not sin: but he that refraineth his lips is wise." (Proverbs 10:19)

"A wise man feareth, and departeth from evil: but the fool rageth, and is confident." (Proverbs 14:16)

"He that is slow to wrath is of great understanding: but he that is hasty of spirit exalteth folly." (Proverbs 14:29)

"A soft answer turneth away wrath: but grievous words stir up anger. The tongue of the wise useth knowledge aright: but the mouth of fools poureth out foolishness." (Proverbs 15:1-2)

"The heart of the righteous studieth to answer: but the mouth of the wicked poureth out evil things." (Proverbs 15:28)

"Even a fool, when he holdeth his peace, is counted wise: and he that shutteth his lips is esteemed a man of understanding." (Proverbs 17:28)

"He that answereth a matter before he heareth it, it is folly and shame unto him." (Proverbs 18:13)

Armed with great knowledge, yet lacking in the wisdom God gave Solomon, Zophar charges straight ahead. With both mouth and throttle wide open, the words come gushing like a Texas oil well strike.

"But oh that God would speak, and open his lips against thee; And that he would shew thee the secrets of wisdom, that they are double to that which is! Know therefore that God exacteth of thee less than thine iniquity deserveth." (Job 11:5-6)

Zophar is calling for God to answer Job. He will in due time. When God does answer Job, Zophar and his colleagues will have long since run out of steam.

In his self-righteous foolishness Zophar gives evidence of just how far the conversation has deteriorated. *"Know therefore that God exacteth of thee less than thine iniquity deserveth."* (Job 11:6)

This is technically true! What we all deserve for our iniquity is to burn forever in hell without God. Yet, one cannot help but see Zophar's lips delicately curled in snarling smugness, convinced that he has placed his finger squarely on Job's problem. While hell is what we have earned for our sin, to tell a man who has just lost his wealth, his health and all of his children all at once that he is getting LESS than what he deserves is not a helpful counseling procedure.

ZOPHAR'S PROBING PHILOSOPHY

7 "Canst thou by searching find out God? canst thou find out the Almighty unto perfection?
8 It is as high as heaven; what canst thou do? deeper than hell; what canst thou know?
9 The measure thereof is longer than the earth, and broader than the sea.
10 If he cut off, and shut up, or gather together, then who can hinder him?
11 For he knoweth vain men: he seeth wickedness also; will he not then consider it?
12 For vain man would be wise, though man be born like a wild ass's colt." (Job 11:7-12)

CONSIDERING THE ALMIGHTY GOD

Emboldened by the harshness of his personal attack on Job, Zophar turns philosophical. Surely he feels that he has been up to the challenge of not letting Job get by with his "secret sin." Inside he is probably saying to himself, "I sure told him!" Having taken the direct approach, he can now afford to back off a little and reflect upon "the issues" involved.

His words in verse 7 embody some of life's great philosophical questions. There are really two parts to his statement. The first is, *"Canst thou by searching find out God?"* (Job 7a)

"Job, do you really think you are going to find God by looking for Him?" Sounds good, and it is a favorite phrase of the philosophical crowd who want to give the impression that knowing God is impossible. The Bible, however, makes it abundantly clear that one CAN find God by looking in the right place which is the Word of God, and by looking before it is too late.

"Seek ye the LORD while he may be found, call ye upon him while he is near." (Isaiah 55:6) Would God ask something of man that could not be done? In the New Testament Jesus said, *"But seek ye first the kingdom of God, and his righteousness; and all these things shall be added unto you."* (Matthew 6:33)

The second philosophical question sounds as sophisticated as the first. *"Canst thou find out the Almighty unto perfection?"* (Job 11:7b) Religious liberals love to concede the existence of a "Higher Power," or a "Superior Being," whoever he or she may be. Yet they are adamant in their contention that no one can truly know this "Ultimate Power," "First Source," or any other of a thousand names. Since he has rejected the names God gives Himself in the Bible, man invents his own names for God.

There is a hidden agenda here that disguises man's sinful pride while espousing high-sounding theology. When a man places God on an unknowable plane, he is also rejecting His authority. What liberal theologians mean to say is "Since God is unknowable, I will tell you what to believe." Elitist scholarship becomes the ultimate authority in place of God's Word.

Again, the question is positively answered in the Bible. God CAN be found out to perfection. Not that finite man could ever exhaust the knowledge of the infinite God, but he definitely can find out all that God wants man to know.

All that is God is totally contained and manifested in the Person of Christ. *"For in him dwelleth all the fulness of the Godhead bodily."* (Colossians 2:9) By knowing Christ, one CAN find out God to perfection.

This was Philip's craving when he blurted out, *"Philip saith unto him, Lord, shew us the Father, and it sufficeth us."* (John 14:8)

The Lord was quick to respond. *"Have I been so long time with you, and yet hast thou not known me, Philip? he that hath seen me hath seen the Father; and how sayest thou then, Shew us the Father?"* (John 14:9)

We must underscore that man's ability to find out God *"unto perfection"* is not limited to warm, fuzzy feelings, but it encompasses definite, hard knowledge. Paul contrasted the wisdom of the world with the wisdom of God as he wrote to the Corinthians. *"But as it is written, Eye hath not seen, nor ear heard, neither have entered into the heart of man, the things which God hath prepared for them that love him."* (1 Corinthians 2:9)

He was quoting Isaiah 64:4, as we saw in our study of Job 9:3. Had he stopped here he would be saying the same thing as Zophar. We hear such things frequently. "You just can't know the deep things of God. Our eyes just can't see what God has prepared."

Actually, Paul is setting us up to say just the opposite. He continues. *"But God hath revealed them unto us by his Spirit: for the Spirit searcheth all things, yea, the deep things of God. For what man knoweth the things of a man, save the spirit of man which is in him? even so the things of God knoweth no man, but the Spirit of God."* (1 Corinthians 2:10-11)

How can we know these things, *"yea, the deep things of God?"* Again, it is by looking in the right place, the Bible, as we are taught by God's Spirit, comparing Scripture with Scripture. *"Now we have received, not the spirit of the world, but the spirit which is of God; that we might know the things that are freely given to us of God. Which things also we speak, not in the words which man's wisdom teacheth, but which the Holy Ghost teacheth; comparing spiritual things with spiritual. But the natural man receiveth not the things of the Spirit of God: for they are foolishness unto him: neither can he know them, because they are spiritually discerned."* (1 Corinthians 2:12-14)

CONSIDERING THE DIMENSIONS OF THE INFINITE

Having carefully built his theological facade, Zophar moves on to wax eloquent about how high and unsearchable God's perfection is. *"It* (the perfection of the Almighty) *is as high as heaven; what canst thou do? deeper than hell; what canst thou know? The measure thereof is longer than the earth, and broader than the sea."* (Job 11:8-9) (Author's note)

Zophar has his facts straight, as usual, yet he doesn't really understand what he is saying. In these two verses he lists the four dimensions of God's cosmos. Physicists list three dimensions of the physical world. The Bible lists four.

The Apostle Paul gives the same four dimensions in his letter to the Ephesians. He is praying for them and says, *"That Christ may dwell in your hearts by faith; that ye, being rooted and grounded in love, May be able to comprehend with all saints what is the BREADTH, and LENGTH, and DEPTH, and HEIGHT."* (Ephesians 3:17-18) (Author's emphasis)

Unfortunately, most modern versions want to connect verse 18 with the verse that follows, in order to lead the reader to mistakenly conclude that the dimensions describe the love of Christ. (Though the love of Christ is certainly without limits!) But here is how they appear in the King James Bible. *"May be able to comprehend with all saints what is the breadth, and length, and depth, and height; And to know the love of Christ, which passeth knowledge, that ye might be filled with all the fulness of God."* (Ephesians 3:18-19)

Notice the semicolon that follows the word *"height."* That means that what follows is an independent clause, complete with its own verb, *"to know."* Paul's prayer for the Ephesians *"to know the love of Christ"* is a separate petition.

The object of the dimensions in Ephesians 3:18 is undefined in the immediate context of verse 18. However, the genitive verb tense of the *"what is"* in this verse demands that it refer to the breadth, length, depth and height of SOMETHING! In such a context the most logical antecedent is the *"heaven and earth"* of Ephesians 3:15. In that context, Paul is praying in verse 3:18 that the Ephesians might be able to comprehend the entire scope of God's creation.

The desire behind Paul's prayer is consistent with the importance he gives to *"heavenly places"* mentioned several times in the epistle. Read and compare Ephesians 1:3, 10, 20; 2:6; 3:10; 4:10 and 6:12. This is also consistent with the content of the Book of Job. When God later speaks, in Job 38, He will immediately take Job into a study of the vastness of His plan for the created universe. I am afraid that the doctrine of creation has received far too little attention today, especially how understanding it affects our daily lives. It is no wonder that this great Bible doctrine has been the subject of such ferocious attack during the last century. Satan doesn't want us modern believers to comprehend the unlimited power of the God who saves us!

This is not the only time Paul uses such dimensions to point to the scope of God's universe. In Romans he spoke in similar language. *"For I am persuaded, that neither death, nor life, nor angels, nor principalities, nor powers, nor things present, nor things to come, Nor height, nor depth, nor any other creature, shall be able to separate us from the love of God, which is in Christ Jesus our Lord."* (Romans 8:38-39)

How amazing that Zophar would use the same language as Paul would use several thousand years later! In the context of his statements Zophar points to the unknowable perfection of God by considering the enormity of the universe.

Zophar won't wander for long in the upper reaches of the universe without seizing the opportunity to take another poke at Job. Having shown that God is beyond human comprehension, Zophar says, not so subtly, *"If he cut off, and shut up, or gather together, then who can hinder him? For he knoweth vain men: he seeth wickedness also; will he not then consider it?"* (Job 11:10-11) The thrust of his argument is that Job cannot fool God, because God knows just how wicked Job really is.

CONSIDERING THE WILD ASS'S COLT

Next, Zophar makes a statement that unlocks a great biblical truth about lost man. *"For vain man would be wise, though man be born like a wild ass's colt."* (Job 11:12)

Two of the most important words in Bible study are "like" and "as." Like any good teacher, God teaches by association. To teach us His great intangible truth, He compares the unknown to the known. He takes what we do understand and relates it to what we need to learn. This is generally indicated by "like" or "as." In the case of Job 11:12, we learn that man is *"born like a wild ass's colt."* What is it about the wild ass's colt that God would compare to man's natural, sinful state at birth?

This is not the only time the comparison will arise in Job. Job himself speaks of the wicked and says, *"Behold, as wild asses in the desert, go they forth to their work; rising betimes for a prey: the wilderness yieldeth food for them and for their children."* (Job 24:5)

God also uses the same figure in His discourse to Job. *"Who hath sent out the wild ass free? or who hath loosed the bands of the wild ass? Whose house I have made the wilderness, and the barren land his dwellings. He scorneth the multitude of the city, neither regardeth he the crying of the driver. The range of the mountains is his pasture, and he searcheth after every green thing."* (Job 39:5-8)

What is it about the wild ass that makes it the object of such comparisons? The answer can be found by looking in the Book of Exodus. There is definitely something special about the wild ass's colt.

When giving the nation instructions about what to do when they entered the land, the Lord told Israel to set apart for Him the first born of every creature. *"And it shall be when the LORD shall bring thee into the land of the Canaanites, as he sware unto thee and to thy fathers, and shall give it thee, That thou shalt set apart unto the LORD all that openeth the matrix, and every firstling that cometh of a beast which thou hast; the males shall be the LORD'S."* (Exodus 13:11-12)

There were only two exceptions to this rule, only two creatures that were not acceptable to the Lord—the firstborn of man, and the firstling of the ass. *"And every firstling of an ass thou shalt redeem with a lamb; and if thou wilt not redeem it, then thou shalt break his neck: and all the firstborn of man among thy children shalt thou redeem."* (Exodus 13:13)

The firstling of the ass is a type of lost man. There is something wrong with his birth. He must be redeemed with the blood of the lamb!!! Any who was not redeemed would be broken at the neck. *"He, that being often reproved hardeneth his neck, shall suddenly be destroyed, and that without remedy."* (Proverbs 29:1)

It was not by accident, but by design that Jesus rode into Jerusalem on the colt of an ass. *"And when they came nigh to Jerusalem, unto Bethphage and Bethany, at the mount of Olives, he sendeth forth two of his disciples, And saith unto them, Go your way into the village over against you: and as soon as ye be entered into it, ye shall find a colt tied, whereon never man sat; loose him, and bring him. And if any man say unto you, Why do ye this? say ye that the Lord hath need of him; and straightway he will send him hither. And they went their way, and found the colt tied by the door without in a place where two ways met; and they loose him. And certain of them that stood there said unto them, What do ye, loosing the colt? And they said unto them even as Jesus had commanded: and they let them go. And they brought the colt to Jesus, and cast their garments on him; and he sat upon him."* (Mark 11:1-7)

Matthew 21:1-3 specifies that it is the colt of an ass. This untamed ass was tamed by Christ, the only One Who can tame lost man. The colt was tied, just as lost man is bound by sin. (John 8:34) The instruction was to loose him, just as lost man needs to be set free.

The disciples found this ass's colt *"by the door without."* In other words, it is outside the door, which is Christ. (John 10:7,9) Not only that, this location is given as *"where two ways meet."* This is a cross, with one wide and broad, and the other straight and narrow. (Matthew 7:13-14) This is the place where lost man must decide whether to let Jesus tame him or not.

Zophar probably doesn't grasp the full significance of his own words, but they open the door to great understanding for us. Great dividends are to be had by those who pay close attention to each and every word of Scripture. Look at the exact words of Scripture if you want to understand exactly what God is saying.

ZOPHAR'S PAT ANSWER

PREPARE YOUR HEART

13 "If thou prepare thine heart, and stretch out thine hands toward him;
14 If iniquity be in thine hand, put it far away, and let not wickedness dwell in thy tabernacles." (Job 11:13-14)

Verse 13 is a "take two aspirins and call me tomorrow" type of comment. Zophar tells Job to *"prepare thine heart,"* in the sense of getting ready to submit to God. In the same breath he advises Job to *"stretch out thine hands toward him."* Stretched out hands are symbolic of openness toward God. Our modern handshake comes from the sign of an open hand, free from weapons or malice.

This is the attitude we are to take before God. *"I will therefore that men pray every where, lifting up holy hands, without wrath and doubting."* (1 Timothy 2:8) Great advice, but not very specific in its application to Job's situation.

The open hands of Job 11:13 are meant to contrast with iniquity in the hand mentioned in the next verse. *"If iniquity be in thine hand, put it far away, and let not wickedness dwell in thy tabernacles."* (Job 11:14)

These guys don't give up, do they? They won't turn loose of the idea that all Job has to do is get his heart right with God, repent, and then everything will be fine.

PURGE YOUR SPOTS

15 "For then shalt thou lift up thy face without spot; yea, thou shalt be stedfast, and shalt not fear:" (Job 11:15)

Job 11:15 is interesting in the Tribulation context of the Book of Job. *"For then shalt thou lift up thy face WITHOUT SPOT; yea, thou shalt be stedfast, and shalt not fear."* (Job 11:15) (Author's emphasis) Zophar is concerned that Job repent so that he will be *"without spot."*

This theme of the *"spot"* of sin is consistent through the Bible. The Antichrist will identify his followers with a mark (or spot). *"And deceiveth them that dwell on the earth by the means of those miracles which he had power to do in the sight of the beast; saying to them that dwell on the earth, that they should make an image to the beast, which had the wound by a sword, and did live. And he had power to give life unto the image of the beast, that the image of the beast should both speak, and cause that as many as would not worship the image of the beast should be killed. And he causeth all, both small and great, rich and poor, free and bond, to receive a mark in their right hand, or in their foreheads: And that no man might buy or sell, save he that had the mark, or the name of the beast, or the number of his name. Here is wisdom. Let him that hath understanding count the number of the beast: for it is the number of a man; and his number is Six hundred threescore and six."* (Revelation 13:14-18)

Jude warns against spots. *"These are SPOTS in your feasts of charity, when they feast with you, feeding themselves without fear: clouds they are without water, carried about of winds; trees whose fruit withereth, without fruit, twice dead, plucked up by the roots. And others save with fear, pulling them out of the fire; hating even the garment SPOTTED by the flesh."* (Jude 12,23) (Author's emphasis)

The entire thirteenth and fourteenth chapters of Leviticus are instructions on dealing with the spot of leprosy. In the Bible, leprosy is a picture of sin and prophetically points to the mark of the beast we saw above in Revelation 13.

James warned, *"Pure religion and undefiled before God and the Father is this, To visit the fatherless and widows in their affliction, and to keep himself UNSPOTTED from the world."* (James 1:27) (Author's emphasis)

Paul spoke of Christ and His bride, the church. *"That he might present it to himself a glorious church, NOT HAVING SPOT, or wrinkle, or any such thing; but that it should be holy and without blemish."* (Ephesians 5:27) (Author's emphasis)

Are YOU unspotted from the world? Zophar may be off base in his application to Job, but his words are just as true today as they were when he spoke them thousands of years ago. If there is iniquity in your hands, you need to get your heart right with God so that you can lift up your face to Him without spot.

16 "Because thou shalt forget thy misery, and remember it as waters that pass away." (Job 11:16)

Here is another apparent reference to Noah's Flood. Zophar's point is that just as God's wrath was poured out on the world in the Flood, and the waters passed away, so God's wrath upon Job would subside if he would just repent. This is Zophar's solution for Job's misery.

POSSESS THE BLESSING

The next few verses reflect the conditions of the Second Coming. Remember that Job is a picture of God's people, Israel, in the time of Tribulation. The message is the same. When Israel gets right with God, the waves of His wrath will pass away, and the world will enter a time of peace and prosperity.

17 "And thine age shall be clearer than the noonday; thou shalt shine forth, thou shalt be as the morning." (Job 11:17)

Malachi 4:1-4 speaks of the dawning of the *"Sun of righteousness,"* a prophecy of the Second Coming of Christ. Like Zophar says of Job, we believers in Christ will also shine forth as the morning sun in that day, for we shall be like Him! The words of Christ in Matthew look forward to this event. *"Then shall the righteous shine forth as the sun in the kingdom of their Father. Who hath ears to hear, let him hear."* (Matthew 13:43)

18 "And thou shalt be secure, because there is hope; yea, thou shalt dig about thee, and thou shalt take thy rest in safety.
19 Also thou shalt lie down, and none shall make thee afraid; yea, many shall make suit unto thee." (Job 11:18-19)

Zophar continues his exhortation which transcends far beyond its direct application to Job. These are precisely the conditions that God promises to His people in Christ's coming earthly reign upon David's throne in the Millennium. Many examples could be given, but consider the similarity of the language of the following prophecies.

"And they shall no more be a prey to the heathen, neither shall the beast of the land devour them; but they shall dwell safely, and none shall make them afraid." (Ezekiel 34:28)

"But they shall sit every man under his vine and under his fig tree; and none shall make them afraid: for the mouth of the LORD of hosts hath spoken it." (Micah 4:4)

"The remnant of Israel shall not do iniquity, nor speak lies; neither shall a deceitful tongue be found in their mouth: for they shall feed and lie down, and none shall make them afraid." (Zephaniah 3:13)

Finally, Zophar contrasts the prosperity and blessing of those who are right with God with the destiny of the wicked.

20 "But the eyes of the wicked shall fail, and they shall not escape, and their hope shall be as the giving up of the ghost." (Job 11:20)

Eyes are an interesting feature of the body. Jesus called them *"the light of the body"* in Matthew 6:22.

Our idiomatic way of saying that someone has an "evil eye" comes straight from the Bible. *"Eat thou not the bread of him that hath an evil eye, neither desire thou his dainty meats."* (Proverbs 23:6)

The Antichrist is distinguished in biblical prophecy by his eyes. Daniel's *"little horn"* is a prophetic picture of the Antichrist. A feature that stands out to Daniel in his vision are the eyes of this *"little horn." "I considered the horns, and, behold, there came up among them another little horn, before whom there were three of the first horns plucked up by the roots: and, behold, in this horn were eyes like the eyes of man, and a mouth speaking great things."* (Daniel 7:8)

Later he said, *"And of the ten horns that were in his head, and of the other which came up, and before whom three fell; even of that horn that had eyes, and a mouth that spake very great things, WHOSE LOOK WAS MORE STOUT than his fellows."* (Daniel 7:20) (Author's emphasis) There is to be something about the eyes of the Antichrist, something about his look.

Just as Zophar said, this wicked one, the Antichrist, will have an eye that fails him according to the prophecy of Zechariah. *"Woe to the idol shepherd that leaveth the flock! the sword shall be upon his arm, and upon his right eye: his arm shall be clean dried up, and his right eye shall be utterly darkened."* (Zechariah 11:17)

Ultimately, the eyes of all wicked will be darkened. *"The eye that mocketh at his father, and despiseth to obey his mother, the ravens of the valley shall pick it out, and the young eagles shall eat it."* (Proverbs 30:17)

The devotional application of these words from Proverbs 30 is obvious. Yet there is a distinctly prophetic feature about them. Eagles and birds of prey have a role in the cleanup operations following the Tribulation. *"And I saw an angel standing in the sun; and he cried with a loud voice, saying to all the fowls that fly in the midst of heaven, Come and gather yourselves together unto the supper of the great God; That ye may eat the flesh of kings, and the flesh of captains, and the flesh of mighty men, and the flesh of horses, and of them that sit on them, and the flesh of all men, both free and bond, both small and great."* (Revelation 19:17-18)

Jesus said, *"For as the lightning cometh out of the east, and shineth even unto the west; so shall also the coming of the Son of man be. For wheresoever the carcase is, there will the eagles be gathered together."* (Matthew 24:27-28)

The carcasses of the wicked will literally have their eyes picked out by these birds of prey following the great slaughter in the Valley of Armageddon. Along with their physical bodies, their hope also perishes. *"And their hope shall be as the giving up of the ghost."* (Job 11:20b)

When the righteous die, their hope lives on. When a wicked man dies, his hope also disappears. *"When a wicked man dieth, his expectation shall perish: and the hope of unjust men perisheth."* (Proverbs 11:7)

What a sad state! Again, the words do not apply to Job, but they just might apply to you, if you don't have the assurance of your eternal salvation. There is no better time than the present to be certain that you have accepted the Lord Jesus Christ as your personal Savior, and have been born again.

"That if thou shalt confess with thy mouth the Lord Jesus, and shalt believe in thine heart that God hath raised him from the dead, thou shalt be saved. For with the heart man believeth unto righteousness; and with the mouth confession is made unto salvation." (Romans 10:9-10)

11

JOB RISES TO HIS OWN DEFENSE

With the ancient is wisdom; and in length of days understanding.
With him is wisdom and strength, he hath counsel
and understanding.
Behold, he breaketh down, and it cannot be built again:
he shutteth up a man, and there can be no opening.

Job 12:12-14

WHEN SNOW BEGINS TO MELT, DRIVING A CAR IS A NASTY, messy chore. A semi truck rushes by and covers your car with a coat of brown slush. You strain to see the road ahead. You push the washer button on your windshield wiper control, praying that there is enough fluid in the reservoir to clean the windshield again. The wipers carve a broad stroke of visibility across the windshield, but it will only be a temporary relief. Soon, the blinding mess will build up again.

Job has had the windshield of his mind clouded with the painful anguish of his tragedy. Yet there comes a time, after receiving a horrible emotional blow, when the panic, denial, anguish and crying temporarily subside. As if the path were cleared by windshield wipers, flashes of reason course through the mind. The anguish, though, can return at any moment.

Job is caught in just such a moment of mental clarity in Job chapter 12. Three of his best friends have just taken turns pounding him. So far, Job has been so consumed with his grief he has not directly dealt with the attacks. His "answers" to their discourses have been more a pouring out of his anguish, than a response. Now for the first time Job rises to his own defense in a calculated manner.

ABSENCE OF WISDOM

1 "And Job answered and said,
2 No doubt but ye are the people, and wisdom shall die with you." (Job 12:1-2)

The sarcasm in Job's words in the first two verses is unmistakable. He has had his fill of "godly counsel" from his friends. Beneath the sarcasm Job has correctly identified the problem. His friends think they are dispensing great wisdom, when wisdom is what they lack.

As evident as the sarcasm is the combative nature of Job's words. Yet do not fail to see that he does not deny the validity of their facts. As we have observed throughout this exchange, these men have great knowledge accompanied by a void of wisdom. Job concedes the truth of their information, as shown by the next verse.

3 "But I have understanding as well as you; I am not inferior to you: yea, who knoweth not such things as these?" (Job 12:3)

"Kid's stuff!" This is what Job is saying. "Who doesn't know these things? Tell me something I don't know."

4 "I am as one mocked of his neighbour, who calleth upon God, and he answereth him: the just upright man is laughed to scorn." (Job 12:4)

Verse 4 is not as easily understood. Carefully examine what is said. Job compares himself to one who is mocked by his neighbor, and who (Job) calls upon the Lord. The *"he"* who answers Job is the neighbor, not God. The result follows on the other side of the colon: *"the just upright man* (Job) *is laughed to scorn* (by his neighbor)." (Author's note)

This is obviously what Job feels. He has called upon God to explain this calamity that has befallen him, yet it is not God Who has answered, but these three "counselors," who are contributing nothing but scorn.

5 "He that is ready to slip with his feet is as a lamp despised in the thought of him that is at ease." (Job 12:5)

Oriental people clothe their thoughts in colorful imagery. Here, Job compares himself to a lamp. He is saying that those who are at ease have no need of a lamp. Since Job is ready *"to slip,"* he is as useless as a lamp is to a man at ease. Who wants to pay attention to any truth that Job would speak, since he is "on his way out."

This is a powerful illustration. Do you remember the teaching of Psalm 119:105? *"Thy word is a lamp unto my feet, and a light unto my path."* When a man is *"at ease"*—not moving, not growing—the *"lamp"* of the Word of God is of no use to him, although it is still Truth.

6 "The tabernacles of robbers prosper, and they that provoke God are secure; into whose hand God bringeth abundantly." (Job 12:6)

Frustration is the operative word to describe Job 12:6. What Job says is not true, but it sure seems like it from his present perspective.

Why do the bad guys get all the breaks? How come the wicked have the nice cars, the big houses and all the finer things of life, when a righteous man like Job is sitting on the ash heap?

Now, be honest. Haven't you ever thought this? Doesn't it seem unfair that drug dealers in large cities live in mansions, while some sincere servant of God struggles to feed his family as he pastors a small, rural church?

Asaph, one of the contributors to the book of Psalms, was honest enough to admit that he harbored such thoughts. He wrote Psalm 73 about this very theme.

"Truly God is good to Israel, even to such as are of a clean heart. But as for me, my feet were almost gone; my steps had well nigh slipped. For I was envious at the foolish, when I saw the prosperity of the wicked. For there are no bands in their death: but their strength is firm. They are not in trouble as other men; neither are they plagued like other men. Therefore pride compasseth them about as a chain; violence covereth them as a garment. Their eyes stand out with fatness: they have more than heart could wish. They are corrupt, and speak wickedly concerning oppression: they speak loftily. They set their mouth against the heavens, and their tongue walketh through the earth. Therefore his people return hither: and waters of a full cup are wrung out to them. And they say, How doth God know? and is there knowledge in the most High? Behold, these are the ungodly, who prosper in the world; they increase in riches. Verily I have cleansed my heart in vain, and washed my hands in innocency." (Psalm 73:1-13)

Asaph was envious of the wicked. He entertained thoughts that his faith in God was in vain. There was just one fact that brought Asaph back to his senses.

"When I thought to know this, it was too painful for me; Until I went into the sanctuary of God; then understood I their end." (Psalm 73:16-17)

No matter how much wealth and blessing the wicked may have in this life, it is ALL they will ever have. Asaph came to understand *"their end."*

Job can be excused for what he said in Job 12:6. Looking out from the depth of his depression, Job can only see the prosperity of robbers and others who provoke God.

Amid this mixture of despair, reason, and sarcasm the main point of the section is that Job's counselors suffer from an absence of wisdom. They have put together a string of facts couched in "God-speak," which fail to address the true nature of Job's sufferings.

ILLUSTRATION OF WISDOM

7 "But ask now the beasts, and they shall teach thee; and the fowls of the air, and they shall tell thee:
8 Or speak to the earth, and it shall teach thee: and the fishes of the sea shall declare unto thee.
9 Who knoweth not in all these that the hand of the LORD hath wrought this?
10 In whose hand is the soul of every living thing, and the breath of all mankind.
11 Doth not the ear try words? and the mouth taste his meat?" (Job 12:7-11)

Having pointed out their own lack of wisdom, Job suggests that his friends look to God's creation to see true wisdom illustrated. Ironically, when God finally speaks to Job in Chapter 38, He is going to give Job a lesson on Creationism.

There is an extremely important biblical truth involved here. Paul expresses it as clearly as anyone.

"For the invisible things of him from the creation of the world are clearly seen, being understood by the things that are made, even his eternal power and Godhead; so that they are without excuse." (Romans 1:20)

In the context of Romans 1:20, Paul is establishing the fact of human sin, and man's guilt before a holy God. Even man without the Bible has the witness of conscience and creation.

For our purposes, we must see that God has illustrated His invisible truths by means of creation—the things He has made. David also understood this great principle.

"The heavens declare the glory of God; and the firmament sheweth his handywork. Day unto day uttereth speech, and night unto night sheweth knowledge. There is no speech nor language, where their voice is not heard. Their line is gone out through all the earth, and their words to the end of the world. In them hath he set a tabernacle for the sun, Which is as a bridegroom coming out of his chamber, and rejoiceth as a strong man to run a race. His going forth is from the end of the heaven, and his circuit

unto the ends of it: and there is nothing hid from the heat thereof." (Psalm 19:1-6)

In these few words David gives us the key to understanding how God has manifested His truth in creation. If you pay close attention to this passage you will see that the tabernacle God has prepared for the sun is the universe. The tabernacle that Moses made according to God's instructions was a type of the universe with its three "rooms," the outer court, the holy place and the holy of holies, corresponding to the three biblical heavens. The sun is likened to a "*bridegroom,*" who is Christ. (Malachi 4:2 and 2 Peter 1:19) The Lord is also likened here to a "*strong man.*" We learn that He travels in space, from one end of heaven to the other. This verse even alludes to the coming judgment of fire by speaking of "*the heat thereof.*"

Job first directs his counselors to the animal world. "*But ask now the beasts.*" (Job 12:7a)

So what can we learn from animals? From Genesis to Revelation God employs animals to illustrate His truth. Often, by learning more about these animals, the Bible will suddenly open in unexpected ways. Things that one has passed over before now take on added meaning.

Examples abound. From the third chapter of Genesis the serpent illustrates sin and Satan. It is no accident that when God sent serpents to judge Israel for murmuring in the wilderness (Numbers 21:4-9), it is a bronze serpent, a type of Christ on the cross made sin for us, that Moses lifted up on a pole. All who looked to the bronze serpent were healed.

Jesus used this same example to teach truth to Nicodemus in John 3. Man has been snake-bit by sin. His only salvation is to look to Jesus, Who became sin for us, and endured God's judgment, which is symbolized in the Bible by bronze.

Sheep are a type of God's people (John 10:1-18). Oxen are a type of God's servants (1 Corinthians 9:1-9). False teachers are pictured by dogs and sows (2 Peter 2:22; Philippians 3:2; Revelation 22:15). We saw in the last chapter that the wild ass is a type of lost sinner (Job 11:12). The lion can either be Christ, the "*Lion of the tribe of Juda*" (Revelation 5:5), or the roaring lion who "*walketh about, seeking whom he may devour*" (1 Peter 5:8).

Birds also have something to tell us in the Bible. Job says to ask "*the fowls of the air, and they shall tell thee.*" (Job 12:7b)

In Leviticus 11, various birds are classified as unclean. When Isaiah describes hell in Isaiah 34, these same unclean birds appear, picturing demons. These are the same "*birds of the air*" that make their nests in Christendom (Matthew 13:32).

The dove is a type of the Holy Spirit, as was confirmed to John the Baptist when he saw the Spirit descend *"like a dove"* upon Jesus. Song of Solomon celebrates the love of Solomon for the Shulamite, picturing the Son of David (Christ) taking a gentile bride (the church). Both are said to have *"dove's eyes"* (Song of Solomon 4:1; 5:12). We, as the bride of Christ, are to see things as He sees them—through the eyes of the Spirit.

Not only beasts and birds, but the very earth itself speaks about God's truth. *"Or speak to the earth, and it shall teach thee."* (Job 12:8a)

The earth is God's creation. Earth also bears the scars of man's sin (Romans 8:22). The great rift that runs from Palestine to Zimbabwe and the great mountain ranges of the earth, give testimony to catastrophic movements. The fossil records do more to substantiate God's judgment than man's inconsistent and unproven theory of evolution. God's handwriting lines the earth.

Job maintains that *"the fishes of the sea shall declare unto thee."* (Job 12:8b)

As part of God's creation, fish also have a contribution to make to our total understanding of God's truth. Besides the obvious lessons to be learned from the literal study of fish, men are compared to fish in the Bible. If you want to understand evangelism, go fishing. Jesus told some commercial fishermen that he would make them *"fishers of men"* (Matthew 4:19).

Peter, a commercial fisherman all his life, still had some things to learn from observing God's fish. The story is found in the Matthew 17.

"And when they were come to Capernaum, they that received tribute money came to Peter, and said, Doth not your master pay tribute? He saith, Yes. And when he was come into the house, Jesus prevented him, saying, What thinkest thou, Simon? of whom do the kings of the earth take custom or tribute? Of their own children, or of strangers? Peter saith unto him, Of strangers. Jesus saith unto him, Then are the children free. Notwithstanding, lest we should offend them, go thou to the sea, and cast an hook, and take up the fish that first cometh up; and when thou hast opened his mouth, thou shalt find a piece of money: that take, and give unto them for me and thee." (Matthew 17:24-27)

Peter found his tax money in the mouth of a fish. There are pastors who complain they never have enough money to do God's work. They need to go fishing. Some of those lost "fish" they need to catch will have enough money in their mouth to supply the needs of the ministry.

This is elementary knowledge according to Job. *"Who knoweth not in all these that the hand of the LORD hath wrought this?"* (Job 12:9) He said much the same thing in verse 3. *"Who knoweth not such things as these?"* (Job 12:3b)

What was common knowledge in Job's day is unknown to even the well-educated of our day. To our shame, we have the Bible, yet most of us seldom read it. When it is read, it is seldom studied. When most of us study it, we seldom believe it.

The essence of Job's message on creation is his remark in verse 10 that the Lord wrought all we see. *"In whose hand is the soul of every living thing, and the breath of all mankind."* (Job 12:10)

Paul made a similar remark in his speech on Mars Hill in Athens. *"For in him we live, and move, and have our being."* (Acts 17:28a)

Since "He's got the whole world in His hands," there isn't much point in arguing with God. In the speeches made against him, Job figures his friends have been imagining that they speak for God. Job has no idea what is happening, but he does understand Who is in charge. This sets up his next remark.

"Doth not the ear try words? and the mouth taste his meat?" (Job 12:11)

Job accuses his friends of hearing without listening, just as some people eat so fast they do not taste their food. Their ears are receiving words and processing them so fast that no understanding is taking place. In this specific context Job has been expounding on God's creation being a witness to God. This truth surrounds his counselors, yet they are not paying attention.

Job's friends suffer from an absence of wisdom in their lives. God has placed them in a world that is saturated with wisdom, as illustrated by beasts, birds and the earth itself. Now, Job points directly to the Source of all wisdom—God Himself.

SOURCE OF WISDOM

THE ANCIENT

12 "With the ancient is wisdom; and in length of days understanding.

13 With him is wisdom and strength, he hath counsel and understanding." (Job 12:12-13)

Job 12:12 is a transition to the One who is the source of wisdom. That the *"he"* of verses 14-25 refers to God is not hard to understand, as we will soon see. The difficulty is the identity of *"the ancient"* mentioned in verse 12. This *"ancient"* is not specifically identified as the *"Ancient of days"* as in Daniel 7:13, or the One who is seen by John in Revelation 1:13-16.

The Hebrew word used here and translated as *"ancient"* appears only four times in the Old Testament, all here in the Book of Job (12:12; 15:10; 29:8; 32:6). The sense of verses 12-13 seems to point to a man who has a great reservoir of wisdom and understanding.

If these words indeed speak of a man, the best candidate to be called *"the ancient"* would appear to be Melchizedek, who is a type of the Lord Jesus Christ (Hebrews 5:6; 6:20; 7:1-21), and still remembered with reverence in Job's day. This would clarify things greatly, since the transition from human to the controlling spiritual power in this passage is similar to the situation we have already examined in Isaiah 14 and Ezekiel 28. There, God begins speaking to a human, then changes and speaks straight to the Devil, who is effectively controlling them. Here, Job would begin speaking of a human and then move on to speak of God.

In the New Testament this technique also has precedent. Shortly after Peter has made a wonderful profession of faith, the Devil begins to control his mouth, as he rebukes Christ for speaking of His crucifixion. Christ looks at Peter but speaks to the Devil. *"But he turned, and said unto Peter, Get thee behind me, Satan: thou art an offence unto me: for thou savourest not the things that be of God, but those that be of men."* (Matthew 16:23)

By comparing Scripture with Scripture, we can propose a solution for our dilemma here in Job 12. Apparently Job refers to *"the ancient,"* thinking of Melchizedek (or at the very least someone of that stature). Speaking under the unction of the Holy Ghost, his words suddenly transcend the mortal priest, and point to the One who Melchizedek typifies. Melchizedek has been a source of fascinating speculation for many. Some have suggested that Melchizedek is none other than Noah's son Shem. He is the likely candidate.

Remember that "Melchizedek" is a title, meaning "king of righteousness." He is also called, in Genesis 14:18, the *"king of Salem,"* meaning "king of peace," which later became "Jeru-SALEM." As king of righteousness, and king of peace, it is no wonder he is a type of Christ.

Following the dates of the Old Testament, Shem does not die until around 1846 B.C., which is around the time Abraham marries Keturah. This date means he is still very much an influence in Job's day.

Noah officiated in priestly functions. *"And Noah builded an altar unto the LORD; and took of every clean beast, and of every clean fowl, and offered burnt offerings on the altar."* (Genesis 8:20)

This priestly knowledge would surely have been passed down to one or more of his three sons. One of his sons, however, was designated by God as the spiritual leader of the three—Shem. "*And he said, Blessed be the LORD God of Shem; and Canaan shall be his servant.*" (Genesis 9:26)

The Jews came from the lineage of Eber, who was a descendant of Shem (Genesis 10:21). The word "Hebrew" (Genesis 14:13) means "descendant of Eber." All great religions of the ancient world came from descendants of Shem.

Considering that Shem would still have been alive in the days of Abraham, who else would have had the priestly stature to be worthy of Abraham's submission in Genesis 14?

"*And the king of Sodom went out to meet him after his return from the slaughter of Chedorlaomer, and of the kings that were with him, at the valley of Shaveh, which is the king's dale. And Melchizedek king of Salem brought forth bread and wine: and he was the priest of the most high God. And he blessed him, and said, Blessed be Abram of the most high God, possessor of heaven and earth: And blessed be the most high God, which hath delivered thine enemies into thy hand. And he gave him tithes of all. And the king of Sodom said unto Abram, Give me the persons, and take the goods to thyself. And Abram said to the king of Sodom, I have lift up mine hand unto the LORD, the most high God, the possessor of heaven and earth, That I will not take from a thread even to a shoelatchet, and that I will not take any thing that is thine, lest thou shouldest say, I have made Abram rich: Save only that which the young men have eaten, and the portion of the men which went with me, Aner, Eshcol, and Mamre; let them take their portion.*" (Genesis 14:17-24)

Such speculation can be stimulating, but the other alternative is quite simple—that Job is speaking of God all along. Whoever "*the ancient*" of Job 12:12-13 may be, the Person of the following verses is without doubt the One Who is the Source of wisdom. Each statement and characteristic attributed to Him can be illustrated in the history of the Old Testament.

THE AWESOME GOD

14 "Behold, he breaketh down, and it cannot be built again: he shutteth up a man, and there can be no opening." (Job 12:14)

God is the only One who can break down something so that it cannot be built again. This is precisely what He promises to do with Babylon. "*Because of the wrath of the LORD it shall not be inhabited, but it shall be wholly desolate: every one that goeth by Babylon shall be astonished, and hiss at all her plagues."* (Jeremiah 50:13)

"And he cried mightily with a strong voice, saying, Babylon the great is fallen, is fallen, and is become the habitation of devils, and the hold of every foul spirit, and a cage of every unclean and hateful bird." (Revelation 18:2)

Also in Job 12:14, when God shuts a man up, there is no getting him out until God is ready. Jesus paraphrased Isaiah 22:22 in His letter to Philadelphia. *"And to the angel of the church in Philadelphia write; These things saith he that is holy, he that is true, he that hath the key of David, he that openeth, and no man shutteth; and shutteth, and no man openeth."* (Revelation 3:7)

15 "Behold, he withholdeth the waters, and they dry up: also he sendeth them out, and they overturn the earth." (Job 12:15)

There is no question that Job's statement in verse 15 refers to the Flood. No one but God has ever sent out the waters to overturn the earth.

16 "With him is strength and wisdom: the deceived and the deceiver are his." (Job 12:16)

Strength and wisdom are certainly *"with him,"* (God) while the last part of the verse is a tremendous promise. Not only are the *"deceived"* under His sovereign power, but also "the deceiver."

The identity of this *"deceiver"* is not hard to learn. He is actively working in Job's life, and continues his same mission today.

Paul describes the Antichrist to the Thessalonians. *"And then shall that Wicked be revealed, whom the Lord shall consume with the spirit of his mouth, and shall destroy with the brightness of his coming: Even him, whose coming is after the working of Satan with all power and signs and lying wonders, And with all deceivableness of unrighteousness in them that perish; because they received not the love of the truth, that they might be saved."* (2 Thessalonians 2:8-10)

The power behind the Antichrist is the very Devil himself. *"Therefore rejoice, ye heavens, and ye that dwell in them. Woe to the inhabiters of the earth and of the sea! for the devil is come down unto you, having great wrath, because he knoweth that he hath but a short time."* (Revelation 12:12)

"And I saw an angel come down from heaven, having the key of the bottomless pit and a great chain in his hand. And he laid hold on the dragon, that old serpent, which is the Devil, and Satan, and bound him a thousand years, And cast him into the bottomless pit, and shut him up, and set a seal upon him, that he should deceive the nations no more, till

the thousand years should be fulfilled: and after that he must be loosed a little season." (Revelation 20:1-3)

Again, we are reminded of the truth of Job 12:14, that God has the power to shut up and to loose according to His will. *"And when the thousand years are expired, Satan shall be loosed out of his prison, And shall go out to deceive the nations which are in the four quarters of the earth, Gog and Magog, to gather them together to battle: the number of whom is as the sand of the sea."* (Revelation 20:7-8)

17 "He leadeth counsellors away spoiled, and maketh the judges fools." (Job 12:17)

The *"counsellors"* Job mentions in Job 12:17 are those in a governmental sense, not like Job's *"counsellors."* This is the same usage of the word we saw earlier. *"With kings and counsellors of the earth, which built desolate places for themselves."* (Job 3:14) Even today we often call an attorney "counselor."

The last part of Job 12:17 says, *"He . . . maketh the judges fools."* This is illustrated by the mighty judge, Samson, reduced to the level of a fool. *"But the Philistines took him, and put out his eyes, and brought him down to Gaza, and bound him with fetters of brass; and he did grind in the prison house."* (Judges 16:21)

When Isaiah thundered the words of God's judgment upon Egypt, his words illustrate both aspects of this truth of God's power over the nations.

"Surely the princes of Zoan are fools, the counsel of the wise counsellors of Pharaoh is become brutish: how say ye unto Pharaoh, I am the son of the wise, the son of ancient kings? Where are they? where are thy wise men? and let them tell thee now, and let them know what the LORD of hosts hath purposed upon Egypt. The princes of Zoan are become fools, the princes of Noph are deceived; they have also seduced Egypt, even they that are the stay of the tribes thereof. The LORD hath mingled a perverse spirit in the midst thereof: and they have caused Egypt to err in every work thereof, as a drunken man staggereth in his vomit." (Isaiah 19:11-14)

18 "He looseth the bond of kings, and girdeth their loins with a girdle." (Job 12:18)

Job continues his illustrations of God's great power and wisdom. The ultimate fulfillment of this verse is recorded in Isaiah, a prophecy of the coming Messiah. The bond of sin upon Israel will be loosed, and the King will be girded with strength.

"And it shall come to pass in that day, that I will call my servant Eliakim the son of Hilkiah: And I will clothe him with thy robe, and strengthen him with thy girdle, and I will commit thy government into his hand: and

he shall be a father to the inhabitants of Jerusalem, and to the house of Judah. And the key of the house of David will I lay upon his shoulder; so he shall open, and none shall shut; and he shall shut, and none shall open. And I will fasten him as a nail in a sure place; and he shall be for a glorious throne to his father's house. And they shall hang upon him all the glory of his father's house, the offspring and the issue, all vessels of small quantity, from the vessels of cups, even to all the vessels of flagons. In that day, saith the LORD of hosts, shall the nail that is fastened in the sure place be removed, and be cut down, and fall; and the burden that was upon it shall be cut off: for the LORD hath spoken it." (Isaiah 22:20-25)

19 "He leadeth princes away spoiled, and overthroweth the mighty." (Job 12:19)

Job 12:19 also deals with the theme of God's sovereignty over human government.

Here, there are also biblical examples. The once mighty kings of Judah are reduced to puppet-princes of Nebuchadnezzar of Babylon, and led away. Here is the fate of one such prince, Jehoiakim: *"Against him came up Nebuchadnezzar king of Babylon, and bound him in fetters, to carry him to Babylon. Nebuchadnezzar also carried of the vessels of the house of the LORD to Babylon, and put them in his temple at Babylon."* (2 Chronicles 36:6-7)

Later, the remaining princes of the royal family suffer the same indignity. *"And all the vessels of the house of God, great and small, and the treasures of the house of the LORD, and the treasures of the king, and of his princes; all these he brought to Babylon."* (2 Chronicles 36:18)

20 "He removeth away the speech of the trusty, and taketh away the understanding of the aged." (Job 12:20)

The first part of Job 12:20 reads, *"He removeth away the speech of the trusty."* (Job 12:20a) Zechariah, John the Baptist's father, had his speech removed as punishment for his unbelief. *"And, behold, thou shalt be dumb, and not able to speak, until the day that these things shall be performed, because thou believest not my words, which shall be fulfilled in their season."* (Luke 1:20)

Senility is the obvious and literal application of the last phrase of Job 12:20. *"He . . . taketh away the understanding of the aged."* (Job 12:20b)

Yet one could also point to the tragic ending of Eli, high priest of Israel. In the third chapter of 1 Samuel, Eli is an overweight old man with failing eyesight, who has lost control of his sons, of his own life, and was seriously deficient in spiritual understanding, in spite of his high office and advanced age. It took three times for him to recognize that God was speaking to young Samuel. Why else would God decline to speak directly to the high priest, choosing rather to give him a message through an unproven young man like Samuel?

21 "He poureth contempt upon princes, and weakeneth the strength of the mighty." (Job 12:21)

We have already seen how God poured contempt on rulers who failed to recognize the true Source of their authority. Again, Samson is the classic example of the mighty made weak.

"But the Philistines took him, and put out his eyes, and brought him down to Gaza, and bound him with fetters of brass; and he did grind in the prison house." (Judges 16:21)

22 "He discovereth deep things out of darkness, and bringeth out to light the shadow of death." (Job 12:22)

The first half of Job 12:22 needs to be considered separately. *"He discovereth deep things out of darkness, and bringeth out to light the shadow of death."* (Job 12:22a)

This is what God did in the creation. The same teaching appears later in Job. *"He stretcheth out the north over the empty place, and hangeth the earth upon nothing."* (Job 26:7)

The same principle can also apply to what is intangible, as God discovers (reveals) what was hidden before. God did this when he revealed the mystery of the church to Paul.

"For this cause I Paul, the prisoner of Jesus Christ for you Gentiles, If ye have heard of the dispensation of the grace of God which is given me to you-ward: How that by revelation he made known unto me the mystery; (as I wrote afore in few words, Whereby, when ye read, ye may understand my knowledge in the mystery of Christ) Which in other ages was not made known unto the sons of men, as it is now revealed unto his holy apostles and prophets by the Spirit; That the Gentiles should be fellow-heirs, and of the same body and partakers of his promise in Christ by the gospel." (Ephesians 3:1-6)

The *"shadow of death"* makes another of its frequent appearances in Job. *"He . . . bringeth out to light the shadow of death."* (Job 12:22b)

We have already mentioned the significance of this *"shadow of death"* in the Tribulation age. Consider these prophetic words of Amos, who is seeing how God will finish this destruction with the dawning of the Sun of righteousness. *"Seek him that maketh the seven stars and Orion, and turneth the shadow of death into the morning, and maketh the day dark with night: that calleth for the waters of the sea, and poureth them out upon the face of the earth: The LORD is his name."* (Amos 5:8)

23 "He increaseth the nations, and destroyeth them: he enlargeth the nations, and straiteneth them again." (Job 12:23)

Again Job turns to God's sovereign power over the nations. The examples already mentioned give ample evidence of this truth. The classic New Testament statement is Paul's word to the Romans. *"Let every soul be subject unto the higher powers. For there is no power but of God: the powers that be are ordained of God."* (Romans 13:1)

24 "He taketh away the heart (courage) of the chief of the people of the earth, and causeth them to wander in a wilderness where there is no way." (Job 12:24) (Author's comment)

The fact that God is in total control of governments and governors is the reason for Job's next truth. *"He taketh away the heart of the chief of the people of the earth."* (Job 12:24a) The Syrians had placed Dothan under siege, and it was only a matter of time before the powerful Syrian armies would annihilate the people of God. God, though, took away the heart of the Syrians.

"For the Lord had made the host of the Syrians to hear a noise of chariots, and a noise of horses, even the noise of a great host: and they said one to another, Lo, the king of Israel hath hired against us the kings of the Hittites, and the kings of the Egyptians, to come upon us. Wherefore they arose and fled in the twilight, and left their tents, and their horses, and their asses, even the camp as it was, and fled for their life." (2 Kings 7:6-7)

The last part of Job 12:24 is not hard to understand. *"He . . . causeth them to wander in a wilderness where there is no way."* (Job 12:24b)

The immediate fulfillment of this verse is the wilderness wandering of Israel during the Exodus. History will repeat itself in the time of Tribulation, as prophesied by Hosea.

"Therefore, behold, I will allure her, and bring her into the wilderness, and speak comfortably unto her. And I will give her her vineyards from thence, and the valley of Achor for a door of hope: and she shall sing there, as in the days of her youth, and as in the day when she came up out of the land of Egypt. And it shall be at that day, saith the LORD, that thou shalt call me Ishi; and shalt call me no more Baali." (Hosea 2:14-16)

The final Tribulation fulfillment of Job 12:24 matches the content of Job's final statement in this chapter.

25 "They grope in the dark without light, and he maketh them to stagger like a drunken man." (Job 12:25)

Isaiah saw this coming event. Isaiah lived centuries after the Exodus, and looked forward to that coming day when the Exodus events would be repeated and magnified immediately before the Second Coming of Christ.

"And it shall come to pass, that he who fleeth from the noise of the fear shall fall into the pit; and he that cometh up out of the midst of the pit shall be taken in the snare: for the windows from on high are open, and the foundations of the earth do shake. The earth is utterly broken down, the earth is clean dissolved, the earth is moved exceedingly. The earth shall reel to and fro like a drunkard, and shall be removed like a cottage; and the transgression thereof shall be heavy upon it; and it shall fall, and not rise again." (Isaiah 24:18-20)

Job will continue his answer to his worthless counselors in the next two chapters. He is finally thinking more clearly, and standing up for the righteousness of his testimony. He still has no clue as to what is happening to him, or why. He began by pointing out his friends' lack of wisdom. Moving next to illustrate God's great wisdom and power, he has closed this chapter in a magnificent strain of divine and prophetic truth, celebrating God as the Source of all wisdom.

If you had suffered the things that befell Job, would YOU have had the presence of mind to still cling to God as the Source of wisdom? Or would you allow yourself to wallow in the pits of self-pity and bitterness? Many things about life we can never understand or change. The one thing we always have complete control over is our attitude of heart. How are you doing in the management of YOUR attitude?

12

JOB PROBES THE NATURE OF LIFE

Wherefore do the wicked live,

become old, yea, are mighty in power?

Job 21:7

"WHAT COMES OUT A LEMON WHEN IT IS SQUEEZED?"

Hesitating for a moment before answering my friend's question, I knew that I was being set up. He had a point to make, however, and I decided to play the role of straight man.

"Lemon juice," I said, giving him the answer that was both obvious, and obviously wrong.

"NO!" he exclaimed. "What comes out, is whatever happens to be inside the lemon. We only ASSUME that it is lemon juice. You can never tell for sure until it is squeezed."

My friend had used this illustration with a chemist, and succeeded in capturing his attention. The chemist, amazed at the coincidence, explained that they were doing an experiment involving lemons in his laboratory. They had removed the juice from some lemons, and filled them with other chemicals, taking advantage of certain properties of lemon skin for their experiment.

"You're quite right," his chemist friend replied. "If you were to squeeze the lemons on the shelf in our lab right now, you'd be very surprised."

My friend was drawing this illustration to show how God uses trials in our lives to reveal the reality of what is inside our lives. When one has made a confession of faith in the Lord Jesus Christ, and gives the outward appearance of living for Him, we must never assume that all is well inside their soul. When squeezed in trials, whatever is on the inside is going to come oozing out into the light.

Job is being squeezed. HARD! What is coming out is what God knew was there all along. Now, we can see that the reality of Job's life matched his confession of faith. He is finishing his response to the third of his three friends who have come to him in his grief.

With remarkable lucidity Job rose to his own defense in chapter 12, in response to Zophar's bitter remarks. Then he launched a marvelous exaltation of God's wisdom and sovereignty. In chapter 13 he continues by again responding directly to these three men, who want to fix the cause for Job's calamity as some secret sin. Next, Job will give a remarkable confession of faith, considering the conditions that afflict him. His remarks will end with another confession—a confession of life's futility.

Don't make the mistake of another unwarranted assumption. Don't assume that there is a conflict between a confession of faith in God, and a confession of life's futility. Immaturity seeks a life free from problems and trial, expecting to make deals with God by a show of piety. Maturity understands that faith in God is totally separate from a world system that is hopelessly twisted by sin. Emerging from the heap of ashes and ruin is a Job who is even stronger and wiser than before.

CHARGES AGAINST HIS COUNSELORS

1 "Lo, mine eye hath seen all this, mine ear hath heard and understood it.

2 What ye know, the same do I know also: I am not inferior unto you." (Job 13:1-2)

Verses 1 and 2 of Job 13 are the same refrain Job sang in chapter 12. *"But I have understanding as well as you; I am not inferior to you: yea, who knoweth not such things as these?"* (Job 12:3)

During Job's time, the remarkable spiritual insight these men have tossed around is viewed as common knowledge. Today we would say something like, "You're not telling me anything I don't already know."

3 "Surely I would speak to the Almighty, and I desire to reason with God." (Job 13:3)

Job is saying that he wants to speak with God, not with them. This is a powerful thought. Job understands that God represents his only court of appeal. No one else can make a difference.

Today, people are far too eager to run to their therapist, their favorite Bible teacher, their pastor, their closest friend and confidant—anyone but God! Those who spend their time talking with God become followers of God rather than followers of men.

4 "But ye are forgers of lies, ye are all physicians of no value." (Job 13:4)

Job wants to plead his case before the Almighty, because he knows the truth. Job will not place his trust in these three men. They are worthless to solve his problem. Those who want to help people with their problems would do well to learn this lesson. All counselors are also helpless to solve people's problems. God alone is the great Physician and He alone can provide for our need. We can only point people to Him, show them His word, love them and comfort them.

Today, men run to the three false counselors of education, religion and science. Like Job's friends, they are also physicians of no value.

Paul was a highly-educated individual. Yet he placed no trust in his education to solve problems or provide strength in trial.

"And I, brethren, when I came to you, came not with excellency of speech or of wisdom, declaring unto you the testimony of God. For I determined not to know any thing among you, save Jesus Christ, and him crucified. And I was with you in weakness, and in fear, and in much trembling. And my speech and my preaching was not with enticing words of man's wisdom, but in demonstration of the Spirit and of power." (1 Corinthians 2:1-4)

In Acts 17 Paul spoke to a group of Greek philosophers on Mars' Hill in Athens. They had an abundance of religion, but no knowledge of the living God. Their faith was placed in a worthless physician—their religion.

Science is another of the darling gods of the Twentieth Century. Paul also warned against trusting in this false physician.

"O Timothy, keep that which is committed to thy trust, avoiding profane and vain babblings, and opposition of science falsely so called: Which some professing have erred concerning the faith. Grace be with thee. Amen." (1 Timothy 6:20-21)

Some will object that Paul's use of the word "science" does not correspond to its modern meaning, that this is the Greek word *"gnosis,"* consistently translated "knowledge" elsewhere in the New Testament. This is certainly true that the word means "knowledge." However it is also true that even in Paul's day there arose a cult of "gnostics," or those who sought to profess Christianity while defining it by their own intellectual terms and arguments. This gnosticism was attacked by Paul, especially in his letter to the Colossians.

Is it not also true that much of what is called modern "science" today is not empirically demonstrated fact, but rather a "scientific" philosophical system? Much "science" today does not really qualify as such, but is merely a system of human "knowledge"—really, idealogy—whereby man controls the power and authority rather than submit to God. The point is that however you want to translate *"gnosis,"* the truth is still the same. Man wants to call the shots, to be in total control. Quite often this is done in the name of "science," but is falsely so called.

To whom do YOU turn first in time of crisis? Are you a follower of God, or a "personality addict" who is dependent upon men? Have you sought the false counselors of education, religion and science? Or, have you run to the secular priesthood of psychology and psychiatry? What kind of juice is coming out of your lemon?

5 "O that ye would altogether hold your peace! and it should be your wisdom." (Job 13:5)

Job anticipates the words Solomon will speak centuries later. *"Even a fool, when he holdeth his peace, is counted wise: and he that shutteth his lips is esteemed a man of understanding."* (Proverbs 17:28)

6 "Hear now my reasoning, and hearken to the pleadings of my lips.

7 Will ye speak wickedly for God? and talk deceitfully for him?

8 Will ye accept his person? will ye contend for God?" (Job 13:6-8)

Job complains that his counselors seem to think they speak for God. This is an accurate analysis of the problem. It is also a valid criticism of many of our best efforts in counseling today.

We are to be God's spokesmen, but this is far different from speaking FOR God, that is to say, in His place. To be a spokesman is to be a communicator, or a facilitator. However, to speak FOR God is to be an intermediary.

God has already spoken for Himself in His Word. There is nothing left for us to add. God has said all He needs to say.

The correct attitude appears in Paul's words to the Corinthians. *"For we are not as many, which corrupt the word of God: but as of sincerity, but as of God, in the sight of God speak we in Christ."* (2 Corinthians 2:17)

Adding to, taking away or twisting the words of Scripture corrupts the Word of God. We are to speak sincerely, and *"as of God"*—in other words, as sent by Him. We shouldn't imagine what God would say, try to speak for Him or invent private interpretations of His words. Our responsibility is simply to speak what He has already said, being led of His Spirit to apply the words of God with all wisdom and understanding.

Churches and Christian organizations are filled with those who speak all manner of fantasy, bitterness, wickedness and malice "in Jesus' name." Christians often vent their own poison, or carry out their personal vendettas by saying that "God impressed this on my heart," or "The Lord told me to tell you this." The message is not Scripture, but venom meted out "in the name of the Lord."

9 "Is it good that he should search you out? or as one man mocketh another, do ye so mock him?
10 He will surely reprove you, if ye do secretly accept persons.
11 Shall not his excellency make you afraid? and his dread fall upon you?
12 Your remembrances are like unto ashes, your bodies to bodies of clay." (Job 13:9-12)

Job's accusations are direct. Looking closely at these verses we can separate four charges Job levels against his counselors. He accuses them of mocking God, of secretly accepting persons, of not fearing God, and failing to remember that they are also mortal bodies of clay that are doomed to return to ashes.

CONFESSION OF FAITH

CONFESSION AND CARNALITY

Job's friends are undoubtedly surprised by his sudden resurgence of energy. No longer sitting despondently on the ash heap, he springs to life, and is responding with this series of stinging accusations we have just examined. Perhaps Job notices that one or more of them are about to respond.

Before the mouth of any one of them can form a word, Job firmly establishes that he still controls the moment. He has patiently listened to them say things that were not only inappropriate, but sometimes cruel. Job is not ready to relinquish the floor until he has had his say. This is the message of the first two verses of this section.

13 "Hold your peace, let me alone, that I may speak, and let come on me what will.
14 Wherefore do I take my flesh in my teeth, and put my life in mine hand?" (Job 13:13-14)

"After all," Job contends, "it is MY flesh that is in question; it is MY life that is affected. You have all had your say. It's MY turn now, and I still have some things I need to say."

The following verse is a classic. Yet in spite of much attention in church circles being given to Job's faith in the first half of the verse, the second half hints at the other side of Job's nature.

15 "Though he slay me, yet will I trust in him: but I will maintain mine own ways before him." (Job 13:15)

This great profession of faith is often quoted. This is the paradox we spoke of earlier in this chapter, when we commented on Job's confession of faith and his confession of life's futility. No matter what happens, no matter whether he understands or not, Job is going to maintain his trust in almighty God.

Many churches today are in the business of accommodation. They will do whatever it takes to make people content and to accommodate their needs, just so they can count them when it comes time to post the attendance. "What's in it for me?" This is the cry of the modern church-goer. If there is ample parking, sparkling nurseries, and services that are "time-sensitive" to the demands of our fast-paced modern society and busy careers, the pampered "baby-boomers" and upscale professionals will do God the favor of gracing the church. All this, provided of course, nothing offensive is said, and no pressure is applied.

Many "megachurches" have been built with this philosophy, but it is questionable whether such Christianity has bred many men with the character of Job, who will say, *"though he slay me, yet will I trust him."*

Job should have stopped with this comment. The second phrase, though, gives evidence that Job still tends to trust in his own righteousness. *"But I will maintain mine own ways before him."*

Job is simply holding tight to his contention that there is no hidden sin in his life. Yet he is dangerously close to trusting in his personal righteousness to stand in God's presence, rather than laying hold of God's grace.

Solomon had some appropriate words if we are tempted to follow Job's thinking. *"Man's goings are of the LORD; how can a man then understand his own way?"* (Proverbs 20:24)

Job has a fundamental, long-term faith in the Lord. Even if the Lord chose to kill him, Job will continue to trust God. Unfortunately, Job's short-term faith is lacking. He trusts God with his life, yet does not trust God with his ways. Job wants to maintain his own ways, instead of recognizing God's control over them.

We ALL have this dual nature and the conflict between flesh and spirit is one that lasts while we are in these *"bodies of clay."* We will see this dichotomy of Job's nature again in the next segment.

16 "He also shall be my salvation: for an hypocrite shall not come before him.

17 Hear diligently my speech, and my declaration with your ears.

18 Behold now, I have ordered my cause; I know that I shall be justified.

19 Who is he that will plead with me? for now, if I hold my tongue, I shall give up the ghost." (Job 13:16-19)

Again, Job is confessing his saving faith in God. He is confident that he is NOT a hypocrite and he implores his three friends to listen to his words. Job simply MUST speak and vent his frustration. Yet he now follows this wonderful confession of faith with two conditions he wants to place upon God.

CONDITIONS AND QUESTIONS

20 "Only do not two things unto me: then will I not hide myself from thee.

21 Withdraw thine hand far from me: and let not thy dread make me afraid.

22 Then call thou, and I will answer: or let me speak, and answer thou me." (Job 13:20-22)

The tremendous effect of Job's confession of faith is dulled by the fleshly self-interest shown by these two conditions. Job will learn that one cannot make deals with God. Nevertheless, Job's two conditions for now are these: 1) "Lay off the tribulation, God." 2) "Let's talk. Either you ask me, or let me ask you to explain what's going on here."

Seeing that God has not yet seen fit to stop his trials, Job opts for the second alternative by listing a series of four questions he wants God to answer. His counselors are no longer the focus of his words as he turns his attention directly to God.

23 "How many are mine iniquities and sins? make me to know my transgression and my sin.

24 Wherefore hidest thou thy face, and holdest me for thine enemy?

25 Wilt thou break a leaf driven to and fro? and wilt thou pursue the dry stubble?" (Job 13:23-25)

Job has consistently maintained that he harbored no secret sin. Not wanting to chance that there is something in his life he is not aware of, Job asks God if there is any sin that needs to be dealt with. This is the point of his first question, and it closely parallels the attitude of the psalmist toward sin.

"Who can understand his errors? cleanse thou me from secret faults.

Keep back thy servant also from presumptuous sins; let them not have dominion over me: then shall I be upright, and I shall be innocent from the great transgression." (Psalm 19:12-13)

"*Examine me, O LORD, and prove me; try my reins and my heart.*" (Psalm 26:2)

"*Search me, O God, and know my heart: try me, and know my thoughts: And see if there be any wicked way in me, and lead me in the way everlasting.*" (Psalm 139:23-24)

Job's second question is in verse 24. "*Wherefore hidest thou thy face, and holdest me for thine enemy?*" (Job 13:24)

Job's question is understandable. God Himself gave testimony that Job was a "*perfect*" man. (Job 1:8; 2:3) Job's question is also unanswerable for now.

As for the Jews in the coming Tribulation, there is no question as to the reason for their suffering, or why God will hide His face from them and hold them as an enemy. The prophetic answer appears in Deuteronomy.

"*And I will surely hide my face in that day for all the evils which they shall have wrought, in that they are turned unto other gods.*" (Deuteronomy 31:18)

Job's final two questions are in Job 13:25. "*Wilt thou break a leaf driven to and fro? and wilt thou pursue the dry stubble?*" (Job 13:25) In other words, "Haven't You done enough, God? Haven't I suffered enough? What's left of me to beat?"

CORNERED AND CONSUMED

26 "For thou writest bitter things against me, and makest me to possess the iniquities of my youth." (Job 13:26)

This verse shows that Job is grasping for answers. Perhaps he thinks all this has come upon him because of sins committed in his youth.

David feared the same thing. He mentioned these youthful sins in the Psalms.

"*Remember not the sins of my youth, nor my transgressions: according to thy mercy remember thou me for thy goodness' sake, O LORD.*" (Psalm 25:7)

27 "Thou puttest my feet also in the stocks, and lookest narrowly unto all my paths; thou settest a print upon the heels of my feet." (Job 13:27)

Job's paranoia grows intense in this verse. God has backed him into a corner. Job feels that God has put his feet in the stocks, like a prisoner. He can't move. He is tied down by the affliction of the Almighty. Job complains that God is looking *"narrowly,"* or intensely upon him. He knows that he is under God's microscope.

The final phrase of this verse should not to be over-looked, considering the prophetic implications of the book, and the fact that Job is a type of Christ in many ways. *"Thou settest a print upon the heels of my feet."*

Watch those heels closely in the Bible! This interest in heels dates from the pronouncement of God upon the occasion of man's fall. God speaks to the serpent, and gives the first promise of a coming Savior.

"And I will put enmity between thee and the woman, and between thy seed and her seed; it shall bruise thy head, and thou shalt bruise his heel." (Genesis 3:15)

Most of us are familiar with the prophecy of the Lord Jesus crushing the head of the serpent beneath his feet. Yet few of us pay much attention to the Lord's heel that is the target of the serpent.

Our Lord paid a dear price on the cross, laying down His life to pay the penalty for our sin. Yet He only received a bruised heel, compared to the bruised head of Satan, crushed beneath the feet of Christ.

"And hath put all things under his feet, and gave him to be the head over all things to the church." (Ephesians 1:22)

"Thou hast put all things in subjection under his feet. For in that he put all in subjection under him, he left nothing that is not put under him. But now we see not yet all things put under him." (Hebrews 2:8)

"For he must reign, till he hath put all enemies under his feet." (1 Corinthians 15:25)

"For he hath put all things under his feet. But when he saith all things are put under him, it is manifest that he is excepted, which did put all things under him." (1 Corinthians 15:27)

Why, then, does the Lord quote Psalm 41:9 when Judas departs from the Last Supper? Judas, not Christ, is the one lifting up his heel.

"I speak not of you all: I know whom I have chosen: but that the scripture may be fulfilled, He that eateth bread with me hath lifted up his heel against me." (John 13:18)

Judas, acting in the spirit of antichrist, lifts up his heel in an attempt to crush the head of Christ. Yet the opposite occurred.

Related to this is the way in which Jacob grabbed hold of Esau's heel at the time of their birth. Watch out for that heel! *"And after that came his brother out, and his hand took hold on Esau's heel; and his name was called Jacob: and Isaac was threescore years old when she bare them."* (Genesis 25:26)

Hosea also mentions this incident. Jacob, from whom the Lord came, marks the heel of Esau, who was a type of antichrist. *"He took his brother by the heel in the womb, and by his strength he had power with God."* (Hosea 12:3)

Yes, Job, God has marked your heel. Right now, Job can see no further than the boils that mark his heel, and the rest of Job's body (Job 2:7). Yet, as a type of One Who will one day crush the Devil beneath His feet, Job is God's instrument in a crucial battle with Satan. Satan thinks that he can make Job curse God. When this battle is over, Satan will be head down in the dust of the earth (Genesis 3:14), and Job will still be standing. In this sense Job's heel has been marked to be firmly placed on the enemy's head.

"Wherefore take unto you the whole armour of God, that ye may be able to withstand in the evil day, and having done all, to stand." (Ephesians 6:13)

Job, understandably, cannot see the larger, prophetic picture. The final verse of the chapter shows his anxiety.

28 "And he, as a rotten thing, consumeth, as a garment that is moth eaten." (Job 13:28)

Job is complaining that he is being consumed by God, as if he were something rotten, or a moth-eaten garment. A similar statement is made by the psalmist.

"Remove thy stroke away from me: I am consumed by the blow of thine hand. When thou with rebukes dost correct man for iniquity, thou makest his beauty to consume away like a moth: surely every man is vanity." (Psalm 39:10-11)

Earlier Job complained about worms. Worms, the worm-like moth, and corruption are connected in Scripture. *"My flesh is clothed with worms and clods of dust; my skin is broken, and become loathsome."* (Job 7:5)

We also see this relationship in Isaiah. *"For the moth shall eat them up like a garment, and the worm shall eat them like wool: but my righteousness shall be for ever, and my salvation from generation to generation."* (Isaiah 51:8)

Here, in chapter 13, he is being consumed as if by a worm-like moth. He will again connect worms and corruption in chapter 17. *"I have said to corruption, Thou art my father: to the worm, Thou art my mother, and my sister."* (Job 17:14)

A graphic picture is painted of Herod's death in the Book of Acts. His body is corrupted by worms. *"And immediately the angel of the Lord smote him, because he gave not God the glory: and he was eaten of worms, and gave up the ghost."* (Acts 12:23)

Herod's death is a superficial illustration of the reality of Satan's doom, as prophesied by Isaiah. As we have seen earlier, Satan is addressed through the king of Babylon, who is the human figure mentioned in this prophecy in Isaiah 14. *"Thy pomp is brought down to the grave, and the noise of thy viols: the worm is spread under thee, and the worms cover thee."* (Isaiah 14:11)

Later in Isaiah's prophecy, God's people, who are called here by the name of Jacob, are seen as corrupted by sin. Notice what God calls them. *"Fear not, thou worm Jacob, and ye men of Israel; I will help thee, saith the LORD, and thy redeemer, the Holy One of Israel."* (Isaiah 41:14)

When Jesus Christ died on the Cross, He had become sin for us (2 Corinthians 5:21). Jesus calls Himself by the appropriate name of corruption, which is recorded by David, who he prophetically gave us the words and thoughts of Christ on the cross. *"But I am a worm, and no man; a reproach of men, and despised of the people."* (Psalm 22:6)

Job has held fast to his confession of faith. Hurricane-force winds are hitting him in the face, and his anxiety is greater than most men could bear. Yet he doesn't move from his position of basic trust in the Almighty.

His flesh keeps reasserting itself, and despair often colors his voice, but Job still stands. Unwittingly, his words paint prophetic pictures of future events of which he knows nothing. From heels to worms, God guides Job's desperate words to give us amazing insight into things to come.

CONFESSION OF LIFE'S FUTILITY

COMPLAINTS ABOUT LIFE'S BREVITY AND INSIGNIFICANCE

This chapter of Job should be read in comparison with the third chapter of Romans, which speaks of the fact of human sin and depravity. Job laments the brevity and futility of life.

1 "Man that is born of a woman is of few days, and full of trouble.

2 He cometh forth like a flower, and is cut down: he fleeth also as a shadow, and continueth not." (Job 14:1-2)

The Bible is filled with warnings about the brevity of human life. A good example, and one that closely corresponds in context and content, is found in Psalm 90.

"Thou turnest man to destruction; and sayest, Return, ye children of men. For a thousand years in thy sight are but as yesterday when it is past, and as a watch in the night. Thou carriest them away as with a flood; they

are as a sleep: in the morning they are like grass which groweth up. In the morning it flourisheth, and groweth up; in the evening it is cut down, and withereth." (Psalm 90:3-6)

Job is still addressing God, as he was in the closing verses of chapter 13. This is evident from the following verse.

3 "And dost thou open thine eyes upon such an one, and bringest me into judgment with thee?" (Job 14:3)

In other words, Job is pondering why God would even bother with him, since his life is nothing anyway. The same thought is expressed by David.

"What is man, that thou art mindful of him? and the son of man, that thou visitest him?" (Psalm 8:4)

4 "Who can bring a clean thing out of an unclean? not one." (Job 14:4)

Job 14:4 is a reminder that Job has never claimed to be sinless. He is very much aware of his sin nature. Yet he steadfastly refuses to concede that some hidden sin is the cause of his problems. This is a paradox because Job tends to trust in his own self-righteousness, yet he freely admits his sin nature.

"Who can bring a clean thing out of an unclean? not one." (Job 14:4) Not one man could ever do such a thing. However, Jesus' words in Matthew are appropriate, though the context has to do with the difficulty of a rich man's salvation, the truth of God's almighty power applies.

"But Jesus beheld them, and said unto them, With men this is impossible; but with God all things are possible." (Matthew 19:26)

5 "Seeing his days are determined, the number of his months are with thee, thou hast appointed his bounds that he cannot pass;

6 Turn from him, that he may rest, till he shall accomplish, as an hireling, his day." (Job 14:5-6)

Since man is corrupted by sin, and since human life is but for a moment of time, Job boldly states his case to the Lord. Job is surely despondent, as we have seen often in these discourses, yet there is another purpose in his words: seeing that we are nothing in the sight of God, who are we to argue with Him, or to attempt to figure out His great plan?

A *"hireling"* is a hired laborer. Job is saying that he has served his time, and it is time for him to "punch out." Job thinks that God surely must be finished with him.

COMPARISONS WITH TREES

Man is often compared to trees in the Bible. We reviewed this truth in chapter 8. The next few verses are a return to this parallel.

7 "For there is hope of a tree, if it be cut down, that it will sprout again, and that the tender branch thereof will not cease.

8 Though the root thereof wax old in the earth, and the stock thereof die in the ground;

9 Yet through the scent of water it will bud, and bring forth boughs like a plant." (Job 14:7-9)

At least a tree has the hope of sprouting again from its stump and root system. Man who is cut down is finished. Job is making this comparison between men and trees to express his frustration at the futility of human life. Job DOES believe in a future resurrection (Job 19:26), but right now he is thinking only of this present life.

In a doctrinal, prophetic sense this passage looks forward to the nation of Israel. Cut down, first by Nebuchadnezzar in 586 B.C., then a second time by the Roman armies of Titus in 70 A.D., Israel is a tree that will blossom again. This is the same figure Paul uses to explain Israel's future to the Romans. He warns them not to boast about the grace of God they had received because of Israel's present separation from blessing. The cut-off tree of Israel will sprout again.

"For if the firstfruit be holy, the lump is also holy: and if the root be holy, so are the branches. And if some of the branches be broken off, and thou, being a wild olive tree, wert grafted in among them, and with them partakest of the root and fatness of the olive tree; Boast not against the branches. But if thou boast, thou bearest not the root, but the root thee. Thou wilt say then, The branches were broken off, that I might be grafted in. Well; because of unbelief they were broken off, and thou standest by faith. Be not highminded, but fear: For if God spared not the natural branches, take heed lest he also spare not thee. Behold therefore the goodness and severity of God: on them which fell, severity; but toward thee, goodness, if thou continue in his goodness: otherwise thou also shalt be cut off. And they also, if they abide not still in unbelief, shall be grafted in: for God is able to graft them in again. For if thou wert cut out of the olive tree which is wild by nature, and wert grafted contrary to nature into a good olive tree: how much more shall these, which be the natural branches, be grafted into their own olive tree? For I would not, brethren, that ye should be ignorant of this mystery, lest ye should be wise in your own conceits; that blindness in part is happened to Israel, until the fulness of the gentiles

be come in. And so all Israel shall be saved: as it is written, There shall come out of Sion the Deliverer, and shall turn away ungodliness from Jacob." (Romans 11:16-26)

So, we again remember that Job is a type not only of Christ, but, at times, also of Israel. A close examination of this passage in Job 14 teaches us how this future restoration will occur. Verse 9 is the answer. Just as water makes a dry tree to bud, "*the washing of water by the word*" (Ephesians 5:26) of God will sanctify and cleanse the church.

In the same restoration context, Isaiah prophesies of that coming day. Notice the connection between budding, water and the Word of God.

"*For as the rain cometh down, and the snow from heaven, and returneth not thither, but watereth the earth, and maketh it bring forth and bud, that it may give seed to the sower, and bread to the eater: So shall my word be that goeth forth out of my mouth: it shall not return unto me void, but it shall accomplish that which I please, and it shall prosper in the thing whereto I sent it. For ye shall go out with joy, and be led forth with peace: the mountains and the hills shall break forth before you into singing, and all the trees of the field shall clap their hands. Instead of the thorn shall come up the fir tree, and instead of the brier shall come up the myrtle tree: and it shall be to the LORD for a name, for an everlasting sign that shall not be cut off.*" (Isaiah 55:10-13)

Israel budded in 1917 when the Balfour Declaration gave the Jewish people the right to establish themselves in their homeland. 1948 was the year when Israel miraculously became a nation once again. The dry branches of the fig tree had put forth its leaves at last, just as Jesus had predicted would occur shortly before His second coming.

"*Now learn a parable of the fig tree; When his branch is yet tender, and putteth forth leaves, ye know that summer is nigh: So likewise ye, when ye shall see all these things, know that it is near, even at the doors. Verily I say unto you, This generation shall not pass, till all these things be fulfilled.*" (Matthew 24:32-34)

Now, those branches are giving forth fruit, as Israel works to make itself a modern day wonder. This means that we should expect to hear our Lord's voice at any moment.

In the elaborate parable that is the Book of Song of Solomon, the love relationship of bride and groom illustrates Christ's love for His bride, the church. It also confirms His wonderful promise in Matthew 24:32-34 about the budding of the fig tree.

"*The flowers appear on the earth; the time of the singing of birds is come, and the voice of the turtle is heard in our land; The fig tree putteth forth her green figs, and the vines with the tender grape give a good smell. Arise, my love, my fair one, and come away.*" (Song of Solomon 2:12-13)

COMMENTS ON THE NATURE OF DEATH

10 "But man dieth, and wasteth away: yea, man giveth up the ghost, and where is he?" (Job 14:10)

In verse 10, Job asks a tremendous question about man who *"giveth up the ghost."* Job asks, *"and where is he?"* The answer to this question may not be as obvious as the New Testament Bible-believer might think. Verse 12 could shed some light on the issue, but first we will glance briefly at verse 11.

11 "As the waters fail from the sea, and the flood decayeth and drieth up." (Job 14:11)

Verse 11 is another of the many references to the Flood that appear in the Book of Job. Remember that such a cataclysmic event was still very fresh in everyone's mind during Job's time. Job thinks there is no more hope for him than for an entire generation leveled by the Flood. No wonder he is pondering the nature of death!

Now, back to what happens to the man who gives up the ghost. The automatic response from those who have been properly schooled in New Testament orthodoxy is that the saved from the Old Testament era go to Paradise, or Abraham's bosom as it is called in Luke 16:22, where Christ compares the eternal destinies of a rich lost man and a poor beggar named Lazarus. The next verse, Luke 16:23, reveals that the lost, as did this rich man, go directly to hell.

This standard answer clarifies what happens to the dead from Abraham forward. Yet what about those who lived before Abraham, and those who lived before the written Word of God? Did Noah, for example, go to ABRAHAM'S bosom? Perhaps Job offers a clue in what he says in verse 12.

12 "So man lieth down, and riseth not: till the heavens be no more, they shall not awake, nor be raised out of their sleep." (Job 14:12)

If Job's understanding is correct, as are most of the other facts he and his friends toss around, perhaps pre-Abraham saints are treated differently from those after the beginning of the Hebrew era when God chose Abraham's descendants, the Hebrews, as His chosen people. Let's compare what John saw in the Revelation.

"And I saw a great white throne, and him that sat on it, from whose face the earth and the heaven fled away; and there was found no place for them. And I saw the dead, small and great, stand before God; and the books were opened: and another book was opened, which is the book of life: and the dead were judged out of those things which were written in the books, according to their works. And the sea gave up the dead which were

in it; and death and hell delivered up the dead which were in them: and they were judged every man according to their works. And death and hell were cast into the lake of fire. This is the second death. And whosoever was not found written in the book of life was cast into the lake of fire." (Revelation 20:11-15)

Will there be those at the Great White Throne Judgment whose names ARE found written in the book of life? What would be the point in the exercise we see in these verses if ALL were condemned?

We know that the Jewish saints remained in Abraham's bosom, or Paradise, until Christ *"led captivity captive"* (Ephesians 4:8), through His finished work on the Cross. This is my speculation, but could it be that those who lived before Abraham will remain in the grave until that day of final judgment, when they will be judged by the criteria explained by Paul in Romans?

"For as many as have sinned without law shall also perish without law: and as many as have sinned in the law shall be judged by the law; (For not the hearers of the law are just before God, but the doers of the law shall be justified. For when the Gentiles, which have not the law, do by nature the things contained in the law, these, having not the law, are a law unto themselves: Which shew the work of the law written in their hearts, their conscience also bearing witness, and their thoughts the mean while accusing or else excusing one another;) In the day when God shall judge the secrets of men by Jesus Christ according to my gospel." (Romans 2:12-16)

CONSIDERATION OF THINGS TO COME

Job's cry in verse 13 is a foreshadow of the cries of men during the coming Tribulation.

13 "O that thou wouldest hide me in the grave, that thou wouldest keep me secret, until thy wrath be past, that thou wouldest appoint me a set time, and remember me!" (Job 14:13)

Job wants God to hide him until His wrath has ended. Consider these two references from Revelation.

"And the kings of the earth, and the great men, and the rich men, and the chief captains, and the mighty men, and every bondman, and every free man, hid themselves in the dens and in the rocks of the mountains; And said to the mountains and rocks, Fall on us, and hide us from the face of him that sitteth on the throne, and from the wrath of the Lamb: For the great day of his wrath is come; and who shall be able to stand?" (Revelation 6:15-17)

"And in those days shall men seek death, and shall not find it; and shall desire to die, and death shall flee from them." (Revelation 9:6)

Job won't find an earthly refuge, but God DOES have a secret place for the Jewish remnant in the Tribulation. Chapter 12 of Revelation describes what will happen to them. *"And the woman fled into the wilderness, where she hath a place prepared of God, that they should feed her there a thousand two hundred and threescore days."* (Revelation 12:6)

Job seemingly already knew the answer to the question he posed in verse 10, about the man who gave up the ghost. *"Where is he?"* Now, he asks another deep question.

14 "If a man die, shall he live again? all the days of my appointed time will I wait, till my change come." (Job 14:14)

Job also knows the answer to this question. He DOES believe in a coming resurrection, as discussed previously in this chapter. Let's look at the passage we mentioned earlier.

"And though after my skin worms destroy this body, yet in my flesh shall I see God: Whom I shall see for myself, and mine eyes shall behold, and not another; though my reins be consumed within me." (Job 19:26-27)

Without doubt, Job holds to a future, literal, bodily resurrection—*"in my flesh shall I see God."* This is why he mentions *"my change"* in verse 14, which is the same change Paul spoke of in Corinthians. *"Behold, I shew you a mystery; We shall not all sleep, but we shall all be changed."* (1 Corinthians 15:51)

Paul also told the Romans about this coming change. *"Because the creature itself also shall be delivered from the bondage of corruption into the glorious liberty of the children of God."* (Romans 8:21)

Though Job is saturated with despair, he returns to his fundamental faith in the next verse. He knows that no matter how far away God may seem, there is coming a day when God is going to call His saints.

15 "Thou shalt call, and I will answer thee: thou wilt have a desire to the work of thine hands." (Job 14:15)

This theme is consistently presented through the Bible. No matter in which dispensation they live, God will call to His saints, be they Old Testament Jews or New Testament Christians.

"He shall call to the heavens from above, and to the earth, that he may judge his people. Gather my saints together unto me; those that have made a covenant with me by sacrifice. And the heavens shall declare his righteousness: for God is judge himself." (Psalm 50:4-6)

"But I would not have you to be ignorant, brethren, concerning them which are asleep, that ye sorrow not, even as others which have no hope.

For if we believe that Jesus died and rose again, even so them also which sleep in Jesus will God bring with him. For this we say unto you by the word of the Lord, that we which are alive and remain unto the coming of the Lord shall not prevent them which are asleep. For the Lord himself shall descend from heaven with a shout, with the voice of the archangel, and with the trump of God: and the dead in Christ shall rise first: Then we which are alive and remain shall be caught up together with them in the clouds, to meet the Lord in the air: and so shall we ever be with the Lord. Wherefore comfort one another with these words." (1 Thessalonians 4:13-18)

Desperate for a face-to-face encounter with God, Job's mind still shows the fruit of the years he dedicated to learning God's truth. God SEEMS to be far away, and Job would love to speak with Him, yet Job knows that God does not miss a thing.

16 "For now thou numberest my steps: dost thou not watch over my sin?" (Job 14:16)

Job knows that God is watching his every step. If there WERE some secret sin, God would be more aware of it than Job's counselors. Nothing gets by God!

Speaking of sin, Job does just that in the next verse. He tells us what God did with sin before Calvary.

17 "My transgression is sealed up in a bag, and thou sewest up mine iniquity." (Job 14:17)

Before Christ paid the penalty of sin with His substitutionary death on the cross, sin could not be dealt with in a final sense. Here, the picture is of God putting it in a bag, and sewing it up.

CONCLUSIONS ABOUT THE FINALITY OF DEATH

18 "And surely the mountain falling cometh to nought, and the rock is removed out of his place." (Job 14:18)

Job finishes his discourse by bringing us back to a common theme in this book—lost man in hell. He is painting a picture of man without hope. He is referring to a time when the mountain falls and the rock is removed out of place. Undoubtedly Job is thinking no further than the boils on his skin and the brokenness of his soul as he speaks these words. Their scope, though, reaches far beyond Job's personal and transitory hell.

19 "The waters wear the stones: thou washest away the things which grow out of the dust of the earth; and thou destroyest the hope of man." (Job 14:19)

We are familiar with the natural erosion process whereby the waters wear down the hardest stones. Job has been overwhelmed by the flood waters of personal disaster. He must feel like a stone worn smooth.

In Job 8:17 we saw *"the place of stones."* Are these the stones worn by the waters?

Man is left without hope, and God washes away those *"things which grow out of the dust of the earth?"* Job knows he came from the dust, and must feel his life is no more permanent than a young seedling in a dusty land, washed away by a spring storm. Yet before the image in your mind turns to the Colorado River wearing down rocks and creating mighty canyons, remember that man is not the only one of God's creatures connected to the dust. Other things come out of this dusty earth.

I try to carefully label everything that is speculation on my part. However, here are a couple of references to ponder as you consider these *"things which grow out of the dust of the earth."*

"They sacrificed unto devils, not to God; to gods whom they knew not, to new gods that came newly up, whom your fathers feared not." (Deuteronomy 32:17)

"And the king said unto her, Be not afraid: for what sawest thou? And the woman said unto Saul, I saw gods ascending out of the earth." (1 Samuel 28:13)

"And out of the ground the LORD God formed every beast of the field, and every fowl of the air; and brought them unto Adam to see what he would call them: and whatsoever Adam called every living creature, that was the name thereof." (Genesis 2:19)

What other things could come out of the dust, considering the things that crawl in it? *"And the LORD God said unto the serpent, Because thou hast done this, thou art cursed above all cattle, and above every beast of the field; upon thy belly shalt thou go, and dust shalt thou eat all the days of thy life."* (Genesis 3:14)

Not only man is mortal. Even the Devil and his legions of angels will be washed away by God's judgment.

Job continues, and his context is eternity.

20 "Thou prevailest for ever against him, and he passeth: thou changest his countenance, and sendest him away." (Job 14:20)

What a shock in the day of judgment for the man who has grown accustomed to wearing the smirk of pride on his face! A millisecond in the presence of almighty God will change his countenance forever, as he is sent away to the lake of fire (Revelation 20:13-15).

21 "His sons come to honour, and he knoweth it not; and they are brought low, but he perceiveth it not of them." (Job 14:21)

Many parents have gone to hell because they were too busy caring for their children to consider the truth of God's words. There are parents who live ONLY for their children. Parental love is a wonderful thing, but nothing is a more important priority than our personal relationship with God. The tragedy of hell for these people is that their labor for their children will be worthless.

The irony is evident. Job was a dedicated parent as we saw in the first chapter. Man's transitory nature means that many who have sacrificed all for the success of their children, die before they can see the fruit of their labor. The irony is that Job's ten children have died before him.

22 "But his flesh upon him shall have pain, and his soul within him shall mourn." (Job 14:22)

The pain and torment of hell will instantly bring everything into proper perspective—though sadly too late. Pain in the flesh and sorrow in the soul will be the order of the day. Job thinks he must be in hell. His suffering is far from hell, but it has certainly brought things into proper perspective.

The experience of the rich man in hell, as told by the Lord Jesus Christ, is a perfect illustration of Job's words. Both torment and sorrow are part of his God-less existence in hell. He is still concerned for his family, yet he has no knowledge of them. The only knowledge he has is that it is too late for him to do anything about it.

"*And in hell he lift up his eyes, being in torments, and seeth Abraham afar off, and Lazarus in his bosom. And he cried and said, Father Abraham, have mercy on me, and send Lazarus, that he may dip the tip of his finger in water, and cool my tongue; for I am tormented in this flame. But Abraham said, Son, remember that thou in thy lifetime receivedst thy good things, and likewise Lazarus evil things: but now he is comforted, and thou art tormented. And beside all this, between us and you there is a great gulf fixed: so that they which would pass from hence to you cannot; neither can they pass to us, that would come from thence. Then he said, I pray thee therefore, father, that thou wouldest send him to my father's house: For I have five brethren; that he may testify unto them, lest they also come into this place of torment. Abraham saith unto him, They have Moses and the prophets; let them hear them. And he said, Nay, father Abraham: but if one went unto them from the dead, they will repent. And he said unto him, If they hear not Moses and the prophets, neither will they be persuaded, though one rose from the dead.*" (Luke 16:23-31)

Job has asked some profound questions in this chapter. Do YOU know where you'll be should you give up the ghost? Do YOU know that you'll live again should you die?

Perhaps the most remarkable thing about Job's speech is the solid, fundamental faith he displays even in the heat of his anxiety. He is like someone who is caught in a pit of quicksand and slime, yet finds a solid rock on which to stand.

This is descriptive of all of us who live in this present world. We are constantly surrounded by things we don't understand, things that hurt, and things that wound us to the depths of our soul. There will always be those moments when God seems so far away.

While we are in this world, we cannot hope to escape the consequences of sin that have corrupted the entire universe, but we CAN find the ROCK on which to stand.

Job has a base—a foundation—that strengthens his character, and equips him to withstand the direct attack of the Devil. You'll probably never be the central piece of a battle between God and Satan, but the Devil has legions of demons seeking to hit believers with the full fury of their might. Be certain your foundation is secure NOW. When the trial comes (and it WILL), you will not have the presence of mind to PREPARE such a foundation. You can only fall back on a solid foundation that has been prepared beforehand.

13

ELIPHAZ STEPS BACK INTO THE RING

What is man, that he should be clean? and he which
is born of a woman, that he should be righteous?
Behold, he putteth no trust in his saints;
yea, the heavens are not clean in his sight.
How much more abominable and filthy is man,
which drinketh iniquity like water?

Job 15:14-16

JOB'S LIFE HAS DETERIORATED TO THE LEVEL OF A TAG-TEAM style boxing match. Eliphaz, the heavy-weight, has just stepped back into the ring, having taken the tag from Zophar. No more dancing around the ring, no more gentle jabs, Eliphaz is "steamed!" He is going for the "knockout."

His head already reeling from satanic blows some days earlier, Job has endured stinging jabs from his three "friends." Poor Job has no one to tag! Having gone down for the count several times, Job has always managed to stagger to his feet, to again endure the solid shots that steadily come his way.

Satan, hovering in the corner of the three counselors, expected this fight to be a knockout in the early rounds. Job's endurance is amazing, and now it looks like he might "go the distance." There will be no more "pulled punches." Satan's team must aggressively land some serious blows to Job's mid-section, and, if he lets down his guard, they will not hesitate to land one squarely on the chin.

Eliphaz begins with a series of questions, peppered with a few strategically spaced accusations. Eliphaz is trying to wear Job down. His goal is to knock the air out of Job—to show that Job is full of hot air. His manager, Satan, failing in his bid for an immediate knockout, is at least hoping that Eliphaz can keep Job on the canvas long enough for Job to curse God.

The first section of the chapter consists of confrontational verbal jabs, and understanding what Eliphaz has to say is not difficult. In the second section, though, his words transcend the historical circumstances, as has so often been the case in our study of Job, and they prophetically look forward to the coming judgment.

CONFRONTATIONAL JABS

HOT AIR

Eliphaz's words are quite easy to understand. He charges out of his corner with a single accusation—Job is full of hot air.

1 "Then answered Eliphaz the Temanite, and said,

2 Should a wise man utter vain knowledge, and fill his belly with the east wind?" (Job 15:1-2)

Eliphaz is quite right in saying that much *"vain knowledge"* has been tossed about in this exchange. Such *"vain"* or empty knowledge is due to the lack of wisdom and understanding displayed by these men. This much is obvious.

What is meant to hurt is the allegation that Job has filled *"his belly with the east wind."* An understanding of the geography and climate of biblical lands is the basis for understanding that Eliphaz claims that Job is full of hot air.

In the United States we chart the Jet Stream on our weather maps to forecast the weather. Sometimes we have our climate affected by a wind off the Pacific coast of South America called El Niño. The Bible speaks of the *"four winds of the earth"* in Revelation 7:1. I suspect that one day scientists will discover that there are four predominant winds that control the earth's climate. God has angels stationed to control these four winds, and He affects the earth's climate as He will.

"And after these things I saw four angels standing on the four corners of the earth, holding the four winds of the earth, that the wind should not blow on the earth, nor on the sea, nor on any tree." (Revelation 7:1)

The Bible also mentions the *"four winds of heaven."* Perhaps the *"four winds of the earth"* are identical with the *"four winds of the heaven,"* understanding that our atmosphere is called a *"heaven"* in the Word of God. What we call outer space is also called *"heaven"* in the Bible (Genesis 1).

"Daniel spake and said, I saw in my vision by night, and, behold, the four winds of the heaven strove upon the great sea." (Daniel 7:2)

"Therefore the he goat waxed very great: and when he was strong, the great horn was broken; and for it came up four notable ones toward the four winds of heaven." (Daniel 8:8)

"And when he shall stand up, his kingdom shall be broken, and shall be divided toward the four winds of heaven; and not to his posterity, nor according to his dominion which he ruled: for his kingdom shall be plucked up, even for others beside those." (Daniel 11:4)

Maybe the *"four winds of the earth"* mirror the *"four winds of heaven,"* which may be winds in outer space. Scientists speak of celestial winds and clouds.

This would make sense, just as the *"wind"* God used to *"pass over the earth"* to dry up the flood waters (Genesis 8:1) mirrors *"the spirit of God"* moving *"upon the face of the waters"* in Genesis 1:2. The Hebrew "rauch" translated "wind" in Genesis 8:1, is the same word translated "spirit" in Genesis 1:2.

Whatever the case, Eliphaz is referring to the famous Sirocco wind of the near East. This is the *"east wind"* of the Bible, over which God exercises His sovereign control. He uses it to execute His will on the earth. Whenever you see the *"east wind"* in the Bible, open your eyes and pay attention. Something transcendental is about to occur.

God used Sirocco to bring the plague of locusts upon Egypt (Exodus 10:13). He used the same *"east wind"* to divide the waters of the Red Sea (Exodus 14:21).

Things have really hit bottom when one "comforts" his friend by telling him that he is full of Sirocco. Yet this is a combination that Eliphaz is throwing at Job. He next tells him that all of his reasoning has been *"unprofitable,"* and his speeches have done "no good."

3 "Should he reason with unprofitable talk? or with speeches wherewith he can do no good?" (Job 15:3)

Not much discernment is required to observe that these questions in the first three verses are thinly-veiled accusations. There is no cover for the next indictments Eliphaz makes.

HIDDEN SIN

4 "Yea, thou castest off fear, and restrainest prayer before God." (Job 15:4)

Pure and simple, Eliphaz says that Job is not right with God. The last part of the verse charges that Job is not praying. In other words, "Job, you don't fear God anymore. This is your problem. If you would just pray, you could get your heart right with God." This is some more "take two aspirins and call me" counseling. Easy, but not effective. Sounds good, sounds spiritual, but fails to address the real issues involved.

5 "For thy mouth uttereth thine iniquity, and thou choosest the tongue of the crafty." (Job 15:5)

The meaning is that Job is not being honest with his words. "Job, you're just trying to cover up the iniquity of your heart." Eliphaz charges that Job has elected to use his tongue in a "*crafty*" manner to disguise the sin that hides in his heart.

6 "Thine own mouth condemneth thee, and not I: yea, thine own lips testify against thee." (Job 15:6)

Job has admitted to being a sinner, as we have observed several times. Yet Eliphaz takes these words to mean that Job is harboring secret sin. This is precisely as Job had prophesied earlier.

"*If I justify myself, mine own mouth shall condemn me: if I say, I am perfect, it shall also prove me perverse.*" (Job 9:20)

No matter what Job said, his words would be used against him. It is clearly true that our own mouth is a witness to the contents of our heart.

"*O generation of vipers, how can ye, being evil, speak good things? for out of the abundance of the heart the mouth speaketh.*" (Matthew 12:34)

No one can claim that if they were in Job's place they would respond better. None of us has ever been in Job's place, and we have no idea what we would do under such pressure. We do learn in the Bible, however, that there are times when it is simply best not to bother trying to defend ourselves in the face of baseless accusations. As Job himself said, whatever we say can and will be held against us. The next time you are tempted to jump to your own defense, consider the mess Job is in, and the following wise counsel.

"*A prudent man concealeth knowledge: but the heart of fools proclaimeth foolishness.*" (Proverbs 12:23)

"*Every prudent man dealeth with knowledge: but a fool layeth open his folly.*" (Proverbs 13:16)

"*The tongue of the wise useth knowledge aright: but the mouth of fools poureth out foolishness.*" (Proverbs 15:2)

"*The heart of the righteous studieth to answer: but the mouth of the wicked poureth out evil things.*" (Proverbs 15:28)

"*He that hath knowledge spareth his words: and a man of understanding is of an excellent spirit. Even a fool, when he holdeth his peace, is counted wise: and he that shutteth his lips is esteemed a man of understanding.*" (Proverbs 17:27-28)

HAUGHTY ATTITUDE

What follows in Eliphaz's discourse in Job 15:7-15 is another series of questions designed not to interrogate, but to intimidate. Most of the section is obvious, and my comments will be limited to the few items that might present some difficulty, or those of special significance.

The thrust of his words is to say "Who are YOU? Job, just who do you think you are? Are you the great and grand guru with all the answers? Do you think you are that much better than everyone else?"

7 "Art thou the first man that was born? or wast thou made before the hills?

8 Hast thou heard the secret of God? and dost thou restrain wisdom to thyself?

9 What knowest thou, that we know not? what understandest thou, which is not in us?" (Job 15:7-9)

Verse 10 is interesting for what it reveals about the relative ages of people in these days when the average life was still much longer than today. Again, Eliphaz's intention is to imply that Job is "just a puppy" in comparison to those who are really wise.

10 "With us are both the grayheaded and very aged men, much elder than thy father." (Job 15:10)

By comparing the information we have, Job would have to be at least 50 to 70 years of age. He had ten grown children. He was a man of immense accomplishment and wealth. He was revered as a wise man. Eliphaz speaks of men who are older than Job's father. Job's father would have to be at least around 100 years old. There were those "*very aged men*" who would be well over 100 years of age.

Remember that Shem died at 600 years of age, living 502 years after the flood (Genesis 11:10-11). The year of his death would have been around 1846 B.C., about the time that Abraham married Keturah, as we commented earlier in this volume.

11 "Are the consolations of God small with thee? is there any secret thing with thee?" (Job 15:11)

This is a strange thing to say to a man who has suffered like Job, but Eliphaz accuses Job of taking the "*consolations*" of God for granted. What he is really saying is that Job should start counting his blessings instead of complaining. "Is nothing sacred with you, Job?" This sounds spiritual, but it is a genuine insult to a man who has just lost his children and life's holdings.

12 "Why doth thine heart carry thee away? and what do thy eyes wink at,

13 That thou turnest thy spirit against God, and lettest such words go out of thy mouth?" (Job 15:12-13)

Eliphaz's intent is obvious. He is saying Job has a heart problem. Job's eyes reveal his deception, his spirit is in rebellion against God, and Job's own words are the proof.

Not to be missed in this statement is the important connection that is made between a man's heart, eyes, spirit and mouth. Despite Eliphaz's faulty application, he understands a very important truth overlooked by many today. A man's heart determines the basic direction of his life, and is revealed by his words. His eyes are the windows of his spirit. Notice the same elements in this passage from Proverbs.

"A naughty person, a wicked man, walketh with a froward MOUTH. He winketh with his EYES, he speaketh with his feet, he teacheth with his fingers; Frowardness is in his HEART, he deviseth mischief continually; he soweth discord." (Proverbs 6:12-14) (Author's emphasis)

The word *"naughty"* comes from the Anglo-Saxon *"naught,"* which means "nothing." A *"naughty man,"* as the word is used in the Bible, is a worthless man, not to be confused with our modern usage of the word, when we tell a three-year-old that he has been a "naughty boy."

A second word to be clarified is *"froward,"* which means "crooked." We would say that a worthless man walks with a crooked mouth.

Notice that this worthless man WALKS with his mouth. Your words take you down certain paths. Your mouth announces the steps your physical body will be taking. Yet this man's mouth is crooked! What he says and what he does are often two distinct things. He is like an old pickup truck that has been wrecked and has a twisted frame, scooting sideways down the road. The hood points to the right, while the truck is veering to the left.

To cover for his insincere words, the worthless man is winking with his eyes. This was Eliphaz's charge against Job. Winking is a sign of deceit, even when done lightly. While telling a fantasy or a "little white lie" to a small child, we tend to wink.

"He that winketh with the eye causeth sorrow: but a prating fool shall fall." (Proverbs 10:10)

"The talking feet" of Proverbs 6:13 are as fantastic as "the walking mouth" in 6:12. Our feet speak volumes by the paths they take. In the same verse, we teach others our outlook on life by what our fingers do.

The real problem is a *"froward"* or crooked heart. Proverbs 6:14 tells us how to diagnose a crooked heart. First, by one's long range plans. A crooked heart devises mischief continually. Second, a heart can be known by what is sown. A crooked heart sows discord.

Eliphaz correctly understands the intricate connection between the various elements of our lives, yet he incorrectly diagnoses Job's problem. Had he spent as much time analyzing Job's life as he did trying to find a cause for Job's circumstances, he would have known that Job had NOT devised mischief continually, nor had he sown discord. Job's problem was not a froward heart.

HUMAN SINFULNESS

14 "What is man, that he should be clean? and he which is born of a woman, that he should be righteous?" (Job 15:14)

This is more orthodox knowledge sliding off Eliphaz's lips. It is great speech material, and clearly true, but Job himself had just said the same thing. Man is born with a sin problem, and is helpless to do anything about it on his own. Job has never denied being a sinner. He has simply and steadfastly denied harboring secret, unconfessed sin, but readily acknowledged man's problem with the sin nature.

"Who can bring a clean thing out of an unclean? not one." (Job 14:4)

Later, Bildad would agree. Have you noticed how much time we waste in our communication saying the same things? Is anyone listening?

Here is how Bildad will express it. *"How then can man be justified with God? or how can he be clean that is born of a woman?"* (Job 25:4)

Fortunately, the New Testament is filled with explicit instruction about how man can be justified with God. With all of their wonderful knowledge, Job and his friends had no clue about what Paul later announced to the Romans.

"Therefore being justified by faith, we have peace with God through our Lord Jesus Christ." (Romans 5:1)

You can spend much time talking about God, life, problems and other great issues. The basic question remains the same in any age. How can sinful man, born of a woman, be justified with God? Perhaps you picked up this book to learn some information about the Book of Job. Yet if you have not been justified by faith, if you do not have the resulting peace with God through our Lord Jesus Christ, you will not understand much. Your reading will be as useless as the talking of these three men. Worse, you will miss heaven and spend eternity in hell.

15 "Behold, he putteth no trust in his saints; yea, the heavens are not clean in his sight." (Job 15:15)

This is the second time Eliphaz has alluded to a problem in outer space, a problem with angels. The first time was in Job 4.

"Behold, he put no trust in his servants; and his angels he charged with folly." (Job 4:18)

In the fifth chapter of this commentary, we briefly discussed this matter. Eliphaz is aware that there has been a rebellion of angels. The angels, who have access to what we would call "outer space," have those among their number who are not clean. Their sin has contaminated the universe.

16 "How much more abominable and filthy is man, which drinketh iniquity like water?" (Job 15:16)

Eliphaz's point is to show that if there is sin even among the angels, who is Job to think that he is so pure? Bildad confirms this truth.

"Behold even to the moon, and it shineth not; yea, the stars are not pure in his sight." (Job 25:5)

Sin is both a personal and a cosmic problem. The next time you become mired down in your problems, remember that we are but small cogs in an entire universe, geared to fulfill God's master plan. This plan has temporarily been deterred due to sin—the sin of angels and the sin of men. One day God will renovate the entire universe, and the problem of sin will be removed forever. When you allow sin in your life, you are out of tune with God's plan. No wonder you feel miserable. Fix your heart with God, and you will find peace and purpose far deeper than the temporal circumstances of your life.

COMING JUDGMENT

Throughout this book we have continually referred to the short span of time and degree of knowledge from Adam to Job. We have marvelled at the incredible information possessed by these men. Here, Eliphaz leaves no doubt as to his source of information.

Eliphaz says that his knowledge comes from wise men who were taught by their fathers. Now this could be variously understood were it not for how Eliphaz identifies these *"fathers."* He says that they were the ones *"unto whom alone the earth was given."*

There are only two fathers *"unto whom alone the earth was given"*—Adam and Noah. Look closely again at verses 17-19.

17 "I will shew thee, hear me; and that which I have seen I will declare;

18 Which wise men have told from their fathers, and have not hid it:

19 Unto whom alone the earth was given, and no stranger passed among them." (Job 15:17-19)

The wise men can be none other than Shem, Ham and Japheth. They are the sons of Noah, unto whom ALONE the earth was given. Noah received his information from the wise sons of Adam, unto whom ALONE the earth was given.

Having identified his source of information, Eliphaz sets out to classify Job as a *"wicked man."* What he does not comprehend is that the Spirit of God is using his words to paint a prophetic picture of THE wicked man, the Antichrist, who is yet to come. Remember that Scripture allows an historical application, a doctrinal application and a personal application. From here until the end of the chapter we are dealing doctrinally with a prophecy of the coming Antichrist, though Eliphaz has only Job in mind. The scope of these words is so deep and broad they far transcend Job's historical situation.

Job is a man whom God called *"perfect,"* and who is the object of satanic attack. His best friends have come to comfort him, and unwittingly become Satan's instruments against Job. Beginning with the best of intentions, they now classify Job with the Antichrist!

Verse 20 contains two remarkable details about the Antichrist, called *"that Wicked"* by Paul in 2 Thessalonians 2:8. Eliphaz means only that Job is wicked, yet the scope of his language is unmistakable, and the cross references too abundant for the student of Scripture to ignore the prophetic tone.

20 "The wicked man travaileth with pain all his days, and the number of years is hidden to the oppressor." (Job 15:20)

In the fourth chapter of this commentary, discussing Job 3:1-10, we learned that the figure of a woman travailing in birth is used in the Bible to describe the anguish of Israel in the coming Tribulation. Israel eventually gives birth. Here, the wicked travails *"with pain all his days,"* yet never gives birth, never escapes the horror of his pain.

The last phrase of verse 20 reveals a great truth—*"the number of years is hidden to the oppressor."* Imagine! The Devil doesn't know everything.

Just as the "wicked" foreshadows THE Wicked, "the oppressor" points to THE Oppressor, as we saw in Job 3:18. The Devil is the ultimate power behind the Wicked, whose goal is to oppress (Isaiah 14:4).

In these final days leading to the Second Coming of Christ, Bible students labor to discover how many years we have left. No one knows the day nor the hour, but we struggle to try to get an idea of the time we have remaining.

Not even the Devil himself knows the number of the years left. Although he is a formidable opponent, we sometimes give him too much credit. Some even make the mistake of imagining him to be all-knowing. Satan cannot figure out the time schedule either, so he is busy redeeming the time. This is precisely what we should be doing (Ephesians 5:16), rather than wasting time trying to pin down a day and an hour that God says will not be revealed to us anyway.

21 "A dreadful sound is in his ears: in prosperity the destroyer shall come upon him." (Job 15:21)

We have spoken of THE Wicked and THE Oppressor. Now Eliphaz mentions *"the destroyer,"* who typifies THE Destroyer. Identifying this one is not difficult. In Revelation 9 the bottomless pit is opened, and a *"king"* comes out who is over a hoard of grisly demonic beings. His name *"in the Hebrew tongue is Abaddon, but in the Greek tongue hath his name Apollyon."* (Revelation 9:11) Both these names have the same meaning—"destroyer." On God's cue this *"destroyer"* is released to wreak havoc upon the world system of the Antichrist. The word is also translated as "perdition," as in the *"son of perdition"* in 2 Thessalonians 2:3, where the context has to do with the Tribulation.

What is this *"dreadful sound?"* It comes upon the *"him"* at the end of verse 21, or the Antichrist in the context of *"in prosperity."* Compare this with what Paul said about these times in Thessalonians.

"For yourselves know perfectly that the day of the Lord so cometh as a thief in the night. For when they shall say, Peace and safety; then sudden destruction cometh upon them, as travail upon a woman with child; and they shall not escape." (1 Thessalonians 5:2-3)

Right when the Antichrist has secured world power, made peace in the Arab world, and proclaimed himself to be god in the Jewish temple (2 Thessalonians 2:3-4), the wrath of God will fall upon the world. The demonic creatures rushing out of the bottomless pit will come upon the world with the fury of battle. There will be a *"dreadful sound"* (Job 15:-21) in that day.

"And they had breastplates, as it were breastplates of iron; and the sound of their wings was as the sound of chariots of many horses running to battle." (Revelation 9:9)

Have you ever heard the sounds of war? I have. During a horrible civil war in El Salvador during the late 1970's and early 1980's, the war was often fought in front of my house. For several years we went to bed each night to the sounds of war. At times the noise was so great we could not sleep. Nothing can compare to the sounds of war, and it is something that those who have heard it will never forget. It is truly a *"dreadful sound."*

22 "He believeth not that he shall return out of darkness, and he is waited for of the sword.

23 He wandereth abroad for bread, saying, Where is it? he knoweth that the day of darkness is ready at his hand." (Job 15:22-23)

This is another confirmation of the terror of *"that day." "The day of the Lord"* is a time of dense darkness. Job fears that darkness. This is *"the day of darkness ready at his hand."* Amos described it as well as anyone.

"Woe unto you that desire the day of the LORD! to what end is it for you? the day of the LORD is darkness, and not light." (Amos 5:18) *"Shall not the day of the LORD be darkness, and not light? even very dark, and no brightness in it?"* (Amos 5:20)

In that dark night the Antichrist will fear assassination, and rightfully so. There is a sword waiting for him—*"he is waited for of the sword."* There will be human assassins lying in wait, but this verse looks to another sword—the same sword of Hebrews 4:12. It is the sword that comes out of the mouth of the coming King.

"And I saw heaven opened, and behold a white horse; and he that sat upon him was called Faithful and True, and in righteousness he doth judge and make war. His eyes were as a flame of fire, and on his head were many crowns; and he had a name written, that no man knew, but he himself. And he was clothed with a vesture dipped in blood: and his name is called The Word of God. And the armies which were in heaven followed him upon white horses, clothed in fine linen, white and clean. And OUT OF HIS MOUTH GOETH A SHARP SWORD, that with it he should smite the nations: and he shall rule them with a rod of iron: and he treadeth the winepress of the fierceness and wrath of Almighty God." (Revelation 19:11-15) (Author's emphasis)

This coming darkness will also be a time when people will be desperate for food. As Job 15:23 expresses it, *"He wandereth abroad for bread, saying, Where is it?"* This is also foreseen in biblical prophecy concerning the Tribulation.

"And when he had opened the third seal, I heard the third beast say, Come and see. And I beheld, and lo a black horse; and he that sat on him had a pair of balances in his hand. And I heard a voice in the midst of the four beasts say, A measure of wheat for a penny, and three measures of barley for a penny; and see thou hurt not the oil and the wine." (Revelation 6:5-6)

The Antichrist's fear is well-founded. He will indeed never return out of darkness. He will be banished forever to the total darkness of the lake of fire. Remember, the hottest fire produces no light.

"And the devil that deceived them was cast into the lake of fire and brimstone, where the beast and the false prophet are, and shall be tormented day and night for ever and ever." (Revelation 20:10)

The Antichrist's fear continues to dominate the next verses. The one who was thought of as fearless, is now consumed with fear.

24 "Trouble and anguish shall make him afraid; they shall prevail against him, as a king ready to the battle.
25 For he stretcheth out his hand against God, and strengtheneth himself against the Almighty." (Job 15:24-25)

We saw this *"king ready to the battle"* in Revelation 19. This KING is ready to come in judgment because the Antichrist has *"stretched out his hand against God, and strengtheneth himself against the Almighty."* We have already seen the first rebellion *"against God"* in Isaiah 14. The Devil will use the Antichrist to continue that rebellion.

"And the king shall do according to his will; and he shall exalt himself, and magnify himself above every god, and shall speak marvellous things against the God of gods, and shall prosper till the indignation be accomplished: for that that is determined shall be done. Neither shall he regard the God of his fathers, nor the desire of women, nor regard any god: for he shall magnify himself above all." (Daniel 11:36-37)

"Now we beseech you, brethren, by the coming of our Lord Jesus Christ, and by our gathering together unto him, That ye be not soon shaken in mind, or be troubled, neither by spirit, nor by word, nor by letter as from us, as that the day of Christ is at hand. Let no man deceive you by any means: for that day shall not come, except there come a falling away first, and that man of sin be revealed, the son of perdition; Who opposeth and exalteth himself above all that is called God, or that is worshipped; so that he as God sitteth in the temple of God, shewing himself that he is God." (2 Thessalonians 2:1-4)

We must observe that the Antichrist is specifically said to stretch out his hand against God. This is much like a story found in 1 Kings. A prophet of Judah has been sent to rebuke King Jeroboam of Israel. Jeroboam becomes angry because of God's Word against him. Look at what he does.

"And it came to pass, when king Jeroboam heard the saying of the man of God, which had cried against the altar in Bethel, that he put forth his hand from the altar, saying, Lay hold on him. And his hand, which he put forth against him, dried up, so that he could not pull it in again to him." (1 Kings 13:4)

Jeroboam learned not to stretch out his hand against God. Compare this story—the story of a man who is a foreshadow of the Antichrist—with Zechariah's prophecy of the Antichrist.

"Woe to the idol shepherd that leaveth the flock! the sword shall be upon his arm, and upon his right eye: HIS ARM SHALL BE CLEAN DRIED UP, and his right eye shall be utterly darkened." (Zechariah 11:17) (Author's emphasis)

26 "He runneth upon him, even on his neck, upon the thick bosses of his bucklers." (Job 15:26)

"He" in this verse is God, the Almighty. The *"bosses"* are the thick metal studs on his shield, or *"buckler."* God will come upon him, breaking his neck. This has been God's promise from his very first prophecy against the Devil.

"And I will put enmity between thee and the woman, and between thy seed and her seed; IT SHALL BRUISE THY HEAD, and thou shalt bruise his heel." (Genesis 3:15) (Author's emphasis)

The wounding of the enemy's head is a consistent theme of Scripture. A sampling of prophecies makes this plain.

"Thou wentest forth for the salvation of thy people, even for salvation with thine anointed; thou woundedst the head out of the house of the wicked, by discovering the foundation unto the neck." (Habakkuk 3:13)

"His mischief shall return upon his own head, and his violent dealing shall come down upon his own pate." (Psalm 7:16)

"But God shall wound the head of his enemies, and the hairy scalp of such an one as goeth on still in his trespasses." (Psalm 68:21)

"Thou didst divide the sea by thy strength: thou brakest the heads of the dragons in the waters. Thou brakest the heads of leviathan in pieces, and gavest him to be meat to the people inhabiting the wilderness." (Psalm 74:13-14)

"He, that being often reproved hardeneth his neck, shall suddenly be destroyed, and that without remedy." (Proverbs 29:1)

Continuing in Job 15:27, the prosperity of the Antichrist had made him fat. More than "chubby," the picture here is one of obesity.

27 "Because he covereth his face with his fatness, and maketh collops of fat on his flanks." (Job 15:27)

This is not without precedent in the Bible. Another man who is a type of the coming Antichrist was Eglon, an oppressor of Israel. The Lord raised up Ehud, a Benjamite, as a judge of Israel to deliver His people. Judges 3:17 points out that *"Eglon was a very fat man."* He was so fat that the Bible graphically tells what happens when Ehud kills him.

"And Ehud came unto him; and he was sitting in a summer parlour, which he had for himself alone. And Ehud said, I have a message from God unto thee. And he arose out of his seat. And Ehud put forth his left hand, and took the dagger from his right thigh, and thrust it into his belly: And the haft also went in after the blade; and the fat closed upon the blade, so that he could not draw the dagger out of his belly; and the dirt came out." (Judges 3:20-22)

The connection with Antichrist continues in Job. This time Eliphaz mentions the dwelling of the wicked.

28 "And he dwelleth in desolate cities, and in houses which no man inhabiteth, which are ready to become heaps." (Job 15:28)

Here, the striking parallel between Eliphaz's words and the prophecies of the Tribulation extends to Babylon, the city of Antichrist. What Eliphaz describes is exactly the doom prophesied to come upon Babylon. Consider the words of the prophets.

"And he cried mightily with a strong voice, saying, Babylon the great is fallen, is fallen, and is become the habitation of devils, and the hold of every foul spirit, and a cage of every unclean and hateful bird." (Revelation 18:2)

"Because of the wrath of the LORD it shall not be inhabited, but it shall be wholly desolate: every one that goeth by Babylon shall be astonished, and hiss at all her plagues." (Jeremiah 50:13)

"Therefore the wild beasts of the desert with the wild beasts of the islands shall dwell there, and the owls shall dwell therein: and it shall be no more inhabited for ever; neither shall it be dwelt in from generation to generation. As God overthrew Sodom and Gomorrah and the neighbour cities thereof, saith the LORD; so shall no man abide there, neither shall any son of man dwell therein." (Jeremiah 50:39-40)

"And Babylon shall become heaps, a dwellingplace for dragons, and astonishment, and an hissing, without an inhabitant." (Jeremiah 51:37)

Earlier, in comments on Job 8:13-18, we discussed how the Antichrist is compared to a tree in Scripture. The same word picture is painted again in the remaining verses of Job 15. There is nothing of great difficulty in this section, but notice the many tree-like references.

In Job 15:30 we see that *"the flame shall dry up his branches."* Nothing like a few milliseconds in the lake of fire to dry up any green branches! Speaking of green branches, Job 15:32 says, *"and his branch shall not be green."*

Verse 15:33 says, *"He shall shake off his unripe grape as the vine, and shall cast off his flower as the olive."* These grapes are the *"grapes of gall"* seen in Deuteronomy. *"For their vine is of the vine of Sodom, and of the fields of Gomorrah: their grapes are grapes of gall, their clusters are bitter."* (Deuteronomy 32:32)

Also in Job 15:33 we learn that the oil of the olive will never anoint him. The Antichrist is empowered by the one who WAS the anointed cherub (Ezekiel 28:14), but no more.

There are things other than references to trees in this passage. Verse 15:29 speaks of his utter ruin.

29 "He shall not be rich, neither shall his substance continue, neither shall he prolong the perfection thereof upon the earth." (Job 15:29)

The spirit of the lost man returns to God (Ecclesiastes 3:21), while his body returns to the dust (Genesis 3:19). His "*substance*" is no more, though his soul suffers eternally in the lake of fire.

In Job 15:31 Eliphaz warns against trusting in the vanity of the deceiver. Those who do are left with nothing but vanity (emptiness).

31 "Let not him that is deceived trust in vanity: for vanity shall be his recompence." (Job 15:31)

Those who follow the vain empire of Antichrist are just more members in the "*congregation of hypocrites*" in Job 15:34. To be part of this vast company, a person has to prostitute himself with innumerable ecclesiastical games and politics. All is played out through sophisticated "*bribery*," as the philosophy of "you scratch my back, I'll scratch yours" prevails.

34 "For the congregation of hypocrites shall be desolate, and fire shall consume the tabernacles of bribery." (Job 15:34)

The maneuvering and manipulations of this evil congregation are seen in the final verse of the chapter. All of their scheming mischief results only in emptiness.

35 "They conceive mischief, and bring forth vanity, and their belly prepareth deceit." (Job 15:35)

Compare these verses with the witness of Scripture. The testimony is clear.

"God judgeth the righteous, and God is angry with the wicked every day. If he turn not, he will whet his sword; he hath bent his bow, and made it ready. He hath also prepared for him the instruments of death; he ordaineth his arrows against the persecutors. Behold, he travaileth with iniquity, and hath conceived mischief, and brought forth falsehood. He made a pit, and digged it, and is fallen into the ditch which he made." (Psalm 7:11-15)

Are you a Jacob? Have you put your faith in "the system?" Do you find yourself following one rainbow after another, only to be left with empty hands and an emptier heart? Eliphaz's application to Job is off by a mile, yet his words are true for those who refuse to believe God's Word and obey it. One simply cannot continue to survive only through manipulations forever. Sooner or later there comes a moment of reckoning. It is Eliphaz's opinion that this is what has happened to his friend Job.

14

THE VIEW FROM THE CROSS

He hath destroyed me on every side, and I am gone:
and mine hope hath he removed like a tree.
He hath also kindled his wrath against me, and he
counteth me unto him as one of his enemies.

Job 19:10-11

UNWANTED AND UNSOLICITED ADVICE IS AS WELCOME AS PIMples on the face of a fashion model. No one enjoys being told what to do, especially by someone who is wrong.

In the first fifteen chapters of the Book of Job, Job's three friends have successfully displayed a total void of wisdom and understanding. Their counsel is unrelenting and consistently off-target.

Job is not yet ready to curse God, but he has had about as much "spiritual counsel" as he can stand. In his discourse that fills chapters 16 and 17, Job unloads his frustration. He will also be God's instrument to provide the careful student of the Bible extraordinary insight into the thoughts of our Lord Jesus Christ as He died on the Cross, having become sin for us.

VENTING HIS IMPATIENCE

1 "Then Job answered and said,
2 I have heard many such things: miserable comforters are ye all.

3 Shall vain words have an end? or what emboldeneth thee that thou answerest?
4 I also could speak as ye do: if your soul were in my soul's stead, I could heap up words against you, and shake mine head at you.
5 But I would strengthen you with my mouth, and the moving of my lips should asswage your grief.
6 Though I speak, my grief is not asswaged: and though I forbear, what am I eased?" (Job 16:1-6)

When the same issues are rehashed repeatedly, it is time to end the discussion, close the meeting, dismiss the committee or whatever you have to do. That time has arrived as far as Job is concerned. He has heard nothing new. His friends' words are empty *("vain")* and endless.

In verse 3 Job demands, *"or what emboldeneth thee that thou answerest?"* He is simply saying, "Who ordained YOU to be God's spokesman? Just who do you think you are?"

Some of the worst torment imaginable is to be the target of a "super-pious" Christian attempting to counsel his suffering victim. His speech is filled with spiritual-sounding "God-speak." No matter what the problem, the answer is always "get your heart right with God," or "you just need more faith."

In verses 4 and 5, Job says that if his friends were in his place, he would try to use his mouth to strengthen them, not tear them down. Job would use his lips to "asswage" their grief. This is an Old English spelling of "assuage," which means to lessen, to mollify, to diminish or to relieve. This is the right idea. Job was already torn down. His great need was for a friend to encourage him, edify him and build him up.

Verse 6 is another eruption of frustration and self-pity. No matter what Job does, he sees no improvement in his miserable situation.

Now we enter another of those great portions of Scripture where the speaker's words far transcend the historical circumstance. No doubt Job has suffered beyond our imagination. His words, though, rise to such a level of intensity, and are filled with such biblical imagery, that even the most critical reader must sense a far-reaching significance. We can almost see the power of God's Spirit sweep across Job's broken body, and take full command of his words. Job, as a type of Christ suffering on the cross, gives a rare glimpse into Christ's thoughts, just as David, another type of Christ, would do centuries later when he wrote Psalm 22.

VIEWING THE CROSS

This chapter is one of six in the Old Testament showing us what was taking place in the heart and mind of the Lord Jesus Christ as He hung on the cross. Before we finish Job we will see another of these chapters, Job 30. The other chapters are Psalm 22 and Isaiah 50, 52 and 53.

God has given us four Gospels. Comparing them, we arrive at a chronology of the life of our Lord, and a complete understanding of what God wants us to know about His life and ministry.

By comparing the chapters listed above, one can discover the chronology of events, and process of thought that occurred when the Lord Jesus Christ died on the cross. The composite of this information, *"comparing spiritual things with spiritual"* (1 Corinthians 2:13), is the way that God reveals to the serious Bible student the *"mind of Christ"* (1 Corinthians 2:16) regarding the Crucifixion.

In the New Testament we have the Crucifixion from man's viewpoint, looking up at the Lord Jesus Christ dying in our place. In the Old Testament God gives us His own perspective of the Crucifixion. It is the sum of these two perspectives that allows one to arrive at a complete understanding of such an important event. Our salvation hinges on the completed work of Christ on the cross, and it is essential to comprehend what took place.

THE ULTIMATE SOURCE OF JOB'S PAIN

Verses 7 to 9 form an important transition. Job leaves off addressing his counselors to speak directly of what God was doing to him. We have observed this phenomenon before in our study. Job is a picture of Christ, deserted by the Father, and hanging on the cross in our stead.

Notice the way in which Job describes the source of his suffering. The key is Job's definitive statement in verse 11—*"God hath delivered me to the ungodly."*

Carefully read verses 7 to 9. Job sees God as the One who is assailing him. Though Satan is the instrument, Job is correct that this trial is the result of divine initiative, as we witnessed in the first two chapters.

7 But now he hath made me weary: thou hast made desolate all my company.

8 And thou hast filled me with wrinkles, which is a witness against me: and my leanness rising up in me beareth witness to my face.

9 He teareth me in his wrath, who hateth me: he gnasheth upon me with his teeth; mine enemy sharpeneth his eyes upon me." (Job 16:7-9)

You can see the transition following the colon in verse 7. Job switches from *"he"* to *"thou"* in the last half of the verse.

Look at the Lord Jesus Christ through these words. He has been up all night. Six times He has stood before the authorities to be condemned for crimes He did not commit. He has been ridiculed and beaten. He was made to carry His heavy cross through the street until He simply could not bear it any longer. He is *"weary,"* and *"desolate,"* having been deserted by even His closest disciples.

His skin is wrinkled by the weight of His own body, pulled by the forces of gravity that want to rip Him from the cross. His lean frame is exposed so that each bone can be counted.

The most startling comment is contained in verse 9, where Job refers to God *"who hateth me."* God is seen as his enemy, pouring out a torrent of wrath upon him. Such a statement would cause many to assume that Job cannot possibly be talking about God. God is love! (1 John 4:8)

"Obviously this cannot be a picture of Christ on the cross," many would wrongfully conclude. We must scrutinize this passage so as not to miss what God has for us.

We must first establish that the loving God, the God Who is love, CAN and DOES hate! There is no contradiction here. God is love. Love is not God. Think about that.

Modern philosophical thought has brainwashed us into thinking that if God is love, then consequently love is God. But this would make God an attribute. The truth is that love is an attribute of God, Who is a personal Being, not a Force, Concept, or Love.

Consider the following references as evidence showing that God does hate. An important part of love is knowing what to hate. When we love someone, we are obligated to hate those things that would destroy those we love.

"The foolish shall not stand in thy sight: thou hatest all workers of iniquity." (Psalm 5:5)

David understood this truth about God's capacity to hate. The Psalms include other references.

"The LORD trieth the righteous: but the wicked and him that loveth violence his soul hateth." (Psalm 11:5)

What is interesting about this statement is the way it shatters one of our pet evangelical maxims. We have often heard, "God hates the sin, but loves the sinner." This sounds very spiritual, yet it is not biblical. Psalm 11:5 clearly states that God's soul HATES *"the wicked and him that loveth violence."*

"Thou lovest righteousness, and hatest wickedness: therefore God, thy God, hath anointed thee with the oil of gladness above thy fellows." (Psalm 45:7)

"These six things doth the LORD hate: yea, seven are an abomination unto him: A proud look, a lying tongue, and hands that shed innocent blood, An heart that deviseth wicked imaginations, feet that be swift in running to mischief, A false witness that speaketh lies, and he that soweth discord among brethren." (Proverbs 6:16-19)

This passage from Proverbs again shows that God can hate both the sinner and his sin. One of the seven things that God hates is *"a lying tongue."* In the same list we see that not only does God hate the *"tongue"* that speaks lies, He hates the one to whom the tongue belongs—*"a false witness that speaketh lies."* As if this were not enough evidence, God also hates *"HE that soweth discord among brethren."* (Author's emphasis)

"Mine heritage is unto me as a lion in the forest; it crieth out against me: therefore have I hated it." (Jeremiah 12:8)

"Howbeit I sent unto you all my servants the prophets, rising early and sending them, saying, Oh, do not this abominable thing that I hate." (Jeremiah 44:4)

"All their wickedness is in Gilgal: for there I hated them: for the wickedness of their doings I will drive them out of mine house, I will love them no more: all their princes are revolters." (Hosea 9:15)

"And I hated Esau, and laid his mountains and his heritage waste for the dragons of the wilderness." (Malachi 1:3)

Lest someone object that these verses are merely the anthropomorphic representation of the "God of the Old Testament," before men had become "enlightened," and religion "evolved" to its contemporary heights, we include a couple of New Testament references. The words are those of our Lord Jesus Christ Himself, as He dictates the letters to the seven churches in Revelation 2.

"But this thou hast, that thou hatest the deeds of the Nicolaitans, which I also hate." (Revelation 2:6)

"So hast thou also them that hold the doctrine of the Nicolaitans, which thing I hate." (Revelation 2:15)

Having established that God can and does hate, we must deal with the picture of Christ on the cross that is drawn. If Job is a type of Christ on the cross, how could it possibly be said that He was the object of God's hate?

The answer is simple—*"For he hath made him to be sin for us, who knew no sin; that we might be made the righteousness of God in him."* (2 Corinthians 5:21)

Not only did Christ bear our sin, He actually BECAME our sin. He was the Object of God's wrath. This is why He cried on the cross, *"My God, my God, why hast thou forsaken me? why art thou so far from helping me, and from the words of my roaring?"* (Psalm 22:1)

These prophetic words were historically uttered by our Lord, as recorded in Matthew 27:46. God the Father turned His back on His own Son, that we might be *"made the righteousness of God in him."* God's hatred of sin was focused on the only One who knew no sin.

THE UNGODLY SCOURGE THAT ADMINISTERS JOB'S PAIN

Should any reader think that seeing the prophetic picture of Jesus dying on the cross in Job 16:7-9 is a little strained, verse 10 closes the door of doubt. These words are unmistakable in their application. The parallel is too close to be coincidence.

10 "They have gaped upon me with their mouth; they have smitten me upon the cheek reproachfully; they have gathered themselves together against me." (Job 16:10)

Compare these words with the following, well-known Messianic prophecies.

"They gaped upon me with their mouths, as a ravening and a roaring lion." (Psalm 22:13)

"I gave my back to the smiters, and my cheeks to them that plucked off the hair: I hid not my face from shame and spitting." (Isaiah 50:6)

"He giveth his cheek to him that smiteth him: he is filled full with reproach." (Lamentations 3:30)

"Now gather thyself in troops, O daughter of troops: he hath laid siege against us: they shall smite the judge of Israel with a rod upon the cheek." (Micah 5:1)

"Then did they spit in his face, and buffeted him; and others smote him with the palms of their hands." (Matthew 26:67)

Ask yourself the question, "Why would God include the words of Job 16:10 in the Bible?" Is it merely to give us some irrelevant historical information about a heated discussion among friends thousands of years ago? Or, is God giving us a picture of something very important to our lives?

The history is certain and true, and we must fully understand the weight of God's wrath that Job feels. Yet this history has been recorded and preserved for more than 3,000 years for a purpose. That purpose is clear from Paul's words in Romans. *"For whatsoever things were written aforetime were written for our learning, that we through patience and comfort of the scriptures might have hope."* (Romans 15:4)

11 "God hath delivered me to the ungodly, and turned me over into the hands of the wicked." (Job 16:11)

This is precisely what God did to His only begotten Son. He turned Him over into the hands of the wicked scribes and Pharisees. They then turned Him over to wicked Herod and ungodly Pilate.

12 "I was at ease, but he hath broken me asunder: he hath also taken me by my neck, and shaken me to pieces, and set me up for his mark.

13 His archers compass me round about, he cleaveth my reins asunder, and doth not spare; he poureth out my gall upon the ground.

14 He breaketh me with breach upon breach, he runneth upon me like a giant." (Job 16:12-14)

Once we grasp the picture that God is painting, these words are not difficult to understand, if we look beyond Job's circumstances and through the eyes of the Lord Jesus as He dies upon the cross. He has become the target *("mark")* of the Father's wrath. God's archers have Him surrounded. We dealt with God's arrows when we studied Job 6:4. Broken, shaken and surrounded, He was torn apart from the inside out—*"he cleaveth* (splits) *my reins* (inner parts) *asunder* (apart)."

The *"gall"* was poured out on the ground. *"Gall"* is bitter and venomous. This Hebrew word appears only here in Job. *"Gall"* is found in other places as the translation of another Hebrew word. One example of this other word is in Psalm 69, where it also is connected to the events of the crucifixion.

"They gave me also gall for my meat; and in my thirst they gave me vinegar to drink." (Psalm 69:21)

Jesus on the cross, broken *"with breach upon breach,"* is seen several places in the Bible. Two Messianic prophecies from Isaiah summarize the issue.

"I gave my back to the smiters, and my cheeks to them that plucked off the hair: I hid not my face from shame and spitting." (Isaiah 50:6)

"As many were astonied at thee; his visage was so marred more than any man, and his form more than the sons of men." (Isaiah 52:14)

THE UNBELIEVABLE STRESS THAT ACCOMPANIES JOB'S PAIN

15 "I have sewed sackcloth upon my skin, and defiled my horn in the dust." (Job 16:15)

In the Bible, one who clothed himself in sackcloth symbolized being stripped of power and authority. The *"horn"* is a biblical symbol of power and authority. In the prophecies of Daniel, "horns" occupy a place of great importance, and personify world leaders, including the Antichrist.

Jeremiah employed this figure to speak of Moab's fall. *"The horn of Moab is cut off, and his arm is broken, saith the LORD."* (Jeremiah 48:25)

The psalmist Asaph warns against self-promotion, or, as we would say today, "blowing your own HORN."

"I said unto the fools, Deal not foolishly: and to the wicked, Lift not up the horn: Lift not up your horn on high: speak not with a stiff neck. For promotion cometh neither from the east, nor from the west, nor from the south. But God is the judge: he putteth down one, and setteth up another." (Psalm 75:4-7)

If anyone is going to blow your horn, let it be God. No one does it better.

"For, lo, thine enemies, O Lord, for, lo, thine enemies shall perish; all the workers of iniquity shall be scattered. But my horn shalt thou exalt like the horn of a unicorn: I shall be anointed with fresh oil." (Psalm 92:9-10)

Here, in Job 16:15, Job pictures the Lord Jesus Christ, hanging on the cross, stripped of His power and authority through His voluntary act of obedience to the Father's will. This is what Paul speaks of to the Philippians.

"Who, being in the form of God, thought it not robbery to be equal with God: But made himself of no reputation, and took upon him the form of a servant, and was made in the likeness of men: And being found in fashion as a man, he humbled himself, and became obedient unto death, even the death of the cross." (Philippians 2:6-8)

16 "My face is foul with weeping, and on my eyelids is the shadow of death." (Job 16:16)

If you have ever wept until you could weep no more, you perhaps can understand what it is to have your face *"foul with weeping."* Jeremiah could identify with a sorrow this great. He is sometimes called the Weeping Prophet. *"Oh that my head were waters, and mine eyes a fountain of tears, that I might weep day and night for the slain of the daughter of my people!"* (Jeremiah 9:1)

In keeping with the consistent theme of this section, Job's sorrow is a foreshadowing of the Man of Sorrows. Isaiah saw Him. *"He is despised and rejected of men; a man of sorrows, and acquainted with grief: and we hid as it were our faces from him; he was despised, and we esteemed him not."* (Isaiah 53:3)

He is the One prophesied of in Psalm 69. Several times we have gone to this psalm to see the sufferings of our Lord. *"When I wept, and chastened my soul with fasting, that was to my reproach."* (Psalm 69:10) *"Reproach hath broken my heart; and I am full of heaviness: and I looked for some to take pity, but there was none; and for comforters, but I found none."* (Psalm 69:20)

The sorrow and crying of the Lord were evident during the time He spent praying in the Garden of Gethsemane shortly before being delivered to judgment. The Book of Hebrews reminds us of what happened that dark night.

"Who in the days of his flesh, when he had offered up prayers and supplications with strong crying and tears unto him that was able to save him from death, and was heard in that he feared." (Hebrews 5:7)

Christ asked the Father to deliver Him from *"death,"* not "dying." He did die, and He did drink from the cup of the Father's wrath. (Matthew 26:39; John 18:11) God answered His prayer in delivering Him from *"death."* (Acts 2:24; Psalm 18:5; 21:4; 49:15; 69:3; Titus 1:2)

The second part of Job 16:16 brings us in contact again with the infamous *"shadow of death."* Historically, Job has in mind the pallor of death that encompasses him. He knows he looks like death. This Tribulation figure has appeared in Job 3:5 and 10:21-22. This will not be the last time that we find it.

17 "Not for any injustice in mine hands: also my prayer is pure." (Job 16:17)

From what we have seen in the preceding verses, comparing Job's condition to that of our Savior on the cross, can there be any reasonable doubt as to the prophecy of this passage? This IS the condition of Christ on the cross. He died not for HIS injustice, but OURS. His prayer was pure.

THE UNMISTAKABLE SYMBOL THAT ACCOUNTS FOR JOB'S PAIN

18 "O earth, cover not thou my blood, and let my cry have no place." (Job 16:18)

Abel was a type of Christ. God tells Cain that Abel's blood cried to Him.

"And he said, What hast thou done? the voice of thy brother's blood crieth unto me from the ground." (Genesis 4:10)

The Book of Hebrews gives us a remarkable commentary, telling us that Abel's blood is STILL speaking!

"By faith Abel offered unto God a more excellent sacrifice than Cain, by

which he obtained witness that he was righteous, God testifying of his gifts: and by it he being dead yet speaketh." (Hebrews 11:4)

Just like Abel, Christ's blood is not silent. Our Savior's blood was not merely absorbed by the ground and covered. It was presented before the throne of the Father by our great High Priest.

"But Christ being come an high priest of good things to come, by a greater and more perfect tabernacle, not made with hands, that is to say, not of this building; Neither by the blood of goats and calves, but by his own blood he entered in once into the holy place, having obtained eternal redemption for us." (Hebrews 9:11-12)

In Deuteronomy 21 and Numbers 35 God told the nation of Israel how to cleanse their hands of innocent blood. The leaders of the nation, who supposedly knew and believed the Scriptures, never followed those instructions. The pagan Pilate washed his hands of the innocent blood, in ignorance following the very instructions of Deuteronomy 21:1-9, as the leaders of the people defiantly shouted their response.

"When Pilate saw that he could prevail nothing, but that rather a tumult was made, he took water, and washed his hands before the multitude, saying, I am innocent of the blood of this just person: see ye to it. Then answered all the people, and said, His blood be on us, and on our children." (Matthew 27:24-25)

God answered their prayer, and will eternally hold them responsible. His blood is still on their hands. Truly the ground did not cover His blood. It continues to speak, to cleanse and to save today.

Occasionally, Bible teachers come along who deny the importance of the physical blood of the Lord Jesus Christ. It is not important to them that the modern versions of the Bible leave out many references to the blood. They see the blood as a symbol only, and one that is offensive to many people. Therefore, they downplay its importance.

"The blood of Christ simply fell on the earth and was absorbed like any other," they say. "Don't attach any undue significance to the blood of Christ. The fact that He died in our place is all that is important."

This does not square with the prophetic message of Job, as a picture of Christ on the cross, who said, *"O earth, cover not thou my blood."* (Job 16:18) Nor does it square with what we read in Acts 20.

"Take heed therefore unto yourselves, and to all the flock, over the which the Holy Ghost hath made you overseers, to feed the church of God, WHICH HE HATH PURCHASED WITH HIS OWN BLOOD." (Acts 20:28) (Author's emphasis)

The Lord Jesus Christ, as our great High Priest, presented His blood, God's blood, in the presence of the Father in the throne room of the third heaven (Hebrews 9). How He collected the blood from the ground and all the technical questions involved are not important here. I would imagine the same God who will know how to set apart 144,000 Jews, 12,000 from each tribe (Revelation 7:1-8), when most Jews do not know their tribe, and the same God who will renovate earthly bodies of believers which have deteriorated to dust, is up to the task of getting the blood to heaven.

Remove the blood, and you remove the power. Take away the blood, and you take away redemption. (Hebrews 9:22)

The last half of Job 16:18 says, *"and let my cry have no place."* This was Christ's cry on the cross. God heard the arrogant cry of the Jewish leaders, yet turned a deaf ear to the cry of His only begotten Son. The reason, as we saw earlier, was that He had become sin for us. This is why His cry found no place. God used David's tongue to express our Lord's grief on the cross.

"My God, my God, why hast thou forsaken me? why art thou so far from helping me, and from the words of my roaring? O my God, I cry in the daytime, but thou hearest not; and in the night season, and am not silent. But thou art holy, O thou that inhabitest the praises of Israel." (Psalm 22:1-3)

19 "Also now, behold, my witness is in heaven, and my record is on high." (Job 16:19)

The life and ministry of the Lord Jesus Christ are a matter of public record. Not only is this witness and record in heaven on high, it is contained in the Word of God. Like that of Abel, Christ's blood is a matter of record and still speaks today.

The same can be said of the record of any human being. For good or bad, our lives are a matter of record.

"And I saw the dead, small and great, stand before God; and the books were opened: and another book was opened, which is the book of life: and the dead were judged out of those things which were written in the books, according to their works." (Revelation 20:12)

THE UTTER SCORN THAT AFFECTED JOB'S PERSPECTIVE

20 "My friends scorn me: but mine eye poureth out tears unto God." (Job 16:20)

Job was subject to the scorn of his closest friends. As he now pours out his heart in tears, he prefigures the Lord Jesus Christ. As our Lord was being scourged in the palace of the high priest, his friend Peter was scorning Him. After three and a half years of intense training and discipleship, the Lord's closest friends were nowhere to be found.

"And as Peter was beneath in the palace, there cometh one of the maids of the high priest: And when she saw Peter warming himself, she looked upon him, and said, And thou also wast with Jesus of Nazareth. But he denied, saying, I know not, neither understand I what thou sayest. And he went out into the porch; and the cock crew. And a maid saw him again, and began to say to them that stood by, This is one of them. And he denied it again. And a little after, they that stood by said again to Peter, Surely thou art one of them: for thou art a Galilaean, and thy speech agreeth thereto. But he began to curse and to swear, saying, I know not this man of whom ye speak." (Mark 14:66-71)

Alone in those final hours, the Lord had no one unto whom He could pour out His tears other than His heavenly Father. When you feel that your *"face is foul with weeping,"* and there is no shoulder on which to cry, remember that our Lord could only turn to the Father to pour out His heart. While the cry of Christ found no place, YOU will never be refused because of what HE did for you.

21 "O that one might plead for a man with God, as a man pleadeth for his neighbour!" (Job 16:21)

Job first expressed his frustration in Job 9:33.

"Neither is there any daysman betwixt us, that might lay his hand upon us both." (Job 9:33)

How wonderful to know that there IS one who pleads for men with God! He is the same One who died on the cross and rose again the third day.

"My little children, these things write I unto you, that ye sin not. And if any man sin, we have an advocate with the Father, Jesus Christ the righteous." (1 John 2:1)

22 "When a few years are come, then I shall go the way whence I shall not return." (Job 16:22)

Job was painfully aware of his mortality. He well understood the common denominator of all men. We have seen this before.

"Before I go whence I shall not return, even to the land of darkness and the shadow of death; A land of darkness, as darkness itself; and of the shadow of death, without any order, and where the light is as darkness." (Job 10:21-22)

"But man dieth, and wasteth away: yea, man giveth up the ghost, and where is he?" (Job 14:10)

Here is the great difference between type and antitype, between Job and the Lord to Whom he points. Our Lord suffered infinitely MORE than Job could dream, and DID return from death! Now, all who believe are spared this journey into everlasting darkness.

VERBALIZING HIS MISERY

READY FOR THE GRAVE

1 "My breath is corrupt, my days are extinct, the graves are ready for me." (Job 17:1)

The bad breath Job mentions in the first verse is typical of one suffering from a terminal illness. Job knows the sign well. He is convinced his time on earth is up. His days are finished, and *"the graves"* ready to receive him.

2 "Are there not mockers with me? and doth not mine eye continue in their provocation?" (Job 17:2)

The mockers, of course, are his counselors, his accusers. When Job says *"doth not mine eye continue in their provocation,"* he is saying, "Do you think I don't understand what you're doing?" They are not ready to let up in their constant *"provocation,"* and Job knows it.

3 "Lay down now, put me in a surety with thee; who is he that will strike hands with me?" (Job 17:3)

A little understanding of the historical background is helpful to see what Job is saying. The three phrases that he speaks all allude to the same thing.

He is asking who is going to *"lay down."* Job wants to know who is going to *"lay down"* his bail, who is going to sign the release to set him free from his misery.

To be a *"surety"* for someone is to be a guarantee. In courtroom terms it is to release someone to the care of another, to one who will be "sure" that the person acts responsibly, and appears in court on the proper day. Often when the word *"surety"* is used in the Bible, we would use the term "cosign" today.

To be *"surety"* for someone, the friend would *"strike hands,"* or "shake on it." This connection between "striking hands" and serving as someone's surety is seen several times in Proverbs, as evidenced by the following examples.

"My son, if thou be surety for thy friend, if thou hast stricken thy hand with a stranger." (Proverbs 6:1)

"Be not thou one of them that strike hands, or of them that are sureties for debts." (Proverbs 22:26)

RETRIBUTION FOR THE MOCKERS

4 "For thou hast hid their heart from understanding: therefore shalt thou not exalt them." (Job 17:4)

Job's use of *"thou"* gives us to understand that he is again addressing God directly. The ones whose heart God has hidden from understanding are the *"mockers"* of verse 2. Not only are they void of understanding, they will not be exalted.

5 "He that speaketh flattery to his friends, even the eyes of his children shall fail." (Job 17:5)

Job introduces the interesting topic of flattery in this verse. Throughout the ages flattery has been a universal instrument to manipulate people.

Here in the Book of Job, Elihu shows that he understands God's disdain for flattery. He has no more wisdom than the three men who precede him, yet he is right on target when he makes the following comments on flattery in Job 32.

"Let me not, I pray you, accept any man's person, neither let me give flattering titles unto man. For I know not to give flattering titles; in so doing my maker would soon take me away." (Job 32:21-22)

God's view of flattery is confirmed both in Psalms and Proverbs. Consider the following verses.

"The LORD shall cut off all flattering lips, and the tongue that speaketh proud things." (Psalm 12:3)

"He that goeth about as a talebearer revealeth secrets: therefore meddle not with him that flattereth with his lips." (Proverbs 20:19)

This verse from Proverbs 20 tells us how to recognize a talebearer, a gossip, one that takes the secrets you tell him, and spreads them in all directions. You can recognize him by his flattering lips. He will make you think that he is your greatest admirer.

"A lying tongue hateth those that are afflicted by it; and a flattering mouth worketh ruin." (Proverbs 26:28)

"A man that flattereth his neighbour spreadeth a net for his feet." (Proverbs 29:5)

Something far darker than the character flaws of a flattering man lurks beneath the surface of God's rejection of flattery. Flattery is a major part of the Antichrist's strategy in his rise to world power, as revealed in Daniel's prophecy.

"And in his estate shall stand up a vile person, to whom they shall not give the honour of the kingdom: but he shall come in peaceably, and obtain the kingdom BY FLATTERIES." (Daniel 11:21) (Author's emphasis)

The Antichrist will be a master diplomat, who, with a golden tongue, will negotiate an end to the Arab-Israeli conflict. His ability to persuade, his personal charisma and his manipulative skills will truly be supernatural. Daniel has more to say about the Antichrist and flattery.

"And such as do wickedly against the covenant shall he corrupt by flatteries: but the people that do know their God shall be strong, and do exploits." (Daniel 11:32)

Seeing that the prophetic context clearly points to the coming Tribulation, and understanding the connection between the Antichrist and flattery, look at the last part of Job 17:5—*"even the eyes of his children shall fail."*

This also has a very literal application to the coming Tribulation, when we see the fruit of a generation of children trained to mock their earthly parents and their heavenly Father. The children of the Antichrist have a horrible end to their earthly existence. (Their eternal end is even worse!)

"THE EYE that mocketh at his father, and despiseth to obey his mother, THE RAVENS of the valley shall pick it out, and the YOUNG EAGLES shall eat it." (Proverbs 30:17) (Author's emphasis)

It would be a mistake to pass by this verse lightly, without considering the cross-references that define it in a literal, prophetic sense. Jesus gives us a clue in His Olivet Discourse, as He lays out the things to come. He has just explained to His disciples the events leading up to His second coming, and the judgment of nations that will follow at the conclusion of the horrible battle of Armageddon.

"And they answered and said unto him, Where, Lord? And he said unto them, Wheresoever the body is, thither will THE EAGLES be gathered together." (Luke 17:37) (Author's emphasis)

Why will these eagles be gathered together in this place of dead bodies? More thorough details appear in Revelation 19, as eagles, vultures and other scavenger fowl will gather to feast upon the carcasses that remain from Armageddon. They will do a lot of "eye-plucking."

"And I saw an angel standing in the sun; and he cried with a loud voice, saying to ALL THE FOWLS that fly in the midst of heaven, Come and gather yourselves together unto the supper of the great God; That ye may eat the flesh of kings, and the flesh of captains, and the flesh of mighty men, and the flesh of horses, and of them that sit on them, and the flesh of all men, both free and bond, both small and great. And I saw the beast, and the kings of the earth, and their armies, gathered together to make war against him that sat on the horse, and against his army. And the beast was taken, and with him the false prophet that wrought miracles before him, with which he deceived them that had received the mark of the beast, and them that worshipped his image. These both were cast alive

into a lake of fire burning with brimstone. And the remnant were slain with the sword of him that sat upon the horse, which sword proceeded out of his mouth: and ALL THE FOWLS WERE FILLED WITH THEIR FLESH." (Revelation 19:17-21) (Author's emphasis)

REASONS FOR THE SORROW

6 "He hath made me also a byword of the people; and aforetime I was as a tabret." (Job 17:6)

Tribulation imagery continues to fill this chapter of Job. The choice of words and the connection between them and other clear prophetic passages cannot be mere coincidence. Job is saying that in the past he made people joyful. He was *"as a tabret."* The *"tabret"* (timbrel or tambourine) is connected with merriment.

"Wherefore didst thou flee away secretly, and steal away from me; and didst not tell me, that I might have sent thee away with mirth, and with songs, with tabret, and with harp?" (Genesis 31:27)

"After that thou shalt come to the hill of God, where is the garrison of the Philistines: and it shall come to pass, when thou art come thither to the city, that thou shalt meet a company of prophets coming down from the high place with a psaltery, and a tabret, and a pipe, and a harp, before them; and they shall prophesy." (1 Samuel 10:5)

Satan, in his original state as the anointed cherub, was the music leader of heaven. God's plan was for him to lead in worship and praise.

"Thou hast been in Eden the garden of God; every precious stone was thy covering, the sardius, topaz, and the diamond, the beryl, the onyx, and the jasper, the sapphire, the emerald, and the carbuncle, and gold: the workmanship of thy TABRETS and of thy pipes was prepared in thee in the day that thou wast created." (Ezekiel 28:13) (Author's emphasis)

Now, this one who was the "life of the party," who made people merry, has become a *"byword of the people."* (Job 17:6)

There is no escaping the Tribulation implication of these words. We first must go to Deuteronomy. God explains the consequences of disobedience, which will be completely fulfilled in the Tribulation.

"And thou shalt become an astonishment, a proverb, and a BYWORD, among all nations whither the LORD shall lead thee." (Deuteronomy 28:-37) (Author's emphasis)

At the time of the dedication of Solomon's temple, God again reminded the nation of Israel of the consequences of disobedience.

"Then will I cut off Israel out of the land which I have given them; and this house, which I have hallowed for my name, will I cast out of my sight;

and Israel shall be a proverb and A BYWORD AMONG ALL PEOPLE." (1 Kings 9:7) (Author's emphasis)

A byword is a proverb, a taunt. It is aimed at an object of scorn. Job fully understands that he is the target of his friends' scorn. He could never have understood that he was a model of the Christ to come.

The leaders of Israel never understood that their Messiah suffered this reproach for them. In Psalm 69 this tag is given prophetically to the Lord Jesus Christ.

"*I made sackcloth also my garment; and I became a proverb to them.*" (Psalm 69:11)

7 "Mine eye also is dim by reason of sorrow, and all my members are as a shadow." (Job 17:7)

The Antichrist and his children are not the only ones whose eyes are affected. Here, Job has his eyesight affected by his great sorrow. The Psalmist also had his eyes affected by his grief. Surely you have been so upset at times you "couldn't see straight." This is Job's condition.

"*Mine eye is consumed because of grief; it waxeth old because of all mine enemies.*" (Psalm 6:7)

"*Have mercy upon me, O LORD, for I am in trouble: mine eye is consumed with grief, yea, my soul and my belly.*" (Psalm 31:9)

When Job says "*all my members are as a shadow,*" he is speaking of his weight loss. He has become "skin and bones."

It is not difficult to see our Lord Jesus Christ consumed with the weight of our sin in this verse. Whether picturing Israel or Christ in this passage, we remember that there are three themes running throughout this book that are impossible to separate totally—Christ on the cross, Israel in the Tribulation and lost man in hell.

REWARD FOR THE RIGHTEOUS

8 "Upright men shall be astonied at this, and the innocent shall stir up himself against the hypocrite." (Job 17:8)

Job says that "*upright men shall be astonied.*" Today, we would say "astonished," but the word means to become like "a stone." One who is "astonished" is one who is so shocked he is like "a stone." The significance and prophetic application are in Isaiah.

"*As many were astonied at thee; his visage was so marred more than any man, and his form more than the sons of men.*" (Isaiah 52:14)

"*The innocent*" is, of course, a reference to the Lord Jesus Christ, Whom Job's innocence foreshadows. He is the innocent Savior who died for the guilty. Judas knew this, and confessed to the priests in horror.

"Saying, I have sinned in that I have betrayed the innocent blood. And they said, What is that to us? see thou to that." (Matthew 27:4)

Judas confessed to the priests. What a shame that he did not confess to God! Millions have made this same mistake throughout history.

Pilate knew that Jesus was the innocent one. Three times he declared that our Savior was innocent. (John 18:38; 19:4,6) Yet he still delivered the Christ to be crucified.

The innocent *"shall stir up himself against the hypocrite."* (Job 17:8) Our Lord certainly stirred up Himself against the hypocritical Pharisees in Matthew 23. THE hypocrite (Who is more of a master of hypocrisy than the Devil himself?) thought that he had won when he had the body of Jesus sealed in the tomb. Yet our Lord stirred up Himself against the hypocrite when He came bursting forth from the grave on the third day, conquering sin, death and the Devil!

The hypocrite assumes that since he is not suffering himself, he must therefore be godly. Paul warned against such a mentality.

"Perverse disputings of men of corrupt minds, and destitute of the truth, SUPPOSING THAT GAIN IS GODLINESS: from such withdraw thyself." (1 Timothy 6:5) (Author's emphasis)

What an interesting world. The godly suffer, while the wicked prosper and assume that they are the godly. Winners do not always win, and losers do not always lose.

9 "The righteous also shall hold on his way, and he that hath clean hands shall be stronger and stronger." (Job 17:9)

Those who are genuinely righteous will not trust the outward and obvious circumstances. They will lock their eyes firmly upon the Lord Jesus Christ and hold their course steady. Not only will they endure suffering, they will be encouraged in their sufferings. They will grow stronger each day in spite of the enemy's best attempts to destroy them. This is precisely the story of Paul's life.

"For all things are for your sakes, that the abundant grace might through the thanksgiving of many redound to the glory of God. For which cause we faint not; but though our outward man perish, yet the inward man is renewed day by day. For our light affliction, which is but for a moment, worketh for us a far more exceeding and eternal weight of glory; While we look not at the things which are seen, but at the things which are not seen: for the things which are seen are temporal; but the things which are not seen are eternal." (2 Corinthians 4:15-18)

VEXING HIS COUNSELORS

10 "But as for you all, do ye return, and come now: for I cannot find one wise man among you." (Job 17:10)

Verse 17:10 brings us back to the historical reality of Job's grief. In his frustration he addresses his counselors, and tells them *"do ye return, and come now"*—or in today's language, "Go back to where you came from!" He has found no wisdom in them. He is right.

11 "My days are past, my purposes are broken off, even the thoughts of my heart.

12 They change the night into day: the light is short because of darkness." (Job 17:11-12)

Job's despair is showing again. He is convinced that his days are over. There is no purpose left in living. His thoughts *"change the night into day."* That is to say his thoughts keep him awake at night. The final phrase of verse 12 is poetic—*"the light is short because of darkness."* In other words, it seems like it is always dark. He cannot see the light for the darkness.

13 "If I wait, the grave is mine house: I have made my bed in the darkness.

14 I have said to corruption, Thou art my father: to the worm, Thou art my mother, and my sister.

15 And where is now my hope? as for my hope, who shall see it?

16 They shall go down to the bars of the pit, when our rest together is in the dust." (Job 17:13-16)

What we have here is an obvious reference to Christ suffering the penalty of our sin, having been made sin for us. Job will say a similar thing in chapter 30.

"I am a brother to dragons, and a companion to owls. My skin is black upon me, and my bones are burned with heat." (Job 30:29-30)

The *"They"* of 17:16, who will *"go down to the bars of the pit,"* are *"corruption"* and *"the worm"* of 17:14.

Compare these words to the well-known Messianic prophecy in Psalm 22. There the context is undisputed.

"Our fathers trusted in thee: they trusted, and thou didst deliver them. They cried unto thee, and were delivered: they trusted in thee, and were not confounded. But I AM A WORM, and no man; a reproach of men, and despised of the people. All they that see me laugh me to scorn: they shoot out the lip, they shake the head, saying, He trusted on the LORD that he

would deliver him: let him deliver him, seeing he delighted in him. But thou art he that took me out of the womb: thou didst make me hope when I was upon my mother's breasts." (Psalm 22:4-9) (Author's emphasis)

Another Messianic type, the prophet Jonah, had his own encounter with death. Notice the similarity of his words.

"I went down to the bottoms of the mountains; the earth with her bars was about me for ever: yet hast thou brought up my life from corruption, O LORD my God." (Jonah 2:6)

In these dark passages, notice that hell has *"bars"*. Hell also has *"gates."* Look at what our Lord said in Matthew.

"And I say also unto thee, That thou art Peter, and upon this rock I will build my church; and THE GATES OF HELL shall not prevail against it." (Matthew 16:18) (Author's emphasis)

Finally, one can also observe that hell has keys. Praise God we know Who has them!

"I am he that liveth, and was dead; and, behold, I am alive for evermore, Amen; and have the keys of hell and of death." (Revelation 1:18)

What a journey we have taken in these two chapters of Job! We have had some of the most remarkable insight into the mind and heart of our Savior to be found in the Bible.

Comprehending a mere portion of what He suffered in our place should bring us to our knees. It should also place us squarely upon our feet to spread the good news of salvation to the uttermost.

15

EYES BIGGER THAN THE BRAIN

Surely such are the dwellings of the wicked, and this is the place of him that knoweth not God.

Job 18:21

"SON, I'M AFRAID YOUR EYES ARE BIGGER THAN YOUR STOMach!"

Sheepishly, his face wearing the chocolate evidence of his defeat, the young lad looks up into the eyes of his father. Still on the plate in front of him is the bigger part of an enormous dessert that the six-year-old just HAD to have all for himself. He has grudgingly come to realize that there is no way for him to finish.

Having "eyes bigger than your stomach" is an expression that most of us heard at least once while growing up. It is such a great line that it has been around for generations, much better than "I told you so." Some parents, though, cannot resist putting both phrases together.

Bildad is now stepping up for his second attempt to convince Job that some secret sin is the cause of his catastrophe. As we examine the words of Bildad, it will become evident that Bildad has a malady far more serious than eyes bigger than his stomach. Bildad's problem is that his eyes are bigger than his brain—he sees far more than he could possibly understand.

By comparing Scripture with Scripture, by prayerfully considering each of Bildad's words that the Holy Spirit has elected to preserve for us, we will be entering a prophetic gold mine. This passage is rich in the information it provides about the coming Antichrist and time of Tribulation.

Bildad obviously had no idea of the prophetic significance of his speech. Motivated to bring Job around to his own point of view, Bildad is the Devil's puppet to pressure Job into cursing God, as the Spirit of the living God sovereignly controls each word to assemble a remarkable glimpse into the coming Tribulation.

PROTEST OF BILDAD

1 "Then answered Bildad the Shuhite, and said,
2 How long will it be ere ye make an end of words? mark, and afterward we will speak.
3 Wherefore are we counted as beasts, and reputed vile in your sight?
4 He teareth himself in his anger: shall the earth be forsaken for thee? and shall the rock be removed out of his place?" (Job 18:1-4)

Bildad beseeches Job to be quiet and listen *("mark")* to what he and the others are saying. He asks Job why he is so upset, why he counts them as brute *"beasts,"* when all they are doing is telling him the truth for his own good.

In the fourth verse Bildad turns to address his companions. Job, he says, is so upset he is doing himself harm. He is only hurting himself.

Then, in the same verse, he again directs his words to Job. *"Shall the earth be forsaken for thee?"* "Job, do you think that God is going to shut down the entire earth just to deal with YOUR problem?"

"And shall the rock be removed out of his place?" "Do you think God is going to start throwing rocks around in an avalanche to prove you are right?"

Not a great deal of genuine communication is taking place in this exchange of words. None of these men is willing to retreat an inch from his position. Despite the argumentative tone of this discussion, the Holy Spirit of God will again transcend these words to masterfully paint a prophetic portrait of future history.

PORTRAIT OF ANTICHRIST

The subject of this passage makes his first appearance in verse 5—*"the wicked."* We have seen before how this representation of *"the wicked"* is a prophetic shadow of *"that Wicked"* whom Paul mentions in 2 Thessalonians.

"And then shall that Wicked be revealed, whom the Lord shall consume with the spirit of his mouth, and shall destroy with the brightness of his coming: Even him, whose coming is after the working of Satan with all power and signs and lying wonders." (2 Thessalonians 2:8-9)

The location that dominates this passages is clearly suggested in verse 18:21, as well as the connection to *"the wicked."* Jump ahead in the chapter for just a moment.

"Surely such are the dwellings of the wicked, and this is the place of him that knoweth not God." (Job 18:21)

We do not have to be great Bible students to calculate that Bildad's words look to the coming Antichrist, and also to a description of hell. Let us be careful, though, to not get ahead of ourselves. We pick up our exposition of the passage in verses 18:5 and 18:6.

LIGHTS OUT

5 "Yea, the light of the wicked shall be put out, and the spark of his fire shall not shine.

6 The light shall be dark in his tabernacle, and his candle shall be put out with him." (Job 18:5-6)

Today, it is not uncommon to hear someone say, "I'm going to punch your lights out!" This is precisely what God is going to do to the Antichrist. *"The light of the wicked shall be put out."*

In the oriental culture of Old Testament times, a light was always left burning in the home, unless the inhabitants were dead or away from home. This explains the promise God made to David.

"And unto his son will I give one tribe, THAT DAVID MY SERVANT MAY HAVE A LIGHT ALWAY BEFORE ME in Jerusalem, the city which I have chosen me to put my name there." (1 Kings 11:36) (Author's emphasis)

God is promising that David's light will never go out, that he will always have someone at home on the throne in Jerusalem. The same "light" principle appears other places in the Bible.

"The light of the righteous rejoiceth: but THE LAMP OF THE WICKED SHALL BE PUT OUT." (Proverbs 13:9) (Author's emphasis)

"For there shall be no reward to the evil man; THE CANDLE OF THE WICKED SHALL BE PUT OUT." (Proverbs 24:20) (Author's emphasis)

Because pagan man lives immersed in a sea of darkness, he has always held a fascination for light. He fears it, worships it and wants it. Spiritually and intellectually his lights are out—there is no life in him. God has given the promise that without saving faith, there is coming a day when man's physical light will be put out. Lost man lights candles as an act of worship, desperately and futilely seeking the immortality of light that will purge away his darkness.

"Behold, all ye that kindle a fire, that compass yourselves about with sparks: walk in the light of your fire, and in the sparks that ye have kindled. This shall ye have of mine hand; ye shall lie down in sorrow." (Isaiah 50:11)

"Go ahead," says God. "Light your candles, set off your fireworks, stage your ceremonies. This is all the light you will ever see without Christ."

The Antichrist will solidify his power over men by exploiting pagan man's fire fetish. The Book of Revelation describes the future.

"And he doeth great wonders, so that he maketh fire come down from heaven on the earth in the sight of men." (Revelation 13:13)

This search for light becomes more significant when we understand that the coming Tribulation will be a time of dense darkness. This was prophetically testified in the exodus of the Israelites from Egypt.

"And the LORD said unto Moses, Stretch out thine hand toward heaven, that there may be darkness over the land of Egypt, even darkness which may be felt. And Moses stretched forth his hand toward heaven; and there was a thick darkness in all the land of Egypt three days: They saw not one another, neither rose any from his place for three days: but all the children of Israel had light in their dwellings." (Exodus 10:21-23)

Amos also foresaw this darkness. His prophecy is frightening.

"Woe unto you that desire the day of the LORD! to what end is it for you? the day of the LORD is darkness, and not light." (Amos 5:18)

"Shall not the day of the LORD be darkness, and not light? even very dark, and no brightness in it?" (Amos 5:20)

The lights are going out. God's hand is cranking back the light, and the darkness is growing denser by the day. Is there light in your soul and spirit? Are you sure? If not, you are really going to be left in the dark!

There is only one sure way to have light in your tabernacle. The Psalmist instructs us.

"Thy word is a lamp unto my feet, and a light unto my path." (Psalm 119:105)

LAID LOW

7 "The steps of his strength shall be straitened, and his own counsel shall cast him down." (Job 18:7)

The idea here is that God is going to narrow, or "straighten," the steps of the wicked, leading him straight into a trap. His own *"counsel"* will be his doom. He will have everything figured out. His own intelligence will lead him into the trap God has laid.

The believer is led of God. The Lord directs his steps and gives him guidance. The wicked sets off on his own path, yet God narrows his steps, putting him in a position from which there is no escape. An excellent example is found in the Book of Numbers.

"And God's anger was kindled because he went: and the angel of the LORD stood in the way for an adversary against him. Now he was riding upon his ass, and his two servants were with him. And the ass saw the angel of the LORD standing in the way, and his sword drawn in his hand: and the ass turned aside out of the way, and went into the field: and Balaam smote the ass, to turn her into the way. But the angel of the LORD stood in a path of the vineyards, a wall being on this side, and a wall on that side. And when the ass saw the angel of the LORD, she thrust herself unto the wall, and crushed Balaam's foot against the wall: and he smote her again. And the angel of the LORD went further, and stood IN A NARROW PLACE, WHERE WAS NO WAY TO TURN EITHER TO THE RIGHT HAND OR TO THE LEFT." (Numbers 22:22-26) (Author's emphasis)

When God narrows, or straightens, the path of the wicked, it is with a particular destination in mind. No matter what course is set by the wicked, no matter in which direction he turns, his path invariably ends in judgment.

8 "For he is cast into a net by his own feet, and he walketh upon a snare.

9 The gin shall take him by the heel, and the robber shall prevail against him.

10 The snare is laid for him in the ground, and a trap for him in the way." (Job 18:8-10)

The first order of business in the exposition of this passage is to define some key words. A *"net"* is a reference to a literal net spread over a pit, and covered with leaves, branches and dirt to await its unsuspecting victim. The *"snare,"* also mentioned in verse 8, is a rope looped on the ground, set to spring around the leg of anyone or anything stepping into its circumference. Verse 10 describes it as *"laid . . . in the ground."*

While most would be familiar with the net or snare described above, fewer will recognize the *"gin."* The *"gin"* is a small trap that catches its victim *"by the heel,"* as we see in verse 9. The *"trap"* of verse 10 is a box-like cage that the victim enters through a door that is operated by a remote line.

Each of these devices speaks of the doom of *"the wicked"* (Job 18:5). God has *"straitened"* the wicked's feet to lead him straight into the net, or snare, or gin, or trap. If he avoids one, another is waiting. *"His own feet"* (Job 18:8) will take him to his doom.

A common theme in Scripture is the irony of the wicked caught in his own trap. This is what happened to the wicked Haman in the Book of Esther. This man, another type of the Antichrist, had built a gallows fifty cubits high for Mordecai the Jew (Esther 5:14). Yet it was Haman who was hung from his own gallows (Esther 7:9-10).

Paul quotes from Psalm 69:22 to show how Israel's unbelief had led them into a trap. Their own *"table,"* or altar of their religion, had become a snare in which they were caught.

"And David saith, Let their table be made a snare, and a trap, and a stumblingblock, and a recompence unto them: Let their eyes be darkened, that they may not see, and bow down their back alway." (Romans 11:9-10)

Another example is found in Proverbs. The point of the following verses is to show that the man who sets out to trap someone else is actually setting a trap for himself.

"My son, if sinners entice thee, consent thou not. If they say, Come with us, let us lay wait for blood, let us lurk privily for the innocent without cause: Let us swallow them up alive as the grave; and whole, as those that go down into the pit: We shall find all precious substance, we shall fill our houses with spoil: Cast in thy lot among us; let us all have one purse: My son, walk not thou in the way with them; refrain thy foot from their path: For their feet run to evil, and make haste to shed blood. SURELY IN VAIN THE NET IS SPREAD IN THE SIGHT OF ANY BIRD. AND THEY LAY WAIT FOR THEIR OWN BLOOD; THEY LURK PRIVILY FOR THEIR OWN LIVES." (Proverbs 1:10-18) (Author's emphasis)

The Psalmist also foresees the same end for the wicked. His own traps will be his doom.

"Let destruction come upon him at unawares; and let his net that he hath hid catch himself: into that very destruction let him fall." (Psalm 35:8)

"Let the wicked fall into their own nets, whilst that I withal escape." (Psalm 141:10)

11 "Terrors shall make him afraid on every side, and shall drive him to his feet." (Job 18:11)

The man who never learns what is called *"the fear of the LORD"* will one day run in fear and terror of the Lord to his own destruction. Like a terrified animal who discovers that he has been cornered, and there is no escape, the wicked will run blindly to his end. This is the scene in Job 18:11.

The terrors mentioned here are those to come in that future seven-year period of Tribulation. The horrors are unlike any ever before experienced. Having seen this portrait of the Antichrist painted prophetically in the words of Bildad, we now enter the final verses of chapter 18, which speak of that time of terror to come.

PREVIEW OF TRIBULATION

HUNGERBITTEN

12 "His strength shall be hungerbitten, and destruction shall be ready at his side." (Job 18:12)

"Hungerbitten"—now THAT is quite a descriptive word! The strength of the Antichrist will be subdued by hunger. Famine definitely has a place in the Tribulation prophecies. The sixth chapter of The Revelation makes this point, looking forward to coming economic disaster and the resulting famine.

"And when he had opened the third seal, I heard the third beast say, Come and see. And I beheld, and lo a black horse; and he that sat on him had a pair of balances in his hand. And I heard a voice in the midst of the four beasts say, A measure of wheat for a penny, and three measures of barley for a penny; and see thou hurt not the oil and the wine. And when he had opened the fourth seal, I heard the voice of the fourth beast say, Come and see. And I looked, and behold a pale horse: and his name that sat on him was Death, and Hell followed with him. And power was given unto them over the fourth part of the earth, to kill with sword, and with hunger, and with death, and with the beasts of the earth." (Revelation 6:5-8)

The second half of Job 18:12 says that *"destruction shall be ready at his side."* Considering the prophetic application of these words, it is easy to see the horrible destruction that will characterize the Tribulation. We have already seen the connection between hunger and destruction in Eliphaz's words Job chapter 5.

"He shall deliver thee in six troubles: yea, in seven there shall no evil

touch thee. In FAMINE he shall redeem thee from death: and in war from the power of the sword. Thou shalt be hid from the scourge of the tongue: neither shalt thou be afraid of DESTRUCTION when it cometh. At DESTRUCTION and FAMINE thou shalt laugh: neither shalt thou be afraid of the beasts of the earth." (Job 5:19-22) (Author's emphasis)

Yet there is another consideration in the use of this word "destruction." In our comments on Job 2:11-13, we saw the incredible prophecy of Revelation 9:11.

"And they had a king over them, which is the angel of the bottomless pit, whose name in the Hebrew tongue is Abaddon, but in the Greek tongue hath his name Apollyon." (Revelation 9:11)

At that time we learned that the Greek word *"Apollyon"* has a related form translated "perdition" in the title *"son of perdition,"* used by Jesus in John 17:12, and by Paul in 2 Thessalonians 2:3. Now, you need to know that the word "Apollyon" in Revelation 9:11 is literally translated as "destroyer." This *"king,"* this *"angel of the bottomless pit,"* will be at the Antichrist's side. If this is indeed a cross-reference to the prophecy of Revelation 9:11, it would certainly explain the next words to come out of Bildad's mouth.

DEVOURED

13 "It shall devour the strength of his skin: even the firstborn of death shall devour his strength." (Job 18:13)

"It" in verse 13 looks back to *"destruction"* of verse 12, and forward to *"the firstborn of death"* in the same verse 13. The attack on *"the wicked's"* skin reminds us that leprosy is often connected with prophetic pictures of the Antichrist in Scripture. His famous "mark" backfires, and he is smitten with the "spot" of leprosy, representing the plague of sin. In our study of Job 11:15 we discussed the importance of being *"without spot."*

Probably this *"destruction,"* or "destroyer," or *"firstborn of death,"* is the same *"destroyer"* who devoured the firstborn of the Egyptians before the exodus of the Israelites from Egypt.

"For the LORD will pass through to smite the Egyptians; and when he seeth the blood upon the lintel, and on the two side posts, the LORD will pass over the door, and will not suffer THE DESTROYER to come in unto your houses to smite you." (Exodus 12:23) (Author's emphasis)

Pharaoh is a type of the Antichrist in the Old Testament. What happened to him and the Egyptians that fateful night in Egypt is a mere foreshadow of what is going to happen to the Antichrist. This will set up the final fulfillment of Hebrews 2:14.

"Forasmuch then as the children are partakers of flesh and blood, he also himself likewise took part of the same; that through death he might destroy him that had the power of death, that is, the devil." (Hebrews 2:14)

The Tribulation connection continues as we look at Job 18:14. *"Destruction,"* the *"destroyer," "the angel of the bottomless pit,"* is also called a *"king"* in Revelation 9:11. We are obviously still speaking of "the wicked" and what "it" will do to him.

ROOTED OUT

14 "His confidence shall be rooted out of his tabernacle, and it shall bring him to the king of terrors." (Job 18:14)

This *"king"* is none other than the same one we will meet in our study of Job 41, a brilliant description of the very Devil. The words in Job 41 are those of God.

"He beholdeth all high things: he is a king over all the children of pride." (Job 41:34)

The Antichrist, "that Wicked," will be possessed by the very Devil, who will be his destruction, just as he has destroyed the seven *"heads"* of state before him, all of whom are types of the Antichrist. (Revelation 17:9-11) He will be *"rooted out of his tabernacle,"* a biblical word for "body." It is this possession of the Antichrist's body that is the topic of the next verse.

15 "It shall dwell in his tabernacle, because it is none of his: brimstone shall be scattered upon his habitation." (Job 18:15)

"It"—call it what you will: destruction, destroyer, firstborn of death, angel of the bottomless pit, king of the children of pride—is going to possess the *"tabernacle,"* or body of "that Wicked".

Yet remember that *"it is none of his."* It does not belong to him. He is merely using it, and will continue until fire and brimstone rains down in the manifestation of God's wrath from heaven.

John foresaw this possession of Antichrist by the Devil. Examine the following verses from Revelation 13.

"And I saw one of his heads as it were wounded to death; and his deadly wound was healed: and all the world wondered after the beast. And they worshipped the dragon which gave power unto the beast: and they worshipped the beast, saying, Who is like unto the beast? who is able to make war with him? And there was given unto him a mouth speaking great things and blasphemies; and power was given unto him to continue forty and two months. And he opened his mouth in blasphemy against God, to blaspheme his name, and his tabernacle, and them that dwell in

heaven. And it was given unto him to make war with the saints, and to overcome them: and power was given him over all kindreds, and tongues, and nations." (Revelation 13:3-7)

"And he had power to give life unto the image of the beast, that the image of the beast should both speak, and cause that as many as would not worship the image of the beast should be killed." (Revelation 13:15)

"Fire and brimstone" are irrevocably connected with images of divine judgment. Such was the fate of Sodom and Gomorrah.

"Then the LORD rained upon Sodom and upon Gomorrah brimstone and fire from the LORD out of heaven." (Genesis 19:24)

Fire and brimstone also await the Antichrist and his followers. One of several references is found in Isaiah.

"And the streams thereof shall be turned into pitch, and the dust thereof into brimstone, and the land thereof shall become burning pitch. It shall not be quenched night nor day; the smoke thereof shall go up for ever: from generation to generation it shall lie waste; none shall pass through it for ever and ever." (Isaiah 34:9-10)

The last scene at the end of the Tribulation includes a vision of this fate. The beast, or Antichrist, and the false prophet that led the world in worshiping him, will be "baptized" in fire and brimstone.

"And the beast was taken, and with him the false prophet that wrought miracles before him, with which he deceived them that had received the mark of the beast, and them that worshipped his image. These both were cast alive into a lake of fire burning with brimstone." (Revelation 19:20)

CHASED OUT

16 "His roots shall be dried up beneath, and above shall his branch be cut off.

17 His remembrance shall perish from the earth, and he shall have no name in the street." (Job 18:16-17)

This is the final end of Antichrist, as well as all who don't know God. Verse 16 is very descriptive, showing him dried up at the roots, and cut off from above. The one who brought the entire world under his spell, will be feared no more. What we see in these two verses perfectly matches other prophecies. Here are two examples.

"For, behold, the day cometh, that shall burn as an oven; and all the proud, yea, and all that do wickedly, shall be stubble: and the day that cometh shall burn them up, saith the LORD of hosts, that IT SHALL LEAVE THEM NEITHER ROOT NOR BRANCH. But unto you that fear my name shall the Sun of righteousness arise with healing in his wings; and ye

shall go forth, and grow up as calves of the stall. And ye shall tread down the wicked; for they shall be ashes under the soles of your feet in the day that I shall do this, saith the LORD of hosts." (Malachi 4:1-3) (Author's emphasis)

"But the wicked shall be CUT OFF from the earth, and the transgressors shall be ROOTED OUT of it." (Proverbs 2:22) (Author's emphasis)

18 "He shall be driven from light into darkness, and chased out of the world." (Job 18:18)

What a remarkable development! The Antichrist is going to be driven into a darkness that is literally "out of this world." Putting together the two phrases of this verse, we arrive at what is called in the Bible *"outer darkness."*

"But the children of the kingdom shall be cast out into OUTER DARKNESS: there shall be weeping and gnashing of teeth." (Matthew 8:12) (Author's emphasis)

"Then said the king to the servants, Bind him hand and foot, and take him away, and cast him into OUTER DARKNESS; there shall be weeping and gnashing of teeth." (Matthew 22:13) (Author's emphasis)

"And cast ye the unprofitable servant into OUTER DARKNESS: there shall be weeping and gnashing of teeth." (Matthew 25:30) (Author's emphasis)

Job's friend Zophar will also comment on this future fate of the Antichrist. We will consider the cross reference, but will wait for complete commentary until we arrive at Job 20. Notice the connection between darkness, fire, and someone's tabernacle.

"All darkness shall be hid in his secret places: a fire not blown shall consume him; it shall go ill with him that is left in his tabernacle." (Job 20:26)

19 "He shall neither have son nor nephew among his people, nor any remaining in his dwellings." (Job 18:19)

What we find in Job 18:19 is a biblical way to say that the Antichrist will have no survivors. A similar prophecy appears in Isaiah, in the same context that deals with the fall of Lucifer, who will one day be incarnate in the Antichrist.

"For I will rise up against them, saith the LORD of hosts, and cut off from Babylon the name, and remnant, and son, and nephew, saith the LORD." (Isaiah 14:22)

Psalm 109 is a prophecy of Judas Iscariot, another of the many Antichrists in the Bible. Peter quoted from verse 8 of this Psalm in Acts 1:20, as he called for the assembled brethren to elect another to take Judas' place in the Twelve.

"Let his days be few; and let another take his office." (Psalm 109:8)

David continues his prophetic utterance. He describes the fate of Judas and his descendants.

"Let his children be continually vagabonds, and beg: let them seek their bread also out of their desolate places." (Psalm 109:10)

"Let there be none to extend mercy unto him: neither let there be any to favour his fatherless children. Let his posterity be cut off; and in the generation following let their name be blotted out." (Psalm 109:12-13)

For the past many centuries Satan has done all he can to infiltrate the human race with his own agents. His angelic followers cohabited with human women in Genesis 6, yet Satan was not able to complete his purposes. Many men have fallen prey to his temptations and have ended as his puppets.

Yet for all of this, there is coming a day when this line of debauchery will be cut off forever. The Antichrist will be bathed in fire and brimstone, and there will be no one to carry on his line.

20 "They that come after him shall be astonied at his day, as they that went before were affrighted." (Job 18:20)

Fear will be the common denominator that unites men's hearts in the Tribulation. The Antichrist's disciples will witness unspeakable horror with wide-eyed terror. Their hearts will be pressurized with terror as they watch the entire world system collapse before them. Life and reality will suddenly spin out of their control, and the result will be unadulterated fear.

Yet the day of the Lord will arrive, payday for Antichrist and his entire tribe. As the events prophesied for centuries unfold, the fear that had once gripped mankind will be converted to pure astonishment. Those who see it happen will emotionally turn to stone, speechless, unable to react, as God's judgment falls upon the neck of the Antichrist.

21 "Surely such are the dwellings of the wicked, and this is the place of him that knoweth not God." (Job 18:21)

The final verse of this chapter removes all doubt as to its subject matter. The statement of verse 21 is clear, requiring little commentary. What we have seen is the destiny of the wicked, and also the place of *"him that knoweth not God."*

Do not fail to comprehend the horrible reality of this statement. The final end of the Antichrist and the Devil is identical to that of the average man who goes to church, lives by the Golden Rule and yet does not know God.

Hell will be filled with deacons, Sunday school teachers, preachers, missionaries and church committee members who played the game of religion, and yet never came to a personal knowledge of Almighty God. If you have come to the pages of this commentary seeking knowledge about the Bible, I pray that if you do not know God, you will find personal knowledge of Him. Intellectual facts about the Book of Job can impress those in your Bible study group or Sunday school class. God will not be impressed if you do not know Him.

Obviously, Bildad cannot possibly grasp the larger, prophetic picture God is drawing with his words. Yet even he realizes, as indicated in verse 21, that his words have passed far beyond a man named Job. He has been caught up in the heat of the moment, and has expounded eloquently upon *"the place of him that knoweth not God."*

16

THIRD TIME'S THE CHARM!

For I know that my redeemer liveth,
and that he shall stand at the latter day upon the earth:
And though after my skin worms destroy this body,
yet in my flesh shall I see God;
Whom I shall see for myself,
and mine eyes shall behold,
and not another;
though my reins be consumed within me.

Job 19:25-27

HOW OFTEN HAVE WE HEARD THIS TIRED REFRAIN? "THIRD time's the charm!"

Perhaps we should give some thought to why it is that the number "3" has held such a fascination for people throughout human history. Could it be that there is some significance deeper than anyone would think?

Everything God is, and everything God has ever made has three dimensions or parts. Think about it.

God Himself is a Trinity—God the Father, God the Son and God the Holy Spirit. The Bible teaches that He made man in His own image. Man is a being with three dimensions—body, soul and spirit.

God gave instructions to Moses to build a tabernacle that would be a model of the created universe (Hebrews 8 and 9). That tabernacle had three parts—the outer court, the holy place and the holiest. These three parts correspond to the three heavens of the Bible—the first is the atmosphere, the second we call outer space, and the third is the very abode of God (2 Corinthians 12:2).

All objects have three dimensions in space—height, width and depth. Every color in the world is a combination of three primary colors. All time is divided into past, present and future. The list could continue, but I trust you are getting the idea.

Philip Elmer DeWitt wrote an article for *Time Magazine* in the October

23, 1989 issue. His article was entitled "A Trinity of Families," with the subtitle "Scientists reduce all matter to three fundamental types."

When my grandfather was in school he was taught to divide matter into animal, vegetable and mineral. In my school days I learned that all matter consisted of atoms, which had three components—electrons, neutrons and protons. As they continued to look, scientists saw even smaller building blocks, such as quarks, neutrinos, taus and muons. Yet no matter how much they look, everything still divides by three, as DeWitt wrote in his article.

We have also commented that all Scripture has three dimensions—historical, doctrinal and personal. This understanding has guided us so far in our study of Job. We start with the historical Job, a man who struggles to trust God in the midst of incredible trials. Then we learned that those things that *"were written aforetime were written for our learning"* (Romans 15:4)—doctrine. We saw that Job is an amazingly accurate illustration of the doctrine of the coming Tribulation. Finally, the personal dimension comes into play as we seek to go beyond mere intellectual learning and apply the spiritual truths of the book of Job to our lives. Among other things in the Book of Job, we learn how to harness these spiritual truths to deal with the trials that come into our lives.

Yet even this doctrinal application of Job has three dimensions. Repeatedly we have observed that in the book of Job there are three things that prophetically are all but impossible to separate—the Jew in Tribulation, Christ on the cross and the lost man in hell. Another clear example of this connection is here in chapter 19. Analyzing Job's words of grief, we will again see the Spirit of God transcend the historical situation to give us a glimpse of the future.

The chapter opens with Job responding to Bildad's discourse. By the time we are four verses into the chapter we will be deep into Tribulation, over our heads in hell and hanging with our Lord on the cross.

TIRED REACTION

1 "Then Job answered and said,
2 How long will ye vex my soul, and break me in pieces with words?" (Job 19:1-2)

Exhausted, Job lashes back at his counselor friends. "How much longer can this go on?" His next phrase is graphic—*"and break me in pieces with words?"*

Satan has tried to attack Job physically on all fronts, and failed. Using these friends as his puppets, Satan has relentlessly smashed and slammed Job with words.

Many people are painfully aware that verbal abuse can be just as damaging as physical violence. We can all conjure up mental images of brutal husbands whose wives and children are crushed under the weight of abusive words. There are other common examples with which we are all familiar—the church gossip, the bitter relative, the filthy-mouthed co-worker, who often leave others bleeding with the sharpness of their words.

Seldom, however, do we consider ourselves capable of verbal abuse. We just want to help people, encourage them, exhort them, edify them. Right? This is exactly what Job's friends had come to do! Look at them now, breaking Job to pieces with their words.

It is disturbing to think about it, but even those of us who minister the Word of God, whose intentions are the best, can be guilty of breaking others to pieces with our words, while thinking we are doing right. We should prayerfully consider the way we use our words, and God's. Remember, Job's friends had their theological facts in order, yet they had no clue how to apply them.

There are frustrated preachers who use the Word of God to hammer their flock on the head, rather than use the two-edged sword to surgically perform life-transforming operations. Reading the words Jesus spoke to Peter, "*feed my sheep*," they incorrectly think He must have meant "beat my sheep."

Some counselors are poor listeners. They are more concerned about using their words to display their great knowledge and their marvelous sense of justice, than they are about ministering grace with what they say. Convinced they are doing a great favor, they are seldom aware their words are breaking their counselee to pieces. The counselee is converted into a victim. These counselors comfort about as well as a clumsy man carrying snow skis through a crystal shop.

There are many places in the Bible where the damaging power of the tongue is exposed. Consider the following.

"*My soul is among lions: and I lie even among them that are set on fire, even the sons of men, whose teeth are spears and arrows, and their tongue a sharp sword.*" (Psalm 57:4)

"*Hide me from the secret counsel of the wicked; from the insurrection of the workers of iniquity: Who whet their tongue like a sword, and bend their bows to shoot their arrows, even bitter words.*" (Psalm 64:2-3)

"*There is that speaketh like the piercing of a sword: but the tongue of the wise is health.*" (Proverbs 12:18)

"There is a generation, whose teeth are as swords, and their jaw teeth as knives, to devour the poor from off the earth, and the needy from among men." (Proverbs 30:14)

Those of us who are spiritual leaders must face the fact that we, too, are in danger of our words breaking to pieces the ones we want to help. In the classic biblical passage on the tongue, James warned those who would be leaders about the grave responsibility that accompanies leadership.

"My brethren, be not many masters, knowing that we shall receive the greater condemnation. For in many things we offend all. If any man offend not in word, the same is a perfect man, and able also to bridle the whole body." (James 3:1-2)

Job has not withheld his frustration with his friends. Following his accusation of having broken him to pieces with their words, he lets them know that he has been keeping a "punch count."

3 "These ten times have ye reproached me: ye are not ashamed that ye make yourselves strange to me." (Job 19:3)

Who has been keeping score? Evidently Job has. When words have pierced your soul, it is hard to forget. With all the indirect blows and insinuations, Job has been slammed many more than ten times.

We, as unofficial scorekeepers, might differ as to the "punch count," but there have been no fewer than ten times that Job has taken a direct hit to a vital area. No one would know better than Job how many hits he has received.

Remember also that we saw in our discussion of Job 1:2 that "10" is the number often associated with completeness and fullness in the Bible. We also saw this number in connection with the fullness of the gentiles. We encounter "10" again. This time, gentile Job has been completely pounded by his friends, and has entered into the fullness of reproach.

Whether your scorecard agrees with Job's, he has been hit enough by these men to spoil the friendship. As Job said, *"ye make yourselves strange to me."* (Job 19:3)

4 "And be it indeed that I have erred, mine error remaineth with myself." (Job 19:4)

Job's point is concise. If there is a sin problem in his life, it is his to deal with. It is not their problem.

This brings us to another key counseling principle. The counselor must realize that it is not his responsibility to force the solution to a problem. If the counselee does not want to do right, all the desire in the world by the counselor is worthless. The problem belongs to the counselee, not the counselor.

The counselor can only expose the real issues, point his counselee to the corresponding biblical teachings, and lay out the options. From that point forward, the decision belongs to the counselee. If there is no willingness to obey God, the counselor cannot make that decision instead. If the Holy Spirit's convicting power is not sufficient to bring the person to repentance, the human counselor is not going to do it by himself.

Here is what Job is saying. "Back off! You've made your point. I hear you loud and clear. If there is a problem in my life, I'll deal with it. This is MY problem. Give me some space."

Those of us who use the Bible to point people to the way of righteousness should take note. There are times when our best intentions push us past the point of our own limitations. There is no sense in pursuing the matter if we have made our point clearly, and the other person is still not willing to make a decision.

Jesus brought people to the point of decision, putting them in a position where they had to answer "yes" or "no." That is where He always left people. He never ran after them insisting that they do what is right. When the rich young ruler refused His instruction and went away sorrowful, Jesus did not chase him. He let him go.

A summary of these truths appears in Romans. Here we see the danger of becoming a stumbling block to others, and the need to step aside to let God do His work.

"Who art thou that judgest another man's servant? to his own master he standeth or falleth. Yea, he shall be holden up: for God is able to make him stand." (Romans 14:4)

"But why dost thou judge thy brother? or why dost thou set at nought thy brother? for we shall all stand before the judgment seat of Christ. For it is written, As I live, saith the Lord, every knee shall bow to me, and every tongue shall confess to God. So then every one of us shall give account of himself to God. Let us not therefore judge one another any more: but judge this rather, that no man put a stumblingblock or an occasion to fall in his brother's way." (Romans 14:10-13)

In a supposed "contradiction," Paul gave paradoxical instructions to the Galatians.

"Bear ye one another's burdens, and so fulfil the law of Christ." (Galatians 6:2)

Then, just three verses later he said what some say is a contradiction.

"For every man shall bear his own burden." (Galatians 6:5)

There is no problem here if we understand the truth we have just been discussing. We all are to be ready to come to the aid of a brother. We should do whatever we can to bear his burden. Yet there is a degree of personal responsibility that each of us must bear alone. We must be willing to help our brother with his load; however, we cannot live his life for him. We can point him to the truth, but we cannot make his decisions for him.

In these cases when we have done all we can, we must trust the matter to God. This is Paul's teaching to the Corinthians.

"Therefore judge nothing before the time, until the Lord come, who both will bring to light the hidden things of darkness, and will make manifest the counsels of the hearts: and then shall every man have praise of God." (1 Corinthians 4:5)

"For we must all appear before the judgment seat of Christ; that every one may receive the things done in his body, according to that he hath done, whether it be good or bad." (2 Corinthians 5:10)

Job's counselors have pushed way beyond the bounds of good taste, good judgment and the limitations of their personal responsibility. Yet they have failed to push Job over the edge of despair. Now, Job's words go past the limitations of his own understanding.

THREEFOLD REPRESENTATION

We now enter that vivid section that is like a triple-exposure picture, showing Christ on the cross, the Jew in Tribulation and the lost man in hell. Job's words etch hard images like acid on metal.

THE NET IS SPREAD

5 "If indeed ye will magnify yourselves against me, and plead against me my reproach:

6 Know now that God hath overthrown me, and hath compassed me with his net." (Job 19:5-6)

While Job was down and hurting, his friends took advantage to magnify themselves. This is not at all an uncommon development. They took his reproach and turned it against him.

David had insight on this point. He pleads for God to answer his prayer, knowing that if he were to fall, there would be those who would immediately *"magnify"* themselves against him. There is nothing like a good trial to show you who your real friends are. *"For I said, Hear me, lest otherwise they should rejoice over me: when my foot slippeth, they magnify themselves against me."* (Psalm 38:16)

Do not fail to notice that in verse 6 Job says that he has fallen into GOD'S net. Satan was the messenger of sorrow and anguish, but God mentioned Job's name first.

When our Lord died on the cross, it was not the Devil who put Him there. He laid His life down voluntarily (John 10:18), and fell into God's net.

In the coming Tribulation the Jew will be drawn into God's net. For centuries God's people have lived religiously in rebellion against the God who loves. Sin will not go unpunished, and the net is being drawn.

The lost man curses God and stays on his own course, the course of his making. His religions, his philosophies and science do not matter a bit. The net is spread.

THE CRY IS IGNORED

7 "Behold, I cry out of wrong, but I am not heard: I cry aloud, but there is no judgment." (Job 19:7)

This is the cry of a deserted man. A man is lost in the desert. He cries till his lungs can take no more, but there is no one to hear his cry.

A time approaches when men will run to hide themselves in dens and caves in the mountains. They will flee in abject terror, crying out to the very dens and rocks themselves, because there is no one to listen—not even God. This is the horror of the Tribulation.

"*And the heaven departed as a scroll when it is rolled together; and every mountain and island were moved out of their places. And the kings of the earth, and the great men, and the rich men, and the chief captains, and the mighty men, and every bondman, and every free man, hid themselves in the dens and in the rocks of the mountains; And said to the mountains and rocks, Fall on us, and hide us from the face of him that sitteth on the throne, and from the wrath of the Lamb: For the great day of his wrath is come; and who shall be able to stand?*" (Revelation 6:14-17)

A crowd has gathered around a Judean hillside. A pathetic figure hangs from a Roman cross as twelve legions of hovering angels pull back from the earth's atmosphere, ending three hours of supernaturally-caused darkness (Matthew 26:53; 27:45).

Criminals were being crucified that day, but the One upon Whom all eyes are fixed is innocent. The man who gave the order to crucify Him said three times that He was innocent (John 18:38; 19:4,6).

In the agony of His innocence He cries with a loud and haunting voice, "*My God, my God, why hast thou forsaken me?*" (Matthew 27:46; Psalm 22:1) There is no one to answer Him—not even God.

Flames so hot they give no light, burn eternally in a lake of fire. Countless millions of souls burn there together, yet each is all alone. In the permanently-hardened human heart dwells an eternal sense of justice. From the depths of this hell comes the gut-wrenching cry of a soul convinced that a great injustice has been done. Yet there is no one to hear—not even God. *"There is no judgment"*—it is past.

Job sits in ashes in the land of Uz. His world has collapsed, and he cries out of wrong, cries that there is no justice. His cry is but a whisper. What must YOUR cry sound like to God? He IS listening, by the way, to Job and to you.

THE WAY IS FENCED

8 "He hath fenced up my way that I cannot pass, and he hath set darkness in my paths." (Job 19:8)

Job has that "fenced-in" feeling. I am sure you can identify. All of us have felt an emotional claustrophobia in the midst of great trial. As we say, your back is up against the wall.

As the Lord Jesus Christ died on the cross, He came to a point of no return. His agony in the garden the previous night revealed that His mission on the cross was purely voluntary. He did not have to die. He died because of His love for lost man.

Just a moment ago we reminded ourselves that the heavenly Father had twelve legions of angels at the ready to rescue Jesus, so many that their massive presence hovering above Palestine blocked the sun's light that day. (No other place on earth reported the intense, mysterious darkness that was experienced in that local region of the Middle East. This is contrary to eclipses, volcanic explosions and other special phenomena that are surprisingly well-documented by comparing ancient records. Such an intense darkness in such a limited area suggests a low altitude obstacle over the affected area.) When the Father turned His back on the Son, Who had become sin for us, the protective angels were withdrawn, and the darkness lifted—*"UNTO the ninth hour"* (Matthew 27:45) (Author's emphasis).

This ninth hour is the hour the angels were withdrawn and the hour He died. This is the moment Jesus cried, *"MY God, my God, why hast thou forsaken me?* (Matthew 27:46)

The decisive moment had been reached. There was no way out. He was fenced in.

Man in the Tribulation will be fenced in. There will be no escape. Many people today consider suicide an escape from a fierce reality more threatening than death. Yet there is coming a day when not even death will be a way out of their constant misery.

"And in those days shall men seek death, and shall not find it; and shall desire to die, and death shall flee from them." (Revelation 9:6)

Hell is securely fenced. Jesus told of the rich man who cried out to Abraham in the agony of his torment. He could see Abraham in Paradise, and sought nothing more than a moist finger on the tip of his tongue.

That in itself tells you something about the horror of hell. A man who has enjoyed a life of riches suddenly has experienced a transformation of values. A man who wore the finest clothes and feasted on gourmet food, now considers a moist finger on his tongue to be the most precious thing he could imagine. Jesus told this story some two thousand years ago. The rich man still has not received even a drop of water. He is fenced in, you see.

"And beside all this, between us and you there is a great gulf fixed: so that they which would pass from hence to you cannot; neither can they pass to us, that would come from thence." (Luke 16:26)

We learned in a previous chapter of this commentary that hell has bars (Jonah 2:6) and gates (Matthew 16:18). Only one man has the key (Revelation 1:18).

Hell is also a place of intense, absolute darkness. Earlier we remarked that the hottest flame gives forth no light. This is the *"outer darkness"* we saw in Job 18:18.

We all have times when it seems we are fenced-in. There are obstacles we come across that are in our way. God does not always remove the obstacles. Sometimes He puts them there because we are in the wrong way! If He is leading us to some place beyond the obstacle, He will surely remove it, or show us the way around it, over it, under it, or through it.

"There hath no temptation taken you but such as is common to man: but God is faithful, who will not suffer you to be tempted above that ye are able; but will with the temptation also make a way to escape, that ye may be able to bear it." (1 Corinthians 10:13)

Similarly, we have all been through those times of great darkness, when we cannot seem to make out the way in front of us. No matter how dark it may seem, it will never be as dark as it was for Christ that day on the cross, or as dark as it will be in the Tribulation. If you know Christ, you can just smile the next time someone says, "It's dark as hell in here!" No. It isn't. Besides, we can always get a light.

"Thy word is a lamp unto my feet, and a light unto my path." (Psalm 119:105)

Not only that, it will be light soon.

"But unto you that fear my name shall the Sun of righteousness arise with healing in his wings; and ye shall go forth, and grow up as calves of the stall." (Malachi 4:2)

THE GLORY IS GONE

9 "He hath stripped me of my glory, and taken the crown from my head." (Job 19:9)

God had promised David a glorious and everlasting kingdom. Sin, however, had toppled that kingdom, and it seemed for many years that all hope was lost. Maschil the Ezrahite lamented the fact.

"Once have I sworn by my holiness that I will not lie unto David. His seed shall endure for ever, and his throne as the sun before me. It shall be established for ever as the moon, and as a faithful witness in heaven. Selah. But thou hast cast off and abhorred, thou hast been wroth with thine anointed. Thou hast made void the covenant of thy servant: thou hast profaned his crown by casting it to the ground. Thou hast broken down all his hedges; thou hast brought his strong holds to ruin. All that pass by the way spoil him: he is a reproach to his neighbours. Thou hast set up the right hand of his adversaries; thou hast made all his enemies to rejoice. Thou hast also turned the edge of his sword, and hast not made him to stand in the battle. Thou hast made his glory to cease, and cast his throne down to the ground. The days of his youth hast thou shortened: thou hast covered him with shame. Selah." (Psalm 89:35-45)

Little did anyone realize that the temporary breach in the glory was but a foreshadow of what David's Seed would suffer to bring the glory of God to all who believe. Voluntarily stripping Himself of His heavenly glory, leaving His crown behind, our Lord became a man. More than that, He became sin for us.

"Let this mind be in you, which was also in Christ Jesus: Who, being in the form of God, thought it not robbery to be equal with God: But made himself of no reputation, and took upon him the form of a servant, and was made in the likeness of men: And being found in fashion as a man, he humbled himself, and became obedient unto death, even the death of the cross." (Philippians 2:5-8)

Since 1948 the world has witnessed an extraordinary development. A people almost two thousand years removed from their homeland gained status as a member of the family of nations again. This reborn nation of Israel has become a model of gritty determination and resourcefulness. The modern Jews have caused the desert to flourish. They have successfully expanded their coasts, and fought off bigger and stronger neighbors.

There have been many sacrifices, to be sure, but the rebirth of the Jewish nation has been glorious. To hear many talk, God has had precious little to do with recent events; instead, this remarkable accomplishment is due to the cunning and courage of the people.

The Bible prophesies a time coming when a brilliant diplomat will even successfully negotiate an end to the ages-long conflict between Jew and Arab. Abraham's sons will begin to lay down their arms, and the world will rejoice at the coming of a New Age of peace.

The glory we now see growing and glowing will come crashing down in a flash. Paul is just one of several biblical writers to see this future event.

"For yourselves know perfectly that the day of the Lord so cometh as a thief in the night. For when they shall say, Peace and safety; then sudden destruction cometh upon them, as travail upon a woman with child; and they shall not escape." (1 Thessalonians 5:2-3)

Our rich friend from Luke 16 has been permanently evacuated from his closets filled with the finest wardrobe. The charismatic air, blown by his riches and influence, that rushed and roared through every room he entered, blows no more. There are no lockers to rent in hell for glory or crowns.

"Go to now, ye rich men, weep and howl for your miseries that shall come upon you. Your riches are corrupted, and your garments are motheaten. Your gold and silver is cankered; and the rust of them shall be a witness against you, and shall eat your flesh as it were fire. Ye have heaped treasure together for the last days. Behold, the hire of the labourers who have reaped down your fields, which is of you kept back by fraud, crieth: and the cries of them which have reaped are entered into the ears of the Lord of sabaoth. Ye have lived in pleasure on the earth, and been wanton; ye have nourished your hearts, as in a day of slaughter. Ye have condemned and killed the just; and he doth not resist you." (James 5:1-6)

Job's glory is gone. He was probably a king of Edom, yet any crown he may have had lies rusting in the ashes of a demolished life. Job's loss of glory is but for a moment, and his recompense is speeding on its way, though he doesn't know it, nor does he care at this point.

Have YOU suffered a loss of glory, or loss of a crown? I doubt it, unless it was a future crown to be rewarded for faithfulness. Whatever problem you may have, I doubt it measures up to the loss that Job has suffered, though his, too, is far less than any loss of glory and crown endured by our Lord.

Perhaps it is a tarnished reputation you have suffered for your Christian witness at work. You were thrilled to share your new faith in Christ with those you love and work with, then, suddenly, you lost your job, were demoted or suffered another trial that you think has stained your sterling status. Here you were, taking your stand for Christ, minding your own business, and, before you knew what was happening, you awoke to discover that you were sitting in ashes. What to do? Read on.

"Wherein ye greatly rejoice, though now for a season, if need be, ye are in heaviness through manifold temptations: That the trial of your faith, being much more precious than of gold that perisheth, though it be tried with fire, might be found unto praise and honour and glory at the appearing of Jesus Christ." (1 Peter 1:6-7)

"When Christ, who is our life, shall appear, then shall ye also appear with him in glory." (Colossians 3:4)

"But we all, with open face beholding as in a glass the glory of the Lord, are changed into the same image from glory to glory, even as by the Spirit of the Lord." (2 Corinthians 3:18)

"For our light affliction, which is but for a moment, worketh for us a far more exceeding and eternal weight of glory." (2 Corinthians 4:17)

"For I reckon that the sufferings of this present time are not worthy to be compared with the glory which shall be revealed in us." (Romans 8:18)

THE HOPE IS REMOVED

10 "He hath destroyed me on every side, and I am gone: and mine hope hath he removed like a tree." (Job 19:10)

Destroyed. Gone. No hope. Job cannot see past his present problems. This is not the first time Job has bemoaned his condition and declared himself hopeless.

"My days are swifter than a weaver's shuttle, and are spent without hope." (Job 7:6)

"And where is now my hope? as for my hope, who shall see it?" (Job 17:15)

Nor did Zophar hesitate to point out that there is no hope for the wicked. His message to Job was an unsubtle call to confess hidden sin, or be left with no hope.

"But the eyes of the wicked shall fail, and they shall not escape, and their hope shall be as the giving up of the ghost." (Job 11:20)

Of the three inseparable things we are considering, only the lost man in hell is totally without hope. We have previously observed how men are often figuratively represented in the Bible as trees. Just as felled tree, when a man dies without Christ, his hope is also dead.

"When a wicked man dieth, his expectation shall perish: and the hope of unjust men perisheth." (Proverbs 11:7)

Lucifer's hope of becoming like God without God was also cut down like a tree.

"How art thou fallen from heaven, O Lucifer, son of the morning! how art thou cut down to the ground, which didst weaken the nations!" (Isaiah 14:12)

Israel, however, is a different story. The horrible, unnatural darkness of the Tribulation will make it seem that all hope is lost (and it will be for those who do not know Christ), but the nation will flourish again like a green tree. Job gave us this possibility earlier.

"For there is hope of a tree, if it be cut down, that it will sprout again, and that the tender branch thereof will not cease." (Job 14:7)

In our study of Job 14 we saw that this is a statement that points forward to Romans 11 and the spiritual rebirth of the nation of Israel. Notice that this theme of lost hope is preserved in the vision of that same spiritual renewal that Ezekiel saw as a valley of dry bones coming to life.

"Then he said unto me, Son of man, these bones are the whole house of Israel: behold, they say, Our bones are dried, and our hope is lost: we are cut off for our parts." (Ezekiel 37:11)

Christ IS our Hope (1 Timothy 1:1; Titus 2:13), and was cut off ON a tree. Because of that we can never honestly say with Job that we have no hope.

THE WAR IS ON

11 "He hath also kindled his wrath against me, and he counteth me unto him as one of his enemies.

12 His troops come together, and raise up their way against me, and encamp round about my tabernacle." (Job 19:11-12)

Here is the common denominator shared by the three inseparable things we are considering. They are all the objects of God's wrath. The Tribulation is the outpouring of God's wrath, and both Christ and the unbeliever receive the brunt of that wrath.

Job says God has counted him as one of his enemies. There is not true, but there was a time when we all were God's enemies.

"For if, when we were enemies, we were reconciled to God by the death of his Son, much more, being reconciled, we shall be saved by his life." (Romans 5:10)

To bring us salvation, the Lord Jesus Christ was counted as God's enemy for our sake. *"For he hath made him to be sin for us, who knew no sin; that we might be made the righteousness of God in him."* (2 Corinthians 5:21)

Job thinks all God's armies have encamped around him, around his tabernacle. All the armies of God were encamped against the One whose tabernacle (body) hung on the cross. A moment earlier legions of God's angels were available to rescue Him. Now, having become a curse, having become sin, He is counted as the enemy.

TRIED REDEEMER

13 He hath put my brethren far from me, and mine acquaintance are verily estranged from me.
14 My kinsfolk have failed, and my familiar friends have forgotten me.
15 They that dwell in mine house, and my maids, count me for a stranger: I am an alien in their sight.
16 I called my servant, and he gave me no answer; I intreated him with my mouth.
17 My breath is strange to my wife, though I intreated for the children's sake of mine own body.
18 Yea, young children despised me; I arose, and they spake against me.
19 All my inward friends abhorred me: and they whom I loved are turned against me." (Job 19:13-19)

Alienation from friends and family is the theme of this passage. Job's family and his friends have deserted him. Even the servants who worked in his house, and reverently snapped to attention when he spoke, consider him to be a stranger. His own wife has offered no comfort—the one who bore his children. She only urged him to curse God and die (Job 2:9). Even little children speak against him and mock him as he passes by. Even those men he counted as intimate friends cannot stand to be around him.

The imagery is not difficult. It shows Israel made a proverb and a byword of reproach. It shows Christ counted as an enemy by the armies of God as He hung on the cross, and it shows lost man in hell forever separated from everyone he knows and loves.

The application to Christ is especially poignant. This alienation is seen in several Messianic prophecies.

"I was a reproach among all mine enemies, but especially among my

neighbours, and a fear to mine acquaintance: they that did see me without fled from me." (Psalm 31:11)

"Thou hast put away mine acquaintance far from me; thou hast made me an abomination unto them: I am shut up, and I cannot come forth." (Psalm 88:8)

"Lover and friend hast thou put far from me, and mine acquaintance into darkness." (Psalm 88:18)

20 "My bone cleaveth to my skin and to my flesh, and I am escaped with the skin of my teeth." (Job 19:20)

This verse, along with Job 30:17, are related to what we find in Psalm 22, describing the crucifixion. The weight of a bloodied body is pulled downward by gravity, skin stretched taut across the skeletal frame. *"I may tell all my bones: they look and stare upon me."* (Psalm 22:17)

The expression "the skin of my teeth" reminds us of the incalculable influence of the King James Bible on our English language. Job may have escaped with the skin of his teeth, but Jesus did not. He tasted death for us.

21 "Have pity upon me, have pity upon me, O ye my friends; for the hand of God hath touched me." (Job 19:21)

In these last few statements of Job, the spotlight has narrowed. All is focused now on the Man of Sorrows. The parallels to the Tribulation and hell fade into the shadows. What Job says here corresponds to a verse from the great Messianic Sixty-Ninth Psalm.

"Reproach hath broken my heart; and I am full of heaviness: and I looked for some to take pity, but there was none; and for comforters, but I found none. They gave me also gall for my meat; and in my thirst they gave me vinegar to drink." (Psalm 69:20-21)

Job was looking for pity, not reproach. He had merely felt the touch of God's hand. Jesus Christ bore the full fury of God's wrath. He who is full of pity found none for Himself that day.

22 "Why do ye persecute me as God, and are not satisfied with my flesh?" (Job 19:22)

Job accuses his counselors of usurping the place of God. Not satisfied with his physical affliction, they are tearing at his very soul.

In our introductory studies we saw that Job is aptly named. His name can be translated as "the persecuted one." As such, he is a fitting picture of Israel persecuted in the Tribulation. John saw this as a "wonder." The woman in the following scene is Israel, which gave us the Lord Jesus Christ.

"And there appeared a great wonder in heaven; a woman clothed with the sun, and the moon under her feet, and upon her head a crown of twelve

stars: And she being with child cried, travailing in birth, and pained to be delivered. And there appeared another wonder in heaven; and behold a great red dragon, having seven heads and ten horns, and seven crowns upon his heads." (Revelation 12:1-3)

"And when the dragon saw that he was cast unto the earth, he persecuted the woman which brought forth the man child." (Revelation 12:13)

From a historical perspective Job does not realize that it is not his friends, but the very Devil who was persecuting him. This is obvious, of course, but we must never forget that it was God Who gave the permission.

Don't think that God is cruel. God does allow the Devil to attack His children. When He does, there is always a purpose beyond our immediate understanding. Sometimes, like Job, we never understand. At other times we become aware of God's greater design, as did Joseph, who was sold into slavery by his own brothers.

"But as for you, ye thought evil against me; but God meant it unto good, to bring to pass, as it is this day, to save much people alive." (Genesis 50:20)

23 Oh that my words were now written! oh that they were printed in a book!

24 That they were graven with an iron pen and lead in the rock for ever!" (Job 19:23-24)

They are! And God has preserved them for our benefit today. Job's words are not the only words written down. Compare what Jeremiah said.

"The sin of Judah is written with a pen of iron, and with the point of a diamond: it is graven upon the table of their heart, and upon the horns of your altars." (Jeremiah 17:1)

TREMENDOUS REALITY

25 For I know that my redeemer liveth, and that he shall stand at the latter day upon the earth:

26 And though after my skin worms destroy this body, yet in my flesh shall I see God:

27 Whom I shall see for myself, and mine eyes shall behold, and not another; though my reins be consumed within me.

28 But ye should say, Why persecute we him, seeing the root of the matter is found in me?

29 Be ye afraid of the sword: for wrath bringeth the punishments of the sword, that ye may know there is a judgment." (Job 19:25-29)

The first three verses of this passage are perhaps the spiritual climax of the book. Job's words form one of the Bible's truly great confessions of faith.

Many years ago as a youth pastor, still a youth myself, I was bothered by a certain teacher at a local high school who relished the opportunity to harass Christian students. For months the teenagers in our group who attended that school had been complaining to me about the critical remarks that continually flowed from his mouth.

One day they told me that he had stated dogmatically that the Old Testament never taught the possibility of future resurrection. He was trying to establish that the resurrection of Christ was a hoax, perpetuated by His followers to bolster His failing popularity.

This was too much. Young as I was, I knew that I had to say something. Making an appointment to speak with the principal, I went with a great confidence in the Word of God and the resurrection, but with a knot in my stomach every time I would consider my ability to express the message of God's Word.

The principal wisely called the teacher in question into his office so that I might offer my complaints face to face. He was a typical little man who enjoyed trying to display what he clearly believed to be his superior intelligence, by attacking the faith of young students. He smugly repeated his claim that biblical teaching on resurrection is non-existent in the Old Testament.

There were several passages I had selected to put in my quiver that day, but the first arrow I drew back in my bow was this one—Job 19: 25-27.

The conversation would go no further than his reply. What he offered was the standard reply that ends any honest discussion about the Bible, showing me his ignorance and intellectual dishonesty—"That's just YOUR interpretation."

What DO these verses say? Let us see exactly what an open mind led by the Holy Spirit can glean (1 Corinthians 2:13-14).

25 "For I know that my redeemer liveth, and that he shall stand at the latter day upon the earth." (Job 19:25)

First, the Redeemer is alive and well. Second, He will physically stand upon the earth in *"the latter day."* In other words, He will be visible, and

He will physically be on this earth, not a "spiritual essence" indwelling all as the New Agers teach.

26 "And though after my skin worms destroy this body, yet in my flesh shall I see God." (Job 19:26)

Not only do we learn that Christ lives and will physically return to earth, we see that the believer has a new physical body coming. Job's body is covered with open sores, and he is convinced that he is at the point of death. Yet he is just as convinced that he will see God *"in my flesh."*

27 "Whom I shall see for myself, and mine eyes shall behold, and not another; though my reins be consumed within me." (Job 19:27)

Though his insides rot away, though his body is eaten by worms, Job knows there is coming a physical resurrection. He is going to see God in the flesh, and it will be with his own eyes. He is not speaking of a reincarnation, but he himself, *"and not another."*

28 "But ye should say, Why persecute we him, seeing the root of the matter is found in me?" (Job 19:28)

Job returns to his original point, made in the first four verses, and reiterated in Job 19:22. What they SHOULD do is to stop persecuting him. If there is a problem in Job's life, it is Job's decision to deal with it, not theirs.

29 "Be ye afraid of the sword: for wrath bringeth the punishments of the sword, that ye may know there is a judgment." (Job 19:29)

God IS just, and will bring judgment—without the help of these three counselors. Rather than constantly hound Job about coming judgment, they should do some fearing themselves.

There are two swords we should all fear. The first is a literal sword, given by God to the human institution of government.

"Let every soul be subject unto the higher powers. For there is no power but of God: the powers that be are ordained of God. Whosoever therefore resisteth the power, resisteth the ordinance of God: and they that resist shall receive to themselves damnation. For rulers are not a terror to good works, but to the evil. Wilt thou then not be afraid of the power? do that which is good, and thou shalt have praise of the same: For he is the minister of God to thee for good. But if thou do that which is evil, be afraid; for he beareth not the sword in vain: for he is the minister of God, a revenger to execute wrath upon him that doeth evil." (Romans 13:1-4)

The other sword to be feared is the sword of the Lord. Never forget it is a *"two-edged"* sword. Not only can we cut with it, it can also cut us to pieces in a split second.

"For the Word of God is quick, and powerful, and sharper than any

twoedged sword, piercing even to the dividing asunder of soul and spirit, and of the joints and marrow, and is a discerner of the thoughts and intents of the heart." (Hebrews 4:12)

We remember James' warning to potential leaders about the awesome responsibility of those who would use their tongue to minister the Word of God. Be very careful. It is but a small step to end like Job's counselors. You begin with the best of intentions, wielding the words of God with a flourish. Soon, your lack of mastery has resulted in some serious self-inflicted wounds with the sword you were so eager to grab, and with which you could not wait to begin slashing any poor victim.

We have come a long way through the Book of Job. There is still a long way to go. We have seen some choice riches that God has stored for us in this book. Always keep present your need to go beyond intellectual assimilation of these truths. The only reason Job could endure such affliction is that his faith was a LIVING faith of the heart.

There is life in this book that YOU desperately need to see you through the trials in your life. That life, not intellectual knowledge, is what will enable you to look disaster in the face and say like Job, "I know that my redeemer liveth."

17

THE LONG SHADOW OF "THE WICKED"

This is the portion of a wicked man from God,

and the heritage appointed unto him by God.

Job 20:29

A FRIEND OF MINE RECENTLY POINTED OUT AN INTERESTING fact. Put an egg and a potato in the same pot of water and gradually turn up the heat. As the water heats, the egg grows hard and the potato becomes soft.

This is not unlike what happens when believers are put in God's pot of trials and temptations. Some grow hard; some grow soft.

We are witnessing the same phenomenon in the drama before us in the book of Job. With each round of discussion the water is steadily heating up. Job is getting softer, while his friends become harder. Zophar, whose turn it is to speak, is nearing the boiling point.

Zophar is determined to convince "wicked" Job of his evil ways. He is satisfied that the disaster that has befallen Job must be due to some specific sin. His words are filed to a sharp edge. More than cutting Job, these words cut through future years to give us yet another glimpse of the one who is called *"that Wicked"* by Paul in 2 Thessalonians 2:8.

Zophar has listened intently to Job's rebuttal to Bildad. Despite the mental and emotional beating he has taken, Job's words reflect a mind that is still functioning rationally. They evidently find a target in Zophar, because he is quick to react.

CHECKMATE IN UZ

1 "Then answered Zophar the Naamathite, and said,
2 Therefore do my thoughts cause me to answer, and for this I make haste.
3 I have heard the check of my reproach, and the spirit of my understanding causeth me to answer." (Job 20:1-3)

Zophar has been thinking things over, and he is anxious to respond. As he listened to Job and the others, he has tried to mentally list all the things he wants to say.

It requires some patience to be part of a group of several people who are all trying to speak their mind to a single individual. Each must wait his turn, hoping that the one speaking does not "steal his thunder." The worst part is having a particularly brilliant point, and then having the conversation change so that your point becomes meaningless before you can make it.

These men are following a strict order—Eliphaz, Bildad and Zophar. Now, Zophar has his chance again. Yet all that Zophar has been storing in his mind melted with Job's last words. Job got his full attention. Zophar feels that Job has put him in checkmate. *"I have heard the check of my reproach."*

Just what had Job said? It will be worth our time to review.

"Be ye afraid of the sword: for wrath bringeth the punishments of the sword, that ye may know there is a judgment." (Job 19:29)

Job has warned his counselors that there is a judgment coming. Zophar considers this an insult to his piety. He will answer out of the abundance of his spirit of understanding that he imagines himself to have.

Observation: Zophar has allowed his emotions to get involved. This is a fatal mistake for any counselor. There comes a time for a counselor to speak loudly, to challenge, to exhort, to refuse to be pushed around by those he wishes to help. Yet above all, he must not take personally the things said to him by the one he tries to help. He must not lose his biblical sense of direction because he feels he has been insulted.

Then again, this discussion between Job and his friends ceased to be a counseling session long ago. As Zophar rushes to defend his honor, the Spirit of God rushes to use his words to give generations of believers a better understanding of *"that wicked,"* whose sinister stature has cast a long shadow across the pages of this book.

CONTENT OF PROPHECY

4 "Knowest thou not this of old, since man was placed upon earth,
5 That the triumphing of the wicked is short, and the joy of the hypocrite but for a moment?" (Job 20:4-5)

The familiar subject of *"the wicked"* comes into view here. We will see it again in this chapter, in verse 29.

"This is the portion of a wicked man from God, and the heritage appointed unto him by God." (Job 20:29)

So, sandwiched between these verses, the subject matter is defined. We will be learning more about the lot of the wicked.

Also, notice that Zophar appeals to knowledge from before the Flood. We have seen this before. Zophar points to a truth that has been known *"since man was placed upon earth."*

The essence of Zophar's point is not difficult. He says simply that any triumph of the wicked is going to be brief—*"but for a moment."*

In the historical sense these words fly directly at Job. Zophar takes Job's warning of coming judgment and shoves them right back in Job's face. He is calling Job a wicked man and a hypocrite.

The memory of the Flood is still clearly etched in the common consciousness. It is the theme of judgment that has prompted this vocal outburst from Zophar. The generation prior to the Flood was saturated with wickedness. God's assessment was plain.

"And GOD saw that the wickedness of man was great in the earth, and that every imagination of the thoughts of his heart was only evil continually." (Genesis 6:5)

The pleasures of sin were as temporary for that generation as for any other. Soon that entire generation was obliterated in the judgment of the Flood. Only the godly Noah and his family were spared.

Yet if we accept these words literally (and there is no reason to do otherwise) there is more to be learned. Zophar says this information has been common knowledge *"since man was placed upon earth."*

Adam clearly discovered that anything gained through his sin, like the knowledge of good and evil, could not last long. The consequences of his sin fell upon him immediately.

Even before his own sin Adam must have understood the truth of God's judgment upon sin. With the communion that he enjoyed with God before his sin, Adam no doubt learned about the rebellion of Lucifer. You and I can read about it in Isaiah 14. Despite Lucifer's great power he could never hope to endure in his fight against the Almighty.

Devotionally, the sense of Zophar's speech is no less obvious. Any wicked man, any hypocrite through the ages would do well to pay heed to the admonition that sin does not pay. The victory of the sinner is temporary at best.

In this book of Job's incredible tribulation it should be apparent that the doctrinal teaching of this passage points prophetically to *"that Wicked,"* the Antichrist. His power will sweep the entire world. Millions will believe he is divine. He will be cheered as no other human has ever been cheered. Yet his triumph and joy will only last for a moment.

COLLAPSE OF ANTICHRIST

6 "Though his excellency mount up to the heavens, and his head reach unto the clouds;
7 Yet he shall perish for ever like his own dung: they which have seen him shall say, Where is he?
8 He shall fly away as a dream, and shall not be found: yea, he shall be chased away as a vision of the night.
9 The eye also which saw him shall see him no more; neither shall his place any more behold him." (Job 20:6-9)

Zophar continues his tirade. For years he has watched Job enjoy the benefits of being the greatest of the men of the East. The vile intensity of venom that flows so easily from his mouth makes it appear that he almost relishes this chance to slam Job. The historical application of these words is not hard to see. We need to look deeper.

The parallels between Zophar's commentary and the incident recorded in Isaiah 14 are striking. Consider what is said above in verse 6, and compare it with the story of Lucifer's fall. He is intent on ascending to heaven and rising above the clouds of God.

"For thou hast said in thine heart, I will ascend into heaven, I will exalt my throne above the stars of God: I will sit also upon the mount of the congregation, in the sides of the north: I will ascend above the heights of the clouds; I will be like the most High." (Isaiah 14:13-14)

These words apply not only to the person of the Antichrist, but to the expanse of his empire, Babylon, and to any subject of the kingdoms of this world down through the ages, who has no hope of eternal life. No matter how high he might rise, his fall will only be that much greater. Read again Job 20:6-9 and again compare Isaiah's prophecy.

"Yet thou shalt be brought down to hell, to the sides of the pit." (Isaiah 14:15)

It would be irresponsible to apply these words to the Antichrist, and then go forward with no regard to their practical application in everyday life. What Zophar says should remind us all of the transitory nature of life, the worthlessness of sin, and the certainty of judgment.

Who are the people who enjoy the spotlight of world fame as you read these words? No doubt the entire world is buzzing about some billionaire, some sports hero, some music or movie star or a politician who dominates this month's news. For all their fame and influence, they will quickly be reduced to nothingness.

Zophar uses imagery that is both gross and graphic. What do dung (20:7) and dreams (20:8) have in common? They mean nothing. They disappear as quickly as they arrive. This is the future of this moment's celebrity hero who does not know Christ. If YOU do not know Christ as your Savior, this is also your future we are discussing.

CONSEQUENCES OF REBELLION

The largest part of this chapter deals with the terrible consequences of the wicked's rebellion against God. This is a good time to remember what was said in comments on Job 20:4-5. The subject of this passage "the wicked." In the historical sense, it is obvious that Zophar wants to categorize Job as a wicked man, and is warning him of the consequences of what he perceives to be Job's rebellion against God. At times, however, Zophar will speak of "the wicked" in general, and not necessarily refer specifically to Job. The context will make this clear.

We have already seen that Zophar's comments about the wicked readily match other biblical passages that prophesy God's judgement to come upon "that Wicked" (2 Thessalonians 2:8), who is also known as the Antichrist. This will be true also in the following verses. We will attempt to locate corresponding prophecies about the Antichrist that parallel Zophar's words concerning the wicked.

Simultaneously, what Zophar says about the wicked also can be directly applied to the life of any individual who lives in rebellion against God. Anyone without God who sets out on a course to be like God, is going to suffer the consequences of rebellion. Rebellion against God has a high price.

Be careful not to get lost as the commentary switches from one application to the other. Remember the threefold application of Scripture. What Zophar has to say about the consequences of the wicked's rebellion against God is true. Though true, his words simply cannot apply to Job. They do apply to anyone who is wicked, and prophetically apply to the Antichrist. The first consequence of rebellion mentioned by Zophar has to do with the family.

RESTITUTION THROUGH THE WICKED'S CHILDREN

10 "His children shall seek to please the poor, and his hands shall restore their goods." (Job 20:10)

The historical meaning of this verse is difficult. It is clear by now that Zophar is talking about "the wicked" in general, of whom Job is seen as representative. This obviously is the case, since Job's children are dead and won't be seeking to please the poor any time soon.

Some say that verse 10 should read "the poor will oppress his children." Yet looking down a little further in the passage, verse 19 speaks of how the wicked has oppressed and forsaken the poor. Putting these things together it appears that Zophar means that the wicked man's children will try to please the poor to compensate for their Father's wickedness. If this is so, the second half of the verse would indicate that they will make restitution to the poor with the riches laid up by the wicked's hands.

Seeing that Zophar is speaking of "the wicked" in a generic sense, with the implication that Job is a wicked man, we then move to see how God uses these words to point to "that Wicked." (2 Thessalonians 2:8) Armed with our knowledge that *"that Wicked"* is the sum of all the wicked of all ages, we compare Scripture with Scripture to make our way through this verse.

Prophetically, we know from what we have learned in this context that we are dealing with God's judgment upon the Antichrist and its results. The time is immediately following the return of our Lord Jesus Christ to earth, since we saw the wicked's doom and disappearance in Job 20:6-9.

The identification of the wicked's children is easy. We listen to the words of Christ as He railed against the religious leaders of His day.

"Ye are of your father the devil, and the lusts of your father ye will do. He was a murderer from the beginning, and abode not in the truth, because there is no truth in him. When he speaketh a lie, he speaketh of his own: for he is a liar, and the father of it." (John 8:44)

Not all the Devil's children are destroyed in the Tribulation. At the conclusion of the Millennium there will still be those who have refused to commit their hearts to the Lord Jesus Christ, even though He will be reigning physically in Jerusalem. While outwardly professing allegiance to Christ, their hearts will be darkened.

They cannot even blame the Devil for their sin, since he will be imprisoned in the bottomless pit for the duration of the Millennium. It will not be until the end of the Millennium that the true condition of their hearts will be revealed. The Book of Revelation teaches that Satan will be released from his imprisonment at the end of the Millennium, and will lead a rebellion against God.

"And when the thousand years are expired, Satan shall be loosed out of his prison, And shall go out to deceive the nations which are in the four quarters of the earth, Gog and Magog, to gather them together to battle: the number of whom is as the sand of the sea. And they went up on the breadth of the earth, and compassed the camp of the saints about, and the beloved city: and fire came down from God out of heaven, and devoured them." (Revelation 20:7-9)

How will these children of the Antichrist disguise their spiritual darkness in the light of Christ's earthly reign? In precisely the same way the Devil's children hide their presence in today's churches—by covering their sinful hearts with the cloak of good works.

Their focus will not be upon the King of kings, but upon the poor. Countless people will be left destitute following the terrible campaign of Armageddon and the corresponding world crisis provoked by the events of the Great Tribulation.

Sometimes we imagine that the Lord Jesus Christ in His second coming will be like a fairy godmother, waving a magic wand and making everything new and sparkling again. The Bible is a realistic book. The prophets speak of the dead bodies remaining from Armageddon and the necessary clean-up time. There will be much work to do. There will also still be those who are poor.

To appease a less than pure conscience, counterfeit believers will express dire concern for the physical needs of mankind, just as they do today. Although it is right and biblical to minister to the poor, the issue here is one of focus and motivation.

This is nothing new. Judas Iscariot was the "bag-carrier," or treasurer of the Twelve. He was a satanic implant. His concern was not to serve Christ, but himself. He camouflaged his self-interest with an expressed concern for the poor. When Mary anointed the Lord with precious ointment, Judas was indignant. The other disciples followed his lead, by the way (Matthew 26:8).

"Then took Mary a pound of ointment of spikenard, very costly, and

anointed the feet of Jesus, and wiped his feet with her hair: and the house was filled with the odour of the ointment. Then saith one of his disciples, Judas Iscariot, Simon's son, which should betray him, Why was not this ointment sold for three hundred pence, and given to the poor? This he said, not that he cared for the poor; but because he was a thief, and had the bag, and bare what was put therein." (John 12:3-6)

Judas' true motivation was exposed. Christ's response is also instructive, for it teaches us the correct focus we are to have.

"Then said Jesus, Let her alone: against the day of my burying hath she kept this. For the poor always ye have with you; but me ye have not always." (John 12:7-8)

Even following Judas' betrayal of the Lord, his wrong focus prevailed. Judas, grieved by what he had done, ran to confess his sin. The problem is that he confessed his sin to the priests, not to God (Matthew 27:3). As the text puts it, Judas *"repented himself,"* rather than responding to the conviction of the Holy Spirit. He then went and hanged himself.

The chief priests and elders were confounded by what to do with the thirty pieces of silver Judas threw down on the floor before them. They could not put it in the treasury because it was "blood money" (Matthew 27:6). This is wildly incredible! They admit they have just paid to assassinate the Messiah, yet they are so concerned about their religious laws they cannot put the money in the treasury.

So what did they do? They did what any good liberal, church-going, religious, spiritual, professing, phoney believer would do. They gave the money to help the poor by buying a plot of ground in which to bury penniless strangers (Matthew 27:7-8).

The spiritual children of the Antichrist will have just witnessed the physical return of Jesus Christ to earth. What will they do? They will express their "sorrow" for the "unfortunate events" during the reign of Antichrist by seeking to please the poor, and using what the hand of the Antichrist had accumulated to make restitution for goods lost in the conflict of the Tribulation.

ROTTEN TO THE BONE IS THE WICKED

11 "His bones are full of the sin of his youth, which shall lie down with him in the dust." (Job 20:11)

Zophar says Job is "wicked to the bone," as someone might say today, and has been since his youth. He will take his sin with him to the grave. However one applies this statement—to the wicked in general, to Job or to Antichrist—the truth concerns man's nature. Man is bad to the bone!

This is the decision that everyone with a load of sin must make. Either we pass that load to the Lord Jesus Christ, and find rest and salvation, or we carry that load of sin to the grave.

While we have emphasized how these truths apply to the Antichrist and his "children," most people would like to avoid the more personal application. Like Zophar, we tend to classify the wicked as anyone but ourselves. The truth of the Bible is that ALL men are wicked by nature. Only the grace of God through Christ's death, burial and resurrection can change that nature.

RANCID SWEETS OF THE WICKED

12 "Though wickedness be sweet in his mouth, though he hide it under his tongue;
13 Though he spare it, and forsake it not; but keep it still within his mouth:
14 Yet his meat in his bowels is turned, it is the gall of asps within him." (Job 20:12-14)

This is a wonderfully graphic description of sin. Though speaking of *"the wicked,"* it obviously applies to any individual in any age who refuses to deal with sin.

Wickedness can be as sweet as a piece of candy in the mouth. There IS pleasure in sin *"for a season"* (Hebrews 11:25).

Have you ever placed a piece of hard candy under your tongue? It makes it last longer, and keeps the sugary sweetness seeping into your system for a long time. You can try to make it last for as long as possible, but it is eventually going to waste away.

In the case of sin, though, the sugary sweetness soon sets the entire digestive system into gyrations. One suddenly discovers that he has been poisoned, as with the *"gall of asps."* Clearly it IS the poison of a serpent (Genesis 3) that has poisoned the system. What one thought to be candy was really poison all along. Paul uses the same imagery to describe sinners.

"Their throat is an open sepulchre; with their tongues they have used deceit; the poison of asps is UNDER THEIR LIPS." (Romans 3:13) (Author's emphasis)

REGURGITATED RICHES OF THE WICKED

15 "He hath swallowed down riches, and he shall vomit them up again: God shall cast them out of his belly." (Job 20:15)

"The wicked" is like a glutton on a food binge, stuffing every delectable delight possible into his mouth. The problem is that what goes down is going to come up! As they say, "you can't take it with you." Yet every day he tries. Man tries to stash away all the riches he can accumulate, yet he has no hope of holding on to them.

Reflecting on the prophetic overtones of verse 15, one has to think of the story of Jonah. The disobedient prophet was swallowed by a whale, only to have God cause the creature to vomit Jonah out upon the dry ground (Jonah 2:10).

Jonah was a Jewish prophet to the gentiles of Nineveh, warning them of great tribulation to follow. He is a picture of 144,000 Jewish witnesses in the time of Tribulation who will cry out to the gentile nations, warning of judgment. The twelfth chapter of Revelation describes the war that the devil wages against this faithful remnant, trying to swallow them up.

Nothing gained by the satanic trinity in the Tribulation will be permanent. God will cause the enemy to vomit up any riches that have been stolen.

16 "He shall suck the poison of asps: the viper's tongue shall slay him." (Job 20:16)

This is a summary statement of what we have just seen. The Antichrist is going to suck on the poison of the serpent, yet will be slain by the very same poison. If you play with fire, you are going to be burned. The Devil's poison is like candy in the mouth. At first, you'll want all you can get. In the end, you discover that the "candy" is deadly poison.

RUINED DREAMS OF THE WICKED

17 "He shall not see the rivers, the floods, the brooks of honey and butter." (Job 20:17)

The figures we see in this verse suggest the coming kingdom, as typified by the promised land of Israel. Here are a few of many examples.

"*And I am come down to deliver them out of the hand of the Egyptians, and to bring them up out of that land unto a good land and a large, unto a land flowing with milk and honey; unto the place of the Canaanites, and the Hittites, and the Amorites, and the Perizzites, and the Hivites, and the Jebusites.*" (Exodus 3:8)

"*And I have said, I will bring you up out of the affliction of Egypt unto the land of the Canaanites, and the Hittites, and the Amorites, and the Perizzites, and the Hivites, and the Jebusites, unto a land flowing with milk and honey.*" (Exodus 3:17)

"*And it shall be when the LORD shall bring thee into the land of the Canaanites, and the Hittites, and the Amorites, and the Hivites, and the*

Jebusites, which he sware unto thy fathers to give thee, a land flowing with milk and honey, that thou shalt keep this service in this month." (Exodus 13:5)

"And they told him, and said, We came unto the land whither thou sentest us, and surely it floweth with milk and honey; and this is the fruit of it." (Numbers 13:27)

"He made him ride on the high places of the earth, that he might eat the increase of the fields; and he made him to suck honey out of the rock, and oil out of the flinty rock; Butter of kine, and milk of sheep, with fat of lambs, and rams of the breed of Bashan, and goats, with the fat of kidneys of wheat; and thou didst drink the pure blood of the grape." (Deuteronomy 32:13-14)

This is the land that God promised to His people, the Jews. It looks forward to the coming kingdom.

In our passage in Job, the prophetic view is the Antichrist *"the wicked"* will never see the fruition of his dream to establish a rival kingdom. As we have previously commented, man's great dream is to get back to the Garden of Eden without going God's way. Yet that dream will never come true.

Are you old enough to remember Woodstock—hippie heaven? Crosby, Stills, Nash and Young recorded a Joni Mitchell song entitled "Woodstock." The song tells of coming upon a child of God and asking him where he is going. Among other things, including joining a rock and roll band, the answer is "to try and get my soul free."

When Joni Mitchell sang the song, the last chorus went,

"We are stardust.
We are golden,
And we've got to get ourselves back to the garden."

Cosby, Stills, Nash and Young added a line:

"We are God in the Devil's body,
And we've got to get ourselves back to the garden."

We would do well to occasionally listen to what the world is singing. The world has been singing this chorus for the last several thousand years, yet most Christians have not figured it out.

All the hard work of the wicked will come tumbling down like a child's playhouse of building blocks. Again, we return to the theme of verses 10 and 15. He will lose what he has. God will cause him to vomit it out of his mouth. What he has hoarded will be used to make restitution to those from whom he has stolen.

Jeremiah saw the same vision. He addresses the earthly puppet that reigned in Babylon.

"Nebuchadrezzar the king of Babylon hath devoured me, he hath

crushed me, he hath made me an empty vessel, HE HATH SWALLOWED ME UP like a dragon, he hath filled his belly with my delicates, HE HATH CAST ME OUT." (Jeremiah 51:34) (Author's emphasis)

"And I will punish Bel in Babylon, and I WILL BRING FORTH OUT OF HIS MOUTH THAT WHICH HE HATH SWALLOWED UP: and the nations shall not flow together any more unto him: yea, the wall of Babylon shall fall." (Jeremiah 51:44) (Author's emphasis)

18 "That which he laboured for shall he restore, and shall not swallow it down: according to his substance shall the restitution be, and he shall not rejoice therein." (Job 20:18)

This was the point that God made with the king of Tyre through His prophet Isaiah. Any ungodly gain will be used to provide for those who love God.

"And her merchandise and her hire shall be holiness to the LORD: it shall not be treasured nor laid up; for her merchandise shall be for them that dwell before the LORD, to eat sufficiently, and for durable clothing." (Isaiah 23:18)

This is a tremendous truth of Scripture. Whatever the wicked lay up for themselves will one day become the possession of the children of God.

This is the prophetic symbolism of Israel coming out of Egypt loaded down with the spoil of the riches of the Egyptians, the just wages for the oppression they had suffered at the Egyptians' hands (Exodus 12:35-36). What man gains today by oppression and injustice is merely transferred to the balance column for God's people. So, go ahead, you sinners. Pile it up higher!

"They are inclosed in their own fat: with their mouth they speak proudly. They have now compassed us in our steps: they have set their eyes bowing down to the earth; Like as a lion that is greedy of his prey, and as it were a young lion lurking in secret places. Arise, O LORD, disappoint him, cast him down: deliver my soul from the wicked, which is thy sword: From men which are thy hand, O LORD, from men of the world, which have their portion in this life, and whose belly thou fillest with thy hid treasure: they are full of children, and leave the rest of their substance to their babes. As for me, I will behold thy face in righteousness: I shall be satisfied, when I awake, with thy likeness." (Psalm 17:10-15)

"For God giveth to a man that is good in his sight wisdom, and knowledge, and joy: but to the sinner he giveth travail, to gather and to heap up, that he may give to him that is good before God. This also is vanity and vexation of spirit." (Ecclesiastes 2:26)

"He that by usury and unjust gain increaseth his substance, he shall gather it for him that will pity the poor." (Proverbs 28:8)

"And the kingdom and dominion, and the greatness of the kingdom under the whole heaven, shall be given to the people of the saints of the most High, whose kingdom is an everlasting kingdom, and all dominions shall serve and obey him." (Daniel 7:27)

REAL MOTIVES OF THE WICKED REVEALED

19 "Because he hath oppressed and hath forsaken the poor; because he hath violently taken away an house which he builded not." (Job 20:19)

It is now clear that all the concern for the poor is a coverup for oppression, to steal that which he has not built. Remember this the next time you listen to a typical politician weeping for the poor, while his hand sneaks the billfold out of his neighbor's pocket. Yet politicians are not the only guilty parties. Our television screens and mailboxes are filled with expensive four-colored ads that picture the poor. These ads are manipulated by those who will use eight cents of every dollar you give to help the poor, and use the rest for "administrative purposes."

Please understand that this knowledge is not designed to give you the excuse not to provide genuine help for the poor as God gives you opportunity. First, here is a sampling of teaching from Proverbs to establish a legitimate responsibility to be sensitive to the poor.

"He that oppresseth the poor reproacheth his Maker: but he that honoureth him hath mercy on the poor." (Proverbs 14:31)

"Whoso stoppeth his ears at the cry of the poor, he also shall cry himself, but shall not be heard." (Proverbs 21:13)

"He that oppresseth the poor to increase his riches, and he that giveth to the rich, shall surely come to want." (Proverbs 22:16)

The New Testament also is clear on the believer's responsibility toward those less fortunate.

"As we have therefore opportunity, let us do good unto all men, especially unto them who are of the household of faith." (Galatians 6:10)

The key to the application of these verses is to see that our responsibility extends only as far as our God-given opportunity. Earlier we saw Jesus' words that we would always have the poor with us in this present world. Some things we cannot change. We must, though, change those things that we have opportunity to change. Our priority is first to the *"household of faith,"* then to *"all men,"* not merely to throw money to the poor.

REJECTION BY THE WICKED'S OWN

20 "Surely he shall not feel quietness in his belly, he shall not save of that which he desired.

21 There shall none of his meat be left; therefore shall no man look for his goods.

22 In the fulness of his sufficiency he shall be in straits: every hand of the wicked shall come upon him." (Job 20:20-22)

"Quietness in his belly"? Hardly! Just about the time he thinks he has reached *"the fullness of his sufficiency,"* his stomach is going to enter into convulsions like a tourist with a belly full of "third world water."

He will have nothing left. Even *"every hand of the wicked,"* for whom he has been a role model, will come upon him. Sinners who refuse to trust God cannot even trust each other.

RIGHTEOUS WRATH OF GOD UPON THE WICKED

23 "When he is about to fill his belly, God shall cast the fury of his wrath upon him, and shall rain it upon him while he is eating." (Job 20:23)

Instead of experiencing *"that which he desired,"* the Antichrist is going to experience the fury of God Almighty. This language is similar to Paul's in his letter to the Thessalonians. Just when the Antichrist and his wicked crowd think that they have brought in the promised kingdom of peace and prosperity, God makes His presence felt.

"For when they shall say, Peace and safety; then sudden destruction cometh upon them, as travail upon a woman with child; and they shall not escape." (1 Thessalonians 5:3)

Obviously, these same words are a solemn warning to any who is wicked and harbors wicked dreams in his heart. Those dreams will be destroyed with the terrible and glorious flash of God's Judgement.

24 "He shall flee from the iron weapon, and the bow of steel shall strike him through.

25 It is drawn, and cometh out of the body; yea, the glittering sword cometh out of his gall: terrors are upon him." (Job 20:24-25)

We broached this subject in our discussion of Job 16:12-13, where Job complained that he was a target for God's archers. Zophar agrees with that assessment, again falsely identifying Job with the Antichrist.

A bowman appears on a white horse in Revelation 6:2. He is often identified in commentaries and sermons as the conquering Christ. However, the context reveals that he is the Antichrist, and he is followed by war, famine, death and hell.

"And I saw, and behold a white horse: and he that sat on him had a bow; and a crown was given unto him: and he went forth conquering, and to conquer." (Revelation 6:2)

The real Christ makes His appearance in chapter 19. He is also riding a white horse and wielding weapons.

"And I saw heaven opened, and behold a WHITE HORSE; and he that sat upon him was called Faithful and True, and in righteousness he doth judge and make war. His eyes were as a flame of fire, and on his head were many crowns; and he had a name written, that no man knew, but he himself. And he was clothed with a vesture dipped in blood: and his name is called The Word of God. And the armies which were in heaven followed him upon white horses, clothed in fine linen, white and clean. And out of his mouth goeth A SHARP SWORD, that with it he should smite the nations: and he shall rule them with a ROD OF IRON: and he treadeth the winepress of the fierceness and wrath of Almighty God." (Revelation 19: 11-15) (Author's emphasis)

The *"iron weapon"* in Job 20:24 could be an allusion to the *"rod of iron"* of Revelation 19:15, or it could be the *"sharp sword"* itself. The *"bow of steel"* is also consistent with the picture of God we have in the Bible. If the Antichrist is a bowman, you can be certain that the Christ is a bowman. Here is one example of God's archery, as he warns Israel against spiritual rebellion.

"I will heap mischiefs upon them; I will spend mine arrows upon them." (Deuteronomy 32:23)

One thing is certain. When all is said and done, the Antichrist will be felled by God's *"glittering sword,"* piercing him through and spilling his *"gall"* upon the ground, just as Job had feared earlier.

"His archers compass me round about, he cleaveth my reins asunder, and doth not spare; he POURETH OUT MY GALL UPON THE GROUND." (Job 16:13) (Author's emphasis)

Job's fears will not be realized, but his sufferings give occasion to illustrate the fate of the Antichrist. Be forewarned that this fate belongs not only to the Antichrist, but to all who reject the truth of God's Word. They will all be pierced by the glittering sword of the Word of God.

26 "All darkness shall be hid in his secret places: a fire not blown shall consume him; it shall go ill with him that is left in his tabernacle." (Job 20:26)

"The wicked" is all darkness. There is no light in him. His *"secret places"* are full of it.

He is consumed by a fire that is definitely NOT made by man *("not blown")*. This being the case, what would be the source of this fire?

"I beheld till the thrones were cast down, and the Ancient of days did sit, whose garment was white as snow, and the hair of his head like the pure wool: HIS THRONE WAS LIKE THE FIERY FLAME, and his wheels AS BURNING FIRE. A FIERY STREAM issued and came forth from before him: thousand thousands ministered unto him, and ten thousand times ten thousand stood before him: the judgment was set, and the books were opened. I beheld then because of the voice of the great words which the horn spake: I beheld even till the beast was slain, and his BODY DESTROYED, and GIVEN TO THE BURNING FLAME." (Daniel 7:9-11) (Author's emphasis)

"For Tophet is ordained of old; yea, for the king it is prepared; he hath made it deep and large: the pile thereof is fire and much wood; THE BREATH OF THE LORD, LIKE A STREAM OF BRIMSTONE, DOTH KINDLE IT." (Isaiah 30:33) (Author's emphasis)

The last phrase of Job 20:26 should not be overlooked—*"it shall go ill with him that is left in his tabernacle."* This takes us back to Job 18:14-15.

"His confidence shall be rooted out of his tabernacle, and it shall bring him to the king of terrors. It shall dwell in his tabernacle, because it is none of his: brimstone shall be scattered upon his habitation." (Job 18: 14-15)

At the time we studied this passage, we learned that the body, or *"tabernacle,"* of the Antichrist will be possessed by the very Devil. Here, we see that the doom of the Devil is sealed also.

27 "The heaven shall reveal his iniquity; and the earth shall rise up against him." (Job 20:27)

It can honestly be said of *"that Wicked"* that heaven and earth will rise up against him. This verse capsulizes the central thought of the last few verses. Sin's cover is pulled back to reveal the reality of sin.

28 "The increase of his house shall depart, and his goods shall flow away in the day of his wrath.

29 This is the portion of a wicked man from God, and the heritage appointed unto him by God." (Job 20:28-29)

In Job 18:21 we saw the *"place of him that knoweth not God."* Here, we see his heritage, or his reward. His heritage is to be stripped naked of all he has worked to accumulate, and burn forever in the pitch-black flames of the eternal fire of God's wrath. This is his *"portion"* and his *"heritage."*

"Then shall he say also unto them on the left hand, Depart from me, ye cursed, into EVERLASTING FIRE, PREPARED FOR THE DEVIL AND HIS ANGELS." (Matthew 25:41) (Author's emphasis)

Would a loving God send sinful man to hell? This verse solemnly reminds us that hell was not prepared for man. Man goes to hell because he stubbornly refuses the grace of God. YOUR eternal destiny is at the mercy of your own free will.

Zophar's words are ended. He will have nothing more to say. When his turn comes up next time, he will pass.

He had come to counsel his friend. He has ended as the Devil's instrument to trap his friend in psychological warfare. Wanting to comfort Job, his words have actually pointed to the coming Antichrist—the personification of the Devil.

The good he wanted to accomplish has come to nothing. The only good realized through his words has been despite both himself and the devil, as God's Spirit has overruled evil intentions to inform believers of coming wickedness.

No matter what you do, God is going to get the glory. Will you be remembered for cooperating with God in that venture, or will you, like Zophar, be remembered for what God did despite your efforts to the contrary?

18

LESSONS FROM FRUSTRATION

Wherefore do the wicked live, become old,

yea, are mighty in power?

Job 21:7

BY LATE IN THE MORNING I WAS BEGINNING TO LOSE CONTROL. Everyone has these days, and today was my turn. Everything I touched crumbled into pieces. I had set out into the freshness of the new day before the sun came up, armed with a full agenda. Little did I know that I was going to be a hot item on the agenda of many others that day.

As I wrestled to juggle calls, interruptions, urgent conversations, and assorted details, my frustration level grew according to the unattended-to items on my list and the fleeting time. Interruptions and unexpected events are a part of life, and normally I calculate room for them in my day. This was one of those special times, though, when everything hit at once, and I was not coping very well.

I rushed out of the office, running late for an appointment. Before I could make it out of the parking lot, I was intercepted by a sweet little old lady who was certain I had time to hear the intimate account of the last several weeks of her life. It is not Christ-like to be rude to little old ladies, and so I found myself stuck, wheels spinning, engine overheating, and going nowhere.

Just when I thought all was lost, my secretary came to my rescue. A major part of her job description is to protect me from situations like this. With a skill that only God could have given her, she quickly sent this lady on her way, and did so in such a pleasant manner that the dear woman thought a great favor had been done to her.

Intuitively sensing the smoke that was beginning to leak from my ears, she sweetly smiled at me and said, "Do you know what this lady represents?"

I stared at her in horror, realizing that it was sermon time! Everything had happened so quickly I was speechless, which is a very uncomfortable position for a preacher.

"This dear lady is a measure of grace. God just wants to measure the level of grace in your life. That's all. And that's your thought for the day. What is the measure of grace in your life?"

All this was said with such natural spontaneity and high level of sugar, that I remained speechless. The man of God had just been rebuked. I was so focused on my personal agenda I had neglected to look for what God was doing in my life that day. I had failed to look for the lessons that frustration always offers.

No frustration in my life could ever measure up to the level of frustration Job was experiencing by this point in his conversation with his three friends. Despite the hopelessness he felt in his heart, there were many lessons God wanted to teach him. There are always blessings hidden behind every frustration, every problem, every affliction.

The lessons offered by these times are not only for our personal edification, but for others also. This was the lesson Paul had learned when he wrote his second letter to the Corinthians.

"Who comforteth us in all our tribulation, that we may be able to comfort them which are in any trouble, by the comfort wherewith we ourselves are comforted of God. For as the sufferings of Christ abound in us, so our consolation also aboundeth by Christ. And whether we be afflicted, it is for your consolation and salvation, which is effectual in the enduring of the same sufferings which we also suffer: or whether we be comforted, it is for your consolation and salvation." (2 Corinthians 1:4-6)

Job doubtless learned more lessons than he could list through this terrible time in his life. It is important for us to understand that Job's frustration is also for our consolation. We can learn from his frustrations, to avoid some of them in our lives.

This is the approach that we will follow in the study of this chapter. As we scrutinize Job's frustrated words, we will see how he confronts his counselors. We will consider a critical question that has relevance for any believer in any age. Also, we will see how his words point to the future judgment and conquest of the system of Antichrist by the Lord Jesus Christ.

CONFRONTED COUNSELORS

1 "But Job answered and said,
2 Hear diligently my speech, and let this be your consolations.
3 Suffer me that I may speak; and after that I have spoken, mock on." (Job 21:1-3)

Job's frustration is no more evident than in the first three verses. He calls upon them to pay attention to what he is about to say, adding, *"and let this be your consolations."* In other words, "Just listen to what I have to say, boys. I hope it makes you happy to torment me like this. But if you're having fun, go at it!"

Verse 3 is the height of sarcasm. "Just let me speak, then go right ahead and mock on, brothers!"

4 "As for me, is my complaint to man? and if it were so, why should not my spirit be troubled?" (Job 21:4)

In the fourth verse Job again defines what has been his position from the beginning. His problem is not with man, but with God.

Job's complaint is NOT to man. Job knows that his conscience is pure. He has done nothing to anyone to bring this tragedy upon himself. God brought all this upon him, yet Job has no idea why.

Even if his problem did have to do with man, he would still have reason to be *"troubled"* in his spirit. Never automatically equate a troubled spirit for sin. There is no question that a man's spirit may be troubled due to sin in his life. Yet there are times when God is dealing with a man and his spirit is troubled.

Ezekiel experienced this sensation. God was mightily dealing with Ezekiel, giving him a charge to deliver to His people. Here is the way Ezekiel himself described it.

"So the spirit lifted me up, and took me away, and I went in bitterness, in the heat of my spirit; but the hand of the LORD was strong upon me." (Ezekiel 3:14)

Job's friends wrongly assumed that his troubled spirit had to point to the presence of guilt. If God gives you the opportunity to minister His Word to others, never leap to this false conclusion. A troubled spirit can suggest many things, not necessarily guilt.

5 "Mark me, and be astonished, and lay your hand upon your mouth." (Job 21:5)

Job is rebuking his friends for having thought evil of him. What he says is a cultural practice as defined in Proverbs 30:32. Laying one's hand upon the mouth was a way to say, "Shame on me!"

"If thou hast done foolishly in lifting up thyself, or if thou hast thought evil, lay thine hand upon thy mouth." (Proverbs 30:32)

He is asking them to *"mark"* him as the object of God's dealings. Such a thing should astonish them and cause them to repent of the bad things they have assumed to be true about Job.

6 "Even when I remember I am afraid, and trembling taketh hold on my flesh." (Job 21:6)

Whatever Job's problems may be, he does not lack the fear of God in his life. Every time he pauses to reflect, he trembles. He has a vivid understanding of the judgment of the Flood. He knows that man cannot sin and escape the wrath of God.

The fear of God is a concept that has been greatly diluted in our day. We limit the fear of God to a mere reverence or respect. It is that, but it is also so much more. One can respect, and even revere presidents, kings and queens. The fear of God is in another category altogether.

The fear of God is not a cowering fear that causes one to slink in the corners. It is a healthy fear that causes one's flesh to tremble upon beholding and contemplating the power and majesty of God Almighty.

"For all those things hath mine hand made, and all those things have been, saith the LORD: but to this man will I look, even to him that is poor and of a contrite spirit, AND TREMBLETH AT MY WORD." (Isaiah 66:2) (Author's emphasis)

It is Job's fear of God that has empowered him to stand up to his counselors. He is grieved, but not intimidated. He hurts, but he has not lost control of his integrity.

There will be times when your life falls apart at the seams. Those who see you judge you, condemn you, mock you. They refuse to understand. No comfort comes from their lips. It is only your righteous fear of the Lord that sustains you in those moments. He is the One to whom you will answer some day. You owe no man a reason for anything. To God you owe everything.

CONCERNED QUESTIONS

7 "Wherefore do the wicked live, become old, yea, are mighty in power?

8 Their seed is established in their sight with them, and their offspring before their eyes.

9 Their houses are safe from fear, neither is the rod of God upon them.
10 Their bull gendereth, and faileth not; their cow calveth, and casteth not her calf.
11 They send forth their little ones like a flock, and their children dance.
12 They take the timbrel and harp, and rejoice at the sound of the organ.
13 They spend their days in wealth, and in a moment go down to the grave.
14 Therefore they say unto God, Depart from us; for we desire not the knowledge of thy ways.
15 What is the Almighty, that we should serve him? and what profit should we have, if we pray unto him?" (Job 21:7-15)

WHY DO THE WICKED PROSPER?

This section begins and ends with two of life's greatest questions. The first appears in verse 7, and is answered in verses 8 to 14. It is a question that men have asked for the entire span of human history. "Why do the wicked seem to prosper?" *"Wherefore do the wicked live, become old, yea, are mighty in power?"* (Job 21:7)

Here lies the key to understanding the verses to follow. Job has apparently been cut in the prime of his life. He has accepted his fate, though he does not understand it. From the first his position has been fixed in the words he spoke to his wife when she implored him to *"curse God and die"* (Job 2:9).

"But he said unto her, Thou speakest as one of the foolish women speaketh. What? shall we receive good at the hand of God, and shall we not receive evil? In all this did not Job sin with his lips." (Job 2:10)

As he sits in his misery, pondering his lot, there is a nagging doubt that continually plagues him. If he has been called upon to suffer this calamity, why is it that the wicked are often the ones who retain all the outward trappings of prosperity? Could this be fair?

A missionary has uprooted his family, taking them to a world that is an ocean away from home. Spending many months living like gypsies, he has traveled from church to church to raise the necessary support. Following the call of God he and his family have gladly made many sacrifices to establish the Gospel in a distant land. By the grace of God they struggle to make ends meet, resourcefully piecing together clothing, food and basic necessities. Health insurance was one of the first items to go, as the family sought to adjust their lifestyle to the budget available. Now, a child has a devastating illness. There is no insurance.

In the bright Miami sun, a figure in a stretch limousine barks orders on his cellular phone. The long drive to his palatial estate is lined with palm trees. Servants await his arrival, running to fulfill his slightest command. A new shipment of cocaine is arriving tonight by clandestine air drop in the everglades. Across the city an impoverished mother mourns the death of a son, killed in a drug deal gone sour. The man responsible soaks in bubbles in a marble tub, basking in the glory of more money and power than he could have imagined.

Where is justice? Where is right? Where is God? Why do the righteous suffer and the wicked prosper? The question is ancient. No one has put it more eloquently than the psalmist Asaph.

"Truly God is good to Israel, even to such as are of a clean heart. But as for me, my feet were almost gone; my steps had well nigh slipped. For I was envious at the foolish, when I saw the prosperity of the wicked. For there are no bands in their death: but their strength is firm. They are not in trouble as other men; neither are they plagued like other men. Therefore pride compasseth them about as a chain; violence covereth them as a garment. Their eyes stand out with fatness: they have more than heart could wish. They are corrupt, and speak wickedly concerning oppression: they speak loftily. They set their mouth against the heavens, and their tongue walketh through the earth. Therefore his people return hither: and waters of a full cup are wrung out to them. And they say, How doth God know? and is there knowledge in the most High? Behold, these are the ungodly, who prosper in the world; they increase in riches. Verily I have cleansed my heart in vain, and washed my hands in innocency. For all the day long have I been plagued, and chastened every morning. If I say, I will speak thus; behold, I should offend against the generation of thy children. When I thought to know this, it was too painful for me." (Psalm 73:1-16)

Asaph not only grappled with the problem, he also came up with the correct answer. To see the prosperity of the wicked is to see only half the picture. Asaph finally saw the other half. *"Until I went into the sanctuary of God; then understood I their end."* (Psalm 73:17)

The prosperity of the wicked is like the pleasures of sin—only transitory. The prosperity of the wicked can never last. A day of reckoning is ahead.

The situation that Asaph describes is remarkably similar to Job's complaint. Not only do the wicked sometimes prosper, they become lifted in pride. They want nothing to do with God. Job also understood this. *"Therefore they say unto God, Depart from us; for we desire not the knowl-*

edge of thy ways." (Job 21:14) Such arrogance as Job describes will be rewarded in due time.

So, why does God allow the wicked to prosper in this life? Like Job, we will never have all of the answers. One who has studied the Bible, though, can offer some educated guesses.

Remember that this sin-corrupted world is the domain of the Devil. Satan is the *"god of this world"* (2 Corinthians 4:4), and the *"prince of the power of the air"* (Ephesians 2:2). The wicked, and all those who do not know God, are the children of the Devil (John 8:44). Sometimes Satan will reward his children, not as a loving father, but to put a carrot on a stick to lead them further down the path of sin.

There are other reasons also. We learned in our study of Job 20:18 that the wicked are mounting up piles of riches to be given to the righteous. The present prosperity of the wicked is God's savings plan for the righteous.

There have been times when the prosperous wicked have been used as powerful testimonies of the grace and mercy of God. This was the case with Nebuchadnezzar, who was incredibly wicked and a type of the coming Antichrist. Daniel 4 gives the testimony of his conversion, showing that even an "impossibly" wicked man can be the recipient of God's grace.

"Now I Nebuchadnezzar praise and extol and honour the King of heaven, all whose works are truth, and his ways judgment: and those that walk in pride he is able to abase." (Daniel 4:37)

Revelation 18 prophesies the coming judgment upon Babylon. God will wait until their prosperity reaches a grand climax, then send them in a spiraling crash to the pit.

The believer looking at God's dealings with the wicked can see His longsuffering in allowing them such a free course in pursuing their sinful ways. In the day of judgment the testimony of God's love, mercy, longsuffering and righteousness will stand intact.

15 "What is the Almighty? that we should serve him? and what profit should we have, if we pray unto him?" (Job 21:15)

This is the second and final question of this section of Job's discourse. The first was "Why do the wicked prosper?" Now, this question gives evidence of the root cause of their problem.

Notice that they do not ask "WHO is the Almighty?" They ask *"WHAT is the Almighty?"* (Author's emphasis) To the wicked God is not a Person, but a thing, or a concept, an idea, a perception.

These are the same people who ask a similar question, recorded by Asaph.

"And they say, How doth God know? and is there knowledge in the most High?" (Psalm 73:11)

False prophets will always lead men to a thing, never to the Person of God. That "thing" may be an idol, a religion, an image, a movement, a concept, or even the person of some false teacher. They know nothing of a personal relationship with God.

Aaron led the children of Israel astray in the wilderness, while Moses was receiving the tables of law from Jehovah. Aaron led the people to "things," not to a closer personal relationship with the living God.

"And he received them at their hand, and fashioned it with a graving tool, after he had made it a molten calf: and they said, THESE be thy gods, O Israel, which brought thee up out of the land of Egypt." (Exodus 32:4) (Author's emphasis)

Why are you studying the Bible? Is it to learn more information about Christianity? Or, is it to know God better? Your motivation reveals your concept of God. Is God a thing? Or, is God a Person? Do you merely have a religion, or a relationship with a personal, living God?

The second half of the verse is a continuation of the same line of questioning. After having asked "What is the Almighty?" lost men want to know what is in it for them. "What profit should we have if we pray unto him?"

False prophets have found great profits in teaching people to worship a variety of "things." Lost man will worship anyone or anything if the price is right.

Don't fail to notice the context and intent of this question. In the next chapter this question will become a point of contention.

COMING JUDGMENT

DESTRUCTION—THE COMMON DOOM OF THE WICKED

16 "Lo, their good is not in their hand: the counsel of the wicked is far from me." (Job 21:16-34)

Job offers a disclaimer in verse 16. He points out that the wicked really don't follow their own best interest. They are short-sighted. *"Lo, their good is not in their hand."* (Job 21:16)

This is not the counsel that Job has followed. He has no part with them. This is his disclaimer. *"The counsel of the wicked is far from me."* (Job 21:16)

17 "How oft is the candle of the wicked put out! and how oft cometh their destruction upon them! God distributeth sorrows in his anger." (Job 21:17)

Earlier, in our study of Job 18:5-6 we learned the cultural significance of having one's candle put out. Those were Bildad's words, and now Job is agreeing with him. No doubt God will "punch out the lights" of the wicked, but Job in his disclaimer is saying that he is not one of them.

God is angry, and will soon be passing out sorrows to the wicked. Destruction is going to fall upon them.

18 "They are as stubble before the wind, and as chaff that the storm carrieth away." (Job 21:18)

The wicked make up the empire of Antichrist that will be destroyed by the Lord Jesus Christ in his return. This empire, depicted by the image that Nebuchadnezzar saw in his dream, is crushed to pieces by the Rock. The same image of stubble and chaff is used.

"Then was the iron, the clay, the brass, the silver, and the gold, broken to pieces together, and became like the chaff of the summer threshing-floors; and the wind carried them away, that no place was found for them: and the stone that smote the image became a great mountain, and filled the whole earth." (Daniel 2:35)

Job says that a storm is coming. What a storm it will be!

"And there fell upon men a great hail out of heaven, every stone about the weight of a talent: and men blasphemed God because of the plague of the hail; for the plague thereof was exceeding great." (Revelation 16:21)

19 "God layeth up his iniquity for his children: he rewardeth him, and he shall know it.

20 His eyes shall see his destruction, and he shall drink of the wrath of the Almighty." (Job 21:19-20)

Judgment day is coming. This is the theme of these verses.

"For the great day of his wrath is come; and who shall be able to stand?" (Revelation 6:17)

God has been laying up the iniquity of the wicked for generations. In a practical, consequential sense, sin is passed from generation to generation, the children suffering the consequences of their parents' sin. In a judicial sense, God lays up iniquity unto the coming day of judgment. Payday is coming.

Do you remember in the movies how the villain wants to draw out the death of the hero? He is concerned that the hero KNOW that he has lost. He wants to make the torture last as long as possible. Have you ever been so mad at someone you wanted to kill them, but kill them SLOWLY? Make them suffer!

If you understand what I'm saying, you will appreciate the fact that the wicked will definitely KNOW that they have drunk of God's wrath. They will see their destruction with their own eyes.

21 "For what pleasure hath he in his house after him, when the number of his months is cut off in the midst?" (Job 21:21)

The wicked, whether any wicked person in any generation or the Antichrist whom they picture, will never experience the joy of seeing his "*house*" established after him. No amount of "empire building" is sufficient to defeat the predetermined counsels of God.

His months are numbered by God, just as the months, days and years of any person are numbered on this earth. Yet Job's statement that the wicked will be "*cut off*" in the midst of his months is enigmatic if one is trying to set dates prophetically. In a purely historical sense, the idea is that the wicked dies before his time.

We know that there are no enigmas in God's mind, and that every problem has a solution. Often God is not ready to reveal certain things to His children. At other times we must work to compare Scripture with Scripture to discover truth that He has hidden from skeptics and nonbelievers.

We know that forty-two months of great tribulation are determined (Revelation 11:2). The Devil knows the facts of the Bible as well as anyone. Revelation 12 confirms that as the Devil unleashes his fury upon Israel, "*he knoweth that he hath but a short time.*"

Anyone can count forty-two months, yet Matthew says, "*But of that day and hour knoweth no man, no, not the angels of heaven, but my Father only.*" (Matthew 24:36) The reason is perhaps to be found in another statement Christ made in this discourse in Matthew.

"*And except those days should be shortened, there should no flesh be saved: but for the elect's sake those days shall be shortened.*" (Matthew 24:22)

This statement, in the context of Israel's elect during the Tribulation, suggests that those days will in some way be shortened, or "*cut off*" in the midst. Neither the Devil, nor anyone else, will figure out the exact length of God's timetable in the Tribulation.

Those who attempt to set dates and make precise charts of Tribulation events are often frustrated by passages such as Daniel, where things just "do not add up." The seven years remaining of the "*seventy weeks,*" or seven units of seven years (490), prophesied in Daniel 9:24-27 do not exactly match the 2,300 days of Daniel 8:14, which supposedly refer to the same period. Daniel 12 deals with the last half of the period, supposedly three and a half years, or "*a time, times, and an half,*" as specified in

Daniel 12:7. Yet Daniel 12:11 speaks of 1,290 days, while Daniel 12:12 mentions a period of 1,335 days.

So, how can we reconcile these apparently conflicting dates? Your guess is as good as mine! That, I believe, is precisely the point. No one, except God Himself, knows the exact timing of the events to come. Just when the Antichrist thinks he may have a chance, he will be *"cut off in the midst."* So will anyone who presumes to get ahead of God, beat His plan and win.

22 "Shall any teach God knowledge? seeing he judgeth those that are high." (Job 21:22)

Do YOU think you can teach God knowledge? This fits the prophetic context mentioned above. God alone knows. He *"judgeth those that are high."* Not only those human beings who are high in their pride are judged by God, but also those who are literally in high places.

"For we wrestle not against flesh and blood, but against principalities, against powers, against the rulers of the darkness of this world, against spiritual wickedness in HIGH PLACES." (Ephesians 6:12) (Author's emphasis)

The context clearly speaks of judgment. When God's judgment comes, it will be without respect of persons. This is the teaching of Job's next words.

DEATH—THE COMMON DENOMINATOR OF ALL

23 "One dieth in his full strength, being wholly at ease and quiet.

24 His breasts are full of milk, and his bones are moistened with marrow.

25 And another dieth in the bitterness of his soul, and never eateth with pleasure.

26 They shall lie down alike in the dust, and the worms shall cover them." (Job 21:23-26)

Death and judgment will come to all alike. Those in their prime, and those in the bitterness of their soul will meet their fate equally.

DEFECTIVE LOGIC—THE COMMON PROBLEM OF JOB'S COUNSELORS

In the following verses Job addresses his counselors directly. He says they have wrongfully judged him.

27 "Behold, I know your thoughts, and the devices which ye wrongfully imagine against me.

28 For ye say, Where is the house of the prince? and where are the dwelling places of the wicked?

29 Have ye not asked them that go by the way? and do ye not know their tokens." (Job 21:27-29)

His point in these words is that even if he were wicked, as they affirm, he could still be wealthy, have his family and his health. So what does it prove that he has lost it all? This has been his theme throughout this entire discourse. The wicked will without doubt be judged. From our present perspective it often seems that the wicked are prospering, yet we fail to consider God's coming judgment. Whether that judgment comes in the prime of prosperity or not, it will come, and without regard for persons.

Job asks his counselors, "Don't you understand? Haven't you talked with anyone on the street to know that there are plenty of wicked men and princes who are flourishing? If they are wicked and still have their power and wealth, what does it prove that I lost mine?"

30 "That the wicked is reserved to the day of destruction? they shall be brought forth to the day of wrath." (Job 21:30)

This verse is the climax of Job's argument. God is going to sort out everything in the *"day of destruction."* Only then will it be possible to determine true "cause and effect." We observe things that happen to people and leap to conclusions. Yet the factors of life are legion, and only God can properly know the reasons for the events that take place in our lives.

God is holding the wicked, and will hold "that Wicked" in reserve unto that *"day of wrath."* This is the scene described in Revelation.

"And I saw a great white throne, and him that sat on it, from whose face the earth and the heaven fled away; and there was found no place for them. And I saw the dead, small and great, stand before God; and the books were opened: and another book was opened, which is the book of life: and the dead were judged out of those things which were written in the books, according to their works. And the sea gave up the dead which were in it; and death and hell delivered up the dead which were in them: and they were judged every man according to their works. And death and hell were cast into the lake of fire. This is the second death." (Revelation 20:11-14)

31 "Who shall declare his way to his face? and who shall repay him what he hath done?" (Job 21:31)

Job is asking his friends if they will be the ones in charge in that day. "Are YOU going to declare to the wicked what he has done? Are YOU going to repay every man according to his works?"

32 "Yet shall he be brought to the grave, and shall remain in the tomb." (Job 21:32)

The doom of the wicked is inescapable. This was also Solomon's final conclusion in Ecclesiastes.

"For God shall bring every work into judgment, with every secret thing, whether it be good, or whether it be evil." (Ecclesiastes 12:14)

33 "The clods of the valley shall be sweet unto him, and every man shall draw after him, as there are innumerable before him." (Job 21:33)

One cannot get much lower than the clods of the valley, yet considering the doom of the wicked, even the clods of the valley will seem sweet.

Jesus said that the way to destruction is broad, and many are on that path (Matthew 7:13). Job knows that every man is drawn after the wicked. This is man's fallen nature, from which the grace of God is the only escape. Just as many are in that way now, there have been *"innumerable before him"* that were also in that way.

34 "How then comfort ye me in vain, seeing in your answers there remaineth falsehood?" (Job 21:34)

This is not the first time Job has bluntly told his counselors they were doing no good. In Job 16:2 he called them *"miserable comforters."*

When one's premise is wrong, his conclusion is necessarily wrong. This is Job's position, and he is right. His counselors, filled with right information, started with the false assumption that since Job has suffered such a tragedy, he must have sin in his life. That is a possibility, but not the only one. Their premise was incomplete. They had no business arriving at the conclusion that Job was in sin.

May this be a lesson for all of us who minister the Word of God. We must be very careful not to place ourselves in the seat of God. God alone will reveal the secrets of hearts in the day of judgment. We apply the Word of God when and where we can, carefully assuring ourselves that the premises for our thoughts are solid. Any conclusion must be subject to the Word of God, recognizing that our comprehension is always limited by our human condition.

19

WHEN COUNSELORS ENGAGE IN SLANDER

Acquaint now thyself with him, and be at peace:
thereby good shall come unto thee.
Receive, I pray thee, the law from his mouth,
and lay up his words in thine heart.

Job 22:21-22

A MAN WHO IS MAD ENOUGH, OR MOTIVATED ENOUGH, WILL lie. Job's counselors have increasingly lost control of their emotions in this discussion. Before, they have twisted words and circumstances to fit their opinions and arguments. Now, Eliphaz will state some things that are blatantly not true.

This is the third and final round of this exchange between Job and the three men who came with the intention of comforting and counseling him in his trial. Eliphaz, probably the eldest and most influential of the group, has led off each round. Ironically, he is the one who completely loses control of his emotions. He will say some things that are simply not true about his friend, Job.

He is undoubtedly a good man. Like all good men, he has feet of clay. He will be guilty of counseling without listening, and prophesying without understanding.

COUNSELING WITHOUT LISTENING

BOLD BLUSTER

In the middle of his rebuttal in chapter 21, Job had asked some pertinent questions. One was, *"what profit should we have, if we pray unto him?"* (Job 21:15b)

Eliphaz has been getting up a head of steam since then, and he opens with his own answer to the question. This is the intent of the first two verses.

1 "Then Eliphaz the Temanite answered and said,

2 Can a man be profitable unto God, as he that is wise may be profitable unto himself?" (Job 22:1-2)

In other words, Eliphaz is accusing Job of serving God for personal profit, although he does not mean that Job is profitable to God. He is putting Job in the same category with the wicked, saying that Job's piety is a cover-up for personal gain. Eliphaz is now hearing only what he wants to hear. He is, in effect, counseling without listening. This is a most dangerous position.

Later, Elihu, the young man listening to all this, is going to say the same thing. He will say it twice.

"For he hath said, It profiteth a man nothing that he should delight himself with God." (Job 34:9)

"If thou be righteous, what givest thou him? or what receiveth he of thine hand? Thy wickedness may hurt a man as thou art; and thy righteousness may profit the son of man." (Job 35:7-8)

This is a bitter pill for a man in Job's position to swallow. He has lived a *"perfect"* life before God, despite his personal prosperity. He has correctly separated that prosperity from his spiritual reality. Having lost it all, he has refused to curse God. He has maintained his spiritual integrity. Now, his best friends tell him to his face that he was only serving God for what he could personally gain.

Fortunately for Job, by this time the sharp, biting accusations of his counselors have had an anesthetic effect upon his soul and spirit. He is so numb he probably doesn't feel the full effect of these words.

3 "Is it any pleasure to the Almighty, that thou art righteous? or is it gain to him, that thou makest thy ways perfect?" (Job 22:3)

This is the continuation of the same thought. Eliphaz argues that God really doesn't have anything to gain by Job's pious facade. It sounds logical, doesn't it? What would Job's righteousness benefit God? Eliphaz is convinced that Job has fabricated a righteous front purely for selfish motives.

Have you noticed that this is precisely the same argument that Satan used in his dialogue with God that led to this entire episode? Satan was also convinced that if God would just withdraw the outward prosperity, Job would soon curse God. The Devil's entire case was constructed around the idea that Job was merely serving God for his own benefit. Who do you suppose has been putting ideas into Eliphaz's head?

There is one fact we must never forget—God mentioned Job's name first. God bragged on Job in the presence of the Devil. Obviously there is some intangible benefit God receives from man's worship. Man was created for God's glory, and in this sense Job has served His Maker well.

4 "Will he reprove thee for fear of thee? will he enter with thee into judgment?
5 Is not thy wickedness great? and thine iniquities infinite?" (Job 22:4-5)

Job has been on the ground for some time. Now, Eliphaz is kicking and stomping on him. There have probably been hyenas that have shown more compassion for a fallen impala than these three men have shown for their friend, Job.

Job has been calling for a meeting with God. Eliphaz is saying, "Why should He bother? Do you think He's afraid of YOU? Do you think God feels a need to settle some things with YOU?"

Eliphaz and Job both know that there is a day of judgment coming soon enough. Eliphaz simply points to Job's "*great*" wickedness and his "*infinite*" iniquities.

This is true. As compared to other men, Job would fare quite well. Yet God does not grade "on the curve," and Job's sin is as real as that of any one of us. We all must plead guilty before the Almighty, and shout an "Amen" to Paul's famous words to the Romans.

"For all have sinned, and come short of the glory of God." (Romans 3:23)

BALD-FACE LIES

6 "For thou hast taken a pledge from thy brother for nought, and stripped the naked of their clothing.
7 Thou hast not given water to the weary to drink, and thou hast withholden bread from the hungry.
8 But as for the mighty man, he had the earth; and the honourable man dwelt in it.

9 Thou hast sent widows away empty, and the arms of the fatherless have been broken." (Job 22:6-9)

Here is the slander. These accusations against Job are not true. There is not a shred of evidence to substantiate them.

In verse 6 Eliphaz accuses Job of making unnecessary demands upon his brethren, and of stripping clothing from the poor. Verse 7 is a condemnation for Job's failure to provide food and water for those in need. The widows and the fatherless were Job's victims, at least according to Eliphaz in verse 9. Verse 8 is a sarcastic remark meant to say that Job wanted things all to himself. He stepped on the poor and helpless to make his position more firm.

This is all contrary to Job's own testimony in his defense. Listen to his words from a later chapter.

"If I have withheld the poor from their desire, or have caused the eyes of the widow to fail; Or have eaten my morsel myself alone, and the fatherless hath not eaten thereof; (For from my youth he was brought up with me, as with a father, and I have guided her from my mother's womb;) If I have seen any perish for want of clothing, or any poor without covering; If his loins have not blessed me, and if he were not warmed with the fleece of my sheep; If I have lifted up my hand against the fatherless, when I saw my help in the gate: Then let mine arm fall from my shoulder blade, and mine arm be broken from the bone." (Job 31:16-22)

Whose testimony should we believe? As Bible-believers the only testimony we should accept is that which is consistent with God's Word. Paul tells us to *"Prove all things; hold fast that which is good."* (1 Thessalonians 5:21)

Our judgment is faulty; our heart is desperately wicked (Jeremiah 17:9). The only way we can obey this instruction is to measure all things by the only absolute standard of measurement that God has provided us—the Word of God.

If only we could learn this as counselors! When Solomon had to decide which of two women was lying about the child that each said was hers, he did the only thing a human being could do—he took out his sword to cut (1 Kings 3:16-28). The drawn, two-edged, sword quickly revealed the truth, just as the living, sharp two-edged sword of God's Word will reveal truth in every situation that confronts us today.

Let's take out that sword right now to see whose testimony we will accept—Eliphaz or Job. The real issue is what God has to say. Listen to the words of God.

"And the LORD said unto Satan, Hast thou considered my servant Job,

that there is none like him in the earth, a perfect and an upright man, one that feareth God, and escheweth evil?" (Job 1:8)

Case closed. Eliphaz is guilty of slander.

BLIND CONCLUSIONS

10 "Therefore snares are round about thee, and sudden fear troubleth thee;

11 Or darkness, that thou canst not see; and abundance of waters cover thee." (Job 22:10-11)

"Therefore," marks the conclusion toward which Eliphaz has been moving with his arguments. The specific sins that Eliphaz has listed are *"therefore"* the cause of the terrible things that have befallen Job. Yet as we have earlier observed, when the premise is wrong, the conclusion will be off by a mile.

Eliphaz is saying that sin has put Job "in the dark," so that he cannot see the reason for his trial. Job is placed under the abundant waters of God's judgment, as Eliphaz considers him in the same category as the sinners destroyed in the Flood. That the memory of the Flood is going through his mind at this time is evident from verse 16, invoking the memory of those *"whose foundation was overflown with a flood."*

This fine, moral, upstanding member of the community has arrived at a false conclusion based upon false information, and a mind that is unwilling to admit any evidence that may contradict his preconceived ideas. His rapid-fire, bitter accusations against Job reveal that he is a mere puppet of the one who is the *"accuser of our brethren,"* as we see in the following text.

"And the great dragon was cast out, that old serpent, called the Devil, and Satan, which deceiveth the whole world: he was cast out into the earth, and his angels were cast out with him. And I heard a loud voice saying in heaven, Now is come salvation, and strength, and the kingdom of our God, and the power of his Christ: for THE ACCUSER OF OUR BRETHREN is cast down, which accused them before our God day and night." (Revelation 12:9-10) (Author's emphasis)

Eliphaz now continues. It is extremely important that you do not lose sight of the context and the flow of his words. Having just concluded (falsely) that Job is under the judgment of the Almighty because of sin, he points to the transcendent majesty and holiness of God in heaven above.

BRILLIANT TRUTH WITHOUT APPLICATION

12 "Is not God in the height of heaven? and behold the height of the stars, how high they are!" (Job 22:12)

He most certainly is! This is a rhetorical question, not meant to be answered by Job, but used to substantiate the argument. No answer is necessary, since God Himself declares His location.

"For thus saith the high and lofty One THAT INHABITETH ETERNITY, whose name is Holy; I DWELL IN THE HIGH AND HOLY PLACE, with him also that is of a contrite and humble spirit, to revive the spirit of the humble, and to revive the heart of the contrite ones." (Isaiah 57:15) (Author's emphasis)

In the earlier round of arguments, Zophar alluded to the same awesome dimensions of the universe. You might want to review what we saw in Job 11:8-9. Paul remarked to the Ephesians (3:18) how important it is for the believer to grasp the enormity of the universe to keep ourselves in proper perspective in relationship to God.

13 And thou sayest, How doth God know? can he judge through the dark cloud?

14 Thick clouds are a covering to him, that he seeth not; and he walketh in the circuit of heaven." (Job 22:13-14)

Eliphaz is again assuming that Job is trying to cover up his sin, thinking that God is not aware of what he is doing. He adds the detail that the face of God is covered by clouds. Knowing that God has covered His presence with thick clouds, Eliphaz affirms that Job thinks he can get away with sin. He is accusing Job of having an idea of an inaccessible, out-of-touch God.

As anyone who has seen a thunderhead knows, thick clouds appear dark, since they block the sun's light. This is not the only time in the Book of Job the matter of clouds appears.

"He stretcheth out the north over the empty place, and hangeth the earth upon nothing. He bindeth up the waters in his thick clouds; and the cloud is not rent under them. He holdeth back the face of his throne, and spreadeth his cloud upon it. He hath compassed the waters with bounds, until the day and night come to an end." (Job 26:7-10)

Back in Job 9:6-8 we talked about the *"waters that be above the heavens"* (Psalm 148:4). There is evidently a vast amount of water somewhere in the universe. These waters are mentioned in Job 26 in the context of creation, and have been bound by God into *"clouds."* In Genesis 1:2, also dealing with creation, this reservoir of water is called *"the deep"* before the Atlantic and Pacific are created.

"And the earth was without form, and void; and darkness was upon the face of THE DEEP. And the Spirit of God moved upon the face of the waters." (Genesis 1:2) (Author's emphasis)

In the first chapter of Genesis these waters are divided. This is NOT the creation of the various oceans on planet earth. Notice that the *"firmament"* that divides the waters is called *"heaven."*

"And God said, Let there be a firmament in the midst of the waters, and let it divide the waters from the waters. And God made the firmament, and divided the waters which were under the firmament from the waters which were above the firmament: and it was so. And God called the firmament Heaven. And the evening and the morning were the second day." (Genesis 1:6-8)

Now, it is in the next verse that the oceans appear. Note carefully.

"And God said, Let the waters under the heaven be gathered together unto one place, and let the dry land appear: and it was so." (Genesis 1:9)

Though the land appears out of the waters that are under the firmament of heaven, we must still reckon with those waters remaining ABOVE the firmament of heaven. God Himself speaks of these waters, the *"deep"* of Genesis 1:2, saying that it's face is frozen.

"The waters are hid as with a stone, and the face of the deep is frozen." (Job 38:30)

Could this be the famous *"sea of glass like unto crystal"* that John saw in Revelation 4:6? We will talk more of this deep with the frozen face when we get to Job 38.

For the present, let us deal specifically with these clouds of water somewhere in the universe, covering the glory of God. Elihu will have something to say about them also in Job 36 and 37.

"Also CAN ANY UNDERSTAND THE SPREADINGS OF THE CLOUDS, or the noise of his tabernacle? Behold, he spreadeth his light upon it, and covereth the bottom of the sea. For by them judgeth he the people; he giveth meat in abundance. WITH CLOUDS HE COVERETH THE LIGHT; and commandeth it not to shine BY THE CLOUD that cometh betwixt." (Job 36:29-32) (Author's emphasis)

"Dost thou know when God disposed them, and caused the light of HIS CLOUD to shine? Dost thou know the balancings of THE CLOUDS the wondrous works of him which is perfect in knowledge? How thy garments are warm, when he quieteth the earth by the south wind? Hast thou with him spread out the sky, which is strong, and AS A MOLTEN LOOKING GLASS? Teach us what we shall say unto him; for we cannot order our speech by reason of darkness. Shall it be told him that I speak? if a man speak, surely he shall be swallowed up. And NOW MEN SEE NOT THE

BRIGHT LIGHT WHICH IS IN THE CLOUDS: but the wind passeth, and cleanseth them. Fair weather cometh out of the north: with God is terrible majesty." (Job 37:15-22) (Author's emphasis)

Speaking of creation, God has more to say later in the book of Job about the matter of clouds. He is in the midst of giving Job a lesson on creation when He makes the following comments.

"Where wast thou when I laid the foundations of the earth? declare, if thou hast understanding. Who hath laid the measures thereof, if thou knowest? or who hath stretched the line upon it? Whereupon are the foundations thereof fastened? or who laid the corner stone thereof; When the morning stars sang together, and all the sons of God shouted for joy? Or WHO SHUT UP THE SEA WITH DOORS, when it brake forth, as if it had issued out of the womb? When I MADE THE CLOUD THE GARMENT THEREOF, and THICK DARKNESS a swaddlingband for it, And brake up for it my decreed place, and set bars and doors, And said, Hitherto shalt thou come, but no further: and here shall THY PROUD WAVES be stayed?" (Job 38:4-11) (Author's emphasis)

On June 23, 1990 the *Economist* of London reported, "Astronomers seem to be missing something: to wit, most of the matter in the universe. Between 90 and 99% of it simply refuses to shine, and is thus invisible to them. They know it is there, but not what sort of stuff it is."

A couple of years later, in the October 19, 1992 issue, U.S. News and World Report ran a story with the headline, "Darkness made visible. Most of the matter in the universe is invisible. What is it, and where?" The story went on to say, "Astronomers have long been puzzled by what they see—and don't see—in the heavens. Based on calculations from the motion of galaxies, they reckon there must be at least 10 times more matter in the universe than what they can actually observe . . . 'I don't think we have a clue what it's made of,' says Anthony Tyson, an astrophysicist at AT&T Bell Laboratories in New Jersey. Yet, he says, 'we've now realized that dark matter dominates and drives the evolution of the universe.' "

TIME magazine ran an article on January 18, 1993 entitled "The Dark Side of the Cosmos." The subtitle read, "As astronomers struggle to illuminate the nature of dark matter, a new report hints that as much as 97% of the universe could be made of the mystery stuff."

The story also said, "When Charles Alcock peers up at the nighttime sky, he wonders not at the luminous stars but at the darkness that enfolds them. The Milky Way, Alcock knows, is like a sprinkling of bright sequins on an invisible cloak spread across the vastness of space. This cloak is woven out of mysterious stuff called dark matter because it emits no discernible light. A sort of shadow with substance, dark matter dominates the universe, accounting for more than 90% of its total mass."

Could it be that this mystery could, in part or in whole, be solved by taking into account what the Bible says about this enormous quantity of water that is called *"the deep,"* whose face is frozen, which shields the light of God's glory that emanates from His throne? Even Alcock's image of an "invisible cloak" matches that used by God in Job 38, and other places. Stay tuned for further developments! Science has been trying to catch up with the Bible for the last several thousand years, and still has a long way to go.

Before leaving this passage, there is another phrase that needs special attention. The last phrase of Job 22:14 says that God *"walketh in the circuit of heaven."* Just as he intended to do with his remarks about God covering Himself with clouds, Eliphaz means to say that Job imagines God to be so busy walking this *"circuit of heaven,"* that He won't bother to deal with Job's sin on earth.

A "circuit" is a way, a path. We speak of an electrical "circuit," referring to the path, or way that the electrical current follows. In the last century it was common to speak of a "circuit-riding preacher." He was one who served several churches, riding a "circuit," way, or route between churches.

Job 22:14 tells us that God has a *"circuit"* He travels in heaven. There is a way, a path, a route in heaven. The living Word walked with Adam in the Garden of Eden (Genesis 3:8). There was probably a "way" in which the Lord walked with man.

When the American frontier was opened, the enormity of the great West must have been overwhelming. It must have seemed that one could just set out walking or riding and travel forever. The vastness of the wide-open spaces must have been intimidating. Even then there were certain routes, ways or trails established. There were the Oregon Trail, the California Trail, the Santa Fe Trail and other such "circuits."

We know very little about the heavens, as evidenced by the magazine articles quoted above. The vastness of space is overwhelming. Job 22:14 is telling us about the circuit of God in heaven. Are there perhaps "circuits," or trails, in the heavens much like our trails on earth, or, in contemporary terms, like our system of interstate highways?

David also spoke of God's heavenly "circuit." In Psalm 19 David celebrates the glory of God as He has revealed Himself in His creation.

"The heavens declare the glory of God; and the firmament sheweth his handywork. Day unto day uttereth speech, and night unto night sheweth

knowledge. There is no speech nor language, where their voice is not heard." (Psalm 19:1-3)

The witness of God's creation is universal. It is understood in any language and culture. The Bible tells us that even the day and night speak, and show the knowledge of God.

"*Their line is gone out through all the earth, and their words to the end of the world. In them hath he set a tabernacle for the sun.*" (Psalm 19:4)

The "line" of day and night reaches around the world. In them—day and night—God has set a "tabernacle for the sun."

"*Which is as a bridegroom coming out of his chamber, and rejoiceth as a strong man to run a race.*" (Psalm 19:5)

Here, David compares the sun to a bridegroom. Malachi prophetically calls the coming Christ the "Sun of righteousness" in Malachi 4:2. Christ, the Sun of righteousness, is returning as a Bridegroom for His bride, the church. Still speaking of this bridegroom, who is also called a "strong man" running a race, David continues.

"*His going forth is from the end of the heaven, and HIS CIRCUIT unto the ends of it: and there is nothing hid from the heat thereof.*" (Psalm 19:6) (Author's emphasis)

Coincidence? I think not. It is amazing how many loose ends of the Bible are tied together by a simple faith that accepts the words of God as they appear. How interesting that David would explain this "circuit" of God the same as Eliphaz had done centuries earlier, and in a similar context.

How much do these men, Job and the others, know about the heavens? Dr. Henry Morris, who has established himself as an authority on the issue of biblical creationism, has written a book called *The Remarkable Record of Job*, in which he points out many amazing scientific facts that these men toss around as common knowledge, facts that have only recently become known to "modern" man.

An earlier work by Dr. Morris is the masterpiece, *The Genesis Flood*. Morris showed mathematically that it would not be unreasonable to imagine that the pre-Flood population of earth was comparable to what it is today. He also reminds us that the long lives of men, lives of up to 900 years or more, would make for an amazing possibility of learning and scientific research. Can you imagine what would happen if Leonardo da Vinci lived for 900 years? How about Einstein?

A scientist by the name of Emil Gaverluk wrote a fascinating book, published in 1974 by Thomas Nelson. Admittedly, it contains much speculation, but it is speculation stimulated by believing the record of the Bible, instead of looking at the Bible through the lens of science. The title of the book is, *Did Genesis Man Conquer Space?* His thoughts are challenging. They point, as does Morris, to the incredible scientific information contained in the Bible.

The purpose of this volume is not to teach science, or even to attempt to show the many instances of good science evidenced by the comments of these men. Dr. Morris' book is highly recommended for those interested in the scientific aspects of the Book of Job.

Nor is the purpose of this volume to speculate. Sometimes, though, it is impossible to resist the temptation to engage in a little sanctified speculation after reading the extraordinary statements flowing from the lips of these men. Because of the ignorance of our own society, we tend to think of anyone who lived very much before Christ as living in caves, scratching out primitive drawings on the walls with a chunk of charcoal. The truth is that man has been degenerating since Adam sinned. The downward spiral of human civilization is explicitly detailed by Paul in the first chapter of Romans.

At the present, we have simply seen that God has a circuit in heaven, a way that He travels. What that way is, where it is and what it is all about will remain a mystery for the moment. In our study of Job 22, carefully note the next verse. Some additional information is given about this *"circuit."*

15 "Hast thou marked the old way which wicked men have trodden?" (Job 22:15)

Eliphaz is asking if Job has noticed, or *"marked"* this *"old way,"* this *"circuit,"* which has been traveled not only by God, but by *"wicked men."* Look at the context! Go back and read it again. Notice the correspondence between God's *"circuit"* and this *"old way."* Who has been on this way? *"Wicked men."* What wicked men? Look at the next verse.

16 "Which were cut down out of time, whose foundation was overflown with a flood." (Job 22:16)

These *"wicked men"* are the same ones whose wickedness caused God's judgment by the Flood. There are some wicked men who have trodden (past tense) the same circuit that God travels in the heavens. They are here identified as those who were destroyed in the Flood.

In the second chapter of this book, we spent some time considering the events recorded in Genesis 6, where the *"sons of God,"* or angels, became intimately involved with the affairs of men. What knowledge might these angels have communicated to men, seeing they were familiar with what we might today call "space travel?" Could it be that the thesis that Gaverluk puts forth in his book, *Did Genesis Man Conquer Space?* have some validity?

Remember that these sons of God are part of the demonic hierarchy of the fallen cherub whose ambitions are recorded in Isaiah 14.

"How art thou fallen from heaven, O Lucifer, son of the morning! how art thou cut down to the ground, which didst weaken the nations! For thou hast said in thine heart, I will ascend into heaven, I will exalt my throne above the stars of God: I will sit also upon the mount of the congregation, in the sides of the north: I will ascend above the heights of the clouds; I will be like the most High." (Isaiah 14:12-14)

Lucifer wanted to ascend above *"the heights of the clouds."* Remember what we just saw concerning the *"clouds"* that cover the throne of God, and that Satan's ambition was to go *"into heaven."* He had set his sights on a throne that is occupied by Another.

Thwarted in his first attempt, as he led a rebellion of angelic beings, was Satan attempting in Genesis 6 to accomplish his ambition vicariously through men? Did Job and his friends know something about pre-Flood ambitions to aspire to the throne of God?

Not long after the Flood man again engages in an attempt to enter God's territory. Gaverluk proposes that the fabled tower of Babel was far more than hanging gardens. Would God have taken such drastic action as dividing men through languages because men simply wanted to make a high tower?

"And they said, Go to, let us build us a city and a tower, whose top may reach unto heaven; and let us make us a name, lest we be scattered abroad upon the face of the whole earth." (Genesis 11:4)

Or, more realistically, was there a residue of knowledge passed on from before the Flood that motivated men to the same sin as their ancestors, prompted by the same spiritual being who has never lost his desire to invade God's throne? Satan knows that *"circuit"* in heaven, as do the *"sons of God,"* since we find them arriving in God's presence in Job chapter one.

BRAZEN RESPONSES

There is much to speculate on in these verses, and one must take care to hedge his suppositions with humility. Regrettably, we have lost much of the information that apparently was commonly available in the days of Job.

Job 22:17-18 are responses to Job's prior statements. In the last chapter Job was pointing out that there are plenty of wicked people who still enjoy prosperity. His point was that loss of prosperity does not automatically imply sin.

"Therefore they say unto God, Depart from us; for we desire not the knowledge of thy ways. What is the Almighty, that we should serve him? and what profit should we have, if we pray unto him?" (Job 21:14-15)

To this Eliphaz replied, *"And thou sayest, How doth God know? can he judge through the dark cloud?"* (Job 22:13)

Now, Eliphaz repeats this thought, again taking Job's words out of context. He refers specifically to the wicked men overthrown in the Flood, but he carefully chooses his words to match Job's.

17 "Which said unto God, Depart from us: and what can the Almighty do for them?" (Job 22:17)

In the previous chapter, Job had offered a disclaimer to protect his own integrity.

"Lo, their good is not in their hand: the counsel of the wicked is far from me." (Job 21:16)

Eliphaz cannot let this comment go by without taking a swing. His next words are obvious sarcasm, as he mocks what Job had earlier said. This is evidently his motive in bringing up the matter of the judgment of the Flood.

18 "Yet he filled their houses with good things: but the counsel of the wicked is far from me." (Job 22:18)

Eliphaz is sarcastically saying, "Yes, Job! You bet that the wicked don't know what is good for them. God knows what is 'good' for them, and filled their houses with this 'good' to the depth of fifteen cubits above the top of the highest mountain. But then I wouldn't know either, for the counsel of the wicked is far from me." (Said with the corners of his mouth twisted.)

19 "The righteous see it, and are glad: and the innocent laugh them to scorn.

20 Whereas our substance is not cut down, but the remnant of them the fire consumeth." (Job 22:19-20)

Eliphaz is on target in saying that there is a day coming when the righteous and the innocent will "have the last laugh." This is reminiscent of prophecies in Psalms and Proverbs.

"He that sitteth in the heavens shall laugh: the Lord shall have them in derision." (Psalm 2:4)

"I also will laugh at your calamity; I will mock when your fear cometh." (Proverbs 1:26)

It is clear, however, that Eliphaz is looking to the future judgment. Earlier he referred to the judgment of the Flood. Now, he speaks of judgment by fire. As usual, Eliphaz has his facts straight, but his application to Job is far from the truth. His "counseling" is done without listening to reason.

PROPHESYING WITHOUT UNDERSTANDING

PIOUS PRESCRIPTION

21 "Acquaint now thyself with him, and be at peace: thereby good shall come unto thee." (Job 22:21)

The advice of Job 22:21 is sound. Basically, it is "Get to know God. He'll give you peace. Good things will happen to you."

It is hard to improve upon this counsel. It is consistent with the testimony of Scripture.

"Great peace have they which love thy law: and nothing shall offend them." (Psalm 119:165)

"Thou wilt keep him in perfect peace, whose mind is stayed on thee: because he trusteth in thee." (Isaiah 26:3)

Yet no matter how good the prescription, it is not much good if the diagnosis is faulty. Though Eliphaz means these words to apply to Job, they are very descriptive of how the remnant of Israel will return to God in the Tribulation. He is being used of God to prophesy, though he understands nothing of this application.

What Eliphaz says next is also perfectly good counsel, and in line with good biblical truth. It also looks forward to the day when the persecuted nation of Israel will follow this advice in a time of great Tribulation.

22 "Receive, I pray thee, the law from his mouth, and lay up his words in thine heart.

23 If thou return to the Almighty, thou shalt be built up, thou shalt put away iniquity far from thy tabernacles." (Job 22:-22-23)

You might summarize this advice as "receive and return." Eliphaz is telling Job that if he will just listen to the Word of God and return to Him, his life will do a turnaround. In the future, the nation of Israel will do just this. They will take God's Word to heart and return to Him. No prophet more than Isaiah saw this aspect of Israel's glorious future.

"The remnant shall return, even the remnant of Jacob, unto the mighty God. For though thy people Israel be as the sand of the sea, yet A REMNANT OF THEM SHALL RETURN: the consumption decreed shall overflow with righteousness." (Isaiah 10:21-22) (Author's emphasis)

"And the LORD shall smite Egypt: he shall smite and heal it: and THEY SHALL RETURN even to the LORD, and he shall be intreated of them, and shall heal them." (Isaiah 19:22) (Author's emphasis)

"And the ransomed of the LORD SHALL RETURN, and come to Zion with songs and everlasting joy upon their heads: they shall obtain joy and

gladness, and sorrow and sighing shall flee away." (Isaiah 35:10) (Author's emphasis)

"*Therefore the redeemed of the LORD SHALL RETURN, and come with singing unto Zion; and everlasting joy shall be upon their head: they shall obtain gladness and joy; and sorrow and mourning shall flee away.*" (Isaiah 51:11) (Author's emphasis)

What follows at the end of Job 22:23 is not hard to understand. These verses outline the blessings that come to those who receive God's Word and return to Him. While Eliphaz is piously thinking of Job's need to get his heart right with God, each blessing listed can be applied properly and prophetically to the remnant of Israel returning to God in the Tribulation.

We have already seen the first of these blessings when Eliphaz said, "*thou shalt be built up.*" (Job 22:23b) Ecclesiastes says that there is "*a time to break down, and a time to build up.*" (Ecclesiastes 3:3b) Having been broken down in the Tribulation, God's people will be built up in the coming kingdom.

The second blessing is also in verse 23. "*Thou shalt put away iniquity far from thy tabernacles.*" (Job 22:23c)

This time is also forecast several times in the Bible. Here is an example.

"*And they shall teach no more every man his neighbour, and every man his brother, saying, Know the LORD: for they shall all know me, from the least of them unto the greatest of them, saith the LORD: for I will forgive their iniquity, and I will remember their sin no more.*" (Jeremiah 31:34)

PRECIOUS PROMISES

24 "Then shalt thou lay up gold as dust, and the gold of Ophir as the stones of the brooks." (Job 22:24)

Job lost his wealth, and Eliphaz believes that all Job needs to do is repent and God will start piling up the gold into Job's account. Eliphaz was a man before his time. He would have been a great television evangelist today!

Seriously, even though prophesying without understanding, Eliphaz has listed another blessing to come upon the remnant of Israel. We saw in Job 20:18 how the prosperity of the wicked is laid up into the account of the righteous.

A further example is to see that the reign of Solomon is a great prophetic type of the coming millennial kingdom of Christ. Solomon's kingdom was characterized by an abundance of gold. The queen of Sheba was overwhelmed by the riches of Solomon, and she added to his prosperity.

"*And when the queen of Sheba heard of the fame of Solomon concerning the name of the LORD, she came to prove him with hard questions. And she came to Jerusalem with a very great train, with camels that bare spices, and very much gold, and precious stones: and when she was come to Solomon, she communed with him of all that was in her heart. And Solomon told her all her questions: there was not any thing hid from the king, which he told her not. And when the queen of Sheba had seen all Solomon's wisdom, and the house that he had built, And the meat of his table, and the sitting of his servants, and the attendance of his ministers, and their apparel, and his cupbearers, and his ascent by which he went up unto the house of the LORD; there was no more spirit in her. And she said to the king, It was a true report that I heard in mine own land of thy acts and of thy wisdom. Howbeit I believed not the words, until I came, and mine eyes had seen it: and, behold, the half was not told me: thy wisdom and prosperity exceedeth the fame which I heard. Happy are thy men, happy are these thy servants, which stand continually before thee, and that hear thy wisdom. Blessed be the LORD thy God, which delighted in thee, to set thee on the throne of Israel: because the LORD loved Israel for ever, therefore made he thee king, to do judgment and justice. And she gave the king an hundred and twenty talents of gold, and of spices very great store, and precious stones: there came no more such abundance of spices as these which the queen of Sheba gave to king Solomon."* (1 Kings 10:1-10)

Solomon had another source of gold, and it happens to be the same gold mentioned by Eliphaz—*"gold of Ophir."*

"And the navy also of Hiram, that brought GOLD FROM OPHIR, brought in from Ophir great plenty of almug trees, and precious stones." (1 Kings 10:11) (Author's emphasis)

The word *"Ophir"* is derived from "gold dust." Its identity as a geographical location is unknown. It was a distant place, as seen by Hiram's navies bringing it to Solomon. Visiting the *Museo de Oro*, or gold museum, in Lima Peru a few years ago, I was amazed to read a plaque that theorized that Ophir was none other than the famous Andean gold source, saying that Hiram's navies made regular trips to bring gold to Solomon. This is ONLY a theory. Whatever the case, remember that these words in Job were written over a thousand years before Solomon, and that they foreshadow future wealth of the nation of Israel in the coming kingdom of the Lord Jesus Christ.

25 "Yea, the Almighty shall be thy defence, and thou shalt have plenty of silver." (Job 22:25)

Two future blessings are foreseen in this verse, as Eliphaz continues to list the good things Job will receive if he will just repent and return to God.

God Himself will be the defense of Israel. No longer will they depend upon their military prowess and the latest in weapons technology. Beyond abundance of gold, they will have *"plenty of silver."*

Isaiah saw this future wealth of silver and gold for the returned remnant. *"Surely the isles shall wait for me, and the ships of Tarshish first, to bring thy sons from far, their silver and their gold with them, unto the name of the LORD thy God, and to the Holy One of Israel, because he hath glorified thee."* (Isaiah 60:9)

26 "For then shalt thou have thy delight in the Almighty, and shalt lift up thy face unto God." (Job 22:26)

The blessing here is that they will be restored to fellowship with their God. This, and other elements in this list, are found in Jeremiah.

"Behold, I will gather them out of all countries, whither I have driven them in mine anger, and in my fury, and in great wrath; and I will bring them again unto this place, and I will cause them to dwell safely: And they shall be my people, and I will be their God." (Jeremiah 32:37-38)

27 "Thou shalt make thy prayer unto him, and he shall hear thee, and thou shalt pay thy vows." (Job 22:27)

This renewed communion with God will result in a life of answered prayer and obedience. This is not unlike the promise that we enjoy as New Testament believers.

"And this is the confidence that we have in him, that, if we ask any thing according to his will, he heareth us: And if we know that he hear us, whatsoever we ask, we know that we have the petitions that we desired of him." (1 John 5:14-15)

28 "Thou shalt also decree a thing, and it shall be established unto thee: and the light shall shine upon thy ways." (Job 22:28)

There is coming a time when believers will live totally according to the will of God. This is the permanent reality of the promise we just saw in 1 John 5:14-15. When we are thinking God's thoughts because we have the mind of Christ. (1 Corinthians 2:16), we declare something so because it is *"according to his will"* (1 John 5:14b), and it is so. When we see in the Bible, for example, that God's will for believers is that the Spirit might control all our lives, we can confidently go to God with a pure heart and ask for His control, knowing that our request is established according to God's will.

There is coming a day when the remnant of Israel will *"walk in the light, as he is in the light"* (1 John 1:7a), just as believers in Christ can do today. The Old Testament prophets saw this day and spoke about it. Isaiah is eloquent as God's spokesman, inviting Israel to walk in this light.

"O house of Jacob, come ye, and let us walk in the light of the LORD." (Isaiah 2:5)

"Then shall thy light break forth as the morning, and thine health shall spring forth speedily: and thy righteousness shall go before thee; the glory of the LORD shall be thy reward. Then shalt thou call, and the LORD shall answer; thou shalt cry, and he shall say, Here I am. If thou take away from the midst of thee the yoke, the putting forth of the finger, and speaking vanity; And if thou draw out thy soul to the hungry, and satisfy the afflicted soul; then shall thy light rise in obscurity, and thy darkness be as the noonday." (Isaiah 58:8-10)

"Arise, shine; for thy light is come, and the glory of the LORD is risen upon thee. For, behold, the darkness shall cover the earth, and gross darkness the people: but the LORD shall arise upon thee, and his glory shall be seen upon thee. And the gentiles shall come to thy light, and kings to the brightness of thy rising." (Isaiah 60:1-3)

The Lord Jesus Christ, the Messiah of God's chosen people, will be the light in that day. Just as the written word is our light today (Psalm 119: 105), the living Word will be the light then.

29 "When men are cast down, then thou shalt say, There is lifting up; and he shall save the humble person." (Job 22:29).

In that coming day of restoration Israel will be God's minister. God's people will speak of His goodness and His *"lifting up."* Those who are burdened ("cast down"), will be "lifted up" by God's people speaking in the name of the Lord.

30 "He shall deliver the island of the innocent: and it is delivered by the pureness of thine hands." (Job 22:30)

In the context *"he"* is still "God." God will deliver the *"island"* of the innocent. A basic rule of Bible study is to take the Bible literally unless it is obvious that figurative language is being employed. Here, it is not a piece of land surrounded by water that is being delivered, but an innocent man who stands as an island of integrity amid the waters that, according to Revelation 17:15, represent the masses of humanity.

The instrument that God will use to do this is Job, in the plain sense of Eliphaz's words. In the prophetic application, Israel will be God's instrument, delivering those in need by the pureness of hands.

Man uses his hands to work. Pureness of hands speaks of the purity of one's works. The content of one's heart is expressed by the work of the hands. More than physically lifting one's hands in a praise service, this is Paul's thought to Timothy.

"I will therefore that men pray every where, lifting up holy hands, without wrath and doubting." (1 Timothy 2:8)

The lifting up of hands is symbolically the presentation of pure works, pure hands to God. We can also see this in Psalms.

"Let my prayer be set forth before thee as incense; and the lifting up of my hands as the evening sacrifice." (Psalm 141:2)

Here, the Psalmist compares the lifting up of hands to the evening sacrifice. This is the commitment of a man's works as a sacrifice to God.

Eliphaz, in challenging Job to get his heart right with God, is telling him the blessings that will result. Again, he sees Job being used as an instrument of God to provide deliverance to those who are an island of innocence in a sea of corruption. When Job's heart is right, his works and his hands will be pure.

Eliphaz is prophesying without understanding that his words also look forward to the day when this will be true of all Israel. Joel saw it.

"And it shall come to pass, that whosoever shall call on the name of the LORD shall be delivered: for in mount Zion and in Jerusalem shall be deliverance, as the LORD hath said, and in the remnant whom the LORD shall call." (Joel 2:32)

Paul took a phrase of this verse to give his clear definition of the means of salvation in Romans 10:9-10. This prophecy is partially fulfilled every time someone comes to Christ for salvation. It will be finally and completely fulfilled in the day that Israel returns to God and becomes His instrument for salvation to the nations of the world.

Eliphaz has said a mouthful in this chapter! God has used his words, although Eliphaz really doesn't grasp their full impact for future generations like us. The prophetic implications are many, and the subject matter Eliphaz so casually mentions is enough to fuel all manner of speculation in those of us who are so many centuries removed from the events of the Flood.

We have learned some principles for effective and biblical counseling. We have dreamed a little. We have seen an illustration of God's future design for Israel following the Tribulation. May we now avail ourselves of God's grace to learn to listen as we counsel those in need, and to correctly understand the biblical meaning of the words that roll off our lips.

20

DESPERATELY SEEKING GOD

But he knoweth the way that I take:

when he hath tried me, I shall come forth as gold.

My foot hath held his steps, his way have I kept,

and not declined.

Neither have I gone back from the commandment of his lips;

I have esteemed the words of his mouth

more than my necessary food.

Job 23:10-12

THE AGONY CONTINUES. WE HAVE HEARD IT ALL BEFORE. WHAT else could be added to the multitude of words? Is it a waste of our time to continue listening to this hopeless deadlock? Job's friends stubbornly insist that there are sins that Job needs to deal with in order to be restored to favor with God. Just as stubbornly, Job continues to refuse to confess sins that do not exist.

Before we conclude that there is nothing more to be gained from this exchange, we need to step back and take a long look at what is happening. Several times we have observed that Job's counselors are becoming more heated with each round of talks, as they lose more control of their emotions.

Job has meted out his share of verbal barbs, and will do so again. Yet, we can observe a solemn resignation forming in the depths of Job's soul. It is a resignation much like that experienced by a seriously injured accident victim, who lays on a table in a hospital emergency room. There is no concern for being naked in the presence of strangers, no more worry that each hair be perfectly in place, that clothes be impeccably draped from the shoulders. There is not much of Job's life left to protect, except his spiritual integrity. Everything else is gone. There is no longer a need to protect his pride, his position or his influence.

Job's position has been punctured; his pride has been pounded. Eliphaz, his friend, has just delivered the most scathing address yet. No biting, sarcastic words explode from Job's mouth in his own defense this time. He is so low he can only look up. Job can only seek desperately for God.

Isn't this the position where God wants Job? Could this be God's "hidden agenda," if there is one? God has not been displeased with Job. We are well-aware of the testimony God gave Satan about his "perfect" man. Was it totally heartless and cold for God to give Satan permission to attack Job? Or, could God have done so because He realized that such an attack would only serve to strengthen Job and deepen his faith?

We would do well to see that many of the trials in our lives have the purpose of forcing us to desperately search for the God of our faith. Is this not what happened to the disciples when they were caught up in a life-threatening storm at sea? They feared for their lives. When they looked for Jesus, he was sleeping below deck! This made it appear that Jesus did not care. *"Master, carest thou not that we perish?"* (Mark 4:38b) The Lord used the trial of the storm to cause His disciples to seek Him, when otherwise they may have taken Him for granted. In the end, they learned some new truth about Him.

"And they feared exceedingly, and said one to another, What manner of man is this, that even the wind and the sea obey him?" (Mark 4:41)

Job has been brought to the lowest point of his life. Nothing else matters now. Job is desperately seeking God.

SEEKING FOR GOD

1 "Then Job answered and said,
2 Even to day is my complaint bitter: my stroke is heavier than my groaning." (Job 23:1-2)

In the first two verses above, Job vents his anguish. Despite all his groanings, Job knows that there is no way to adequately express the bitterness of his soul. Whatever complaint, whatever bitterness that may come out of his mouth, Job says that his *"stroke is heavier."*

Here, the New Testament believer can find solace. There are also times in our lives when we simply cannot find the words to express the anguish of our hearts. Paul offers an amazing promise to the Christians at Rome.

"Likewise the Spirit also helpeth our infirmities: for we know not what we should pray for as we ought: but the Spirit itself maketh intercession for us with groanings which cannot be uttered." (Romans 8:26)

Job is desperate to talk with God, but he has no promise of the indwelling Holy Spirit of God as we do. He can only cry out in his misery.

3 "Oh that I knew where I might find him! that I might come even to his seat!" (Job 23:3)

At least Job is looking for HIM! In Job 21:15 he mentioned the wicked who say, *"What is the Almighty, that we should serve him?"* Job knows that God is a Person. He just doesn't know where to find Him.

God DOES have a seat. This is where Job wants to come, to God's seat. In the Bible a "seat" is a place of judgment. Today, we speak of believers appearing before the *"judgment seat of Christ"* (Romans 14:10).

4 "I would order my cause before him, and fill my mouth with arguments.

5 I would know the words which he would answer me, and understand what he would say unto me.

6 Will he plead against me with his great power? No; but he would put strength in me." (Job 23:4-6)

Job just wants to get on with it. He is anxious to hear what God would say to him. His boldness here is greater than it was earlier. In the ninth chapter, Job had nothing to say to God.

"How much less shall I answer him, and choose out my words to reason with him? Whom, though I were righteous, yet would I not answer, but I would make supplication to my judge." (Job 9:14-15)

There, in the ninth chapter, Job was speechless. Now, in Job 23, he has had time to think about it, and says that he knows what he would say, and even imagines that he knows what God would reply.

There is no conflict, or contradiction in these two passages. In Job 9:14-15, though Job had no idea what he would say to God, he was willing simply to throw himself on the mercy of the court. *"But I would make supplication to my judge."* Here, though he now has some words picked out, he is still confident that he would find mercy with God. He is convinced that God would not come against him with His great power, but rather God would strengthen him.

This is the answer of a good conscience, and it is also consistent with what we see elsewhere in the Bible. Daniel had a similar experience, having received divine revelation.

"For how can the servant of this my lord talk with this my lord? for as for me, straightway there remained no strength in me, neither is there breath left in me. Then there came again and touched me one like the appearance of a man, and he strengthened me, And said, O man greatly beloved, fear not: peace be unto thee, be strong, yea, be strong. And when he had spoken unto me, I was strengthened, and said, Let my lord speak; for thou hast strengthened me." (Daniel 10:17-19)

Job wants a chance to speak his mind, and a chance to let God strengthen him. His attitude is remarkable, considering what he has been through. He still knows that God loves him, that God is fair, and that God wants to make him strong.

7 "There the righteous might dispute with him; so should I be delivered for ever from my judge." (Job 23:7)

Here is another remarkable fact about our God. He DOES allow the righteous to dispute with Him. You can tell God anything with confidence. God is never afraid to field questions or complaints from the righteous. David knew this confidence. He was not afraid to dispute with God, and the Psalms contain many examples.

"How long wilt thou forget me, O LORD? for ever? how long wilt thou hide thy face from me? How long shall I take counsel in my soul, having sorrow in my heart daily? how long shall mine enemy be exalted over me?" (Psalm 13:1-2)

"For thou art the God of my strength: why dost thou cast me off? why go I mourning because of the oppression of the enemy?" (Psalm 43:2)

The righteous can dispute with God, but the only way to win is to agree with Him. In Job 9:14-15 Job wanted to plead his case, and put himself at the mercy of his *"judge."* Here, Job seeks deliverance from his "judge." The first passage appears to make God Job's judge. Here, the *"judge"* appears to be Job's accuser.

Again, there is no conflict. Satan is the attacker who has brought such woe to Job's life, and Job understands this.

"God hath delivered me to the ungodly, and turned me over into the hands of the wicked." (Job 16:11)

Yet God mentioned Job's name first to Satan! Satan is nothing more than an errand boy, doing God's work unwittingly. Ultimately, God is THE JUDGE. At times Satan and his underlings set themselves up as judges, yet it all works to fulfill God's master plan. Whatever the case, Job wants deliverance. All he knows to do is to cast himself at God's feet, plead for mercy, and trust in God's goodness. Rather than fight the Devil, make excuses or try to put up a false front, Job continues his desperate search for God.

Job has selected the right course of action. Not even Michael the archangel dared to take on the Devil.

"Yet Michael the archangel, when contending with the devil he disputed about the body of Moses, durst not bring against him a railing accusation, but said, The Lord rebuke thee." (Jude 9)

When YOUR life falls apart, and you have no idea what is happening, or why, don't take matters into your own hands. Have the faith and patience of Job. Trust in the fact that God is good, and that He loves you and wants to strengthen you. Let HIM deal with the Devil; you worry about your own life. If your heart is pure, know that when you DO hear from God, it will be to strengthen you, not to condemn you. Don't be afraid to "dispute" with God by pouring out your complaint before Him. Immerse yourself in the Word of God to learn God's truth. You will win by agreeing with God, by acknowledging who He is.

8 "Behold, I go forward, but he is not there; and backward, but I cannot perceive him:

9 On the left hand, where he doth work, but I cannot behold him: he hideth himself on the right hand, that I cannot see him." (Job 23:8-9)

Job has done nothing specifically to deserve the tragedy that has befallen him, and this sense of being cut off from God's presence. He is, however, a picture of Israel in the coming Tribulation. His desperate search for God prefigures the desperation of Israel to find God. Their isolation from the Almighty, though, is the result of their sin.

"Then my anger shall be kindled against them in that day, and I will forsake them, and I will hide my face from them, and they shall be devoured, and many evils and troubles shall befall them; so that they will say in that day, ARE NOT THESE EVILS COME UPON US, BECAUSE OUR GOD IS NOT AMONG US? AND I WILL SURELY HIDE MY FACE IN THAT DAY for all the evils which they shall have wrought, in that they are turned unto other gods." (Deuteronomy 31:17-18) (Author's emphasis)

SETTING FORTH FAITH

JOB'S CONFIDENCE IN HIS INTEGRITY

Job's attitude has led him to a rich vein of gold. He does not understand all that has happened. He would love to sit down with God and talk about it. Yet, there is one thing he does understand, and it is the most important thing of all.

10 "But he knoweth the way that I take: when he hath tried me, I shall come forth as gold." (Job 23:10)

This is all we mortal men need to know—that God is in control and knows our way. No matter what happens, all we must do is trust in Him and we will *"come forth as gold."*

This is God's will for Israel in the Tribulation. He is going to purge them so that they come forth as gold.

"And he shall sit as a refiner and purifier of silver: and he shall purify the sons of Levi, and purge them as gold and silver, that they may offer unto the LORD an offering in righteousness." (Malachi 3:3)

This is also God's will for the New Testament believer in every trial. Listen to Peter's teaching, who knew a thing or two about trials, as he reminds us that we are worth far more than literal gold.

"That the trial of your faith, being much more precious than of gold that perisheth, though it be tried with fire, might be found unto praise and honour and glory at the appearing of Jesus Christ." (1 Peter 1:7)

Later Peter added more truth about trials. Job would have cherished a book like I Peter to cling to in the moment of his trial. He may not have had the Bible in his hand, but it is obvious Job had the Word of God in his heart.

"Beloved, think it not strange concerning the fiery trial which is to try you, as though some strange thing happened unto you: But rejoice, inasmuch as ye are partakers of Christ's sufferings; that, when his glory shall be revealed, ye may be glad also with exceeding joy." (1 Peter 4:12-13)

This is what Job was coming to understand. This is what you and I must understand. Even in trials, God loves us and wants only our good. Trials are the Refiner's fire to purify the gold of our lives.

James 5:11 points out the *"patience of Job."* That same book, in James 1:2-4, tells us how it is that God develops that patience in our lives.

"My brethren, count it all joy when ye fall into divers temptations; Knowing this, that the trying of your faith worketh patience. But let patience have her perfect work, that ye may be perfect and entire, wanting nothing." (James 1:2-4)

There have been some brilliant flashes of faith and spiritual insight displayed by Job in this book. None other is deeper or more significant than his words in Job 23:10. Understanding this truth led him to the following testimony.

11 "My foot hath held his steps, his way have I kept, and not declined." (Job 23:11)

Job's body is broken, but he is still standing tall in a spiritual sense. He clings to his spiritual integrity. Job knows that he is not off course. *"My foot hath held his steps."*

The same testimony appears in the Psalms. The sons of Korah said the same thing in time of trial.

"Our heart is not turned back, neither have our steps declined from thy way." (Psalm 44:18)

There is tremendous spiritual power in such a testimony. It is the power of knowing that despite appearances and the circumstances, you know that you have not detoured from the course that God set for you. It was God's way that Job had kept, not his own. God decides the way of the believer, and He does so as we are in His Word.

"Order my steps in thy word: and let not any iniquity have dominion over me." (Psalm 119:133)

We set the direction of our heart, and God determines our steps. Consider the teaching of God's Word.

"A man's heart deviseth his way: but the LORD directeth his steps." (Proverbs 16:9)

"The steps of a good man are ordered by the LORD: and he delighteth in his way." (Psalm 37:23)

Job had an unshakable confidence in God. That unshakable confidence in God, fueled by his unassailable integrity, led to Job's inalterable walk, and his belief in the blessing that would ultimately come from his trial. His remarkable testimony continues.

12 "Neither have I gone back from the commandment of his lips; I have esteemed the words of his mouth more than my necessary food." (Job 23:12)

Job expresses his commitment to obey the Word of God. His view of God's words is that they were more important than food. This is not gourmet food of which he is speaking; this is his *"necessary food."*

We all have a list of things we "just can't live without." What could possibly be more important than food? You can go without it for a time, but you cannot live without it. Job says that God's words mean more to him than the food that is necessary for his survival. Can YOU honestly say that the Word of God means that much to you? Job did not have a physical Bible like you do, yet he still valued God's Word above all else. How much MORE should you and I, who have the completed Bible, value God's Word?

Jesus voluntarily went without physical food for forty days in the wilderness (Matthew 4:1-11). When weak, He was tempted by a Bible-quoting Devil. Though deprived of his "necessary food," His response was to carefully aim specific verses of the Bible right back at the Devil. The Devil left.

JOB'S COMMITMENT TO GOD'S SOVEREIGNTY

13 "But he is in one mind, and who can turn him? and what his soul desireth, even that he doeth.

14 For he performeth the thing that is appointed for me: and many such things are with him." (Job 23:13-14)

If we were asked to label these verses with the name of a biblical doctrine, we would choose the "sovereignty of God." When Job says that *"he is in one mind,"* he means that God is His own counsel. God has no need to look elsewhere to know what to think. God is self-sufficient in His thinking. Besides that, there is no one who can *"turn Him,"* or change His mind.

Paul knew this truth. He mentions it to the Roman Christians as he explains to them God's plan for Israel. God has a plan for Israel, for the gentiles, for everyone. No one is going to change that plan.

"Thou wilt say then unto me, Why doth he yet find fault? For who hath resisted his will? Nay but, O man, who art thou that repliest against God? Shall the thing formed say to him that formed it, Why hast thou made me thus? Hath not the potter power over the clay, of the same lump to make one vessel unto honour, and another unto dishonour?" (Romans 9:19-21)

Job's point in speaking of the sovereignty of God is to lay bare his own helplessness. His suffering is not necessarily because of specific sin. God does what He wants to do, and no one can stop Him. He has a plan for man, a plan that Job says *"is appointed for me."*

Job's grief cannot be denied, but his strength to hold up under such incredible pressure is this basic faith in God's sovereignty. He knows that God is there, and that God is good. He knows that God has a master plan, and that it is futile to try to change Him. Job does not understand what is happening to him, and would love to talk to God about it. Yet he is resigned to "wait it out," knowing that God is going to do what He is going to do.

When YOUR life is falling apart, remember this—God is sovereign. Don't panic; don't try to change His mind. You are part of a master plan, and the less you fight it, the easier it will be. He loves you.

Does this conflict with Job's attitude in the next verse? Is Job really "resting" in God's sovereignty?

JOB'S CONSOLATION IN HIS TRIALS

15 "Therefore am I troubled at his presence: when I consider, I am afraid of him." (Job 23:15)

Thinking over these things makes Job fear God. As we have commented before, this is a healthy, biblical fear of God, not the desperate terror of a cornered animal. It is the awe-filled, wide-eyed fear of God who is the Boss, the Master, the Lord, the King.

Philippians is a book of abundant, overflowing joy. Yet it is also a book that speaks of the fear of God. There is no conflict between rejoicing in God's great love and provision, and living in the fear of the Lord.

"Wherefore, my beloved, as ye have always obeyed, not as in my presence only, but now much more in my absence, work out your own salvation with fear and trembling." (Philippians 2:12)

This is not an admonition to work FOR salvation, but to work OUT salvation. Because of what God has done IN our lives, we need to let that work OUTWARD through our lives and the lives of others. We do this "with fear and trembling." Could this be a conflict with what we read in 1 John 4:18?

"There is no fear in love; but perfect love casteth out fear: because fear hath torment. He that feareth is not made perfect in love." (1 John 4:18)

In 1 John the context is the security of our salvation in the day of judgment. In Philippians the context is our service to God BECAUSE OF our salvation. The issue is in knowing when, what and Whom to fear.

16 "For God maketh my heart soft, and the Almighty troubleth me:

17 Because I was not cut off before the darkness, neither hath he covered the darkness from my face." (Job 23:16-17)

Here are a pair of paradoxes. The first, in verse 16, is that God both made Job's heart soft, and troubled him. There is no contradiction. God did not let Job's heart get bitter, since Job had maintained a good heart attitude toward God and His Word. Yet God loved Job enough to allow him to be troubled for a time to make him stronger.

We need to learn the same lesson. If we will keep our heart attitude right toward Him, He will keep our heart from growing cold, hard and bitter. We should not be surprised, though, when He allows us to be troubled. It is part of His master plan, and He, in His sovereignty, is working to make us stronger.

"Beloved, think it not strange concerning the fiery trial which is to try you, as though some strange thing happened unto you: But rejoice, inasmuch as ye are partakers of Christ's sufferings; that, when his glory shall be revealed, ye may be glad also with exceeding joy." (1 Peter 4:12-13)

The second paradox is in verse 17. God did not allow Job to be "cut off" before the darkness. Job's troubles did not "finish him off," in other words. Yet God did not hide Job from the darkness, or keep it from him. YOU can rest in this truth, and no one is better qualified to tell you about it than Job.

SEEING FORWARD THROUGH THE AGES

The apocalyptic language of chapter 24 is an indicator that this section is another look at a future time, and is using Job's experience as a picture. Job, of course, is undergoing some very apocalyptic experiences. Beyond the historical framework of Job's story, the language is so severe that we must understand this chapter to be a general description of the ultimate fate of the wicked. It is also a futuristic glimpse of the coming Tribulation in particular.

THE WAY OF THE WICKED

1 "Why, seeing times are not hidden from the Almighty, do they that know him not see his days?" (Job 24:1)

The *"times"* that Job mentions in Job 24:1 are the times of judgment in the context of his remarks. The Almighty knows the times of judgment. This being the case, why do those *"that know him not"* continue to go on living, and seeing days?

To answer this question Job is going to set the stage by characterizing the wicked. Then, he will put them in proper perspective by showing that they are part of a larger picture, and by pointing to their sure end.

Job is doing this because his friends have wrongly accused him of being part of the ranks of the wicked. His aim is to show that temporal problems in this life are not a sure indicator of wickedness, any more than the temporal prosperity of the wicked is an indicator of blessing.

2 "Some remove the landmarks; they violently take away flocks, and feed thereof." (Job 24:2)

A great cultural sin in Job's day was to remove the landmarks of another person's property. In a fenceless society, landmarks were a foundation of life. The wicked would remove landmarks with the goal of stealing livestock. The severity of this sin is underscored by being mentioned twice in the Book of Proverbs.

"Remove not the ancient landmark, which thy fathers have set." (Proverbs 22:28)

"Remove not the old landmark; and enter not into the fields of the fatherless." (Proverbs 23:10)

The 1990's have seen the collapse of world communism. This should not prevent the believer from seeing the confiscation of personal property in the future. Such tactics have characterized dictatorial regimes for centuries. There is no reason to suppose that the coming kingdom of Antichrist will be any different.

Already we can see the removal of ancient landmarks in a symbolic sense. We can see this in history, where it is impossible to have a complete understanding of any period, without first understanding what is happening with the nation of Israel. Most history texts, however, make only passing reference to the Jews, if they are mentioned at all. Yet God intends Israel to be a landmark of history. Even texts on church history tend to forget that God is not finished with His people.

Another form of removing landmarks is the abandonment of the absolute standard of God's Word in favor of either experience or scholarship. Yet God tells us in Job that removing ancient landmarks is a characteristic of the wicked.

3 "They drive away the ass of the fatherless, they take the widow's ox for a pledge.
4 They turn the needy out of the way: the poor of the earth hide themselves together.
5 Behold, as wild asses in the desert, go they forth to their work; rising betimes for a prey: the wilderness yieldeth food for them and for their children.
6 They reap every one his corn in the field: and they gather the vintage of the wicked.
7 They cause the naked to lodge without clothing, that they have no covering in the cold." (Job 24:3-7)

These verses speak of the wicked's heartless oppression of the poor. The wicked have always made their fortunes at the expense of those who are poor.

In Egypt, Pharaoh destroyed Israel's economy. He used their bondage and made it impossible for them to make any economic progress. Pharaoh is a biblical picture of a coming pharaoh (Antichrist) who will be worse than anyone could imagine. The Antichrist will feed upon the poor. Those who refuse his mark will not be allowed to buy or sell (Revelation 13:16-17). He will reduce the world to economic slavery.

People who are the oppressed in such a system go about their work *"as wild asses"* (Job 24:5). Remember that we learned in Job 11:12 that the lost man is portrayed in biblical symbolism as a wild ass.

8 "They are wet with the showers of the mountains, and embrace the rock for want of a shelter." (Job 24:8)

The pronoun *"they"* undergoes a shift in this verse. It is important that the Bible student continually survey the context of the passage to pick up on these subtle and continual changes, especially in portions like this speech of Job's. In the previous verses *"they"* were the wicked. Now, *"they"* are those who are oppressed. The context of any passage in the Bible is the key to understanding it. The serious Bible student must pay close attention to the flow of thought and what is being said.

Looking to the future, we can see it being described in Revelation 6. The scene is of massive panic and terror, when oppressor and oppressed alike stand in terror of God's wrath.

"And the kings of the earth, and the great men, and the rich men, and the chief captains, and the mighty men, and every bondman, and every free man, hid themselves in the dens and in the rocks of the mountains; And said to the mountains and rocks, Fall on us, and hide us from the face of him that sitteth on the throne, and from the wrath of the Lamb: For the great day of his wrath is come; and who shall be able to stand?" (Revelation 6:15-17)

Job's words also remind us of past events. Consider, for example, this passage from Hebrews.

"And others had trial of cruel mockings and scourgings, yea, moreover of bonds and imprisonment: They were stoned, they were sawn asunder, were tempted, were slain with the sword: they wandered about in sheepskins and goatskins; being destitute, afflicted, tormented; (Of whom the world was not worthy:) they wandered in deserts, and in mountains, and in dens and caves of the earth." (Hebrews 11:36-38)

History reminds us just how much things never change concerning the nature of lost man. The wickedness of the ages is on a perilous downhill slide, with the promise that it will all culminate in the coming kingdom of Antichrist.

9 "They pluck the fatherless from the breast, and take a pledge of the poor.
10 They cause him to go naked without clothing, and they take away the sheaf from the hungry;
11 Which make oil within their walls, and tread their winepresses, and suffer thirst.
12 Men groan from out of the city, and the soul of the wounded crieth out: yet God layeth not folly to them." (Job 24:9-12)

As Job describes the ways of the wicked, we can prophetically see more of the barbaric deeds that will take place in the Tribulation.

Job 24:9 describes the breakup of the family, and the plight of the poor, enslaved by debt. The poor will be without even life's most basic necessities, according to verse 10, and the poor will have the fruit of his labor taken right out of his hand.

The reference to oil and wine in verse 11 reminds us that the empire of Antichrist will hoard both commodities. They will both be in short supply.

"And I heard a voice in the midst of the four beasts say, A measure of wheat for a penny, and three measures of barley for a penny; and see thou hurt not the oil and the wine." (Revelation 6:6)

The agony and groaning of verse 12 will be experienced globally in the Tribulation. God knows exactly the cause of this misery, and whom to blame and whom not to blame. Many gentiles paid with their lives, or suffered incredibly, for their deeds of kindness to Jews in Europe during the Second World War. In Christ's second coming, He will judge the nations according to their treatment of the Jews. He will know how His witnesses have been treated. The Second World War was a foreshadowing of things to come in this regard.

The words of Christ that follow describe similar heroism in the coming Tribulation, as many risk their lives to protect and provide for God's faithful remnant.

"For I was an hungered, and ye gave me meat: I was thirsty, and ye gave me drink: I was a stranger, and ye took me in: Naked, and ye clothed me: I was sick, and ye visited me: I was in prison, and ye came unto me. Then shall the righteous answer him, saying, Lord, when saw we thee an hungered, and fed thee? or thirsty, and gave thee drink? When saw we thee a stranger, and took thee in? or naked, and clothed thee? Or when saw we thee sick, or in prison, and came unto thee? And the King shall answer and say unto them, Verily I say unto you, Inasmuch as ye have done it unto one of the least of these my brethren, ye have done it unto me. Then shall he say also unto them on the left hand, Depart from me, ye cursed, into everlasting fire, prepared for the devil and his angels: For I was an hungered, and ye gave me no meat: I was thirsty, and ye gave me no drink: I was a stranger, and ye took me not in: naked, and ye clothed me not: sick, and in prison, and ye visited me not. Then shall they also answer him, saying, Lord, when saw we thee an hungered, or athirst, or a stranger, or naked, or sick, or in prison, and did not minister unto thee? Then shall he answer them, saying, Verily I say unto you, Inasmuch as ye did it not to one of the least of these, ye did it not to me. And these shall go away into everlasting punishment: but the righteous into life eternal." (Matthew 25:35-46)

13 "They are of those that rebel against the light; they know not the ways thereof, nor abide in the paths thereof." (Job 24:13)

In this verse *"they"* have switched again. Now, *"they"* are the wicked. Job leaves no doubt about their identity. Their rebellion is *"against the light."* This is a light that has *"ways"* and *"paths."* This light is a Person.

"Then spake Jesus again unto them, saying, I am the light of the world: he that followeth me shall not walk in darkness, but shall have the light of life." (John 8:12)

14 "The murderer rising with the light killeth the poor and needy, and in the night is as a thief.

15 The eye also of the adulterer waiteth for the twilight, saying, No eye shall see me: and disguiseth his face." (Job 24:14-15)

We know who their father is. Jesus told us.

"Ye are of your father the devil, and the lusts of your father ye will do. He was a murderer from the beginning, and abode not in the truth, because there is no truth in him. When he speaketh a lie, he speaketh of his own: for he is a liar, and the father of it." (John 8:44)

Three sins are listed: murder, theft and adultery. Could you think of three other sins to better characterize city life in the modern world?

Also seen in this passage is how darkness has always been a cover for sin. Jesus said, *"and men loved darkness rather than light, because their deeds were evil."* (John 3:19)

16 "In the dark they dig through houses, which they had marked for themselves in the daytime: they know not the light.

17 For the morning is to them even as the shadow of death: if one know them, they are in the terrors of the shadow of death." (Job 24:16-17)

Why would someone scope out the house of another person, mark it, then return that night to rob it? The answer is simple, and given in this passage. "They know not the light."

For wicked people, the *"morning"* is like the *"shadow of death."* This *"morning"* points to the morning of Malachi 4:2, when the Lord Jesus Christ, the "Sun of righteousness," returns to put an end to the dark night of the Tribulation. Yet that morning will be like the *"shadow of death"* to the wicked. We have seen this *"shadow of death"* before. What the dawn of a new day is for some, the nightfall of judgment is for others.

THE KING OF THE WICKED

18 "He is swift as the waters; their portion is cursed in the earth: he beholdeth not the way of the vineyards." (Job 24:18)

It is very easy to become confused by Job's pronouns. Now, Job throws in the *"he"* of Job 24:18, mixing it with *"their"* portion in the same verse. Reading forward a few verses leads us to conclude that the best explanation is that Job speaks of the wicked in a singular, or generic sense, while he uses "*they*" to mean the wicked masses of humanity. Prophetically, the "*he*" is fulfilled in the person of Antichrist.

The references fit. The Antichrist is certainly "*swift as the waters.*" His rise to world power will be meteoric. Before anyone has a chance to see it coming, a global empire will be established.

The only consolation is to understand that the Antichrist will not be around to see the way of his vineyards, or the fruit of his master plan. This has been mentioned before in Job—how the wicked will not see the completion of his goal. Here are a couple of examples from Job 20.

"*Yet he shall perish for ever like his own dung: they which have seen him shall say, Where is he?*" (Job 20:7)

"*The increase of his house shall depart, and his goods shall flow away in the day of his wrath.*" (Job 20:28)

19 "Drought and heat consume the snow waters: so doth the grave those which have sinned.

20 The womb shall forget him; the worm shall feed sweetly on him; he shall be no more remembered; and wickedness shall be broken as a tree." (Job 24:19-20)

The fate of the wicked is "*the grave.*" There will be no need to remember the wicked, because they, and "*he,*" will be forgotten. The one who threw the entire world into terror will be nothing more than worm food!

Watch out for the worms! We last commented on worms in Job 17:14, and will have more to say about worms in the very next chapter, in remarks on Job 25:6.

Comparing the wicked to a tree is in keeping with another figure we have seen before. Daniel 4 and Ezekiel 31 both speak of the Antichrist through the figure of a tree. David uses the same image.

"*I have seen the wicked in great power, and spreading himself like a green bay tree.*" (Psalm 37:35)

21 "He evil entreateth the barren that beareth not: and doeth not good to the widow." (Job 24:21)

Another of the great themes of Scripture appears in this verse. The barren woman is a figure that is repeated throughout the Bible. There are seven barren women prominently positioned in the Bible, who miraculously give birth by the grace of God. They are Sarah, Rebekah, Rachel, Hannah, Manoah's wife, who gave birth to Samson, the Shunammite in Elisha's day, and Elisabeth, mother of John the Baptist. All are poignant reminders of a miraculous birth that was to come—the virgin birth of the Messiah.

These literal women, who gave birth miraculously, point to Israel symbolically as well as to Mary literally. Israel was barren. Several times Israel is said to be Jehovah's wife. The third chapter of Jeremiah is one example. Yet, Israel bore God no fruit. In Isaiah we find this wonderful prophecy.

"Sing, O barren, thou that didst not bear; break forth into singing, and cry aloud, thou that didst not travail with child: for more are the children of the desolate than the children of the married wife, saith the LORD." (Isaiah 54:1)

In Galatians 4:27 Paul quotes this verse from Isaiah as support for an allegory he drew, contrasting law and grace. When it appeared that Israel was hopelessly barren, the nation gave birth to the Messiah. Though rejected by His own, the Messiah opened the way to the "heavenly Jerusalem" for all who believe.

Job's point in Job 24:21 is to give another characteristic of the wicked, in showing his evil treatment of barren women and widows. These two classes are singled out several places in the Bible to receive the special interest and protection of God.

22 "He draweth also the mighty with his power: he riseth up, and no man is sure of life." (Job 24:22)

The literal application of these words has been played out by wicked men throughout human history. What we loosely call "civilization" is one continuous power struggle among *"the mighty."* Wicked men, motivated by their sin nature, resort to any means to gain control over other men. The mighty fight it out while the masses suffer. *"No man is sure of life"* is one of the truest phrases ever uttered.

It does not matter when you are reading these words. I can confidently say that at this moment most people on earth live in uncertainty and fear, pawns in the power struggle to see who is the mightiest. This is the story of human life on earth since sin.

All of this will one day culminate when the Antichrist draws the mighty to him with his power. He will draw the mighty into his conspiracy against the Almighty. There will be no certainty in that day. Men will fear for their lives. The earth will be plunged into total chaos.

23 "Though it be given him to be in safety, whereon he resteth; yet his eyes are upon their ways." (Job 24:23)

The Antichrist will appear to succeed in assembling his empire, drawing the mighty into it, as he seeks to fulfill the wish of his father (John 8:44) by being "like the most High" (Isaiah 14:14). God will grant him *"to be in safety."* Peace and prosperity will characterize the first three and a half years of his reign, and he will rest upon the false security of that safety.

It is a false security, because *"his"* (God's) eyes are continually upon the ways of the wicked. No one will get by with sin.

"The eyes of the LORD are in every place, beholding the evil and the good." (Proverbs 15:3)

Just when the wicked are resting in their safety, their final doom will arrive. Paul prophecies this time.

"For yourselves know perfectly that the day of the Lord so cometh as a thief in the night. For when they shall say, Peace and safety; then sudden destruction cometh upon them, as travail upon a woman with child; and they shall not escape." (1 Thessalonians 5:2-3)

THE END OF THE WICKED

24 "They are exalted for a little while, but are gone and brought low; they are taken out of the way as all other, and cut off as the tops of the ears of corn.

25 And if it be not so now, who will make me a liar, and make my speech nothing worth?" (Job 24:24-25)

This needs little explanation. Job is answering the question he began this chapter with—"Why does God allow the wicked to continue in their lives and prosperity?" Job worded it this way:

"Why, seeing times are not hidden from the Almighty, do they that know him not see his days?" (Job 24:1)

The answer is to see that their rest or safety is only temporary. It cannot last. *"They are exalted for a little while."* (Job 24:24a) There is coming a day when the wicked will be "brought low," "taken out of the way," "cut off."

Job is confident in his conclusion. He challenges his friends to deny the truth of what he has spoken. He knows they cannot because the truth is obvious, whether they admit it or not.

This tendency to judge things and people according to external manifestations is a part of our human nature. When we have "things" we suppose that God is blessing us. When we do not have the "things" we think we should, we assume that we have done something wrong. We judge ourselves, and others, by this set of external criteria. Our measure is wrong.

We must learn to measure things and people by the absolute measure of the Word of God. This is the only eternal, secure and absolute measure we have. Despite how things look to us, we are to judge by the Word. We are all guilty of judging others by appearances, and we are all guilty of judging ourselves by the same standards. May we learn from Job by faith, so that we can avoid learning by experience, like Job did.

21

FINAL SERVE AND VOLLEY

He stretcheth out the north over the empty place,

and hangeth the earth upon nothing.

He bindeth up the waters in his thick clouds;

and the cloud is not rent under them.

He holdeth back the face of his throne,

and spreadeth his cloud upon it.

He hath compassed the waters with bounds,

until the day and night come to an end.

Job 26:7-10

LITTLE REMAINS TO BE SAID. BOTH JOB AND HIS COUNSELORS stubbornly refuse to budge from the position each side has taken. The three friends are convinced that Job has some hidden sin that has caused his calamity. Job knows that is not so.

Eliphaz opened the third round in the twenty-second chapter. Job's rebuttal appears in chapters 23 and 24. Now, it is Bildad's turn.

One of the most effective forms used to conclude a speech is to offer a reflective question. During the body of the speech the major thrust of the message has been established. To motivate the audience to action, the speaker leaves a final question with them that is designed to make them think seriously about what has been said. This is the technique Bildad uses.

He opens his final remarks by stating an indisputable truth, followed by a leading question, which leads to a series of questions that form his conclusion.

Job's response in Job 26 will be to ask some questions of his own. Six of the most probing questions ever asked form the opening words of Job's rebuttal. Those questions will then be followed by a truly remarkable cosmological discourse, one that has proven to be several thousand years ahead of "modern" science. But let's not jump ahead.

FACT AND QUESTION

1 "Then answered Bildad the Shuhite, and said,
2 Dominion and fear are with him, he maketh peace in his high places.
3 Is there any number of his armies? and upon whom doth not his light arise?" (Job 25:1-3)

Bildad opens with a pair of facts that will not be disputed by anyone. Dominion and fear belong to God. This speaks of God's sovereignty, and is seen throughout the Bible. Nowhere is this truth more clearly expressed than in Daniel's prophecy.

"Nebuchadnezzar the king, unto all people, nations, and languages, that dwell in all the earth; Peace be multiplied unto you. I thought it good to shew the signs and wonders that the high God hath wrought toward me. How great are his signs! and how mighty are his wonders! his kingdom is an everlasting kingdom, and his dominion is from generation to generation." (Daniel 4:1-3)

Nebuchadnezzar was the most powerful man in the world. He was arrogant and subject to no one. The fourth chapter of Daniel is the story of this man, who was brought to his knees by Almighty God. Nebuchadnezzar learned to fear God, and learned that dominion belongs to God alone. After living a beast-like existence for seven years, prophetically picturing the Antichrist, Nebuchadnezzar gave this testimony.

"And at the end of the days I Nebuchadnezzar lifted up mine eyes unto heaven, and mine understanding returned unto me, and I blessed the most High, and I praised and honoured him that liveth for ever, whose dominion is an everlasting dominion, and his kingdom is from generation to generation: And all the inhabitants of the earth are reputed as nothing: and he doeth according to his will in the army of heaven, and among the inhabitants of the earth: and none can stay his hand, or say unto him, What doest thou?" (Daniel 4:34-35)

The second part of Bildad's opening statement is to say that God makes peace in *"high places."* Whether you see those *"high places"* as positions of authority on earth, or the *"high places"* in the universe, the truth is the same—God makes peace.

The Apostle Paul wrote to the Ephesians about spiritual warfare in *"high places,"* where we do battle against principalities, powers and rulers (Ephesians 6:12). It was in high places that a ferocious battle broke out before man was created. Lucifer, the anointed cherub (Ezekiel 28:11-19), sought to invade the very throne room of God (Isaiah 14:12-19). God ended that rebellion.

There is still sin in the universe that must be dealt with in a final way. We learned in Job 15:15 that *"the heavens are not clean in his sight."* We will see this same truth here in Job 25:5.

Revelation 12:1-10 speaks of another rebellion in high places that is to occur during the Tribulation. God will again make peace, ushering in His millennial kingdom.

In a spiritual sense, God made the ultimate peace in high places, when He sent His only-begotten Son to die in our place. The atoning death of Christ makes it possible for lost man to have peace with God.

"Therefore being justified by faith, we have peace with God through our Lord Jesus Christ." (Romans 5:1)

Who could argue with Bildad's facts? No one would be so foolish as to deny the sovereignty of God.

These opening remarks set the stage for Bildad's first question. It is a rhetorical question, one that is not designed to provoke an audible answer. It is a question whose answer is obvious. Based on the fact of God's sovereignty, Bildad asks a two-part question in the next verse.

3 "Is there any number of his armies? and upon whom doth not his light arise?" (Job 25:3)

His armies, the heavenly host, are without number. Can you count them? Of course not!

This is the meaning of God's name, the "Lord of hosts." This is the "Lord of sabaoth" of James 5:4. When the "Lord of hosts" appears in the Old Testament, it is the translation of "Jehovah-sabaoth."

Again, the answer to Bildad's question is not in dispute.

"A fiery stream issued and came forth from before him: thousand thousands ministered unto him, and ten thousand times ten thousand stood before him: the judgment was set, and the books were opened." (Daniel 7:10)

The innumerable heavenly host includes more than angelic beings. Add to that the company of saints who will return with Him to rule.

"As the host of heaven cannot be numbered, neither the sand of the sea measured: so will I multiply the seed of David my servant, and the Levites that minister unto me." (Jeremiah 33:22)

Just as no one answers the first part of Bildad's question, no one steps forward to answer the second part either. Is there someone upon whom God's light does not shine? Of course not!

Physically, this truth is outlined in Psalm 19. The whole earth is illuminated by His light, crossing all barriers of geography, language and culture.

"The heavens declare the glory of God; and the firmament sheweth his handywork. Day unto day uttereth speech, and night unto night sheweth

knowledge. There is no speech nor language, where their voice is not heard. Their line is gone out through all the earth, and their words to the end of the world. In them hath he set a tabernacle for the sun, Which is as a bridegroom coming out of his chamber, and rejoiceth as a strong man to run a race. His going forth is from the end of the heaven, and his circuit unto the ends of it: and there is nothing hid from the heat thereof." (Psalm 19:1-6)

The physical light from God's sun is a mere picture of the spiritual light that similarly illuminates every man that comes into the world. This is the message found in the opening verses of John's Gospel, speaking of the Lord Jesus Christ.

"That was the true Light, which lighteth every man that cometh into the world." (John 1:9)

To this point, no one would dare argue with the validity of Bildad's reasoning. God is sovereign. His armies are innumerable, and His light has shined on all.

QUESTIONS AND CONCLUSION

4 "How then can man be justified with God? or how can he be clean that is born of a woman?" (Job 25:4)

This question is not answered in full until God uses Paul to set forth the doctrine of justification. A man can only be justified with God because God was just and justified man when He dealt with sin in the Person of His Son Jesus Christ. The climax of this argument can be seen in the third chapter of Romans.

"To declare, I say, at this time his righteousness: that he might be just, and the justifier of him which believeth in Jesus." (Romans 3:26)

The second part of Bildad's question was answered by our Lord Jesus Christ, as He explained the new birth to Nicodemus in the third chapter of John. The only way for a man born of woman to be clean is to be born again.

Of course, Bildad's purpose in asking the question is not to get an answer. His intention is to show that Job cannot possibly be justified before God.

5 "Behold even to the moon, and it shineth not; yea, the stars are not pure in his sight." (Job 25:5)

The first part of verse 5 is an accurate scientific statement. The moon does NOT shine. It reflects the light that shines forth from the sun.

Even allowing for the scientific aspect of Bildad's comment, there is far more implied. Bildad knows that there is something desperately wrong in the universe. This is evidenced in the final part of the verse, when he mentions that not even the stars are pure in the sight of God.

Space, which is the second heaven, is the domain of Satan and his hordes. The sin-stained creation of the universe is still awaiting the final purifying made possible by the sacrifice of Christ on the cross. Eliphaz mentioned earlier the impurity of space.

"Behold, he putteth no trust in his saints; yea, the heavens are not clean in his sight." (Job 15:15)

All this is a foretaste of darkness yet to come, a darkness that has been prophesied for centuries. The prophet Joel represents this as well as anyone, as he looks forward through the centuries to the coming Tribulation. Perhaps it will be by divine decree, or perhaps God will use a cloud of radioactive dust obscuring the light of sun and moon, but that day will certainly be a day of darkness. It will be a time when the moon shines not.

"The earth shall quake before them; the heavens shall tremble: the sun and the moon shall be dark, and the stars shall withdraw their shining." (Joel 2:10)

We have commented before about the many parallels between the Exodus and the Tribulation. This is another aspect of the Tribulation that is prophesied by the events of the Exodus.

"And Moses stretched forth his hand toward heaven; and there was a thick darkness in all the land of Egypt three days." (Exodus 10:22)

By his sweeping reference to the impurity of the heavens, Bildad means to show how foolish it is for Job to think that he, a mere man, could be pure in God's sight.

6 "How much less man, that is a worm? and the son of man, which is a worm?" (Job 25:6)

Bildad's point is obvious. Man is nothing more than a worm. The word "worm" is used in the colloquial sense to speak of man's sperm, which appears to have a worm-like appearance. What could be lower than that?

In remarks on Job 17:14, we saw how the reference to the worm has a prophetic meaning when viewed in the light of Psalm 22 that gives us the thoughts of Christ on the cross.

"But I AM A WORM, and no man; a reproach of men, and despised of the people." (Psalm 22:6) (Author's emphasis)

We also ran into worms in Job 24:20. More than the worm-like sperm that gives life, the "worm" also appears to have a definite connection with the final state of lost man. Jesus said He was reduced to a worm on the cross. Consider the following references that have to do with judgment. Jesus spoke of the destination of condemned man.

"Where their worm dieth not, and the fire is not quenched." (Mark 9:46)

Isaiah saw the same thing. He saw man's final state as a worm, looking forward to the time of judgment.

"And they shall go forth, and look upon the carcases of the men that have transgressed against me: for their worm shall not die, neither shall their fire be quenched; and they shall be an abhorring unto all flesh." (Isaiah 66:24)

Modern science offers the wisdom that man has merely evolved from the lowest forms of life. Science teaches that from a worm-like life form, man is the crowning achievement thus far in the evolutionary process. How ironic it is that the Bible sees a worm-like state as lost man's final condition!

Bildad's speech has been brief. There is no way he can properly answer what Job has said. He can only hold to his position that Job cannot be right with God. Nothing more can be added. Zophar does not even try. This is the end of the remarks by the three counselors. They came to counsel and to comfort, but they each crashed and burned. They utterly failed in their attempts to help Job, and instead they became the unwitting instruments of the Devil's psychological warfare.

Job will offer one final rebuttal to his friends. His remarks comprise Job 26 to 31. We will begin by examining what he has to say in chapter 26.

QUESTIONS AND COSMOLOGY

Bildad has used a rhetorical question as the central technique in his closing arguments. Job now offers his rebuttal, and serves up a few questions of his own. Far from being rhetorical, Job's questions are probing in nature, cutting deep into the heart.

Job displays great technique as a debater, and as a man of God. So many debates about "religion" or "spiritual matters" degenerate into an exchange of trite answers, Bible facts and "proof texts." Nothing is ever settled.

How many man hours have been wasted by sincere believers tossing Bible verses back and forth with Mormons and Jehovah's Witnesses? You have your proof texts; I have mine. You attack with this verse; I counter with mine. You make your point; I make mine. Again, there are no winners in this type of exchange. No one ever wins arguments about religion.

Much of what we have seen in the preceding chapters has been on this level. Both sides have resolutely held their ground, offering up standard theological textbook positions to prove their arguments. As we have often observed, the spiritual truth offered up is not disputed by either side.

Now, however, Job, who has been stuck face-down in the dust, suddenly takes up eagle's wings and soars to the heights. He rises far above the sphere of intellectual arguments that have been the realm of his counselors.

Job earlier offered his own position, and was right, but facts do not persuade religious fanatics. This is why nothing has been accomplished.

Job's sudden rise is due to the series of questions that flow from his mouth. Bildad's questions were rhetorical, designed to prove a point. Job's questions are designed to probe the heart. THIS is the route to take in any argument with religious fanatics or misguided counselors. Get out of the realm of Bible trivia and get into the heart!

Job asks a series of six questions that are so penetrating that a religious phony would not dare to answer any of them. Zophar has another turn coming, but after these questions there is no way he is going to open his mouth. These six questions stop the mouths of any religious fake.

These six questions are so piercing that they would stop any serious person dead in his tracks. Bob Alexander, who serves with me at the Baptist Temple as co-pastor, has a powerful message he preaches on this passage. He approaches this text asking what would be our response if the Lord Jesus Christ asked these same six questions of us at the Judgment Seat of Christ.

JUDGMENT SEAT QUESTIONS

1 "But Job answered and said,
2 How hast thou helped him that is without power? how savest thou the arm that hath no strength?
3 How hast thou counselled him that hath no wisdom? and how hast thou plentifully declared the thing as it is?
4 To whom hast thou uttered words? and whose spirit came from thee?" (Job 26:1-4)

These four verses are said to be part of a parable. We learn this by looking carefully at Job 27:1. Then, we see that this parable continues even through chapter 29.

"Moreover Job continued his parable, and said." (Job 27:1)

"Moreover Job continued his parable, and said." (Job 29:1)

A parable is called a "dark saying" in the Psalms. Two references give us this detail.

"I will incline mine ear to a PARABLE: I will open my DARK SAYING upon the harp." (Psalm 49:4) (Author's emphasis)

"I will open my mouth in a PARABLE: I will utter DARK SAYINGS of old." (Psalm 78:2) (Author's emphasis)

This is reminiscent of our Lord's remarks about the purpose of parables in Matthew 13. When questioned by His disciples about why He suddenly began to speak in parables, He told them that it was to hide His truth from unbelievers and reveal it to those who were spiritually discerning.

"And the disciples came, and said unto him, Why speakest thou unto them in parables? He answered and said unto them, Because it is given unto you to know the mysteries of the kingdom of heaven, but to them it is not given. For whosoever hath, to him shall be given, and he shall have more abundance: but whosoever hath not, from him shall be taken away even that he hath. Therefore speak I to them in parables: because they seeing see not; and hearing they hear not, neither do they understand." (Matthew 13:10-13)

All this should suggest that Job's words must be spiritually discerned. There is depth here, and we must not miss the message that God has for us. Job effectively silences his accusers. Will it be questions like this that will stop every mouth when we stand before our Lord? How would YOU answer these questions?

The questions themselves are not hard to understand. They all have to do with the APPLICATION of God's truth. Three of the questions relate directly to our spoken words, reminding us of Christ's words in Matthew.

"But I say unto you, That every idle word that men shall speak, they shall give account thereof in the day of judgment. For by thy words thou shalt be justified, and by thy words thou shalt be condemned." (Matthew 12:36-37)

The only question that requires some explanation is the last one, where Job asks, *"and whose spirit came forth from thee?"* You must remember that this question has three possible answers. Man has a human spirit that can control his life. Or, he can yield his life to the Holy Spirit of God, so that He can flow forth out of his life. Finally, there are demonic spirits that strive to control the lives of men. This is the reason for John's instruction.

"Beloved, believe not every spirit, but try the spirits whether they are of God: because many false prophets are gone out into the world." (1 John 4:1)

JOB'S COSMOLOGY

DEAD THINGS

Having finally shut the mouths of his friends, Job draws his own conclusions. Far from being "out of gas," Job begins his longest discourse in the book, continuing through chapter 31. His topic in chapter 26 is "cosmology," the study of how God's universe fits together. His appeal is to the power and sovereignty of God. Job concludes with a flourish! But we will still see flashes of the old Job we have seen all along. Amid wonderful passages containing divine insight, we will also find Job's same old frustration, confusion and self-pity. Yet, on the whole, Job has held up remarkably well!

5 "Dead things are formed from under the waters, and the inhabitants thereof." (Job 26:5)

Having just listed six questions that deliver a "knock-out blow" to any contender, Job moves directly to the place of the dead. Job 26:5 is as enigmatic as any statement in the book. Normally, one thinks of living things being formed, but Job speaks of *"dead things"* that are *"formed from under the waters."* He then mentions the inhabitants thereof—of under the waters.

What does this mean? All I can offer is an educated guess. I am NOT expecting to discover a lost, underwater continent of Atlantis! We will examine a few Scriptures that might shed some light on an otherwise dark subject. First, as we attempt to learn who these inhabitants from under the waters are, we remember that there is a *"congregation of the dead."*

"The man that wandereth out of the way of understanding shall remain in the congregation of the dead." (Proverbs 21:16)

Yet, this congregation is not necessarily in any special place *"under the waters."* Any individual who is not in the way of understanding (the position of the saved person) is going to remain in the *"congregation of the dead."* If you would like to see this *"congregation,"* simply look out your window. Any man without Christ is born dead.

Perhaps Job has in mind the special place for imprisoned spirits, the bottomless pit that is in the center of the earth. This would be a place beneath the waters. Furthermore, if this place is indeed in the center of the earth, perhaps the "great gulf fixed" (Luke 16:26) between hell and paradise, it would literally have no bottom. Every direction would be "up."

"And they had a king over them, which is the angel of the bottomless pit,

whose name in the Hebrew tongue is Abaddon, but in the Greek tongue hath his name Apollyon." (Revelation 9:11)

There are angels who died like men. We learn this in the Psalms.

"I have said, Ye are gods; and all of you are children of the most High. But ye shall die like men, and fall like one of the princes." (Psalm 82:6-7)

There are also angels who are imprisoned in a special place due to their sin. Consider the following.

"For if God spared not the angels that sinned, but cast them down to hell, and delivered them into chains of darkness, to be reserved unto judgment." (2 Peter 2:4)

"And the angels which kept not their first estate, but left their own habitation, he hath reserved in everlasting chains under darkness unto the judgment of the great day." (Jude 6)

In the day of the "Great White Throne Judgment" (Revelation 20:11) there will be those who come forth from under the waters. Perhaps this has to do with these fallen angels.

"And the sea gave up the dead which were in it; and death and hell delivered up the dead which were in them: and they were judged every man according to their works." (Revelation 20:13)

Is it possible that this famous verse deals with more than sailors lost at sea? Is the "sea" the Mediterranean, the Atlantic or Pacific? Or, is it *"the deep"?* (Genesis 1:2, 7:11) These are questions that are yet to be answered.

NAKED HELL

6 "Hell is naked before him, and destruction hath no covering." (Job 26:6)

The context here remains the same as Job 26:5. Job is obviously dealing with judgment and God's sovereign power. This would support some of our speculation above, that the congregation of the dead and those who come forth from beneath the sea have something to do with the bottomless pit. From a historical perspective, Job's point in mentioning hell and destruction is the same as that found in Proverbs.

"Hell and destruction are before the LORD: how much more then the hearts of the children of men?" (Proverbs 15:11)

Job's reference to "hell" needs no clarification, but it is fascinating that he mentions *"destruction"* in the same breath. *"Destruction"* is the name of the angel of the bottomless pit. We need to review what we just saw in Revelation 9:11.

"And they had a king over them, which is the angel of the bottomless pit,

whose name in the Hebrew tongue is Abaddon, but in the Greek tongue hath his name Apollyon." (Revelation 9:11) Both the Hebrew "*abaddon,*" and the Greek "*Apollyon*" mean "destruction."

Fire, water, and God's judgment are intricately connected in the Word of God. Some examples from the Psalms help us see that connection.

"*Then the channels of waters were seen, and the foundations of the world were discovered at thy rebuke, O LORD, at the blast of the breath of thy nostrils. He sent from above, he took me, he drew me out of many waters.*" (Psalm 18:15-16)

"*Thou hast caused men to ride over our heads; we went through fire and through water: but thou broughtest us out into a wealthy place.*" (Psalm 66:12)

"*Thy wrath lieth hard upon me, and thou hast afflicted me with all thy waves.*" (Psalm 88:7)

God safely taking His people through the waters of judgment is typified in the Flood, the crossing of the Red Sea and the crossing of the Jordan River, and is celebrated in the Psalms.

"*The Lord said, I will bring again from Bashan, I will bring my people again from the depths of the sea.*" (Psalm 68:22)

"*Then the waters had overwhelmed us, the stream had gone over our soul: Then the proud waters had gone over our soul.*" (Psalm 124:4-5)

Jonah went "under the waters," and came back describing hell itself.

"*Then Jonah prayed unto the LORD his God out of the fish's belly, And said, I cried by reason of mine affliction unto the LORD, and he heard me; out of the belly of hell cried I, and thou heardest my voice. For thou hadst cast me into the deep, in the midst of the seas; and the floods compassed me about: all thy billows and thy waves passed over me. Then I said, I am cast out of thy sight; yet I will look again toward thy holy temple. The waters compassed me about, even to the soul: the depth closed me round about, the weeds were wrapped about my head. I went down to the bottoms of the mountains; the earth with her bars was about me for ever: yet hast thou brought up my life from corruption, O LORD my God.*" (Jonah 2:1-6)

From speaking about the depths of hell and destruction, Job now leaps to the heavens above. The statement he makes is amazing! Job's next remarks are scientifically accurate and several thousand years ahead of modern science. They totally debunk the image that he and his friends had just emerged from the caves where they spent their time drawing stick figures on the wall with charcoal.

THE EMPTY PLACE

7 "He stretcheth out the north over the empty place, and hangeth the earth upon nothing." (Job 26:7)

The Hebrew word for "heaven" means a "beaten-out expanse." The idea of stretching out the north over the empty place fits perfectly well with the description of creation we find in the first chapter of Genesis, which tells of God stretching out the expanse of heaven.

"In the beginning God created the heaven and the earth. And the earth was without form, and void; and darkness was upon the face of the deep. And the Spirit of God moved upon the face of the waters. And God said, Let there be light: and there was light. And God saw the light, that it was good: and God divided the light from the darkness. And God called the light Day, and the darkness he called Night. And the evening and the morning were the first day. And God said, Let there be a firmament in the midst of the waters, and let it divide the waters from the waters. And God made the firmament, and divided the waters which were under the firmament from the waters which were above the firmament: and it was so. And God called the firmament Heaven. And the evening and the morning were the second day." (Genesis 1:1-8)

Astronomers tell us that the area of space in the universe directly to the north, relative to earth's perspective, is a void. There appears to be nothing there. Our North Star, Alpha Draconus, is not perfectly in the north. It has not even always been our North Star. The universe is constantly in motion, and positions of heavenly bodies change relative to one another.

North is where heaven is said to be.

"Beautiful for situation, the joy of the whole earth, is mount Zion, on the sides of the north, the city of the great King." (Psalm 48:2)

"For thou hast said in thine heart, I will ascend into heaven, I will exalt my throne above the stars of God: I will sit also upon the mount of the congregation, in the sides of the north." (Isaiah 14:13)

The phrase *"the sides of the north"* is interesting, since the north is said to be stretched out over *"the empty place."* Countless believers will be sucked up into that apparent vacuum in the coming rapture of the church!

The last part of Job 26:7 says that God hung the earth upon nothing. This simply does not square with the image we have of primitive man thinking that the earth rested upon the back of a giant turtle, or some such thing. Where did Job get his information? Is it possible that these men had much more information than we could imagine?

HEAVENLY CLOUDS

8 "He bindeth up the waters in his thick clouds; and the cloud is not rent under them.
9 He holdeth back the face of his throne, and spreadeth his cloud upon it.
10 He hath compassed the waters with bounds, until the day and night come to an end." (Job 26:8-10)

In comments on Job 22:13-14 we discussed the issue of the waters that Psalm 148:1-4 says are above the heavens. We also saw how God binds up water in clouds, and that there are clouds not only in the atmosphere, but also in space. A review of those comments in Job 22:13-14 might be helpful at this point.

Whether Job has in mind the function of atmospheric clouds or galactic clouds, his knowledge is amazing. This truth of God binding up waters in the clouds is seen also in Proverbs.

"Who hath ascended up into heaven, or descended? who hath gathered the wind in his fists? WHO HATH BOUND THE WATERS IN A GARMENT? who hath established all the ends of the earth? what is his name, and what is his son's name, if thou canst tell?" (Proverbs 30:4) (Author's emphasis)

Piecing together the information we have so far, it would appear that in some way God uses these heavenly waters and His clouds to hide the face of His throne. This would correspond to the veil in the temple, that separated the holy place and the outer court from the holiest, the abode of God. This veil of waters, or clouds, veils the throne of God, isolating the third heaven from the contamination of sin.

DIVINE REPROOF

11 "The pillars of heaven tremble and are astonished at his reproof." (Job 26:11)

We don't know what they are, but heaven has pillars. Earth also has pillars.

"Which shaketh the earth out of her place, and the pillars thereof tremble." (Job 9:6)

God has some sort of pillars on earth. We find more information in 1 Samuel.

"He raiseth up the poor out of the dust, and lifteth up the beggar from the dunghill, to set them among princes, and to make them inherit the throne of glory: for THE PILLARS OF THE EARTH ARE THE LORD'S, and he hath set the world upon them." (1 Samuel 2:8) (Author's emphasis)

Though we do not know the nature of these pillars, we must give God some leeway in His use of language. Pillars do not have to be literal in nature, as we can see from the following example from Exodus, when God used special forms of pillars to guide the Israelites.

"And the LORD went before them by day in a pillar of a cloud, to lead them the way; and by night in a pillar of fire, to give them light; to go by day and night." (Exodus 13:21)

12 "He divideth the sea with his power, and by his understanding he smiteth through the proud." (Job 26:12)

In our study of Job 26:5 we saw that the literal dividing the waters of the Red Sea and Jordan River was also used in a symbolic way to picture a future time when our Lord will return to smite the proud, and to lead His people to the presence of God through the waters of the *"deep."* In his prophecy of coming judgment, Habakkuk saw the same thing.

"Thou didst walk through the sea with thine horses, through the heap of great waters." (Habakkuk 3:15)

The *"proud"* that our Lord will smite in His coming have a king. This king is mentioned in the next verse as *"the crooked serpent."*

CROOKED SERPENT

13 "By his spirit he hath garnished the heavens; his hand hath formed the crooked serpent." (Job 26:13)

Before dealing with this crooked serpent, notice the wonderful way in which Job describes God's work in creation. He says that God has *"garnished the heavens."* To garnish something is to adorn it or decorate it. One garnishes a Christmas tree, or a plate of gourmet food. Many passages of Scripture come to mind, the foremost being Psalm 19, to which we have referred several times.

"The heavens declare the glory of God; and the firmament sheweth his handywork. Day unto day uttereth speech, and night unto night sheweth knowledge. There is no speech nor language, where their voice is not heard. Their line is gone out through all the earth, and their words to the end of the world. In them hath he set a tabernacle for the sun, Which is as a bridegroom coming out of his chamber, and rejoiceth as a strong man to run a race. His going forth is from the end of the heaven, and his circuit unto the ends of it: and there is nothing hid from the heat thereof." (Psalm 19:1-6)

The crooked serpent is clearly identified in the Bible. From Genesis 3 to Revelation 12, there is no doubt as to his identity.

"And the great dragon was cast out, that old serpent, called the Devil,

and Satan, which deceiveth the whole world: he was cast out into the earth, and his angels were cast out with him." (Revelation 12:9)

He also appears in Isaiah. "*In that day the LORD with his sore and great and strong sword shall punish leviathan the piercing serpent, even leviathan that crooked serpent; and he shall slay the dragon that is in the sea.*" (Isaiah 27:1)

The context of this verse is important. Consider the final two verses of the preceding chapter. The coming day of the Lord is in view, a time of judgment.

"*Come, my people, enter thou into thy chambers, and shut thy doors about thee: hide thyself as it were for a little moment, until the indignation be overpast. For, behold, the LORD cometh out of his place to punish the inhabitants of the earth for their iniquity: the earth also shall disclose her blood, and shall no more cover her slain.*" (Isaiah 26:20-21)

When we remember the waters in the universe, discussed above, this "sea monster," leviathan, seems much less mythological and more real. The Psalmist also knew him.

"*Thou brakest the heads of leviathan in pieces, and gavest him to be meat to the people inhabiting the wilderness.*" (Psalm 74:14)

This same leviathan is the subject of much attention by God Himself, when He finally answers Job. Job 41 is entirely dedicated to him. There will be time to study leviathan in greater detail when we arrive at Job 41, but notice for now a very important fact about this crooked serpent.

"*He beholdeth all high things: he is a king over all the children of pride.*" (Job 41:34)

Job has just rattled off an astounding list of cosmological information. The chapter closes with Job's humble opinion of these facts.

THE THUNDER OF HIS POWER

14 "Lo, these are parts of his ways: but how little a portion is heard of him? but the thunder of his power who can understand?" (Job 26:14)

There is so much more that could be said. One thing is certain, Job says. When God does speak and move, there is no one who can understand.

God WILL finally speak in the last chapters of this book. When he does, the prophecy of Job is fulfilled in his very own person. Job has no answer. He is awed by the wonderful thunder of God's power.

How little we really understand about God! This is the lesson we must carry away from this chapter. God's Word is settled in heaven (Psalm 119:89); man's opinions about God's Word are always tentative.

We have seen some astounding cosmological information rolling off the lips of these men. Some things are clearly confirmed by science. At other times we have engaged in sanctified speculation. Yet for all of it, we remain fundamentally ignorant of the grand power of God. How unfortunate that Job's counselors think they have figured out everything. How much more unfortunate if you and I do not learn from their example.

22

JOB'S ACHING HEART

My righteousness I hold fast,

and will not let it go: my heart shall not reproach

me so long as I live.

Job 27:6

IN THE LAST CHAPTER WE COMPARED JOB TO AN ACCIDENT VICtim stretched out on a gurney in the emergency room. His pride, concern for appearance, and social status had all been reduced to nothing. His nakedness was displayed in sharp, vivid lines of contrast under the bright lights that patrol emergency rooms like sentries.

As we enter Job 27, the context continues, and we will borrow the same illustration. Any medical doctor will tell you that after medical science has offered its best, there is an internal quality within the individual patient that often decides life or death in extreme cases. Some patients possess a will to live that empowers them to smash medical statistics and odds that are stacked against them. These special patients can conquer situations that would kill others. The only explanation has nothing to do with the quality of medical care, but with the "heart"—the fighting spirit of the patient.

Job has a will to survive, despite his desperate comments about being ready to meet his Maker, and cursing the day he was born. Those remarks are screams of intense emotional and spiritual pain. They do not negate the amazing internal fortitude of this man, who, despite all that he has endured, refuses to budge from his commitment to God, or from his own integrity.

As we move through the next two chapters, we will see glimpses of

Job's remarkable spirit. He will refuse to budge from his position of being right with God. He will respond powerfully to his critics. God's Spirit will speak through him with more prophetic images, and he will also offer an astounding analysis of the value of righteousness and wisdom.

As you work through his speech, ask yourself if you could hold on so doggedly to your integrity, as Job has done. If not, you must remember that God has equipped us all with a free will. You are the only one who can flip the switch within your soul to make such a powerful commitment to God. It is a choice you make. God will give you the power, the grace and the strength to endure as Job has endured. Yet only you can make the choice to commit so totally to Him.

REFUSING TO BUDGE FROM HIS RIGHTEOUSNESS

1 "Moreover Job continued his parable, and said." (Job 27:1)

We are reminded that Job's speech is called a "parable." It is a teaching to be applied to those who believe. It is a "dark saying" that requires spiritual discernment to discover the deeper truth.

2 "As God liveth, who hath taken away my judgment; and the Almighty, who hath vexed my soul." (Job 27:2)

We must be careful to understand how the word *"judgment"* is used in this context. When Job complains that God has taken away his judgment, he is simply saying that God has not given him his "day in court." He is not saying that God's judgment, in the sense of punishment, has been lifted from him.

Job's soul has been *"vexed."* There can be no doubt about it. Nor can there be any doubt about God allowing it to take place, although the Devil was the executor. Not only has Job been vexed, Job has been allowed no voice in the judgment.

3 "All the while my breath is in me, and the spirit of God is in my nostrils." (Job 27:3)

Job's soul is vexed, yet he correctly understands the source of life. The same God who has allowed the vexing, also gives him breath. The inseparable connection between man's breath and the Spirit of God is seen from the Genesis account of man's creation.

"And the LORD God formed man of the dust of the ground, and

breathed into his nostrils the breath of life; and man became a living soul." (Genesis 2:7)

This is the dilemma of Job's existence. On one hand, Job's soul is vexed. On the other, Job recognizes that the same God who allows him to be vexed, also gives him breath.

Denied direct access to God for the moment, Job adamantly clings to his own righteousness and integrity. He IS righteous, and he DOES have integrity. There is, however, a fine line between confidence in one's own righteousness and the very carnal self-righteousness of the New Testament Pharisees. Listen to Job's testimony.

4 "My lips shall not speak wickedness, nor my tongue utter deceit.

5 God forbid that I should justify you: till I die I will not remove mine integrity from me.

6 My righteousness I hold fast, and will not let it go: my heart shall not reproach me so long as I live." (Job 27:4-6)

Job will state something similar before this discourse is finished. Look ahead to Job 29.

"I put on righteousness, and it clothed me: my judgment was as a robe and a diadem." (Job 29:14)

We have said there is a fine line between truly being righteous and merely trusting in one's own self-righteousness, and Job might be teetering on the edge. Yet we must remember that Job has the testimony of God in the first two chapters to confirm that he is righteous, and that his tragedy is not due to any particular sin on his part.

Hearing these words of Job, it is easy to wonder whether Job is trusting in God, or trusting in his own righteousness, even though he IS a righteous man. A young man named Elihu is listening intently to Job. Later he will conclude that Job has crossed the line, making himself more righteous than God.

Elihu will confront Job and ask, *"Thinkest thou this to be right, that thou sadist, My righteousness is more than God's?"* (Job 35:2)

Many of us would be tempted to agree with Elihu, concluding that Job has crossed the line into self-righteousness. It is a natural and human thing to see someone else as a self-righteous Pharisee, or as being "holier than thou." This is especially true if the other person IS holier than we are, and we are motivated by jealousy. There is a fine line between correctly assessing the other person's spiritual condition, and falsely condemning him.

Fortunately, the responsibility to judge the heart attitude and motives of others is not ours. That responsibility belongs to God alone. God will deal with Job when He is ready to speak in Job 40. Our instruction in such matters is clearly outlined by Paul.

"But with me it is a very small thing that I should be judged of you, or of man's judgment: yea, I judge not mine own self. For I know nothing by myself; yet am I not hereby justified: but he that judgeth me is the Lord. Therefore judge nothing before the time, until the Lord come, who both will bring to light the hidden things of darkness, and will make manifest the counsels of the hearts: and then shall every man have praise of God." (1 Corinthians 4:3-5)

Job is correct in maintaining that there is no specific sin in his life that brought judgment from God. Whether he is trusting excessively in his self-righteousness is for God to decide.

What we do know is that Job pictures the self-righteousness of Israel as they go from this present age into the time of Tribulation. Job at least can hold onto his integrity. The nation of Israel has a history of rejecting God's truth in favor of their own tradition and self-righteousness. This is Paul's message to the Romans regarding their attitude.

"Brethren, my heart's desire and prayer to God for Israel is, that they might be saved. For I bear them record that they have a zeal of God, but not according to knowledge. For they being ignorant of God's righteousness, and going about to establish their own righteousness, have not submitted themselves unto the righteousness of God. For Christ is the end of the law for righteousness to every one that believeth." (Romans 10:1-4)

The key for our lives is to submit to God's righteousness, not to try to establish our own. This is the lesson we need to glean from Job's words.

RESPONDING TO HIS COUNSELORS

7 "Let mine enemy be as the wicked, and he that riseth up against me as the unrighteous." (Job 27:7)

This will be Job's final shot at his counselors. In essence, he is accusing them of hypocrisy. Job is convinced that he is on God's side, and that means that whoever is not on Job's side is siding with the wicked.

The questions that follow are all rhetorical. Job is using the same tactic Bildad employed in Job 25. Every one of these questions has an obvious answer, and every answer is negative.

8 "For what is the hope of the hypocrite, though he hath gained, when God taketh away his soul?

9 Will God hear his cry when trouble cometh upon him?

10 Will he delight himself in the Almighty? will he always call upon God?" (Job 27:8-10)

Of course not! You had no trouble answering these questions, did you? Having set the stage, Job now declares that what he is about to say is common knowledge. He is going to point them to something they have all seen.

11 "I will teach you by the hand of God: that which is with the Almighty will I not conceal.

12 Behold, all ye yourselves have seen it; why then are ye thus altogether vain?" (Job 27:11-12)

There is no way to respond to Job's words. Again, we are reminded of his debating skills. He points to those things that are obvious, then draws the logical conclusion.

Job's counselors have used the same technique, yet there is a flaw in their arguments. Although they begin with what is common knowledge, like many people today, they take an erroneous course. They draw a conclusion that appears obvious and logical to them, yet is not correct and biblical.

This is an effective tactic if the conclusion genuinely follows from a biblical perspective. Paul used this method also. In his letter to the Romans, Paul began his teaching by first establishing those things that everyone can "see."

"For the wrath of God is revealed from heaven against all ungodliness and unrighteousness of men, who hold the truth in unrighteousness; Because that which may be known of God is manifest in them; for God hath shewed it unto them. For the invisible things of him from the creation of the world are clearly seen, being understood by the things that are made, even his eternal power and Godhead; so that they are without excuse." (Romans 1:18-20)

After revealing "by the hand of God" those things that can be seen, Paul moves to establish the fact of human sin. He does so with a combination of logic and Scriptural support.

He used the same method in his sermon on Mars Hill in Athens. Beginning with the daily lives of the Athenians and the fact of creation, he went on to show how God supernaturally intervened in human history through His incarnation in Jesus Christ.

Paul's logic was always impeccable, and his biblical support was thorough. We would do well to observe and learn from him. Often our discussions about spiritual matters degenerate into cheap interchanges of theological clichés and proof texts, with no understanding taking place on either side.

Job has held firmly to his integrity, he has refused to be swayed by faulty logic, and he has used his own knowledge of God and His ways to finally silence his accusers. Just what is this common knowledge that Job says all have seen, and why is it so important?

REVEALING MORE PROPHECY

THE WICKED'S PORTION

13 "This is the portion of a wicked man with God, and the heritage of oppressors, which they shall receive of the Almighty." (Job 27:13)

There is no question about Job's purpose in the words that follow. This is a discourse on the inheritance of the wicked. Historically, Job brings his counselors face to face with the facts about the wicked. His goal is to show conclusively that he is not among "the wicked," and that if they do not back off, they are in danger of being classified with the wicked themselves.

Prophetically, we will again see an insightful picture of God's coming judgment upon Antichrist, "that Wicked." This sets the subject matter for the rest of Job 27.

A key to Bible study is to look for those clues within the context of Scripture itself that give us the meaning of the passage. John 20:31 is a classic example.

"But these are written, that ye might believe that Jesus is the Christ, the Son of God; and that believing ye might have life through his name." (John 20:31)

This one verse gives us a valuable key to understand the purpose of John's gospel. It is the evangelistic gospel. There is no wonder why so many evangelists take their texts from John's gospel. That is the intended purpose.

Here, in the Book of Job, we have statements that provide us with similar insight into God's purpose. We saw one such example in Job 18:21, and again in Job 20:29.

"Surely such are the dwellings of the wicked, and this is the place of him that knoweth not God." (Job 18:21)

"This is the portion of a wicked man from God, and the heritage appointed unto him by God." (Job 20:29)

Job 27:13 brings us back to the same purpose. What we are going to read will be very instructive about the fate of the wicked. It will prophetically take us forward to see what awaits the Antichrist in particular, and lost men in general.

THE WICKED'S PEOPLE

14 "If his children be multiplied, it is for the sword: and his offspring shall not be satisfied with bread." (Job 27:14)

Countless people through the ages could testify that this verse is an apt description of life. They have brought their children into the world to perish through the violence and wars of sinful men, and through the devastated economy of a creation tainted by man's sin.

Prophetically, of course, this is the literal doom of the children of Antichrist's generation. They will perish by the sharp, two-edged sword that goes out of the mouth of the returning Lord Jesus Christ in Revelation 19: 15. Even before that, they will have suffered the worst famine in the history of mankind, the one prophesied in Revelation 6.

"And when he had opened the third seal, I heard the third beast say, Come and see. And I beheld, and lo a black horse; and he that sat on him had a pair of balances in his hand. And I heard a voice in the midst of the four beasts say, A measure of wheat for a penny, and three measures of barley for a penny; and see thou hurt not the oil and the wine." (Revelation 6:5-6)

15 "Those that remain of him shall be buried in death: and his widows shall not weep." (Job 27:15)

There is no escape. Any survivors will meet a certain death. Notice that the *"widows"* that survive will be in such a state of shock, they will be numb. They will not weep.

Notice also that the word *"widows"* is plural. Does this mean that *"the wicked man"* will have multiple wives? Does this mean that *"the wicked man"* is indeed a prophetic reference to the Antichrist, and that the reference is to the widows that remain from his empire? Whatever the case, the outlook is staggering, and the situation somber indeed.

THE WICKED'S POSSESSIONS

16 "Though he heap up silver as the dust, and prepare raiment as the clay;

17 He may prepare it, but the just shall put it on, and the innocent shall divide the silver." (Job 27:16-17)

"Raiment," you remember, is an old word for "clothing." It does not matter how much money, or how fine the clothes that the wicked amass, it will all be divided by the just and the innocent.

We have seen this truth earlier in our study of Job, in remarks made regarding Job 20:18. Let us remind ourselves of this incredible truth—that the wicked are busy laying up treasures for the righteous, though he doesn't know it.

"For God giveth to a man that is good in his sight wisdom, and knowledge, and joy: but to the sinner he giveth travail, to gather and to heap up, that he may give to him that is good before God. This also is vanity and vexation of spirit." (Ecclesiastes 2:26)

"A good man leaveth an inheritance to his children's children: and the wealth of the sinner is laid up for the just." (Proverbs 13:22)

18 "He buildeth his house as a moth, and as a booth that the keeper maketh." (Job 27:18)

A moth makes a house that is both intricate and delicate. It is made with amazing skill. Yet the structure is temporary and fragile.

The booth that the keeper makes refers to a shack that provides temporary shelter for the man who watches over a field. In both cases the idea is something that is easily torn down.

The Antichrist will construct a great empire, and will undoubtedly live in a great palace. Yet, for all its glory, will provide no more security than a moth's house or a shack in the field.

Centuries ago God told Israel that their sins had reduced them to the level of a cottage in the middle of a cucumber field. Isaiah is the prophet who recorded these words.

"And the daughter of Zion is left as a cottage in a vineyard, as a lodge in a garden of cucumbers, as a besieged city." (Isaiah 1:8)

Many good believers labor to keep up social appearances. They overextend themselves financially to live in the finest house possible. Not only do they limit their flexibility and tie up resources that could be used for things more important, the finest house offers no security. It can be gone in the time it takes a tornado to cross the street, or with the huffing a puffing of the Santa Ana winds pushing a mighty fire in Southern California. In seconds an earthquake can reduce a mansion to mush, or a hurricane can rip a coastal palace from its pilings.

If God provides for you to live in a fine house, you should feel no guilt. You should be thankful to God for the provision, and should put it at His disposal to be used as a tool for ministry. Yet realize that He can take it back from you just as fast as he did in Job's case. Will you have the same attitude that Job displayed?

"And said, Naked came I out of my mother's womb, and naked shall I return thither: the LORD gave, and the LORD hath taken away; blessed be the name of the LORD." (Job 1:21)

THE WICKED'S PLACE

19 "The rich man shall lie down, but he shall not be gathered: he openeth his eyes, and he is not." (Job 27:19)

In Old Testament terminology, this "gathering" refers to the death of saints. Here are a couple of examples of this usage.

"And Isaac gave up the ghost, and died, and WAS GATHERED UNTO HIS PEOPLE, being old and full of days: and his sons Esau and Jacob buried him." (Genesis 35:29) (Author's emphasis)

"And when Jacob had made an end of commanding his sons, he gathered up his feet into the bed, and yielded up the ghost, and WAS GATHERED UNTO HIS PEOPLE." (Genesis 49:33) (Author's emphasis)

In other words, the wicked will not experience the death of a believer. He will open his eyes, and though conscious, will not possess life. This was the experience of the rich man who opened his eyes in hell. Jesus told the story in Luke 16.

Also in Luke is a parable Jesus told, remembering that Job's words here are called a "parable." The circumstance in Luke is similar to that described by Job.

"And he said, This will I do: I will pull down my barns, and build greater; and there will I bestow all my fruits and my goods. And I will say to my soul, Soul, thou hast much goods laid up for many years; take thine ease, eat, drink, and be merry. But God said unto him, Thou fool, this night thy soul shall be required of thee: then whose shall those things be, which thou hast provided?" (Luke 12:18-20)

20 "Terrors take hold on him as waters, a tempest stealeth him away in the night." (Job 27:20)

Again, we see the connection between waters and God's judgment. We explained this in the previous chapter in our discussion of Job 26:5.

"Dead things are formed from under the waters, and the inhabitants thereof." (Job 26:5)

The Psalmist also spoke of those waves, or waters, of God's judgment.

"I sink in deep mire, where there is no standing: I am come into deep waters, where the floods overflow me." (Psalm 69:2)

21 "The east wind carrieth him away, and he departeth: and as a storm hurleth him out of his place." (Job 27:21)

The *"east wind"* makes another cameo appearance in Job's story. We saw in Job 15:2 that it is in some way connected with God's judgment. It also blew back the waters of the Red Sea and has performed other key feats during the course of history.

"Should a wise man utter vain knowledge, and fill his belly with the east wind?" (Job 15:2)

Through Job, we are seeing that the wicked man will be carried away by the east wind. Furthermore, this will be *"as a storm hurleth him out of his place."*

In our study of Job 8:18 we saw that the phrase *"his place"* offers some interesting speculation regarding Judas Iscariot, Satan's failed attempt at Antichrist. Acts 1:25 tells us that Judas went to *"his own place."*

It is difficult to arrive at any solid conclusions, yet it is fascinating to see these same phrases that appear in other biblical passages on judgment appear here in the same context. What we can conclude is that the wicked will not be able to stand against the east wind of God's judgment, and that God has a place prepared for those who rebel against Him, just as surely as our Lord has gone to prepare a place for those who believe in Him.

22 "For God shall cast upon him, and not spare: he would fain flee out of his hand." (Job 27:22)

It is not difficult to capture the meaning of this verse. Though the wicked would try to flee from the hand of God, it is of no use. There is no way out. God will be upon him, and will *"not spare."*

23 "Men shall clap their hands at him, and shall hiss him out of his place." (Job 27:23)

Clapping the hands and hissing comprise an oriental form of expressing contempt, like a middle-eastern "Bronx cheer." One example is found in the little book of Lamentations.

"All that pass by clap their hands at thee; they hiss and wag their head at the daughter of Jerusalem, saying, Is this the city that men call The perfection of beauty, The joy of the whole earth?" (Lamentations 2:15)

The wicked enjoy the fruit of their wickedness, yet their transitory joy is all they will ever have. There is coming a day when they will be held in contempt, from the lowest sinner to the Antichrist himself.

Isaiah saw the future of the king of Babylon, one of the richest and powerful men of his day. He spoke of impending judgment to come upon this powerful individual.

"Hell from beneath is moved for thee to meet thee at thy coming: it stirreth up the dead for thee, even all the chief ones of the earth; it hath raised up from their thrones all the kings of the nations. All they shall speak and say unto thee, Art thou also become weak as we? art thou become like unto us?" (Isaiah 14:9-10)

Just a few verses later Isaiah's prophecy obviously transcends the human king of Babylon, and addresses the spiritual power behind his throne. We have spoken before of this critically important description of the fall of Lucifer in Isaiah 14. This time, notice the contempt with which this mighty one is regarded.

"Yet thou shalt be brought down to hell, to the sides of the pit. They that see thee shall narrowly look upon thee, and consider thee, saying, Is this the man that made the earth to tremble, that did shake kingdoms; That made the world as a wilderness, and destroyed the cities thereof; that opened not the house of his prisoners?" (Isaiah 14:15-17)

Job has spoken of the *"portion of a wicked man with God."* It is continually astounding to observe that whenever Job enters this mode of forecasting doom upon the wicked, the images he uses are totally consistent with those found other places in the Bible, most written centuries later. We need to remember that God is the Author of this Book.

RELATING THE VALUE OF RIGHTEOUSNESS AND WISDOM

MORE PRECIOUS THAN THE THINGS OF THIS WORLD

1 "Surely there is a vein for the silver, and a place for gold where they fine it.

2 Iron is taken out of the earth, and brass is molten out of the stone." (Job 28:1-2)

These strange words are the beginning of a section that is working toward a climax in the concluding verses of Job 28. The idea is that Job is contrasting these metals with the incomparable value of righteousness and wisdom. We will not reach the climax of Job's arguments until the next chapter of this commentary. For the moment we will concern ourselves with the first eleven verses of Job 28.

It is extremely interesting to observe that the four metals, silver, gold, iron and brass, are the same that appear in the image of Nebuchadnezzar's dream in Daniel 2. As we have seen, these Tribulation images just keep popping up in Job!

Job is not ignorant of how iron is produced. He says that iron is taken out of the earth. Obviously, the ingredients that are processed to produce iron ARE taken out of the earth.

The greatest difficulty that many scholars have with this passage is with the word "brass." They do not want to think that the "ancients" had the knowledge to produce brass. Brass is also mentioned as early as Genesis 4:22, listing Tubal-cain as an *"instructor of every artificer in brass and iron."* Both metals are products of processes performed on ingredients that occur naturally in nature. These same scholars want to change the translation of "brass" in Genesis 4:22 also.

This is why many want to translate *"brass"* as "copper," which appears in nature without any man-made intervention. If they believe otherwise it would throw off their entire evolutionary scheme, and would require that history books be rewritten.

The famous LXX Greek version of the Hebrew Old Testament, uses the same word here that is translated universally as *"brass"* in Revelation 1:15. The problem is not linguistic, but rather is not wanting to accept the possibility that historical calculations on the arrival of brass to human civilization may be wrong.

Also, there is an unwillingness to accept that iron and brass—metals that require processing—are really intended here, when silver and gold are mentioned in the same verse. The idea of many scholars is to make everything match, so that all might refer to metals in their natural state. Yet it is seldom mentioned that the word translated *"gold"* is usually used to speak of gold in its refined, not raw, state.

Failure to appreciate the consistent Tribulation imagery in Job has led most commentators to see the first eleven verses of this chapter as a human mining operation, rather than allowing themselves to believe that the technology of Job's day was so advanced. Yet if we follow their reasoning through these verses, we are confronted in Job 28:9-10 with the problem of man overturning mountains by their roots, cutting rivers through rock, and having an eye that sees every precious thing. However, by comparing Scripture with Scripture, the Tribulation imagery emerges in sharp focus.

These four metals are not the only Tribulation figures that appear in this passage. There are several of them that we will encounter in our journey through the rest of Job 28. We will also see many images that we have already discussed in our previous studies in the Book of Job.

MORE PRECIOUS THAN THINGS OUT OF THIS WORLD

3 "He setteth an end to darkness, and searcheth out all perfection: the stones of darkness, and the shadow of death." (Job 28:3)

As we continue reading Job 28, it will be clear that the *"he"* of verse 28:3 is God. It is God who searches out all perfection, and it is God who will put an end to darkness.

"And there shall be no night there; and they need no candle, neither light

of the sun; for the Lord God giveth them light: and they shall reign for ever and ever." (Revelation 22:5)

Here in this verse we also find two of those familiar figures associated with the judgment of the coming Tribulation. The first is the phrase *"stones of darkness."* We first talked about the series of strange stones in the Bible back in Job 8:17-18.

"His roots are wrapped about the heap, and seeth the place of stones." (Job 8:17)

Next, we again see the *"shadow of death."* Earlier we traced a series of references to this shadow of death through the Scriptures, to show how it is related to the Tribulation. It made its first appearance in Job back in Job 3:5.

A quick review of these two phrases as they appear in Job, and the corresponding cross references, will confirm their consistent connection with God's judgment and the Tribulation. That is, of course, the context here in Job 28.

4 "The flood breaketh out from the inhabitant; even the waters forgotten of the foot: they are dried up, they are gone away from men." (Job 28:4)

If God is the subject of this discussion, this could possibly be another of the frequent references to the Flood that we have seen in Job. The Genesis flood did break out "from the inhabitant," in the sense that the inhabitant of the earth was the cause of God's judgment.

"The earth also was corrupt before God, and the earth was filled with violence. And God looked upon the earth, and, behold, it was corrupt; for all flesh had corrupted his way upon the earth. And God said unto Noah, The end of all flesh is come before me; for the earth is filled with violence through them; and, behold, I will destroy them with the earth." (Genesis 6:11-13)

These flood waters were *"forgotten of the foot"* in that they had no contact with men for the 370-day duration of the waters upon the earth. They also *"dried up"* as we read in Genesis 8:1.

Wait! The next verse gives us something to think about, and reminds us just how difficult this passage is to understand.

5 "As for the earth, out of it cometh bread: and under it is turned up as it were fire." (Job 28:5)

What does this mean, when Job says *"as for the earth?"* We have spoken on several occasions of the waters in the heavens. Perhaps Job, in 28:4, is talking about a "heavenly flood," like the state described in the first chapter of Genesis with the waters below and above the heavens.

Peter describes the same thing when he talks about the *"earth standing out of the water and in the water."*

Whatever Job means by this statement, we can know that it is true. Our understanding of the Bible is not always correct. We must realize that God's Word is true despite what we believe or understand.

In a figurative way one can correctly say, as Job does, that bread comes out of the earth. It is also correct to say that fire is *"under it."* The only thing that scientists know for sure about the center of the earth is that it is extremely hot. They cannot simply accept the testimony of the Bible which speaks of the fires of hell, but we can, as believers in the Word of God.

6 "The stones of it are the place of sapphires: and it hath dust of gold." (Job 28:6)

The stones of *"it"* obviously refer to the subject *"earth"* of the preceding verse, Job 28:5. Again we run into these strange stones that keep popping up in the Bible.

Consider the following cross references to strange stones. The first is in the prophecy concerning the fall of Satan.

"By the multitude of thy merchandise they have filled the midst of thee with violence, and thou hast sinned: therefore I will cast thee as profane out of the mountain of God: and I will destroy thee, O covering cherub, from the midst of THE STONES OF FIRE." (Ezekiel 28:16) (Author's emphasis)

God will mention these stones Himself, when He speaks with Job. He mentions them with Leviathan, the very Devil.

"SHARP STONES are under him: he spreadeth sharp pointed things upon the mire." (Job 41:30) (Author's emphasis)

"And the streams thereof shall be turned into pitch, and the dust thereof into brimstone, and the land thereof shall become burning pitch. It shall not be quenched night nor day; the smoke thereof shall go up for ever: from generation to generation it shall lie waste; none shall pass through it for ever and ever. But the cormorant and the bittern shall possess it; the owl also and the raven shall dwell in it: and he shall stretch out upon it the line of confusion, and THE STONES OF EMPTINESS." (Isaiah 34:9-11) (Author's emphasis)

If you are wondering what conclusion we came to about these stones in Job 8:17, the answer is easy—none! We can say that it appears these strange stones have something to do with the fires of hell, but beyond that we have nothing but speculation.

The *"dust of gold"* is equally enigmatic. From a purely human point of view, precious stones are found *"in the earth,"* as is gold dust.

MORE PRECIOUS THAN ANYTHING YOU HAVE EVER KNOWN

7 There is a path which no fowl knoweth, and which the vulture's eye hath not seen:

8 The lion's whelps have not trodden it, nor the fierce lion passed by it." (Job 28:7-8)

These two verses introduce the subject of the rest of the chapter, the way of wisdom. The context is seamless, concluding with these words in verse 28.

"And unto man he said, Behold, the fear of the Lord, that is wisdom; and to depart from evil is understanding." (Job 28:28)

This path is unknown, not only to the fowl, the vulture, the lion's whelps and the fierce lion, but also to all living creatures, as we see in Job 28:21.

"Seeing it is hid from the eyes of all living, and kept close from the fowls of the air." (Job 28:21)

Only God knows this way.

"God understandeth the way thereof, and he knoweth the place thereof." (Job 28:23)

9 "He putteth forth his hand upon the rock; he overturneth the mountains by the roots.

10 He cutteth out rivers among the rocks; and his eye seeth every precious thing." (Job 28:9-10)

We mentioned earlier in regard to Job 28:1-2 that many only want to see a human miner in these verses. Yet God is the only one who overturns mountains by the roots, and whose eye sees every precious thing. According to 2 Chronicles 16:9 God uses His supernatural powers *"to shew himself strong in the behalf of them whose heart is perfect toward him"*.

"For the eyes of the LORD run to and for throughout the whole earth, to shew himself strong in the behalf of them whose heart is perfect toward him. Herein thou hast done foolishly: therefore from henceforth thou shalt have wars." (2 Chronicles 16:9)

Job's idea in these two verses, Job 28:9-10, is to contrast the power of God as manifested in nature, with the excellency of this way of wisdom. A lost man can appreciate God's power. But he cannot find the way of wisdom by his power of reasoning, nor by his good works.

11 "He bindeth the floods from overflowing; and the thing that is hid bringeth he forth to light." (Job 28:11)

Here is another theme we have examined before. Remember what we saw in Job 26:10.

"He hath compassed the waters with bounds, until the day and night come to an end." (Job 26:10)

We will see the same thing when God speaks.

"Or who shut up the sea with doors, when it brake forth, as if it had issued out of the womb? When I made the cloud the garment thereof, and thick darkness a swaddlingband for it, And brake up for it my decreed place, and set bars and doors, And said, Hitherto shalt thou come, but no further: and here shall thy proud waves be stayed?" (Job 38:8-11)

The power of God over the celestial flood waters appears elsewhere, not only in the Book of Job. Consider the following cross references.

"When he uttereth his voice, there is a multitude of waters in the heavens, and he causeth the vapours to ascend from the ends of the earth; he maketh lightnings with rain, and bringeth forth the wind out of his treasures." (Jeremiah 10:13)

"When he uttereth his voice, there is a multitude of waters in the heavens; and he causeth the vapors to ascend from the ends of the earth: he maketh lightnings with rain, and bringeth forth the wind out of his treasures." (Jeremiah 51:16)

God promised Noah in Genesis 9 that He would not again judge the earth with a great flood, as He did in Genesis 7-8.

"And I will establish my covenant with you; neither shall all flesh be cut off any more by the waters of a flood; neither shall there any more be a flood to destroy the earth." (Genesis 9:11)

The information we have here in Job implies that God also will not again cause the waters to overflow from the great *"deep,"* as He did in Genesis 1:1-7, and as described by Peter in 2 Peter 3:6-7.

Job understands that God's power is great. He understands that there is a way of wisdom that is known only to God. Job, with all his knowledge, integrity and commitment to God, would love to know that way. He needs wisdom from God in this moment of trial.

Although this way is hidden, Job also understands that God can bring it to light. He says, *"and the thing that is hid bringeth he forth to light"*. (Job 28:11b) This is the same thing Jesus said.

"For there is nothing covered, that shall not be revealed; neither hid, that shall not be known." (Luke 12:2)

The way of God's wisdom HAS been revealed. That *"way"* is a Person.

"Jesus saith unto him, I am the way, the truth, and the life: no man cometh unto the Father, but by me." (John 14:6)

Do YOU know this way? If you do, are you walking in it? Job is correctly cutting through the external circumstances of his trial and seeing the far more important purpose of God. He is looking to walk in that way that is hidden from most, yet revealed to those who love God.

23

JOB'S LAST STAND

And unto man he said, Behold, the fear of the Lord, that is wisdom; and to depart from evil is understanding.

Job 28:28

THIS CHAPTER WILL COVER A LARGE PORTION OF SCRIPTURE. WE will pick up our study in Job 28:12, where we left off in the preceding chapter. Our goal for this chapter is to complete our study of Job's final discourse, which will extend through Job 31.

The final part of Job 28 is dedicated to discussing the answer to two powerful questions posed in verse 28:12. Job 29 finds Job in a reflective mood, talking about how good life used to be. Then, Job begins to complain again about his present condition in chapter 30. Finally, Job 31 contains the last words of Job's rebuttal, which is fittingly a defense of his personal righteousness.

We have attempted to give due attention the words of Scripture in their historical, doctrinal and devotional applications. There have been times in our study where we have entered lengthy discussions revolving around meaning of the contents of the Book of Job. For the most part, the concluding remarks of Job offer no great difficulties in understanding. There will be a few issues we must deal with in some detail, but the primary thrust of our study here will be to put these remarks in their proper context. Rather than pause to consider each word, we will survey the main flow of thought as Job concludes his arguments.

POWERFUL QUESTIONS

THE PLACE OF WISDOM AND UNDERSTANDING

12 "But where shall wisdom be found? and where is the place of understanding?" (Job 28:12)

It is hard to imagine two questions that have more direct bearing upon our lives and eternity than the two that Job submits in verse 12. Most people think of wisdom and understanding as slippery and elusive. Is there a place where one can find them in a tangible way?

This is the main point of Job's words. He has been leading up to these two questions in 28:12. This is the *"path which no fowl knoweth, and which the vulture's eye hath not seen"* (Job 28:7). He will repeat the question in Job 28:20.

The remainder of Job 28 explores the implications of this question, leading to the great conclusion that Job reaches in verse 28:28. Job's words are worthy to be compared to the other great wisdom passages of the Bible, such as Proverbs chapters 8 and 9.

13 "Man knoweth not the price thereof; neither is it found in the land of the living." (Job 28:13)

Man has no earthly idea of the price of wisdom or understanding. In the verses ahead Job will make it clear that there simply is no price tag that can be attached to either. No billionaire can purchase wisdom. No one can put together anything that would be valuable enough to buy understanding. They are not for sale.

Not only are wisdom and understanding far above any price, *"it,"* referring to the place where wisdom and understanding can be found, is not located *"in the land of the living."* Such incalculable treasure cannot be found among our contemporaries.

14 "The depth saith, It is not in me: and the sea saith, It is not with me." (Job 28:14)

We have sailed the great deep together in an earlier discussion. We saw its face covered with darkness in Genesis 1:2. We have seen in Job 38:30 that its face is frozen. There is so much we do not know about *"the depth,"* or *"the deep."* However, one thing we know with certainty—one cannot find the place of wisdom or understanding there.

Do not let someone tell you that some extra-terrestrial is going to reveal the secrets of life. No space alien knows the place of wisdom and understanding, despite the many popular books that are written to the contrary.

We also cannot find the place of wisdom and understanding in the sea. Not even the lost continent of Atlantis can offer the place of wisdom and understanding.

THE PRICE OF WISDOM AND UNDERSTANDING

15 "It cannot be gotten for gold, neither shall silver be weighed for the price thereof." (Job 28:15)

This verse logically concludes the thought put forth in Job 28:13. The way of wisdom and understanding cannot be purchased. There is no currency in the world sufficient to close the deal. No checks are accepted; no credit cards, wire transfers, stock options, cashier's checks or bank notes have the financial clout to buy wisdom and understanding

16 "It cannot be valued with the gold of Ophir, with the precious onyx, or the sapphire.

17 The gold and the crystal cannot equal it: and the exchange of it shall not be for jewels of fine gold.

18 No mention shall be made of coral, or of pearls: for the price of wisdom is above rubies.

19 The topaz of Ethiopia shall not equal it, neither shall it be valued with pure gold.

20 Whence then cometh wisdom? and where is the place of understanding?" (Job 28:16-20)

Several precious metals and stones are listed. None of them is sufficient to purchase the way of wisdom. In Job 22:24 we first encountered this mysterious "*gold of Ophir*." Whatever the historical explanation is for this very special gold, not even it can buy wisdom.

In Job 28:20 Job returns to the original question. His point is made. No man can buy wisdom or understanding. There is no way to amass a sufficient quantity or quality of physical material to obtain what every man needs—wisdom and understanding.

THE PUZZLE OF WISDOM AND UNDERSTANDING

21 "Seeing it is hid from the eyes of all living, and kept close from the fowls of the air.

22 Destruction and death say, We have heard the fame thereof with our ears.

23 God understandeth the way thereof, and he knoweth the place thereof.

24 For he looketh to the ends of the earth, and seeth under the whole heaven." (Job 28:21-24)

There is nothing hard to understand about these verses. This way of wisdom and understanding is hidden from *"the eyes of all living."* Even from the airborne perspective of the *"fowls of the air,"* we cannot discover this *"way."* We cannot follow some yellow brick road that leads to the great Oz, who can dispense wisdom to whom he will.

Destruction and death have heard of the fame of this *"way."* The inhabitants of hell know that there is a *"way"* to wisdom, yet they will never walk that way.

The rich man, whose tragic death Jesus spoke of in Luke 16, yearned to come back and be an evangelist five minutes after arriving in hell. He was five minutes too late.

Paul told the Philippians that every knee would bow and every tongue confess that Jesus Christ is Lord (Philippians 2:10-11). They will have heard the fame of this way of wisdom, yet never have the chance to walk in it.

God is the only one who understands this way and knows where it is to be found. Job knew a great deal about God and His truth. He did not know, as we now do, that God would one day reveal that Way.

"Jesus saith unto him, I am the way, the truth, and the life: no man cometh unto the Father, but by me." (John 14:6)

In Job's day, God alone knew the way. He alone has those eyes that constantly scan the entire universe.

25 "To make the weight for the winds; and he weigheth the waters by measure." (Job 28:25)

Here is another scientific gem that destroys our image of ancient times. Job possesses a bit of scientific information that was not confirmed by modern science until some 300 years ago. Job knows that winds have weight!

Understanding the relative weights of winds allows scientists to predict storms and climatic changes. Hot air rises, because it has less weight than cold air.

It is obvious that waters have weight. This information would appear to have been more accessible to "ancient" men like Job. Yet Job mentions the weight of winds and water in the same breath. Could he possibly understand, as modern scientists do, that there is a crucial difference between the total weights of air and water, and that without this balance life could not exist on this planet? The parallels between wind and water, with their respective weights, form the basis for the modern science of aerodynamics.

The weight of salt also explains how salt water becomes fresh water, the water evaporating in the sunlight and falling to earth. Perhaps ancient men were not as "primitive" as we have been led to believe.

26 "When he made a decree for the rain, and a way for the lightning of the thunder." (Job 28:26)

Ask any farmer, and he will tell you that man still cannot control the rain. Rain is controlled by divine decree, something that Elijah understood by faith.

"Elias was a man subject to like passions as we are, and he prayed earnestly that it might not rain: and it rained not on the earth by the space of three years and six months." (James 5:17)

Job also understood that there is a *"way for the lightning of thunder."* More than a good guess on Job's part, God Himself confirms this scientific fact in Job 38, several thousand years before "modern" science caught up.

"Who hath divided a watercourse for the overflowing of waters, or a way for the lightning of thunder." (Job 38:25)

Today we know that there IS a way for the lightning of thunder. A path DOES open from cloud to ground BEFORE the lightning.

Scientists still lack a complete understanding of all the complexities of lightning and thunder. Most would agree that the most familiar lightning strokes are those that extend from a cloud that has a negative electrically-charged base to the ground. This spectacular phenomenon begins with an invisible discharge, called a stepped leader. Free, negatively charged electrons rush downward along a path. Once they reach a short distance from the ground, another leader, positively charged and attracted by the negative electrons, moves upward from the ground to meet the oncoming electrons.

The contact between these two leaders, one moving upward, the other moving downward, produces the visible "lightning," called the return stroke. This return stroke flies upward to the cloud along this "way" opened by the stepped leader.

In less than a second several strokes can move along this "way," until the imbalance of electrical charges is neutralized. The heating and expansion of air along this path that occurs with the electrical discharges is an explosive shock known as "thunder." There is, you see, a *"way for the lightning of the thunder."*

THE PROCLAMATION OF WISDOM AND UNDERSTANDING

27 "Then did he see it, and declare it; he prepared it, yea, and searched it out." (Job 28:27)

When God made this decree for the rain and the way for the lightning (Job 28:26), He saw, declared and prepared the way of wisdom and understanding. Yes, He even searched it out.

What is this way? Job's next words are among the most important in this book. They define wisdom and understanding.

Job is quoting what God said to man. Again, we observe that God had ways of communicating His word to men before the Scriptures were committed to writing.

28 "And unto man he said, Behold, the fear of the Lord, that is wisdom; and to depart from evil is understanding." (Job 28:28)

There is nothing complicated about these definitions. Volumes of philosophical musing have been written attempting to define wisdom and understanding, yet they only confirm the truth of Job's words—man doesn't know the price of this way, and it is not to be found in the land of the living (Job 28:13).

Wisdom is the fear of the Lord. This is not a cowering fear that drives one into a corner to tremble. Nor is it the anemic, watered-down "respect, or reverence" that appears in modern versions of the Bible and many commentaries. The truth contains elements of both extremes, but is not limited to either.

The fear of the Lord is modeled by the relationship between a father and child. In a healthy family there is a love, trust, respect and reverence that a child holds toward his father. There is also a healthy fear, causing the heart to sink when the child knows that he has disobeyed.

The fear of the Lord can be learned. Specifically, the fear of the Lord can be learned in the Word of God, as suggested by this verse in Deuteronomy.

"Specially the day that thou stoodest before the Lord thy God in Horeb, when the Lord said unto me, Gather me the people together, and I WILL MAKE THEM HEAR MY WORDS, THAT THEY MAY LEARN TO FEAR ME all the days that they shall live upon the earth, and that they may teach their children." (Deuteronomy 4:10) (Author's emphasis)

Understanding is *"to depart from evil."* While wisdom has to do with one's relationship with God, understanding is connected to obedience. Both are part of a trinity that occurs with frequency in the Bible—wisdom, knowledge and understanding.

The three are intricately connected. Consider the following biblical instruction.

"The fear of the LORD is the beginning of knowledge: but fools despise wisdom and instruction." (Proverbs 1:7)

In Job 28:28 we just learned that the fear of the Lord is wisdom. Here in Proverbs 1:7, it is the beginning of knowledge. This common use of contrasts in Proverbs implies that wisdom and knowledge are linked as though interchangeable.

"The fear of the LORD is the beginning of wisdom: and the knowledge of the holy is understanding." (Proverbs 9:10)

In Proverbs 9:10 the fear of the Lord is defined as Job defined it. Here, too, wisdom is connected with knowledge and understanding.

"The fear of the LORD is the beginning of wisdom: a good understanding have all they that do his commandments: his praise endureth for ever." (Psalm 111:10)

In this verse from the Psalms we again see the relationship between the fear of the Lord and wisdom. We also see understanding equated to obedience.

These three concepts are so simply defined in Scripture, they have eluded most men through the centuries. They are so deep, they can never be exhausted by those who choose to pursue them.

The "way" to them can only be revealed by God Himself, and He has chosen to reveal this way in His Word. No amount of money on earth can buy these qualities, nor the way to them, yet multitudes have lost their souls because they did not have them.

PAST BLESSINGS

DAYS OF DIVINE PRESERVATION

1 "Moreover Job continued his parable, and said,

2 Oh that I were as in months past, as in the days when God preserved me." (Job 29:1-2)

In Job 29:1 we are reminded that this is a parable. This is material that is recorded to instruct believers and hide God's truth from skeptics. (Matthew 13:11)

This has been quite a discourse! In Job 26, Job laid out some incredible cosmological information. In Job 27, he successfully defended his personal righteousness and forecast the doom of the wicked, while in Job 28 he dealt with two of life's greatest questions. He also defined wisdom and understanding and the source of them as well as any human being has ever done.

Now, in Job 29 Job is going to reflect upon the "good old days." For most of us the "good old days" are a fantasy that never existed. We all share the tendency to selectively remember things, and think that our contemporary problems are unique. For most of us the "good old days" were no better than the days we are presently living, but in Job's case they really were better!

It is good for Job to give God credit for the blessings in life that he had enjoyed. He attributes them to the fact that God had *"preserved"* him. (Job 29:2)

3 "When his candle shined upon my head, and when by his light I walked through darkness." (Job 29:3)

In our study of Job 18:5-6 we saw the cultural significance of the candle in the middle eastern homes of Job's day. We learned that the lighted candle or lamp signified life in the home. In Job 18:5 Bildad declared that God would put out the light of the wicked.

Satan has unleashed his full fury upon Job, destroying every outward aspect of his life. Yet, internally, inside Job's soul, the light is still on.

It is the darkness that surrounds him that has Job confused. Through every other time of darkness in his life, God had caused His light to shine down upon Job, showing him the way through the darkness. It has never been this dark for Job before, nor for this long.

The sensitive and mature believer understands that God's light is the only way to get through the darkness. There are many places in the Bible that teach this, but let's consider these words of the psalmist.

"The LORD is my light and my salvation; whom shall I fear? The LORD is the strength of my life; of whom shall I be afraid?" (Psalm 27:1)

"O send out thy light and thy truth: let them lead me; let them bring me unto thy holy hill, and to thy tabernacles." (Psalm 43:3)

What has happened to this light in Job's life? Perhaps you are asking, "What happened to this light in MY life?"

God has never left Job. God allowed the Devil to try him, but God never deserted him. God WILL speak and give Job light. It is simply not God's time yet.

Sometimes we remove ourselves from God's light through sin. Sometimes we find ourselves in darkness because we get out of God's Book.

"Thy word is a lamp unto my feet, and a light unto my path." (Psalm 119:105)

"The entrance of thy words giveth light; it giveth understanding unto the simple." (Psalm 119:130)

Today, we have a hand-held light that Job did not have available—the

Bible. There is no reason for the New Testament believer to be in total darkness. We have a light to guide our feet. If the lights have gone out in your life, grab the Word of God!

We have the possibility of a life of fellowship and light that was not possible in Job's day, because of what Christ accomplished on the cross.

"This then is the message which we have heard of him, and declare unto you, that God is light, and in him is no darkness at all. If we say that we have fellowship with him, and walk in darkness, we lie, and do not the truth: But if we walk in the light, as he is in the light, we have fellowship one with another, and the blood of Jesus Christ his Son cleanseth us from all sin. If we say that we have no sin, we deceive ourselves, and the truth is not in us. If we confess our sins, he is faithful and just to forgive us our sins, and to cleanse us from all unrighteousness." (1 John 1:5-9)

The issue for us is simple. If we are left in the dark, we do not have fellowship with God. The solution is also clear. We must confess our sins to God to restore that fellowship. The more we walk with Him, the more light we have.

"But the path of the just is as the shining light, that shineth more and more unto the perfect day." (Proverbs 4:18)

4 "As I was in the days of my youth, when the secret of God was upon my tabernacle." (Job 29:4)

Job is still casting a wistful glance backward over his shoulder to his younger days, when God's light guided him through darkness. A *"tabernacle"* is a dwelling place. Paul used the word figuratively in 2 Corinthians 5:1 to refer to his earthly body.

Job had the confidence of knowing that the *"secret of God"* rested upon him and his dwelling. What is this *"secret of God?"*

"The secret things belong unto the LORD our God: but those things which are revealed belong unto us and to our children for ever, that we may do all the words of this law." (Deuteronomy 29:29)

It is easy for the believer to understand that those things which are not revealed, those things which are hidden, or "secret," belong to God. God reveals to His children what He chooses.

Earlier, in a heated exchange of words, Eliphaz accused Job of an "holier-than-thou" attitude, because Job thought the secret of God had been revealed to him.

"Hast thou heard the secret of God? and dost thou restrain wisdom to thyself?" (Job 15:8)

The truth is, Job says, that there was a time when he knew that God's secret was upon him. This does not mean that Job thinks he knows something that others do not. He is only saying that he rested in the confidence that the secret things of God were hidden in God, and that God and His secret were available as a constant resource.

David, another man who enjoyed a remarkable and intimate fellowship with God, trusted in this same truth. Here are his words in the Psalms.

"What man is he that feareth the LORD? him shall he teach in the way that he shall choose. His soul shall dwell at ease; and his seed shall inherit the earth. The secret of the LORD is with them that fear him; and he will shew them his covenant." (Psalm 25:12-14)

David taught his son Solomon the same confidence. Solomon expressed it this way.

"For the froward is abomination to the LORD: but his secret is with the righteous." (Proverbs 3:32)

Daniel also availed himself of this resource. Again, the idea is not that Daniel was made privy to all the hidden counsel of God. It is only that the secret of God rested upon Daniel as a righteous man, and when he had need, the hidden things of God were there for him. Here is what Daniel said when trusting God to reveal to him Nebuchadnezzar's dream.

"He revealeth the deep and secret things: he knoweth what is in the darkness, and the light dwelleth with him." (Daniel 2:22)

Tragically, Job thinks that those days are gone. Unknown to Job, God is shortly going to reveal to him things that had before been hidden.

How easy the fires of affliction rob us of our confidence!

"But as it is written, Eye hath not seen, nor ear heard, neither have entered into the heart of man, the things which God hath prepared for them that love him. But God hath revealed them unto us by his Spirit: for the Spirit searcheth all things, yea, the deep things of God." (1 Corinthians 2:9-10)

Job's character, integrity and ability to survive Satanic attack are admirable. Yet there is no reason for you, as a New Testament believer, to experience such darkness and hopelessness. Rather than sink in the muck of despair and doom, the believer can go directly to the Book that has been provided to reveal the secret of God, *"yea, the deep things of God."*

DAYS OF DEFERENTIAL PRAISE

5 "When the Almighty was yet with me, when my children were about me;

6 When I washed my steps with butter, and the rock poured me out rivers of oil;

7 When I went out to the gate through the city, when I prepared my seat in the street!

8 The young men saw me, and hid themselves: and the aged arose, and stood up." (Job 29:5-8)

Job fondly remembers the times of prosperity. There were times when he knew that God was with him, and he was surrounded by his children. Verse 6 paints the image of prosperity. In verse 7, he speaks of a seat in the street, located in the gate of the city, which belongs to a government official. This is in keeping with the idea that Job was one of the kings of Edom. Or, as said in Job 1:3, he was *"the greatest of all the men of the east."*

His power intimidated the young, he says in verse 8. The elderly gave him the respect usually reserved for them. Clearly, Job was a man of immense power and influence.

9 "The princes refrained talking, and laid their hand on their mouth." (Job 29:9)

Returning to our original speculation that Job was a duke, or king, of Edom, this verse confirms that even the princes of the land held their peace when Job walked into the room. In our study of Job 1, we commented how Job could easily be the king Jobab, mentioned in Genesis 36:-33.

10 "The nobles held their peace, and their tongue cleaved to the roof of their mouth.

11 When the ear heard me, then it blessed me; and when the eye saw me, it gave witness to me:

12 Because I delivered the poor that cried, and the fatherless, and him that had none to help him.

13 The blessing of him that was ready to perish came upon me: and I caused the widow's heart to sing for joy.

14 I put on righteousness, and it clothed me: my judgment was as a robe and a diadem.

15 I was eyes to the blind, and feet was I to the lame.

16 I was a father to the poor: and the cause which I knew not I searched out.

17 And I brake the jaws of the wicked, and plucked the spoil out of his teeth." (Job 29:10-17)

Job continues his recollections. There is nothing hard to understand about his words. He points to the days when he sat in the seat of power and prosperity.

His words, however, are so grand that they remind us of the times in the book when Job has been a prophetic illustration of the Lord Jesus

Christ. Verse 14 especially prefigures Christ, as Job says that he wore righteousness as his clothing, and judgment as a robe and crown, or diadem. In a chapter that the Lord Jesus Christ applied to Himself, we read these words of the prophet.

"I will greatly rejoice in the LORD, my soul shall be joyful in my God; for he hath clothed me with the garments of salvation, he hath covered me with the robe of righteousness, as a bridegroom decketh himself with ornaments, and as a bride adorneth herself with her jewels." (Isaiah 61:10)

Do not think it presumptuous of Job to speak this way. You, as a New Testament believer, can give the same testimony. You are clothed in Christ's righteousness, or you would still be in the putrid rags of sin. You were given a change of clothing at the time of salvation. Wear them.

"That ye put off concerning the former conversation the old man, which is corrupt according to the deceitful lusts; And be renewed in the spirit of your mind; And that ye put on the new man, which after God is created in righteousness and true holiness." (Ephesians 4:22-24)

"And be found in him, not having mine own righteousness, which is of the law, but that which is through the faith of Christ, the righteousness which is of God by faith." (Philippians 3:9)

"For he hath made him to be sin for us, who knew no sin; that we might be made the righteousness of God in him." (2 Corinthians 5:21)

"Let us be glad and rejoice, and give honour to him: for the marriage of the Lamb is come, and his wife hath made herself ready. And to her was granted that she should be arrayed in fine linen, clean and white: for the fine linen is the righteousness of saints." (Revelation 19:7-8)

While rejoicing in the splendid way in which we can adorn ourselves as the bride of Christ, let us never forget the Lord Jesus Christ stripped Himself of His heavenly garb and glory to die in our place on the cross. (Philippians 2:6-8) This is the picture that is painted as Job laments his lost glory.

DAYS OF DECEPTIVE PERMANENCE

18 "Then I said, I shall die in my nest, and I shall multiply my days as the sand." (Job 29:18)

The nesting instinct is in all of us. We also have the tendency to think we are immortal. This was the case with Job. When things are going well, we want to think it will last forever. David felt the same way.

"And in my prosperity I said, I shall never be moved." (Psalm 30:6)

Never forget that good times can be more dangerous and deceitful than bad times. I look back upon years spent in a civil war in El Salvador. We had some tough times, but I now recognize that they were some of the most precious years in my life. It is easy to go to sleep spiritually when things are comfortable.

19 "My root was spread out by the waters, and the dew lay all night upon my branch.

20 My glory was fresh in me, and my bow was renewed in my hand." (Job 29:19-20)

Job employs the tree figure so commonly used to represent men in the Bible. Just before the rug was pulled out from under his feet, King Nebuchadnezzar enjoyed the same false feelings of security, comparing himself to the flourishing of a tree.

"I Nebuchadnezzar was at rest in mine house, and flourishing in my palace." (Daniel 4:4)

The word *"flourishing"* means "to be green" as in a "tree." Job is a tree blown by a fierce hurricane.

21 "Unto me men gave ear, and waited, and kept silence at my counsel.

22 After my words they spake not again; and my speech dropped upon them." (Job 29:21-22)

Job is not comfortable being in a position where he has no clue about what is happening. He is accustomed to being the one who has all the answers. It was to him that men came for counsel, and they hung upon every word.

23 "And they waited for me as for the rain; and they opened their mouth wide as for the latter rain." (Job 29:23)

We are accustomed to seeing Tribulation images in the Book of Job. Here is a reference to the *"latter rain"* that is often mentioned in connection with end time prophecies. We associate this with the last days because of a prophecy in Joel.

"Be glad then, ye children of Zion, and rejoice in the LORD your God: for he hath given you the former rain moderately, and he will cause to come down for you the rain, the former rain, and the latter rain in the first month." (Joel 2:23)

In Palestine there were two rainy periods, the former and the latter rain. What Joel is really prophesying is a future time when God will cause both to come together in the first month. It will be a real "gully-washer!"

Job's point is to say that men waited for his words with great anticipation. What Job had to say was as refreshing as the rain after a long dry spell.

24 "If I laughed on them, they believed it not; and the light of my countenance they cast not down.
25 I chose out their way, and sat chief, and dwelt as a king in the army, as one that comforteth the mourners." (Job 29: 24-25)

Job was so respected that no one would dream that he would seriously make fun of anyone, or take him lightly. They cherished the chance to be in the *"light of his countenance."*

For his part, Job made himself available, "choosing out their way." When he sat down among his contemporaries, it was chief, or as a king. He was someone who had the right words to comfort the heavy heart.

What a life! It is no wonder he would want to think it would last forever.

Perhaps your life is going so well you have trouble identifying with the trials of Job. Pay heed. Everything you cherish can come tumbling down in a moment's time. What will be your spiritual attitude then? Will you still love God as you do now? Will you still give Him glory?

PRESENT PROBLEMS

Suddenly, Job awakes to the terrible reality of his condition. The memories of past glory fade against the backdrop of his present problems. He describes the misery of his sorry state in Job 30.

DISDAINED BY MEN

1 "But now they that are younger than I have me in derision, whose fathers I would have disdained to have set with the dogs of my flock.
2 Yea, whereto might the strength of their hands profit me, in whom old age was perished?
3 For want and famine they were solitary; fleeing into the wilderness in former time desolate and waste.
4 Who cut up mallows by the bushes, and juniper roots for their meat.
5 They were driven forth from among men, (they cried after them as after a thief;)
6 To dwell in the clifts of the valleys, in caves of the earth, and in the rocks.

7 Among the bushes they brayed; under the nettles they were gathered together.

8 They were children of fools, yea, children of base men: they were viler than the earth." (Job 30:1-8)

Now, those young men, who before would have trembled in his presence, have him *"in derision."* Job says that he would have considered their fathers no better than his dogs.

In the first verses of this chapter Job describes the outcasts of society, and marvels that he is now lower than they. The people he describes were those who had no strength, no value, no resources and no place.

How quickly things can change! Job has fallen from one end of the social pole to the other. The truth is that God's people have historically spent more time as social outcasts than as social leaders.

The very words Job uses to portray these people who now hold him in derision compare to words used to describe the heroes of the faith.

"And others had trial of cruel mockings and scourgings, yea, moreover of bonds and imprisonment: They were stoned, they were sawn asunder, were tempted, were slain with the sword: they wandered about in sheepskins and goatskins; being destitute, afflicted, tormented; (Of whom the world was not worthy:) they wandered in deserts, and in mountains, and in dens and caves of the earth. And these all, having obtained a good report through faith, received not the promise." (Hebrews 11:36-39)

This will be the state to which God's people, the Jews, will be reduced in the Tribulation to come. Jesus prophesied this in Matthew 24.

"Then shall they deliver you up to be afflicted, and shall kill you: and ye shall be hated of all nations for my name's sake." (Matthew 24:9)

"Then let them which be in Judaea flee into the mountains." (Matthew 24:16)

We are reminded of the conditions of the "judgment of nations" in Matthew 25:32-46. All revolves around the treatment given to those who are forced to live as the "scum of the earth" due to their faith in Christ. Revelation 12 is another prophecy of the incredible persecution to which God's people will be subjected in the days of Tribulation.

Now, we enter another of those passages in Job that is simultaneously a prophetic shadow of Christ on the cross, the coming Tribulation and of lost man in hell. This change is evident from Job 30:9.

9 "And now am I their song, yea, I am their byword." (Job 30:9)

In Job 17:6 Job complained that he was made a *"byword."* Then, we looked at the prophetic reference in Deuteronomy 28:37.

"And thou shalt become an astonishment, a proverb, and a byword,

among all nations whither the LORD shall lead thee." (Deuteronomy 28:37)

This has been the case for over two thousand years, and will be finally and completely fulfilled in the Tribulation. Israel is certainly a proverb and a byword all over the world.

We also saw how the same prophecy is fulfilled in Christ, Who was rejected of men. Psalm 69 is Messianic without a doubt. Job is in good company, and again he is a type of Christ in this regard.

"I made sackcloth also my garment; and I became a proverb to them." (Psalm 69:11)

10 "They abhor me, they flee far from me, and spare not to spit in my face." (Job 30:10)

The apparent parallel to Christ is again striking. Consider the following. No one would doubt that Isaiah's prophecy points to Christ, as fulfilled in Matthew's gospel.

"I gave my back to the smiters, and my cheeks to them that plucked off the hair: I hid not my face from shame and spitting." (Isaiah 50:6)

"Then did they spit in his face, and buffeted him; and others smote him with the palms of their hands." (Matthew 26:67)

11 "Because he hath loosed my cord, and afflicted me, they have also let loose the bridle before me." (Job 30:11)

The *"cord"* that Job speaks of is a tent cord, the cord of his tabernacle or body. In other words, he is holding onto life "by a thread," as we would say today, and God has just loosened his cord. Those who would afflict Job are ready to put him under the control of their bridle. They think they have him where they can control him.

12 "Upon my right hand rise the youth; they push away my feet, and they raise up against me the ways of their destruction.

13 They mar my path, they set forward my calamity, they have no helper.

14 They came upon me as a wide breaking in of waters: in the desolation they rolled themselves upon me.

15 Terrors are turned upon me: they pursue my soul as the wind: and my welfare passeth away as a cloud." (Job 30: 12-15)

These verses continue the tale of Job's horror, and they also continue to preview the plight of Christ on the cross, God's people in the Tribulation, and the lost man in hell. The image they present is similar to the one painted in Isaiah 53.

DEBILITATED BY AFFLICTION

16 "And now my soul is poured out upon me; the days of affliction have taken hold upon me." (Job 30:16)

To speak of pouring out one's soul is graphic indeed. The psalmist uses the same notion.

"When I remember these things, I pour out my soul in me: for I had gone with the multitude, I went with them to the house of God, with the voice of joy and praise, with a multitude that kept holyday." (Psalm 42:4)

17 "My bones are pierced in me in the night season: and my sinews take no rest." (Job 30:17)

No thoughtful believer could read these words without thinking of our Lord Jesus Christ as He hung upon the cross in those dark hours. Many would criticize me for reading too much into the words of Job's book. Yet words, phrases and portraits keep flooding these pages that are consistent with the "big picture," as we compare Scripture with Scripture.

"I am poured out like water, and all my bones are out of joint: my heart is like wax; it is melted in the midst of my bowels. My strength is dried up like a potsherd; and my tongue cleaveth to my jaws; and thou hast brought me into the dust of death. For dogs have compassed me: the assembly of the wicked have inclosed me: they pierced my hands and my feet. I may tell all my bones: they look and stare upon me." (Psalm 22:14-17)

18 "By the great force of my disease is my garment changed: it bindeth me about as the collar of my coat.

19 He hath cast me into the mire, and I am become like dust and ashes." (Job 30:18-19)

The saga continues. Also, the comparisons to the crucifixion continue. The next verse is truly remarkable for its similarity to another famous phrase.

DESERTED BY GOD

20 "I cry unto thee, and thou dost not hear me: I stand up, and thou regardest me not." (Job 30:20)

We just looked at Psalm 22. Do you remember how that Psalm opens? These are the very words quoted by Jesus on the cross, as recorded in the gospels.

"My God, my God, why hast thou forsaken me? why art thou so far from helping me, and from the words of my roaring? O my God, I cry in the daytime, but thou hearest not; and in the night season, and am not silent." (Psalm 22:1-2)

The next verses follow with the agony of Job's soul. All, of course, is a mere shadow of what our Lord experienced in His passion on the cross. Read them carefully. There is nothing hard to understand as far as the meaning is concerned. You can NEVER comprehend their depth and reality.

21 "Thou art become cruel to me: with thy strong hand thou opposest thyself against me.
22 Thou liftest me up to the wind; thou causest me to ride upon it, and dissolvest my substance.
23 For I know that thou wilt bring me to death, and to the house appointed for all living.
24 Howbeit he will not stretch out his hand to the grave, though they cry in his destruction.
25 Did not I weep for him that was in trouble? was not my soul grieved for the poor?
26 When I looked for good, then evil came unto me: and when I waited for light, there came darkness.
27 My bowels boiled, and rested not: the days of affliction prevented me.
28 I went mourning without the sun: I stood up, and I cried in the congregation." (Job 30:21-28)

Can you see a fraction of Job's fractured soul? Can you catch a glimpse of our Lord as He suffered in our place?

29 "I am a brother to dragons, and a companion to owls.
30 My skin is black upon me, and my bones are burned with heat.
31 My harp also is turned to mourning, and my organ into the voice of them that weep." (Job 30:29-31)

Dragons are mentioned several times in the Bible. They are never the product of ignorant Hebrew superstition as sometimes speculated. They are always associated with THE dragon, who is clearly identified in Revelation 12.

"And the great dragon was cast out, that old serpent, called the Devil, and Satan, which deceiveth the whole world: he was cast out into the earth, and his angels were cast out with him." (Revelation 12:9)

The owls of Job 30:29 are unclean birds according to Leviticus 11, types of demons. They appear with other unclean birds and animals in Isaiah 34, which paints a graphic picture of hell.

Job's *"black skin"* condition and the burning in his bones are evidence of a very sick man. Figuratively, this description fits with the threefold prophetic picture of Christ on the cross, God's people in the Tribulation, and lost man in hell. Being accompanied by Satan's hordes and a burning from within and without aptly portray the condition of all three. There is no wonder that joy is converted to mourning and tears, as Job laments in Job 30:31.

PERSONAL RIGHTEOUSNESS

The tone changes abruptly in Job 31. From his unimaginable abyss of agony, Job draws a deep breath, lifts his head and bravely puts his personal righteousness on the line. This entire chapter, comprising Job's final remarks, is a grand tribute to Job's own righteousness.

Nothing Job says requires much explanation or commentary. We will simply lay it out before us, examine how it fits the context, and stand back in awe, considering how this man has managed to hold fast to his integrity through the relentless physical and psychological pounding he has received.

1 **"I made a covenant with mine eyes; why then should I think upon a maid?**
2 **For what portion of God is there from above? and what inheritance of the Almighty from on high?**
3 **Is not destruction to the wicked? and a strange punishment to the workers of iniquity?**
4 **Doth not he see my ways, and count all my steps?" (Job 31:1-4)**

Job's covenant with his eyes in verse 1 is sound advice for any young man (or old man for that matter). This is a very practical application of the truth that Jesus expounded in the Sermon on the Mount.

"Ye have heard that it was said by them of old time, Thou shalt not commit adultery: But I say unto you, That whosoever looketh on a woman to lust after her hath committed adultery with her already in his heart. And if thy right eye offend thee, pluck it out, and cast it from thee: for it is profitable for thee that one of thy members should perish, and not that thy whole body should be cast into hell." (Matthew 5:27-29)

Obviously, this is an example of oriental hyperbolic teaching. Plucking out the eye to avoid dangerous temptation is not to be taken literally. Yet Job's practice of seriously guarding what entered his mind through the eye gate is a pragmatic approach to a dangerous source of temptation. The reason for such care is also articulated by Jesus in the same Sermon on the Mount.

"The light of the body is the eye: if therefore thine eye be single, thy whole body shall be full of light. But if thine eye be evil, thy whole body shall be full of darkness. If therefore the light that is in thee be darkness, how great is that darkness!" (Matthew 6:22-23)

Job's reason for zealously standing sentry over his eyes is his knowledge that God's omniscient eye sees his every move. He also knows that God is faithful to reward *"workers of iniquity."*

The next 36 verses consist of a series of questions regarding Job's personal testimony, marked by the 20 times the word *"if"* appears. If Job has been guilty of any of the accusations he mentions, he is ready to bear the full brunt of God's judgment. Some of these accusations were hurled at Job by his counselors. Others are suggested here by Job himself. This is the biggest bite of Scripture we have attempted to swallow at one time in our study. There is nothing here, however, that requires much explanation.

5 "If I have walked with vanity, or if my foot hath hasted to deceit;

6 Let me be weighed in an even balance, that God may know mine integrity.

7 If my step hath turned out of the way, and mine heart walked after mine eyes, and if any blot hath cleaved to mine hands;

8 Then let me sow, and let another eat; yea, let my offspring be rooted out.

9 If mine heart have been deceived by a woman, or if I have laid wait at my neighbour's door;

10 Then let my wife grind unto another, and let others bow down upon her.

11 For this is an heinous crime; yea, it is an iniquity to be punished by the judges.

12 For it is a fire that consumeth to destruction, and would root out all mine increase.

13 If I did despise the cause of my manservant or of my maidservant, when they contended with me;

14 What then shall I do when God riseth up? and when he visiteth, what shall I answer him?

15 Did not he that made me in the womb make him? and did not one fashion us in the womb?

16 If I have withheld the poor from their desire, or have caused the eyes of the widow to fail;

17 Or have eaten my morsel myself alone, and the fatherless hath not eaten thereof;

18 (For from my youth he was brought up with me, as with a

father, and I have guided her from my mother's womb;)

19 If I have seen any perish for want of clothing, or any poor without covering;

20 If his loins have not blessed me, and if he were not warmed with the fleece of my sheep;

21 If I have lifted up my hand against the fatherless, when I saw my help in the gate:

22 Then let mine arm fall from my shoulder blade, and mine arm be broken from the bone.

23 For destruction from God was a terror to me, and by reason of his highness I could not endure.

24 If I have made gold my hope, or have said to the fine gold, Thou art my confidence;

25 If I rejoiced because my wealth was great, and because mine hand had gotten much;

26 If I beheld the sun when it shined, or the moon walking in brightness;

27 And my heart hath been secretly enticed, or my mouth hath kissed my hand:

28 This also were an iniquity to be punished by the judge: for I should have denied the God that is above.

29 If I rejoiced at the destruction of him that hated me, or lifted up myself when evil found him:

30 Neither have I suffered my mouth to sin by wishing a curse to his soul.

31 If the men of my tabernacle said not, Oh that we had of his flesh! we cannot be satisfied.

32 The stranger did not lodge in the street: but I opened my doors to the traveller.

33 If I covered my transgressions as Adam, by hiding mine iniquity in my bosom:

34 Did I fear a great multitude, or did the contempt of families terrify me, that I kept silence, and went not out of the door?

35 Oh that one would hear me! behold, my desire is, that the Almighty would answer me, and that mine adversary had written a book.

36 Surely I would take it upon my shoulder, and bind it as a crown to me.

37 I would declare unto him the number of my steps; as a prince would I go near unto him.

38 If my land cry against me, or that the furrows likewise thereof complain;

39 If I have eaten the fruits thereof without money, or have caused the owners thereof to lose their life:
40 Let thistles grow instead of wheat, and cockle instead of barley. The words of Job are ended." (Job 31:5-40)

None of us would dare to compare our own troubles with the terrible calamity suffered by Job. Nor would we want to compare our personal righteousness to his. If Job's testimony is correct, and God said that it was, then few men have approached a life of such moral uprightness.

Despite such worthiness, the Bible is clear in teaching that self-righteousness alone is not sufficient to gain eternal life. Luke 18 records the story of the Pharisee who felt secure in comparing his righteousness to that of a publican whom he saw praying in the temple. The same chapter tells of the rich young ruler, who also wanted to think that his personal righteousness was enough to impress God.

Acts 10 is the tale of Cornelius, the morally correct and religious centurion. He was not only personally righteous, he had a pure heart as well. Still, even that was not enough. It was enough, though, for God to send him more light, in the person of Peter, who proclaimed the gospel to Cornelius and his household. Only his faith in the gospel could gain him entry into eternal life.

Job 31 is another classic portion of the Bible which teaches that one's own righteousness alone is not sufficient. We must admire Job for his righteousness. Yet when all is said and done, there is still something lacking.

Job 31:40 says that *"The words of Job are ended."* There is no final peace in his heart. The matter has still not been resolved. Something is missing and God will supply it. He alone can supply what is lacking in Job's life, and in yours and mine.

Reflecting on what Job has spoken, I think of the stinging words that Jesus said to the Pharisees in Matthew's Gospel.

"Woe unto you, scribes and Pharisees, hypocrites! for ye pay tithe of mint and anise and cummin, and have omitted the weightier matters of the law, judgment, mercy, and faith: these ought ye to have done, and not to leave the other undone." (Matthew 23:23)

One could not possibly accuse Job of the hypocrisy of the Pharisees. Yet the situation is similar to Job's. He has done what he ought to have done. He SHOULD have had a life this righteous. The fact that his righteousness is greater than most men's, does not negate the fact that such righteousness is what God requires.

Even at that, there is still something "undone." The undone will not be done until Calvary. Job cannot understand this as we can, but he must finally come to realize that he must lean upon God alone to have hope of eternal life and deliverance.

24

THE EXPLOSION OF ELIHU

Behold, now I have opened my mouth,
my tongue hath spoken in my mouth.
My words shall be of the uprightness of my heart:
and my lips shall utter knowledge clearly.
The Spirit of God hath made me,
and the breath of the Almighty
hath given me life.

Job 33:2-4

THE WORDS OF JOB ARE ENDED, AND THE DUST IS SETTLING from the animated conversation that has filled the air. Four great men sit silent, each disconcerted in his inability to convince the others of his point of view.

The battle has been intense. From the beginning, no pleasantries have been exchanged. No sympathetic words of understanding came from the mouths of these men who had supposedly come to comfort and to counsel. Job heard not one comforting phrase such as "Sorry to hear about your family, Job."

These men immediately vaulted into the debate arena, as though life and death depended upon what they were going to say. They spoke with an intensity that underscored the depth of their conviction. At times heated, at times insightful or even grand, their speeches covered the entire panorama of human emotion and thought.

So, who won? No one won. No one ever wins when "spiritual" matters are debated.

This is like much of our "witnessing" to people of other faiths. We throw out-of-context proof texts at each other, each holding firm to his convictions, while absolutely no communication takes place.

It also resembles much of our "counseling." Highly qualified individuals dispense facts they have found through years of preparation. Desperately frustrated individuals hear this knowledge, and perceive it to be a threat to what little security they have remaining. Positions are defended, while little truth is wisely applied with understanding.

Job and his three friends can go no further. They all four sit silently, reflecting upon the stubbornness of the other. All are "great men," in the sense of position and worldly knowledge. They are highly respected. None, however, could prevail against the others.

So, the debate is over. No one has "won," except each in his own mind. These men are not alone, however.

It is impossible to say how many spectators made up the gallery that day. Four men of the stature of these would undoubtedly cause a stir, especially when their words were forceful and heated.

There is at least one spectator who has been present from the beginning. He has carefully listened to every word. Since he is younger than the other men, he has kept silent out of respect. Yet within him a fire is raging. He can keep silent no longer. His name is Elihu.

ELIHU'S ANGER REACHES THE BOILING POINT

1 "So these three men ceased to answer Job, because he was righteous in his own eyes." (Job 32:1)

There have been three cycles of exchanges between Job and his friends. Each has spoken his mind three times, and three times Job has rebutted each of them. Zophar is the only exception, as we have previously noted. He has one turn left, yet denies himself the opportunity. What more could be said?

None of the three has been able to budge Job from holding onto his personal righteousness. God has already given us His testimony in the first chapter of the Book of Job. Job IS a righteous man.

If Job has a problem, it is the tendency to trust more in his own righteousness than in God's. Yet that is pure speculation on our part. We have seen how these three men shared that speculation, carried it to an extreme, and refused to move from it.

2 "Then was kindled the wrath of Elihu the son of Barachel the Buzite, of the kindred of Ram: against Job was his wrath kindled, because he justified himself rather than God." (Job 32:2)

Elihu is now formally introduced. He is a Buzite, which would trace his family back to Buz in Genesis 22.

"And it came to pass after these things, that it was told Abraham, saying, Behold, Milcah, she hath also born children unto thy brother Nahor; Huz his firstborn, and Buz his brother, and Kemuel the father of Aram." (Genesis 22:20-21)

This passage shows that Elihu is descended from the same family from which Abraham came. Jeremiah 25:23 mentions a city called "Buz," which is connected with Dedan and Tema, two towns in Edom. It would appear that the Buzite, coming out of Mesopotamia, like Abraham, would have settled in the area of Edom. Remember that Abraham sent his servant back to his family in search of a wife for Isaac. This continued contact could have resulted in the migration of Buzites to Edom, where we find Elihu in the days when Esau's sons ruled.

The "Ram" mentioned in Job 32:2 may be the "Aram" of Genesis 22:21. Others would identify him as "Abraham." In any case, these names probably all share a common origin.

Whatever conclusions we might draw concerning Elihu's parentage and identity, we have no difficulty taking his emotional temperature. He is steamed!

The reason is clearly stated—*"Because he (Job) justified himself rather than God."* Elihu is highly offended by Job's act of defending his own righteousness. Elihu thinks that Job should allow God to come to his defense and justify him.

While this sounds logical, good and even "spiritual," it is a dangerous trap for a counselor, or anyone for that matter. Elihu has jumped into the fray to defend God. God needs no defense!

Which is worse? To justify yourself rather than God, or to defend God rather than allow Him to defend Himself?

When one steps in to defend God, he is stepping into the place of God. This is always a precarious place to be. We must learn this lesson well.

Our job as counselors is to minister the Word of God. (I much prefer the term minister over counselor). We have used the other because of the fact that Job's three friends are so often called his "counselors.") As biblical counselors we are only here to put forth the truth of God. We do NOT have to defend God. God needs no secret police.

All four men who approach Job are guilty of this mistake. They are so offended "for God's sake," that they miss God altogether.

One who would minister the Word of God should learn that things are to be taken seriously, but not TOO seriously. We lay out God's truth, then allow God to be God. There is only one mediator between God and man. The position has already been filled by the Lord Jesus Christ. No one else need apply.

3 "Also against his three friends was his wrath kindled, because they had found no answer, and yet had condemned Job." (Job 32:3)

At least Elihu is fair and doesn't take sides. He is just as angry with the other three men as he is at Job.

He has seen through the shallowness of their arguments. He is right, of course, that *"they had found no answer, and yet had condemned Job."* In speaking himself, however, he becomes guilty of the same thing. He will continue the same thesis—that Job has some uncovered sin in his life. The sum of his arguments will be the same total as the men before him—nothing.

Elihu illustrates another common snare that awaits those who want to minister to others. In condemning the other men, Elihu, in his super-piety, becomes guilty of the same sin. Paul warned the Romans of this frequent human weakness.

"Therefore thou art inexcusable, O man, whosoever thou art that judgest: for wherein thou judgest another, thou condemnest thyself; for thou that judgest doest the same things." (Romans 2:1)

Paul makes this statement while establishing the fact of human sin. He cautions against looking down on others, thinking that one has an exclusive right to God.

The correct attitude is also taught by Paul. We find this instruction in his letter to the Galatians.

"Brethren, if a man be overtaken in a fault, ye which are spiritual, restore such an one in the spirit of meekness; considering thyself, lest thou also be tempted." (Galatians 6:1)

Elihu is obviously a brilliant young man. As we read the words he spoke, though, I think you will agree that there is not much *"spirit of meekness."*

4 "Now Elihu had waited till Job had spoken, because they were elder than he.

5 When Elihu saw that there was no answer in the mouth of these three men, then his wrath was kindled." (Job 32:4-5)

Respect for age is still a vital part of oriental society. Elihu is obviously aware of the age and social position of the four men who have exchanged words. He would not have dared to interrupt them.

That he would even speak now is a significant thing in that culture. Either he has some age and status himself, or he is REALLY upset. Probably both are true.

He has patiently waited to see if they would come to a conclusion, a consensus, or anything. Seeing that so many words have been tossed about without accomplishing a thing has only increased his fury.

ELIHU'S JUSTIFICATION FOR SPEAKING REVEALS HIS MOTIVATION

6 "And Elihu the son of Barachel the Buzite answered and said, I am young, and ye are very old; wherefore I was afraid, and durst not shew you mine opinion.
7 I said, Days should speak, and multitude of years should teach wisdom." (Job 32:6-7)

There is nothing hidden or hard here. Elihu is simply showing some respect before slam-dunking these men through the basket of life.

8 "But there is a spirit in man: and the inspiration of the Almighty giveth them understanding." (Job 32:8)

To overstate the importance of this verse would be impossible. This is one of two places in the Bible where the word *"inspiration"* appears.

A great debate rages today concerning the inspiration of the Bible. Major denominations, such as the Southern Baptists, have suffered division over this issue. Theologians laboriously weigh each word in preparing their definitions of *"inspiration."* All this work is terribly important. Yet in their passion to be theologically correct, men tend to ignore the obvious—the simple testimony of Scripture itself. Before defining inspiration we should listen carefully to the two times the word is used in Scripture.

Here, in Job 32:8, *"inspiration"* has to do with God giving understanding to man's spirit. In Job 28:28 understanding was defined as departing from evil. Though the context does not directly deal with the process of writing Scripture, it would not be stretching the meaning of these words to see them applied to that process. Peter explains how that process worked.

"For the prophecy came not in old time by the will of man: but holy men of God spake as they were moved by the Holy Ghost." (2 Peter 1:21)

These holy men of God were not sanctified dictation machines; they were no robots engaged in what some have called "automatic writing." They were men just like us, whose spirit was the recipient of God's inspiration as they were moved by the Holy Ghost.

The second, and final, occurrence of the word *"inspiration"* in 2 Timothy 3:16, refers to the way in which the Scriptures came to us.

"All scripture is given by inspiration of God, and is profitable for doctrine, for reproof, for correction, for instruction in righteousness." (2 Timothy 3:16)

The process by which Scripture comes to us, or *"is given,"* is through inspiration. Many have pointed to the Greek word *"theopneustos,"* translated *"inspiration"* and meaning "God-breathed." Without question, it is a wonderful truth to know that the Bible has been breathed out of the mouth of God!

Before we nail down our "confessions of faith" and defend the Bible, inspired by God in the original manuscripts, notice that the same "Scriptures" inspired by God in 2 Timothy 3:16, were in Timothy's house in 2 Timothy 3:15, and responsible for his conversion. I seriously doubt that the early church chose to store the "original manuscripts" in Timothy's house.

My purpose is not to cause you to doubt the inspiration of Scripture, but merely to suggest that the word may be a bit broader than we usually think.

Could the word *"inspiration"* as found in Scripture also extend to God's grace given to man to "understand" the Scriptures He has breathed out of His mouth? We remember that 1 Corinthians 2:14 tells us that the Scriptures are to be *"spiritually discerned."* Elihu uses the word *"inspiration"* in just that sense.

The debate over the Bible will continue. It is vitally important that we hold to a Bible given to us directly from God, divinely inspired. Yet no matter how precise and theologically correct your definition of inspiration may be, it is worthless unless God infuses your human spirit to understand it. Your correct theology is also impotent if the Bible is not the final authority in your life. I propose that while many of us exchange words over the precise meaning of inspiration, the real issue is authority. Will you *"understand,"* as Job 28:28 explains it and obey the Word of God?

9 "Great men are not always wise: neither do the aged understand judgment." (Job 32:9)

Earlier we commented that all four men involved in this debate were *"great"* men. The world labels *"great men"* as those who profoundly influence the course of human civilization. Benjamin Franklin, Thomas Jefferson, Thomas Edison, Alexander Graham Bell and others would be included in a list of great Americans. As Bible believers, we know there is absolutely no automatic correlation between being a great individual and having biblical wisdom. We know that Elihu's assertion is totally correct.

The second half of the verse is equally true. A good share of grey hair is no guarantee of good judgment. There are plenty of golden-agers who possess horrible judgment.

This reality is confirmed in Psalm 119. The psalmist lets us know how it is possible to have wisdom far beyond our years.

"I understand more than the ancients, because I keep thy precepts." (Psalm 119:100)

The opposite is also true. Elderly people who do not obey the precepts of the Word of God display their lack of wisdom and understanding, no matter how much knowledge they may have accumulated over the years.

10 "Therefore I said, Hearken to me; I also will shew mine opinion.

11 Behold, I waited for your words; I gave ear to your reasons, whilst ye searched out what to say.

12 Yea, I attended unto you, and, behold, there was none of you that convinced Job, or that answered his words." (Job 32:10-12)

With these words, Elihu feels confident that he is justified in adding his two-cents worth. He has patiently and carefully listened to all that has been said. Yet he is sure that none of these men has gotten his point across to Job, or answered his rebuttals.

13 "Lest ye should say, We have found out wisdom: God trusteth him down, not man." (Job 32:13)

Here is Elihu's real motivation. He simply cannot stand to think that these men will go away convinced they are right.

Elihu is not really concerned with WHAT is right. He is bothered about what people THINK is right.

Elihu, for all his obvious intelligence, has not learned the lesson we just discussed—no one wins spiritual or religious arguments. No matter what we say, there is no convincing someone who does not want to be convinced.

Be careful not to get caught up in the mentality of thinking that you have the responsibility to convince others of the truth. Such thinking is an intellectual "black hole," which sucks up all those who venture too close.

Truth is truth. Truth does not need anyone to defend it. Truth stands alone without assistance due to the very fact that it is true. Truth does not need anyone to believe it in order for it to be true.

Jesus simply spoke the truth and left it there. He was never seen chasing after truth, trying to convince everyone in its path to believe.

Elihu's main interest is not getting to the truth. He is angry because these men have not done a better job of convincing Job of secret sin. He is not only frustrated by Job's stubborn refusal to confess his secret sin, he is also angry that these three men would walk away thinking they had done God a favor.

14 "Now he hath not directed his words against me: neither will I answer him with your speeches." (Job 32:14)

Before setting forth his own argument, Elihu wants to protect himself. He disassociates himself from the heat of all that was said previously. He makes it clear that nothing has been directed at HIM. This is not HIS problem. Job has not spoken to HIM. Also, he works to draw a line separating himself from the other men. He is not going to take their side, or answer their speeches.

Elihu wants everyone to think that he is only concerned for the truth, yet we have already seen otherwise. He wants everyone to think that he is finally going to resolve the real issues. We will soon see that he has nothing new to add.

ELIHU'S AUTHORSHIP IS SEEN IN HIS PREAMBLE

15 "They were amazed, they answered no more: they left off speaking.
16 When I had waited, (for they spake not, but stood still, and answered no more)." (Job 32:15-16)

These two verses are the basis for our earlier assertion that Elihu is the best candidate as author of the Book of Job. This is the only example of narrative in the first person that we find in the book.

These words do not record the speech that Elihu made. They are the author's reflections upon the hearers' reaction to what he has just said. Here the author appears to be Elihu. He says that he was waiting for them to speak, but they did not.

Again, these are not words that form part of his speech to the other men. They are his impressions of how the men responded to his remarks.

The other men are speechless. Perhaps they think Elihu is being presumptuous in speaking. Maybe they are so shocked they do not know what to say. Anyway, there is nothing left for them to say that they have not already said.

17 "I said, I will answer also my part, I also will shew mine opinion.
18 For I am full of matter, the spirit within me constraineth me.
19 Behold, my belly is as wine which hath no vent; it is ready to burst like new bottles.
20 I will speak, that I may be refreshed: I will open my lips and answer." (Job 32:17-20)

In these verses also Elihu seems to be recording what he is thinking to himself. He claims to be so full of the matter being discussed, he just cannot hold it in any longer. He says his inner spirit is motivating him to speak. The comparison he makes is to a new bottle of wine that is ready to burst. The only relief he is going to have will come from venting his pent-up feelings.

21 "Let me not, I pray you, accept any man's person, neither let me give flattering titles unto man.

22 For I know not to give flattering titles; in so doing my maker would soon take me away." (Job 32:21-22)

Now, there is no doubt that Elihu is again speaking directly to the other men. Simply put, he is advising them that he will be blunt and will not make allowances because of their age, influence or position.

To do otherwise, he says, would be to invite God's wrath. While we might question his motives (and we have), Elihu shows his understanding of a truth that later appears in the Book of Proverbs.

"*These things also belong to the wise. It is not good to have respect of persons in judgment.*" (Proverbs 24:23)

ELIHU'S AUDACITY SHINES THROUGH HIS WORDS

1 "Wherefore, Job, I pray thee, hear my speeches, and hearken to all my words.

2 Behold, now I have opened my mouth, my tongue hath spoken in my mouth." (Job 33:1-2)

Elihu now singles out Job, and urges him to listen carefully and weigh every word. Elihu is primed to speak, and he wants Job to know that he is choosing his words carefully.

3 "My words shall be of the uprightness of my heart: and my lips shall utter knowledge clearly." (Job 33:3)

Elihu claims to speak from a pure heart. Would you expect anything different?

He also says that he will speak clearly. Clear knowledge will definitely flow from his lips. Unfortunately, he will often show himself deficient in wisdom and understanding.

4 "The Spirit of God hath made me, and the breath of the Almighty hath given me life." (Job 33:4)

In remarks concerning Job 3:11 and 27:3, we considered how the Spirit of God and the breath of God are used in a synonymous sense to speak of the unique nature of human life. We saw how Genesis 2:7 describes the way in which God gave this life to man.

"*And the LORD God formed man of the dust of the ground, and breathed into his nostrils the breath of life; and man became a living soul."* (Genesis 2:7)

Elihu obviously understands this unique feature of human life. Notice how he parallels God having MADE him, with God having given him life. The Spirit of God breathed into man is what makes him human. There are many creatures that God has made, as testified by the first chapter of Genesis. Only man had God breathe life into his nostrils.

When we consider the context and flow of Elihu's words, apparently he means something more by this comment than a reference to creation. In Job 32:8 Elihu mentioned this spirit in man, and then he drew the conclusion that *"the inspiration of the Almighty giveth them understanding."*

Making the connection between Job 33:4 and 32:8, it seems that Elihu is claiming divine inspiration. He set the foundation in Job 32:8, and now makes the application. He has just said that he is going to speak clearly from a pure heart in Job 33:3. In Job 33:5 he will challenge these men to answer him if they can. In Job 33:6 he makes the audacious claim to be speaking *"in God's stead"*!

Putting the pieces together in the proper frame, Elihu's intentions are clear. He asserts that God's Spirit will be speaking through him.

5 "If thou canst answer me, set thy words in order before me, stand up." (Job 33:5)

Can he really be serious? Is Job going to stand up and answer a man who claims to be speaking on God's behalf?

This adds a new dimension to the scene. The four men we have listened to have all had some thought-provoking things to say. None of them, though, has claimed to have spoken with divine inspiration.

Before you become indignant at the thought of this man daring to make such a claim, remember that the same thing goes on in many Christian circles today. Charismatics, Pentecostals and many from the mainline denominations believe there is a modern revival of signs and wonders. While giving lip service to the Bible, and using it as a devotional resource, many believe that God is giving revelations today that are at least equal to Scripture in their authority.

When someone in these denominations says they got a "word of knowledge," a "word of faith," a "word from God," or whatever the catch phrase of the moment, it is accepted unquestionably. Since they believe these new revelations can come from God, who is going to question God? Yet what is to prevent someone from just saying that God has spoken through them? Obviously, there is nothing to prevent that, and it happens constantly.

What can prevent such confusion and chaos? Only one thing—the authority of the Bible. This is the reason God has given us a single voice of authority, not several competing ones. With a Bible in our hand we can measure everything that is said, and reject without apology those things that do not line up with the teaching of God's Word.

Before becoming too judgmental, remember that even those of us who do not believe in additional revelation sometimes tend to pepper our speech with careless phrases. "God told me," "The Lord said to me," or other phrases often casually slide from our lips and we don't really stop to consider how others may interpret them.

As you have opportunity to minister the Word of God, be careful to place the emphasis upon the authority of the Bible, not upon your own words. God has already spoken His mind and placed it in your hands. He does not need you to speak on His behalf. He has only commanded that you communicate with the power of the Spirit the words He has already spoken.

6 "Behold, I am according to thy wish in God's stead: I also am formed out of the clay." (Job 33:6)

Several times Job has verbally expressed his wish to speak with God. In Job 9:32-33 he laments the fact that there is no *"daysman"* between him and God who could mediate whatever differences existed.

Now, Elihu claims to be the answer to Job's prayers! Elihu proudly announces that he will be speaking to Job *"in God's stead,"* that is to say "in God's place."

He is careful to clothe this in appropriate humility, of course. He adds *"I also am formed out of the clay,"* to remind these men that he is just as human as they are. Thanks for the reminder, Elihu!

7 "Behold, my terror shall not make thee afraid, neither shall my hand be heavy upon thee." (Job 33:7)

All along Job has complained about the heavy hand of God upon him, and the terror that has taken hold of him. As if what he has said already was not outrageous enough, Elihu now claims to be able to do a better job of ministering to Job than God. He will get his point across without all the terror and heavy-handed approach.

Plainly, Elihu does not intend for his words to sound so harsh and arrogant. It just goes to confirm the words of Christ in Luke 6:45, that a man speaks out of the abundance of his heart, whether good or evil.

Many a Christian counselor in the abundance of sincerity presumes to place himself in the seat of God, or at least to become His mediator, speaking in His stead. Be very careful if you are in this position.

Elihu also illustrates a second error in ministering the Word of God. Like Elihu, we often want to soften what God is doing in someone's life.

At times God finds it necessary to deal harshly with us. The reasons belong to Him alone. Who are we to think that God is too hard? Be very careful not to attempt to blunt the edge of the sharp, two-edged sword. You will not succeed anyway.

ELIHU'S ANALYSIS DEPICTS JOB'S CONDITION

8 "Surely thou hast spoken in mine hearing, and I have heard the voice of thy words, saying,
9 I am clean without transgression, I am innocent; neither is there iniquity in me." (Job 33:8-9)

Elihu acknowledges that he has listened carefully to Job. He understands that Job claims to be innocent of hidden sin.

10 "Behold, he findeth occasions against me, he counteth me for his enemy,
11 He putteth my feet in the stocks, he marketh all my paths." (Job 33:10-11)

Elihu has also picked up on another constant theme as he listened to Job's anguish. He sees that Job blames God for his problems. This is important, because it sets up Elihu's basic thesis as expressed in the following verse.

12 "Behold, in this thou art not just: I will answer thee, that God is greater than man." (Job 33:12)

Here is the problem according to Elihu. He, the same as the others, is convinced that Job's problems are due to Job's sins. The difference between Elihu and the others is that Elihu is certain he knows the exact sin.

The sin is in having blamed God for his problems. *"Behold, in this thou art not just."*

Elihu's doctrinal view centers on the sovereignty of God. He accuses Job of failing to understand *"that God is greater than man."* According to Elihu, if Job would just submit himself to the sovereignty of God, resolve himself to a fatalistic view of life, and stop complaining, all would be well.

Job should not try to figure out God, Elihu says, because He is sovereign. God can never be fully understood by His creation. Elihu continues this thought in the next verse.

13 "Why dost thou strive against him? for he giveth not account of any of his matters." (Job 33:13)

Well, isn't that comforting? Elihu certainly has things calculated. God is sovereign. Sometimes tragedy falls within the sovereign plan of the sovereign God. That is all there is to it. He doesn't have to account for what he does, nor answer to anyone. There is no use fighting Him.

A couple of observations need to be addressed. First, Job has never denied God's sovereignty. Job has never said he wants to understand everything, only to know what God is doing now in his life. He has refused to curse God. He has refused to rebel against God's sovereignty, though his wife tried to talk him into it.

Second, Elihu is a perfect illustration of how a man with only intellectual knowledge of God's attributes is powerless to deal with life's problems. For many, the sovereignty of God is a way to escape from dealing with life's difficult situations and questions. It is not so much meekly accepting an attribute of God, as it is a theological sheet to be pulled over the head in time of trial.

Like so many have done since, Elihu's counseling method is to toss out theological facts, thinking that their mere mention is enough to solve any problem. Theological data is worthless to help another's painful reality.

Who would be so foolish as to deny God's sovereignty? Surely not Job! Job doesn't need a course in systematic theology. He doesn't even need all the answers. What he desperately needs is a real friend to put his arm around him, keep his mouth shut for a while, and radiate a genuine love that is much louder than words.

ELIHU'S ARGUMENTS DETAIL GOD'S COMMUNICATION WITH MEN

14 "For God speaketh once, yea twice, yet man perceiveth it not.
15 In a dream, in a vision of the night, when deep sleep falleth upon men, in slumberings upon the bed;
16 Then he openeth the ears of men, and sealeth their instruction." (Job 33:14-16)

Read these words carefully. They are a correct description of God's manner of communicating with man. We again remember that these men, Elihu included, have access to wonderful information about God and His creation.

Before God chose to reduce His communication with man to written form, He used a variety of methods to communicate. We have already learned that Job is the oldest Bible book in terms of chronological age.

Next come the five books of Moses that begin our Old Testament, Genesis, Exodus, Leviticus, Numbers and Deuteronomy.

Even after God had begun to speak through His prophets who reduced His words to writing, He still used other ways of speaking from time to time. Hebrews makes this clear.

"God, who at sundry times and in divers manners spake in time past unto the fathers by the prophets, Hath in these last days spoken unto us by his Son, whom he hath appointed heir of all things, by whom also he made the worlds." (Hebrews 1:1-2)

Numbers 12:6 is one of several Old Testament references that confirms God had ways to communicate to His people other than the written word.

"And he said, Hear now my words: If there be a prophet among you, I the LORD will make myself known unto him in a vision, and will speak unto him in a dream." (Numbers 12:6)

Obviously, God employed some of these diverse methods to teach much of His truth to men like Job and his friends.

Whether by vision, dream or other method, God was able to work in man's subconscious to speak His word. Often, as Elihu suggests, God would speak to men as they quieted their souls in restful sleep. God first spoke to young Samuel this way in 1 Samuel 3.

Today, however, we have something far superior—the written Word of God. We do not have to use our subjective judgment about whether a man is speaking on God's behalf or not. Fragile feelings and impressions no longer need to be our guide. The passage we just saw in Hebrews 1:1-2 announces that in these last days God has spoken to us by His Son, first as the living Word (as a man), and now as the written Word.

Paul tells the Corinthians in 1 Corinthians 2:16 that they have the mind of Christ. He makes this statement in the context of telling them that the Word of God must be spiritually discerned.

Peter proclaimed that the written Word of God is far more certain than seeing God with your own eyes and hearing His voice with your own ears.

"For we have not followed cunningly devised fables, when we made known unto you the power and coming of our Lord Jesus Christ, but were eyewitnesses of his majesty. For he received from God the Father honour and glory, when there came such a voice to him from the excellent glory, This is my beloved Son, in whom I am well pleased. And this voice which came from heaven we heard, when we were with him in the holy mount. We have also a more sure word of prophecy; whereunto ye do well that ye take heed, as unto a light that shineth in a dark place, until the day dawn, and the day star arise in your hearts: Knowing this first, that no prophecy of the scripture is of any private interpretation. For the prophecy came not

in old time by the will of man: but holy men of God spake as they were moved by the Holy Ghost." (2 Peter 1:16-21)

Though God has spoken today with the authoritative voice of His Word, Elihu's words still offer some enlightening instruction for us. According to Elihu, God speaks to men when deep sleep falls upon them. Sleep typifies death for the New Testament believer. God best speaks to us today when we learn to die to self.

In Job 33:16 Elihu said, "*THEN he openeth the ears of men, and sealeth their instruction.*" It is when we die to self that God can open our ears of faith. (Author's emphasis)

Paul teaches in Romans that faith comes by hearing, and, specifically, by hearing the Word of God.

"*So then faith cometh by hearing, and hearing by the word of God.*" (Romans 10:17)

Now, go back and reread Job 32:8. Is not this what Elihu means by "*inspiration?*"

"*But there is a spirit in man: and the inspiration of the Almighty giveth them understanding.*" (Job 32:8)

Whether God's work in man's spirit is to WRITE the words of God, to SPEAK the words of God in a dream or vision, or to UNDERSTAND the words of God, it is all God's work, not man's. This is God's inspiration that gives man understanding.

Sometimes definitions that may be theologically correct can plant images and prejudice in our minds. These make it difficult to understand the clear, teaching of the Bible in its own context. Please understand that I am not minimizing the need to be precise in our theological definitions. I am only reminding that there is a time and place to speak theology, and a time to let God speak. We need to give God the freedom to speak, giving words the meanings that He intends, and not limiting Him to our own, carefully-conceived definitions. We must be careful that our definitions are those we read out of the Bible, not those we read INTO the Bible.

17 "That he may withdraw man from his purpose, and hide pride from man.

18 He keepeth back his soul from the pit, and his life from perishing by the sword.

19 He is chastened also with pain upon his bed, and the multitude of his bones with strong pain:

20 So that his life abhorreth bread, and his soul dainty meat.

21 His flesh is consumed away, that it cannot be seen; and his bones that were not seen stick out.

22 Yea, his soul draweth near unto the grave, and his life to the destroyers." (Job 33:17-22)

These verses outline the purpose of God's communication. Elihu has just explained HOW God communicates with man; now he explains WHY. Five specific reasons are listed.

The first is to *"withdraw man from his purpose"* (Job 33:17a). In other words, God wants to show man how to leave his own purpose to follow God's purpose for his life.

Second, God wants to deal with man's pride problem. Elihu says God wants to *"hide pride from man"* (Job 33:17b).

God also wants to keep man from eternal damnation. *"He keepeth back his soul from the pit"* (Job 33:18a).

The fourth purpose is to keep man's *"life from perishing by the sword"* (Job 33:18b). Physical safety is an obvious application. Yet man giving heed to God's communication will also keep him from being cut by that sharp, two-edged sword (Hebrews 4:12).

Fifth, in Job 33:19-22 is for man to come to the end of self. Elihu describes a man who is brought to the end of self by whatever means. This is a portrait of Job, and Elihu's obvious application. Elihu is saying that God has spoken through him so that Job might see that all his trials have been to bring him to the end of self.

In this point, Elihu is closer to the truth than any of the men have been. It is tragic that Elihu cannot just leave it there, and let God's Word speak for itself.

Elihu reaches an eloquence in the next few verses that is as rich as any in this book. It is clear that whatever motivation, fleshly or otherwise, may be at work in Elihu's soul, God's Spirit has overshadowed Elihu in order to communicate His truth to man.

These words are a beautiful picture of God's plan of salvation. Elihu establishes the fact and manner of God's communication, as well as His purposes in this communication. He shows how God has brought Job to the end of self. Now, Elihu says, all that is worthless if there is no one to explain to Job what God has done. Elihu believes, of course, that he should be the self-appointed interpreter. Yet the magnificence of his words still have value for all of us.

23 "If there be a messenger with him, an interpreter, one among a thousand, to shew unto man his uprightness." (Job 33:23)

Quite simply, Elihu sets forth the need for a messenger, a missionary to make man aware of God's message. Someone needs to show lost men God's righteousness.

24 "Then he is gracious unto him, and saith, Deliver him from going down to the pit: I have found a ransom." (Job 33:24)

Here is the message of salvation that calls for a messenger and an interpreter. This is the message of a ransom paid to deliver man from the pit of hell. Just when all seems hopeless, a ransom is found. The ransom is our Lord Jesus Christ.

"Who gave himself a ransom for all, to be testified in due time." (1 Timothy 2:6)

25 "His flesh shall be fresher than a child's: he shall return to the days of his youth." (Job 33:25)

Elihu is looking at a man whose flesh is covered with open sores, a man who has lost the glory that has surrounded him since his youth. We look at these same words, and place our hope in a future day when our Lord returns. In that day, our physical bodies will be glorified, with flesh *"fresher than a child's."*

26 "He shall pray unto God, and he will be favourable unto him: and he shall see his face with joy: for he will render unto man his righteousness." (Job 33:26)

Job has lamented the fact that God seems so distant in these days of trial. Elihu holds out the hope that if Job will just confess his sin, he will again enjoy God's favor, and rejoice in the presence of His face.

We have a similar hope. Paul, in Titus 2:13, says that we are looking for that blessed hope, and defines it as the return of our Lord Jesus Christ. We WILL see His face in the day of His return.

27 "He looketh upon men, and if any say, I have sinned, and perverted that which was right, and it profited me not;

28 He will deliver his soul from going into the pit, and his life shall see the light." (Job 33:27-28)

According to Elihu's theory of Job's circumstance, this is all Job has to do to be restored. Job just has to confess his sin of blaming God for his problems.

Looking from the perspective of the New Testament and 1 John 1:9 in particular, we can see in Job 32:27-28 what some have called the "sinner's prayer." All it takes for a lost man to be born again is to confess his sin. That is what delivers man from the pit, and gives him the light of life.

29 "Lo, all these things worketh God oftentimes with man,

30 To bring back his soul from the pit, to be enlightened with the light of the living." (Job 33:29-30)

Elihu returns to the purpose of God in all that has happened. He argues that God wants to bring Job back from the pit and enlighten him.

This is God's purpose in His love manifested toward us. He wants us to have life, and to have it more abundantly (John 10:10).

31 "Mark well, O Job, hearken unto me: hold thy peace, and I will speak.

32 If thou hast any thing to say, answer me: speak, for I desire to justify thee.

33 If not, hearken unto me: hold thy peace, and I shall teach thee wisdom." (Job 33:31-33)

Elihu now addresses Job formally, offering him the opportunity to respond. Well, not really. How is Job going to debate a man who thinks he speaks *"in God's stead"*?

Everything Elihu has said has been squarely in the bull's eye as far as accuracy is concerned. The only problem is that the bull's eye has been on the wrong target. No matter that Elihu's theology is correct, the problem is not Job's sin.

Elihu adds, *"for I desire to justify thee."* How nice! That makes me want to ask where are the Pharisees when you really need them? Someone needs to stand up and say, *"Who can forgive sins but God only?"* (Mark 2:7).

Job has nothing to worry about. Elihu is going to teach him wisdom. Right.

Elihu will teach a great deal of knowledge. Wisdom, though, will not be seen.

25

THE COUNSELOR WHO WAS SO SMART HE DID NO GOOD

For his eyes are upon the ways of man,
and he seeth all his goings.
There is no darkness, nor shadow of death,
where the workers of iniquity may hide themselves.
For he will not lay upon man more than right;
that he should enter into judgment with God.

Job 34:21-23

WHEN I WAS YOUNG, I HAD ALL THE ANSWERS. THE IDEALISM of youth drove me right past my own faults to concentrate on the problems of others. I found it far easier to deal with their problems than to deal with my own.

Something strange happened as I grew older. The more I studied the Bible, the dumber I became.

Today, I have been intensely studying the Bible for over a quarter of a century. I now realize how little I understand about it and about God.

Oh, I haven't lost my faith in God's Word! It is still as real and true as ever. I have lost faith in me. More than ever I believe God's Word when it tells me that my heart is wicked and deceitful.

I trust that I've not lost all my idealism. Idealism is not all bad. It only needs to be tempered with reality and humility.

We will never understand all God was doing in Job's life through his incredible testings. However, it's been obvious so far, that Elihu needed to learn some of the realism and humility I mentioned above.

No one would argue against the brilliance of Elihu. He has mastered the language of "God-speak," and learned to pepper his conversation with abundant "God-facts."

So convinced of his own rightness is Elihu, he has no room for mercy. He knows so much, he is no good as a counselor. He will fail as utterly and miserably as the three men before him.

Elihu has concluded his opening remarks. Having established that he is God's spokesman, he explained the process of inspiration by which he believes he received his information. While the other men all pointed to some secret sin in Job's life as the cause of his calamity, Elihu claims to know what the specific sin is. He says that Job has simply not submitted himself to the sovereignty of God, but is wrestling instead against God's work in his life. Elihu now proceeds to the main body of his arguments.

THE CONCLUSIONS OF ELIHU

CONCLUSIONS ABOUT JOB

1 "Furthermore Elihu answered and said,

2 Hear my words, O ye wise men; and give ear unto me, ye that have knowledge." (Job 34:1-2)

Elihu already gave these men proper deference as he began his remarks in chapter 32. He has acknowledged their age, social stature and wisdom.

What he is really saying between the lines is more than common courtesy. He is implying that if they are really wise and really have understanding, they will obviously agree with his conclusions.

3 "For the ear trieth words, as the mouth tasteth meat." (Job 34:3)

The comparison between words and food is made several times in Scripture. Job had earlier said that God's words were more important than his "necessary food" (Job 23:12).

Again, we must consider what Elihu really means to say. To properly enjoy and digest food, the food must be thoroughly chewed and tasted, not gulped down without a chance to taste. Words have the same need to be considered individually, with the ear trying each one.

Elihu announced in Job 32:4 that this is what he had done with each word during the long exchange among the four men. Now, he implies that they should do the same thing with his words.

4 "Let us choose to us judgment: let us know among ourselves what is good.

5 For Job hath said, I am righteous: and God hath taken away my judgment.

6 Should I lie against my right? my wound is incurable without transgression." (Job 34:4-6)

Now that he has admonished them to tune their ears to try each word, Elihu asks them to go back and consider what they have heard Job say. Elihu's conclusion is that Job is guilty of self-righteousness.

Let's give Elihu the benefit of the doubt for the moment. Let's go back and try the words of Job.

"Behold, I cry out of wrong, but I am not heard: I cry aloud, but there is no judgment." (Job 19:7)

"As God liveth, who hath taken away my judgment; and the Almighty, who hath vexed my soul; All the while my breath is in me, and the spirit of God is in my nostrils; My lips shall not speak wickedness, nor my tongue utter deceit. God forbid that I should justify you: till I die I will not remove mine integrity from me. My righteousness I hold fast, and will not let it go: my heart shall not reproach me so long as I live. Let mine enemy be as the wicked, and he that riseth up against me as the unrighteous." (Job 27:2-7)

So far, what Elihu has said closely resembles Job's own words. If we did not know better, we would be tempted to think that Job was trusting in his own self-righteousness. The difference is that Job had the life to back up his words. God Himself gave clear testimony as to Job's righteousness.

We have followed Elihu's instruction. So far his representation of Job's words is fair enough. He turns the fire up a notch.

7 "What man is like Job, who drinketh up scorning like water?
8 Which goeth in company with the workers of iniquity, and walketh with wicked men." (Job 34:7-8)

These are heavy words that flow from Elihu's mouth. Before even coming to a conclusion, it is not hard to see where Elihu is going with all this. He is convinced that Job is guilty as charged.

By comparing Scripture with Scripture, we see that Elihu has placed Job squarely in the first verse of the first Psalm. Try these words with your ears.

"Blessed is the man that walketh not in the counsel of the ungodly, nor standeth in the way of sinners, nor sitteth in the seat of the scornful." (Psalm 1:1)

Clearly Job is not blessed, Elihu argues, because he is the antithesis to the conditions of this verse. Now, having laid this base, Elihu moves to his conclusion. Job is getting just what he deserves.

9 "For he hath said, It profiteth a man nothing that he should delight himself with God." (Job 34:9)

Wait! Job has said no such thing!

Profit has never been Job's motivation, nor has it been his question. This is the man whose wife told him to curse God and die.

"But he said unto her, Thou speakest as one of the foolish women

speaketh. What? shall we receive good at the hand of God, and shall we not receive evil? In all this did not Job sin with his lips." (Job 2:10)

This is the same man who professed his great faith in God. The man who lost his children, his wealth, his influence and his health, made the following confession.

"For I know that my redeemer liveth, and that he shall stand at the latter day upon the earth: And though after my skin worms destroy this body, yet in my flesh shall I see God: Whom I shall see for myself, and mine eyes shall behold, and not another; though my reins be consumed within me." (Job 19:25-27)

Elihu is guilty of the same faulty logic that plagued the others. He begins with a solid premise, yet leads to a false conclusion, because his mind is already made up before he begins.

CONCLUSIONS ABOUT GOD

Elihu's mind is made up concerning Job's guilt. Next, he sets forth a series of basic theological facts about God. His intent is to reinforce his argument against Job. We will examine these facts and see that they cannot be denied. However, the error has already been committed.

There is a flaw in Elihu's logic. He started from a right premise and drew a false conclusion. Remember, no matter how many theologically correct footnotes he adds to his thesis, he will still be wrong.

10 "Therefore hearken unto me, ye men of understanding: far be it from God, that he should do wickedness; and from the Almighty, that he should commit iniquity.

11 For the work of a man shall he render unto him, and cause every man to find according to his ways.

12 Yea, surely God will not do wickedly, neither will the Almighty pervert judgment." (Job 34:10-12)

Is any man of understanding going to argue with this? Will God do wickedness? Will God commit iniquity?

Verse 10 stands. Now, considering verse 11, will any argue that God does not deal with men according to their ways? Of course not! Proverbs tells it straight.

"If thou sayest, Behold, we knew it not; doth not he that pondereth the heart consider it? and he that keepeth thy soul, doth not he know it? and shall not he render to every man according to his works?" (Proverbs 24:12)

This is great debating technique. Begin with a solid premise. Slip in a false conclusion. Then, before anyone has a chance to think it through, begin to tack on every commonly-accepted theological fact you can muster. The more "God-facts" you can pile on, the more impressive your argument appears to those who do not think things through. Elihu is a master at this technique.

"Yea," Elihu billows in verse 12, "God would never do wickedly. How could God do something unfair?"

13 "Who hath given him a charge over the earth? or who hath disposed the whole world?" (Job 34:13)

Does God have a boss? Did anyone put God in charge? Is there anyone ahead of Him in the chain of command?

"Amen!" shouts the congregation. Would anyone like to argue this fact?

14 "If he set his heart upon man, if he gather unto himself his spirit and his breath;

15 All flesh shall perish together, and man shall turn again unto dust." (Job 34:14-15)

God is in charge of life and death. God is sovereign. If it were any different, God would not be God.

All who minister the Word of God should cringe in fear upon seeing the above verses. No one could accuse Elihu of insincerity. There is no malice or conspiracy in his heart as he pours forth these words with the full force of his conviction.

How easy it is to possess many facts about the Bible, and still come to faulty conclusions. It is also easy to know key words, phrases and arguments that are certain to elicit loud choruses of "Amen's" from the congregation.

We must study to show ourselves workmen that need not be ashamed, rightly dividing the word of truth (2 Timothy 2:15). Being mostly right is never good enough when we deal with the Word of God and the souls of men.

THE CONFIDENCE OF ELIHU

Having set us up to follow his faulty logic, Elihu will fill the arena with the smoke of fiery truths with which no one could disagree. A series of spiritual ideas is laid down by Elihu, as he does his best to push Job into a corner from which there is no escape. Clearly Elihu is confident in the case he is building, and there is no one to contradict him—yet.

CONFIDENCE IN GOD'S FAIRNESS

16 "If now thou hast understanding, hear this: hearken to the voice of my words.

17 Shall even he that hateth right govern? and wilt thou condemn him that is most just?" (Job 34:16-17)

Elihu's thought is easy to follow. Will you trust government to someone who hates righteousness? Will you speak against a ruler who is most just? Of course not!

18 "Is it fit to say to a king, Thou art wicked? and to princes, Ye are ungodly?" (Job 34:18)

How many men have the courage to stand up in the face of a king or prince, and accuse them of wickedness or ungodliness? Not many.

Not even Michael the archangel dared to rail against the Devil. Jude tells us this somber fact.

"Yet Michael the archangel, when contending with the Devil he disputed about the body of Moses, durst not bring against him a railing accusation, but said, The Lord rebuke thee." (Jude 1:9)

Now, if all this is true (who would dispute it?), who would dare to rail against God? Who is going to tell God that He is not fair?

19 "How much less to him that accepteth not the persons of princes, nor regardeth the rich more than the poor? for they all are the work of his hands." (Job 34:19)

Will the creature tell the Creator that He is not fair? Will you dare tell that to God, who cares not whether you are rich, poor, influential or powerful? Obviously, you will not, nor will anyone else.

Even if there were one with such audacity to challenge the Almighty God, there is coming a day of reckoning. This is the continuation of Elihu's case.

20 "In a moment shall they die, and the people shall be troubled at midnight, and pass away: and the mighty shall be taken away without hand." (Job 34:20)

Whatever men may say is irrelevant considering the coming day of judgment. The mighty of this world will be taken away *"without hand,"* felled by the Word of God alone. This phrase *"without hand"* also reminds us of the prophecy of Daniel, when he foresaw the final destruction of gentile dominion.

"Forasmuch as thou sawest that the stone was cut out of the mountain without hands, and that it brake in pieces the iron, the brass, the clay, the silver, and the gold; the great God hath made known to the king what shall come to pass hereafter: and the dream is certain, and the interpretation thereof sure." (Daniel 2:45)

At midnight the mighty will be troubled. This, and the reappearance of the *"shadow of death"* in verse 22 alert us to the prophetic application of these words to the coming time of Tribulation.

At midnight the Bridegroom is coming. This is the prophecy of our Lord Himself.

"And at midnight there was a cry made, Behold, the bridegroom cometh; go ye out to meet him." (Matthew 25:6)

21 "For his eyes are upon the ways of man, and he seeth all his goings.

22 There is no darkness, nor shadow of death, where the workers of iniquity may hide themselves." (Job 34:21-22)

Elihu offers up a truth of God that has been loudly proclaimed through the ages. God's omniscience and omnipresence are seen here. God never loses track of anyone; there is nowhere to hide from His all-seeing eyes.

Not even in the darkness of the coming Tribulation, nor under the terrible shadow of death will sinners be able to hide from the Almighty. Consider a few of the places in Scripture where this truth is witnessed.

"Whither shall I go from thy spirit? or whither shall I flee from thy presence? If I ascend up into heaven, thou art there: if I make my bed in hell, behold, thou art there. If I take the wings of the morning, and dwell in the uttermost parts of the sea; Even there shall thy hand lead me, and thy right hand shall hold me." (Psalm 139:7-10)

"For the eyes of the LORD run to and fro throughout the whole earth, to shew himself strong in the behalf of them whose heart is perfect toward him. Herein thou hast done foolishly: therefore from henceforth thou shalt have wars." (2 Chronicles 16:9)

"The eyes of the LORD are in every place, beholding the evil and the good." (Proverbs 15:3)

"For mine eyes are upon all their ways: they are not hid from my face, neither is their iniquity hid from mine eyes." (Jeremiah 16:17)

To this truth, Elihu adds another, also indisputable truth. God is fair in all His judgment.

23 "For he will not lay upon man more than right; that he should enter into judgment with God.

24 He shall break in pieces mighty men without number, and set others in their stead." (Job 34:23-24)

By this time Elihu has piled up so many indisputable facts about God, and the "Amen's" are becoming so loud, that no one considers if his primary conclusion about Job is valid or not. It is not, but how could anyone argue with all this wonderful truth about God?

25 "Therefore he knoweth their works, and he overturneth them in the night, so that they are destroyed.

26 He striketh them as wicked men in the open sight of others;
27 Because they turned back from him, and would not consider any of his ways:
28 So that they cause the cry of the poor to come unto him, and he heareth the cry of the afflicted." (Job 34:25-28)

There is no mystery about where Elihu is going with all this. The transparent application is that God has been perfectly fair in raining down judgment upon Job. Who cares what Job says about his own personal righteousness and testimony. God would not bring this judgment if it were not called for, and who is going to argue with God?

God obviously knows Job's works, Elihu reasons, and has brought upon him this horrible calamity *"in the open sight of others."* Elihu believes that Job has rebelled against God and His ways. God is simply taking up the cause of those Job must have afflicted and oppressed to gain his wealth and position.

Beyond the obvious historical applications, the words of Elihu will be finally and completely fulfilled when God overturns the works of the wicked in the night of the Tribulation, all in the open sight of others. The poor and afflicted of His people will be avenged in that day.

CONFIDENCE IN GOD'S PEACE

29 "When he giveth quietness, who then can make trouble? and when he hideth his face, who then can behold him? whether it be done against a nation, or against a man only." (Job 34:29)

Now, if no one can argue with God's judgment, the same can be said of His peace. When God gives peace and quietness, who can make trouble?

Job has repeatedly complained that he had received no communication from God. Elihu reminds him that when God wants to hide His face, it is of no use to look for Him. These truths, Elihu proclaims, are just as applicable to nations as they are to individuals. God Himself made this very promise to Israel if they were to violate His law.

"And I will surely hide my face in that day for all the evils which they shall have wrought, in that they are turned unto other gods." (Deuteronomy 31:18)

In *"that day"* of the coming Tribulation, God will keep His promise. Those who have turned from God will discover that He has turned from them.

From the vantage point of biblical prophecy, it is interesting that immediately following God's midnight judgment, Elihu follows with the theme of God's quietness. Immediately following the judgment of the Tribulation comes the quietness and peace of the millennial reign.

In a purely devotional sense, no believer should fail to claim this wonderful promise of God's quietness and peace that follows tribulation of any kind. Isaiah lays down the truth in a wonderful way.

"Thou wilt keep him in perfect peace, whose mind is stayed on thee: because he trusteth in thee." (Isaiah 26:3)

Our Lord Jesus Christ gave us the same promise. He also promised persecution and trials, but to the believer He holds out the guarantee of victory.

"These things I have spoken unto you, that in me ye might have peace. In the world ye shall have tribulation: but be of good cheer; I have overcome the world." (John 16:33)

Paul personally knew the peace of the quietness God gives. At a time when he was imprisoned in Rome, he wrote to the Philippians about God's quietness that no one can trouble.

"And the peace of God, which passeth all understanding, shall keep your hearts and minds through Christ Jesus." (Philippians 4:7)

Still in prison, he wrote to Timothy. Everyone except Luke had abandoned Paul in his trial. Here is what he wrote from the quietness of his heart.

"Notwithstanding the Lord stood with me, and strengthened me; that by me the preaching might be fully known, and that all the gentiles might hear: and I was delivered out of the mouth of the lion." (2 Timothy 4:17)

Elihu has spoken well. No matter how dark it may be, you can always know that there is a quietness that God gives to the righteous. When God's quietness comes, there is no one who can make trouble.

CONFIDENCE IN CONFESSION OF SIN

30 "That the hypocrite reign not, lest the people be ensnared." (Job 34:30)

From the time he first opened his mouth, this has been Elihu's battle cry. He is obsessed with not letting anyone get away with anything.

In his mind, of course, the master hypocrite is Job. What he does not realize is that there is a hypocrite still to come on the world stage who will be beyond his wildest imagination. The Antichrist will be a hypocrite so polished, that he will pass himself off as God. He will be so good at it, that he will convince himself! (2 Thessalonians 2:3-4)

31 "Surely it is meet to be said unto God, I have borne chastisement, I will not offend any more:

32 That which I see not teach thou me: if I have done iniquity, I will do no more.

33 Should it be according to thy mind? he will recompense it, whether thou refuse, or whether thou choose; and not I: therefore speak what thou knowest." (Job 34:31-33)

Here is Elihu's cure-all remedy—just confess your sin to God and everything will be just fine. But we have heard this before, haven't we? Same song, fourth verse.

He is absolutely right—again. This is nothing short of good, solid preaching. The one problem is the faulty assumption that Job's problems must be due to sin.

CONFIDENCE IN HIS CHALLENGE

34 "Let men of understanding tell me, and let a wise man hearken unto me." (Job 34:34)

Will any of these men answer him? Will the wise man, Job, have anything to say?

Job is silent. The other three will not open their mouths either.

Who would be foolish enough to quarrel with the commonly-accepted information Elihu has been preaching? After all, who would dare to answer the man who is God's self-appointed spokesman?

35 "Job hath spoken without knowledge, and his words were without wisdom." (Job 34:35)

Confident that no one is going to reply, Elihu takes another step. "Job simply does not know what he's talking about!"

Even THIS is true! God will say the same thing himself.

"Who is this that darkeneth counsel by words without knowledge?" (Job 38:2)

36 "My desire is that Job may be tried unto the end because of his answers for wicked men.

37 For he addeth rebellion unto his sin, he clappeth his hands among us, and multiplieth his words against God." (Job 34:36-37)

Emboldened and encouraged by the fact that no one had the courage to speak up, Elihu presses his point even more.

Job not only deserves what he has received, he still doesn't have a repentant attitude. Therefore, God would be just in bringing even more disaster down upon his head. He wants Job to be tried *"unto the end."*

Elihu now announces that what Job has spoken reveals that he is in a state of rebellion against God. His words have insulted the Almighty. (Remember the cultural significance of clapping hands? See Job 27:23.) From an initial accusation of blaming God for his problems, Elihu has accelerated the charges to outright rebellion.

Job has got quite a mess on his hands! I am sure he feels that he HAS been tried unto the end.

When we compare our problems to Job, we are encouraged. Yet were Job to compare his situation to that of believers in the Tribulation, even HE would feel fortunate. They WILL be tried unto the end.

In words that are often incorrectly applied to believers in this age, Jesus prophesies the excruciating trials of those who will come to Christ in the coming Tribulation.

"But he that shall endure unto the end, the same shall be saved." (Matthew 24:13)

Many wrongly think that Jesus was speaking of those who could hold out and live a good, Christian life until the end of their lives. Yet the end of an individual's life was not the topic He was discussing. He was speaking of the *"beginning of sorrows,"* a time also foreseen by the Old Testament prophets (Isaiah 13:6-11; Jeremiah 13:21; 49:24; Hosea 13:13).

"And Jesus answered and said unto them, Take heed that no man deceive you. For many shall come in my name, saying, I am Christ; and shall deceive many. And ye shall hear of wars and rumours of wars: see that ye be not troubled: for all these things must come to pass, but THE END IS NOT YET. For nation shall rise against nation, and kingdom against kingdom: and there shall be famines, and pestilences, and earthquakes, in divers places. ALL THESE ARE THE BEGINNING OF SORROWS." (Matthew 24:4-8) (Author's emphasis)

Those that endure unto the end, mentioned by Jesus in Matthew 24:13, are those who endure to the end of this time of sorrows. This is the end Jesus speaks of in the very next verse.

"And this gospel of the kingdom shall be preached in all the world for a witness unto all nations; and THEN SHALL THE END COME." (Matthew 24:14) (Author's emphasis)

Job has wished for the end of his life. The coming Tribulation will be so horrible that men will want to die, yet *"death shall flee from them"* (Revelation 9:6).

In those days the end is not the end of any individual life. It is simply "the end" of the Tribulation. The same phraseology is found in Daniel's prophecy, dealing with the same subject matter.

"And he said, Go thy way, Daniel: for the words are closed up and sealed till THE TIME OF THE END." (Daniel 12:9) (Author's emphasis)

The moral of all this is simple. Just when you think no one has ever suffered more than you, there is always a worse case. Even Job's suffering pales when compared to those who WILL be tried unto the end during the Tribulation.

THE COUNSEL OF ELIHU

Elihu has the confidence of an attorney who believes there is no way he can lose his case. He has set forth facts that are beyond doubt. But Elihu doesn't know that all of his facts are based on a primary conclusion that is dead wrong. No one has noticed this except the Judge, and He is not yet ready to offer an opinion. This perfect Judge will allow Elihu more time to publicly display his lack of wisdom.

Elihu now makes it clear that his remarks are aimed directly at Job. He has also made it clear to all that he is the only one who understands Job's root sin that has caused this colossal downfall. In his mind he is convinced that no one else could present this case in such an air-tight manner.

Any biblical counselor should remember that biblical knowledge alone is insufficient. No counselor can soothe the hurts of life without the anointing of the Holy Spirit, which gives him wisdom and understanding to apply the Word of God to each specific heart.

On the receiving side, when you are the one who is misunderstood and unappreciated, when you are the target of unjust condemnation, you must hold tight to your spiritual integrity. Hold tight to the Word of God. Worry about your own obedience to the Word. You have nothing to prove. You have no argument to win. God has already done that. Rest in Him.

This is precisely the situation we see at this point in Job. Job is silent. He has already said everything he can think to say. He has NOT denied his Lord and God, and he will not.

Job's silence will not deter Elihu. No one could tell Job what to do better than Elihu. Job 35 is dedicated to this end. It will be clear that Elihu is from what I call the direct, "in-your-face" school of counseling.

1 "Elihu spake moreover, and said,

2 Thinkest thou this to be right, that thou saidst, My righteousness is more than God's?" (Job 35:1-2)

No! Job did NOT say this.

Yes, Job did claim to be righteous. Yes, you could even suspect that he was bordering on becoming a little "self-righteous" under the pressure he was receiving from his friends. Let's look again at what Job really said.

"My righteousness I hold fast, and will not let it go: my heart shall not reproach me so long as I live." (Job 27:6)

"I put on righteousness, and it clothed me: my judgment was as a robe and a diadem." (Job 29:14)

He did NOT say that his righteousness exceeded God's. I cannot give you a reference, because it is not there.

Tragically, no one is paying any attention to what was, and what was not said. Once a preacher gets up a full head of steam, and has convinced his audience that 99 percent of what he says is the gospel truth, it is not too difficult to pass off blatant lies.

Wait a minute! Does not this sound vaguely familiar? Can you think of someone else who has the same method of operation? How about the Devil?

Take the time to probe beneath the surface for a moment, and there you will find him—the prince of darkness. Never forget how this story began, and what is at stake. This is something far deeper than a heated discussion among friends. Someone is coaching from the sidelines.

Satan met Eve in the garden as a Bible-quoting preacher of righteousness, an angel of light. He quoted God's words ALMOST word for word. He just removed a word here, added a word there. Then, as Eve shouted "Amen!" he pulled the rug out from under her, as he proclaimed, "Ye shall not surely die" (Genesis 3:1-4).

By this time Eve was convinced this must be the most spiritual, knowledgeable preacher she had ever heard. Never mind that this "angel of light" had just directly contradicted what God said, and passed off a lie as the truth.

As a preacher myself, I am painfully aware that the same human weakness exists today. One who speaks with confidence, and is right most of the time, has a powerful influence over the masses of people who do NOT think, or carefully consider what they hear.

We should appreciate the testimony of the Bereans. They searched the Scriptures daily to see whether the teaching of Paul and his missionary team lined up with God's Word. They did not have a cynical, critical spirit, doubting what Paul preached. They possessed receptive hearts, yet discerning minds. They recognized God's authority as supreme, not the preacher's.

Let me take this occasion to remind you of that very truth. In a commentary like this one that offers so many "against-the-grain" observations, you must realize that the only standard we can measure by is the Bible. God's Word is true; my comments are always subject to analysis and correction.

My motives are pure, but my understanding is limited. God's Word is absolute. Search the Scriptures to see if what I say rings true.

"Prove all things; hold fast that which is good." (1 Thessalonians 5:21)

Elihu is the one who is operating by false assumptions. He is correct that many men consider their righteousness to exceed God's. This is why many go to hell.

He is wrong to think that this is Job's position. The same man who held to his own righteousness was just as quick to confess his sinful nature before a holy God.

"If I be wicked, why then labour I in vain? If I wash myself with snow water, and make my hands never so clean; Yet shalt thou plunge me in the ditch, and mine own clothes shall abhor me." (Job 9:29-31)

3 "For thou saidst, What advantage will it be unto thee? and, What profit shall I have, if I be cleansed from my sin?" (Job 35:3)

Elihu has returned to a reasonable approximation of the truth, just as the master deceiver, Satan, never wanders far from the truth. We return to the record to check things out for ourselves.

"What is the Almighty, that we should serve him? and what profit should we have, if we pray unto him?" (Job 21:15)

That is a fair enough representation of what Job said. There is, however, one slight problem. Job says these words, but not about himself. The preceding verse, Job 21:14, shows that Job is talking about "them," the wicked. They are the ones, according to Job, who say such things. Taking words out of context is fatal both to good communication and good Bible study.

4 "I will answer thee, and thy companions with thee." (Job 35:4)

Ever thinking, ever building his case, Elihu is moving toward even more conclusions. There is still no voice raised to search the Scriptures, so he continues.

5 "Look unto the heavens, and see; and behold the clouds which are higher than thou." (Job 35:5)

Elihu invites Job to turn his eyes heavenward. The point is to remind him that God is higher than man. God has a perspective that allows Him to see everything. What Elihu means to say is eloquently expressed by God speaking through his prophet Isaiah.

"For as the heavens are higher than the earth, so are my ways higher than your ways, and my thoughts than your thoughts." (Isaiah 55:9)

6 "If thou sinnest, what doest thou against him? or if thy transgressions be multiplied, what doest thou unto him?" (Job 35:6)

Elihu is still on his crusade to get Job to confess his sin. Having pointed to the all-powerful, all-seeing God, he is asking Job to consider how useless it is to cling to his sin.

"What harm could you ever do to God with your sin? You're only hurting yourself."

7 "If thou be righteous, what givest thou him? or what receiveth he of thine hand?" (Job 35:7)

Now, Elihu swings back to the other side of the argument. Obviously one's sin cannot hurt God. Yet it must also be true that one's righteousness cannot help Him. Why, then, should anyone cling so tenaciously to his righteousness? God will not benefit from it, any more than He would be harmed by one's sin.

8 "Thy wickedness may hurt a man as thou art; and thy righteousness may profit the son of man." (Job 35:8)

One's sin CAN hurt other men, just as one's righteousness CAN help another. God, though, is above it all. He cannot be harmed or helped by mortal man.

9 "By reason of the multitude of oppressions they make the oppressed to cry: they cry out by reason of the arm of the mighty.

10 But none saith, Where is God my maker, who giveth songs in the night." (Job 35:9-10)

This is another well-taken point. The only time most men cry out to God is when they are in trouble, when the hand of the most high God is upon them.

Elihu knows what the correct response to trial should be. Genuine fellowship with God is manifested by the heart that cries *"Where is God my maker, who giveth songs in the night?"*

Job is not far from this. He has loudly cried, *"Where is God my maker!"* Nevertheless, there is no sign of singing in his heart.

Only David seemed to find those songs in the night. Sometimes in a minor key, at other times triumphant, David explored every avenue of fellowship with God. The results we know as the Book of Psalms.

In New Testament times we have more information available for nighttime songwriting. Paul and Silas sang songs to God at midnight in prison. (Acts 16:25)

Those psalms of David are a precursor of the songs that will resonate in the hearts of God's children in the dark night of the Tribulation. Reading many of David's psalms, one can see an immediate application to the horrible days to come.

"For in the time of trouble he shall hide me in his pavilion: in the secret of his tabernacle shall he hide me; he shall set me up upon a rock. And

now shall mine head be lifted up above mine enemies round about me: therefore will I offer in his tabernacle sacrifices of joy; I will sing, yea, I will sing praises unto the LORD." (Psalm 27:5-6)

11 "Who teacheth us more than the beasts of the earth, and maketh us wiser than the fowls of heaven?" (Job 35:11)

Unpolluted by the modern "science" of evolution, Elihu knows enough to draw a clear distinction between man and beast. This is an obvious fact, and none of the learned men present raise their voice in protest.

That these men knew so much truth about God and His creation is a constant source of wonder to us. Could it be that modern man, by placing himself on a level equal to animals, has neatly cut himself off from God's truth? Elihu was a counselor who was so smart, he did no good. There is much we can learn from his example.

12 "There they cry, but none giveth answer, because of the pride of evil men." (Job 35:12)

Elihu is unconditionally correct. Prideful men always place themselves in a position of no escape. Man's pride will reach a fearful climax in the days of the coming Tribulation. The book of Proverbs gives witness to the same truth.

"Then shall they call upon me, but I will not answer; they shall seek me early, but they shall not find me." (Proverbs 1:28)

The reason is explicitly defined in the next verse. Here is why there will be no answer from God for the wicked.

13 "Surely God will not hear vanity, neither will the Almighty regard it." (Job 35:13)

Man apart from God is vanity—nothing more than whipped cream over frothed milk. Solomon preached it and wrote a book about it.

"Vanity of vanities, saith the Preacher, vanity of vanities; all is vanity." (Ecclesiastes 1:2)

Now, Elihu issues another call for Job to mend his ways before it is too late. This is a final chance to get right with God before the judgment.

14 "Although thou sayest thou shalt not see him, yet judgment is before him; therefore trust thou in him." (Job 35:14)

The message is transparent. One day Job is going to be in the presence of God. Elihu calls for him to trust in God now, before he stands before Him in final judgment.

We have here yet another example of careless quotation. Elihu accuses Job of saying he would not see God. Job DID say that he would stand in God's presence. Don't you remember this great passage?

"For I know that my redeemer liveth, and that he shall stand at the latter day upon the earth: And though after my skin worms destroy this body, yet in my flesh shall I see God." (Job 19:25-26)

Job has been misquoted, misunderstood and maligned, but why should Job bother replying to one who speaks *"in God's stead?"* Elihu claims to have heard each word. What could Job say he has not already said? So, as the organ begins to softly play "Just As I Am" in the background, Job sits still in his pew. He will not respond to Elihu's invitation. How often have we preachers missed the mark just as completely, though our sermons are full of Bible truth.

15 "But now, because it is not so, he hath visited in his anger; yet he knoweth it not in great extremity." (Job 35:15)

What Elihu is saying is that God's final judgment has not yet come. God has merely visited Job in anger. Although his present trials are great, Job knows it *"not in great extremity."* In other words, "Job, you ain't seen nothin' yet!"

16 "Therefore doth Job open his mouth in vain; he multiplieth words without knowledge." (Job 35:16)

We are right back in Job 34:35. Elihu charges that Job does not know what he is saying. Nothing but hot air has poured from his mouth. Elihu believes that Job is piling up a mountain of words that has no meaning.

There is more to come from Elihu. He has waited a long time for his chance to speak, and he is not ready to let it slip by before he has completely ventilated.

We have heard enough, however, to know that we do not want to end in the same self-deluded condition. Elihu fancies himself as a defender of truth and righteousness, a champion for God. He is nothing more than another well-intentioned individual who unwittingly becomes the dupe of Satan.

Careless listening, biased analysis, faulty logic, knowledge without wisdom and understanding, flagrant misrepresentation and bold conclusions with no foundation—the list of potential lessons to be learned from the bad example of Elihu could continue. Perhaps most important of all is to remember that no human is the final authority. No one of us is qualified to offer opinions *"in God's stead."* Only God's Word is the final word.

26

THE MAN WHO PRESUMED TO SPEAK FOR GOD

Behold, God exalteth by his power: who teacheth like him?

Who hath enjoined him his way?

or who can say, Thou hast wrought iniquity?

Remember that thou magnify his work,

which men behold.

Every man may see it; man may behold it afar off.

Behold, God is great, and we know him not,

neither can the number of his years be searched out.

Job 36:22-26

HOW QUICK WE ARE TO SPEAK FOR GOD! WE OFTEN THINK that nothing gives a little credibility to our opinions more than tagging them with a "God revealed to me," or "the Lord spoke to me and said. . . ."

The doctrinal anarchy that plagues Christianity today is due in large part to the way many Christians appoint themselves as God's spokesmen. As I mentioned earlier, it is essential that those who want to minister the Word of God to others should be careful not to play this game.

When you speak for God, be certain that you have a chapter and verse to support your claim. Those of us who have the completed Bible in our hands have no excuse for creating such confusion by pretending to have exclusive rights to God's opinions about everything. God has already expressed His opinion, and it is found in the pages of the Bible.

While Elihu did not have a Bible, no one has ever developed the practice of speaking for God to such an art form as he. The two chapters we will now consider, Job 36 and 37, are the conclusion of Elihu's remarks.

As we make our way through Elihu's pronouncements on a variety of subjects, we will see that as usual, he has his facts in order. Yet since his basic assumption is wrong, the great information he lays out is of no practical use to Job.

There is much that we can learn, though, as we examine his words.

Before applying anything to our lives, we will attempt to be certain that our presuppositions are in line with the Word of God.

Approaching the words of Scripture, we go forward with a prayer for God's wisdom. Repeatedly, we have seen the folly of information without wisdom and understanding.

GOD'S TREATMENT OF HIS OWN

1 "Elihu also proceeded, and said,
2 Suffer me a little, and I will shew thee that I have yet to speak on God's behalf.
3 I will fetch my knowledge from afar, and will ascribe righteousness to my Maker.
4 For truly my words shall not be false: he that is perfect in knowledge is with thee." (Job 36:1-4)

Pausing only to catch his breath, Elihu continues. When he says, *"Suffer me a little,"* he means, "Allow me just a little more time." This must have had the same effect as listening to a long-winded, pompous preacher, who says for the fifth or sixth time, "In conclusion, just let me say this and I'm finished."

He is still claiming to be God's spokesman, and says that his words will prove it. Elihu's knowledge comes from *"afar."* When a man is convinced he has a hot line from heaven, he becomes much better at speaking than listening.

In Job 36:3 Elihu proclaims that his purpose is *"to ascribe righteousness"* to his Maker. Of course it is! When one speaks on God's behalf, doing "all for the glory and honor of God" is just part of the package.

Elihu's outrageous affirmations to be God's earthly representative are bad enough, but in verse 4 he clearly breaches all biblical protocol. He claims that his words are infallible, since he is perfect in knowledge. It sounds like Elihu is a candidate for Pope!

Before dismissing Elihu as an arrogant, bombastic fool, we should reflect for a moment on how easy it is to give others the same impression when we minister the Word of God. Those of us who believe in the inerrancy and infallibility of the divinely-inspired Word of God possess a SOURCE of perfect knowledge. This does NOT mean that WE are perfect in knowledge, nor does it mean that OUR words *"shall not be false."*

While agreeing that the Bible is without error, we must also agree that our human understanding is NOT without error. We must always hold out the possibility that our ability to understand the inerrant Word of God leaves room for growth and improvement.

We begin with a true premise—the Word of God is infallibly true. But then, our human logic can lead us wrong. We figure that since we have access to the Word of God, can read it and understand it, that when we speak about biblical matters, we, too, are infallible. True premise, false conclusion.

This is precisely the problem of Elihu. He begins with a true premise—God judges sinners. He leaps to a false conclusion—Job is a sinner, since he is suffering what seem to be the consequences of God's judgment.

Barely four verses into Job 36, and we are reminded of our need for wisdom and understanding to accompany our biblical knowledge. There is always something to learn from everyone, even those who operate from a wrong conclusion like Elihu.

5 "Behold, God is mighty, and despiseth not any: he is mighty in strength and wisdom.

6 He preserveth not the life of the wicked: but giveth right to the poor." (Job 36:5-6)

In his quest to ascribe righteousness to God, Elihu calls attention to God's might, His fairness in not despising or favoring any particular individual, and His strength and wisdom. No one, of course, can argue with these attributes of God.

Next, Elihu concludes that while the poor are the recipients of what is "*right*," the wicked get what they deserve. A theological degree is not necessary to see where Elihu is going with all these lofty pronouncements of God's greatness. His aim is to show that Job's terrible condition is no less than what he deserves. As far as Elihu is concerned, Job IS "*the wicked.*"

What irony! We recall that we have often seen Job as a picture of Christ in the throes of His passion on the cross. Just as Job was falsely accused, our Lord was accused of casting out demons in the power of Beelzebub, the prince of the devils (Matthew 12:24). He was despised, rejected, and hung on a cross. When the Antichrist appears, he will be proclaimed and received as the very Christ.

7 "He withdraweth not his eyes from the righteous: but with kings are they on the throne; yea, he doth establish them for ever, and they are exalted." (Job 36:7)

This is obviously true. God does indeed keep His eyes upon the righteous, just as His eyes are on the sparrow (Matthew 6:25-26).

God does establish the righteous with kings. New Testament believers are called kings in Revelation 1:6 and 5:10. We WILL reign with Him eternally according to 2 Timothy 2:12 and Revelation 5:10, 20:6 and 22:5.

8 "And if they be bound in fetters, and be holden in cords of affliction;

9 Then he sheweth them their work, and their transgressions that they have exceeded.

10 He openeth also their ear to discipline, and commandeth that they return from iniquity." (Job 36:8-10)

Here is a note of grace that springs from Elihu's lips. He is not accusing Job of being a lost unbeliever. In these verses Elihu holds out the possibility of the righteous being *"bound in fetters"* and tied in *"cords of affliction"* because of transgression. We have heard all this before from the three men who have spoken before him. The major thesis has not changed. Job has sinned. Therefore, he has suffered this calamity.

We are again confronted with a biblical truth. Even believers can be bound and fettered. A good reference for anyone to study is Isaiah 58, where God shows that the correct use of the fast is to free believers from the binding effects of sin.

Job's problems, however, aren't due to some specific sin in his life. He is not bound by sin, contrary to Elihu's inaccurate assumption.

A biblical example of this truth in operation is that of Manasseh, a most horrible and wicked king of Judah. Because of his sin, this man was literally bound and fettered and carried away to Babylon (2 Chronicles 33:-11).

Just as Elihu has been saying, 2 Chronicles 33:12-16 tells how God showed Manasseh his sin, and how Manasseh repented of his sin and was restored.

Elihu is convinced that God is simply showing Job the fruit of his *"work"* and his many transgressions. Yet he offers the hope that God also opens the sinner's ear to receive divine discipline as a motivation to repent from this great iniquity. This, too, we heard from the first three men who spoke. They have all said that if Job will confess his sin and repent, God will restore him.

11 "If they obey and serve him, they shall spend their days in prosperity, and their years in pleasures." (Job 36:11)

Another true statement is added to Elihu's pile of God-facts. Yet even here we must be careful in our understanding and application.

It is true that God blesses the righteous with prosperity and pleasure. The psalmist promises that the man who meditates day and night in the Word of God will have prosperity in all he does.

"Blessed is the man that walketh not in the counsel of the ungodly, nor standeth in the way of sinners, nor sitteth in the seat of the scornful. But his delight is in the law of the LORD; and in his law doth he meditate day and night. And he shall be like a tree planted by the rivers of water, that bringeth forth his fruit in his season; his leaf also shall not wither; and whatsoever he doeth shall prosper." (Psalm 1:1-3)

Yet one must carefully define prosperity and pleasure from a biblical perspective. The little epistle of 3 John, in the second verse, distinguishes between physical prosperity and prosperity of soul.

"Beloved, I wish above all things that thou mayest prosper and be in health, even as thy soul prospereth." (3 John 1:2)

The believer in Christ can prosper in poverty! Paul knew this truth from personal experience.

"Not that I speak in respect of want: for I have learned, in whatsoever state I am, therewith to be content. I know both how to be abased, and I know how to abound: every where and in all things I am instructed both to be full and to be hungry, both to abound and to suffer need." (Philippians 4:11-12)

Pleasure is another often misunderstood concept. Paul could find pleasure in suffering! The reason for this amazing and seemingly contradictory attitude was Paul's ability to lay hold of the grace of God.

"And he said unto me, My grace is sufficient for thee: for my strength is made perfect in weakness. Most gladly therefore will I rather glory in my infirmities, that the power of Christ may rest upon me. Therefore I take pleasure in infirmities, in reproaches, in necessities, in persecutions, in distresses for Christ's sake: for when I am weak, then am I strong." (2 Corinthians 12:9-10)

All this underscores what we have seen all along. Elihu and the others know a lot of correct truth about God and His ways. The breakdown comes from their lack of wisdom and understanding, not knowing how to correctly apply this truth.

No one could fault the correctness of what Elihu says in these verses. However, he is operating under a false assumption, namely that Job has harbored some sin that has resulted in his grief.

When one's basic conclusion is wrong, it doesn't matter how many correct facts are hung on that conclusion to decorate it in a godly fashion. This is the pattern of so much discussion about spiritual matters and religion. Men with wrong presumptions and conclusions exchange facts about God, throwing biblical references back and forth.

12 "But if they obey not, they shall perish by the sword, and they shall die without knowledge." (Job 36:12)

We have seen the consequences of obedience. Now, come the consequences of disobedience. Those who do not repent will perish. They will die never knowing the beauty of God's grace, *"without knowledge."*

We must remember that Elihu has defined his remarks as applying to the righteous who have become bound and fettered by their own sin. Even for the New Testament believer there IS a sin unto death. This is the object of John's attention.

"If any man see his brother sin a sin which is not unto death, he shall ask, and he shall give him life for them that sin not unto death. There is a sin unto death: I do not say that he shall pray for it." (1 John 5:16)

The issue here is not one's eternal salvation. John is dealing with the consequence of sin in our earthly lives. There comes a time when man crosses the line of God's patience. His continued unrepentant attitude moves God to take him home. Sin that is not corrected on earth will be dealt with in the presence of God.

This is not the penalty of sin, which was dealt with once for all by our Lord upon the cross. At stake here are the practical consequences of sin in everyday living.

GOD'S TREATMENT OF THE LOST

13 "But the hypocrites in heart heap up wrath: they cry not when he bindeth them." (Job 36:13)

Elihu must present the other alternative also. It could be that Job is not a genuine believer. As God's spokesman, Elihu has held out the possibility that Job is a good man who has suffered the consequence of unrepented sin. If so, Job must only confess and repent to be restored.

Now, the words of Elihu turn ominous, like the black and green clouds that push away the sunshine before a severe thunderstorm. Elihu wants Job to know that if he does not repent, it is good evidence that he is really a hypocrite.

When God binds hypocrites, they do not cry out to God for His mercy and grace. Instead, they heap more wrath upon the wrath already reserved for them.

This is, of course, true for any lost sinner in any age, although Job is not a lost sinner.

Paul also understands this truth. Unlike Elihu, he correctly applies it. In

Romans 2, he is speaking of religious men who are lost and refuse to turn from their religion to God.

"But after thy hardness and impenitent heart treasurest up unto thyself wrath against the day of wrath and revelation of the righteous judgment of God." (Romans 2:5)

14 "They die in youth, and their life is among the unclean.
15 He delivereth the poor in his affliction, and openeth their ears in oppression." (Job 36:14-15)

Elihu warns Job of a premature death, and of a life lived among the unclean to contrast with his past riches. Twisting the knife, Elihu points out how God delivers those who are poor and afflicted. When they are oppressed, God opens THEIR ears.

All four men have made much to do about the poor and afflicted in their comments to Job. Could it be that they are a bit jealous of Job's former wealth and prominence? Could it be that some of our own "biblical counsel" is sometimes motivated by our envies and prejudice?

16 "Even so would he have removed thee out of the strait into a broad place, where there is no straitness; and that which should be set on thy table should be full of fatness.
17 But thou hast fulfilled the judgment of the wicked: judgment and justice take hold on thee." (Job 36:16-17)

Had Job just repented, God would have done the same for him. A *"strait"* place in 1611 English is a "narrow" place, or "between a rock and a hard place." If Job had repented, God would have led Job into a *"broad"* place and set him down at a table *"full of fatness."*

That Job did not repent is evidence to Elihu that Job has become the object of God's judgment. He is getting exactly what he deserves. Tragically, Elihu has never considered that Job has not repented, because he has done nothing requiring repentance.

18 "Because there is wrath, beware lest he take thee away with his stroke: then a great ransom cannot deliver thee." (Job 36:18)

The wrath of God is real. When God swings His mighty club, one does not want to be in the path.

There is no ransom man can offer to escape God's wrath. God cannot be bought or bribed. Only One has offered a ransom sufficient to keep God's wrath from lost man.

"For even the Son of man came not to be ministered unto, but to minister, and to give his life a ransom for many." (Mark 10:45)

Even then, the ransom offered by Christ did NOT prevent the wrath of

God from falling upon sin. Our Lord and Savior bore that wrath Himself, in His body. This was the ransom He offered for us. God's wrath fell on Him in our stead.

"Who gave himself a ransom for all, to be testified in due time." (1 Timothy 2:6)

A man is a fool who understands what Christ did on the cross, and yet refuses the grace of God. Unlike Job, such a man is guilty as charged.

All the terrible consequences of God's wrath, detailed here by Elihu, by all rights should have fallen upon us. They fell on the Lord Jesus Christ instead.

Reject His offer of grace, and what He did for you is in vain. God's wrath WILL come upon you. The words of Elihu will apply to you.

19 "Will he esteem thy riches? no, not gold, nor all the forces of strength." (Job 36:19)

This verse continues the thought of the preceding verse. There is no ransom man can offer for his sin to escape the wrath of God.

God is not impressed with human riches. Nor is He impressed with our *"forces of strength."* Not even the supernatural forces of satanic strength can resist the wrath of God.

The same thought is put forth by both Solomon and Ezekiel.

"Riches profit not in the day of wrath: but righteousness delivereth from death." (Proverbs 11:4)

"They shall cast their silver in the streets, and their gold shall be removed: THEIR SILVER AND THEIR GOLD SHALL NOT BE ABLE TO DELIVER THEM IN THE DAY OF THE WRATH OF THE LORD: they shall not satisfy their souls, neither fill their bowels: because it is the stumblingblock of their iniquity." (Ezekiel 7:19) (Author's emphasis)

20 "Desire not the night, when people are cut off in their place." (Job 36:20)

The coming *"day of the LORD"* will be a time of darkness, not light according to Amos 5:18-20. It is not to be desired.

"WOE UNTO YOU THAT DESIRE the day of the LORD! to what end is it for you? THE DAY OF THE LORD IS DARKNESS, and not light. As if a man did flee from a lion, and a bear met him; or went into the house, and leaned his hand on the wall, and a serpent bit him. Shall not the day of the LORD be darkness, and not light? even very dark, and no brightness in it?" (Amos 5:18-20) (Author's emphasis)

In the coming darkness of the Tribulation many will be "cut off." They will be cut off "in their place," right where they are. It will be sudden and final.

Dark bars, dark dance floors and a dark ally, are only a few of the dark things we associate with debauchery. Why? The reason why some men desire darkness is conclusively defined by the Lord Himself.

"And this is the condemnation, that light is come into the world, and men loved darkness rather than light, because their deeds were evil." (John 3:19)

21 "Take heed, regard not iniquity: for this hast thou chosen rather than affliction." (Job 36:21)

Here is another call to Job to repent. Elihu contends that Job has a problem with sin. He wants Job to understand that his affliction is merely evidence that he has chosen the way of sin. Obviously, no one in his right mind would choose affliction like that of Job.

Elihu calls on Job to *"regard not iniquity."* If Job would just repent, his affliction could be alleviated.

Before passing on we should recall that there was a man in his right mind who chose affliction. His name was Moses, who is spoken of in the great "faith chapter" of Hebrews 11.

"Choosing rather to suffer affliction with the people of God, than to enjoy the pleasures of sin for a season." (Hebrews 11:25)

GOD'S TERRIBLE GLORIES

22 "Behold, God exalteth by his power: who teacheth like him?
23 Who hath enjoined him his way? or who can say, Thou hast wrought iniquity?" (Job 36:22-23)

To speak of God's glories, and use the adjective "terrible" seems to many to be a poor choice of words. Yet this passage, whose context continues through the remainder of the chapter, directly points the reader to God's glories, and they are terrible in the sense of their power and majesty.

There is no contradiction between destructive power and beauty. A line of thunderstorms can display an awesome beauty against the backdrop of a spring sky. From those thunderstorms can drop deadly tornados.

God's glory is beautiful and majestic. It fills the soul of any creature with awe. Elihu's line of reasoning is to show how God's majestic glory can spell doom for the unrepentant sinner.

In these two verses, Job 36:22-23, Elihu directs Job's attention to God' power and sovereignty. Can anyone teach like God? Can anyone tell God what to do? Can anyone accuse God of wrong-doing?

24 "Remember that thou magnify his work, which men behold.

25 Every man may see it; man may behold it afar off.

26 Behold, God is great, and we know him not, neither can the number of his years be searched out." (Job 36:24-26)

Elihu enjoins Job to turn his thoughts from his personal problems to the mighty work of God. Instead of complaining so loudly, Job should be loudly praising God for His work.

Elihu's point is evident in Job 36:26, when he says, *"Behold, God is great."* He is the almighty, infinite, unknowable God. No man can ever comprehend the depths of God's Person, nor can we answer the child's simple question "how old is God?"

27 "For he maketh small the drops of water: they pour down rain according to the vapour thereof:

28 Which the clouds do drop and distil upon man abundantly." (Job 36:27-28)

Again, our stereotype of "primitive" man is shattered by this remarkable summary of the rain process. Elihu knows that rain is dependent upon *"vapour"* in the air. Water on earth is vaporized by the energy of the sun. This is necessary, since water is heavier than air, and normally could not remain aloft. It is possible, because the vapor is lighter than air. As this moisture is gathered together in clouds, small drops of water form.

When they grow heavy enough, the clouds do drop and *"distil"* them upon man *"abundantly."* Their size when they reach the ground is *"according to the vapour thereof,"* picking up size according to the amount of moisture in the atmosphere.

Reading the remaining verses of Job 36, the theme that predominates this passage concerns God's clouds. While Elihu's remarks in Job 36:27-28 can be fully explained as referring to the natural process of rain, the *"clouds"* in the following verses will stretch our thinking.

Some *"clouds"* mentioned in this passage may not be explained as airborne water droplets. The word *"cloud"* admits a variety of meanings. A cloud can be a concentration of airborne moisture that floats through the earth's atmosphere. A cloud can be a large mass of almost anything, as in the *"cloud of witnesses"* mentioned in Hebrews 12:1. There are galactic clouds of stars in the universe. In a figurative sense, a cloud can be any mystery, doom or uncertainty that hangs above something or someone.

A review of comments on Job 22:13-14 is in order for the reader to fully appreciate what Elihu is saying here, and to avoid a duplicity of comments. In the biblical context, there are also different usages of the word *"cloud."*

29 "Also can any understand the spreadings of the clouds, or the noise of his tabernacle?" (Job 36:29)

Monitor any television or radio meteorologist for a month, and it will be clear that there is still no one who understands *"the spreadings of the clouds,"* so as to accurately predict the weather. From a purely conventional viewpoint, the first part of this verse presents no difficulty.

To speak of the *"noise of his tabernacle"* is a different matter. Elihu clearly understands the rain process. He has listened with care to a discussion among learned men who have tossed around amazing cosmological facts like so many children's building blocks. Why would we imagine that Elihu means only thunder when he mentions the *"noise of his tabernacle?"*

God's tabernacle is the universe, though many limit Elihu's remarks to the sky, where thunder and lightning take place. To see only thunder and lightning in the atmosphere as the noise in *"God's tabernacle"* is clearly a logical application. Yet there are other remarks in this context that are not so easily understood if we limit God's tabernacle to only what man can see in the storm clouds above his head.

We do know that in this passage God's "tabernacle" is not a reference to a tent on the Palestinian plain. Remember that the events of Job take place centuries before Moses.

There is much we do not understand about thunder. Yet Elihu's words imply a noise far higher than thunder. In Elihu's day God's tabernacle was creation, not a tent. Any astronomer will tell you that space is a noisy place, and we do not have a clue as to the source of many of those noises that fill God's tabernacle.

We must therefore be open to consider the various possibilities of meaning for the *"clouds"* Elihu mentions. Already in this book, we have seen how God spread out *"clouds"* to cover His face. We discussed this in connection with Job 22:13-14, and have just recommended above that you review those comments.

30 "Behold, he spreadeth his light upon it, and covereth the bottom of the sea." (Job 36:30)

The *"it"* upon which God spreads His light, must point back to His tabernacle of the preceding verse, Job 36:29. Some see this as a reference to lightning, since God does spread out His lightning upon the sky.

Yet, again, we recall the incredible cosmological and scientifically-correct information these men possessed, and we wonder if Elihu speaks of God's greater tabernacle, which is the universe. A careful review of Genesis 1:3-4 reveals that God spread His light across the universe before He created the sun, moon and stars in Genesis 1:14-18. The light of Genesis

1:3-4 cannot be explained by celestial bodies, since it was there before God created them. This light is the light God spread out across His *"tabernacle."*

Understanding the second part of Job 36:30 presents greater difficulty. Elihu says, *"and covereth the bottom of the sea."* If we limit God's tabernacle, the light He spreads, and the noise of His tabernacle to lightning and thunder in the sky, we can only say that this statement is hyperbole. This phrase would merely be an exaggeration, to say that lightning even shines down below the surface of the sea, all the way to the bottom.

Analyzing what these men have said, and comparing what we have found elsewhere in the Bible, leads to a mass of circumstantial evidence that should be seriously considered. If, for example, the *"sea"* that Elihu mentions is a reference to *"the deep,"* loose ends begin to fit together. Just as Genesis 1 tells of that light God created, which does not emanate from celestial bodies such as sun and stars, there are celestial waters which are not the Atlantic and Pacific.

We have encountered these waters of *"the deep"* before in our journey through Job. In comments on Job 9:6-8, and especially Job 26:7-10, we assessed evidence pointing to the existence of a large body of water called *"the deep."* We will shortly see, in Job 38:30, that the face of the deep is frozen. This would perhaps account for the *"sea of glass like unto crystal"* that appears before the throne of God in Revelation 4:6.

In our study of Job 26:7-10, we saw how God has spread His cloud across the face of His throne, preventing man from seeing it. Like the veil in the holiest place in the tabernacle, separating God from sinful man, God's cloud veils His physical presence. The direct access to God that Christ provided spiritually will be true in a physical sense when our Lord returns.

Such speculations are just that—speculations. Lest we get carried away on a journey through space, it is time again to plant our feet firmly on the ground. The next verse does just that.

31 "For by them judgeth he the people; he giveth meat in abundance." (Job 36:31)

Literally, through His sovereign control of clouds, rain, lightning and thunder, God brings judgment upon people, and provides for food ("meat"). Yet even this truth has a broader application to God's master plan for all creation. The coming day of judgment will most assuredly be accompanied by heavenly signs. And clouds, lightning and thunder consistently appear in those biblical prophecies that speak of God's coming judgment. Clouds, lightning and thunder were also associated with the judgment of the Flood, both in the earth's atmosphere and beyond. This purifying judgment ushered in God's provision for future generations, providing their *"meat."*

It is difficult at times to follow whether Elihu is speaking of things on earth or things in the heavens. The truth is that it makes little difference, since one is a mirror of the other, as we have consistently seen.

Do you really understand this principle? An example is the tabernacle. The earthly tabernacle was only a shadow of the heavenly reality (Hebrews 8:1-5; 9:11-12, 23-24). Yet both, earthly and heavenly, picture what God does within the tabernacle of the believer's body. Again, we see the threefold application of Scripture.

Paul reveals in Romans 1:20 that God illustrates His invisible truth by means of what can be physically observed. All this is truth to be applied internally by the believer.

32 "With clouds he covereth the light; and commandeth it not to shine by the cloud that cometh betwixt.

33 The noise thereof sheweth concerning it, the cattle also concerning the vapour." (Job 36:32-33)

Here come the lightning and thunder again. From our earthly perspective, Elihu tells how God sometimes hides lightning from man's view by covering it with clouds. Its presence is known by the noise of the thunder. Even the cattle are aware of its presence by the noise of the thunder.

Following the truth we mentioned above, every time the lightning and thunder fill the sky, God is painting a prophetic reminder of a coming day of judgment. When God speaks through His prophets in the Bible, He frequently mentions lightning and thunder. When He speaks, He thunders. Remember the various levels of application, and notice the language of Psalm 29.

"The voice of the LORD is upon the waters: THE GOD OF GLORY THUNDERETH: the LORD is UPON MANY WATERS. The voice of the LORD is powerful; the voice of the LORD is full of majesty. The voice of the LORD breaketh the cedars; yea, the LORD breaketh the cedars of Lebanon. He maketh them also to skip LIKE A CALF; Lebanon and Sirion like a young unicorn. The voice of the LORD divideth the flames of fire. The voice of the LORD shaketh the wilderness; the LORD shaketh the wilderness of Kadesh. The voice of the LORD maketh the hinds to calve, and discovereth the forests: and in his temple doth every one speak of his glory." (Psalm 29:3-9) (Author's emphasis)

GOD'S TRIBULATION ACTIVITIES

Elihu has worked himself into a frenzy. The chapter division between Job 36:33 and 37:1 is only so that the reader might catch his breath. Elihu has not stopped to take a breath yet. He continues to speak of heavenly phenomena such as thunder and lightning.

Now, however, it becomes clearer that his scope is broader than what is directly above his head. Elihu may be thinking of summer thunderstorms, but God is using his words to draw prophetic images and illustrate future judgment.

1 "At this also my heart trembleth, and is moved out of his place." (Job 37:1)

Anyone who has had his heart jump at the lightning and thunder of a terrible storm, can only imagine what it will be like when the voice of God thunders from heaven in judgment. It will definitely be a moving experience, with men's hearts failing them for fear (Luke 21:26).

The believer's heart will also be moved in the day of our Lord's coming, but in a different way. The "daystar," our Lord Jesus Christ (Malachi 4:2; Luke 1:78-79; Revelation 22:16), will arise in our hearts.

"We have also a more sure word of prophecy; whereunto ye do well that ye take heed, as unto a light that shineth in a dark place, until the day dawn, and the day star arise in your hearts." (2 Peter 1:19)

12 "Hear attentively the noise of his voice, and the sound that goeth out of his mouth." (Job 37:2)

The noise that Elihu has been describing since Job 36:29 is defined here as the *"noise of his voice."* Just a couple of verses later, in Job 37:4, we will see the same comparison made between this noise Elihu speaks of, and the voice of God.

Here, some commentaries describe pagan attitudes that they believe influenced these men. People of this age, we are told, believed that thunder was the voice of the gods speaking.

Say what?! Elihu has just delivered a perfectly acceptable explanation of the rain process. He and these men have exchanged information about the weight of winds, constellations, the *"way for the lightning of thunder,"* the fact that the moon does not shine but reflects the light of the sun, and other scientific truths. How can we believe that these men are ignorant savages, who are committed to superstition and mythology?

No. Elihu uses thunder as an image to describe the awesome voice of God Almighty. His images of lightning and thunder are to point toward a coming day of judgment. These are word-pictures. Their accuracy and consistency with the witness of the rest of scripture are so complete, that they continue to minister to us several thousand years later.

3 "He directeth it under the whole heaven, and his lightning unto the ends of the earth." (Job 37:3)

The context requires that *"it"* be God's voice that He directs *"under the whole heaven."* Here is that broad scope mentioned earlier. The omnipresence of God's voice is in view.

This is the same message that David expresses so eloquently in Psalm 19. We saw this reference earlier concerning comments on Job 22:13-14. Notice that the context of that Psalm also mentions a heavenly *"tabernacle,"* just as we have been dealing with in Job 36:29.

"The heavens declare the glory of God; and the firmament sheweth his handywork. Day unto day uttereth speech, and night unto night sheweth knowledge. THERE IS NO SPEECH NOR LANGUAGE, WHERE THEIR VOICE IS NOT HEARD. Their line is gone out THROUGH ALL THE EARTH, and their words TO THE END OF THE WORLD. In them hath he set A TABERNACLE FOR THE SUN, Which is as a bridegroom coming out of his chamber, and rejoiceth as a strong man to run a race. His going forth is FROM THE END OF THE HEAVEN, and HIS CIRCUIT UNTO THE ENDS OF IT: and there is nothing hid from the heat thereof." (Psalm 19:1-6) (Author's emphasis)

There is more in Job 37:3 than the noise of God's voice that stretches out *"under the whole heaven."* Elihu also mentions God's lightning as having that same boundless character—*"his lightning unto the ends of the earth."*

A comparison of other scriptures that look to the coming of Christ show that they use similar language. Here is an example from Matthew.

"For as the lightning cometh out of the east, and shineth even unto the west; so shall also the coming of the Son of man be." (Matthew 24:27)

An amazing attribute of the Bible is the way its many authors, whose writing is often separated by centuries and civilizations, use the same imagery in similar contexts. The only logical explanation for this phenomenon is to look to God as the Author, whose Spirit moved these human authors to speak and write.

4 "After it a voice roareth: he thundereth with the voice of his excellency; and he will not stay them when his voice is heard." (Job 37:4)

After *"it,"*—God's lightning—a voice roars. When God's lightning comes out of the east and extends its powerful fingers to the west, when the Lord of glory appears with a sword (Hebrews 4:12) coming out of His mouth (Revelation 19:15), a voice will roar. When God speaks, He thunders!

"Father, glorify thy name. Then came there a voice from heaven, saying, I have both glorified it, and will glorify it again. The people therefore, that stood by, and heard it, said that it thundered: others said, An angel spake to him." (John 12:28-29)

"And I saw another mighty angel come down from heaven, clothed with a cloud: and a rainbow was upon his head, and his face was as it were the sun, and his feet as pillars of fire: And he had in his hand a little book open: and he set his right foot upon the sea, and his left foot on the earth, And cried with a loud voice, as when a lion roareth: and when he had cried, seven thunders uttered their voices. And when the seven thunders had uttered their voices, I was about to write: and I heard a voice from heaven saying unto me, Seal up those things which the seven thunders uttered, and write them not." (Revelation 10:1-4)

When the voice of God roars and thunders, He (God) *"will not stay them."* (Job 37:4) To stay is "to hold back, to prevent." Just who are *"them"* who will not be held back by God? When God speaks, someone is leaving, and God will not prevent them or hold them back.

Figuring out who they are from the historical context of Elihu's words is difficult. Are they the lightning and thunder? It is impossible to say.

When we consider the prophetic picture that is drawn of the coming of God in judgment, there is also someone who will not be kept from leaving. This exodus of believers is sometimes called "the rapture," and is foreseen in 1 Corinthians 15:51-54 and 1 Thessalonians 4:13-18. The Lord will descend from heaven with a shout (1 Thessalonians 4:16) and He will not *"stay"* His saints when His voice thunders *"come up hither!"* (Revelation 4:1)

5 "God thundereth marvellously with his voice; great things doeth he, which we cannot comprehend." (Job 37:5)

There can be no question that the thunder or the voice being discussed is the voice of God. The only further comment we can make regarding this verse is to add a firm "amen" to the fact that we simply cannot comprehend fully the great things that God does. Elihu continues by giving examples of these great things that God does.

6 "For he saith to the snow, Be thou on the earth; likewise to the small rain, and to the great rain of his strength." (Job 37:6)

God controls snow and rain. Here, Elihu distinguishes between *"the small rain"* and the *"great rain of his strength."*

There is a rain phenomenon connected with the Second Coming. Joel prophesies about it, as we have seen earlier, looking to the time when the latter rain and the former rain come in the first month (Joel 2:23).

7 "He sealeth up the hand of every man; that all men may know his work." (Job 37:7)

Most commentators have seen this as God using winter weather to cause men's hands to be idle, *"sealing them up."* This provides opportunity for them to reflect upon the work of God. This fits the context nicely.

Yet these same scholars will also tell you that this is literally "He puts a seal upon the hand of every man." Is there not another possible meaning that is far more extraordinary? Consider the following possibility.

Here is a truly remarkable work of God, and one that definitely lies beyond the range of our comprehension. As a testimony of the great things He does, (which is the context) God sealed up the hand of every man. There is a seal on the hand of every man. Law officials around the world are well-aware of the individuality of every man's fingerprints.

This explanation also fit the context of snow and rain. Was Elihu aware of the snowflake-like uniqueness of every man's fingerprints?

If this is the case, unlike many modern men, Elihu had reflected upon the significance of this marvel, and correctly ascribed it to God's power. Men employ fingerprints in many ways, yet rarely pause to ponder why it is that men are born with such individualities. Elihu correctly says that the mighty works of God should motivate us to ponder the wonders of the God who did them.

8 "Then the beasts go into dens, and remain in their places." (Job 37:8)

"Then" probably refers prophetically to this time of coming Tribulation when God begins to crank up His working of nature. Elihu has mentioned thunder and lightning, snow and rain. In the following verse he will speak of the whirlwind and cold. At least the beasts have the sense to come in out of the rain, going into their dens and places, which is more than can be said for many men!

Then, when the REAL storm clouds gather, when the Lord Jesus Christ makes His appearance in the power of His glory, there will be some REAL scurrying for cover! Both man and beast will flee in panic.

"And the heaven departed as a scroll when it is rolled together; and every mountain and island were moved out of their places. And the kings of the earth, and the great men, and the rich men, and the chief captains, and the mighty men, and every bondman, and every free man, hid themselves in the dens and in the rocks of the mountains; And said to the mountains and rocks, Fall on us, and hide us from the face of him that

sitteth on the throne, and from the wrath of the Lamb: For the great day of his wrath is come; and who shall be able to stand?" (Revelation 6:14-17)

"And they shall go into the holes of the rocks, and into the caves of the earth, for fear of the LORD, and for the glory of his majesty, when he ariseth to shake terribly the earth." (Isaiah 2:19)

In the preceding verses from Revelation and Isaiah, we see men in that day desperately looking for shelter from the storm of God's wrath. Elihu specifically mentions the beasts in Job 37:8. The connection of animal activity to the events of that day is also made by the prophet Ezekiel.

"So that the fishes of the sea, and the fowls of the heaven, and the beasts of the field, and all creeping things that creep upon the earth, and all the men that are upon the face of the earth, shall shake at my presence, and the mountains shall be thrown down, and the steep places shall fall, and every wall shall fall to the ground." (Ezekiel 38:20)

9 "Out of the south cometh the whirlwind: and cold out of the north." (Job 37:9)

As Elihu said, we cannot understand completely the things God does. What we do know is that Elihu is giving examples of natural phenomena that are subject to God's power, and that these phenomena are prophetically associated with the second coming of Christ.

The whirlwind has some connection with the appearance of the Lord. When God speaks in the next chapter, Job 38:1, it will be *"out of the whirlwind."* The Lord appears to Ezekiel in the same fashion.

"And I looked, and, behold, a whirlwind came out of the north, a great cloud, and a fire infolding itself, and a brightness was about it, and out of the midst thereof as the colour of amber, out of the midst of the fire." (Ezekiel 1:4)

Isaiah and Jeremiah both mention the whirlwind. Both associate it with the coming wrath of God.

"For, behold, the LORD will come with fire, and with his chariots like a whirlwind, to render his anger with fury, and his rebuke with flames of fire." (Isaiah 66:15)

"Thus saith the LORD of hosts, Behold, evil shall go forth from nation to nation, and a great whirlwind shall be raised up from the coasts of the earth." (Jeremiah 25:32)

We must not forget that when the heavenly delegation came for the prophet Elijah, there was a whirlwind along with that famous chariot of fire. Could it be that the whirlwinds mentioned in these passages have something to do with the swirling effect of God's chariots that transport the cherubs mentioned by Ezekiel, or His angels?

"And it came to pass, as they still went on, and talked, that, behold,

there appeared a chariot of fire, and horses of fire, and parted them both asunder; and Elijah went up by a whirlwind into heaven." (2 Kings 2:11)

Elihu says that the whirlwind comes out of the south. (Job 37:9) The whirlwind that swirled around the Lord's appearance to Ezekiel came out of the north.

Commenting on Job 26:7, we mentioned the significance of north. North, in relationship to earth, is the direction of the third heaven. The whirlwind of the Lord's return will come from the north.

What is going through Elihu's mind as he reminds his hearers that the whirlwind comes out of the south, is impossible to say. There could be a prophetic meaning if we remember the Second Coming prophecy of Habakkuk.

The third chapter of Habakkuk's prophecy looks forward to the coming of the Lord. He says here that *"God came from Teman, and the Holy One from mount Paran."* (Habakkuk 3:3) Teman was a duke from Esau, while Paran is a wilderness area in the vicinity Sinai.

Putting these things together, convinced that there are no contradictions in the Bible, and convinced that the Bible contains no "filler" or "fluff," but only that which God wants us to know, the following scenario emerges. The Lord returns to earth from the "north." Once on earth, he traces the route of the exodus from Sinai to Jerusalem in His triumphant conquest, accompanied by the whirlwinds of the south. As did our great Joshua, He crosses Jordan, climbs the Jericho pass toward the heights of Jerusalem, where He triumphantly sets His feet upon the mount of Olives as promised (Zechariah 14:4; Acts 1:11).

In fact, this prophecy of Zechariah, which centers on Christ's return, also connects this great event with the *"whirlwinds of the south."*

"Turn you to the strong hold, ye prisoners of hope: even to day do I declare that I will render double unto thee; When I have bent Judah for me, filled the bow with Ephraim, and raised up thy sons, O Zion, against thy sons, O Greece, and made thee as the sword of a mighty man. And the LORD shall be seen over them, and his arrow shall go forth as the lightning: and the Lord GOD shall blow the trumpet, and shall go with WHIRLWINDS OF THE SOUTH. The LORD of hosts shall defend them; and they shall devour, and subdue with sling stones; and they shall drink, and make a noise as through wine; and they shall be filled like bowls, and as the corners of the altar. And the LORD their God shall save them in that day as the flock of his people: for they shall be as the stones of a crown, lifted up as an ensign upon his land." (Zechariah 9:12-16) (Author's emphasis)

Perhaps the whirlwinds of the south are the swirling, twisting air currents produced by the angelic host accompanying the Lord. The prophets who "saw" these future events through the inspiration of the Holy Spirit had to describe them in the limited language of their day.

What Elihu has in mind is probably nothing more than what people in the southwest United States would call "dust devils," little swirls of dust swept up by churning air currents in the wide-open spaces of arid plains. This is the same type of territory in the Sinai peninsula.

Whatever is running through Elihu's mind, we may never know. What is certain is that he makes these remarks while describing to Job the mighty works of God, warning him of judgment to come. Prophetically, these same images are employed by successive generations of prophets, right up to New Testament times, to speak of the Lord's return.

Elihu mentions not only the whirlwind of the south, but also the cold that comes from the north. This is a meteorologically-correct statement. That is where the cold weather comes from in that part of the world. Elihu continues the theme of God's control over weather, and cold in particular, in the next verse.

10 "By the breath of God frost is given: and the breadth of the waters is straitened." (Job 37:10)

The cold that comes from the north, bringing the frost and freezing the waters, is called here the *"breath of God."* This is what Elihu means to say by *"the breadth of the waters is straitened."* The edges of the waters are fixed, that is to say "frozen."

The theme is still God's control over the elements, as Elihu warns Job not to mess with God. Prophetically, we are reminded of God's coming judgment. The elements of nature are a reflection of God's control of the entire universe, which will be shaken in the day of His return.

11 "Also by watering he wearieth the thick cloud: he scattered his bright cloud." (Job 37:11)

As moisture continues to build up in clouds, they grow thicker. These clouds finally build up so much moisture—they grow "weary" from the weight of the water vapor—until they can no longer contain it. God's watering of the earth by rain begins.

The first part of the verse is easy to understand. It is harder to understand what Elihu means when he says, *"he scattereth his bright cloud."*

Some suggest that this is a reference to lightning in the clouds. Others point to the clouds that are illuminated by the rays of the setting sun.

The expression *"his bright cloud"* seems to be pointing to a specific cloud, not clouds. Again, we are confronted with the impossibility of getting inside the head of Elihu. Seeing the passage as a prophetic illustration of coming judgment, and recognizing the same elements used to symbolize that coming day enables us to make some observations.

There IS a bright cloud associated with the coming Christ. We will examine some references. The first is from the Revelation, as John tells about the returning Lord.

"And I looked, and behold a white cloud, and upon the cloud one sat like unto the Son of man, having on his head a golden crown, and in his hand a sharp sickle." (Revelation 14:14)

"And I looked, and, behold, a whirlwind came out of the north, a great cloud, and a fire infolding itself, and a brightness was about it, and out of the midst thereof as the colour of amber, out of the midst of the fire." (Ezekiel 1:4)

We just cited this verse to point out the whirlwind from the north. The passage describes how the Lord appeared to Ezekiel in a prophetic vision that looks forward to the millennial reign of Christ.

In the same sentence we find a *"great cloud."* This cloud has a brightness about it. The *"fire infolding itself"* is a way to speak of a light that is self-contained, not a blazing fire. Isn't it interesting that the whirlwind and the bright cloud appear together in the same context of the Lord coming to earth?

In the exodus, as described in Exodus 19, the Lord manifested His presence to Israel for guidance as a cloud by day and a fire by night. The precise form of cloud and fire is not given. Could they be of the type seen by Ezekiel?

There are several mentions of clouds in the Bible in connection with the Lord's glory. Here are a few.

"Who layeth the beams of his chambers in the waters: WHO MAKETH THE CLOUDS HIS CHARIOT: who walketh upon the wings of the wind." (Psalm 104:3) (Author's emphasis)

"The burden of Egypt. Behold, THE LORD RIDETH UPON A SWIFT CLOUD, and shall come into Egypt: and the idols of Egypt shall be moved at his presence, and the heart of Egypt shall melt in the midst of it." (Isaiah 19:1) (Author's emphasis)

"I saw in the night visions, and, behold, one like the Son of man CAME WITH THE CLOUDS OF HEAVEN, and came to the Ancient of days, and they brought him near before him. And there was given him dominion, and glory, and a kingdom, that all people, nations, and languages, should serve him: his dominion is an everlasting dominion, which shall not pass away, and his kingdom that which shall not be destroyed." (Daniel 7:13-14) (Author's emphasis)

"And then shall appear the sign of the Son of man in heaven: and then shall all the tribes of the earth mourn, and they shall see THE SON OF MAN COMING IN THE CLOUDS OF HEAVEN with power and great glory." (Matthew 24:30) (Author's emphasis)

"And when he had spoken these things, while they beheld, he was taken up; and A CLOUD RECEIVED HIM out of their sight." (Acts 1:9) (Author's emphasis)

"Behold, HE COMETH WITH CLOUDS; and every eye shall see him, and they also which pierced him: and all kindreds of the earth shall wail because of him. Even so, Amen." (Revelation 1:7) (Author's emphasis)

"And they heard a great voice from heaven saying unto them, Come up hither. And THEY ASCENDED UP TO HEAVEN IN A CLOUD; and their enemies beheld them." (Revelation 11:12)

We keep coming back to this issue of clouds. Draw your own conclusions, but be open to the possibility of clouds being more than fluffy, white collections of water vapor blowing across the overhead sky. Could these *"clouds"* have something to do with the transport of angelic beings who accompany our Lord? Is there a special *"cloud"* for the Lord?

12 "And it is turned round about by his counsels: that they may do whatsoever he commandeth them upon the face of the world in the earth." (Job 37:12)

"It" is His bright cloud. He turns it where He wants *"by his counsels."* In other words, He does with it what He wants to do. He is His own counselor.

In the middle of the sentence the number of the subject changes from *"it"* to *"they."* Clearly *"it"* points back to the bright cloud. Just who *"they"* are is not at all clear. The antecedent cannot be definitely decided.

Does it refer to the various elements of weather mentioned above, to the rain, snow, whirlwind and cold? Or, does it stand for the clouds of Job 37:11 collectively, the thick cloud and His bright cloud? Whatever or whoever *"they"* may be, God is in charge. They do whatever and wherever He commands them.

13 "He causeth it to come, whether for correction, or for his land, or for mercy." (Job 37:13)

The only logical antecedent for *"it"* is again the bright cloud. Possibly, you could view *"it"* as the collective group of elements we have been discussing. God DOES control the weather. He also controls His bright cloud.

This verse is instructive in that it shows us that God uses *"it"* for correction, that is to bring judgment, or for His land, to cause it to produce fruit. He also uses *"it"* for mercy, to bring relief from drought, for example, if we are talking about weather. He uses *"it"* to manifest His glory, if we are talking about His cloud. Either the elements of weather or God's bright cloud fit the context.

14 "Hearken unto this, O Job: stand still, and consider the wondrous works of God." (Job 37:14)

This is Elihu's invitation to Job. He calls upon Job to pause long enough to consider the majesty and power of God. Remember that Elihu has accused Job of wrestling against God. He wants Job to understand that to do so is futile.

15 "Dost thou know when God disposed them, and caused the light of his cloud to shine?" (Job 37:15)

Professor Elihu is ready to administer Job's final exam. He initiates a series of unanswerable questions.

The first question asks if Job knows when God put all these wondrous works into effect. The second comes back to God's bright cloud. Obviously Job cannot tell when God caused the light of His cloud to shine.

It does appear, though, that it is a specific cloud in view. This adds to the balance of evidence we studied above. He contrasts this particular bright cloud with the clouds of the next verse.

16 "Dost thou know the balancings of the clouds, the wondrous works of him which is perfect in knowledge?" (Job 37:16)

No man has ever fully understood the *"balancings of the clouds."* In our analysis of Job 36:27-28 and Job 37:11 we saw a rudimentary explanation of the rain process.

We know that heat from the sun converts liquid water to vapor that rises into atmospheric clouds. Those small drops are held aloft through a complex combination of electrical charges, wind currents, altitude and temperature changes. When the clouds are thick and heavy, the water droplets become large enough to fall back to earth as rain, snow or some combination such as sleet. Then, the whole process begins again.

Despite our research and knowledge of this process, how is earth's climate maintained in some sort of balance? This is the balancing of the clouds, and only God fully comprehends the way it works. He is in control. He is *"perfect in knowledge."*

17 "How thy garments are warm, when he quieteth the earth by the south wind?" (Job 37:17)

Elihu wants to know if Job really understands how God warms him and quiets the earth with the south wind? That is what happens, of course, when the famous *Sirocco* wind blows its southerly breezes across the Middle East. HOW it all happens is something only understood by God.

18 "Hast thou with him spread out the sky, which is strong, and as a molten looking glass?" (Job 37:18)

Obviously, Job did not help God spread out the sky. Something *"molten"* is "poured out." We have already seen that *"heaven"* in Genesis 1 is a beaten-out, spread-out expanse. The *"sky"* that Elihu speaks of could be either the atmosphere, the heavens, or both.

This sky is strong, and as a poured-out mirror. Remembering earlier comments on *"the deep,"* and the reference in Revelation 4:6 about the *"sea of glass like unto crystal,"* we can then move to God's statement in Job 38:30, that the face of the deep is frozen. Putting this together, may suggest that Elihu's *"sky"* extends upward to quite a height.

19 "Teach us what we shall say unto him; for we cannot order our speech by reason of darkness." (Job 37:19)

Elihu is taunting Job about his earlier wish to have his "day in court," to stand face-to-face with God. "What would you say, Job?"

Now, we see where Elihu has been going with all this talk about God's mighty works. His point is that man doesn't even know enough to order his thoughts so that he can converse intelligently with God.

20 "Shall it be told him that I speak? if a man speak, surely he shall be swallowed up." (Job 37:20)

This is a really sarcastic slam to Job. Elihu believes that Job has been terribly presumptuous in wanting to speak to God.

"Why, I wouldn't dare think of asking to speak to God! What would I say? Whatever I say would swallow me up." This is the sense of Elihu's words, and quite an admission from the man who claims to be God's spokesman.

21 "And now men see not the bright light which is in the clouds: but the wind passeth, and cleanseth them." (Job 37:21)

Here we are again, back to that bright light in the clouds. This time, though, it is not His *"cloud,"* but *"clouds."*

Here is another reason I believe that this whole issue of clouds and lights transcends the earth's atmospheric weather. This bright light is not lightning, since it is a bright light that *"now men see not."*

We saw repeated references linking the physical appearance of God's glory to clouds. Now, God is not physically manifest on earth. Men now do not see the bright light in the clouds. Following the flow of Elihu's arguments, he has just been speaking of being in the presence of God.

The force of these words, then, is that now it is not possible to be in the presence of God. What is possible is a wind that cleanses. This is Job's need according to Elihu's thinking. The wind separates the wheat from the chaff. This is a common theme in the Bible.

"The ungodly are not so: but are like the chaff which the wind driveth away." (Psalm 1:4)

"Let them be as chaff before the wind: and let the angel of the LORD chase them." (Psalm 35:5)

On the day of Pentecost, it was a sound from heaven *"as of a rushing mighty wind,"* that ushered in the power of the Holy Spirit (Acts 2:2). Wind cleanses and purifies. Just as the wind blows up a storm, it also blows it away.

22 "Fair weather cometh out of the north: with God is terrible majesty." (Job 37:22)

The image of the terrible majesty of God is beyond dispute. This is the image that Elihu wants to leave burned into Job's consciousness.

While impressing God's holiness upon Job, Elihu also aims to leave a message of hope contingent upon Job's repentance. This is the reason for the *"fair weather"* comment. Job has surely had enough "stormy weather!"

"The north wind driveth away rain: so doth an angry countenance a backbiting tongue." (Proverbs 25:23)

Here *"north"* and *"wind"* are combined to confirm the same message.

Consider the scope of Elihu's words: he mentions God's mighty works, the inadvisability of being in God's presence, and the coming judgment. All point to *"fair weather"* from the *"north"* that concerns more than climate.

Job told us in Job 26:7 that God stretched the *"north"* out over the empty place. We saw that God's throne *"in the sides of the north"* was Lucifer's target in Isaiah 14:12-14. Psalm 48:2 taught us that *"the city of the great King"* is *"on the sides of the north."*

Psalm 75:6 says that promotion comes neither from the east, nor the west, nor the south. The only direction left is north. Job is in need of promotion, and it comes from the north.

23 "Touching the Almighty, we cannot find him out: he is excellent in power, and in judgment, and in plenty of justice: he will not afflict.

24 Men do therefore fear him: he respecteth not any that are wise of heart." (Job 37:23-24)

Here is the conclusion of the whole matter from Elihu's perspective. God is simply beyond the reach of man's comprehension. Logic and reasoning alone are not sufficient to *"find him out."*

He is matchless in His power, judgment and justice. That is to say He is God, and there is none like Him.

Having said this, Elihu reminds, *"he will not afflict."* This is not affliction like Job has experienced, but means that he will not respond to man's petty approaches. In other words, He does not have to offer man any explanations for what He does.

This is the same thought he carries over into his final words, counseling men simply to fear God. God shows no partiality to men who think they are wise in their own hearts.

While Elihu has been administering his sophomoric exam to Job, a whirlwind has been racing in from the north. A bright cloud is just beyond the sight of these pathetic figures by the ash heap of Uz.

The One who will speak from the whirlwind in the next heartbeat has His own exam prepared. No scientist in the history of human civilization has ever passed it.

Men have spoken, and have nothing left to say. God is about to speak, and no one will be able to answer.

27

THE WORLD'S MOST DIFFICULT EXAMINATION

Where wast thou when I laid the foundations of the earth?
declare, if thou hast understanding.
Who hath the measures thereof, if thou knowest?
or who hath stretched the line upon it?
Whereupon are the foundations fastened?
or who laid the corner stone thereof;
When the morning stars sang together,
and all the sons of God shouted for joy?

Job 38:4-7

ELIHU IS LIKE A BOTTLE OF SODA POP VIGOROUSLY SHAKEN ON A hot, summer afternoon. When opened, there is an explosion of built-up pressure, a virtual frenzy of fizz. Some of the contents spills out onto the ground. Soon, the fizz is gone. Allowed to stand for a few minutes, what is left in the bottle has a stale taste.

Elihu's fizz is gone. He has "blown off steam," as we say. Now, all that remains is the stale taste of misapplied words. After the initial explosion, he is quiet at last.

No one moves to break the silence. Four men sit in speechless tension. From the perspective of the late 20th Century, what happens next is impossible to describe fully. All we know for certain is that the next voice to break the silence is God's.

QUESTIONS ABOUT WORDS WITHOUT KNOWLEDGE

1 "Then the LORD answered Job out of the whirlwind, and said." (Job 38:1)

Perhaps storm clouds had been churning in the distance, at last charging in to punctuate this dramatic pause, dropping down a whirlwind (or swirling cloud) to announce that God was about to speak. Is this that same *"cloud?" "God's cloud,"* that seems to keep popping up in the context of God's appearing? Is it an audible voice that blasts forth from the whirlwind like a loudspeaker?

In our study of Job 37:9, we speculated on the nature of this whirlwind. We compared the experience of Ezekiel in Ezekiel 1:4, and that of Elijah in 2 Kings 2:11. Other prophets, Isaiah, Jeremiah, Amos, Nahum and Zechariah saw the same *"whirlwind"* image in Advent prophecies. We examined some of them in the previous chapter.

The first time a *"whirlwind"* is mentioned in the English Bible is in 2 Kings, and we will review this event to make a point.

The mighty prophet Elijah is going to heaven without dying first. His "flight" has arrived, and he is at the gate. His apprentice Elisha is there to see him off on his northward journey.

"And it came to pass, as they still went on, and talked, that, behold, there appeared a chariot of fire, and horses of fire, and parted them both asunder; and Elijah went up by a whirlwind into heaven." (2 Kings 2:11)

You don't need to imagine that the chariot and horses of fire necessarily look like they are sometimes depicted by artists. Our understanding of the account is limited by the language. We should suppose that some sort of apparatus is used to transfer Elijah to the presence of God in the third heaven.

Perhaps the "takeoff" of this heavenly vehicle kicks up a whirlwind of dust, like a modern helicopter. You do NOT have to imagine that this IS a modern day helicopter, nor do you need to see UFO's and cute little extra-terrestrials of modern legend.

That God would employ physical, visible means to transport Elijah should not disrupt your faith any more than to imagine that Elijah was instantly transported to heaven, like Scotty beaming up Captain Kirk to the Spaceship Enterprise of "Star Trek" fame. We don't know what that apparatus might be. God has always employed physical means, or methodology in His dealings with mankind. Examples are His use of men to preach the gospel, and controlling the elements of nature to provide food for men.

It is beyond dispute that Elijah goes into heaven in a *"whirlwind"*. Whether this whirlwind is a storm cloud, "dust devil," or the swirl of a heavenly vehicle, is not of critical concern. Yet the consistency of similar accounts leads to speculation that God's *"chariots"* and the inseparable whirlwinds are some type of transport for angelic beings.

Modern UFO literature gives many wild and speculative theories for UFO sightings, often quoting Bible passages such as these to show that earth is being invaded by extraterrestrials. You can be certain that this modern confusion is not caused by God's heavenly hosts. There IS an author of confusion, and he is not God. If God does employ *"chariots"* in His earthly visitations, rest assured that the enemy has counterfeited them to create chaos, especially when we consider the soon return of our Lord to earth.

Putting aside the troublesome identity of the whirlwind, observe that however God stages His arrival, the purpose is clear. He is there to end Job's tribulation. One future day the skies will fill with the heavenly hosts and the glorious appearing of our Lord Himself, coming to finish the Tribulation prophesied so many times in both Testaments.

2 "Who is this that darkeneth counsel by words without knowledge?" (Job 38:2)

This is the first time God has spoken since the second chapter of Job. To whom is He speaking? Job 38:1 says that *"the Lord answered Job."*

Some have suggested that the one who was *"darkeneth counsel by words without wisdom"* was Elihu. While there is ambiguity, the context seems to require that God be dealing only with Job. Job is specifically addressed in Job 38:1. The words that follow Job 38:2 are to display Job's lack of knowledge. Therefore, God must be referring to Job in 38:2. Most commentators agree.

3 "Gird up now thy loins like a man; for I will demand of thee, and answer thou me." (Job 38:3)

This is God's wake-up call to Job. In biblical times, men wore long, flowing robes. To work or run, a man would *"gird up"* his robe around his loins to have freedom of movement.

Today, we would use a similar idiom, saying "roll up your sleeves." The idea is simply to get ready to go to work.

Perhaps you would imagine that God's first words after Job's agonizing ordeal would be empathetic words of comfort and reassurance. Not so! The voice of God thunders authoritatively from the whirlwind, demanding that Job prepare to do hard labor.

God is going to give Job the most difficult test you have ever seen. Specifically, it is a science test focusing on creation. There is not a scientist alive who could score a passing grade on this exam. Job 38 consists of a series of at least 35 questions, depending on how you want to divide them.

Isn't this remarkable? JOB is the one who has had the questions! Now that God finally breaks His silence, He begins by administering this examination.

There will be more questions in Job 39, but they will all share a common denominator, and we will deal with them separately. For the sake of organization, we will divide these questions into groups based on common denominators.

QUESTIONS ABOUT CREATION

4 "Where wast thou when I laid the foundations of the earth? declare, if thou hast understanding." (Job 38:4)

There is no possible response. Obviously, Job was not around to witness God's creative work.

Speaking of being around when the earth's foundations were laid, we often hear believers say that "we were in Christ before the foundation of the world." This statement comes from a misunderstanding of a passage in Ephesians, and it would be worthwhile to correct this common error while we focus on the time when earth's foundations were laid.

"Blessed be the God and Father of our Lord Jesus Christ, who hath blessed us with all spiritual blessings in heavenly places in Christ: According as he hath chosen us in him before the foundation of the world, that we should be holy and without blame before him in love." (Ephesians 1:3-4)

The verse says that *"he hath chosen us in him"* before the foundation of the world, not that "we were in him before the foundation of the world." This is a significant difference.

Paul is simply saying that God made a decision before He laid the foundation of the world. That decision, following the information in this verse, was no one could be *"holy and without blame before him in love"* without being in Christ. Ephesians 1:3-4 describes how God, before He laid the world's foundation, elected to make it possible for us to be a part of His plan in Christ.

Otherwise, we have a conflict with the rest of Scripture. Paul, in 1 Corinthians 15:22, says that we died *"in Adam"* when he sinned. We get "in Christ" by accepting His gracious offer of salvation, as Paul explains in the remainder of Ephesians 1 and in chapter 2. If we were "in Christ" before the foundation of the world, we would have to get out of Christ, to get in Adam to die in sin, then get back in Christ at salvation.

The point to be made here is that we are just as mute as Job when confronted with this question. Were YOU there when God laid the foundations of the earth? Do YOU have some special understanding that you would like to share?

5 "Who hath laid the measures thereof, if thou knowest? or who hath stretched the line upon it?" (Job 38:5)

The second and third questions appear in this verse. God is asking if Job knows who *"laid the measures"* of the earth. Who was there to explain to the chief Architect the size, shape and orientation of this orb that He hung upon nothing? (Job 26:7)

Do you know someone who has actually measured, *"stretched the line"* upon the earth? There are many who can answer that the earth has a diameter of 7,927 miles and an equator of 24,894 miles. Yet who among them has stretched out the line?

6 "Whereupon are the foundations thereof fastened? or who laid the corner stone thereof;

7 When the morning stars sang together, and all the sons of God shouted for joy?" (Job 38:6-7)

The fourth question is the first part of Job 38:6, and it boggles the mind! Do you know where the earth's foundations are fastened? This is particularly difficult in light of Job 26:7 we just mentioned. If the earth is hung upon nothing, then what are we talking about? How could the foundations of the earth be fastened to nothing?

Perhaps God has in mind the fastening of the continents to whatever is below the surface of the earth. No one really knows what is beneath the surface of the earth. We know more about outer space than we know about the interior of our own planet. Drilling has only penetrated the mere surface of the earth. The only thing scientists know assuredly about the center of the earth is that it is extremely hot. (Think about it!)

Again, Job is not quick to fill in the blanks with quick answers to God's questions. The best guess is that God has in mind the truth expressed in Colossians 1:16-17, that Christ Himself is the anchor upon which the earth's foundations are fastened.

"For by him were all things created, that are in heaven, and that are in earth, visible and invisible, whether they be thrones, or dominions, or principalities, or powers: all things were created by him, and for him: And he is before all things, and by him all things consist." (Colossians 1:16-17)

The next question concerns the corner stone of the earth. Did Job lay that corner stone? Of course not!

Yet, someone was there when it was laid. The parallelism of Job 38:7 suggests that these *"morning stars"* are the same *"sons of God"* who shouted for joy.

From a purely literal point of view, this IS a noisy universe that God has created. Physical stars DO have a tonal quality in the sounds they emit, and one could speak of them "singing."

Symbolically, stars are identified as a symbol of angels in Revelation 1:20. These *"sons of God"* are the same ones who show up in Genesis 6, intermarrying with the *"daughters of men."*

These are the same sons of God who present themselves before God in the first two chapters of Job. They are not alone, because Satan is among them. It should come as no surprise, therefore, that Satan is connected with the earliest history of earth. Look again at this remarkable reference to Satan, the power behind the human king of Tyre.

"Thou hast been in Eden the garden of God; every precious stone was thy covering, the sardius, topaz, and the diamond, the beryl, the onyx, and the jasper, the sapphire, the emerald, and the carbuncle, and gold: the workmanship of thy tabrets and of thy pipes was prepared in thee in the day that thou wast created. Thou art the anointed cherub that covereth; and I have set thee so: thou wast upon the holy mountain of God; thou hast walked up and down in the midst of the stones of fire." (Ezekiel 28:13-14)

The reference to tabrets and pipes implies a connection with music. Maybe Lucifer was the song leader in that day when the morning stars sang together in praise when God laid earth's corner stone.

QUESTIONS ABOUT THE WATERS

8 "Or who shut up the sea with doors, when it brake forth, as if it had issued out of the womb?
9 When I made the cloud the garment thereof, and thick darkness a swaddlingband for it,
10 And brake up for it my decreed place, and set bars and doors,
11 And said, Hitherto shalt thou come, but no further: and here shall thy proud waves be stayed?" (Job 38:8-11)

The question asks who shut off the gush of water at the time of creation, setting limits for it. Most see this *"sea"* as earth's waters. God's creative work, therefore, put limits to the waters by the complex system of tides. From a literal and earthly standpoint, there is no man who can completely explain the connection between the pull of the moon, gravity and the ocean tides. Much less could one claim to have issued the decree that they come into existence. We know that there IS a connection, but no one can claim authorship for this grand scheme, other than the one who is now speaking.

Considering the cosmological references scattered through this book, and the immediate context of these questions, it is more likely that God is speaking of setting the bounds of those waters that are called *"the deep,"* the waters above the heavens found in Psalm 148:4. We have encountered these waters several times in the Book of Job. The figure of waters issuing forth as if out of the womb, obviously points to birth, quite fitting the context of creation.

God says this flow of water was clothed with the cloud, perhaps the cloud of Job 36:29-32. Newborn babies in biblical times were wrapped in swaddling clothes. Here, God says the infant creation was swaddled in thick darkness. The language used here is quite similar to that of Psalm 18.

"He made darkness his secret place; his pavilion round about him were dark waters and thick clouds of the skies. At the brightness that was before him his thick clouds passed, hail stones and coals of fire. The LORD also thundered in the heavens, and the Highest gave his voice; hail stones and coals of fire. Yea, he sent out his arrows, and scattered them; and he shot out lightnings, and discomforted them. Then the channels of waters were seen, and the foundations of the world were discovered at thy rebuke, O LORD, at the blast of the breath of thy nostrils." (Psalm 18:11-15)

When these waters cascaded forth in creation, God established their limits, shutting it up with bars and doors, according to Job 38:8-11. We don't know what these bars and doors may be. Genesis 7:11 speaks of the *"windows of heaven"* that were opened to allow the waters of the *"great deep"* to flood the earth.

There is a fascinating account in 2 Kings 7 about a certain lord of Samaria in the days of Elisha. This man publicly scoffed at the idea of windows in heaven. Shortly, he lay dead, trampled by the people who saw the fulfillment of the prophecy made by the man of God.

Isaiah continues with a similar imagery of heaven's windows and earth's foundations. The whole idea of this section is to reveal man's shallow understanding. We make no attempt to answer these questions God poses to Job. What is important to see is the consistency and continuity of truth.

"And it shall come to pass, that he who fleeth from the noise of the fear shall fall into the pit; and he that cometh up out of the midst of the pit shall be taken in the snare: for THE WINDOWS FROM ON HIGH ARE OPEN, and THE FOUNDATIONS OF THE EARTH do shake." (Isaiah 24:18) (Author's emphasis)

We have also seen this truth of God setting limits for these heavenly waters elsewhere in this Book of Job. Consider these remarks of Job.

"He bindeth up the waters in his thick clouds; and the cloud is not rent under them. He holdeth back the face of his throne, and spreadeth his cloud upon it. He hath compassed the waters with bounds, until the day and night come to an end." (Job 26:8-10)

Though Job was aware of God's creative decree establishing limits for the waters, whether earthly or heavenly, he cannot respond to the question. God's question is rhetorical. Obviously, God issued the decree.

QUESTIONS ABOUT THE SUN'S LIGHT

12 "Hast thou commanded the morning since thy days; and caused the dayspring to know his place?" (Job 38:12)

Consider the question in the first phrase of Job 38:12. God wants to know if Job, in his lifetime, has ever managed to control the rising of the sun, or *"dayspring."*

God is the only one to readjust the rising or setting of the sun. There are two times recorded in the Bible when God did just this. The first is in the Book of Joshua, when God delayed the setting of the sun for almost an entire day. Then, in Isaiah 38:8, He added an extra 20 minutes to the day by causing the sun to go back 10 degrees on the sundial as a sign of Hezekiah.

We remember the great prophecy of Malachi 4:2, likening the soon coming of Christ to the rising of the *"Sun of righteousness."* There is no man who can control the rising of that Sun either.

Many think that their labors for the cause of Christ are bringing in His kingdom. They quote Matthew 24:14, saying that *"this gospel of the kingdom shall be preached in all the world for a witness unto all nations; and then shall the end come."*

While not questioning their sincerity, note that they fail to observe the context of Matthew 24, which has to do with signs of the Second Coming to Christ's Jewish disciples, not signs of the rapture of believers. They incorrectly think that someone is going to "win that last soul" that makes possible the return of Christ.

There is nothing that blocks the coming of Christ for His church, other than His own timetable. The kingdom will come when the King comes, and not before. No man can cause the Sun of righteousness to rise, any more than he could cause the physical star we call the sun to peek out from the eastern horizon, scattering the night.

Several questions have been posed. Job is still silent. Our comments are limited to understanding the remarkable scope of the questions, not to answering them.

The second half of Job 38:12 introduces a question whose context continues through verse 15.

12 "Hast thou commanded the morning since thy days; and caused the dayspring to know his place;
13 That it might take hold of the ends of the earth, that the wicked might be shaken out of it?
14 It is turned as clay to the seal; and they stand as a garment.
15 And from the wicked their light is withholden, and the high arm shall be broken." (Job 38:12-15)

The first part of Job 38:12 concerns God's regulation of the rising sun. The second half of the verse also has to do with the rising sun, called here the *"dayspring,"* but the following context reveals a change of emphasis. The first half relates to the fact of the sunrise, while the second half looks beyond that to the effects of the sunrise based on the unique orientation of earth upon its axis.

It is this slight tilt of the earth that causes the dayspring *"to know his place."* It is this tilt that allows for every bit of the earth to be exposed to the Sun at one time or another. This inclination of the planet enables the sun to *"take hold of the ends of the earth."*

Job 38:14 graphically illustrates this truth by comparing it to the way a metal seal completely presses out the clay as it rolls on a document to leave its distinctive mark. This is the meaning of *"It is turned as clay to the seal."* Every part of that seal presses upon the clay.

The last part of Job 38:14 says *"they stand as a garment." "They"* refers back to *"the ends of the earth"* in Job 38:13. In other words, this total exposure to the light of the sun causes the light to cover the entire globe like a garment, from pole to pole. Therefore, the wicked have no place to hide.

The inclusion of the wicked in this passage gives it a sense of meaning beyond the material. It is a good reminder of the constant connection between God's physical creation and His spiritual truth. This is why God constantly and consistently uses His creation to illustrate His will for man. Notice how God naturally and easily moves from one dimension to the other, from physical reality to spiritual truth.

We have cited Malachi 4:2 several times to show that the coming of Christ in glory is illustrated by the figure of the rising sun. We see God compared to the sun other places in the Bible.

"For the LORD God is a sun and shield: the LORD will give grace and glory: no good thing will he withhold from them that walk uprightly." (Psalm 84:11)

The *"dayspring"* is another word that is specifically applied to Christ in a prophetic way. Zacharias, filled with the Holy Spirit, prophesies over his newborn son, John the Baptist.

"And thou, child, shalt be called the prophet of the Highest: for thou shalt go before the face of the Lord to prepare his ways; To give knowledge of salvation unto his people by the remission of their sins, Through the tender mercy of our God; whereby THE DAYSPRING FROM ON HIGH hath visited us." (Luke 1:76-78) (Author's emphasis)

So what happens when this Dayspring appears? The answer is included in the words of God.

"That it might take hold of the ends of the earth, that the wicked might be shaken out of it?" (Job 38:13)

"And from the wicked their light is withholden, and the high arm shall be broken." (Job 38:15)

This is a universal truth, whether in the material or the spiritual realm. Light exposes darkness.

Another point to observe is that *"their light is withholden."* Though the wicked are exposed by the light, the light does not penetrate their wicked hearts. Not only are the wicked IN darkness, they ARE darkness. This is why their light is withheld, even when they stand in the presence of the One who is the Light of the world. *"For ye were sometimes darkness."* (Ephesians 5:8)

A final phrase in this passage is worthy of comment. In verse 15 it is said that *"the high arm shall be broken."* That is to say that the strength, the high arm, of the wicked will be broken. This is another common figure in Scripture, and it applies in a very specific way to the high arm of the Antichrist. His right arm will be withered according to this prophecy of Zechariah, called here the *"idol shepherd."*

"Woe to the idol shepherd that leaveth the flock! the sword shall be upon his arm, and upon his right eye: his arm shall be clean dried up, and his right eye shall be utterly darkened." (Zechariah 11:17)

QUESTIONS ABOUT STRANGE PLACES

16 "Hast thou entered into the springs of the sea? or hast thou walked in the search of the depth?" (Job 38:16)

It was not until this century that "modern" man discovered the *"springs of the sea."* We now know that there are literally springs, sources of water, bubbling up from the ocean bottoms. Here is another amazing scientific fact revealed in Job that we can add to our collection.

Whether this information also applies to the heavenly waters, mentioned so frequently, we do not know. We simply point to the consistent parallel between things on earth and things in the heavens, just like the earthly tabernacle reflected the heavenly model showed to Moses on the mount.

We do know that the great *"deep"*, that massive body of waters above the heavens, has *"fountains."* We read about it in the Genesis account of the flood.

"In the six hundredth year of Noah's life, in the second month, the seventeenth day of the month, the same day were ALL THE FOUNTAINS OF THE GREAT DEEP broken up, and the windows of heaven were opened." (Genesis 7:11) (Author's emphasis)

The Hebrew words are different. The word in Job translated as *"springs"* occurs only there in the Old Testament. The word translated *"fountains"* in Genesis 7:11 is also translated *"springs."* So we could legitimately speculate that a parallel exists between earthly and heavenly waters.

Obviously, Job has never entered these springs. Nor has he walked *"in the search of the depth."* This is the second part of Job 38:16, and the third question of the group.

Again, there is no possibility of response on Job's part. It is understood that he has never walked in search of the heavenly deep, and no man has ever walked the bottom of earthly oceans.

We can survey the oceans, and we can send probes to certain depths. Man can only go a few feet below the surface of ocean waters with his diving gear, and even submarines have their limits. To this day, no man has ever *"walked in the search of the depth."*

17 "Have the gates of death been opened unto thee? or hast thou seen the doors of the shadow of death?" (Job 38:17)

The two questions contained in this verse are powerful. In the first, God asks if Job has ever had death's gates opened to him. As bad as things have been for Job, he still cannot answer affirmatively.

Not only have these gates not been opened unto him, neither Job nor we can understand fully what they are. We know that hell has gates, as we learn from Christ in Matthew's Gospel.

"And I say also unto thee, That thou art Peter, and upon this rock I will build my church; and THE GATES OF HELL shall not prevail against it." (Matthew 16:18) (Author's emphasis)

So, both death and hell have gates. It is comforting to know who has the keys to these gates. We find the answer in the Book of Revelation.

"I am he that liveth, and was dead; and, behold, I am alive for evermore, Amen; and have the keys of hell and of death." (Revelation 1:18)

The second part of Job 38:17 moves from the gates of death to *"the doors of the shadow of death."* Job has not seen them, nor have we.

We just cannot get away from this shadow of death. We have observed it's Tribulation connection. With all this talk about death and hell, gates, doors and keys, I wonder what relationship this has to the events foreseen in Revelation 9:1-11. There, an angel is given the key to the bottomless pit, and he opens it. Out come the very forces of hell, led by their "king," whose name is given as "Destroyer," both in Hebrew and Greek *(Abaddon* and *Apollyon).*

18 Hast thou perceived the breadth of the earth? declare if thou knowest it all." (Job 38:18)

Today, it is possible to measure such things as the earth's breadth by satellite. The word, however, is "perceive," which is much more than to "measure." To perceive implies understanding, comprehension. Though we can measure many things with great technical precision, there is still much we do not perceive, even the breadth of the earth.

Job, despite his great knowledge of heaven, earth and cosmology, does not perceive the full scope of God's plan for earth.

19 "Where is the way where light dwelleth? and as for darkness, where is the place thereof?" (Job 38:19)

The next question is found in the first part of verse 19. Notice very carefully that God asks Job if he knows the *"way"* where light dwells, not the "place."

This is a extraordinary bit of scientific information to be found in such an ancient document. We now know that light is constantly moving. We measure distances by the speed of light. In the past few years we have only begun to take our first baby steps in the exciting field of lasers and fiber optics. Never before has the *"way where light dwelleth"* been more relevant than today.

There is only one "place" where light can legitimately be said to dwell, and that is in the third heaven. Light dwells there, because God is light. Listen to Daniel's words.

"He revealeth the deep and secret things: he knoweth what is in the darkness, and the light dwelleth with him." (Daniel 2:22)

We are only beginning our knowledge of the way where light dwells. Neither we nor Job can respond to the Almighty who MADE the way where light dwelleth. After asking if Job can tell the way where light dwells, he now asks about darkness. *"Where is the way where light dwelleth? and as for darkness, where is the place thereof,"* (Job 38:19)

Not the *"way"* but the *"place"* of darkness is the object of the question. Light is dynamic; darkness is static. Light is connected with the nature of God; darkness is connected with sin and evil.

Is this *"place"* of darkness hell? Is it the pit? The lake of fire? From a scientific perspective, what connection might this have with the "black holes" astronomers speak of in their theories of the universe?

Whatever it may be, there IS a place of darkness. God knows where it is.

20 "That thou shouldest take it to the bound thereof, and that thou shouldest know the paths to the house thereof?" (Job 38:20)

The context is still the place of darkness. After asking Job if he knew this place, God now asks another question about *"it"* (darkness).

From what we see here, darkness has a *"bound"* (boundary), and there are paths to its house. Just what is God talking about? We could speculate endlessly. Does this boundary have something to do with the edge of the deep, whose face is frozen (Job 38:30), this sea of glass? Could it have something to do with what Job said earlier?

"Before I go whence I shall not return, even to the land of darkness and the shadow of death; A land of darkness, as darkness itself; and of the shadow of death, without any order, and where the light is as darkness." (Job 10:21-22)

If we knew the answers to these questions, there would be no point in God asking them. God's aim is to readjust Job's perspective, and ours.

21 "Knowest thou it, because thou wast then born? or because the number of thy days is great?" (Job 38:21)

Speaking of an attitude adjustment, God's next questions are pointed. He asks if Job knows these things just from being born. Job's silence is his answer. The answers that God demands are NOT common knowledge meted out to all humans at birth.

Or, God asks, does Job know these things because he has enjoyed a long life? No matter how long you have been around, grey hair does not assure that you can ever pass this examination that God is giving.

QUESTIONS ABOUT THE WEATHER

22 "Hast thou entered into the treasures of the snow? or hast thou seen the treasures of the hail,
23 Which I have reserved against the time of trouble, against the day of battle and war?" (Job 38:22-23)

The enigmas intensify. What are these *"treasures of the snow"* and *"treasures of the hail?"*

It is no mystery that snow symbolizes purity and holiness in the Bible. One need think no further than the well-known invitation of Isaiah 1:18 to see this truth.

"Come now, and let us reason together, saith the LORD: though your sins be as scarlet, they shall be as white as snow; though they be red like crimson, they shall be as wool." (Isaiah 1:18)

The holiness of our God is likened to snow in Daniel's prophecy. In the Book of Revelation, John uses the same figure to describe the Lord Jesus Christ who appears to him.

"I beheld till the thrones were cast down, and the Ancient of days did sit, whose garment was white as snow, and the hair of his head like the pure wool: his throne was like the fiery flame, and his wheels as burning fire." (Daniel 7:9)

"His head and his hairs were white like wool, as white as snow; and his eyes were as a flame of fire." (Revelation 1:14)

Have YOU entered into the *"treasures of the snow"*? From a purely devotional standpoint, entering into the *"treasures of the snow"* is entering into the holiness of God.

Yet what can we say about the *"treasures of the hail"*? Hail has played a role or two in history. In the Book of Joshua, five Amorite kings had come against the Gibeonites, who had just deceived the Israelites into forming an alliance with them. Joshua had to honor the agreement he had made, and God supernaturally intervened through nature.

"And it came to pass, as they fled from before Israel, and were in the going down to Bethhoron, that the LORD cast down great stones from heaven upon them unto Azekah, and they died: they were more which died with hailstones than they whom the children of Israel slew with the sword." (Joshua 10:11)

Neither we nor Job may know what the *"treasures of the hail"* may be, but you can be sure God does. He has drawn upon these treasures in critical times. A survey of history reveals that God has used snow and hail often to influence the outcome of battles and wars.

Again, we are left to speculation, in the face of our helplessness to answer God's questions. Yet before passing on, we have not yet commented on Job 38:23. The phrases used there suggest that, in a prophetic sense, God has reserved the treasures of snow and hail for the coming Tribulation.

God's question concerning these treasures continues in Job 38:23, when He says, *"Which I have reserved against the time of trouble."* The time of trouble is associated with the coming Tribulation. The phrase is used eight times in the Old Testament, but never more forcefully than in Daniel. This prophecy is alluded to by Christ in Matthew 24:21.

"And at that time shall Michael stand up, the great prince which standeth for the children of thy people: and there shall be a TIME OF TROUBLE, such as never was since there was a nation even to that same time: and at that time thy people shall be delivered, every one that shall be found written in the book." (Daniel 12:1) (Author's emphasis)

Clearly that time of trouble, that Tribulation, will be a time of *"battle and war,"* as indicated in Job 38:23. That turbulent time is foreseen in the Book of Revelation. There, we find hail right in the middle of it all.

"And the nations were angry, and thy wrath is come, and the time of the dead, that they should be judged, and that thou shouldest give reward unto thy servants the prophets, and to the saints, and them that fear thy name, small and great; and shouldest destroy them which destroy the earth. And the temple of God was opened in heaven, and there was seen in his temple the ark of his testament: and there were lightnings, and voices, and thunderings, and an earthquake, AND GREAT HAIL." (Revelation 11:18-19) (Author's emphasis)

There are treasures in the snow and hail that no scientist understands. God understands, and will make them known in due time.

24 "By what way is the light parted, which scattereth the east wind upon the earth?" (Job 38:24)

We now know that light can be divided, or *"parted."* This is what causes the rainbow, as the light is divided into its individual colors. What does this have to do with scattering the east wind upon the earth? Our modern science has seen only a fraction of God's truth.

25 "Who hath divided a watercourse for the overflowing of waters, or a way for the lightning of thunder;

26 To cause it to rain on the earth, where no man is; on the wilderness, wherein there is no man;

27 To satisfy the desolate and waste ground; and to cause the bud of the tender herb to spring forth?" (Job 38:25-27)

These verses pose God's question to Job about the process of rain. Is this *"watercourse"* (waterway) for the overflowing of waters a reference to the overflowing of waters from the clouds that pour down upon the earth? Does it have to do with the way that waters course their way toward the sea? Or, could this be some cosmological reference to the overflowing of waters from the *"deep"* at the time of the Great Flood?

The *"way for the lightning of thunder"* was discussed in our study of Job 28:26. A path DOES open from cloud to ground before the lightning of thunder. Lightning and thunder DO have effect upon the cloud formations, causing rain. Just how all this fits together is still an uncertain infant science for man, yet elementary truth for God.

We can see how God uses the rain to satisfy the thirst of parched land and to cause the vegetation of that land to bud, as described in Job 38:27. Yet what is that wilderness where no man is, mentioned in the preceding verse, Job 38:26? How will we answer, when we do not even understand the question?

28 "Hath the rain a father? or who hath begotten the drops of dew?

29 Out of whose womb came the ice? and the hoary frost of heaven, who hath gendered it?" (Job 38:28-29)

These questions do not represent a stretch of the imagination. God is the source of both rain and dew, and also ice and hoary (white) frost.

Isaac knew this. We see the answer in his words to Jacob, whom he mistook for his other son, Esau.

"Therefore God give thee of the dew of heaven, and the fatness of the earth, and plenty of corn and wine." (Genesis 27:28)

Job is still speechless, however, since he well knows that HE has nothing to do with any of these things. God is the Father. Sometimes the most difficult questions are the ones for which you know the answers.

30 "The waters are hid as with a stone, and the face of the deep is frozen." (Job 38:30)

Now, it appears that God's focus moves to the second heaven. We have commented several times on the frozen face of the *"deep"*, as recently as Job 37:18. Yet the first part of the verse is a mystery. Notice also that this is a declarative statement, not a question.

In Job 22:13-14 we speculated that the *"deep"* is a vast body of celestial waters, seen by John as a sea of glass like crystal. If it is true that the *"deep"* is a vast, heavenly body of water whose face is frozen, these waters are hidden. Here, God says they are hidden *"as with a stone."* God Himself is the stone of Israel (Genesis 49:24) and He is the Rock (Deuteronomy 32:4).

Does God mean that these waters are hidden as if by Himself? Whatever He means, clearly these waters are hidden, and will stay hidden until He chooses to reveal them.

QUESTIONS ABOUT THE HEAVENS

Job 38:30 formed an abrupt transition from questions about weather, to a new series of questions about the cosmos. God seems to make such jumps naturally. His mind has no trouble seeing how everything is tied together.

31 "Canst thou bind the sweet influences of Pleiades, or loose the bands of Orion?" (Job 38:31)

Pleiades is the tightly-formed group of seven stars in the constellation of Orion. This is why they would be mentioned in the same breath. They are visible in spring and summer.

"Seek him that maketh the seven stars and Orion, and turneth the shadow of death into the morning, and maketh the day dark with night: that calleth for the waters of the sea, and poureth them out upon the face of the earth: The LORD is his name." (Amos 5:8)

So, the question is whether Job can bind *"the sweet influences"* of Pleiades, or the pleasant weather they usher in with their appearing. In other words, can Job bind them to make spring last all year? Or, can he *"loose the bands,"* making winter come?

Orion is the constellation sometimes called the Strong Man, or The Hunter. The first hunter in the Bible is Nimrod, founder of Babel.

The one Nimrod represents, the Antichrist, is now loose on the earth, and in the second heaven. He is the *"god of this world"* (2 Corinthians 4:4), and the *"prince of the power of the air"* (Ephesians 2:2). One day, he will be bound for a thousand years (Revelation 20:1-3).

32 "Canst thou bring forth Mazzaroth in his season? or canst thou guide Arcturus with his sons?" (Job 38:32)

Mazzaroth means the twelve signs of the Zodiac with their related 36 constellations. Arcturus is another name for Ursa Major, the big bear, better known as the "Big Dipper."

Does Job have any influence over the times and seasons of the constellations? Can he decide the course of the stars in the heavens? Of course not!

33 "Knowest thou the ordinances of heaven? canst thou set the dominion thereof in the earth?" (Job 38:33)

An *"ordinance"* is something prescribed, a statute. God set the universe in motion according to predetermined ordinances or laws of nature. Job doesn't know them all, nor do we.

"Thus saith the LORD, which giveth the sun for a light by day, and the ordinances of the moon and of the stars for a light by night, which divideth

the sea when the waves thereof roar; The LORD of hosts is his name: If those ordinances depart from before me, saith the LORD, then the seed of Israel also shall cease from being a nation before me for ever. Thus saith the LORD; If heaven above can be measured, and the foundations of the earth searched out beneath, I will also cast off all the seed of Israel for all that they have done, saith the LORD." (Jeremiah 31:35-37)

God also knows that Job cannot set the dominion of these heavenly ordinances in earth. The implication is, of course, that God has done just that.

Modern astrologers claim to predict the future by their study of the constellations. There is nothing biblical about their claims. In Isaiah 47:13 God challenges those who trust in astrologers.

While astrology is resolutely condemned in the Bible, it is also certain that there is a connection between things in heaven and things on earth. Job and his friends were keenly aware of the heavenly signs.

Much of human myth and legend is based upon a kernel of truth. The closer to the truth without being the truth, the more dangerous something is. Satan was not far from the truth in what he said in the Garden. He was just far enough from the truth to plunge the human race on a course toward hell. Perhaps there is a grain of truth that fuels man's interest in astrology.

Whatever the case, God has established ordinances of heaven. In some way, they have some sort of dominion on earth. Figuratively, God's Word that He has given us from heaven teaches us the ordinances by which we are to live.

QUESTIONS IN GENERAL

The amazing thing about God's questioning is the way He has consistently been drawing lines from heaven to earth, naturally and without the slightest strain. He has just spoken of the signs of the Zodiac and the constellations, and, without pausing for breath, He suddenly asks Job about rain and lightning in the next two verses.

34 "Canst thou lift up thy voice to the clouds, that abundance of waters may cover thee?" (Job 38:34)

God is in control of the universe. From the outermost constellations to the clouds that shower an abundance of rain upon the earth, God has spoken into existence an interdependent universe that meshes better than the many parts of a complicated Swiss watch.

Does Job have control of the clouds to cause them to unleash their rain.

No. Armed with our "advanced" technology, not only can we not cause rain in any consistent manner, we cannot even forecast consistently when God is going to cause it to rain.

Elijah, the mighty prophet of God, prayed that it would not rain, and God answered his prayer. Then, when God's purposes had been accomplished, Elijah prayed again and it rained (1 Kings 18).

"Elias was a man subject to like passions as we are, and he prayed earnestly that it might not rain: and it rained not on the earth by the space of three years and six months. And he prayed again, and the heaven gave rain, and the earth brought forth her fruit." (James 5:17-18)

The fact that God would answer a man's earnest prayer who is engaged in spiritual combat with the priests of Baal, does not weaken the force of God's question to Job. Elijah's prayer is the exception, not the rule. Even under such special circumstances, God is ultimately the one who controls the weather.

We should also remember the many prophetic images in this book that point to the coming Tribulation. The events of Elijah's day will be repeated in the Tribulation by God's two witnesses, as foretold in Revelation 11:6.

"These have power to shut heaven, that it rain not in the days of their prophecy: and have power over waters to turn them to blood, and to smite the earth with all plagues, as often as they will." (Revelation 11:6)

35 "Canst thou send lightnings, that they may go, and say unto thee, Here we are?" (Job 38:35)

If Job has no control over the rain, he certainly has no control over the lightning. There is, though, a sense in which modern man has learned to control certain aspects of the lightning, if we understand lightning to be connected with electricity.

Through electricity, man has learned in the last century how to make it "talk" to us through applications such as radio and telephone. There is a great leap between using electricity in applied situations and controlling the lightning, or even understanding precisely what it is and how it works.

36 "Who hath put wisdom in the inward parts? or who hath given understanding to the heart?" (Job 38:36)

Now, God moves from His control of nature and the universe to the depths of the human soul. Even there God is sovereign.

Men can teach other men knowledge, but only God gives true wisdom. Paul eloquently describes the difference between the world's wisdom and God's wisdom in the second chapter of 1 Corinthians. The wisdom that God gives cannot be found in a book or classroom. God gives wisdom *"in the inward parts."*

Understanding was defined in Job 28:28 as *"to depart from evil."* To give man the grace in his heart to depart from evil is something only God can do. Lost men are slaves to sin, as Jesus said in John 8:34.

37 "Who can number the clouds in wisdom? or who can stay the bottles of heaven

38 When the dust groweth into hardness, and the clouds cleave fast together?" (Job 38:37-38)

Man has managed to classify some types of clouds, but no one has ever counted them. God even has the stars numbered according to Psalm 147:4.

God asks who can "*stay*" (prevent) the bottles of heaven in a time of drought, when the ground is hard and the clods stick together. When God wants it to rain, it is going to rain.

In Job 38:34 we referred to Elijah's prayer that shut off the rain for three and a half years. When he prayed again, the rain came in buckets! We also saw how this was prophetic of a similar time in the coming Tribulation, when God's two witnesses will shut off the rain for the three-and-a-half-year time of their ministry. Then, the rains will come. It will be a rain like never seen since the days leading to Noah's flood. Joel says it will be a combination of the former and the latter rains, the two primary rains that feed the soil of Palestine.

"Be glad then, ye children of Zion, and rejoice in the LORD your God: for he hath given you the former rain moderately, and he will cause to come down for you the rain, the former rain, and the latter rain in the first month." (Joel 2:23)

Hosea saw the same vision. He described it in his prophecy.

"Then shall we know, if we follow on to know the LORD: his going forth is prepared as the morning; and he shall come unto us as the rain, as the latter and former rain unto the earth." (Hosea 6:3)

Could Job, or we, prevent this from happening? Of course not. Speaking of the Tribulation, there are some bottles (vials) that are going to be poured out beginning in Revelation 16. God's wrath is meted out upon the earth, described in Revelation 16 as a series of seven vials. Again, man is helpless to prevent (stay) these bottles of heaven.

39 "Wilt thou hunt the prey for the lion? or fill the appetite of the young lions,

40 When they couch in their dens, and abide in the covert to lie in wait?

41 Who provideth for the raven his food? when his young ones cry unto God, they wander for lack of meat." (Job 38:39-41)

God has covered the entire span of His creation in this series of questions to Job. God reigns supreme over it all, from the heights of the third heaven, to earthly weather, the inner parts of men's souls and even animal life.

These last verses of Job 38 challenge Job to consider God's ability to provide for the creatures He has created. It is the same truth Jesus expressed in the Sermon on the Mount.

"Behold the fowls of the air: for they sow not, neither do they reap, nor gather into barns; yet your heavenly Father feedeth them. Are ye not much better than they?" (Matthew 6:26)

Even in the coming millennial reign of Christ, God will be concerned to take care of His animals. Hosea saw that in his prophecy.

"And in that day will I make a covenant for them with the beasts of the field, and with the fowls of heaven, and with the creeping things of the ground: and I will break the bow and the sword and the battle out of the earth, and will make them to lie down safely." (Hosea 2:18)

These questions about the animals provide a transition to the subject matter of the next chapter. In Job 39 God will continue His questioning. All will revolve around animal life. The lion and the raven are the first two of fourteen animals God will parade in front of Job.

This section of the exam, though, is over. Job cannot respond. No matter how hard he studied or prepared for this exam, he would still fail miserably. God is still God.

From Job 3 through Job 37 these men had been involved in a ferocious debate. Each set forth great truth about God and His creation. We saw that the overwhelming majority of what they said was true, in line with the rest of the Bible. Yet for all their talk, nothing was decided, nothing accomplished.

When God finally spoke, He began by asking questions, all designed to show man that he really knows nothing at all. God did not declare anything; He merely asked some questions which ended the debate.

We spend an inordinate amount of time debating information about God and His creation. We know no more than Job or his friends. Let us learn a great lesson from what we have witnessed. We do not need more information about God. We need God.

28

LESSONS FROM GOD'S ZOO

Knowest thou the time when the wild goats
of the rock bring forth?
or canst thou mark when the hinds do calve?
Canst thou number the months that they fulfil?
or knowest thou the time when they bring forth?
They bow themselves,
they bring forth their young ones,
they cast out their sorrows.
Their young ones are in good liking,
they grow up with corn; they go forth,
and return not unto them.

Job 39:1-4

GOD HAS A STRANGE WAY OF RESPONDING TO QUESTIONS WITH questions of His own. Jesus used the technique often. We now see it here in the Book of Job. Job has had many questions about the series of calamities that has claimed the joy of his life. Now, God finally speaks, but He does nothing more than ask questions.

God's questions are so potent, they silence Job's. Job has wondered about the tragic events that shook his life. God has asked questions about creation and the universe. Job's questions took him on a bitter inward journey. God's questions have redirected Job's attention outward and upward.

Now, matters take an even stranger turn from man's natural perspective. Having laid down a series of cosmological and natural questions, God now asks questions about animals. What could this possibly have to do with Job's life?

Job's friends came to comfort and counsel him. They were armed with weighty theological knowledge and arguments. The precision of their words was impressive. Rarely did they stray from a theologically-correct position.

God is speaking now. He bypasses the many sincere and honest questions that have percolated in Job's heart. He sweeps by the grandiose theology of the counselors. With only a handful of declarative statements and many questions, God has established His sovereignty over creation. None of these men has uttered a word in reply.

Once we catch the drift of the questions, we can see the wisdom in pointing Job to God's plan for the universe. The implication is that Job should be concerned with the whole of God's design, not merely his own bit part in the drama. But animals? What is happening here?

Before we consider Job 39 verse by verse, we will make a series of observations. We have already seen two animals in our study of Job 38, the lion and the raven. Here, in Job 39, we will examine a series of ten animals. Both Job 40 and 41 feature the appearance of a strange animal. In all, there are fourteen animals mentioned from Job 38 through Job 41.

Seven is God's number of completion, the number associated with His perfect works, just as in the seven days of creation. Two is the number of witness, or confirmation. We are considering a list of fourteen animals, for whatever reason. Could it be that God wants to confirm the perfection of His work to Job? Is there valuable truth to be learned from God's zoo?

Most of the animals mentioned are found among the unclean animals in Leviticus 11 and Deuteronomy 14. Here, they appear in a setting that is a prophetic portrayal of Tribulation and Second Coming (Advent).

We have already commented on the singular way God has directed Job's attention to creation. Job has the testimony by God that he is a "perfect" man. In that, he shares a common attribute with the man who was the heir to God's creation—Adam. Adam was perfect in his ways until the day that sin corrupted the human race.

Following creation, God caused all the animals to pass before Adam to see what he would call them (Genesis 2:19-20). Now, in a scene that is eerily reminiscent of that famous time in the Garden, God is addressing a man who has been tempted by the Devil as no man other that the Lord Jesus Christ Himself. Yet, unlike Adam, Job has stubbornly clung to his spiritual integrity.

God has offered no word of comfort to Job, nor has He even addressed the issue of Job's suffering. Instead, He immediately administered an impossibly tough exam concerning the creation of the universe, and the workings of nature.

Now, immediately after directing Job's attention to creation, God parades these animals before Job to see how he will respond. The parallels to the story of Adam are too profound to be mere coincidence. God's counseling procedure is so diametrically opposed to what WE think best, that we must pay close attention to what He is saying.

So, what does all this mean? To be brutally honest, I don't understand even a fraction of what is taking place here in the last chapters of Job. Yet, we must be consistent in the application of the rules of Bible study, and comparing Scripture with Scripture is foundational to all correct understanding of the Bible. Words, phrases, scenarios and situations that are consistently repeated in the Bible must bear our intense scrutiny. Our God is a consistent God, and a God of order. There are patterns to be discerned in the Word of God. These are the "ways of God."

Having confessed my own insufficiency to exhaust the truth of God in this passage, allow me to offer some concrete ways in which we can begin to grow in our understanding of the meaning and application of this Scripture. First, any man who is "perfect" will definitely be tested to his maximum limit. No sooner had Adam begun to explore the paradise in which God had placed him, than he was face to face with the most critical test of his existence. Job gains an incredible testimony with God due to his upright life, and suddenly he finds himself the object of intense spiritual warfare.

We often fail to remember this most basic truth. Our tendency is to think that bad things happen to people who are bad, that every bad thing in life is merely a "payback" from God. This is precisely the one thing that all four of Job's counselors overlooked in their basic assumptions. Despite their advanced theology and science, they neglected a foundational truth that undergirds human life—we are in a spiritual war. Their error in this one point rendered their weighty pronouncements worthless.

Second, don't fail to observe that God is not at all concerned with getting into the details of Job's suffering. He immediately points Job to the whole of His creation, to His grand design for His kingdom. Job must lift up his eyes to see how God's master plan unfolds, not bury himself in self-pity.

Many professing Christians today have conceded the debate over creation. They have succumbed to the claims of "*science falsely so called*" (1 Timothy 6:20). Instead, they build "church-growth" strategies around the accommodation of man's wants and desires, focusing on man's inner hurts and struggles. They have lost the biblical perspective of God's grand plan. Concerned with what they can get from God, they have lost sight of how they fit into God's total design.

The debate about whether God created by the fiat of His word has become irrelevant to modern man. With so much suffering in the world, the argument goes, why should energy be spent on such trivial and unimportant issues?

Truly God's ways are not our ways. There is much we can learn simply from observing how God deals with this situation. Even if we cannot understand some of God's questions, we can still learn from paying close attention to His ways.

Now, what about those animals?

PREGNANT GOATS AND HINDS

1 "Knowest thou the time when the wild goats of the rock bring forth? or canst thou mark when the hinds do calve?
2 Canst thou number the months that they fulfil? or knowest thou the time when they bring forth?
3 They bow themselves, they bring forth their young ones, they cast out their sorrows.
4 Their young ones are in good liking, they grow up with corn; they go forth, and return not unto them." (Job 39:1-4)

The essence of God's question in these verses has to do with the gestation times of these two animals. Can Job know or mark the time, or number the months when wild goats and hinds *"bring forth?"*

Contrary to some of God's questions on cosmology, this question is not that hard to answer. Any observer with a sharp eye and an abundance of patience, could study these animals, noting their mating habits and the length of the gestation periods.

God's purpose in asking this question is not so much to stump Job, as to cause him to reflect upon times and seasons. We must be constantly aware that we are in a book rich in prophetic imagery. It is a book that paints colorful and graphic portraits of those three things that are often so hard to distinguish—Christ on the cross, God's people in tribulation, and the sinner in hell. Each of these items is inseparably tied to times and seasons.

God's point is that He alone is in charge of times and seasons. Job can observe them, mark them and number them, but he has no control over them.

Just as God firmly controls the gestation periods of wild goats and hinds, He controls the times and seasons of everything. Christ came to die on the cross in "the *fulness of the time*" (Galatians 4:4). The Bible says that there is a time *"appointed unto men once to die, but after this the judgment"* (Hebrews 9:27). There is also a day when the dead without Christ will appear before God in judgment (Revelation 20:11-12). The coming Tribulation, when hell will be let loose upon earth, also has a precise time set. Daniel 9 gives understanding as to the times and seasons that are yet to come upon Israel.

God is calling Job to pay attention to the times. We would be wise to do the same.

Speaking of prophetic images, a graphic image employed by several writers compares the coming Tribulation, or time of Jacob's trouble, to the excruciating pains of birth. This figure is employed by several of the prophets, whether in reference to the immediate fulfillment in captivity, or the long range fulfillment in the Tribulation. Here is a sampling.

"Fear took hold upon them there, and pain, AS OF A WOMAN IN TRAVAIL." (Psalm 48:6) (Author's emphasis)

"Therefore are my loins filled with pain: pangs have taken hold upon me, AS THE PANGS OF A WOMAN THAT TRAVAILETH: I was bowed down at the hearing of it; I was dismayed at the seeing of it." (Isaiah 21:3) (Author's emphasis)

"We have heard the fame thereof: our hands wax feeble: anguish hath taken hold of us, and pain, AS OF A WOMAN IN TRAVAIL." (Jeremiah 6:24) (Author's emphasis) (See also Jeremiah 4:31 and 22:23)

"The sorrows of A TRAVAILING WOMAN shall come upon him: he is an unwise son; for he should not stay long in the place of the breaking forth of children." (Hosea 13:13) (Author's emphasis)

"Now why dost thou cry out aloud? is there no king in thee? is thy counsellor perished? for pangs have taken thee AS A WOMAN IN TRAVAIL." (Micah 4:9) (Author's emphasis)

A biblical truth is established. The tribulation and anguish of birth bring forth new life. If we understand nothing else, we can begin to see that God's words about animals are not totally irrelevant to Job's tribulation.

The tribulation of the Jew's seventy year captivity in Babylon was a purifying time for the nation, in just the same way that the coming Tribulation will also have a purifying effect to restore the nation to God's favor. Jesus' pain and anguish on the cross brought forth our new life. Job has known pain like he never imagined possible, but this, too, will ultimately result in his restoration and purification.

The exception to this rule is the case of the man who is lost without Christ. He will experience unbelievable anguish, yet birth will never come, only the eternal tribulation of hell.

This is because of another basic biblical truth, namely that everything reproduces after its own kind (Genesis 1:12,24-25; John 3:6). Only life survives the pangs of birth to reproduce new life. Job's endurance of this incredible experience only serves to show the reality of his spiritual life. The lost man has no life to begin with.

We have seen that God is in control of the times and seasons, and that the birth pangs of tribulation lead to newness of life. There are also lessons to learn from the very animals that God names here.

The wild goat was classified as a clean animal according to Deuteronomy 14:5. Wild goats were connected with a place of refuge in the wilderness when David was fleeing for his life from the evil hand of Saul, who was a type of Antichrist at that moment of his life. The story of David's flight from Saul is told in the Book of 1 Samuel, but notice especially this passage.

"And it came to pass, when Saul was returned from following the Philistines, that it was told him, saying, Behold, David is in the wilderness of En-gedi. Then Saul took three thousand chosen men out of all Israel, and went to seek David and his men upon the rocks of the wild goats." (1 Samuel 24:1-2)

Wild goats were also connected to a place of refuge in the Psalms.

"The high hills are a refuge for the wild goats; and the rocks for the conies." (Psalm 104:18)

There is coming a day when the real Antichrist will pass himself off to be God in the holy place of the temple in Jerusalem (2 Thessalonians 2:3-4). This is what Daniel called the *"abomination that maketh desolate"* (Daniel 9:27; 11:31; 12:11), and that Jesus Himself referred to in Matthew 24:15.

Jesus told His Jewish disciples that when they saw this abomination of desolation, they were to immediately flee to the mountains (Matthew 24: 16). There, God will have a place of refuge prepared for them in the rocks and mountains of the wilderness, the place of the wild goats. (Isaiah 33: 15-16; Revelation 12:14) They, like Job, should pay close attention to what time it is. Neither they, nor Job, can control the times and seasons that God alone has established, but they had best keep a watchful eye upon God's clock.

The hind (a type of deer) is also an interesting animal, and has a varied history in the Bible. Naphtali is likened to a hind in the prophecy Jacob pronounces upon him shortly before his death.

"Naphtali is a hind let loose: he giveth goodly words." (Genesis 49:21)

A man's wife is also compared to a hind in the Book of Proverbs.

"Let her be as the loving hind and pleasant roe; let her breasts satisfy thee at all times; and be thou ravished always with her love." (Proverbs 5:19)

There is something special about the hind's feet. Three times in the Bible we are told that it is a good thing to have feet like the hind, to get up to high places.

David said it in Psalm 18:33: *"He maketh my feet like hinds' feet, and setteth me upon my high places."* This is repeated in 2 Samuel 22:34. Habakkuk said the same thing in Habakkuk 3:19.

That faithful remnant in the Tribulation will want to have hind's feet, as they scramble for cover in the rocky refuge that God has prepared for them. God's question, however, has to do with the reproductive cycles of wild goats and hinds. Interestingly enough, there is something very specific said about the reproduction of hinds in the Bible.

"The voice of the LORD shaketh the wilderness; the LORD shaketh the wilderness of Kadesh. The voice of the LORD maketh the hinds to calve, and discovereth the forests: and in his temple doth every one speak of his glory." (Psalm 29:8-9)

Here we are in the wilderness again. God's voice is thundering forth and the hinds are calving. From a purely devotional standpoint, God's word is what causes believers in Christ to reproduce spiritually also.

Speaking of devotional applications, notice what is said in Job 39:4. The offspring of these creatures are well fed, and therefore able to *"go forth, and return not unto them."*

This is a wonderful illustration of the goal of discipleship. We are to feed our spiritual offspring well. The object is for them to stand on their own. Instead of being continually dependent, they must be able to go forth, and reproduce themselves.

A complete understanding of God's intent in mentioning the wild goats and hinds to Job is beyond our level of comprehension. It is interesting to notice, though, the many connections and parallels as we compare Scripture with Scripture.

A time of trouble is coming which will make Job's suffering look paltry. This time is clearly marked by times and seasons established and controlled by God alone. Just like goats, God will lead His people to a rocky place of refuge in the wilderness to find safety from the attacks of Antichrist. To get there, they will need feet like those of hinds. The voice of God will thunder forth in judgment, and will also bring forth new life to those who have placed their faith in Him.

Passages like John 3 and Ephesians 2 are so clear and plain. This is a passage that stretches our understanding. There is much left for us to discover, but we must be careful not to invent fanciful doctrines rooted in speculation. We compare Scripture with Scripture, make dutiful note of similarities and context, attempt to assimilate what we can, and make every effort to see the lessons that God would have us apply to our personal lives. Beyond that, we patiently wait. Like Mary, when presented with things that went beyond her ability to fully comprehend, we must simply ponder these things in our hearts (Luke 2:19).

WILD ASSES

5 "Who hath sent out the wild ass free? or who hath loosed the bands of the wild ass?
6 Whose house I have made the wilderness, and the barren land his dwellings.
7 He scorneth the multitude of the city, neither regardeth he the crying of the driver.
8 The range of the mountains is his pasture, and he searcheth after every green thing." (Job 39:5-8)

This is not the first time the wild ass has made an appearance in our study of Job. We first met this unlikely creature as we considered the words of Job 11:12. We learned that the wild ass is a Bible picture of lost man. In Exodus 13:13 we saw how the wild ass was singled out by God as in need of redemption. There is something wrong with his birth.

There is also something wrong with man's birth. This is why man must be born again. We are not fit to be in God's presence, and must be redeemed by the blood of the Lamb.

Now, we encounter the wild ass again, as part of this remarkable series of questions that God poses to Job. Understanding the typology of the wild ass, there are some valuable lessons we can learn in these words.

The wild ass that God pictures here has been freed. His bands have been loosed. God asks if Job knows who did it.

Lost man has the same need. He is bound by sin, and needs to be set free. The bands of sin must be loosed.

When we recognize the typology, the answer becomes clear. Only God can set man free. No one else can loose the bands of sin. This need is clear when we survey the condition of the wild ass (or lost man) in these verses.

Job 39:6 reveals that the natural dwelling of the wild ass is in the wilderness, in a barren land. Lost man also lives there, in the barren wilderness of sin.

In Job 39:7 we see that the wild ass scorns the multitudes of the city, and pays no attention to anyone who would try to tame, or *"drive"* him. Is this not a perfect portrait of lost man? Lost man scorns the multitudes, not caring who gets in his way. He pays no attention to his Master. He is beyond domestication by the Master in his natural state.

The picture painted in Job 39:8 is of a wild ass who roams the high places of the mountains in search of any green thing he can find to eat. This is the pilgrimage of lost man, who roams the high places of the earth seeking anything he can find to fill the spiritual void within.

Such has been the condition of man without God through these many centuries. Imagine the sad state of man without Christ in the coming Tribulation, wandering aimlessly seeking food, yet stubbornly refusing to submit to the Master.

The only solution is to be set free. God wants Job to reflect on the state of the wild ass. Who can set the wild ass free and loose his bonds? The only one who is capable is the One who is speaking to Job.

9 "Will the unicorn be willing to serve thee, or abide by thy crib?
10 Canst thou bind the unicorn with his band in the furrow? or will he harrow the valleys after thee?
11 Wilt thou trust him, because his strength is great? or wilt thou leave thy labour to him?
12 Wilt thou believe him, that he will bring home thy seed, and gather it into thy barn?" (Job 39:9-12)

Not only does this passage stretch our understanding, it can be said that this passage is truly obscure. While the Bible isn't hard to understand when it concerns the basic issues of life and death, it IS a living and infinite book. There ARE some truly difficult passages, and we have one before us now.

Obviously, the difficulty concerns the identity of the unicorn. There are those who point to this passage to show that the Bible is not above mythology. They operate from the presupposition that the Bible is NOT the divinely inspired Word of God, and this is merely fuel for the fire.

Others are quick to assure us that this is obviously a mistranslation. Yet no one can tell us what the correct translation should be. Check out some modern English Bible versions, and you will find an entire zoo in the many "translations" they offer. The truth is that no one knows what this animal really is. One's guess is as good as the other's. Some think it is a wild bull or the great auroch, which are extinct.

A basic Bible study truth that we have followed in this study is to compare Scripture with Scripture to arrive at a better understanding of the Word of God. Unicorns make other appearances in the Bible. Let us consider the evidence before we come to any conclusions.

"God brought them out of Egypt; he hath as it were the strength of an unicorn." (Numbers 23:22)

"God brought him forth out of Egypt; he hath as it were the strength of an unicorn: he shall eat up the nations his enemies, and shall break their bones, and pierce them through with his arrows." (Numbers 24:8)

"His glory is like the firstling of his bullock, and his horns are like the horns of unicorns: with them he shall push the people together to the ends

of the earth: and they are the ten thousands of Ephraim, and they are the thousands of Manasseh." (Deuteronomy 33:17)

"Save me from the lion's mouth: for thou hast heard me from the horns of the unicorns." (Psalm 22:21)

"He maketh them also to skip like a calf; Lebanon and Sirion like a young unicorn." (Psalm 29:6)

"But my horn shalt thou exalt like the horn of an unicorn: I shall be anointed with fresh oil." (Psalm 92:10)

"And the unicorns shall come down with them, and the bullocks with the bulls; and their land shall be soaked with blood, and their dust made fat with fatness." (Isaiah 34:7)

Did you realize that there were so many unicorns in the Bible? Before abandoning the King James Bible's unicorn, consider a few things. There is nothing wrong with the translation *"unicorn."* The Hebrew word used here comes from a primitive root, giving the sense of something "risen up," as a horn that rises up on the animal. *"Unicorn"* means "single horn." That same verb root is translated as *"lifted up"* in Zechariah 14:10.

What is wrong with the translation is simply that we do not want to accept the existence of a *"unicorn,"* since the animal has become the subject of mythology. Stars have become the object of astrology. Should we reject them simply because we really don't understand them?

All the Bible says is that there is a single-horned animal. Call it what you like (your guess is as good as any), but the *"unicorn"* is merely presented as another of the animals. God speaks of it as naturally as He does any of the other identifiable animals in the passage.

Perhaps the unicorn is extinct. This is not without precedent. The *"serpent"* that spoke with Eve in the Garden bears little resemblance to the serpents that crawl in your garden today. Scientists tell us that the skeletal structure of the modern snake suggests the presence of limbs in earlier times.

Analyzing what we have read about unicorns in the biblical references before us, we can conclude that unicorns, whatever they may be, are characterized by great strength. From what God says about the unicorn, it is totally untrustworthy and cannot be tamed. Furthermore, there is the implication that the unicorn can communicate, when God asks in Job 39:12 *"Wilt thou believe him?"*

We do not have anything to compare to the unicorn in our contemporary world. When we consider the context of the Bible, however, there is a single, little horn which appears in the prophecy of Daniel. This little horn is symbolic of the Antichrist. He is *"lifted up;"* he rises up from among other *"horns,"* or governmental rulers (Daniel 7:8,20,24-25). He is characterized by great strength, is an excellent communicator and is never to be trusted!! (Daniel 8:9-12)

Everything we have seen so far about these animals seems to coincide with prophetic images of the coming Tribulation. Do you think that this unicorn could have some connection with the Antichrist?

PEACOCKS AND OSTRICHES

13 "Gavest thou the goodly wings unto the peacocks? or wings and feathers unto the ostrich?
14 Which leaveth her eggs in the earth, and warmeth them in dust,
15 And forgetteth that the foot may crush them, or that the wild beast may break them.
16 She is hardened against her young ones, as though they were not hers: her labour is in vain without fear;
17 Because God hath deprived her of wisdom, neither hath he imparted to her understanding.
18 What time she lifteth up herself on high, she scorneth the horse and his rider." (Job 39:13-18)

Again, we must confess our ignorance as we consider the words God speaks to Job. Precisely what He means by calling Job's attention to these two birds we do not know.

We do know that what God says about these two birds is correct from a naturalistic, scientific perspective. We also know that no portion of the Bible is fluff. We began with the presupposition that the Bible is the divinely-inspired, inerrant, infallible Word of God. There is nothing in it by chance, or for the sake of intellectual curiosity.

When we come to a portion of the Bible that is beyond our full understanding, there are several truths that we must bear in mind. First, we cannot violate the teaching of clear passages of Scripture in order to force some meaning on the portion that is obscure. By comparing Scripture with Scripture, by prayer, by meditation and analysis, we can do the best we can to find the truth that God has reserved for us.

Second, it could be that we are not mature enough to comprehend this passage. A third possibility is that God has not chosen to reveal the basic meaning of the passage yet. Daniel 12 is an example of a passage that God says is sealed until the time of the end.

Applying these principles to our present study, there is not much Scripture for comparison with our peacocks and ostriches. Peacocks are only mentioned in 1 Kings 10:22 and 2 Chronicles 9:21 as part of a list of goods imported by the ships of Tarshish in Solomon's reign.

The one thing that stands out about the peacock is the beauty of its feathers. This is precisely the feature that God singles out when He asks if Job was the one who gave the peacock *"the goodly wings"* (Job 39:13). The answer is no, of course. God gave the beautiful plumage to the peacock.

The only portion of the Bible that reminds me of peacocks is found in Isaiah. God is pronouncing His coming judgment upon Judah. One of the characteristics of that ungodly, apostate society was an obsession of women to dress in an extravagant fashion.

"In that day the Lord will take away the bravery of their tinkling ornaments about their feet, and their cauls, and their round tires like the moon, The chains, and the bracelets, and the mufflers, The bonnets, and the ornaments of the legs, and the headbands, and the tablets, and the earrings, The rings, and nose jewels, The changeable suits of apparel, and the mantles, and the wimples, and the crisping pins, The glasses, and the fine linen, and the hoods, and the vails. And it shall come to pass, that instead of sweet smell there shall be stink; and instead of a girdle a rent; and instead of well set hair baldness; and instead of a stomacher a girding of sackcloth; and burning instead of beauty. Thy men shall fall by the sword, and thy mighty in the war. And her gates shall lament and mourn; and she being desolate shall sit upon the ground." (Isaiah 3:18-26)

Unfortunately, this passage has a most contemporary ring to it! This is even more significant when we consider that this is a prophecy of what is to take place in *"that day."* Consistently through the prophecy of Isaiah the prophet speaks of the coming judgment of *"that day,"* as do others of the prophets. This prophecy found a partial fulfillment in the captivity of Israel, but awaits a complete fulfillment in the coming Tribulation.

Isn't it interesting that Isaiah saw a society totally given to an obsession with appearances, particularly evident in female fashion? Can it be mere coincidence that those of us who believe that we are living in the last days before the coming of the Lord Jesus Christ, also find ourselves in a similar society? Does this not fit with the many other Tribulation images we have noted in this study of Job? While the wild ass represented lost man in general in these turbulent times, can it be that the peacock speaks to us of human preoccupation with exterior beauty in those same times?

Like the peacock, the ostrich has feathers that are valued for certain uses even today, as in dusters made of ostrich feathers. God mentions this by asking Job if he gave *"feathers unto the ostrich"* (Job 39:13).

The next three verses, Job 39:14-17, isolates a distinct quality of the ostrich, namely her seeming cruelty to her young, and her fame as an irresponsible mother. God says that He has deprived her of wisdom and understanding (Job 39:17).

Although this same Hebrew word is translated three times as *"feathers,"* the only other time the ostrich is specifically named is in Lamentations 4:3, where, again, her bad standing as a mother is mentioned.

"Even the sea monsters draw out the breast, they give suck to their young ones: the daughter of my people is become cruel, like the ostriches in the wilderness." (Lamentations 4:3)

This is a correct assessment of the ostrich from a literal standpoint, as naturalists would confirm. The spiritual truth that God would illustrate is what interests us. If we are correct in comparing the peacock to a lost woman, the ostrich would illustrate another characteristic of women in the last days.

Like the ostrich leaves her eggs in the earth, not concerned whether they will be stepped on and crushed, many a modern mother willingly relinquishes the upbringing of her young for day care, often more concerned about going further in her career than what will happen to her offspring. More than one modern mother has sold her young for a fix of drugs. We live in a time when motherly love is in danger of becoming the exception rather than the rule.

Please remember that the yellow flag of caution is up regarding the interpretation of these verses. They are difficult, with precious little scriptural evidence to help us in our understanding. These thoughts, however, are the only suggestions that may help us on our way to a better grasp of God's purpose in including them in the Bible.

We do know that they are there for a definite purpose, and that purpose is not to teach us zoology. It is fascinating how the images and characteristics of the coming Tribulation keep occurring as common denominators. While we cannot speak dogmatically about these verses, the images they suggest provide material for prayerful meditation.

The only verse we have not commented on is verse 39:18, which describes the ostrich as lifting herself up against the horse and rider. This is a big bird, and has a reputation for being contrary. The Book of Revelation has something to say about horses and riders. Perhaps, again, there is some connection. This verse also serves as a transition to the next section.

HORSES AND GRASSHOPPERS

19 "Hast thou given the horse strength? hast thou clothed his neck with thunder?
20 Canst thou make him afraid as a grasshopper? the glory of his nostrils is terrible.
21 He paweth in the valley, and rejoiceth in his strength: he goeth on to meet the armed men.
22 He mocketh at fear, and is not affrighted; neither turneth he back from the sword.
23 The quiver rattleth against him, the glittering spear and the shield.
24 He swalloweth the ground with fierceness and rage: neither believeth he that it is the sound of the trumpet.
25 He saith among the trumpets, Ha, ha; and he smelleth the battle afar off, the thunder of the captains, and the shouting." (Job 39:19-25)

We just saw a mention of a horse and rider in God's words about the ostrich, saying that the ostrich scorned them. Now, God directly addresses the subject of the horse.

The horse is renowned as an animal of great strength. His strong neck is singled out here. He is fearless, rushing forth to battle.

The Book of Revelation gives prominence to horses and riders. Chapter 6 presents a series of four horses with their riders. The rider on the white horse in Revelation 6:2 is a prophetic picture of the conquering Antichrist in the early part of his reign. He is much like the white horse and rider that appear in Revelation 19, which are often confused with the conquering Christ. That great similarity is why he is called the Antichrist.

The rider in Revelation 6 has a crown and a bow. He is followed by horses and riders that respectively represent war, economic disaster, famine, death and hell.

The rider in Revelation 19 has many crowns, and has a sharp, two-edged sword coming out of His mouth, instead of a bow in His hand. He is followed by the armies of God and a thousand-year reign of peace. He is the Lord Jesus Christ.

Now, follow what God said in Job 39:19-25, as I describe what will happen when the rider on the white horse of Revelation 19 comes to earth. He will come to a valley where armed men have gathered (Job 39:21). This is the *"valley of decision"* mentioned in Joel 3:13-15, also called the valley of Megiddon (Zechariah 12:11), or Armageddon (Revelation 16:16), the *"place of slaughter."*

Just as God tells Job that the horse's neck is clothed with *"thunder"* (Job 39:19), Joel says that the Lord will *"roar,"* and that the *"heavens and the earth shall shake"* (Joel 3:16). That roaring voice of God is called "thunder" by the psalmist (Psalm 77:18; 104:7), Isaiah (Isaiah 29:6), and John (Revelation 14:20).

The rest of God's description focuses on the fearlessness of this horse that rushes forth to the battle, smelling it *"afar off"* (Job 39:25). Like the other animal descriptions we have seen in this chapter, most of what God says is still shrouded in mystery yet to be revealed. It does not take much of a stretch to see how this description, too, could legitimately be connected in some way with the events of Armageddon and the Second Coming of our Lord.

Another animal is mentioned in this passage. Specifically, it is an insect. God asks Job if he could make this horse *"afraid as a grasshopper"* (Job 39:20).

The grasshopper is classified as clean according to Leviticus 11:22. In the literature of the prophets, though, the grasshopper is seen as an instrument of God's wrath in judgment. Amos saw grasshoppers this way in Amos 7:1, executing God's judgment.

Nahum saw a similar image as he pronounced God's judgment upon wicked Nineveh. Nineveh is a type of another wicked city, Babylon, which will soon be the object of God's wrath (Revelation 17-18). The third chapter of Nahum is filled with familiar prophetic pictures, including horses and horsemen, ripe fig trees, locusts and GRASSHOPPERS that flee at the rising of the sun (Malachi 4:2).

Even Ecclesiastes has an obscure reference to grasshoppers in the context of coming judgment. Ecclesiastes 12 begins with an admonition to *"Remember now thy Creator in the days of thy youth."* This is defined as a time before the evil days come, when the sun, moon and stars still give their light. There is coming a day when they will not give their light (Amos 5:18,20). In the picture of coming judgment painted in Ecclesiastes 12, the grasshopper jumps into the picture.

"Remember now thy Creator in the days of thy youth, while the evil days come not, nor the years draw nigh, when thou shalt say, I have no pleasure in them; While the sun, or the light, or the moon, or the stars, be not darkened, nor the clouds return after the rain: In the day when the keepers of the house shall tremble, and the strong men shall bow themselves, and the grinders cease because they are few, and those that look out of the windows be darkened, And the doors shall be shut in the streets, when the sound of the grinding is low, and he shall rise up at the voice of the bird, and all the daughters of musick shall be brought low; Also when they shall be afraid of that which is high, and fears shall be in the way, and the

almond tree shall flourish, and the grasshopper shall be a burden, and desire shall fail: because man goeth to his long home, and the mourners go about the streets: Or ever the silver cord be loosed, or the golden bowl be broken, or the pitcher be broken at the fountain, or the wheel broken at the cistern. Then shall the dust return to the earth as it was: and the spirit shall return unto God who gave it." (Ecclesiastes 12:1-7)

Obviously, there is more we don't understand than what we do understand. We are still observing, though, that the animals mentioned by God, as He ends Job's tribulation, are among the same animals that appear in the prophetic images concerning that time when our Lord returns to earth to end THE Tribulation. While admitting our ignorance at every turn, the circumstantial evidence connecting these animals to prophecy of the coming Tribulation is too consistent to be dismissed out of hand.

HAWKS AND EAGLES

26 "Doth the hawk fly by thy wisdom, and stretch her wings toward the south?
27 Doth the eagle mount up at thy command, and make her nest on high?
28 She dwelleth and abideth on the rock, upon the crag of the rock, and the strong place.
29 From thence she seeketh the prey, and her eyes behold afar off.
30 Her young ones also suck up blood: and where the slain are, there is she." (Job 39:26-30)

By His questions in Job 39:26, God attributes the wisdom of the hawk's flight and southward migration to Himself. The spectacular flight of the eagle and its tendency to make nests in the high places are also God's doings, not Job's or ours.

We learn in Leviticus 11 that both the hawk and the eagle are considered unclean, since they, along with the other birds on the unclean list, are ravenous birds of prey. As such, they are often considered as a group to picture unclean spirits, as in Isaiah 34, where the prophet takes us to the coming doom of the nations at Armageddon. Many unclean birds are seen there, feeding upon the carcasses of the fallen, and picturing in type, the unclean spirits of hell.

The *"birds of the air"* is an expression used several times in Scripture to refer to demonic forces. The Lord used the phrase that way in Matthew

13:32 when He spoke of the spectacular, unnatural growth of Christendom, and the fact that demonic forces would build their nests in its branches.

In this regard, we can understand what is happening in Revelation 19, when the Lord will gather all the armies of the world at Armageddon for their doom. The Rider on the white horse will appear with all the heavenly host, and this sharp sword fells the enemies of the Lord.

"And I saw an angel standing in the sun; and he cried with a loud voice, saying to all the fowls that fly in the midst of heaven, Come and gather yourselves together unto the supper of the great God; That ye may eat the flesh of kings, and the flesh of captains, and the flesh of mighty men, and the flesh of horses, and of them that sit on them, and the flesh of all men, both free and bond, both small and great." (Revelation 19:17-18)

Jesus spoke of the same time in His prophetic discourse on the Mount of Olives. Notice the specific reference to eagles.

"For wheresoever the carcase is, there will the eagles be gathered together." (Matthew 24:28)

The eagle presents a strange case, in that while it is associated with the unclean birds, it can also have a very positive application. God compares Himself to the eagle.

"Ye have seen what I did unto the Egyptians, and how I bare you on eagles' wings, and brought you unto myself." (Exodus 19:4)

"He found him in a desert land, and in the waste howling wilderness; he led him about, he instructed him, he kept him as the apple of his eye. As an eagle stirreth up her nest, fluttereth over her young, spreadeth abroad her wings, taketh them, beareth them on her wings: So the LORD alone did lead him, and there was no strange god with him. He made him ride on the high places of the earth, that he might eat the increase of the fields; and he made him to suck honey out of the rock, and oil out of the flinty rock." (Deuteronomy 32:10-13)

In this Deuteronomy passage, we see some elements God mentions in connection with eagles in His comments to Job. God, comparing Himself to an eagle, speaks of taking His people to the *"high places of the earth."* The rock is mentioned as a place of refuge. Only here in Deuteronomy, the eagle's young suck honey and oil out of the rock, while in Job, God speaks of them sucking the blood of the slain.

The fact that one of the four faces of the cherubim is that of an eagle, also carries good connotations (Ezekiel 1:10; Revelation 4:7). Another positive reference to the eagle is found in Revelation 12, as God relates how He will preserve the faithful remnant of Israel from the attacks of the Devil during the Tribulation.

"And to the woman were given two wings of a great eagle, that she

might fly into the wilderness, into her place, where she is nourished for a time, and times, and half a time, from the face of the serpent." (Revelation 12:14)

In all this, we are again face to face with a Tribulation application of the creatures God lists in Job 39. In Revelation 12:14, we remember what we have spoken of several times: God will provide a place of refuge in the rocky wilderness of Edom for Israel during the reign of terror of Antichrist. "*Rocks*", "*high places*", "*nesting places*", the eagle "*mounting up*" at God's command, "*seeking the prey*", "*sucking the blood of the slain*"—all God says about eagles has the possibility of finding a final fulfillment in the coming Tribulation, as does everything God has said about all the creatures in this chapter.

We are confronted with the limits of our understanding. Like Job we must bow down before the unanswerable questions of the Almighty. The more we hear from the mouth of God, the more we recognize our ignorance.

We can see the correctness of what God has spoken. Also, we can see how all this can very well have a prophetic fulfillment in the Tribulation. We leave this passage with a notable absence of dogmatism.

One temptation of a Bible passage such as this is to frustrated that we cannot get a complete grasp of what God has spoken. Another is simply to ignore it. The proper course is to prayerfully consider what is said, carefully compare it to other similar passages, and humbly ponder these things in our hearts until God would reveal to us the full extent of the meaning.

Surely, God, the almighty God of heaven, the sovereign King, who spoke the universe into existence, would not answer a man who has experienced all Job has with a study of animals, unless there was something profound to be discovered in His words. There is more here than naturalistic curiosities. Perhaps those Bible students who see only irrelevant animals would perceive much more if subjected to a dose of Job's tribulation!

29

NOTHING LEFT TO SAY

Behold now behemoth,

which I made with thee; he eateth grass

as an ox.

Lo now, his strength is in his loins,

and his force is in the navel of his belly.

Job 40:15-16

I ENJOY TALKING WITH PEOPLE ABOUT THE BIBLE. NOTHING motivates me more.

I avoid pastors' conferences and fellowships whenever possible, because it is a colossal bore to stand around comparing notes on attendance figures, budget amounts, and everyone's favorite horror story about problem people in ministry. Unfortunately, it is often hard to find pastors who just want to sit around talking about the Bible.

Give me someone who wants to learn the Bible, and I'll sit up all night trying to answer their questions, and throw in a few questions of my own. I believe every church ought to have a time when people can come together and try to find answers for their questions about the Word of God.

Invariably, though, someone will ask one of those unanswerable questions. I probably can offer some educated guesses, or toss out a couple of suggestions. Ultimately, I must confess my ignorance.

Often, the questioner will say, "When I see the Lord, that's the first question I'm going to ask Him." Others say, "I have this list of questions I'm going to ask God when I get to heaven."

I don't think anyone will ask God questions, at least not right away. The reason is what we find in this chapter.

Job had his own list of questions. These were not mere theological questions. Job didn't have a shred of interest in how many angels fit on the head of a pin. He really was not concerned to discover whether God is a Calvinist or arminianist.

Job's questions were authentic, legitimate questions. He burned inside to know the answers. He has longed for and pleaded for his day in court. He has cried for a mediator. He has rehearsed what he would say; he had his list ready.

The day has come. The list is gone.

JOB'S DAY IN COURT

1 "Moreover the LORD answered Job, and said,
2 Shall he that contendeth with the Almighty instruct him? he that reproveth God, let him answer it." (Job 40:1-2)

How interesting! The Lord ANSWERED Job, although Job has not yet said a word to God. Furthermore, God's ANSWER is a QUESTION. Most everything God has said so far has been a question.

Yet, God is clearly answering Job's questions. This is one of the "ways of God" that we have pointed out before. God knows the questions before we ask them. He often answers them with a question, as we learned studying Job 38.

These first two verses should not be too hard to understand. God is saying that no one is going to convince Him of anything. In modern speech we might put it this way. "Do you really think that you are going to argue with Me until you bring Me around to your point of view? Whoever has a gripe with Me, let him step right up and give Me his best shot!"

Job's response is predictable to anyone who has read the Bible with even a shred of spiritual sensitivity. He comes to the only right conclusion for an intelligent man.

3 "Then Job answered the LORD, and said,
4 Behold, I am vile; what shall I answer thee? I will lay mine hand upon my mouth.
5 Once have I spoken; but I will not answer: yea, twice; but I will proceed no further." (Job 40:3-5)

Here is the evidence of a just man, a truly just man. It is the response that will echo out through eternity countless times in the day when believers stand before the Lord, *"Behold, I am vile."*

Isaiah lived hundreds of years after Job, yet this truth had not changed. He was ushered into the presence of God to receive God's call, and here was his response.

"Then said I, Woe is me! for I am undone; because I am a man of unclean lips, and I dwell in the midst of a people of unclean lips: for mine eyes have seen the King, the LORD of hosts." (Isaiah 6:5)

The difference between the man who has a sensitive heart toward God and the hypocrite is conspicuous. The Lord Jesus Christ gave us an idea of a hypocrite's typical response in the day of reckoning.

"Not every one that saith unto me, Lord, Lord, shall enter into the kingdom of heaven; but he that doeth the will of my Father which is in heaven. Many will say to me in that day, Lord, Lord, have we not prophesied in thy name? and in thy name have cast out devils? and in thy name done many wonderful works? And then will I profess unto them, I never knew you: depart from me, ye that work iniquity." (Matthew 7:21-23)

Job finally has his day in court, but has nothing left to say. All the arguments, all the many questions have no more relevance.

At first it was hard to see where God was going with His questions on creationism. Now, His wisdom is apparent.

Job's focus was squarely on his personal problems. God redirected his focus to see the big picture. Suddenly, Job's problems are not as big as he thought. They don't really make any difference as far as God's perspective is concerned.

Stop. What are the problems you are wrestling with in your own life? Could it be that your real need is to refocus your vision? Have you recently taken the time to meditate upon God's overall plan?

This is why it is always good for the believer to be reading Scripture from beginning to end, from Genesis to Revelation, no less than once a year. We often become too focused even in our Bible study. We become so caught up in the wonders of Ephesians, Philippians, or even Job, that we lose our sense of perspective.

Every believer should have a daily time to scrutinize the riches of the Word of God. There should be a structured approach in every life to plumb the depths of God's Word, breaking down the meaning of specific verses, words and events. Yet there must also be a time to put the mind on cruise control, and simply enjoy a ride through the entire Bible, if only three or four chapters a day. There is no better way to maintain a proper perspective of how the whole Bible fits together, and see that our own personal problems are not the center of the universe.

SPEECHLESS BEFORE THE BENCH

Like a condemned prisoner before the judge's bench with no more appeals, Job knows that there is nothing to say, no further recourse. God has given him a chance to speak his mind, but Job wisely elected to shut his mouth. The Judge continues.

6 "Then answered the LORD unto Job out of the whirlwind, and said,

7 Gird up thy loins now like a man: I will demand of thee, and declare thou unto me." (Job 40:6-7)

We are again reminded that God is speaking to Job *"out of the whirlwind,"* whatever that may be. We may not understand all about the physical scene that Job is viewing, but there is no doubt about God's words.

God is telling Job to get ready, to gird up his loins. This girding up the loins is familiar to us now. God is going to make some demands of Job, and Job should be ready to respond.

Job has had precious little to say up to this point. There is no reason to believe that he will have much more to say later.

God follows with a series of four questions. They are so powerful that an answer would be meaningless. The only possible way that any man could answer these questions would be with a simple "no." Even that, however, would be almost sacrilegious, considering the circumstances.

8 "Wilt thou also disannul my judgment? wilt thou condemn me, that thou mayest be righteous?

9 Hast thou an arm like God? or canst thou thunder with a voice like him?" (Job 40:8-9)

God's *"judgment"* is what He has pronounced, what He has said. The first question is if Job can *"disannul"* that judgment? The wording is legal, but the meaning is obvious. There is no way Job, or any man, could ever cancel God's Word. One may not believe God's Word, but there is nothing he can do to make it any less true.

"Wilt thou condemn me, that thou mayest be righteous?" The second question in Job 40:8 encapsulates the problem of the self-righteous. By making themselves to be righteous, they are really saying that God is not righteous. When God has spoken a thing, and declared every man guilty before Him, for a man to presume to become righteous by his works is to deny what God has already spoken.

This question at the end of Job 40:8 really follows from the question about disannulling God's judgment that starts verse 8. Most self-righteous individuals never see this side of the equation, because they are too self-centered in their entire outlook. They would be mortified if someone told them their self-righteousness was really condemning God.

"Hast thou an arm like God?" Of course not! Again, the question that starts Job 40:9 follows from those before. Is there anyone who could consider himself more powerful that God?

Let's examine the evidence to see what God's arm has accomplished.

"Wherefore say unto the children of Israel, I am the LORD, and I will bring you out from under the burdens of the Egyptians, and I will rid you out of their bondage, and I will redeem you with a stretched out arm, and with great judgments." (Exodus 6:6)

"Or hath God assayed to go and take him a nation from the midst of another nation, by temptations, by signs, and by wonders, and by war, and by a mighty hand, and by a stretched out arm, and by great terrors, according to all that the LORD your God did for you in Egypt before your eyes?" (Deuteronomy 4:34)

"The great temptations which thine eyes saw, and the signs, and the wonders, and the mighty hand, and the stretched out arm, whereby the LORD thy God brought thee out: so shall the LORD thy God do unto all the people of whom thou art afraid." (Deuteronomy 7:19)

"The LORD hath made bare his holy arm in the eyes of all the nations; and all the ends of the earth shall see the salvation of our God." (Isaiah 52:10)

"I have made the earth, the man and the beast that are upon the ground, by my great power and by my outstretched arm, and have given it unto whom it seemed meet unto me." (Jeremiah 27:5)

These are some of Scripture's testimonies about the power of God's arm. Anyone want to arm wrestle with God?

"Canst thou thunder with a voice like him?" (Job 40:9b) You may have a big mouth, but it is a certainty that you cannot *"thunder"* forth with a voice like God's! Listen to His voice.

"God thundereth marvellously with his voice; great things doeth he, which we cannot comprehend." (Job 37:5)

"Who laid the foundations of the earth, that it should not be removed for ever. Thou coveredst it with the deep as with a garment: the waters stood above the mountains. At thy rebuke they fled; at the voice of thy thunder they hasted away." (Psalm 104:5-7)

10 "Deck thyself now with majesty and excellency; and array thyself with glory and beauty.

11 Cast abroad the rage of thy wrath: and behold every one that is proud, and abase him.

12 "Look on every one that is proud, and bring him low; and tread down the wicked in their place.
13 Hide them in the dust together; and bind their faces in secret.
14 Then will I also confess unto thee that thine own right hand can save thee." (Job 40:10-14)

What a thing for God to say to man sitting on an ash heap, scraping his oozing wounds with a broken piece of pottery! This is the height of irony.

Obviously Job cannot deck himself with majesty, excellency, glory and beauty. Furthermore, Job is certainly not in the position to take charge of the judgment of the proud and wicked.

All this leads to God's conclusion in Job 40:14. Only if he could do those other things, would Job be able to save himself. God's point in this entire section is to reveal the futileness of man's self-righteousness.

We have seen Job walk the line between faith in God and self-righteousness. We have been careful not to accuse Job of self-righteousness, as did his counselors.

God is not even accusing Job of being self-righteous. He is just making sure that Job is properly focused. He wants Job to understand that the only alternative to a proper focus on God's righteousness is self-righteousness, and that is a dead-end street.

The lesson is unforgettable. Job, sitting in ashes and covered with sores, his life in ruin, is helpless. Man at his very best is no more than this in the sight of God, whether he is decked in regal robes and firmly in charge of his life, or sitting in the midst of ruin. Man in all his glory is no more righteous than Job on the ash heap. It is just as absurd for a man to imagine decking himself in righteousness, as it would be for Job to try to deck himself in majesty and glory in his present condition.

How far removed are God's ways from our ways. What would we say today to a man who lost all his children in a day, who lost all his earthly possessions, and who then was stricken with a horrible, publicly-humiliating illness? Would we be concerned that his self-image suffer? Would we hold his hand and try to empathize? Would we order a psychological evaluation to see if Job were choleric, phlegmatic, melancholy or sanguine? Would we try to decide if the right or the left side of Job's brain had been more affected? Perhaps we could show Job how to blame everything on some long-forgotten childhood trauma.

Enter God. Has God spent much time pumping up Job's self-image? How many sweet, empathetic words of encouragement have come out of God's mouth?

I am NOT recommending that anyone attempt such a counseling

methodology. This works for God, but won't for you. Unless, of course, you are God, which you are not.

What I AM recommending is that we reevaluate our focus and priorities. There is nothing wrong with empathetic words of encouragement from a sincere heart. Yet, we must not become so caught up in our counseling technique that we forget to point our patient to the big picture. Perhaps the best we could do for one whose suffering is unbearable is to point them to the only One who can speak to their need, and show them their place in His total plan.

THE MYSTERY OF BEHEMOTH

In Job 40:7 God told Job to gird up his loins. The solemn tone of the words shows God had something very important to say. God said that He would demand an answer from Job. The four unanswerable questions we have seen earlier and the ironic challenge to clean himself up and take charge of judging the wicked, seem only to set the stage for the declarative section that now follows.

This is a most enigmatic passage. The best approach will be to reproduce the section in its entirety, so that you can have an idea of the context and subject matter, then take it apart verse by verse.

ONE BEAST THAT IS SEVERAL

15 "Behold now behemoth, which I made with thee; he eateth grass as an ox.

16 Lo now, his strength is in his loins, and his force is in the navel of his belly.

17 He moveth his tail like a cedar: the sinews of his stones are wrapped together.

18 His bones are as strong pieces of brass; his bones are like bars of iron.

19 He is the chief of the ways of God: he that made him can make his sword to approach unto him.

20 Surely the mountains bring him forth food, where all the beasts of the field play.

21 He lieth under the shady trees, in the covert of the reed, and fens.

22 The shady trees cover him with their shadow; the willows of the brook compass him about.

23 Behold, he drinketh up a river, and hasteth not: he trusteth that he can draw up Jordan into his mouth.

24 He taketh it with his eyes: his nose pierceth through snares." (Job 40:15-24)

Who in the world, or what in the world is "*behemoth?*" The word itself is not a translation, but a transliteration. That is to say that the translators elected to simply give the Hebrew word an equivalent spelling in English so we could read it, but did not translate it. "*Behemoth*" is a Hebrew word that most scholars believe to be of Egyptian derivation.

Those who do dare to translate the word are really guessing at best. Survey a handful of commentaries or modern translations, and you will see a wild range of such guesses.

Some think that behemoth is an elephant or hippopotamus. Others see a water ox. A thoughtful reading of the context shows that these guesses are not satisfactory.

Still others think this must be an extinct dinosaur, or perhaps a mythological beast. Now, honestly, do you really think that the God who has just laid down such an incredible and scientific account of creation, would announce that He had something really important to say, and then talk about a mythological creature? Or an extinct dinosaur? Really?

What do we know for sure about this word? "*Behemoth*" is the feminine plural form of the word that is commonly translated as "cattle," or "beast." ("Beast" in the old English sense for "animal.") The confusion is that this plural noun is followed by singular pronouns and verbs.

Think! Can you remember a place in the Bible where a single animal is really "animals?" Let us jog our memories in the Book of Revelation.

"*And I stood upon the sand of the sea, and saw a beast rise up out of the sea, having seven heads and ten horns, and upon his horns ten crowns, and upon his heads the name of blasphemy. And the beast which I saw was like unto a leopard, and his feet were as the feet of a bear, and his mouth as the mouth of a lion: and the dragon gave him his power, and his seat, and great authority.*" (Revelation 13:1-2)

Here is a single "*beast*" which is really a combination of "beasts." We see the leopard, the bear and the lion, yet the whole is much more than the parts.

Daniel had a vision of the coming gentile powers. The first three he saw were represented by the lion, bear and leopard respectively. The fourth beast was unlike anything he had ever imagined, and most commentators equate it with the strange beast John saw in Revelation 13. Here is the interpretation of Daniel's vision.

"I came near unto one of them that stood by, and asked him the truth of all this. So he told me, and made me know the interpretation of the things. These great beasts, which are four, are four kings, which shall arise out of the earth. But the saints of the most High shall take the kingdom, and possess the kingdom for ever, even for ever and ever. Then I would know the truth of the fourth beast, which was diverse from all the others, exceeding dreadful, whose teeth were of iron, and his nails of brass; which devoured, brake in pieces, and stamped the residue with his feet; And of the ten horns that were in his head, and of the other which came up, and before whom three fell; even of that horn that had eyes, and a mouth that spake very great things, whose look was more stout than his fellows. I beheld, and the same horn made war with the saints, and prevailed against them; Until the Ancient of days came, and judgment was given to the saints of the most High; and the time came that the saints possessed the kingdom. Thus he said, The fourth beast shall be the fourth kingdom upon earth, which shall be diverse from all kingdoms, and shall devour the whole earth, and shall tread it down, and break it in pieces. And the ten horns out of this kingdom are ten kings that shall arise: and another shall rise after them; and he shall be diverse from the first, and he shall subdue three kings. And he shall speak great words against the most High, and shall wear out the saints of the most High, and think to change times and laws: and they shall be given into his hand until a time and times and the dividing of time. But the judgment shall sit, and they shall take away his dominion, to consume and to destroy it unto the end. And the kingdom and dominion, and the greatness of the kingdom under the whole heaven, shall be given to the people of the saints of the most High, whose kingdom is an everlasting kingdom, and all dominions shall serve and obey him." (Daniel 7:16-27)

The prophetic Tribulation images in Job have been consistent. Then why would we think that the climax of the book would showcase an extinct dinosaur or mythological beast?

God's manner of speech and the space dedicated to this beast point to a matter of great importance. Who—except Satan himself—would want us to think that all we had here was an elephant or water ox?

Daniel's prophecy shows us that God uses animals to represent gentile world powers. The beast John describes in Revelation is obviously not a literal animal, but the representation of the power of Antichrist. Wouldn't it be strange to think that the Book of Job, which has so illustrated the coming Tribulation, would close without including one of the main characters of that time? Why should we think that what we have here in Job 40 is a mythological monster, when we have biblical precedence for a prophetically symbolic beast?

Unless we understand that *"behemoth"* is the same beast seen by Daniel and John, God's great climax degenerates into nothing more than devotional drivel about some unidentifiable animal. Otherwise, this great book that steadily swells to this climatic moment when God finally speaks, becomes nothing more than an interesting story.

When we see that this is the same beast that Daniel and John saw, we understand that God really IS, in a sense, answering the question of Job's suffering by pointing him to the source. The same spiritual power that engineered Job's pain, will mastermind even more intense suffering on a worldwide level in the coming Tribulation.

Now that we have an idea of the identity of this behemoth, we can review the individual verses of this passage. Like the Bereans of the Book of Acts, check for yourself to see if the identity matches the description of this beast given by God.

ONE MYSTERIOUS AND MONSTROUS BEAST

15 "Behold now behemoth, which I made with thee; he eateth grass as an ox." (Job 40:15)

God directs Job's attention to this strange beast. Job does not interrupt to ask God what He is talking about. It seems that Job understands. If this IS an extinct beast, known to Job but not to us, there is also biblical precedent for using such a beast as a vehicle for Satan's work, such as happened with the serpent in the Garden.

As God asks Job to *"behold,"* or consider this beast, He mentions that the behemoth was made with Job. This statement seems most curious at first glance, because most would likely see this to mean that Job and behemoth were "hatched out of the same egg," so to speak.

That behemoth was made with Job does not necessarily refer to the chronological event, but more probably to mean simply that they were both *"made."* Just as Job is the result of God's creation, so is behemoth.

This is a most important detail, since it separates the Book of Job from the "dualism" of the ancient Greeks and other peoples. Dualism sees the forces of good and evil as having been eternally coexistent. History is the account of the everlasting duel between the two, the god of good and the god of evil.

The problem of dualism for the Bible-believer is that God is reduced to the level of the Devil. This is NOT the teaching of the Bible. God is above and separate from His creation.

Nor is the struggle between good and evil an eternal one. There was a definite point in space and time when sin entered God's creation by the act of Lucifer's free will. There will also be a definite end to sin, as God's plan for His kingdom comes to final fruition.

The second part of Job 40:15 connects behemoth to oxen through the analogy used, that *"he eateth grass as an ox."* If we understand behemoth to be a shadow of the beast yet to come, the gentile world dominion of Antichrist, this connection is not without biblical precedent.

In Genesis 3, the serpent was classified with *"cattle."* The word God uses is the same from which behemoth is derived.

"And the LORD God said unto the serpent, Because thou hast done this, thou art cursed ABOVE ALL CATTLE, and above every beast of the field; upon thy belly shalt thou go, and dust shalt thou eat all the days of thy life." (Genesis 3:14) (Author's emphasis)

In Ezekiel 28:14, the Devil is called the *"anointed cherub."* In the same book, Ezekiel 1:7, cherubs are said to have split hoofs like those of a calf. In Revelation 4 there are four beasts, supposedly cherubs, before the throne of God. One of them is likened to a calf.

"And before the throne there was a sea of glass like unto crystal: and in the midst of the throne, and round about the throne, were four beasts full of eyes before and behind. And the first beast was like a lion, and the second beast like a calf, and the third beast had a face as a man, and the fourth beast was like a flying eagle." (Revelation 4:6-7)

The reason that most believe that these four beasts are cherubs, is because the cherubs described in Ezekiel 1 and 10 are said to have four faces (manifestations? appearances?) that correspond to these same figures. The only difference is that the calf figure of Revelation 4:7 is called the *"face of a cherub"* in Ezekiel 10:14. What calls our attention is the correspondence between cherubs and cattle, and the connection we have seen here in Job 40:15.

Another singular connection is made in Daniel's prophecy. Nebuchadnezzar is a clear foreshadowing of the Antichrist in Daniel. God condemns Nebuchadnezzar to suffer seven years of an affliction called lycanthropy or boanthropy, where a person becomes like an animal. For seven years Nebuchadnezzar lived a beast-like existence, as a type of the beast to come. Notice, though, the similarity to what we have seen in Job 40:15.

"The same hour was the thing fulfilled upon Nebuchadnezzar: and he was driven from men, AND DID EAT GRASS AS OXEN, and his body was wet with the dew of heaven, till his hairs were grown like eagles' feathers, and his nails like birds' claws." (Daniel 4:33) (Author's emphasis)

16 "Lo now, his strength is in his loins, and his force is in the navel of his belly." (Job 40:16)

Both bodily locations are identified with power. Strong loins are characteristic of any "beast." Man's strength is there also. God smote Jacob there, in the strongest part of his body, to make him dependent on the power of the Almighty (Genesis 32:25).

Anyone who has studied the martial arts, or is familiar with oriental culture, understands that the "life force" of man is in the area of his navel. Western man tries to pump up his chest and biceps to give the appearance of strength. The oriental man looks to the force within him, *"in the navel,"* as his source of inner strength.

17 "He moveth his tail like a cedar: the sinews of his stones are wrapped together." (Job 40:17)

Again, the picture painted is of great strength and power. A tail with the smashing force of a cedar log swung in the hand of a giant. His masculine organ is tightly held by the force of his muscular structure.

18 "His bones are as strong pieces of brass; his bones are like bars of iron." (Job 40:18)

Brass and iron are mentioned in the same breath 36 times in Scripture. Often they appear in the context of man's rebellion and God's judgment.

"And I will break the pride of your power; and I will make your heaven as IRON, and your earth as BRASS." (Leviticus 26:19) (Author's emphasis)

"And thy heaven that is over thy head shall be BRASS, and the earth that is under thee shall be IRON." (Deuteronomy 28:23) (Author's emphasis)

"Because I knew that thou art obstinate, and thy neck is an IRON sinew, and thy brow BRASS." (Isaiah 48:4) (Author's emphasis)

"Then I would know the truth of the fourth beast, which was diverse from all the others, exceeding dreadful, whose teeth were of IRON, and his nails of BRASS; which devoured, brake in pieces, and stamped the residue with his feet." (Daniel 7:19) (Author's emphasis)

Yet where does this beast get such incredible strength and power? That is precisely the point of the next verse, Job 40:19.

ONE WAY TO APPROACH THIS BEAST

19 "He is the chief of the ways of God: he that made him can make his sword to approach unto him." (Job 40:19)

This behemoth is the *"chief of the ways of God."* Can this really be an elephant, water ox, hippopotamus, or mythological creature? Has the animal that is the *"chief of the ways of God"* become extinct?

Only if we see that this is Daniel and John's beast, can we make sense of this statement. There is only one of God's created creatures that is recipient of such exalted language—none other than the Devil himself. Ezekiel saw him as the power behind the king of Tarsus. We have examined this passage before to see how Ezekiel's prophecy obviously transcends the human kind.

"Son of man, take up a lamentation upon the king of Tyrus, and say unto him, Thus saith the Lord GOD; THOU SEALEST UP THE SUM, FULL OF WISDOM, AND PERFECT IN BEAUTY. Thou has been in Eden the garden of God; every precious stone was thy covering, the sardius, topaz, and the diamond, the beryl, the onyx, and the jasper, the sapphire, the emerald, and the carbuncle, and gold: the workmanship of thy tabrets and of thy pipes was prepared in thee in the day that thou wast created. Thou art the anointed cherub that covereth; and I have set thee so: thou wast upon the holy mountain of God; thou hast walked up and down in the midst of the stones of fire. THOU WAST PERFECT IN THY WAYS FROM THE DAY THAT THOU WAST CREATED, till iniquity was found in thee." (Ezekiel 28:12-15) (Author's emphasis)

Behemoth is a symbol of the most powerful beast this world has ever seen, a beast that is soon to come. The source of great power is rooted in the ruler of hell.

This beast is so powerful, that the only way to approach him is through the sword of the God who made him, as stated in the final phrase of Job 40:19. We again see the importance of God specifying that this is a created, *"made,"* beast. The imagery of the sword is consistent through Scripture.

Not even Michael the archangel would stand up to him verbally, as we see in Jude. *"Yet Michael the archangel, when contending with the Devil he disputed about the body of Moses, durst not bring against him a railing accusation, but said, The Lord rebuke thee."* (Jude 9)

No mere man can take on this beast in combat. We are to stand in God's strength alone. He is the only one able to approach him, and He does so with His mighty sword.

20 "Surely the mountains bring him forth food, where all the beasts of the field play." (Job 40:20)

God tells us here where the beast receives his nourishment. He gets it from the mountains. Are we to accept this literally or symbolically? Mountains in Scripture often appear as emblematic of authoritative power.

Is God talking about the gentile world powers nourishing this beast, just as the beast of Revelation 17 sits upon seven mountains? (Revelation 17:9) If this is true, it is certainly true that the *"beasts of the field,"* prey upon the nations of the world, in the sense of Satan's hordes using them to work out their mischief.

ONE DANGEROUS AND DECEITFUL BEAST

21 "He lieth under the shady trees, in the covert of the reed, and fens.

22 The shady trees cover him with their shadow; the willows of the brook compass him about." (Job 40:21-22)

Trees are another common symbol in the Bible. We have already seen how they represent men, either individually or collectively as nations. This beast slyly hides behind "trees" by using men and nations to do his bidding. He hides in their shadow instead of appearing in an outward manifestation.

His demons, the *"birds of the air,"* come and make their nests in the branches of these trees. This is what Jesus foresaw in Matthew 13:31-32.

"Another parable put he forth unto them, saying, The kingdom of heaven is like to a grain of mustard seed, which a man took, and sowed in his field: Which indeed is the least of all seeds: but when it is grown, it is the greatest among herbs, and becometh a tree, so that the birds of the air come and lodge in the branches thereof." (Matthew 13:31-32)

23 "Behold, he drinketh up a river, and hasteth not: he trusteth that he can draw up Jordan into his mouth.

24 He taketh it with his eyes: his nose pierceth through snares." (Job 40:23-24)

Another very enigmatic statement is better understood if we see behemoth as the beast of Daniel and Revelation. In Revelation 12 we see the Devil pursuing the remnant of Israel. Part of his attack is with a *"flood."*

"And the serpent cast out of his mouth water as a flood after the woman, that he might cause her to be carried away of the flood." (Revelation 12:15)

The connection becomes even stronger when we compare what Daniel saw. A flood appears in his prophecy also.

"And after threescore and two weeks shall Messiah be cut off, but not for himself: and the people of the prince that shall come shall destroy the city and the sanctuary; and the end thereof shall be with a flood, and unto the end of the war desolations are determined." (Daniel 9:26)

Just how this will be, and exactly what this will be, only God knows. Again we are confronted with the truth that the more we see about the future in the Bible, the more we understand how little we know.

This side of eternity we will never know the full details about behemoth. What we have tried to establish is simply that this passage makes little sense in the context, unless we see behemoth as the beast that John and Daniel saw. Even then, there is so much we still cannot comprehend.

The most important truth to take away from this chapter is to come to grips with the source of evil in this world. There is a *"god of this world"* (2 Corinthians 4:4).

I believe that God was revealing to Job the source of his problems. He still has not answered the "why," nor will He.

The application is simple. Don't blame God for everything. God is sovereign; this is true. Yet the sovereign God has elected to allow sin to run its course for a season. There is an evil personality who seeks to devour (1 Peter 5:8).

Realize that there is a spiritual war raging. You may often be a victim. Don't worry so much about the "why." The best we can do is recognize where evil originates, and turn our eyes upward to our Lord Jesus Christ. Only His sword is able to approach this enemy.

"Finally, my brethren, be strong in the Lord, and in the power of his might. Put on the whole armour of God, that ye may be able to stand against the wiles of the devil. For we wrestle not against flesh and blood, but against principalities, against powers, against the rulers of the darkness of this world, against spiritual wickedness in high places. Wherefore take unto you the whole armour of God, that ye may be able to withstand in the evil day, and having done all, to stand." (Ephesians 6:10-13)

30

THE LEGACY OF LEVIATHAN

Upon earth there is not his like,

who is made without fear.

He beholdeth all high things:

he is a king over all the children of pride.

Job 41:33-34

LANGUAGES ARE BOTH FASCINATING AND FRUSTRATING. SINCE the tower of Babel, men have struggled to understand them.

My wife and I raised two daughters in Latin America. Our family is bilingual. Sometimes the decision of which language to use is a matter of convenience. There are words and phrases that are easier to say in one language than the other. Some words simply do not translate.

It is not uncommon for us to speak to each other in one language, slipping in an occasional word or phrase in the other language. At such times we don't translate, since we easily roll back and forth from one language to the other. There are things, which, if translated, would lose their zip, their punch, or even their full meaning.

Our parents taught us that some things are better left unsaid. As far as the Bible is concerned, some things are better left untranslated.

We saw that this was true in the previous chapter, Job 40, when we met behemoth the beast. Now, we find the fourteenth of the creatures God parades before Job for his careful consideration. Again, the word is better left untranslated—*"leviathan."*

THE MYSTERY REVEALED

"Leviathan" comes from the Hebrew root that means "joined together," or "united." *"Leviathan"* is a composite of this root, and the root meaning "serpent." Leviathan is the "united serpent." Though not the same word, Job 41:15 tells us that his scales are tightly *"shut up,"* or joined.

There are as many guesses as to the identity of leviathan as there are with behemoth. Some say it is a crocodile, others a whale, sea monster or mythological beast. A reading of the chapter before us along with comparing the Scripture here with other Scripture makes it clear that such guesses fall far short of resolving the real issues. The student of Scripture should reject any such guesses for the same reasons given in the study of behemoth. Some things are better left untranslated.

We have an advantage in dealing with leviathan that we did not have in our study of behemoth. We could peg behemoth to the beasts that Daniel and John saw, but we did so purely by comparing Scripture with Scripture. In this case, we have several direct Bible references to leviathan in the same transliterated form. A study of these verses will make it possible to identify this beast also.

"Thou brakest the heads of leviathan in pieces, and gavest him to be meat to the people inhabiting the wilderness." (Psalm 74:14)

This beast has multiple heads. This beast also has some connection with the food that God gave to the children of Israel in the wilderness.

"In that day the LORD with his sore and great and strong sword shall punish leviathan the piercing serpent, even leviathan that crooked serpent; and he shall slay the dragon that is in the sea." (Isaiah 27:1)

Isaiah calls leviathan a *"crooked serpent,"* and a *"dragon."* By comparing Scripture with Scripture it is not hard to identify this being. We turn to the words John recorded in the Book of Revelation.

"And the great DRAGON was cast out, that old SERPENT, called the DEVIL, and SATAN, which deceiveth the whole world: he was cast out into the earth, and his angels were cast out with him." (Revelation 12:9) (Author's emphasis)

We have seen this being before in Job, when Job himself mentioned this crooked serpent.

"By his spirit he hath garnished the heavens; his hand hath formed the crooked serpent." (Job 26:13)

Leviathan is the Devil. The repeated references, the correlation of Scripture and the evidence that we will see in Job 41 add up to a conclusion much more solid than that of some mythological beast, an extinct dinosaur or a crocodile. He is called *"a king over all the children of pride."* (Job 41:34)

Failure to see this clear connection is due to a mind more enamored with Hebrew etymologies than with the God of the Bible, a mind more open to myth than the simple fact of the existence of a personal devil.

The sea where this dragon dwells is the mighty *"deep"* we have mentioned so often. This is confirmed in Job 41:31-32, as God describes his activities in the *"deep."* We will have more to say later, as we examine this passage verse by verse.

It is revealing that God spends no time convincing Job of this beast's existence. As we saw above, Job himself mentions this crooked serpent. God simply draws Job's attention to leviathan to continue His list of unanswerable questions.

To think that God Almighty would finally respond to Job's trials by pointing out characteristics of a crocodile or mythological dragon is absurd!—More than that, it reduces God to the level of a tribal deity, and borders on blasphemy. Only by understanding that God is pointing Job to the one who is responsible for his pain, is it possible to make sense of the flow of God's words.

THE MYSTERY EXAMINED

NOT YOUR AVERAGE SEA MONSTER

1 "Canst thou draw out leviathan with an hook? or his tongue with a cord which thou lettest down?

2 Canst thou put an hook into his nose? or bore his jaw through with a thorn?

3 Will he make many supplications unto thee? will he speak soft words unto thee?" (Job 41:1-3)

The point of these first three verses is to show that leviathan is no fish! God is reminding Job that this is not your normal underwater creature.

No fisherman has ever snared this dragon with a hook. This is NOT the "big one that got away." No fisherman has ever let down a cord to haul this serpent on board.

No one will ever put a hook through this nose and drag leviathan triumphantly from the side of a little fishing boat. No thorn will ever pierce this jaw to string him up with the other trophies of the day's catch.

God is asking Job if he thinks that leviathan is going to softly beg him to leave him alone. This beast knows no fear (Job 41:33), and dares to walk into the very presence of God (Job 1:6).

NOT TO BE TRUSTED

4 "Will he make a covenant with thee? wilt thou take him for a servant for ever?" (Job 41:4)

Job won't make a covenant, pact or agreement with this beast, but Israel will. We must always remember that Job is a prophetic picture of God's people in the Tribulation, persecuted by the Devil.

The Antichrist comes to power by bringing peace to the Middle East. Treaties will be signed between the political coalitions engineered by Antichrist and the Jews. Daniel foresees this in his famous prophecy of the "*seventy weeks*" of years, or 490 of Jewish history.

Without taking the time to set the complete background, notice this part of Daniel's prophecy that pertains to the Antichrist and his "*covenant*" with God's remnant. These prophetic words stretch from the decree of Artaxerxes to rebuild Jerusalem in 445 B.C. to the Tribulation. The church age is not seen, as is usual in Old Testament prophecy, since it appears as a parenthesis in God's plan to establish His kingdom through Israel.

"*Know therefore and understand, that from the going forth of the commandment to restore and to build Jerusalem unto the Messiah the Prince shall be seven weeks, and threescore and two weeks: the street shall be built again, and the wall, even in troublous times. And after threescore and two weeks shall Messiah be cut off, but not for himself: and the people of the prince that shall come shall destroy the city and the sanctuary; and the end thereof shall be with a flood, and unto the end of the war desolations are determined. And he shall confirm THE COVENANT with many for one week: and in the midst of the week he shall cause the sacrifice and the oblation to cease, and for the overspreading of abominations he shall make it desolate, even until the consummation, and that determined shall be poured upon the desolate.*" (Daniel 9:25-27) (Author's emphasis)

Daniel returns to the theme of Antichrist in Daniel 11. Notice the mention of the covenant in this account of Antichrist's attempt to control the remnant of believers.

"*And arms shall stand on his part, and they shall pollute the sanctuary of strength, and shall take away the daily sacrifice, and they shall place the abomination that maketh desolate. And such as do wickedly against THE COVENANT shall he corrupt by flatteries: but the people that do know their God shall be strong, and do exploits."* (Daniel 11:31-32) (Author's emphasis)

Isaiah also received revelation about this covenant between Israel and Antichrist. A portion of Isaiah's prophecy beginning in Isaiah 27 is sometimes called the "Little Apocalypse," because of its strong prophetic content and many parallels to the material found in the Book of Revelation.

"Wherefore hear the word of the LORD, ye scornful men, that rule this people which is in Jerusalem. Because ye have said, We have made A COVENANT WITH DEATH, and with hell are we at agreement; when the overflowing scourge shall pass through, it shall not come unto us: for we have made lies our refuge, and under falsehood have we hid ourselves." (Isaiah 28:14-15) (Author's emphasis)

God asks Job, ironically, *"wilt thou take him for a servant forever?"* (Job 41:4b) No, Job will not make the Devil his servant, nor will we. Israel will see the Antichrist as the Messiah when the *"covenant"* is signed, but it will be Israel who will end up in a subservient position to the Antichrist.

Sometimes we lift ourselves up in our own minds, thinking that since we are the children of God, the Devil has no power over us. His power is certainly limited, but don't think for a minute that you will place the Devil in a subservient relationship, now that you are God's child. Not even the archangel Michael dared to take on the Devil himself, but said, *"The Lord rebuke thee."* (Jude 9)

NOT TO BE PLAYED WITH

5 "Wilt thou play with him as with a bird? or wilt thou bind him for thy maidens?" (Job 41:5)

The Devil is not to be played with. He is not a participant in wild "revival" meetings, where arrogant evangelists claim to be chasing him across the platform.

God asks Job if he will *"bind"* him for his maidens. Job is wise enough not to answer.

Sincere, but less wise Christians think they "bind" the Devil, belting out trendy "faith" formulas at the top of their lungs. When they think the proper incantations have been invoked, they feel they can rest securely in the knowledge that they have bound the Devil.

The truth is, the flesh is more than sufficient to bind most Christians. The Devil doesn't have time to bother with most "revivals" or prayer meetings. If the flesh is already doing a good job of neutralizing Christ's power in the believer, why should the Devil waste energy?

God's question implies presumption on the part of one who would attempt to bind the Devil. The Devil WILL be bound, but the binding will be done by the only one qualified for the job—God. Revelation 20:2 tells how God will bind the Devil for a thousand years, ushering in the thousand-year reign of Christ. He will do so for the benefit of the *"maidens,"* believers who accompany the bride of Christ.

6 "Shall the companions make a banquet of him? shall they part him among the merchants?" (Job 41:6)

Job's companions will not dare to approach the Devil. They will neither use him for their own purposes (make a banquet of him), nor will they try to make profit from him *"part him among the merchants"*.

Sadly, there are those who DO try to use the Devil for personal gain, playing on people's fears in order to "market" Satan. There are extreme pockets of Christianity where people possess an obsession for things about the Devil. Newsletters, tapes and courses are peddled by merchants of demonic lore, and snatched up by those who find more comfort in them than in garlic cloves and silver crosses.

God is asking Job if he would dare to do those things that only God is qualified to do. Job obviously cannot bind the Devil. He can't make a banquet out of him, or make merchandise out of him.

Observing the pattern in God's questioning, this verse would suggest an interesting connection to an earlier question. Researching biblical information about leviathan, a verse in the Psalms offered a challenge.

"Thou brakest the heads of leviathan in pieces, and gavest him to be meat to the people inhabiting the wilderness." (Psalm 74:14)

While not understanding the full meaning of this verse, it would appear that God has made or will make a banquet of leviathan. In what way leviathan is connected to God's provision of food ("meat") to His wilderness generation of Israelites, is open to question. Perhaps there will be some fulfillment in the coming Tribulation when God again provides food for the remnant in the wilderness.

NOT TO BE MESSED WITH

7 "Canst thou fill his skin with barbed irons? or his head with fish spears?

8 Lay thine hand upon him, remember the battle, do no more." (Job 41:7-8)

Obviously, leviathan is not subject to ordinary barbed irons and fish spears. This is why God advises Job against engaging in battle with leviathan.

The idea of Job 41:8 is that if Job were to ever lay his hand upon leviathan in battle, he would surely remember the battle and do it no more.

Earlier we referred to Jude 1:9, showing how even Michael the archangel did not dare to engage in battle with the Devil. Mess with him once, and you won't do it again!

9 "Behold, the hope of him is in vain: shall not one be cast down even at the sight of him?" (Job 41:9)

This is not a crocodile or a sea monster. This is the creature who has nothing but an empty (vain) hope. The fierce fighting of the Devil is motivated by the empty hope that he can somehow thwart God's plan and maintain his control over the kingdom of men.

He disguises himself as an *"angel of light"* (2 Corinthians 11:14). If a man could see him for what he really is, that man would be *"cast down."* That is to say that the very sight of the Devil is enough to cause you to faint! It would be a sight more frightening than anything the wizards of Hollywood could conjure up with their technological wonders. While he appears as a godly religious leader to men, an angel of light, God sees him as a repulsive, seven-headed reptile.

10 "None is so fierce that dare stir him up: who then is able to stand before me?" (Job 41:10)

Is there anyone who thinks he can stir up the Devil? Unfortunately, there are numbers of Christians who seem to think that is their mission in life. When you play with fire, you will surely be burned. No wonder there are so many problems in Christianity today. We cannot stir up the Devil without suffering dire consequences.

Why, then, would anyone think he could stand up to God? *"Who then is able to stand before me?"* God has demonstrated great grace in not saying so specifically, but the comment is directly applicable to Job's desire to stand before God and find out the reason for his trial.

NOT TO BE MISUNDERSTOOD

11 "Who hath prevented me, that I should repay him? whatsoever is under the whole heaven is mine.

12 I will not conceal his parts, nor his power, nor his comely proportion.

13 Who can discover the face of his garment? or who can come to him with his double bridle?

14 Who can open the doors of his face? his teeth are terrible round about." (Job 41:11-14)

"Prevented" in verse 11 is used in the sense of going before someone. Idiomatically, God is saying, "Who thinks he can get up in the morning before me? Everything under heaven belongs to me."

Contextually, God is still speaking of leviathan. Taking the idiomatic expression of Job 41:11 into account, God is simply asking Job if there is anyone who thinks he knows enough to tell God something about leviathan.

For His part, God has nothing to hide about the Devil. He vows to reveal his makeup *("his parts")*, his power and his beauty *("comely proportions")*.

God is certainly speaking the truth! He reveals volumes about the Devil right here in Job 41. This is more than we can say for those scholars who tell us that *"leviathan"* means nothing more than a crocodile or sea monster. That makes a great chapter on the Devil become nothing more than a literary curiosity. God says He WANTS to reveal the full truth about this creature. Some try to obscure this truth. Who could possibly be behind this scheme?

In the passage before us, Job 41:11-14, we can learn a great deal about the Devil. In verse 12 we see that he has power and beauty. Verse 13 shows that the Devil has a garment, a covering or disguise (2 Corinthians 11:13-15), as well as a double bridle. In verse 14 we see that he has a face with doors and terrible teeth.

NOT TO BE MOVED

15 "His scales are his pride, shut up together as with a close seal.

16 One is so near to another, that no air can come between them.

17 They are joined one to another, they stick together, that they cannot be sundered." (Job 41:15-17)

What a revealing statement! *"His scales are his pride, shut up together as with a close seal."*

His pride is so great that it forms an armor like the scales of a sea creature. Yet these scales are so tight, that they are air-proof! Leviathan is impenetrable due to his incredible pride. No wonder he is called a king over all the children of pride (Job 41:34).

Only one thing can penetrate such pride. Only one thing can *"sunder,"* or pry apart those scales.

"For the word of God is quick, and powerful, and sharper than any two-edged sword, piercing even to the dividing asunder of soul and spirit, and of the joints and marrow, and is a discerner of the thoughts and intents of the heart." (Hebrews 4:12)

18 "By his neesings a light doth shine, and his eyes are like the eyelids of the morning.

19 Out of his mouth go burning lamps, and sparks of fire leap out.
20 Out of his nostrils goeth smoke, as out of a seething pot or caldron.
21 His breath kindleth coals, and a flame goeth out of his mouth.
22 In his neck remaineth strength, and sorrow is turned into joy before him.
23 The flakes of his flesh are joined together: they are firm in themselves; they cannot be moved." (Job 41:18-23)

These verses reveal a regular fire-breathing dragon! When the Devil appears to man, it is as an *"angel of light"* (2 Corinthians 11:14). This is the passage where God describes him as he really is. To maintain his effective disguise, the Devil has worked overtime to assure that this description is passed off as quaint musing about a mere animal.

No, this is not the fire-breathing dragon of mythology, but the authentic fire-breathing dragon which forms the grain of truth around which mythology is built. The biblical concept of a personal Devil is not the evolutionary product of ancient Canaanite myth. Mythology is the product of the biblical concept of a personal Devil. This is a terrifying, grotesque, awesomely-powerful beast, the result of the anointed cherub's sin. Leviathan is not a symbolic representation of the "force of evil," but a genuine being consumed with the sin of pride.

The *"neesings"* of Job 41:18 is an antiquated way to say "sneezings." Even the sneezings of this wide-eyed, fire-breathing creature are fiery.

Smoke curls up from his nostrils and his breath ignites coals. His thick neck swings in an awesome display of force.

God has already described his tightly-knit scales of pride. Now, He says that the skin not covered with scales is flaky, hard and just as tightly-matted as his scales.

Another component of this description is the statement in Job 41:22 that *"sorrow is turned into joy before him."* Most modern scholarship is quick to point out that the phrase would be better translated to give the idea of sorrow or terror dancing before him. This would then express the same idea as Job 41:9, where God says that one is *"cast down"* at the very sight of him.

The Hebrew word rendered as *"turned into joy"* in the King James Bible is found only here. The definition usually given is to dance or to leap.

The average student confronted with this information is tempted to think that the translation in the King James Bible is dead wrong. In defense of our standard English translation for the last 400 years, there is another sense to *"sorrow is turned into joy before him."*

Considering that dancing and leaping are usually associated with joy, it is not a stretch of the imagination to see why the translators would have interpreted it as they did. This would be especially true if they were trying to communicate the idea of leviathan thriving on turning the sorrow of others into his own joy. Not only does this fit the context and the thought of Job 41:9 mentioned above, it is complementary to that and stronger still.

24 "His heart is as firm as a stone; yea, as hard as a piece of the nether millstone." (Job 41:24)

Talk about a hard heart! There is no wonder that the children of leviathan (John 8:44) are noted for having hard hearts.

Not only is leviathan's heart hard as a stone, it is as hard as a *"piece of the nether millstone." "Nether"* is old English for "lower." The nether millstone is the bottom and hardest grinding stone in a mill. That is about as hard as you can get!

25 "When he raiseth up himself, the mighty are afraid: by reason of breakings they purify themselves." (Job 41:25)

When leviathan raises up his seven ugly heads (Revelation 12:3), even the mighty are terrified. So terrified are they, that they try to purify themselves *"by reason of breakings."* "Breakings" are also translated as "affliction," "hurt" or "vexation."

The prophets of Baal, in 1 Kings 18:28, thought to get their god's attention through their self-inflicted wounds. So powerful is leviathan (Baal, Zeus, Tamuz or any other pagan god you would want to substitute), that his children are still afflicting themselves to this very day. They crawl on their knees to gold-gilded cathedrals, tighten knotted cords around their waists until they bleed, or have themselves nailed to crosses during "Holy Week."

Pick your religion; self-inflicted wounds and self-mutilation are common human ideas of how to gain favor of the gods. From Genesis 3 to Revelation 17, there is only one true source of all false religion. Men see him as an angel of light; God sees him as a seven-headed beast He calls leviathan.

NOT TO BE FACED WITH ORDINARY WEAPONS

26 "The sword of him that layeth at him cannot hold: the spear, the dart, nor the habergeon.

27 He esteemeth iron as straw, and brass as rotten wood.

28 The arrow cannot make him flee: slingstones are turned with him into stubble.

29 Darts are counted as stubble: he laugheth at the shaking of a spear." (Job 41:26-29)

The essence of these words is easy to discern. No ordinary weapon is sufficient against this beast. No matter what you throw at him, he is not impressed, intimidated or threatened.

The only way to wage battle against leviathan is with supernatural weapons. We are engaged in a supernatural warfare with supernatural beings, according to Paul's words in Ephesians 6:12. Paul also tells us that we have available supernatural weapons.

"For the weapons of our warfare are not carnal, but mighty through God to the pulling down of strong holds." (2 Corinthians 10:4)

In the same discussion regarding spiritual warfare in Ephesians 6, Paul lists the only sword that can penetrate the airtight scales of leviathan's pride. It is the sword of the Spirit, the Word of God.

As we reflect upon the lengthy discussions we have just studied, there is a great lesson we can learn. Job and his friends have tossed God's words back and forth at each other. Tragically, they never learned how to effectively use the sword of the Lord against the Devil.

We see the same tendency in our day, using the Bible more effectively against each other than against the Devil. We need to use the Bible to edify each other, and to stand against the Devil.

NOT TO BE COMPARED TO ANYONE OR ANYTHING ELSE

30 "Sharp stones are under him: he spreadeth sharp pointed things upon the mire." (Job 41:30)

Here are those stones again! We have seen this singular connection with stones and the Devil, hell and destruction, without coming to a satisfactory understanding of them.

Job 8:17 speaks of the place of stones. We found the stones of darkness in Job 28:3. Isaiah spoke of the stones of emptiness in Isaiah 34:11. Ezekiel told how the anointed cherub had every precious stone for his covering in Eden before his fall.

Here, we are again reminded of the yet unrevealed mystery of the stones as they relate to the Devil. We are also reminded of how much we have yet to learn.

31 "He maketh the deep to boil like a pot: he maketh the sea like a pot of ointment.

32 "He maketh a path to shine after him; one would think the deep to be hoary." (Job 41:31-32)

Earlier in this chapter we commented that this *"deep"* is not the Mediterranean or the Atlantic, but the deep of Genesis 1:2, whose face is frozen (Job 38:30).

God is saying in Job 41:31-32 that the Devil is constantly "stirring the pot." He is, after all, the prince of the power of the air. He can travel through the deep to the very throne room of God (Job 1-2). This is why *"the heavens are not clean in his sight"* (Job 15:15).

When he moves, he leaves a white *("hoary")* wake behind him. (Job 41:32) What this tangibly means is beyond our current level of comprehension.

Viewing the record of scientific investigation, it is not unreasonable to hold to the biblical account despite the questions that remain. Scientific theory changes as often as the winds in Kansas. ALL scientific theory is based on certain sets of presuppositions.

The believer's presuppositions are that there is a God, and that this God has chosen to communicate with man in a written record called the Bible. If these presuppositions are correct (and they are no more preposterous than to believe that all life accidentally resulted from a chemical explosion), it makes sense that God knows more about the universe than we do.

33 "Upon earth there is not his like, who is made without fear." (Job 41:33)

"On earth is not his equal" is the way that Martin Luther's famous hymn "A Mighty Fortress is Our God" expresses this truth. The Devil is unique.

He is fearless. Yet the text says he was *"made"* that way. It was not the result of his creation by God, but the result of his sin that made him without fear.

Proverbs 1:7 teaches that the fear of the Lord is the beginning of knowledge. Leviathan has no fear of the Lord. There is a great difference between intelligence and biblical knowledge. The same verse in Proverbs says that fools despise wisdom and knowledge. There are many intelligent, well-educated people who are biblical fools. They have wonderful information, yet are void of true wisdom and knowledge.

The Devil is wonderfully intelligent. He has more information about the universe than we could hope to learn in multiple lifetimes. Yet he is without fear. He is, therefore, a fool. Do not, though, make the mistake of trying to mix it up with this fool. He will burn you to a crisp with the slightest puff out of his mouth. His powerful neck will send you reeling into eternity.

34 "He beholdeth all high things: he is a king over all the children of pride." (Job 41:34)

We have seen that he has access to the very presence of God. There is nothing higher for him to behold. There is, however, a significant difference between beholding and controlling.

He is the king over all the children of pride. John 8:44, where Jesus says that the Devil is the father of unbelievers, has already been offered as a cross-reference in the process of identifying this beast. It is obvious that this is not a crocodile. This is the Devil.

Commentaries suggest a multitude of ideas about the meaning of "*leviathan.*" We have already considered some of the theories. Considering all that has happened in this book—the exchange between God and Satan, the attacks on Job, the series of verbal exchanges—it seems incredible to me to suggest that after all is said and done, God wants to talk to Job about a hippopotamus and a crocodile!

Many scholars have been so obsessed with tracing vocabulary, word usages, cultural practices and the like, that they have lost sight of the whole. Rather than standing in awe of the Almighty God who transcends time and space to speak to Job, and learning from His divine perspective of what has taken place, man has opted to look at God through the cloudy lens of pagan ritual and culture. The result is a vision of a god no bigger than the ones worshipped by Job's pagan neighbors.

A just man has lost his ten children. He has lost his earthly possessions and been physically attacked by the Devil himself. His best friends have become satanic tools in a psychological war against him. Will the God of heaven have nothing more to say to him than to quiz him on cosmological curiosities and characteristics of natural animals? Is that all God has to offer? Is that all there is to life?

Failure to see where God is leading with this monologue, is failure to understand the purpose of the book. Job, like his colleagues, has command of an impressive body of God-facts. What they all fail to see is the "big picture."

God began his remarks by pointing Job to the beginning, to the creation itself. With ages-wide brush strokes, God paints the picture of creation and the natural processes He has established. At issue are not Job's particular perils, but God's plan as a whole.

God then calls Job's attention to the living beings He made to inhabit this wondrous creation. Each has a distinct purpose and nature. Each is pregnant with symbolism, consistently witnessed throughout the Scriptures.

The climax of God's discourse is to point to two powerful beasts. One is a prophetic representation of Satan's plan to subdue the earth under his control, while the other is the source of the first beast's power. This latter beast is the very one who is responsible for Job's tragedy.

God has not directly addressed Job's problem, but has answered it for anyone who can see the big picture. Job's need was to see his own insignificance in light of God's grand design. Job had done a good job of living a life of righteousness upon the earth. He had been faithful to cling to his faith while enduring intense attack. Yet like so many righteous-living believers today, Job failed to comprehend the big picture.

God's manner of "answering" Job is so typical of His ways. Jesus often answered a question with a question, as we have previously observed. To set forth profound truth, He often employed parables. He defined the purpose of parables Himself in Matthew 13:10-17, when He said that they were to hide his truth from the unbelievers, but reveal it to those who had eyes and ears of faith.

The voice of Almighty God has thundered. Job's trial has come to its conclusion. Job's focus is directed upward. For the first time in his life he has seen that he is only a bit player in an epic drama larger than he had ever imagined.

The mask has been stripped from the villain's face. The *"angel of light"* has been exposed. A loathsome, repulsive, vile and odious beast stands naked before Job's gaze. Here is the issue. Here is the source of the problem.

Yet some see only a hippopotamus or a crocodile.

31

WHEN YOU DON'T HAVE ALL THE ANSWERS

Then came there unto him all his brethren,

and all his sisters, and all they that had

been of his acquaintance before,

and did eat bread with him in his house:

and they bemoaned him, and comforted him over all the evil

that the LORD had brought upon him:

every man also gave him a piece of money,

and every one an earring of gold.

So the LORD blessed the latter end of Job more than his beginning:

for he had fourteen thousand sheep, and six thousand camels,

and a thousand yoke of oxen, and a thousand she asses.

Job 42:11-12

BASIC TRUTH ABOUT LIFE AND SALVATION IS FREELY AVAILABLE. Advanced truth requires a stretch.

"For whosoever shall call upon the name of the Lord shall be saved." (Romans 10:13) This truth is not difficult to understand, though many stumble over it because they don't want to believe it.

To understand the ways of God requires sacrifice by the disciple. This is why the nation of Israel saw the works of God, while only Moses understood God's ways. (Psalm 103:7)

Jesus spoke clearly concerning His mission. Yet once He was rejected by the leaders of the nation, He began to give His truth in parables. (Matthew 13) He said that He did this to hide His truth from nonbelievers, and to reveal it to those who believed. (Matthew 13:10-17)

Job's basic faith in God was solid and unshakable. Not even the Devil could pry Job's fingers from his grip on God.

Job has just been through the most horrible trial imaginable. He has been stripped of everything except his basic faith in God and countless questions. Yet the answers to Job's questions have been anything but obvious. This is what I mean by advanced truth—basic faith in God and trusting God with everything else, as He stretches us to new levels of understanding.

Throughout his debate with the counselors, Job cried for a meeting with God, for answers, for reasons, for purpose. God has made His appearance, but He offered no direct answers.

Neither empathy nor sympathy has oozed from God's mouth. He has offered Job no direct explanation about His earlier dialogue with Satan and the resulting attack on Job. God has not outlined for Job all the many benefits of passing through this trial. God has not so much as spoken a word of encouragement.

God has simply pointed Job to the grandness of His creation. He has spoken specifically about fourteen of His created beings, concluding with the Devil himself. God has not spoken what Job wanted to hear, but what he needed to hear. Job will now have to deduce his own conclusions.

For centuries believers have found solace in Job, realizing that even the righteous suffer. Understanding that righteous people suffer is not the problem. What eludes us are those answers we all crave when we are in the fiery furnace.

This is the reason I said from the beginning that the Book of Job is not the book that tells us WHY the righteous suffer; it is the book to instruct the righteous HOW to suffer.

Now, from our perspective as unattached observers, it is easier to speculate what God is doing. We have commented that God is pointing Job to the big picture, to see that his personal suffering is only a minor piece in the major puzzle. He has drawn Job's attention to His purposes in all created life, leading to a climatic description of the infamous leviathan.

With the information we were provided in the first two chapters of the book, we can conclude that leviathan has lashed out in furious anger at the righteous Job. We can see where God is leading Job because we can read about the discussion between God and Satan. Coming to those conclusions must be much harder from Job's side of the fire.

What do you do when you don't have all the answers? What can we learn from Job?

You continue to hold to your basic faith in God. You refuse to allow anyone or anything to shake you from your solid stance. Realizing that you may never have all the answers, you allow God to direct your attention to His total plan. Instead of fretting over what you don't know, understand that your petty questions are only a fraction of what you do not comprehend about God's plan. Then, stand in awe of God. Confess that He is in control. That is all you need to know for the moment.

At some point, God revealed this story to someone. If, as we have speculated, Elihu is the author, he heard the rest of the story from Job or from God. If Job is the author, God later gave him additional revelation. Whoever wrote the book received additional information not available to Job at this point in the history we are considering.

When you are in the trial, there may come a point when God will give you additional understanding. He may give that understanding to another, and never to you. None of this matters, however, if we have mastered the essence of God's words to Job in Job 38-42.

This chapter is the conclusion to our adventures in the land of Uz. Like a chromatic musical scale slowly ascending through its web of sharps and flats, this chapter is the major chord that is finally struck, resolving the tension.

The pieces of Job's life will now be carefully glued together. The pain will become a memory; the patience will remain.

This chapter naturally divides into three sections. Job speaks and has nothing to add. God speaks to Job's friends and they have nothing to answer. God restores what Job lost, and we realize that the man who is committed to God has nothing to lose.

NOTHING TO ADD

1 "Then Job answered the LORD, and said,
2 I know that thou canst do every thing, and that no thought can be withholden from thee." (Job 42:1-2)

Job's questions have vanished in the radiant glory of God's omnipotence. When God is God, personal questions lose their relevance. The situation is as follows.

Is God God? Yes. Is He omnipotent, omniscient and omnipresent? Yes, of course. Is there any thought held back from Him? No. Can He reveal to us whatever we need to know, when we need to know it? Certainly. Does He have an overall purpose and fit everything to it? Yes. Does it matter whether I like His plan or agree with it? Not in the least. Questions? No.

Job's need was not for more information. His problem was an undersized vision of God.

3 "Who is he that hideth counsel without knowledge? therefore have I uttered that I understood not; things too wonderful for me, which I knew not.
4 Hear, I beseech thee, and I will speak: I will demand of thee, and declare thou unto me." (Job 42:3-4)

Job repeats God's question of Job 38:2, *"Who is he that hideth counsel without knowledge?"* then gives the answer. Job confesses that he is the one who is speaking without knowledge.

No time is wasted in futile self-justification. Job does not even try to point an accusing finger at his worthless counselors. When one has seen God in His proper perspective, no circumstance or person has any bearing on God's plan for that individual. Nothing matters now but God.

Job boldly announces that he has something to say. He tells God that he will "*demand*" of him, then wait for His answer.

This is not said insultingly. Job is merely stating how important it is for him to say this, and to hear God's response.

5 "I have heard of thee by the hearing of the ear: but now mine eye seeth thee." (Job 42:5)

Job has only heard about God. Now, he has seen God.

Obviously, Job is seeing a physical manifestation, as we commented in our analysis of Job 38:1. This is a Christophany, an appearance of the preincarnate Christ. Job is looking at God, as surely as Peter looked into the face of the Lord Jesus Christ.

6 "Wherefore I abhor myself, and repent in dust and ashes." (Job 42:6)

Here is Job's conclusion, and it is in direct contrast to much of today's popular counseling. Humanistic counseling tells us that many of man's woes are directly related to a poor self-image. Some "Christian leaders" have even defined sin as a negative self-image. Job's self-image is none too positive!

Clearly there are many who needlessly wrestle with false guilt, inferiority complexes and the like. Yet the answer is not "within ourselves," as Shakespeare and many modern psychologists tell us. Within man is only the deceitful, desperately wicked heart of which Jeremiah wrote. (Jeremiah 17:9)

A "positive self-image" is obtained through a thorough recognition of our helplessness and need for total dependency on God's power alone. The only way up is down.

No matter how righteous a man may be, he is nothing apart from God. No matter how bright his light, it is invisible in the light of God's glory. A lighted candle gives no light when held against the high beam of a car headlight.

Job's reaction is no different than other holy men who suddenly found themselves in God's presence. Consider Isaiah.

"In the year that king Uzziah died I saw also the Lord sitting upon a throne, high and lifted up, and his train filled the temple. Above it stood the seraphims: each one had six wings; with twain he covered his face, and with twain he covered his feet, and with twain he did fly. And one cried unto another, and said, Holy, holy, holy, is the LORD of hosts: the whole earth is full of his glory. And the posts of the door moved at the voice of him that cried, and the house was filled with smoke. Then said I, Woe is me! for

I am undone; because I am a man of unclean lips, and I dwell in the midst of a people of unclean lips: for mine eyes have seen the King, the LORD of hosts." (Isaiah 6:1-5)

When confronted with the miraculous power of Christ, Peter instantly came to the same conclusion. The Lord had just produced a miraculous catch of fishes, and Peter *"fell down at Jesus' knees, saying, Depart from me; for I am a sinful man, O Lord."* (Luke 5:8)

Earlier in the book, Job's dreadful trials drove him to the ash heap. Now, it is the honest recognition of his own sinfulness that drives him to sackcloth and ashes.

This is the key to victory. One must be horrified not at trials, but at one's own sinful nature.

This is similar to the lesson Paul teaches to the Corinthians. He distinguishes between a repentance that is genuine sorrow for one's sin, and a false repentance that is sorrow only for having been caught.

"For godly sorrow worketh repentance to salvation not to be repented of: but the sorrow of the world worketh death." (2 Corinthians 7:10)

Genuine repentance is not just being sorry for what you have done, but being sorry for what you are. This is God's lesson for Job, and he has learned it well.

Job insisted throughout that he was innocent of any specific sin. There is no doubt that this was true. God Himself gave testimony of Job.

Job freely admitted his sinful nature. Yet only now, faced with the stark comparison of God's omnipotence, does the full force of horrible reality of his sinful nature grip Job's soul.

There is nothing left for Job to add. God has spoken. Job has understood that he does not understand.

No plea, no questions, no further comments.

NOTHING TO ANSWER

7 "And it was so, that after the LORD had spoken these words unto Job, the LORD said to Eliphaz the Temanite, My wrath is kindled against thee, and against thy two friends: for ye have not spoken of me the thing that is right, as my servant Job hath." (Job 42:7)

Attitude of heart, not knowledge alone, is God's basic concern when dealing with man. God is neither impressed with the knowledge of Job's counselors, nor does He accept their "secret sin" theory. The Almighty has seen through their pious facade, and His wrath is kindled against them.

Confirming what we said earlier about Eliphaz being the eldest and most influential of the group, God addresses him as the representative. With his position, he will now accept the corresponding responsibility.

This verse also confirms the idea that God's words were directly addressed to Job from the beginning of His speech. Some see Elihu as the one who *"darkeneth counsel by words without knowledge."* (Job 38:2) Yet this is exactly what Job confessed to do in Job 42:3. Here, in Job 42:7, we read that God had spoken these words *"unto Job."*

God is upset because these men have not spoken what is right of Him. They have been more concerned with making their own arguments than with speaking what is right about God.

Job's redeeming personal quality was his immediate humility when confronted with the presence of God. He freely confessed his own unworthiness, and pointed to the holiness of God. This confirms the confidence God had placed in Job from the beginning of His dialogue with Satan.

This is a good rule of thumb for a question to ask ourselves in any situation of life—what is our motivation when speaking of God? Are we more concerned with being right, or speaking what is right about God?

8 "Therefore take unto you now seven bullocks and seven rams, and go to my servant Job, and offer up for yourselves a burnt offering; and my servant Job shall pray for you: for him will I accept: lest I deal with you after your folly, in that ye have not spoken of me the thing which is right, like my servant Job." (Job 42:8)

We must again remind ourselves that these men are not Jews. What God is requiring of them cannot be compared to the levitical system of sacrifice.

However, the message of the need for a substitutionary sacrifice is the common denominator, both, in gentile sacrifice and the later Jewish system. Most important, the substitutionary sacrifice was initiated by God.

God sacrificed animals to provide skins to clothe Adam and Eve's nakedness following their fall. (Genesis 3:21) When Cain and Abel came before the Lord with their sacrifices (Genesis 4), it was not because of their quest for God. They came because God had instructed them.

Not only that, it is clear from the context that God had been specific in His instructions regarding the substitutionary nature of the sacrifice required, and the need for the shedding of blood. Cain brought the fruit of the ground, which God had cursed. He pictures man who tries to work his way to God. Abel brought sacrifices from his flocks. God accepted Abel's offering, but rejected Cain's. Cain was furious.

"And the LORD said unto Cain, Why art thou wroth? and why is thy countenance fallen? If thou doest well, shalt thou not be accepted?" (Genesis 4:6-7a)

God had previously revealed a way to do well, or these words would have no meaning. Man takes God's instructions and corrupts them in a prideful attempt to design his own religions. Yet the seed of the substitutionary sacrifice was planted by God Himself.

It is remarkable to notice that the sacrifice offered by the gentile priest Baalam, is the same sacrifice required by God of Eliphaz and his colleagues. God asks the men for seven bullocks and seven rams. Now, look at what Baalam did.

"And Balaam said unto Balak, Build me here seven altars, and prepare me here seven oxen and seven rams." (Numbers 23:1)

Balaam was a religious prostitute, a false prophet, selling his services to the highest bidder. Yet hundreds of years before Balaam, we see evidence of a pattern of gentile sacrifice that is required of Eliphaz and company.

These men believed that Job was a sinner who was getting what he deserved. Now, God sets Job up to be their mediator. *"And my servant Job shall pray for you: for him will I accept."* (Job 42:8b)

Following the Tribulation, of which the Book of Job is a prophetic image, sacrifices will again be restored, even among the gentiles on earth. In this millennial kingdom, Israel will be the center of the earth. When the Tribulation ends, Christ will reign on earth and the peoples of the world will come to Jerusalem to worship. Isaiah saw this coming period. Just as Job mediated for his friends, the Jews will mediate for the nations.

"And it shall come to pass in the last days, that the mountain of the LORD'S house shall be established in the top of the mountains, and shall be exalted above the hills; and all nations shall flow unto it. And many people shall go and say, Come ye, and let us go up to the mountain of the LORD, to the house of the God of Jacob; and he will teach us of his ways, and we will walk in his paths: for out of Zion shall go forth the law, and the word of the LORD from Jerusalem. And he shall judge among the nations, and shall rebuke many people: and they shall beat their swords into plowshares, and their spears into pruninghooks: nation shall not lift up sword against nation, neither shall they learn war any more." (Isaiah 2:2-4)

Ezekiel also saw this coming day. Ezekiel 45 is a prophecy of that future time. We should not, therefore, be surprised by the similarity of what we see in Ezekiel 45, and what we have seen in Job 42 concerning God's requirements for these gentiles.

"In the first month, in the fourteenth day of the month, ye shall have the passover, a feast of seven days; unleavened bread shall be eaten. And upon

that day shall the prince prepare for himself and for all the people of the land a bullock for a sin offering. And seven days of the feast he shall prepare a burnt offering to the LORD, SEVEN BULLOCKS AND SEVEN RAMS without blemish daily the seven days; and a kid of the goats daily for a sin offering. And he shall prepare a meat offering of an ephah for a bullock, and an ephah for a ram, and an hin of oil for an ephah. In the seventh month, in the fifteenth day of the month, shall he do the like in the feast of the seven days, according to the sin offering, according to the burnt offering, and according to the meat offering, and according to the oil." (Ezekiel 45:21-25) (Author's emphasis)

The restoration of the sacrificial system is not a "plan of salvation" for those in the millennial kingdom, any more than it was for the Jews of the Old Testament. There was never any power to save from sin in the blood of animals. The Book of Hebrews makes that very clear.

The Old Testament sacrifices pointed to God and pointed to the Lamb of God to come. They were an educational system, as Paul explained to the Galatians, beset by false teachers who were trying to convince them of the need to become Jewish to be good believers in Christ. (Galatians 3:24-25)

In the future, such a system of worship will also be educational and inspiration, not redemptive. To both Jewish and gentile believers in the millennium, these sacrifices will be much like the Lord's Table for us in this present age. There is no redemptive power, nor is there grace to be imparted in this ceremony. As Paul explains in 1 Corinthians 11, it points us back to what Christ did for us, and points us forward to the promise of His return.

The Colossians had also been infiltrated by those who would force them to return to the Old Testament ritual. They wanted to keep the Jewish festivals and holy days. Paul's advice to them was just as clear as to the Galatians. Notice carefully the exact words.

"Let no man therefore judge you in meat, or in drink, or in respect of an holyday, or of the new moon, or of the sabbath days: WHICH ARE A SHADOW OF THINGS TO COME; but the body is of Christ." (Colossians 2:16-17) (Author's emphasis)

These things, Paul says, still point to the future. There is coming a day when they will be valid. What we see here in Job, in God's requirement of sacrifices from these gentiles, is a prophetic glimpse of what is in store following the Tribulation.

9 "So Eliphaz the Temanite and Bildad the Shuhite and Zophar the Naamathite went, and did according as the LORD commanded them: the LORD also accepted Job." (Job 42:9)

These men who had all the answers now have nothing to answer. There is no record of any verbal response. They simply went and did what God told them to do.

The section closes with the wonderful testimony, *"the LORD also accepted Job."* Job is now in the position of blessing again. How quickly things have turned around.

NOTHING TO LOSE

The remainder of the book is the record of how God restored to Job double what he had before. The man who lost it all got it all in the end. In the process, however, the man who had it all learned that in reality, he had nothing to lose. His relationship with God was all he needed to sustain him through life's darkest hours.

We grow attached to things. In times of trial we waste much energy worrying about WHAT THINGS we might lose. Victory comes from recognizing that when our relationship with God is on solid ground, we have NOTHING to lose that is worth worrying about. Whatever we may lose, God can restore double any time He sees fit.

10 "And the LORD turned the captivity of Job, when he prayed for his friends: also the LORD gave Job twice as much as he had before." (Job 42:10)

The Bible's use of key words and phrases is as amazing as it is supernatural. The evidence of the single authorship of Scripture is abundant to anyone who is looking for it. God, using multiple authors in many places over the course of centuries, wrote a single, unified, harmonious book. He did so, even preserving the personalities and styles of the human writers.

In this verse is one of those key phrases—*"turned the captivity."* Such an expression is used elsewhere only to speak of the restoration of Israel. This is meaningful to us only when we see that Job is a prophetic image of Israel in the Tribulation. Consider some evidence.

"Oh that the salvation of Israel were come out of Zion! when the LORD bringeth back the captivity of his people, Jacob shall rejoice, and Israel shall be glad." (Psalm 14:7)

"Turn again our captivity, O LORD, as the streams in the south." (Psalm 126:4)

"And I will cause the captivity of Judah and the captivity of Israel to return, and will build them, as at the first." (Jeremiah 33:7)

"The voice of joy, and the voice of gladness, the voice of the bridegroom, and the voice of the bride, the voice of them that shall say, Praise the LORD of hosts: for the LORD is good; for his mercy endureth for ever: and of them that shall bring the sacrifice of praise into the house of the LORD. For I will cause to return the captivity of the land, as at the first, saith the LORD." (Jeremiah 33:11)

"Then will I cast away the seed of Jacob, and David my servant, so that I will not take any of his seed to be rulers over the seed of Abraham, Isaac, and Jacob: for I will cause their captivity to return, and have mercy on them." (Jeremiah 33:26)

"And the coast shall be for the remnant of the house of Judah; they shall feed thereupon: in the houses of Ashkelon shall they lie down in the evening: for the LORD their God shall visit them, and turn away their captivity." (Zephaniah 2:7)

"At that time will I bring you again, even in the time that I gather you: for I will make you a name and a praise among all people of the earth, when I turn back your captivity before your eyes, saith the LORD." (Zephaniah 3:20)

Job's captivity is turned after seven days of being humiliated in the presence of his friends. Israel's captivity will be turned after seven years of Tribulation.

Job is restored to the place of blessing when he mediates for his friends. Israel will be restored to the place of blessing, and will represent God to the nations of the earth.

11 "Then came there unto him all his brethren, and all his sisters, and all they that had been of his acquaintance before, and did eat bread with him in his house: and they bemoaned him, and comforted him over all the evil that the LORD had brought upon him: every man also gave him a piece of money, and every one an earring of gold.

12 So the LORD blessed the latter end of Job more than his beginning: for he had fourteen thousand sheep, and six thousand camels, and a thousand yoke of oxen, and a thousand she asses." (Job 42:11-12)

The ones who had rejected Job in his tribulation now come to him. We just saw in Isaiah 2 how the nations will come to Jerusalem to seek the Lord in that day. Other prophecies also look forward to that day, when the scene in Job's house will be amplified on a worldwide level.

"And it shall come to pass in that day, that the Lord shall set his hand again the second time to recover the remnant of his people, which shall be left, from Assyria, and from Egypt, and from Pathros, and from Cush, and

from Elam, and from Shinar, and from Hamath, and from the islands of the sea." (Isaiah 11:11)

Finally, Job is comforted. *"They bemoaned him, and comforted him over all the evil that the LORD had brought upon him."*

This, too, is consistent with the position of Israel following the Tribulation. For these many centuries Israel has lived through countless sorrows. Leviticus 26 lists the many consequences of sin that have characterized the existence of God's people. Yet all this is a foreshadow of the Tribulation to come. On the other side of the time of sorrows comes the consolation, as testified by the prophets.

"Comfort ye, comfort ye my people, saith your God. Speak ye comfortably to Jerusalem, and cry unto her, that her warfare is accomplished, that her iniquity is pardoned: for she hath received of the LORD'S hand double for all her sins." (Isaiah 40:1-2)

"Sing, O heavens; and be joyful, O earth; and break forth into singing, O mountains: for the LORD hath comforted his people, and will have mercy upon his afflicted." (Isaiah 49:13)

"Then shall the virgin rejoice in the dance, both young men and old together: for I will turn their mourning into joy, and will comfort them, and make them rejoice from their sorrow." (Jeremiah 31:13)

Before going any further, there is one more thing we need to weigh. Those who have come to comfort Job, do so *"over all the evil the LORD had brought upon him."*

This doesn't mean that God is the origin of evil. We saw in the first two chapters of this book that God mentioned Job's name first. Satan executed the attacks against Job, yet did nothing without God's permission.

At issue is simply God's sovereignty. The Lord brought all Job's trials upon him. The Devil DID the evil that Job suffered, because he IS evil.

There is another fascinating element of this verse. Those who came to Job each brought him a piece of money and an earring of gold.

Again, Job serves as a type of Israel in oppression. Emerging from his tribulation, Job is enriched by those around him. When God turned Israel's captivity in Egypt, the Hebrews left enriched in the exodus.

"And the children of Israel did according to the word of Moses; and they borrowed of the Egyptians jewels of silver, and jewels of gold, and raiment." (Exodus 12:35)

Solomon extended the kingdom to its maximum limits in the Old Testament monarchy. Those glory days of Solomon's kingdom look forward to the millennial reign of Christ. At the height of his glory, the Queen of Sheba comes to him bearing gentile riches, as recorded in 2 Chronicles 9:1-12.

All this confirms the picture we have already seen in passages such as Isaiah 2 and 11. God will turn the captivity of Israel. The nation will enter a period of unprecedented prosperity, with the nations bringing their gifts to Jerusalem.

12 "So the LORD blessed the latter end of Job more than his beginning: for he had fourteen thousand sheep, and six thousand camels, and a thousand yoke of oxen, and a thousand she asses." (Job 42:12)

Job's *"latter end"* is even better than the former years of blessing—doubly so! Job's *"latter end"* is another phrase that reminds us of the similarity to the *"latter days"* of Israel.

"Afterward shall the children of Israel return, and seek the LORD their God, and David their king; and shall fear the LORD and his goodness in the latter days." (Hosea 3:5)

A comparison with the first inventory of Job's possessions, listed in Job 1:3, confirms that Job's new wealth is exactly double. He was rich before; now, his wealth is spectacular.

13 "He had also seven sons and three daughters.

14 And he called the name of the first, Jemima; and the name of the second, Kezia; and the name of the third, Keren-happuch.

15 And in all the land were no women found so fair as the daughters of Job: and their father gave them inheritance among their brethren.

16 After this lived Job an hundred and forty years, and saw his sons, and his sons' sons, even four generations.

17 So Job died, being old and full of days." (Job 42:13-17)

Not only does Job receive double his material possessions, his family is restored. Since a child who dies is still the child of the parents, even in this area of his life has Job received double. He originally had seven sons and three daughters, and received exactly the same in the latter end, which makes the double.

Some have suggested that Job's original children are resurrected. They point out that Job's wife is never mentioned again after telling Job to curse God and die in Job 2:9. Nothing is said about Job marrying again.

In Job 1:2 it specifically says that these seven sons and three daughters were BORN unto Job. Here, in Job 42:13 it simply says that Job "had" these sons and daughters.

The purpose in attempting to resurrect Job's children is to see in them a prophetic type of the coming resurrection of those saints martyred in the Tribulation. (Matthew 24:31) Such a resurrection is not without precedent in the Old Testament. The ministries of both Elijah and Elisha record the resurrection of young men. Job professed to believe in a coming physical resurrection. (Job 19:26)

The actual resurrection of the same children who died in Job 1 is not necessary to fulfil the prophetic image of the resurrection of the Tribulation martyrs. Though Job is a mature man when his tragedy strikes, it is not that uncommon for a fifty- or sixty-year-old man to have children.

Job 42:16 tells us that Job lived 140 years after the events of this book. Job would have been around 200 years old when he died, which would qualify as *"being old and full of days,"* as we read in Job 42:17. Abraham lived to be 175. (Genesis 25:7) Clearly, this is enough time to see four generations as recorded in Job 42:16.

I recently took part in a five-generation photo of my family, ranging from my grandmother to my granddaughter. My grandmother has lived to see the fourth generation from her, though she is still in her nineties. Job had 140 years to see four generations.

The singular thing about this passage is to see the names Job gives to his daughters. Why would they be named now if they were the same ones? Not only that, why are their names given, and not those of the sons? Why does it also say that they were given inheritance among their brethren, which was very unusual in oriental culture of that day?

The names are Jemima, Kezia and Keren-happuch. Jemima probably means "day by day," or "fair as the day." Others think the meaning is from the word for "dove." In either case, the emphasis is upon beauty, as indicated in Job 42:15.

Kezia means "cassia," after the family of trees and sweet-smelling spices, so important in oriental society. Keren-happuch means "horn of antimony." Antimony is the principal ingredient in the eye makeup used by the women of that day. She would probably be the classic "painted" beauty. The three names are complimentary, and confirm the claim of Job 42:15 about these girls being the best looking of the Eastern women of the day.

This "and they lived happily ever-after" ending eliminates this story from being a candidate for a major motion picture from modern Hollywood. It does serve as a model of encouragement for any believer of any age who is struggling through trials beyond comprehension.

Our adventures in the land of Uz have ended. It has been quite a journey!

I pray that all the speculations and staggering truth we have explored have been as challenging to you as to me. I trust that the practical application of the truth we have seen will stick in your heart above all. If the study of Job has only puffed up your mind, I have failed as a teacher. May your heart be touched and transformed! Only if your life is different from having plowed through these pages, will I consider that my mission has been fulfilled.

If it were possible to summarize the many truths we should take with us from this study, I would reduce it all to a list of eight:

1. Some questions will never be answered in this life, if ever. God owes us no explanations.
2. Some believers suffer for no reason of their own making.
3. We are but a small part of an immense spiritual war that has been raging since the fall of Lucifer, a war of which we have little understanding.
4. Unless we exercise great caution and discernment, even our best intentions to minister to those who suffer can be easily seized by the enemy to use to his advantage in this spiritual war.
5. An abundance of facts about God does not necessarily qualify anyone to understand God's purposes, especially to diagnose His workings in the life of another.
6. Our need is not just for more information about God; our need is to know God.
7. When baffled and overwhelmed by trials that are not of our own creation, we should lift up our eyes to see the big picture of God's plan for the universe. We should simply stand in awe of God's great power, and simply let Him be God.
8. Finally, as we have just seen, all trials for righteousness' sake ultimately lead to new beginnings.

No one can fully understand what Job has experienced. Not even Job had all his questions answered.

However, his excruciating pain and anguish have now been replaced by the warm glow of God's blessings. Job has lived a long life filled with power, influence and wealth.

Yet, for the last 140 years of his life, none of these things ever held the same appeal. Job's priorities had been permanently rearranged.

The sun sets in the land of Uz. An old man closes his eyes for the last time in the flesh. His tribulation had taught him many things, and led to a fulfilled life. His legacy continues to enrich our lives several thousand years later.

Books of the Old Testament

GENESIS

Genesis 1, 262
Genesis 1:1-2, 186
Genesis 1:1-8, 428
Genesis 1:2, 381, 426
Genesis 1:6-8, 381
Genesis 1:9, 381
Genesis 1:20-21, 156
Genesis 2:7, 98, 121, 197, 437, 488
Genesis 3, 180
Genesis 3:1-4, 511
Genesis 3:5, 184
Genesis 3:14, 255, 601
Genesis 3:15, 245, 273
Genesis 3:19, 197, 275
Genesis 4:6-7a, 631
Genesis 4:22, 445, 446
Genesis 6:1-6, 54
Genesis 6:4, 56
Genesis 6:5, 341
Genesis 6:8-9, 49
Genesis 6:11-13, 447
Genesis 7:11, 426, 553, 557
Genesis 8:1, 263
Genesis 8:20, 226
Genesis 9:11, 450
Genesis 9:26, 227
Genesis 10:23, 38
Genesis 11:4, 386
Genesis 11:10-11, 265
Genesis 13:17, 59
Genesis 14:17-24, 227
Genesis 15:12, 119
Genesis 19:24, 310
Genesis 22:5, 66
Genesis 22:20-21, 481
Genesis 25:1-2, 36
Genesis 25:15, 36
Genesis 25:26, 245
Genesis 27:28, 562
Genesis 31:27, 294
Genesis 32:25, 602
Genesis 35:29, 443
Genesis 36:1, 110
Genesis 36:8, 38, 110
Genesis 36:9-11, 111
Genesis 36:33, 36
Genesis 37:9, 89
Genesis 46:13, 36
Genesis 49:21, 576
Genesis 49:24, 562
Genesis 50:20, 332

EXODUS

Exodus 3:5, 60
Exodus 3:8, 348
Exodus 3:17, 348
Exodus 6:6, 595
Exodus 10:21-23, 96, 304
Exodus 10:22, 421
Exodus 12:23, 192, 308
Exodus 12:35, 635
Exodus 13:5, 349
Exodus 13:11-12, 211
Exodus 13:13, 211
Exodus 13:21, 430

Exodus 15:26, 75
Exodus 19:4, 587
Exodus 32:4, 366
Exodus 34:6-7, 102

LEVITICUS

Leviticus 26:19, 602

NUMBERS

Numbers 12:6, 118, 492
Numbers 13:27, 349
Numbers 22:22-26, 305
Numbers 23:1, 631
Numbers 23:22, 579
Numbers 24:8, 579

DEUTERONOMY

Deuteronomy 4:10, 458
Deuteronomy 4:34, 595
Deuteronomy 7:19, 595
Deuteronomy 28:23, 602
Deuteronomy 28:37, 32, 294, 468
Deuteronomy 28:58-61, 74
Deuteronomy 29:29, 461
Deuteronomy 31:17-18, 401
Deuteronomy 31:18, 244, 506
Deuteronomy 32, 41
Deuteronomy 32:4, 562
Deuteronomy 32:8-13, 41
Deuteronomy 32:10-13, 587
Deuteronomy 32:13-14, 349
Deuteronomy 32:15-30, 42
Deuteronomy 32:17, 255
Deuteronomy 32:23, 353
Deuteronomy 32:31-33, 42
Deuteronomy 32:32, 274
Deuteronomy 32:39, 136
Deuteronomy 33:17, 580

JOSHUA

Joshua 1:3, 60
Joshua 10:11, 560

JUDGES

Judges 3:17, 273
Judges 3:20-22, 273
Judges 16:21, 229, 231

I SAMUEL

1 Samuel 2:8, 429
1 Samuel 10:5, 294
1 Samuel 24:1-2, 576
1 Samuel 28:13, 255

II SAMUEL

2 Samuel 23:2-4, 132

I KINGS

1 Kings 9:7, 32, 295
1 Kings 10:1-10, 390
1 Kings 10:11, 390
1 Kings 11:36, 303

II KINGS

2 Kings 2:11, 537, 548
2 Kings 7:6-7, 232

II CHRONICLES

2 Chronicles 16:9, 449, 505
2 Chronicles 36:6-7, 230
2 Chronicles 36:18, 230
2 Chronicles 36:22-23, 22

EZRA

Ezra 1:1-3, 25

ESTHER

Esther 4:1, 65
Esther 7:9-10, 306

JOB

Job 1:3, 75, 112
Job 1:5, 163
Job 1:6, 53, 57
Job 1:7, 58
Job 1:8, 49, 244, 379
Job 1:12, 62
Job 1:18, 191
Job 1:20-22, 73, 131
Job 1:21, 442
Job 1:22, 66, 148
Job 2:1, 53
Job 2:2-3a, 70
Job 2:3, 191, 244
Job 2:3b, 70
Job 2:9, 77, 363
Job 2:10, 78, 88, 363, 502
Job 2:11, 35, 83, 163
Job 3:1-3, 52, 73
Job 3:14, 229
Job 3:18, 102
Job 3:19, 103
Job 3:23, 104
Job 3:24, 104
Job 3:25-26, 114
Job 4:9, 114
Job 4:13, 119
Job 4:18, 119, 267
Job 4:19, 120
Job 4:20, 121
Job 4:21, 121
Job 5:3, 128
Job 5:7, 131
Job 5:19-22, 308
Job 5:26, 139
Job 6:14, 149
Job 7a, 207
Job 7:5, 246
Job 8:1-2, 162
Job 8:3, 162
Job 8:4, 163
Job 8:5, 163
Job 8:5-7, 163
Job 8:6, 164
Job 8:7, 164
Job 8:9, 165
Job 8:10, 166
Job 8:11, 166
Job 8:12, 166
Job 8:13, 167
Job 8:14, 167
Job 8:15, 167
Job 8:16-18, 168
Job 8:17, 255
Job 8:17-18, 170, 172
Job 8:18, 444
Job 9:2, 180, 181
Job 9:6, 184, 429
Job 9:14-15, 399
Job 9:20, 264
Job 9:20-21, 49
Job 9:24, 193
Job 9:25-26, 193
Job 9:28, 194
Job 9:29-31, 512
Job 9:31, 194
Job 9:32, 194
Job 9:33, 195, 290
Job 9:34, 195
Job 10:1, 196
Job 10:2, 196
Job 10:21-22, 92, 290, 559
Job 11:2a, 205
Job 11:3, 205
Job 11:2b, 205
Job 11:4, 205
Job 11:5-6, 206

Job 11:6, 206
Job 11:7b, 207
Job 11:8-9, 209
Job 11:10-11, 210
Job 11:12, 210
Job 11:14, 212
Job 11:15, 213
Job 11:20, 328
Job 11:20b, 216
Job 12:9, 224
Job 12:10, 225
Job 12:11, 225
Job 12:22, 92
Job 12:3b, 224
Job 12:3, 238
Job 12:7a, 223
Job 12:7b, 223
Job 12:8a, 224
Job 12:8b, 224
Job 12:20a, 230
Job 12:20b, 230
Job 12:22a, 231
Job 12:22b, 231
Job 12:24a, 232
Job 12:24b, 232
Job 13:24, 244
Job 13:25, 244
Job 14:4, 248, 267
Job 14:7, 329
Job 14:10, 290
Job 15:15, 126, 419, 421, 620
Job 15:21, 270
Job 15:22-23, 199
Job 15:30, 199, 274
Job 15:31, 275
Job 15:32, 274
Job 15:33, 274
Job 16:11, 400
Job 16:13, 353
Job 16:16, 92
Job 16:18, 288, 289
Job 17:5, 293
Job 17:6, 32, 294
Job 17:8, 296
Job 17:14, 246
Job 17:15, 328
Job 18:5, 306
Job 18:8, 306
Job 18:12, 307
Job 18:14-15, 354
Job 18:18, 325
Job 18:21, 303, 354, 440
Job 19:3, 320
Job 19:7, 501
Job 19:9, 36
Job 19:25-26, 514
Job 19:25-27, 502
Job 19:26-27, 253
Job 19:29, 340
Job 20:7, 411
Job 20:26, 311
Job 20:28, 411
Job 20:29, 341, 440
Job 21:7, 363
Job 21:14, 365
Job 21:14-15, 387
Job 21:15, 512
Job 21:15b, 376
Job 21:16, 366, 387
Job 22:13, 387
Job 22:15-17, 165
Job 22:23b, 389
Job 22:23c, 389
Job 23:12, 500
Job 23:15, 114
Job 24:1, 413
Job 24:5, 211
Job 24:17, 92
Job 24:24a, 413
Job 25:4, 267
Job 25:5, 268
Job 26:5, 443

Job 26:7, 231
Job 26:7-10, 380
Job 26:8-10, 554
Job 26:10, 449
Job 26:13, 610
Job 27:1, 423
Job 27:2-7, 501
Job 27:3, 98
Job 27:6, 511
Job 27:18, 121
Job 28:3, 92, 171
Job 28:6-8, 171
Job 28:7, 454
Job 28:11b, 450
Job 28:21, 449
Job 28:23, 449
Job 28:28, 122, 449
Job 29:1, 423
Job 29:2, 460
Job 29:14, 437, 511
Job 30:29-30, 297
Job 31:6, 144
Job 31:16-22, 378
Job 31:40, 474
Job 32:2, 35
Job 32:8, 488, 493
Job 32:15, 35
Job 32:16-17, 35
Job 32:21-22, 292
Job 32:27-28, 495
Job 33:4, 98
Job 33:6, 488
Job 33:14-16, 119
Job 33:16, 493
Job 33:17a, 494
Job 33:17b, 494
Job 33:18a, 494
Job 33:18b, 494
Job 34:9, 376
Job 34:22, 92
Job 35:2, 437
Job 35:7-8, 376
Job 36:29-32, 381
Job 36:29, 532
Job 37:3, 533
Job 37:4, 534
Job 37:5, 595
Job 37:15-22, 382
Job 38:1-7, 53
Job 38:2, 508, 630
Job 38:4-7, 185
Job 38:4-11, 382
Job 38:8-11, 450
Job 38:8, 156
Job 38:13, 556
Job 38:15, 556
Job 38:16, 156
Job 38:17, 92
Job 38:19, 559
Job 38:25, 457
Job 38:30, 381
Job 39:5-8, 211
Job 39:12, 580
Job 39:13, 582
Job 39:19, 585
Job 39:20, 585
Job 39:25, 585
Job 40:9b, 595
Job 40:15, 601
Job 41:18, 617
Job 41:30, 171, 448
Job 41:34, 309, 431, 611
Job 41:4b, 613
Job 42:7, 630
Job 42:17, 637
Job 42:8b, 631

PSALMS

Psalm 1:1, 501
Psalm 1:1-3, 523
Psalm 1:4, 542

Psalm 2:4, 387
Psalm 6:7, 295
Psalm 7:11-15, 275
Psalm 7:16, 273
Psalm 8:4, 157, 248
Psalm 11:3, 162
Psalm 11:5, 282
Psalm 12:3, 292
Psalm 13:1-2, 400
Psalm 17:10-15, 350
Psalm 18:2, 41
Psalm 18:11-15, 553
Psalm 18:15-16, 427
Psalm 19:1-2, 187
Psalm 19:1-3, 384
Psalm 19:1-6, 188, 223, 420, 430, 533
Psalm 19:4, 384
Psalm 19:5, 384
Psalm 19:6, 384
Psalm 19:12-13, 244
Psalm 22:1, 284, 323
Psalm 22:1-2, 469
Psalm 22:1-3, 289
Psalm 22:4-9, 298
Psalm 22:6, 154, 247, 421
Psalm 22:13, 284
Psalm 22:14-17, 469
Psalm 22:17, 331
Psalm 22:21, 580
Psalm 23:4, 93
Psalm 25:7, 244
Psalm 25:12-14, 462
Psalm 26:2, 244
Psalm 27:1, 460
Psalm 27:5-6, 514
Psalm 29:3-9, 531
Psalm 29:6, 580
Psalm 29:8-9, 577
Psalm 30:6, 464
Psalm 31:9, 295
Psalm 31:10, 190
Psalm 31:11, 331
Psalm 32:3, 104
Psalm 33:16, 190
Psalm 35:1-7, 71
Psalm 35:5, 542
Psalm 37:1-2, 168
Psalm 37:23, 403
Psalm 37:35, 168, 411
Psalm 37:35-36, 129
Psalm 38:2, 145
Psalm 38:16, 322
Psalm 39:10-11, 246
Psalm 39:11, 121
Psalm 42:4, 469
Psalm 43:2, 400
Psalm 43:3, 460
Psalm 44:13-14, 32
Psalm 44:18, 402
Psalm 44:19, 93
Psalm 45:7, 283
Psalm 48:2, 428, 543
Psalm 48:6, 575
Psalm 49:4, 424
Psalm 49:12, 122
Psalm 49:16-17, 122
Psalm 49:20, 122
Psalm 50:4-6, 253
Psalm 51:5, 131
Psalm 52:1-7, 129
Psalm 57:4, 319
Psalm 64:2-3, 319
Psalm 66:12, 427
Psalm 68:9, 132
Psalm 68:18, 103
Psalm 68:21, 273
Psalm 68:22, 427
Psalm 69:2, 443
Psalm 69:4, 71
Psalm 69:10, 287
Psalm 69:11, 295

Psalm 69:20, 287
Psalm 69:20-21, 331
Psalm 69:21, 285
Psalm 72:16, 139
Psalm 73:1-13, 221
Psalm 73:1-16, 364
Psalm 73:11, 366
Psalm 73:17, 364
Psalm 73:16-17, 221
Psalm 74:13-14, 273
Psalm 74:14, 431, 610, 614
Psalm 75:4-7, 286
Psalm 77:18; 104:7, 585
Psalm 78:2, 424
Psalm 78:39, 155
Psalm 82:6-7, 426
Psalm 84:11, 556
Psalm 88:7, 427
Psalm 88:8, 331
Psalm 88:18, 331
Psalm 89:35-45, 326
Psalm 90:3-6, 248
Psalm 92:9-10, 286
Psalm 92:10, 580
Psalm 103:13-14, 155
Psalm 103:15-16, 155
Psalm 104:3, 539
Psalm 104:5-7, 595
Psalm 107:10, 93
Psalm 109:1-5, 71
Psalm 109:8, 167, 312
Psalm 109:10, 312
Psalm 109:12-13, 312
Psalm 109:13, 167
Psalm 111:10, 459
Psalm 112:2, 139
Psalm 119:100, 484
Psalm 119:105, 304, 325, 460
Psalm 119:130, 460
Psalm 119:133, 403
Psalm 119:165, 388
Psalm 120:4, 145
Psalm 124:4-5, 427
Psalm 138:8, 196
Psalm 139:7-10, 505
Psalm 139:9-11, 197
Psalm 139:14-16, 197
Psalm 139:23-24, 244
Psalm 141:2, 393
Psalm 141:3, 66
Psalm 144:3, 157
Psalm 144:6, 145
Psalm 148:4, 187, 380

PROVERBS

Proverbs 1:7, 127, 458
Proverbs 1:10-18, 306
Proverbs 1:26, 387
Proverbs 1:28, 514
Proverbs 2:22, 129, 311
Proverbs 3:11, 136
Proverbs 3:32, 462
Proverbs 4:18, 461
Proverbs 5:19, 576
Proverbs 6:1, 291
Proverbs 6:12-14, 266
Proverbs 6:16-19, 283
Proverbs 9:10, 459
Proverbs 10:10, 266
Proverbs 10:19, 66, 206
Proverbs 10:28, 167
Proverbs 11:4, 526
Proverbs 11:7, 216, 328
Proverbs 12:13, 66
Proverbs 12:18, 319
Proverbs 12:23, 264
Proverbs 13:9, 303
Proverbs 13:16, 264
Proverbs 13:22, 442
Proverbs 14:16, 206
Proverbs 14:29, 206

Proverbs 14:31, 351
Proverbs 15:1-2, 206
Proverbs 15:2, 264
Proverbs 15:3, 505
Proverbs 15:11, 426
Proverbs 15:28, 206, 264
Proverbs 16:9, 403
Proverbs 17:27-28, 264
Proverbs 17:28, 206, 240
Proverbs 18:13, 206
Proverbs 20:19, 292
Proverbs 20:24, 242
Proverbs 21:13, 351
Proverbs 21:23, 66
Proverbs 22:8, 114
Proverbs 22:16, 351
Proverbs 22:28, 406
Proverbs 23:6, 215
Proverbs 24:12, 502
Proverbs 24:20, 304
Proverbs 25:23, 543
Proverbs 26:28, 292
Proverbs 28:8, 350
Proverbs 29:1, 182, 211, 273
Proverbs 29:5, 292
Proverbs 30:14, 320
Proverbs 30:17, 215, 293
Proverbs 30:32, 362

ECCLESIASTES

Ecclesiastes 1:2, 514
Ecclesiastes 1:9, 23, 120, 204
Ecclesiastes 2:14-16, 192
Ecclesiastes 2:26, 350, 442
Ecclesiastes 3:3b, 389
Ecclesiastes 3:20, 121
Ecclesiastes 3:21, 275
Ecclesiastes 12, 585
Ecclesiastes 12:1-7, 586
Ecclesiastes 12:14, 371

SONG OF SOLOMON

Song of Solomon 2:12-13, 250

ISAIAH

Isaiah 1:5-8, 77
Isaiah 1:8, 442
Isaiah 1:18, 196, 560
Isaiah 2:2-4, 631
Isaiah 2:5, 392
Isaiah 2:19, 536
Isaiah 3:18-26, 582
Isaiah 4:2, 169
Isaiah 5:20, 128
Isaiah 6:1-5, 629
Isaiah 6:5, 593
Isaiah 9:2, 93
Isaiah 10:21-22, 388
Isaiah 11:1, 168
Isaiah 11:1-9, 138
Isaiah 11:4, 115
Isaiah 11:11, 635
Isaiah 14:4, 269
Isaiah 14:9-10, 444
Isaiah 14:12, 329
Isaiah 14:12-14, 386, 543
Isaiah 14:12-17, 184
Isaiah 14:13, 428
Isaiah 14:13-14, 342
Isaiah 14:14, 412
Isaiah 14:15, 343
Isaiah 14:15-17, 445
Isaiah 14:22, 311
Isaiah 19:1, 539
Isaiah 19:11-14, 229
Isaiah 19:22, 388
Isaiah 21:3, 575
Isaiah 22:20-25, 230
Isaiah 23:18, 350
Isaiah 24:18, 553

Isaiah 24:18-20, 233
Isaiah 24:19-21, 186
Isaiah 26:3, 388, 507
Isaiah 26:20-21, 431
Isaiah 27:1, 431, 610
Isaiah 27:10, 100
Isaiah 28:14-15, 613
Isaiah 28:15-18, 192
Isaiah 29:6, 585
Isaiah 30:33, 354
Isaiah 34:7, 580
Isaiah 34:9-10, 310
Isaiah 34:9-11, 171, 448
Isaiah 35:3, 112
Isaiah 35:10, 389
Isaiah 41:14, 247
Isaiah 48:4, 602
Isaiah 49:13, 635
Isaiah 50:6, 284, 285, 468
Isaiah 50:11, 304
Isaiah 51:6, 121
Isaiah 51:8, 246
Isaiah 51:11, 389
Isaiah 52:10, 595
Isaiah 52:14, 81, 285, 295
Isaiah 53:3, 287
Isaiah 54:1, 412
Isaiah 55:6, 207
Isaiah 55:9, 512
Isaiah 55:10-13, 250
Isaiah 57:15, 380
Isaiah 58:8-10, 392
Isaiah 60:1-3, 392
Isaiah 60:9, 391
Isaiah 61:10, 464
Isaiah 63:1, 40
Isaiah 64:1-2, 183
Isaiah 65:20, 139
Isaiah 66:2, 362
Isaiah 66:7-8, 89
Isaiah 66:15, 536
Isaiah 66:24, 154, 422

JEREMIAH

Jeremiah 2:6, 93
Jeremiah 4:31, 575
Jeremiah 6:24, 575
Jeremiah 9:1, 286
Jeremiah 9:23, 190
Jeremiah 10:13, 450
Jeremiah 12:8, 283
Jeremiah 13:16, 93
Jeremiah 13:21, 97
Jeremiah 16:17, 505
Jeremiah 17:1, 332
Jeremiah 20:14-15, 90
Jeremiah 20:18, 90, 99
Jeremiah 22:23, 575
Jeremiah 23:5-6, 168
Jeremiah 25:32, 536
Jeremiah 27:5, 595
Jeremiah 30:6-9, 90
Jeremiah 31:13, 635
Jeremiah 31:34, 389
Jeremiah 31:35-37, 564
Jeremiah 33:7, 633
Jeremiah 33:11, 634
Jeremiah 33:22, 419
Jeremiah 33:26, 634
Jeremiah 44:4, 283
Jeremiah 48:25, 286
Jeremiah 49:7, 111
Jeremiah 50:13, 274
Jeremiah 50:39-40, 274
Jeremiah 51:16, 450
Jeremiah 51:20-23, 195
Jeremiah 51:34, 350
Jeremiah 51:37, 274
Jeremiah 51:44, 350

LAMENTATIONS

Lamentations 2:15, 444
Lamentations 3:37-41, 78
Lamentations 4:3, 583
Lamentations 4:21, 38

EZEKIEL

Ezekiel 1:4, 536, 539
Ezekiel 3:14, 361
Ezekiel 3:15, 80
Ezekiel 7:19, 526
Ezekiel 10:14, 601
Ezekiel 14:20, 27
Ezekiel 15:29, 275
Ezekiel 17:24, 168
Ezekiel 20:33-38, 39
Ezekiel 26:19, 101
Ezekiel 27:30, 75
Ezekiel 28:11-14, 172
Ezekiel 28:12, 185
Ezekiel 28:12-15, 603
Ezekiel 28:13, 185, 294
Ezekiel 28:13-14, 552
Ezekiel 28:14, 274, 601
Ezekiel 28:14-15, 185
Ezekiel 28:16, 448
Ezekiel 34:28, 214
Ezekiel 37:11, 329
Ezekiel 38:10-13, 116
Ezekiel 38:20, 536
Ezekiel 45:21-25, 632

DANIEL

Daniel 2:22, 462, 559
Daniel 2:35, 367
Daniel 2:45, 504
Daniel 4:1-3, 418
Daniel 4:4, 465
Daniel 4:10-17, 169
Daniel 4:20-26, 170
Daniel 4:33, 601
Daniel 4:34-35, 418
Daniel 4:37, 365
Daniel 7:1-4, 116
Daniel 7:2, 262
Daniel 7:8, 215
Daniel 7:8, 20, 24-25, 580
Daniel 7:9-11, 354
Daniel 7:10, 419
Daniel 7:13-14, 539
Daniel 7:16-27, 599
Daniel 7:19, 602
Daniel 7:20, 215
Daniel 7:27, 351
Daniel 9:24-27, 137
Daniel 9:25-27, 612
Daniel 9:26, 604
Daniel 9:27; 11:31; 12:11, 576
Daniel 10:17-19, 399
Daniel 11:4, 263
Daniel 11:21, 292
Daniel 11:31-32, 613
Daniel 11:32, 293
Daniel 11:36-37, 272
Daniel 12:1, 561
Daniel 12:8-9, 171
Daniel 12:9, 509

HOSEA

Hosea 2:14-15, 39
Hosea 2:14-16, 232
Hosea 2:18, 567
Hosea 3:5, 636
Hosea 6:3, 133, 566
Hosea 9:15, 283
Hosea 10:13, 114
Hosea 12:3, 246
Hosea 13:13, 575

JOEL

Joel 2:2, 135
Joel 2:10, 421
Joel 2:23, 132, 465, 566
Joel 2:32, 393
Joel 3:16, 585

AMOS

Amos 1:11-12, 111
Amos 5:8, 93, 231, 563
Amos 5:18, 135, 304
Amos 5:18-20, 91, 526
Amos 5:20, 135, 271, 304

OBADIAH

Obadiah 1-4, 40

JONAH

Jonah 1:17, 156
Jonah 2:1-6, 427
Jonah 2:6, 298
Jonah 3:6, 75

MICAH

Micah 1:16, 65
Micah 4:9-10, 97
Micah 4:9, 575
Micah 5:1, 284
Micah 7:14-15, 39

NAHUM

Nahum 1:7, 117
Nahum 2:11-12, 117

HABAKKUK

Habakkuk 3:3, 537
Habakkuk 3:11, 145
Habakkuk 3:13, 273
Habakkuk 3:15, 430

ZEPHANIAH

Zephaniah 1:15, 91
Zephaniah 2:7, 634
Zephaniah 3:13, 215
Zephaniah 3:20, 634

ZECHARIAH

Zechariah 3:8, 169
Zechariah 4:11-14, 96
Zechariah 6:12-13, 169
Zechariah 7:14, 101
Zechariah 9:12-16, 537
Zechariah 9:14, 145
Zechariah 11:17, 215, 272, 556
Zechariah 12:11, 584

MALACHI

Malachi 1:3, 283
Malachi 3:3, 402
Malachi 4:1-3, 311
Malachi 4:2, 22, 326

Books of the New Testament

MATTHEW

Matthew 3:10, 170
Matthew 4:8-10, 59
Matthew 4:19, 224
Matthew 5:27-29, 471
Matthew 6:19-20, 100
Matthew 6:22, 215
Matthew 6:22-23, 472
Matthew 6:26, 567
Matthew 6:33, 207
Matthew 7:21-23, 593
Matthew 8:12, 311
Matthew 12:34, 264
Matthew 12:36-37, 424
Matthew 13:10-13, 424
Matthew 13:31-32, 604
Matthew 13:43, 214
Matthew 16:16, 82
Matthew 16:18, 298, 558
Matthew 16:23, 82, 226
Matthew 17:24-27, 224
Matthew 19:26, 248
Matthew 22:13, 199, 311
Matthew 22:30, 55
Matthew 23:23, 474
Matthew 24:4-8, 509
Matthew 24:9, 467
Matthew 24:9-11, 129
Matthew 24:13, 509
Matthew 24:14, 509, 554
Matthew 24:15-21, 40
Matthew 24:21, 95
Matthew 24:22, 368
Matthew 24:23-24, 129
Matthew 24:27-28, 216
Matthew 24:27, 533
Matthew 24:28, 587
Matthew 24:30, 539
Matthew 24:32-34, 250
Matthew 24:36, 368
Matthew 24:37-39, 57
Matthew 25:6, 505
Matthew 25:30, 311
Matthew 25:35-46, 409
Matthew 26:50, 58
Matthew 26:67, 284, 468
Matthew 27:4, 296
Matthew 27:24-25, 288
Matthew 27:39-44, 78
Matthew 27:42, 113
Matthew 27:45, 324
Matthew 27:46, 323, 324

MARK

Mark 2:7, 496
Mark 4:41, 398
Mark 4:38b, 398
Mark 7:21-23, 130
Mark 9:45-48, 154
Mark 9:46, 422
Mark 10:45, 525
Mark 11:1-7, 211
Mark 14:66-71, 290

LUKE

Luke 1:20, 230
Luke 1:76-78, 556
Luke 1:78-79, 94

Luke 4:5-7, 193
Luke 4:23, 113
Luke 5:8, 629
Luke 12:2, 450
Luke 12:18-20, 443
Luke 16:22, 102
Luke 16:23-31, 256
Luke 16:26, 325
Luke 17:37, 293

JOHN

John 1:9, 420
John 3:19, 410, 527
John 5:45-46, 30
John 6:70-71, 83
John 8:12, 410
John 8:44, 344, 410, 412
John 9:1-3, 76
John 12:3-6, 346
John 12:7-8, 346
John 12:28-29, 534
John 13:18, 245
John 13:27, 173
John 14:6, 450, 456
John 14:8, 208
John 15:25, 71
John 16:12, 171
John 16:33, 507
John 17:12, 83, 174
John 18:38, 190
John 19:9, 58
John 20:31, 440

ACTS

Acts 1:9, 540
Acts 1:24-25, 83, 172
Acts 1:25, 444
Acts 2:19-20, 186
Acts 12:23, 246
Acts 17:28a, 225
Acts 17:31, 152, 190
Acts 20:28, 288

ROMANS

Romans 1:18-20, 439
Romans 1:20, 222
Romans 2:1, 482
Romans 2:5, 525
Romans 2:12-16, 252
Romans 2:14-16, 191
Romans 3:13, 347
Romans 3:13-14, 191
Romans 3:23, 377
Romans 3:24-26, 181
Romans 3:26, 181, 420
Romans 4:25, 181
Romans 5:1, 267, 419
Romans 5:3-5, 79, 105
Romans 5:10, 329
Romans 5:16-18, 181
Romans 6:23, 181
Romans 8:18, 328
Romans 8:21, 253
Romans 8:26, 398
Romans 8:28, 78, 176
Romans 8:28-29, 184
Romans 8:38-39, 210
Romans 9:19-21, 404
Romans 10:1-4, 152, 438
Romans 10:9-10, 216
Romans 10:13, 625
Romans 10:17, 493
Romans 11:9-10, 306
Romans 11:16-26, 250
Romans 11:33, 188
Romans 13:1, 232
Romans 13:1-4, 334
Romans 14:4, 321
Romans 14:10, 399

Romans 14:10-13, 321
Romans 15:4, 29, 285, 318

I CORINTHIANS

1 Corinthians 2:1-4, 239
1 Corinthians 2:9, 182, 208
1 Corinthians 2:9-10, 462
1 Corinthians 2:10, 182
1 Corinthians 2:10-11, 208
1 Corinthians 2:12-14, 209
1 Corinthians 2:13, 30, 281
1 Corinthians 2:16, 118, 281
1 Corinthians 3:19, 134
1 Corinthians 4:3-5, 438
1 Corinthians 4:5, 322
1 Corinthians 9:7-9, 29
1 Corinthians 9:10, 29
1 Corinthians 10:1-11, 29
1 Corinthians 10:11, 31
1 Corinthians 10:13, 61, 155, 325
1 Corinthians 14:32, 112
1 Corinthians 15:8, 101
1 Corinthians 15:25, 245
1 Corinthians 15:27, 245
1 Corinthians 15:51, 253

II CORINTHIANS

2 Corinthians 1:4-6, 360
2 Corinthians 2:17, 240
2 Corinthians 3:18, 328
2 Corinthians 4:4, 59, 193, 365, 605
2 Corinthians 4:7, 121
2 Corinthians 4:15-18, 296
2 Corinthians 4:17, 144, 328
2 Corinthians 5:10, 322
2 Corinthians 5:21, 284, 330, 464
2 Corinthians 7:10, 629
2 Corinthians 10:4, 619
2 Corinthians 11:14, 615, 617
2 Corinthians 11:23-28, 144
2 Corinthians 12:7-10, 61, 76
2 Corinthians 12:9-10, 523

GALATIANS

Galatians 2:20, 157
Galatians 4:4, 574
Galatians 6:1, 482
Galatians 6:2, 321
Galatians 6:5, 321
Galatians 6:7-8, 114
Galatians 6:10, 351

EPHESIANS

Ephesians 1:3, 60
Ephesians 1:3-4, 550
Ephesians 1:22, 245
Ephesians 2:2, 59, 365, 563
Ephesians 3:1-6, 231
Ephesians 3:17-18, 209
Ephesians 3:18-19, 209
Ephesians 4:8, 102, 252
Ephesians 4:22-24, 464
Ephesians 5:8, 556
Ephesians 5:25-27, 49
Ephesians 5:26, 250
Ephesians 5:27, 213
Ephesians 6:10-12, 131
Ephesians 6:10-13, 605
Ephesians 6:12, 369
Ephesians 6:13, 246
Ephesians 6:16, 145

PHILIPPIANS

Philippians 1:15-18, 79
Philippians 1:21, 157

Philippians 2:5-8, 326
Philippians 2:6-8, 286
Philippians 2:12, 405
Philippians 3:9, 464
Philippians 4:7, 507
Philippians 4:11-12, 523

COLOSSIANS

Colossians 1:16-17, 551
Colossians 2:9, 208
Colossians 2:16-17, 632
Colossians 3:4, 328

I THESSALONIANS

1 Thessalonians 4:13-18, 254
1 Thessalonians 5:1-2, 91
1 Thessalonians 5:2-3, 270, 327, 413
1 Thessalonians 5:3, 352
1 Thessalonians 5:21, 512

II THESSALONIANS

2 Thessalonians 2:1-4, 272
2 Thessalonians 2:3, 174
2 Thessalonians 2:3-4, 83, 270
2 Thessalonians 2:8, 114, 175, 344
2 Thessalonians 2:8-9, 303
2 Thessalonians 2:8-10, 228

I TIMOTHY

1 Timothy 2:5, 195
1 Timothy 2:6, 526
1 Timothy 2:8, 212, 392
1 Timothy 6:5, 296
1 Timothy 6:20, 573
1 Timothy 6:20-21, 239

II TIMOTHY

2 Timothy 1:7, 105
2 Timothy 2:15, 204
2 Timothy 3:16, 483
2 Timothy 3:16-17, 49, 191
2 Timothy 4:17, 507

HEBREWS

Hebrews 1:1-2, 118, 492
Hebrews 1:10-12, 187
Hebrews 1:14, 119
Hebrews 2:6, 157
Hebrews 2:8, 245
Hebrews 2:14, 62, 309
Hebrews 4:12, 147, 335, 494, 616
Hebrews 4:15-16, 197
Hebrews 5:7, 287
Hebrews 9:11-12, 288
Hebrews 9:16, 20
Hebrews 9:27, 152, 574
Hebrews 11:4, 288
Hebrews 11:25, 347, 527
Hebrews 11:36-38, 408
Hebrews 11:36-39, 467
Hebrews 12:1, 528
Hebrews 12:5, 136
Hebrews 12:12, 113
Hebrews 13:3, 149

JAMES

James 1:2-4, 402
James 1:3, 180
James 1:27, 213
James 3:1-2, 320
James 4:1, 130
James 4:14, 154, 193
James 5:1-6, 327
James 5:11, 27, 79, 179, 402

James 5:17, 457
James 5:17-18, 565

I PETER

1 Peter 1:7, 402
1 Peter 2:4-8, 42
1 Peter 2:20-23, 73
1 Peter 2:23, 73
1 Peter 3:18-20, 56
1 Peter 4:12-13, 402, 405
1 Peter 5:8, 58, 59, 115

II PETER

2 Peter 1:16-21, 493
2 Peter 1:19, 532
2 Peter 1:21, 483
2 Peter 2:4-6, 57
2 Peter 2:4, 120, 426
2 Peter 2:17, 199

I JOHN

1 John 1:5-9, 461
1 John 1:7a, 391
1 John 1:8, 192
1 John 2:1, 195, 290
1 John 4:1, 424
1 John 4:18, 105, 405
1 John 5:14-15, 391
1 John 5:14b, 391
1 John 5:16, 524

III JOHN

3 John 1:2, 523

JUDE

Jude 1:9, 504
Jude 6-7, 56
Jude 7, 120
Jude 9, 400, 603, 613
Jude 12,23, 213

REVELATION

Revelation 1:7, 540
Revelation 1:14, 560
Revelation 1:15, 446
Revelation 1:18, 298, 558
Revelation 1:20, 54
Revelation 2:6, 283
Revelation 2:15, 283
Revelation 3:7, 228
Revelation 4:1, 534
Revelation 4:6-7, 601
Revelation 4:7, 601
Revelation 5:5, 104, 115, 223
Revelation 6:2, 353
Revelation 6:5-6, 271, 441
Revelation 6:5-8, 307
Revelation 6:6, 409
Revelation 6:12, 91
Revelation 6:14-17, 323, 536
Revelation 6:15-17, 252, 408
Revelation 6:17, 367
Revelation 7:1, 262
Revelation 9:1-10, 173
Revelation 9:6, 104, 253, 325, 509
Revelation 9:9, 270
Revelation 9:11, 83, 173, 192, 270, 308, 427
Revelation 10:1-4, 534
Revelation 11:6, 565
Revelation 11:12, 540
Revelation 11:18-19, 561
Revelation 12:1-3, 332
Revelation 12:1-4, 120
Revelation 12:1-5, 89
Revelation 12:5, 89
Revelation 12:6, 38, 253
Revelation 12:7-9, 120
Revelation 12:9, 431, 470, 610

Revelation 12:9-10, 379
Revelation 12:9-13, 33
Revelation 12:10, 62
Revelation 12:12, 228
Revelation 12:13, 332
Revelation 12:14, 588
Revelation 12:15, 604
Revelation 13:1-2, 598
Revelation 13:3-7, 310
Revelation 13:13, 64, 304
Revelation 13:14-18, 213
Revelation 13:15, 310
Revelation 14:4, 90
Revelation 14:14, 539
Revelation 14:20, 585
Revelation 16:2, 74
Revelation 16:9, 95
Revelation 16:10, 91
Revelation 16:11, 74
Revelation 16:13-14, 82
Revelation 16:20, 183
Revelation 16:21, 367
Revelation 17:9-11, 309
Revelation 18:2, 274
Revelation 19:11-15, 271, 353
Revelation 19:11-21, 175
Revelation 19:15, 135, 534
Revelation 19:17-18, 216, 587
Revelation 19:17-21, 294
Revelation 19:20, 310
Revelation 20:1-3, 229
Revelation 20:7-8, 229
Revelation 20:7-9, 345
Revelation 20:10, 271
Revelation 20:11-14, 370
Revelation 20:11-15, 252
Revelation 20:12, 289
Revelation 20:13-15, 255
Revelation 21:1-4, 139
Revelation 22:5, 447